Concise Dictionary of British Literary Biography
Volume Five

Late Victorian and Edwardian Writers, 1890-1914

Concise Dictionary of British Literary Biography
Volume Five

Late Victorian and Edwardian Writers, 1890-1914

A Bruccoli Clark Layman Book
Gale Research Inc.
Detroit, London

The paper used in this publication meets the minimum requirements
of American National Standard for Information Sciences—Permanence
Paper for Printed Library Materials, ANSI Z39.48-1984. ∞™

Matthew J. Bruccoli and Richard Layman, *Editorial Directors*
Karen L. Rood, *Senior Editor*

Printed in the United States of America

Published simultaneously in the United Kingdom
by Gale Research International Limited
(An affiliated company of Gale Research Inc.)

ISBN 0-8103-7980-5
ISBN 0-8103-7985-6

10 9 8 7 6 5 4 3

Contents of Volume 5

Authors Included in This Series

Volume 1
Writers of the Middle Ages and Renaissance Before 1660

Francis Bacon
Francis Beaumont & John Fletcher
Beowulf
Thomas Campion
Geoffrey Chaucer
Thomas Dekker
John Donne
John Ford
George Herbert
Ben Jonson
Sir Thomas Malory
Christopher Marlowe
Sir Walter Ralegh
William Shakespeare
Edmund Spenser
Henry Howard Surrey
Izaak Walton
John Webster
Thomas Wyatt

Volume 2
Writers of the Restoration and Eighteenth Century, 1660-1789

Joseph Addison
James Boswell
John Bunyan
William Congreve
Daniel Defoe
John Dryden
Henry Fielding
Oliver Goldsmith
Thomas Gray
Samuel Johnson
Andrew Marvell
John Milton
Samuel Pepys
Alexander Pope
Samuel Richardson
Richard Brinsley Sheridan
Tobias Smollett
Richard Steele
Laurence Sterne
Jonathan Swift
William Wycherley

Volume 3
Writers of the Romantic Period, 1789-1832

Volume 4
Victorian Writers, 1832-1890

Volume 6
Modern Writers, 1914-1945

Volume 7
Writers After World War II, 1945-1960

Volume 8
Contemporary Writers, 1960-Present

Plan of the Work

The eight-volume *Concise Dictionary of British Literary Biography* was developed in response to requests from school and college teachers and librarians, and from small- to medium-sized public libraries, for a compilation of entries from the standard *Dictionary of Literary Biography* chosen to meet their needs and their budgets. The *DLB*, which comprises more than one hundred volumes as of the end of 1991, is moving steadily toward its goal of providing a history of literature in all languages developed through the biographies of writers. Basic as the *DLB* is, many librarians have expressed the need for a less comprehensive reference work which in other respects retains the merits of the *DLB*. The *Concise DBLB* provides this resource.

The *Concise* series was planned by an eight-member advisory board, consisting primarily of secondary-school educators, who developed a method of organization and presentation for selected *DLB* entries suitable for high-school and beginning college students. Their preliminary plan was circulated to some five thousand school librarians and English teachers, who were asked to respond to the organization of the series. Those responses were incorporated into the plan described here.

Uses for the Concise DBLB

Students are the primary audience for the *Concise DBLB*. The stated purpose of the standard *DLB* is to make our literary heritage more accessible. *Concise DBLB* has the same goal and seeks a wider audience. What the author wrote; what the facts of his or her life are; a description of his or her literary works; a discussion of the critical response to his or her works; and a bibliography of critical works to be consulted for further information: these are the elements of a *Concise DBLB* entry.

The first step in the planning process for this series, after identifying the audience, was to contemplate its uses. The advisory board acknowledged that the integrity of *Concise DBLB* as a reference book is crucial to its utility. The *Concise DBLB* adheres to the scholarly standards established by the parent series; the *Concise DBLB* is a ready-reference source of established value, providing reliable biographical and bibliographical information.

It is anticipated that this series will not be confined to uses within the library. Just as the *DLB* has been a tool for stimulating students' literary interests in the college classroom—for comparative studies of authors, for example, and, through its ample illustrations, as a means of invigorating literary study—the *Concise DBLB* is a primary resource for high-school and junior-college educators.

Organization

The advisory board further determined that entries from the standard *DLB* should be presented complete—without abridgment. The board's feeling was that the utility of the *DLB* format has been proven, and that only minimal changes should be made.

The advisory board further decided that the organization of the *Concise DBLB* should be chronological to emphasize the historical development of British literature. Each volume is devoted to a single historical period and includes the most significant literary figures from all genres who were active during that time.

The eight period volumes of the *Concise DBLB* are: *Writers of the Middle Ages and Renaissance Before 1660; Writers of the Restoration and Eighteenth Century, 1660-1789; Writers of the Romantic Period, 1789-1832; Victorian Writers, 1832-1890; Late Victorian and Edwardian Writers, 1890-1914; Modern Writers, 1914-1945; Writers After World War II, 1945-1960; Contemporary Writers, 1960-Present.*

Form of Entry

The form of entry in the *Concise DBLB* is substantially the same as in the standard series. Entries have been updated and, where necessary, corrected.

It is anticipated that users of this series will find it useful to consult the standard *DLB* for information about those writers omitted from the *Concise DBLB* whose significance to contemporary readers may have faded but whose contribution to our cultural heritage remains meaningful.

Comments about the series and suggestions for its improvement are earnestly invited.

A Note to Students

The purpose of the *Concise DBLB* is to enrich the study of British literature. Besides being inherently interesting, biographies of writers provide a basic understanding of the various ways writers react in their works to the circumstances of their lives, the events of their times, and the cultures that envelop them.

Concise DBLB entries start with the most important facts about writers: what they wrote. We strongly recommend that you also start there. The chronological listing of an author's works is an outline for the examination of his or her career achievements. The biography that follows sets the stage for the presentation of the works. Each of the author's important works and the most respected critical evaluations of them are discussed in *Concise DBLB*. If you require more information about the author or fuller critical studies of the author's works, the references section at the end of the entry will guide you.

Illustrations are an integral element of *Concise DBLB* entries. Photographs of the author are reminders that literature is the product of a writer's imagination; facsimiles of the author's working drafts are the best evidence available for understanding the act of composition—the author in the process of refining his or her work and acting as self-editor; dust jackets and advertisements demonstrate how literature comes to us through the marketplace, which sometimes serves to alter our perceptions of the works.

Literary study is a complex and immensely rewarding endeavor. Our goal is to provide you with the information you need to make that experience as rich as possible.

Acknowledgments

This book was produced by Bruccoli Clark Layman, Inc. Karen L. Rood is senior editor for the *Dictionary of Literary Biography* series. David Marshall James was the in-house editor.

Production coordinator is James W. Hipp. Projects manager is Charles D. Brower. Photography editors are Edward Scott and Timothy C. Lundy. Permissions editor is Jean W. Ross. Layout and graphics supervisor is Penney L. Haughton. Copyediting supervisor is Bill Adams. Typesetting supervisor is Kathleen M. Flanagan. Systems manager is George F. Dodge. Charles Lee Egleston is editorial associate. The production staff includes Rowena Betts, Teresa Chaney, Patricia Coate, Gail Crouch, Margaret McGinty Cureton, Sarah A. Estes, Robert Fowler, Mary L. Goodwin, Cynthia Hallman, Ellen McCracken, Kathy Lawler Merlette, Laura Garren Moore, Catherine A. Murray, John Myrick, Pamela D. Norton, Cathy J. Reese, Laurrè Sinckler-Reeder, Maxine K. Smalls, Teri C. Sperry, and Betsy L. Weinberg.

Walter W. Ross and Timothy D. Tebalt did library research. They were assisted by the following librarians at the Thomas Cooper Library of the University of South Carolina: Jens Holley and the interlibrary-loan staff; reference librarians Gwen Baxter, Daniel Boice, Faye Chadwell, Jo Cottingham, Cathy Eckman, Rhonda Felder, Gary Geer, Jackie Kinder, Laurie Preston, Jean Rhyne, Carol Tobin, Virginia Weathers, and Connie Widney; circulation-department head Thomas Marcil; and acquisitions-searching supervisor David Haggard.

Concise Dictionary of British Literary Biography
Volume Five

Late Victorian and Edwardian Writers, 1890-1914

Concise Dictionary of British Literary Biography

James M. Barrie

(9 May 1860 - 19 June 1937)

This entry was updated by Valerie C. Rudolph (Purdue University) from her entry in DLB 10: Modern British Dramatists, 1900-1945: Part One.

SELECTED BOOKS: *Better Dead* (London: Swan Sonnenschein, 1888);

Auld Licht Idylls (London: Hodder & Stoughton, 1888; New York: Cassell, 1891);

When a Man's Single (London: Hodder & Stoughton, 1888; New York: Harper, 1889);

A Window in Thrums (London: Hodder & Stoughton, 1889; New York: American Publishers, 1889);

Richard Savage (London: Privately printed, 1891);

The Little Minister (Boston: Estes, 1891; London: Cassell, 1896);

Sentimental Tommy (London: Cassell, 1896);

Margaret Ogilvy (New York: Scribners, 1896; London: Hodder & Stoughton, 1896);

Tommy and Grizel (London: Cassell, 1900; New York: Scribners, 1900);

The Wedding Guest (London: Chapman & Hall, 1900; New York: Scribners, 1900);

The Little White Bird, or Adventures in Kensington Gardens (London: Hodder & Stoughton, 1902; New York: Scribners, 1902);

Peter Pan in Kensington Gardens (London: Hodder & Stoughton, 1906; New York: Scribners, 1906);

Walker, London (London & New York: French, 1907);

Peter and Wendy (London: Hodder & Stoughton, 1911; New York: Scribners, 1911);

Quality Street (London: Hodder & Stoughton, 1913);

The Admirable Crichton (London & New York: Hodder & Stoughton, 1914);

Half Hours (London: Hodder & Stoughton, 1914; New York: Scribners, 1914)—includes *Pantaloon, The Twelve-Pound Look, Rosalind,* and *The Will*;

Der Tag; or, The Tragic Man (New York: Scribners, 1914);

Echoes of the War (London & New York: Hodder & Stoughton, 1918)—includes *The New Word, The Old Lady Shows Her Medals, A Well-Remembered Voice,* and *Barbara's Wedding*;

The Works of J. M. Barrie, 16 volumes (New York: Scribners, 1929-1940);

The Plays of James M. Barrie (New York: Scribners, 1930)—includes *Alice-Sit-by-the-Fire, What Every Woman Knows, Old Friends, Seven Women, Half an Hour, The New World, A Kiss for Cinderella, Dear Brutus, Mary Rose, Peter Pan, Quality Street, The Admirable Crichton, Pantaloon, Rosalind, The Will, The Twelve-Pound Look, A Well-Remembered Voice, Barbara's Wedding, The Old Lady Shows Her Medals,* and *Shall We Join the Ladies?*;

The Greenwood Hat (Edinburgh: A. & T. Constable, 1930);

The Boy David (London: Davies, 1938; New York: Scribners, 1938);

M'Connachie and J. M. B. (London: Davies, 1938; New York: Scribners, 1939);

Letters of J. M. Barrie, edited by Viola Meynell (London: Davies, 1942; New York: Scribners, 1947);

When Wendy Grew Up: An Afterthought (New York: Dutton, 1957);

Ibsen's Ghost; or, Toole Up-to-Date (London: Cecil Woolf, 1975).

PLAY PRODUCTIONS: *Bandolero, the Bandit*, Dumfries, Scotland, Dumfries Academy, 1877;

Richard Savage, by Barrie and H. B. Marriott Watson, London, Criterion Theatre, 16 April 1891;

Ibsen's Ghost; or, Toole Up-to-Date, London, Toole's Theatre, 30 May 1891;

Walker, London, London, Toole's Theatre, 25 February 1892, 511 [performances];

Jane Annie; or, The Good Conduct Prize, by Barrie and Sir Arthur Conan Doyle, music by E. Ford, London, Savoy Theatre, 13 May 1893;

Becky Sharp, adapted from William Makepeace Thackeray's *Vanity Fair*, New York, Star Theatre, 3 June 1893;

The Professor's Love Story, New York, Star Theatre, 13 December 1893; London, Comedy Theatre, 25 June 1894;

The Little Minister, adapted from Barrie's novel, New York, Empire Theatre, 27 September 1897, 300;

The Wedding Guest, London, Garrick Theatre, 27 September 1900, 100;

Quality Street, New York, Knickerbocker Theatre, 11 November 1901, 459;

The Admirable Crichton, London, Duke of York's Theatre, 4 November 1902, 328;

Little Mary, London, Wyndham's Theatre, 24 September 1903, 208;

Peter Pan; or, The Boy Who Wouldn't Grow Up, adapted from Barrie's *The Little White Bird, or Adventures in Kensington Gardens*, London, Duke of York's Theatre, 27 December 1904, 145;

Pantaloon, London, Duke of York's Theatre, 5 April 1905;

Alice-Sit-by-the-Fire: A Page from a Daughter's Diary, London, Duke of York's Theatre, 5 April 1905, 115;

Josephine, London, Comedy Theatre, 5 April 1906;

Punch: A Toy Tragedy, London, Comedy Theatre, 5 April 1906;

What Every Woman Knows, London, Duke of York's Theatre, 3 September 1908, 384;

The Twelve-Pound Look, London, Duke of York's Theatre, 1 March 1910;

Old Friends, London, Duke of York's Theatre, 1 March 1910;

A Slice of Life: An Advanced Drama, London, Duke of York's Theatre, 7 June 1910;

Rosalind, London, Duke of York's Theatre, 14 October 1912;

The Dramatists Get What They Want, London, Hippodrome Theatre, 23 December 1912;

The Adored One, London, Duke of York's Theatre, 4 September 1913; first act revised and produced as *Seven Women*, London, New Theatre, 7 April 1917;

The Will, London, Duke of York's Theatre, 4 September 1913;

Half an Hour, London, Hippodrome Theatre, 29 September 1913;

Der Tag; or, The Tragic Man, London, Coliseum Theatre, 21 December 1914;

The New Word, London, Duke of York's Theatre, 22 March 1915;

Rosy Rapture, the Pride of the Beauty Chorus, music by H. Darewski and J. D. Kern, London, Duke of York's Theatre, 22 March 1915;

The Fatal Typist, London, His Majesty's Theatre, 19 November 1915;

The Real Thing at Last, London, Coliseum Theatre, 7 March 1916;

A Kiss for Cinderella, London, Wyndham's Theatre, 16 March 1916, 156;

Shakespeare's Legacy, London, Drury Lane Theatre, 14 April 1916;

Reconstructing the Crime, London, Palace Theatre, 16 February 1917;

The Old Lady Shows Her Medals, London, New Theatre, 7 April 1917;

Dear Brutus, London, Wyndham's Theatre, 17 October 1917, 365;

La Politesse, London, Wyndham's Theatre, 28 June 1918;

A Well-Remembered Voice, London, Wyndham's Theatre, 28 June 1918;

The Truth About the Russian Dancers, London, Coliseum Theatre, 15 March 1920;

Mary Rose, London, Haymarket Theatre, 22 April 1920, 399;

Shall We Join the Ladies?, London, Royal Academy of Dramatic Arts, 27 May 1921;

Barbara's Wedding, London, Savoy Theatre, 23 August 1927;

The Boy David, Edinburgh, King's Theatre, 21 November 1936; London, His Majesty's Theatre, 21 December 1936, 55.

If Sir James M. Barrie had written no play other than *Peter Pan* (1904), the extraordinary and enduring popularity of this single work would testify to his talents as a dramatist. As it stands, however, the more than forty plays he wrote also manifest his creativity, albeit a creativity often marred by excessive sentimentality. Barrie's fifty-year career as a playwright exposed him to the whimsy of W. S. Gilbert, the problem plays of Henrik Ibsen and George Bernard Shaw, and the social comedy of Oscar Wilde. Indeed, his plays taken as a whole form a compendium of late-nineteenth- and early-twentieth-century dramatic and theatrical conventions—a virtue which paradoxically also makes his works seem dated.

James Matthew Barrie was the third son and youngest child of David and Margaret Ogilvy Barrie, born on 9 May 1860 in Kirriemuir, Forfarshire, Scotland. Barrie's somewhat austere father seems not to have been nearly so important to Barrie as his mother, whom he idolized and immortalized in his prose work *Margaret Ogilvy* (1896). His excessive attachment to his mother led to lifelong problems in Barrie's relationships with women, including his wife, actress Mary Ansell, whom he married in 1894 and divorced in 1909. Barrie's other strong attachment was to his older brother David, whose accidental death at thirteen sent Margaret Ogilvy to bed for the remainder of her life and set Barrie to acting the role of the lost brother in order to win maternal attention and affection.

From 1873 to 1878 Barrie attended Dumfries Academy in Dumfries, Scotland, where his first play, *Bandolero, the Bandit,* was presented in 1877. Its hero was a composite of Barrie's fantasy heroes, gleaned from his reading of adventure stories. In 1878 he enrolled at Edinburgh University, taking his M.A. in 1882. Upon leaving the university, he became an editor for the *Nottingham Journal* and in 1885 became a journalist in London. In 1888 his first book, *Better Dead,* whose title echoed Barrie's own later appraisal of the work, was published. As a journalist Barrie had written several successful sketches of life in his birthplace, Kirriemuir, especially of the Auld Licht religious sect, to which his mother had belonged before her marriage. As the fictional village of Thrums, Kirriemuir provided the background for a succession of popular Scottish novels: *Auld Licht Idylls* (1888), *When a Man's Single* (1888), *A Window in Thrums* (1889), *The Little Minister* (1891), *Sentimental Tommy* (1896), and

James M. Barrie

Tommy and Grizel (1900). In these early works, Barrie explored many of the themes and techniques that he would later transfer successfully to the stage.

If Barrie's plays expound one consistent notion, it is that social conventions, especially those of marriage and of class distinction, are necessary to channel energies that might otherwise disrupt society. Barrie's dramas often portray characters who have not yet found, or who contemplate changing, their proper social roles. Those whose energies society needs to channel appropriately include children who are becoming adults, spinsters desperate to escape spinsterhood, bachelors reluctant to leave bachelorhood, husbands and wives contemplating affairs or divorce, and servants who would be equal to their masters. In the later plays, the shadow of World War I often influences the actions and decisions of the characters.

When he turned from newspaper work to the drama, Barrie collaborated with H. B. Marriott Watson on his first London play, *Richard Savage* (1891)—a four-act drama (laced with eighteenth-century dialogue) about the British satirist whose *"Life"* Dr. Johnson had written more than a century earlier. The play itself, however, lasted only one performance. Undiscouraged, a month later on 30 May 1891, Barrie, without the aid of collaborator, brought out his burlesque of Ibsenism, which was then fashionable in London. *Ibsen's Ghost; or, Toole Up-to-Date* caricatured Ibsen's Nora Helmer and Hedda Gabler, poked fun at Ibsen's fondness for repetitious phrases, such as "fancy that" or "ghosts," and burlesqued Hedda's suicide by having all the remaining characters imitate her and shoot themselves simultaneously. This play, while amusing, was hardly sufficient to establish Barrie as a playwright.

His first successful play, *Walker, London*, opened at Toole's Theatre on 25 February 1892 and ran for 511 performances. "Walker," in London slang, meant someone who was lying. "Walker, London" is the address given by the play's chief dissembler, Jasper Phipps, a reluctant bridegroom who must be brought to matrimony. Posing as a famous African explorer and the rescuer of Bell Golightly, Jasper joins the Golightly family. The Golightly surname aptly reflects the placid, innocent life aboard their houseboat, a forerunner of the magical islands or enchanted woods Barrie was to use in subsequent plays as a device to enable his characters to gain new self-knowledge and greater awareness of their appropriate social roles. This setting also liberated him from the drawing room so that his characters might analyze what otherwise would have escaped their attention. Thus Jasper returns to the fiancée he has jilted, and the intellectual Bell, still affirming that woman is not man's "plaything" but his "equal in mind," marries Kit Upjohn, the fiancé who addresses her in baby talk. Whereas Jasper deliberately deceives the Golightlys, Bell is self-deceived. Both forms of deception are used to frustrate as well as to accomplish the goals of Barrie's characters. In fact, Jasper's deception leads to his awareness that "it's just the same, all the world over, the men run after the women—and the women run after the men" and catch them. Affirming the convention of matrimony, Jasper returns to his fiancée Sarah, leaving only his fictitious address to comment on the deception necessary to channel youthful exuberance and sexuality into holy wedlock.

Barrie's future wife, Mary Ansell, played Bell's cousin Nancy O'Brien. Often infatuated with actresses, Barrie pursued Mary but was as reluctant as Jasper Phipps to marry, though the wedding did take place more than two years later under circumstances not altogether clear to Barrie's biographers, perhaps more at the insistence of Mary Ansell than of Barrie himself. Barrie was far too attached to his mother ever to permit his wife to displace her in his affections; the marriage was both unhappy and childless, ending in divorce in October 1909.

Barrie's single foray into comic opera (in collaboration with Sir Arthur Conan Doyle) was commissioned by Richard D'Oyly Carte as insurance against the threatened collapse of the collaboration between the feuding William Gilbert and Arthur Sullivan. *Jane Annie; or, The Good Conduct Prize*, with music by E. Ford, opened at the Savoy Theatre on 13 May 1893, but was unsuccessful, lasting only seven weeks. Barrie was no Gilbert, even though his plays sometimes exhibit Gilbertian wit. Sir Arthur Conan Doyle was obviously more at home on Baker Street.

A month later, Barrie followed this failure with *Becky Sharp*, a condensation of the final three chapters of William Makepeace Thackeray's *Vanity Fair*. This work formed part of a quintuple bill presented at New York's Star Theatre on 3 June 1893, where it was received as the worst of a bad lot. Mercifully it quickly faded into oblivion.

Not so with *The Professor's Love Story*, which opened in New York on 13 December 1893 and after a successful run opened in London on 25 June 1894 for more than 140 performances. In this play the hero is yet another reluctant bridegroom, Prof. Tom Goodwillie, a famous inventor and author of books on electricity. A mysterious illness—later diagnosed as love—imperils the professor's creativity and threatens to destroy it. Lucy White, the professor's new secretary and the cause of his illness, effects his cure when she tricks him into acknowledging his love and proposing to her. Lucy becomes the prototype of the manipulative woman who often appears in Barrie's plays. Her machinations help her both to get a husband and also to retain power over him in the marriage. It is possible to see in this stereotypical character a reflection of Barrie's relationship with his soon-to-be wife, Mary Ansell. Though the Barries' love ultimately proved destructive, in *The Professor's Love Story* love becomes creative, but only when it is acknowledged, expressed, and safely channeled into matrimony. Like the isolated houseboat in *Walker, London*, the professor's summer cottage in Scotland provides the essential change of location necessary to alter the perceptions of both major and minor characters. It also offers the playwright a chance to indulge in Scottish dialect, to exult in Scottish wit, and to depict Scottish village life.

In 1894 the newlywed Barries returned from their honeymoon in Switzerland to settle near Kensington Gardens, a popular place for parents to stroll and play with their children. There the childless Barrie met George Davies, the first of five sons born to Arthur Llewelyn and Sylvia DuMaurier Davies. Barrie, acutely sensitive about his diminutive stature—he was barely five feet tall—often had difficulty communicating with adults but seldom with children. His critics accused Barrie of being himself childlike, but Barrie paid little heed. He continued to develop his friendship with the Davies family to the neglect of his wife and the chagrin of the boys' father. The five Davies boys—George, Jack, Peter, Michael, and Nicholas—were models for several of the characters in *Peter Pan*. After the deaths of Arthur and Sylvia Davies, Barrie became the children's guardian, much to his delight. Tragedy, however, soon marred his satisfaction. George was killed in World War I; Michael, long subject to fits of depression, apparently drowned himself; and Jack eventually became estranged from Barrie. In 1960, years after Barrie's own death, Peter threw himself in front of a London subway train.

During the years preceding *Peter Pan* (1904), Barrie deepened his friendship with the Davies family and also produced a succession of popular plays, beginning with *The Little Minister*. This adaptation of Barrie's 1891 novel of the same title opened on 27 September 1897 at the Empire Theatre, New York, with Maude Adams as the exotic gypsy, Babbie. It ran for three hundred performances, but, more importantly, it introduced Barrie to impresario Charles Frohman, who was to produce many of his plays, including *Peter Pan*. Their exceptionally cordial relationship lasted until 1915, when, responding to an invitation from Barrie, Frohman set sail on the *Lusitania*, which was sunk by a torpedo from a German U-boat off the Irish coast on 7 May 1915, killing 1,195.

In *The Little Minister*, matrimony once again channels potentially destructive energies. The excessive piety of Gavin Dishart, the little minister of Thrums (the Kirriemuir of Barrie's boyhood), and the excessive frolicsomeness of Lady Barbara (Babbie), daughter of the local British nobleman, must both be subjected to the corrective of marriage. Disguised as the captivating gypsy Babbie, Lady Barbara not only enthralls the pious Gavin but also saves the town from persecution by British troops, since her marriage allies a British lord, her father, with the town's minister.

The dialogue between the main characters exhibits the same charm and wit as that between the title characters in Shaw's *Caesar and Cleopatra* (1899). Babbie's exotic costume, vivaciousness, and puckish flaunting of social convention made her role much sought after by actresses of the period. Ironically, however, the very social conventions that Babbie flaunts save the day. Gavin is about to be turned out of his parish for falling in love with a gypsy, whose unconventional life-style represents a natural religion and an uncontrolled sexuality that are threatening to Gavin's congregation. As Babbie, his bride is unacceptable; revealed as Lady Barbara, her rank confers distinction on the townspeople, who cheer the match they had earlier condemned. Gavin, in the end, becomes more spontaneous, compassionate, and less rigidly pious while Barbara is glad to put her exuberance under the "control" of a strong husband, but one whom she will still manage to manipulate through wit and charm.

The Wedding Guest (1900), Barrie's chief foray into Ibsenism, asserts the power of the past upon the present to bring unhappiness and destruction. Mrs. Ommaney, a woman with a "past," turns up on the wedding day of her former lover, Paul Digby, who is also the father of her child. Paul attempts to bribe Mrs. Ommaney, and Mrs. Ommaney tries to blackmail Paul, who is finally forced to confess to his new bride that he is a man with a "past." Such are the bitter fruits of love not properly channeled through matrimony. Paul's bride Margaret leaves him but is convinced by her aunt, Lady Jane, to return because of her "duty" to her husband—another idea much discussed in Ibsen's plays. Lady Jane, who once spurned a man with a "past," never had another chance to marry and convinces Margaret that an imperfect husband is better than no husband at all. Paul and Margaret resume a marriage of duty and convention. A bitter Mrs. Ommaney abandons her blackmail scheme and departs. Having defied social convention, she is left alone and unprotected, to survive as best she can. Though Barrie treats Mrs. Ommaney with understanding and sympathy, she still remains guilty of an unforgivable moral lapse, which justifies her suffering. Although Barrie's overreliance on dramatic clichés led to the play's poor reception, it did run for at least one hundred performances, many more than some of Barrie's other "failures."

In contrast, the uncontestably successful *Quality Street,* after a tryout in Toledo, Ohio, opened 11 November 1901 at the Knickerbocker Theatre, where it ran for 459 performances. The Misses Phoebe and Susan Throessel live on Quality Street, a quaint lane in a country town. The sensible and always proper Miss Phoebe, disappointed at not receiving a marriage proposal from the dashing young surgeon Valentine Brown, observes that it is a world where the empty-headed marry the empty-headed. As a "woman of sense" she has no chance for the social, emotional, and economic security of a husband, so, on the spur of the moment, she flings aside the conventional behavior of the over-twenty spinster to masquerade as the Throessels' imaginary, flirtatious young niece, Miss Livvy. However, Miss Phoebe thoughtfully rejects the marriage proposals she receives in this guise because she must find her identity as Miss Phoebe, not as Miss Livvy. Fortunately, Brown, whose head has also been turned momentarily by Miss Livvy, comes to his senses, preferring the proper Miss Phoebe to the flighty Miss Livvy. He proposes and she accepts.

Although the play ends sentimentally and conventionally with the marriage of two people whose love triumphs over both internal and external obstacles, the play also raises an interesting question: how is a "woman of sense" to deal with the restrictiveness and emptiness of the social conventions which seem to prevent her finding a "man of sense"? For example, Miss Phoebe never hints of her love to Brown for fear her declaration would be unseemly. Ironically, it is only when the woman of sense acts irrationally and unconventionally that the man of sense finally comes to his senses, spurning Miss Livvy for Miss Phoebe. Marriage itself is never questioned. Indeed, spinsterhood is a horror to be avoided at all costs by Barrie's heroines. Only the basis for choosing a partner is questioned. In the end, both Miss Phoebe and Brown come to a realistic assessment of the deleterious effects of social conventions on human relationships. The same social conventions that expect their love to be channeled into marriage in turn almost prevent the occurrence of that very marriage. It is the couple's awareness of the paradox that gives their relationship a chance to succeed.

One of Barrie's early novels, *When a Man's Single,* introduced the fantasy island that was to become a convention of several Barrie plays, including *The Admirable Crichton* and the later play *Mary Rose* (1920). *The Admirable Crichton,* one of Barrie's most popular works, opened 4 November 1902 at the Duke of York's Theatre, running for 328 performances. This play deals with a perennially favorite British subject—the necessity for and the inevitability of class distinctions, defended here by the title character as perfectly "natural."

Crichton, the conventional gentleman's gentleman, despises the attempts of his employer, Lord Loam, to level class distinctions. Crichton sees these efforts as violations of nature, which ultimately governs the establishment of class structure. Nature, says Crichton, will assert itself according to circumstances.

Crichton's observation is tested when he and his employer are shipwrecked on a remote island. Nature does reassert class distinctions, but this time with Crichton as governor because he has the survival skills the others lack. Lord Loam and his family become the servants.

Crichton's adherence to the upper-class convention of sportsmanship brings about his downfall. True to this convention, Crichton insists on "playing the game," inventing and igniting the signal flare that eventually leads to the company's rescue and to his return to his former rank as Lord Loam's butler. Whether on the island or in London, social order is maintained by class considerations, which are in no way indicative of the worth of individuals. The servants as well as the gentry have their share of useless snobs. In the end the better man is not necessarily the one so designated by society but the one who, as Harry M. Geduld observes, "knows his place in society and respects the limitations imposed on him by class barriers."

Barrie's next play, *Little Mary,* opened at Wyndham's Theatre on 24 September 1903 and ran for 208 performances. It was less than popular because of its outrageous premise: Moira Loney, granddaughter of an eccentric Scottish pharmacist, dedicates herself to curing the sickly British with the aid of a three-volume compendium, written by her late grandfather and a medium she has named "Little Mary." "Little Mary," one of Barrie's less fortunate whimsies, turns out to be a euphemism for the stomach. Moira's grandfather had deduced that poor diet is responsible for the enfeebled condition of the British and also for their stuffiness and bad temper. Moira cures her clients by restricting them to one full

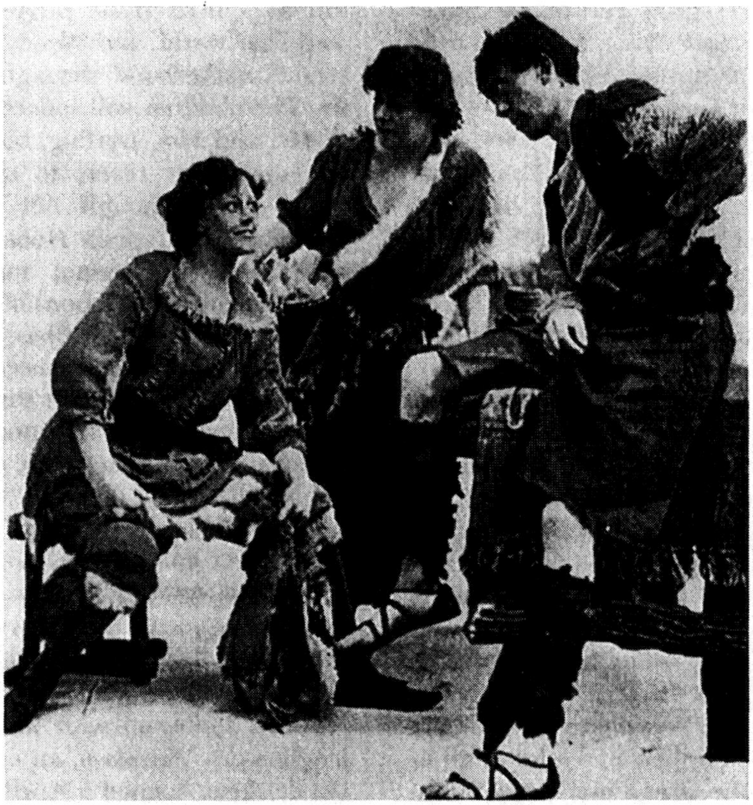

A scene from the 1902 London production of The Admirable Crichton

meal a day and by designing diets that improve their temperament. However, she cures a British lord old enough to be her father by crossing class barriers to marry him. Justifiably, Barrie's critics were dissatisfied with the play.

Barrie atoned for this theatrical peccadillo by writing *Peter Pan; or, The Boy Who Wouldn't Grow Up*, the play on which his reputation rests. Although the play opened on 27 December 1904 at the Duke of York's Theatre, its subsequent production history as well as its genesis are far from simple. Several elements of the play originate in the Thrums novels, and several can be traced back to *The Boy Castaways of Black Lake Island* (1901), a privately printed photographic record, with appropriate titles, of the fantasy games Barrie and the Davies boys played at their summer vacation spot. The boys' nurse, Mary Hodgson, anticipates Wendy; the Barries' St. Bernard, Porthos—Nana; the pirate fantasies and a local resident nicknamed Captain Swarthy—Captain Hook (also partially derived from Hooky Crewe, driver of the Thrums mail coach); and the use of lanterns to light their way—the sparkling Tinker Bell.

Barrie was fond of making up tales to amuse the Davies boys. Elements of these fantasies eventually found their way into the Peter Pan narrative. For example, Barrie's assertion that children were once birds who could fly away led to the creation of Peter Pan himself as an alter ego for the earthbound infant Peter Davies. This second Peter, according to Andrew Birkin, was "named after the Greek God who symbolized nature, paganism, and the amoral world," perhaps as a joke on the boys' nurse, Mary Hodgson, who had earlier chastised Barrie for filling the boys' heads with amoral tales.

Peter Pan made his first literary appearance in a six-chapter story within Barrie's novel *The Little White Bird, or Adventures in Kensington Gardens* (1902). In 1904 the story was produced as a three-act play. Nina Boucicault played Peter Pan, and Sylvia Davies's brother, Gerald DuMaurier, doubled as Mr. Darling and Captain Hook. *Peter Pan* opened in New York on 6 November 1905 with Maude Adams as Peter, and the production shattered all previous engagement records at the Knickerbocker Theatre. Despite the play's astounding success, Barrie continued to revise *Peter Pan* almost every time it began a new run; thus the play's definitive text (in five acts) was not published until 1928.

In 1906 Barrie slightly revised the Peter Pan chapters in *The Little White Bird* and published them as an illustrated children's story, *Peter Pan in Kensington Gardens*. In 1911 the play was converted into another children's story, with an additional chapter, "When Wendy Grew Up." This new chapter, in turn, was based on *When Wendy Grew Up: An Afterthought*—a 1908 addendum to Barrie's play. This dramatic sequel, performed only once (in 1908 as a tribute to Charles Frohman), was not published until 1957, completing the Peter Pan story.

The play opens at the home of Mr. and Mrs. Darling (modeled upon Arthur and Sylvia Davies), who talk of business and of children. The entrance of Nana, the St. Bernard Nursemaid, immediately suggests the intrusion of fantasy into the conventionality of middle-class family life. As the Darlings leave for the evening, Peter Pan, seeking his missing shadow, encounters the Darling children, whom he convinces to fly with him to the Never Land. This land is the home of the "lost boys"—orphans and others somehow separated from their parents and all in need of mothers. If one takes a psychological approach to *Peter Pan*, it is possible to see in this element the loss of the playwright's brother David as well as Barrie's own longing for acceptance by his mother.

The Never Land is also the home of the notorious pirate Captain Hook, pursued by a crocodile who has swallowed a ticking clock; of Tiger Lily and her band of marauding Indians; and of the fairy Tinker Bell, who is insanely jealous of Wendy. Andrew Birkin remarks perceptively that staging *Peter Pan* is like staging "a Barnum and Bailey circus extravaganza." Indeed, he has understood the play better than those readers who insist on deeper meaning. The play is like a multiring circus, with wild animals, ladies in exotic costumes, danger, daring, and flying above all, like a trapeze artist, is Peter Pan. As the ringmaster always says, the circus is a fantasy for "ladies and gentlemen and children of all ages." It captures children's fantasies and offers grownups a chance to relive momentarily the fantasies of their own youth. The play offers the message that growing up is clearly viewed as necessary, but a loss. Thus, the lost boys are not only orphans but also those about to trade their boyhoods for adult roles as businessmen, husbands, and fathers.

Perhaps in no other Barrie play is the necessity to accept one's proper role so evident. The lost boys must trade pirate adventures for the workaday world, and Wendy must realize her potential motherhood through marriage and family. The children will indeed grow into the roles of Mr. and Mrs. Darling, but Mr. and Mrs. Darling can never revert to their childhood. The Never Land, though not without its dangers (for example, Captain Hook and Tiger Lily), remains only a pleasant fantasy long ago exchanged for the responsibilities of middle-class life. In *When Wendy Grew Up: An Afterthought*, Wendy is offered a chance to return to Never Land with Peter Pan, but she refuses because she "is no longer young and innocent." However, she permits her daughter Jane to accompany Peter, hoping that Jane, in turn, "will have a daughter, who will fly away with him" and thus it will "go on for ever and ever . . . so long as children are young and innocent."

Barrie's next play after *Peter Pan* was one of the several half-hour playlets he wrote and his first attempt at pantomime. *Pantaloon* formed part of a double bill with *Alice-Sit-by-the-Fire*, a full-length work. *Pantaloon*, an essay into the commedia dell'arte, opened 5 April 1905 at the Duke of York's Theatre. Columbine, pressured by her father, Pantaloon, to marry Joey the clown, whom she does not love, elopes with Harlequin, whom she does love. Their marriage produces destitution for both the couple and for Pantaloon, but it also produces a son—a natural clown whose talent will eventually rescue the family from its poverty. Unlike most people who must grow into their proper roles, this child is born into his. Obviously, the commedia dell'arte tradition underlying *Pantaloon* dictates a half-hour filled with physical comedy as the play's stock characters act out the roles assigned to them by centuries of dramatic convention.

Physical comedy carries over into the second half of the double bill, *Alice-Sit-by-the-Fire: A Page from a Daughter's Diary*. The madcap heroine of the title returns from India with her husband to the London flat where her seventeen-year-old daughter Amy has been caring for her two younger brothers. Among the most manipulative of Barrie's heroines, Alice desires to resume her proper maternal role but has to resort to deception to gain control over her independent daughter, her indifferent sons, and her conventional husband. The play is filled with misunderstandings, deliberate and accidental, and with people hiding in closets or behind curtains. Although the play has moments of genuine wit and charm, its first run lasted only 115 performances, almost 100 fewer than the first run of the disastrous *Little Mary. Alice-Sit-by-the-Fire* has never been one of Barrie's most popular works.

The following year, two Barrie playlets, *Punch* and *Josephine*, opened 5 April 1906 at the Comedy Theatre. Both pieces were revuelike satires; *Punch* poked fun at George Bernard Shaw while *Josephine* lampooned the statesman Joseph Chamberlain. The audience, however, was not amused, and Barrie's playlets ran less than three weeks. Barrie's next success was *What Every Woman Knows*, which opened 3 September 1908 at the Duke of York's Theatre, where it ran for 384 performances. John Shand, a poor young scholar, marries Maggie Wylie in a match arranged by her wealthy brothers to prevent her remaining a spinster. Through the talented Maggie's efforts, Shand, totally unaware of his wife's contribution, is elected to Parliament. Indeed, it is Maggie who writes his speeches, but she does this so cleverly that Shand believes he is solely responsible for his success. Thus, when he becomes infatuated with the empty-headed but beautiful Lady Sybil, Shand intends to divorce Maggie, but a month's separation convinces him that he cannot function without her, and the couple is reconciled. As the play ends, Maggie reminds her husband, "It's nothing unusual I've done, John. Every man who is high up loves to think that he has done it all himself; and the wife smiles, and lets it go at that. It's our only joke. Every woman knows that."

Understanding one's proper role is vital in this play. For example, Maggie's brothers, former workmen, now wealthy, try uncomfortably to adjust to upper-middle-class life. Maggie, who escapes spinsterhood, becomes a wife and her husband a member of Parliament. Matrimony once again channels both talent and sexual energy. Maggie's talents help John succeed, and once he realizes Maggie's worth, he sensibly terminates his brief infatuation with Lady Sybil. Lady Sybil has charm, which Maggie defines as "a sort of bloom on a woman," but Maggie has self-sacrificing love and consistent good humor that in the end convert a reluctant husband into a willing one.

Barrie himself was never completely satisfied with this play. All but the first act seemed artificial to him. Given the deterioration of his marriage to Mary Ansell—whom he divorced slightly more than a year later—the reconciliation of Maggie and Shand must have seemed contrived, indeed. In fact, his wife's affair with critic Gilbert Cannan, whom she later married, was neither so innocent nor so brief as that of John Shand and Lady Sybil. Thus, this play's light, witty dialogue and happy ending produced a cheerfulness onstage almost completely antithetical to its playwright's somber mood.

Barrie soon went to Switzerland to await his divorce. While there, he wrote another of his half-hour playlets, *The Twelve-Pound Look*, which formed a double bill with a second playlet, *Old Friends*. It opened 1 March 1910 at the Duke of York's Theatre. Sir Harry Sims, an eminently successful man, modeled on Barrie himself, is confronted by his ex-wife Kate, who has left him because she could not endure his success. Having felt suffocated by Harry's materialism, Kate had resolved to leave him as soon as she was sure that she could survive on her own, i.e., as soon as she could earn twelve pounds. Kate had rented a typewriter, learned to type, gotten work through friends, earned her twelve pounds, and left. Although she has given up all her past luxuries, she tells Harry that she now feels more human living among people of modest means. Her parting advice is that Harry should watch his new wife carefully "to see whether the twelve-pound look" is "not coming into her eyes," too.

Old Friends concerns alcoholism. In the manner of Ibsen's *Ghosts*, Mr. Brand, a reformed alcoholic, leaves his daughter Carry a legacy—a predisposition toward alcoholism. The "old friends" of the title are Mr. Brand and his bottle. In the end, Mrs. Brand sets about curing her daughter as she has her husband. Father and daughter thus become "old friends" through shared suffering.

If Barrie uses seriously the dramatic cliché of "ghosts" in *Old Friends*, he burlesques the convention of characters with a "past" in *A Slice of Life: An Advanced Drama*, which opened 7 June 1910 at the Duke of York's Theatre. Reacting to a contrivance of their female butler Fredrika, Mr. and Mrs. Hyphen Brown, speaking as "one erring slice of life to another," reveal their several pasts. Each is shocked to discover that the other has been absolutely moral, since social and dramatic conventions dictate that each must have a "past." The play's deliberate incongruities of speech and action reach beyond fantasy, almost into theater of the absurd.

A slice from Barrie's own life between 1909 and 1913 reveals, in addition to his divorce, several noteworthy events. On 2 April 1909 Edinburgh University conferred on him an honorary

LL.D. In November of that year, his move to a new apartment in Adelphi Terrace, London, made him a neighbor of George Bernard Shaw. In May 1911 a statue of Peter Pan, sculpted by Sir George Frampton and paid for by Barrie, was erected in Kensington Gardens. Finally, in May 1913 George V made him a baronet.

Barrie's dramatic output during these years consisted chiefly of half-hour playlets in the vein of *The Twelve-Pound Look* and *Old Friends*. *Rosalind*, which opened 14 October 1912 at the Duke of York's Theatre, again picks up Barrie's theme of role-playing. Mrs. Page is a middle-aged actress who must play the parts of twenty-nine-year-old women because dramatists do not write parts for those "between the ages of twenty-nine and sixty." When Charles, a stagestruck young man, calls at her vacation cottage in search of Mrs. Page's "daughter," she explains that she is herself the young lady. Insisting that "all life's a game," she tells Charles to "blame the public of whom you are one; the pitiless public that has made me what I am." Nevertheless, with the still-adoring Charles accompanying her, Mrs. Page returns to London to play Rosalind. As she leaves for the "Forest of Arden," she observes, "Rosalind is real and I am Rosalind, [and] . . . everything is real except middle age."

Barrie's own middle age was real enough, however. Confined to his bed with bronchitis, he nevertheless managed to write a sketch, *The Dramatists Get What They Want*. Originally inserted into the British/American revue *Hullo, Ragtime*, it was dropped from the longer piece and produced by itself on 23 December 1912 at the Hippodrome Theatre, London. The playlet satirized both contemporary dramatists and the British censor. Though this sketch was not well received, it suggested to Barrie creative possibilities within the format of the English music hall.

Also not successful was *The Adored One*, which opened 4 September 1913 but was withdrawn after only two weeks. Barrie reworked the first act of this play and retitled it *Seven Women*. As such it premiered 7 April 1917 at the New Theatre, London. The play emphasizes the amazing capacity of women for playing multiple roles, much to the bewilderment of men. Mr. Torvay, a practical joker, tells his dinner guest, Captain Rattray, that seven women will be joining them that evening. Only one woman, Leonora, actually arrives, but during her conversation with Captain Rattray, she exhibits the distinguishing characteristic of each of the seven women mentioned earlier by their host. Eventually Rattray deduces that all seven women are, in truth, different aspects of the same woman. Charmed and intrigued, the bachelor captain decides to add "wife" to Leonora's repertoire.

On the same bill with the original production of *The Adored One* was *The Will* (1913), a play that shares the skepticism about wealth of *The Twelve-Pound Look*. As wealth destroyed the marriage of Harry and Kate Sims, so also it destroys the love of Philip and Emily Ross. The play's opening brings the young couple to the law office of Mr. Devizes Senior to draw up a will out of concern for each other. After having been married some years, the couple return to update their will, but their concern has shifted to their money, and their love has been reduced to mere tolerance. Finally the widowed Ross, now Sir Philip, again comes to revise the will. Recalling his first visit when the couple was genuinely in love, he likens wealth to a black spot "no bigger than a pin's head," like the cancer which spread and destroyed the Devizes' former clerk, Surtees. A wiser Philip desires to help other young couples but realizes "it can't be done with money." The stage directions call for him to go off, "God knows where." Obviously this play is another reflection on Barrie's relationship with Mary Ansell—a relationship he was to agonize over all of his life.

Barrie presents still another version of marriage gone sour in *Half an Hour*, a three-scene playlet that opened 29 September 1913 at the Hippodrome Theatre. Feeling trapped in her stultifying marriage to the wealthy Richard Garson, Lady Lillian decides to elope with her lover, Hugh Paton. Leaving her wedding ring and a note in her husband's desk drawer, she crosses the street to Hugh's house to announce that she will go to Egypt with him. The elated Hugh, on his way to call a taxi, is run over by a bus. Fearing scandal, Lady Lillian returns home, and after some tense moments succeeds in retrieving both her ring and her note. Safe but frustrated, she resumes her empty marriage to Richard. Dramatic contrivances abound in this piece, but perhaps the worst contrivance is the marriage in name only—a domestic situation Barrie once shared with the Garsons.

With the start of World War I, Barrie responded to the tensions of the conflict with propaganda pieces and also with four one-act plays, *The New Word*, *The Old Lady Shows Her Medals*, *A Well-Remembered Voice*, and *Barbara's Wedding*,

Barrie in 1904, portrait by Sir William Nicholson

which were published as *Echoes of the War* (1918). *Der Tag; or, The Tragic Man* opened at the Coliseum Theatre, London, on 21 December 1914. "Der Tag," as Dennis Mackail explains, was "the toast . . . of the German army and navy." Barrie uses a dream within a dream as the Spirit of Culture confronts the emperor (Kaiser Wilhelm), warning him that he has miscalculated both England's will to fight and the effects of the war on his own country and people. She leaves, giving the perplexed emperor a pistol—a silent suggestion that he end the war by committing suicide.

In *The New Word* the war helps a father and son achieve new intimacy. This playlet opened 22 March 1915 at the Duke of York's Theatre. Roger Torrence, a lieutenant, is to leave for duty the next morning. Though Roger and his father have never openly expressed affection for each other for fear of seeming effeminate, their awkward but honest parting conversation leads to Roger's calling his father "dear"—a new word for a new understanding of their relationship. The traditional masculine roles have obscured an affection already present, but another masculine role—that of soldier—finally permits that affection to be expressed. Indeed, only a week before this play opened, Barrie's favorite of the Davies boys, George, had been killed in France, leaving much between them unsaid.

Sharing the bill with *The New Word* was *Rosy Rapture, the Pride of the Beauty Chorus*, a revue written to showcase the dubious talents of the Parisian dancer Gaby Deslys, with whom Barrie was inexplicably fascinated. Even the patriotism of the revue's one wartime scene was insufficient to rescue the work itself. Barrie's own sense of patriotism led him to turn his theatrical talents to raising money for charitable causes. On 19 November he presented a sketch, *The Fatal Typist*, to benefit the Australian wounded. The following spring, 7 March 1916, he presented *The Real Thing at Last*, described by Mackail as "a burlesque, modern, motion picture version of *Macbeth*," for the benefit of the YMCA.

The war also formed the backdrop for Barrie's next full-length play, *A Kiss for Cinderella*, which opened 16 March 1916 at Wyndham's Theatre. Miss Jane Thing, "a slavey," escapes the bleakness of her life by fantasizing that she is Cinderella, awaiting an invitation from the Prince of Wales to a ball at which she will become engaged to him. In her poor living quarters, Jane cares for four children—one of whom is German. Her efforts to communicate with the German child's family on the Continent raise official suspicions, and Robert, the policeman, comes to investigate. He is touched by Jane's lovingness and also by her seemingly harmless fantasy, as she sits outside on her doorstep waiting for the coveted invitation she is sure will arrive that very evening. Her fantasy is indeed realized but only in the long dream scene that follows, wherein the characters are slightly altered versions of those outside her dream. Jane's long sleep in the London chill results in a fatal illness. Before she dies, however, Robert arrives to propose, not with an engagement ring, but with a pair of slippers. "Cinderella" accepts the proposal of her "Prince" and receives her first and only kiss.

Criticized as a superimposition of the pathos of "The Little Match Girl" over the happy ending of "Cinderella," Cinderella's death, nevertheless, is necessary to assure that her newly realized fantasy will not be spoiled by the realities of marriage. Given Barrie's growing cynicism about wedlock, "they lived happily ever after" would have been the truly unrealizable fantasy for Cinderella and her Prince.

Over the next year, Barrie wrote two more pieces for charity benefits. The first, *Shakespeare's Legacy*, was performed 14 April 1916 at Drury Lane Theatre, London, to benefit the YWCA. Its two jokes concerned a heroine who could box and the revelation that Shakespeare was a Scotsman. The second, *Reconstructing the Crime*, was performed 16 February 1917 at the Palace Theatre, London, to benefit the Cavendish Square War Hospital Depot. The piece consisted of six scenes plus a ballet—*The Origin of Harlequin*. Mackail describes the work as "a series of personal and professional jokes" with an all-star cast that included H. B. Irving and Irene Vanbrugh.

Barrie followed these skits with another echo of the war—*The Old Lady Shows Her Medals*, which opened at the New Theatre on 7 April 1917. In this play another Barrie heroine realizes a fantasy and finds her proper role when the soldier "son" she has invented unexpectedly materializes. Mrs. Dowey, a Scottish charwoman from Thrums, feels left out when her friends brag about their soldier sons, so she scavenges envelopes from wastebaskets and pretends they are letters from her son Kenneth—a hero with the elite Black Watch. Mrs. Dowey has selected her "son's" name from newspaper reports, never dreaming that the real Kenneth will appear in London, still less on her own doorstep through the misguided intervention of the local clergyman. Since Kenneth is conveniently an orphan, one of the "lost boys," he is in need of a mother. As his leave draws to a close, he finally accepts the old lady in that role, remarking that women earn their medals as well as men. Kenneth returns to duty and is killed at the front, leaving Mrs. Dowey with happy memories and genuine letters.

This play incorporates three sets of tensions: tension between Mrs. Dowey and her friends as they brag about their sons; tension between Mrs. Dowey and Kenneth as they tentatively explore the possibilities of a mother-son relationship; and tension caused by the war, which leads Mrs. Dowey to invent her son and also leads to Kenneth's death. As in *A Kiss for Cinderella*, the fantasy comes true, and Kenneth's death allows the mother-son relationship to remain an idyllic memory, unscarred by the realities of family life.

By 1917 Mary Ansell's marriage to Gilbert Cannan was nearly over. In fact, Cannan had deserted her for another woman. Barrie, touched by his former wife's distress, offered financial aid but had no intention of trying marriage a second time, thereby crushing her hopes for a reconciliation. One of Barrie's characters had earlier remarked that "in this world there are no second chances" (*The Little White Bird*), and what was true for the Barries was also true for the couples in *Dear Brutus*, which opened 17 October 1917 at Wyndham's Theatre, running for 365 performances. A decade earlier Barrie had sketched out a play to be called "The Second Chance." Its main point, carried over into *Dear Brutus*, was that if people were given second chances, they would simply repeat past mistakes because, as Shakespeare had already observed, "The fault, dear Brutus, is not in our stars, / But in ourselves. . . ." An enchanted wood, similar to that of *A Midsummer Night's Dream*, allows the characters—eight houseguests of the enigmatic Mr. Lob—to live out the "second chance" each has fantasized. But the realization of their fantasies does not bring satisfaction because the characters remain the same. Hence there are no genuine second chances for them, not because of fate or chance, but because the characters themselves are incapable of creating them.

After the success of *Dear Brutus*, Barrie again turned to writing playlets about the war. *La Politesse* and *A Well-Remembered Voice* opened 28 June 1918 at Wyndham's Theatre, forming two-thirds of a triple bill that included a revival of *The Origin of Harlequin* (the ballet sequence from *Reconstructing the Crime*, 1917). The first performance was to benefit the Countess of Lytton's hospital.

La Politesse is a sketch concerning two British soldiers who take refuge in a French house on its owner's wedding night. The comedy depends on the soldier's misinterpretation of their hosts' marital status and also on the soldier's subsequent misadventures in the pigsty on the property. Although six different typescripts testify to the care Barrie devoted to this piece, its first performance was also its last.

A Well-Remembered Voice opens with a séance at which Mrs. Don is trying to make contact with her dead soldier son, Dick, while a skeptical Mr. Don looks on. Mr. Don, who has always felt excluded from his son's affections, is surprised when, after the séance has broken up, Dick materializes to him. Dick explains that he can return from the dead to appear to only one person and that he is aware that it is really his father who misses him most. The scene is reminiscent of the final conversation between father and son in *The New Word*. Decades earlier George Davies as a child had uttered a line that ever afterward intrigued Barrie—"to die will be an awfully big adventure." In this play, Dick recounts his death on the battlefield. He is at first hardly aware of it, but then joins the dead of both sides in a camaraderie that crosses barriers of nationality. Indeed, they are all "lost boys," and the land of the dead, not surprisingly, is like the Never Land. The living, however, must put aside memories and continue to live, and Dick's visit—albeit brief and not to be repeated—gives Mr. Don the courage to pick up his life once again.

Barrie, too, had to put aside memories of George, and his new secretary, Lady Cynthia Asquith, helped him to do so. She soon became Barrie's friend and confidante and remained so for the rest of his life. In 1919, the year after he met Lady Cynthia, he was elected to the largely ceremonial office of Rector of Saint Andrews University in Scotland, an honor that greatly pleased him.

In 1920 Barrie once again became infatuated with a dancer, Mlle Lydia Lopokova, a member of Diaghilev's Russian ballet. Barrie began to write a play for her about the life of a Russian dancer. When Mlle Lopokova mysteriously disappeared for a short time, Barrie condensed his intended three-act play into a one-act ballet along the same lines as the original, and *The Truth About the Russian Dancers* opened 15 March 1920 at the Coliseum Theatre.

Barrie followed this slight piece with perhaps his most enigmatic play, *Mary Rose*, which opened 22 April 1920 at the Haymarket Theatre, where it ran for 399 performances. Much earlier in his career, Barrie had toyed with the idea of writing a play based on the notion that all ghosts are really women looking for their lost children. However, as *Mary Rose* opens, a now-grown-up son is looking for his parents. He returns to the old family home, haunted by the ghost of his mother, Mary Rose. Flashbacks reveal Mary Rose's involvement with the mysterious "Island that Likes to be Visited." People vanish suddenly on this island, only to come back years later unchanged and unaware of where they have been. This island calls only to a select few, and Mary Rose is among those. As a girl, she had disappeared for several months on the island, and years later, as a wife with a young son, she returns to visit the island and disappears for twenty-five years. When Mary Rose returns, she is as youthful as when she disappeared, but her husband and parents have aged. Her son Harry has run away to sea, and the news kills Mary Rose, whose ghost continues to search for him. When the action returns to the present, it focuses on the adult Harry, who expects his presence to end his mother's search. However, Mary Rose has been searching for so long that she no longer remembers the object of her search; called by celestial music, she walks off into the empyrean.

Interpreted psychologically, this play reflects Barrie's inability to win the attention and affection of his mother, who is now forever lost to him. Dennis Mackail, on the other hand, calls the play "magic" and "a tremendous frontal assault on the emotions." Not even Barrie himself, Mackail asserts, knew what the play meant.

Barrie had begun incubating the idea for *Mary Rose* some fifteen years earlier when, according to Mackail, he became intrigued by two lines in the Scottish ballad *Kilmeny*: "For Kilmeny had been she ken'd not where / And Kilmeny had seen what she could not declare." Such disappearances, says Mackail, were an established part of Scottish legend and always inexplicable—the result of supernatural forces working out their own purposes. In *Mary Rose*, therefore, the fault lies in the stars and not in ourselves as it did in *Dear Brutus*.

Discovering where the fault lay was precisely the problem in Barrie's only murder mystery, *Shall We Join the Ladies?* Performed at the Royal Academy of Dramatic Arts on 27 May 1921, this playlet was but the first act of a projected mystery that Barrie was never able to finish. It exploits all the conventions of the tradition, including a house full of guests, one of whom is a murderer. Since the play was unfinished, the murderer could never be known, so the playlet's attraction was its star-studded cast, including Irene Vanbrugh, Fay Compton, Dion Boucicault, and Sybil Thorndike. Two years later a revival of this playlet at Saint Martin's Theatre ran for 407 performances.

It was Michael Davies who had asked Barrie to write a mystery play for him. On 19 May 1921, little more than a week before *Shall We Join the Ladies?* was performed, Michael had committed suicide, plunging Barrie into years of almost unmitigated gloom. These same years brought many honors, however, including the Order of Merit in 1922, an honorary D.Litt. from Oxford in 1926, an honorary LL.D. from Cambridge in 1930, and installation as Chancellor of Edinburgh University in that same year.

Eventually Barrie emerged sufficiently from his depression and reclusiveness to become a much-sought-after speaker and to host famous politicians and entertainers in his London apartment. He had become well-known as a public personality. His years as a dramatist, however, were nearly over.

From 1921 until his death in 1937 only two new Barrie plays were produced. The first of these, *Barbara's Wedding*, was another echo of the war that Barrie had actually written shortly before the Armistice had been signed. In this play, which opened 23 August 1927 at the Savoy Theatre, the colonel, Barbara's senile father, cannot adjust to the present. Instead, he imagines that Barbara is married to her childhood sweetheart Billy, who has been killed in the war. Barbara is actually married to the family's former gardener—another sign that times have changed. In the end the young couple move into the future while the colonel remains imprisoned in the past.

Barrie's last play, *The Boy David* (1936), was not well received. After a premiere performance at the King's Theatre, Edinburgh, it was taken to London, where it ran for only fifty-five performances. The play, however, deserves more credit than has customarily been given to it. Based on material from 1 Samuel, the play captures the young David at his critical transition from boy to man to king of Israel. It is the same transition that Michelangelo has captured in his statue of David. Barrie shows that he has not lost his understanding of children in the scenes between Saul and David, which are as entrancing as any in the canon of Barrie's plays. The use of a dream to recount David's history is both economical and effective. The dialogue retains the wit of Barrie's best efforts, although there are some lapses into sentimentality and preciosity. This play also recapitulates Barrie's preoccupation with the discovery and acceptance of one's proper role; for David that role is the kingship of Israel. David's mother must lose her son; David must lose his boyhood; and Saul, who has already lost his way, must also lose his throne. As in *Dear Brutus*, so in this play: there are no second chances.

In failing health, the seventy-seven-year-old Barrie died on 19 June 1937, with Cynthia Asquith at his bedside. In accordance with his wishes, Barrie was buried next to his mother, Margaret Ogilvy, and his brother David in Kirriemuir.

Barrie's accomplishment was not so much the wealth he himself detested but rather the fantasies he created, his legacy to the theater. Unfortunately, these fantasies captured the realities of an era no longer recognizable to a new generation. Except for the universal fantasy of *Peter Pan*, most of the plays of the once-celebrated Barrie are today seldom produced and just as seldom read. Ironically, this neglect may have resulted from the extraordinary success of *Peter Pan*, for its popularity seems to have marked Barrie, indeed almost indelibly, as an author of children's plays and also as a writer whose fantasies were too sentimental. Certainly Barrie could be childlike. What other playwright could have termed dying "an awfully big adventure"? However, he could also be sophisticated, and in those parts of his more intellectual comedies—for example, *What Every Woman Knows* and *The Admirable Crichton*—where sentimentality does not intrude, his work compares favorably with that of his neighbor, George Bernard Shaw. Like Shaw, Barrie's sense of character is sure, his dialogue is witty, and his analysis of social roles, while not iconoclastic, is nevertheless intriguing. Moreover, Barrie, like Shaw, wrote plays that work onstage, despite sometimes obvious weaknesses in their scripts.

Thus, a reconsideration of Barrie's achievements as a dramatist seems in order. Any such critical reappraisal of Barrie's work must first abandon the presupposition that *all* of his plays are inferior to *Peter Pan* and, second, must subordinate the author's psychological problems to his literary aesthetic, which transcends them. Though Barrie's own characters were given no second chances, perhaps their author deserves one.

Bibliographies:

B. D. Cutler, *Sir James M. Barrie: A Bibliography* (New York: Greenberg, 1931);

Allardyce Nicoll, "Hand-List of Plays, 1850-1900," in his *A History of English Drama, 1660-1900*, volume 5, second edition (Cambridge: Cambridge University Press, 1959), pp. 250-251;

Nicoll, "Hand-List of Plays, 1900-1930," in his *English Drama: 1900-1930* (Cambridge: Cambridge University Press, 1973), pp. 496-497.

References:

Andrew Birkin, *Barrie and his Lost Boys* (New York: Clarkson N. Potter, 1979);

William Blackburn, "*Peter Pan* and the Contemporary Adolescent Novel," in *The Child and the Story: An Exploration of Narrative Forms*, edited by Priscilla Ord (Boston: Children's Literature Association, 1983), pp. 47-53;

Janet Dunbar, *J. M. Barrie. The Man Behind the Image* (Boston: Houghton Mifflin, 1970);

Michael Egan, "The Neverland of Id: Barrie, *Peter Pan*, and Freud," *Children's Literature*, 10 (1982): 37-55;

Michael Foster, "*Peter Pan*: The Lost Act," *Mythlore*, 14 (Summer 1988): 27-32;

Harry M. Geduld, *James Barrie* (New York: Twayne, 1971);

Lois Rauch Gibson, "Beyond the Apron: Archetypes, Stereotypes, and Alternative Portrayals of Mothers in Children's Literature," *Children's Literature Association Quarterly*, 13 (Winter 1988): 177-181;

Martin Green, "The Charm of *Peter Pan*," *Children's Literature*, 9 (1981): 19-27;

R. D. S. Jack, "Barrie as Journey-Dramatist: A Study of 'Walker, London,' " *Studies in Scottish Literature*, 22 (1987): 60-77;

Jack, "From Novel to Drama: J. M. Barrie's *Quality Street*," *Scottish Literary Journal*, 14 (November 1987): 48-61;

Dennis Mackail, *The Story of J. M. B.* (New York: Scribners, 1941);

Patricia Read Russell, "Parallel Romantic Fantasies: Barrie's *Peter Pan* and Spielberg's *E. T.: The Extraterrestrial*," *Children's Literature Association Quarterly*, 8 (Winter 1983): 28-30.

Papers:

The largest collection of Barrie materials is in the Beinecke Library at Yale University. The original draft of *Peter Pan* is in the Lilly Library Collection at the University of Indiana. Other materials are held at the New York Public Library in its Berg Collection and by the Scottish National Trust.

Arnold Bennett

(27 May 1867 - 27 March 1931)

This entry was written by Anita Miller for DLB 34: British Novelists, 1890-1929: Traditionalists.

See also the Bennett entries in DLB 10: Modern British Dramatists, 1900-1945: Part One *and* DLB 98: Modern British Essayists: First Series.

Arnold Bennett, 1928 (Collection of Richard Bennett)

BOOKS: *A Man from the North* (London & New York: John Lane / Bodley Head, 1898);

Journalism for Women: A Practical Guide (London: John Lane / Bodley Head, 1898);

Polite Farces for the Drawing Room (London: Lamley, 1900 [i.e., 1899]);

Fame and Fiction: An Enquiry into Certain Popularities (London: Richards, 1901; New York: Dutton, 1901);

The Grand Babylon Hotel: A Fantasia on Modern Themes (London: Chatto & Windus, 1902); republished as *T. Racksole and Daughter: Or, the Result of an American Millionaire Ordering Steak and a Bottle of Bass at the Grand Babylon Hotel, London* (New York: New Amsterdam Book Company, 1902);

Anna of the Five Towns (London: Chatto & Windus, 1902; New York: McClure, Phillips, 1903);

The Gates of Wrath: A Melodrama (London: Chatto & Windus, 1903);

The Truth About an Author, anonymous (London: Constable, 1903; New York: Doran, 1911);

How to Become an Author: A Practical Guide (London: Pearson, 1903);

Leonora: A Novel (London: Chatto & Windus, 1903; New York: Doran, 1910);

A Great Man: A Frolic (London: Chatto & Windus, 1904; New York: Doran, 1911);

Teresa of Watling Street: A Fantasia on Modern Themes (London: Chatto & Windus, 1904);

Tales of the Five Towns (London: Chatto & Windus, 1905);

The Loot of Cities: Being Adventures of a Millionaire in Search of Joy (A Fantasia) (London: Rivers, 1905); enlarged as *The Loot of Cities: Being the Adventures of a Millionaire in Search of Joy (A Fantasia) and Other Stories* (London: Nelson, 1917);

Sacred and Profane Love: A Novel in Three Episodes (London: Chatto & Windus, 1905); republished as *The Book of Carlotta: Being a Revised Edition (With New Preface) of Sacred and Profane Love . . .* (New York: Doran, 1911);

Hugo: A Fantasia on Modern Themes (London: Chatto & Windus, 1906; New York: Buckles, 1906);

Whom God Hath Joined (London: Nutt, 1906; New York: Doran, 1911);

The Sinews of War: A Romance of London and the Sea, by Bennett and Eden Phillpotts (London: Laurie, 1906); republished as *Doubloons* (New York: McClure, Phillips, 1906);

Things That Interested Me: Being Leaves from a Journal (Burslem: Privately printed, 1906);
The Ghost: A Fantasia on Modern Themes (London: Chatto & Windus, 1907; Boston: Turner, 1907);
The Reasonable Life: Being Hints for Men and Women (London: Fifield, 1907); revised as *Mental Efficiency, and Other Hints to Men and Women* (New York: Doran, 1911; London: Hodder & Stoughton, 1912);
The Grim Smile of the Five Towns (London: Chapman & Hall, 1907);
The City of Pleasure: A Fantasia on Modern Themes (London: Chatto & Windus, 1907; New York: Doran, 1915);
Things Which Have Interested Me: Being Leaves from a Journal, Second Series (Burslem: Privately printed, 1907);
The Statue, by Bennett and Phillpotts (London: Cassell, 1908; New York: Moffatt Yard, 1908);
Buried Alive: A Tale of These Days (London: Chapman & Hall, 1908; New York: Brentano's, 1910);
How to Live on 24 Hours a Day (London: New Age Press, 1908; New York: Doran, 1910);
The Old Wives' Tale: A Novel (London: Chapman & Hall, 1908; New York: Doran, 1911);
The Human Machine (London: New Age Press, 1908; New York: Doran, 1911);
Things Which Have Interested Me, Third Series (Burslem: Privately printed, 1908);
Literary Taste: How to Form It, with Detailed Instructions for Collecting a Complete Library of English Literature (London: New Age Press, 1909; New York: Doran, 1911; revised, with an American book list by John Farrar, New York: Doran, 1927; revised edition, with additional lists by Frank Swinnerton, London: Hodder & Stoughton, 1937; revised, London: Hodder & Stoughton, 1912; New York: Doran, 1927);
Cupid and Commonsense: A Play in Four Acts (London: New Age Press, 1909);
What the Public Wants: (A Play in Four Acts) (London: Duckworth, 1909; New York: Doran, 1911);
The Glimpse: An Adventure of the Soul (London: Chapman & Hall, 1909; New York: Appleton, 1909);
The Present Crisis (Burslem: Privately printed, 1910);
Helen with the High Hand: An Idyllic Diversion (London: Chapman & Hall, 1910; New York: Doran, 1910);
Clayhanger (London: Methuen, 1910; New York: Dutton, 1910);
The Card: A Story of Adventure in the Five Towns (London: Methuen, 1911); republished as *Denny the Audacious* (New York: Dutton, 1911);
Hilda Lessways (London: Methuen, 1911; New York: Dutton, 1911);
The Honeymoon: A Comedy in Three Acts (London: Methuen, 1911; New York: Doran, 1912);
The Feast of St. Friend (London: Hodder & Stoughton, 1911; New York: Doran, 1911); republished as *Friendship and Happiness: A Plea for the Feast of St. Friend* (London: Hodder & Stoughton, 1914);
The Matador of the Five Towns, and Other Stories (London: Methuen, 1912; with somewhat different contents, New York: Doran, 1912);
Milestones: A Play in Three Acts, by Bennett and Edward Knoblock (London: Methuen, 1912; New York: Doran, 1912);
Those United States (London: Secker, 1912); republished as *Your United States: Impressions of a First Visit* (New York & London: Harper, 1912);
The Regent: A Five Towns Story of Adventure in London (London: Methuen, 1913); republished as *The Old Adam: A Story of Adventure* (New York: Doran, 1913);
The Great Adventure: A Play of Fancy in Four Acts (London: Methuen, 1913; New York: Doran, 1913);
The Plain Man and His Wife (London: Hodder & Stoughton, 1913); republished as *Married Life: The Plain Man and His Wife* (New York: Doran, 1913); republished as *Marriage (The Plain Man and His Wife)* (London: Hodder & Stoughton, 1916);
Paris Nights and Other Impressions of Places and People (London: Hodder & Stoughton, 1913; New York: Doran, 1913);
The Author's Craft (New York: Doran, 1914; London, New York & Toronto: Hodder & Stoughton, 1915 [i.e., 1914]);
The Price of Love: A Tale (London: Methuen, 1914; New York & London: Harper, 1914);
Liberty! A Statement of the British Case (London: Hodder & Stoughton, 1914; New York: Doran, 1914);
From the Log of the Velsa (New York: Century, 1914; London: Chatto & Windus, 1920);

Bennett's birthplace, 90 Hope Street, Hanley, over his father's pawnshop, and the bigger house at 205 Waterloo Road, Burslem, where the Bennett family moved in 1878, two years after Enoch Bennett became a solicitor

Over There: War Scenes on the Western Front (London: Methuen, 1915; New York: Doran, 1915);

These Twain (New York: Doran, 1915; London: Methuen, 1916);

The Lion's Share (London: Cassell, 1916; New York: Doran, 1916);

Books and Persons: Being Comments on a Past Epoch, 1908-1911 (London: Chatto & Windus, 1917; New York: Doran, 1917);

The Pretty Lady: A Novel (London: Cassell, 1918; New York: Doran, 1918);

The Title: A Comedy in Three Acts (London: Chatto & Windus, 1918; New York: Doran, 1918);

Self and Self-Management: Essays About Existing (London: Hodder & Stoughton, 1918; New York: Doran, 1918);

The Roll-Call (London: Hutchinson, 1919; New York: Doran, 1919);

Judith: A Play in Three Acts, Founded on the Apocryphal Book of "Judith" (London: Chatto & Windus, 1919; New York: Doran, 1919);

Sacred and Profane Love: A Play in Four Acts Founded Upon the Novel of the Same Name (London: Chatto & Windus, 1919; New York: Doran, 1920);

Our Women: Chapters on the Sex-Discord (London: Cassell, 1920; New York: Doran, 1920);

Things That Have Interested Me (London: Chatto & Windus, 1921; New York: Doran, 1921);

Body and Soul: A Play in Four Acts (New York: Doran, 1921; London: Chatto & Windus, 1922);

The Love Match: A Play in Five Scenes (London: Chatto & Windus, 1922; New York: Doran, 1922);

Mr. Prohack (London: Methuen, 1922; New York: Doran, 1922);

Lilian (London: Cassell, 1922; New York: Doran, 1922);

Things That Have Interested Me, Second Series (London: Chatto & Windus, 1923; New York: Doran, 1923);

How to Make the Best of Life (London: Hodder & Stoughton, 1923; New York: Doran, 1923);

Don Juan de Marana: A Play in Four Acts (London: Laurie, 1923);

Riceyman Steps: A Novel (London: Cassell, 1923; New York: Doran, 1923);

London Life: A Play in Three Acts and Nine Scenes, by Bennett and Knoblock (London: Chatto & Windus, 1924; New York: Doran, 1924);

Marguerite Soulie Bennett, whom Bennett married in Paris, 4 July 1907 (photograph by H. C. Murcott)

The Bright Island (London: Golden Cockerel Press, 1924; New York: Doran, 1925);

Elsie and the Child: A Tale of Riceyman Steps and Other Stories (London: Cassell, 1924); republished as *Elsie and the Child, and Other Stories* (New York: Doran, 1924);

The Clayhanger Family. I. Clayhanger. II. Hilda Lessways. III. These Twain. (London: Methuen, 1925);

Things That Have Interested Me, Third Series (London: Chatto & Windus, 1926; New York: Doran, 1926);

Lord Raingo (London: Cassell, 1926; New York: Doran, 1926);

The Woman Who Stole Everything and Other Stories (London: Cassell, 1927; New York: Doran, 1927);

Mr. Prohack: A Comedy in Three Acts, by Bennett and Knoblock (London: Chatto & Windus, 1927; Garden City, N.Y.: Doubleday, Doran, 1928);

The Vanguard: A Fantasia (New York: Doran, 1927); republished as *The Strange Vanguard: A Fantasia* (London: Cassell, 1928);

The Savour of Life: Essays in Gusto (London: Cassell, 1928; Garden City, N.Y.: Doubleday, Doran, 1928);

Mediterranean Scenes: Rome—Greece—Constantinople (London: Cassell, 1928);

Accident (Garden City, N.Y.: Doubleday, Doran, 1928; London: Cassell, 1929);

The Religious Interregnum (London: Benn, 1929);

"Piccadilly": The Story of the Film (London: Readers Library, 1929);

Journal 1929 (London: Cassell, 1930); republished as *Journal of Things New and Old* (Garden City, N.Y.: Doubleday, Doran, 1930);

Imperial Palace (London: Cassell, 1930; Garden City, N.Y.: Doubleday, Doran, 1930);

Venus Rising from the Sea (London: Cassell, 1931);

The Night Visitor and Other Stories (London: Cassell, 1931; Garden City, N.Y.: Doubleday, Doran, 1931);

Dream of Destiny: An Unfinished Novel and Venus Rising from the Sea (London: Cassell, 1932); republished as *Stroke of Luck and Dream of Destiny: An Unfinished Novel* (Garden City, N.Y.: Doubleday, Doran, 1932);

The Journals of Arnold Bennett, 1896-1928, 3 volumes, edited by Newman Flower (London: Cassell, 1932-1933; revised edition, New York: Viking, 1932-1933); republished with additions from the years 1906-1907 and with the *Florentine Journal* (London: Penguin, 1971);

Florentine Journal, 1st April 25-May 1910, edited by Dorothy Cheston Bennett (London: Chatto & Windus, 1967);

The Author's Craft and Other Critical Writings of Arnold Bennett, edited by Samuel Hynes (Lincoln: University of Nebraska Press, 1968);

Arnold Bennett: The Evening Standard Years. Books & Persons, 1926-1931, edited by Andrew Mylett (London: Chatto & Windus, 1974; Hamden, Conn.: Shoe String Press, 1974);

Sketches for Autobiography, edited by James Hepburn (London & Boston: Allen & Unwin, 1980).

Straw was laid in the streets outside Chiltern Court, to deaden sounds, while Arnold Bennett lay dying in his flat there. It was the last time the city of London was to pay such respect to a public figure. To some extent this respect was nostalgic because by 1931 Bennett's reputation was already considerably frayed. He had been too successful; he had written too much. His short stories and his journalism were appearing in magazines and newspapers on both sides of the Atlantic; his novels *The Old Wives' Tale* (1908) and the Clayhanger trilogy—*Clayhanger* (1910), *Hilda Lessways* (1911), and *These Twain* (1915)—were considered to be masterpieces; *Riceyman Steps* came close to being a best-seller and in 1924 won the James Tait Black Memorial Prize for fiction published in 1923. His book reviews, which appeared each Thursday in the London *Evening Standard*, were so influential that he was at his death far and away the most important literary critic in Europe.

If all this success were not enough to invite envy and spite, Bennett was also a member of the establishment: he served in 1918 as Director of Propaganda for the Ministry of Information, his opinion on political matters was sought and given, and he visited Checquers with Lord Beaverbrook, his close friend. He lived well, traveled extensively, often in his own yacht, and kept servants. He was thus a target for ambitious young writers; Virginia Woolf in particular attacked him in her essay *Mr Bennett and Mrs. Brown*, published as a pamphlet in 1924. He was made to look old-fashioned by Woolf and was caricatured as the philistine Mr. Nixon by Ezra Pound in his poem *Hugh Selwyn Mauberley* (1920). Pound admitted decades later that he had never read Arnold Bennett's work and knew nothing about him, except that he was rich and owned a yacht.

This reputation for good living damaged Bennett's credibility as a writer. The Bloomsbury set ridiculed him because he came from the pottery district and retained his Northern accent throughout his life. His father had kept a pawnshop before qualifying as a lawyer in early middle age. This sort of thing was used as a weapon against Bennett by people too young or too careless to remember that he had fought the good fight against English philistinism all his life; his tastes were sophisticated, encompassing painting, music, architecture, and interior decoration, and especially French literature. Long before Pound discovered French poet Paul Verlaine, Bennett was attempting to bring his work to the attention of the English public.

Enoch Arnold Bennett was born on 27 May 1867 in Hanley, one of the six Staffordshire towns which were later to become federated into Stoke-on-Trent, and which he was to make famous as—for purposes of euphony—the Five

Bennett in Paris, 1907. Marguerite Bennett kept this photograph, inscribed "A son coeur, Marguerite. Arnold," on her dressing table until her death.

Towns. He was the eldest of nine children of Enoch and Sarah Ann Bennett, the son and daughter, respectively, of a potter and a tailor. Enoch Bennett, a pawnbroker, was a man of iron will and strong ambition: he studied law at night, and in 1876 he became a solicitor and moved his family to Burslem, another of the six towns. In 1878 they moved to a larger house at 205 Waterloo Road in the Cobridge neighborhood of Burslem. Until recently this house was the site of the Arnold Bennett Museum.

In 1883 Enoch Arnold Bennett left school (Middle School, Newcastle-under-Lyme) to clerk in his father's law office. It was his father's wish that the boy become a lawyer. Enoch Arnold had literary interests, however; he continued his studies at night at the Wedgwood Institute and in 1885 passed matriculation examinations for London University. His father did not wish him to attend university. In 1888 Enoch Arnold twice failed his legal examinations; in November of that year he began to write weekly columns for two Staffordshire newspapers. He read voraciously and taught himself to read French. He admired French novelists Honoré de Balzac and

Gustave Flaubert, and among English writers, he was impressed with the works of George Moore and Thomas Hardy. He often said that it was Moore's *A Mummer's Wife* which awakened him to the "romantic" possibilities of the pottery district in which he had spent his formative years.

After Bennett secured a position as a shorthand clerk in a London law office in 1889, his father reluctantly consented to his move to London. Once there he began to move in "cultural" circles and to put his considerable knowledge of books to use: he collected and sold, by mail order, old and rare books and sent his stories to London periodicals.

In 1894 he gave up the law, which held little interest for him, and, with his father's help, became assistant editor of the weekly ladies' magazine *Woman*. The following year the *Yellow Book* published his story "A Letter Home," which he had written in 1893; and he began work on a serious novel, *A Man from the North* (1898), a realistic picture of the attempts of a young man from the pottery district to adjust to life in London as an office clerk. Carefully and sensitively written, without sentimentality or self-conscious passages, the book is an impressive debut.

His first London publication had been in *Tit-Bits* magazine: a prizewinning parody of Grant Allen's *What's Bred in the Bone* (1891). Critics have been fond of contrasting *Tit-Bits* and *Yellow Book* as examples of a striking split in Bennett's intellectual processes between serious literary and crass commercial production. The impression they give is that these stories appeared at the same time: in fact the *Tit-Bits* parody appeared in December of 1891, nearly three and one half years before the *Yellow Book* story. In any case Bennett saw no difficulty in writing serious fiction, light or sensational fiction, and journalism, all at more or less the same time. In 1898 *Journalism for Women* was published in March, a month after John Lane brought out *A Man from the North*; in the same year he began a series of critical articles (published in 1901 as *Fame and Fiction*) for the literary weekly *Academy*, and he began work on a series "Love and Life" (published as *The Ghost* in 1907), which was to run in 1900 in the English woman's magazine *Hearth & Home*. Thus at the outset of his career Bennett set a pattern of work: he financed his elegant style of living and his serious work by journalism and light popular work. This is not to say that he did not respect his popular pieces; he took great pride in his journalism and enjoyed writing it, and his sensational or light novels as well.

In 1900 he gave up the editorship of *Woman*, to which he had succeeded in November of 1896, in order to concentrate all of his considerable energies on writing. The following year he began his association with the literary agent J. B. Pinker, which was to last until Pinker's death in 1922. While he continued to contribute signed and unsigned pieces of journalism (book and play reviews and comments on literature, art, travel, and social phenomena such as insurance companies) to various London periodicals, he continued also his pattern of publishing both serious and sensational fiction by producing in 1902 his second serious novel, *Anna of the Five Towns*, and his second sensational novel, *The Grand Babylon Hotel*. *Anna of the Five Towns* is written in the same restrained, unsentimental style as *A Man from the North*, but it is a more ambitious and interesting book, the first to be written in the Five Towns setting. Here is Bennett's first use of the Northern characters he knew so well: their materialism and the narrowness of their lives. The restraint and meticulous craftsmanship of the novel were undoubtedly Bennett's legacy from George Moore, Ivan Turgenev and Guy de Maupassant, the Goncourts, and Flaubert. There is strength and vigor as well in the portrait, for instance, of Anna's father, Ephraim Tellwright: the first of many such portraits in Bennett's gallery of grotesques. Both *Anna of the Five Towns* and *The Grand Babylon Hotel*, a lively, amusing thriller, received good critical notices.

In 1902 Bennett's father died at the farm in Bedfordshire which Bennett had rented for himself, his parents, and his sister Tertia. A year later Tertia became engaged to be married, and Sarah Ann Bennett returned to Staffordshire to live. Bennett had long wanted to live in France, the home of his literary mentors, and he felt free to move there. Before he left England he wrote his autobiographical book *The Truth About an Author*, which appeared anonymously in 1903. The tone of the book is light; Bennett's intention was to tease literary pomposity and pretentiousness. But the effect was unfortunate: Bennett's biographer Reginald Pound says that this book "struck a bounderish note in the ears of critics . . . because it linked the sanctities of authorship with the crudities of commerce." The book hurt Bennett, just as Anthony Trollope's *An Autobiography* (1883) hurt Trollope (with its revelation that the Victorian novelist wrote every day for a set

Bennett at work on his 1908 novel The Old Wives' Tale

number of hours and went on to begin a new novel if he finished writing one before his time was up). After its appearance Bennett's book was taken by critics to be a literal description of his attitude toward his craft and not at all as what it was: an amusing fragment by a cocky and insecure neophyte of twenty-seven.

Bennett lived in France, with intermittent trips to England and elsewhere abroad, from 1903 to 1912. This was a crucial period in his life. He continued his journalism, contributing long series of articles to the English periodicals *T. P.'s Weekly, PTO,* the *London Evening News,* and the *Manchester Daily Dispatch.* He continued his examinations of life in the Five Towns, which he had marked out as a territory for himself, with his third serious novel, *Leonora* (1903), the story of a middle-aged wife and mother and the second in an intended series of books about women, of which *Anna of the Five Towns* was the first. He contributed also a series of stories to the *Windsor Magazine,* which were collected and published in 1905 as *Tales of the Five Towns.* His third novel about a woman—this one a singer—also appeared in 1905. *Sacred and Profane Love,* which has a Five Towns setting, suffers from a melodramatic heavy-handedness. It is probably Bennett's least attractive serious novel.

By 1906 his career had begun to blossom. In June of that year he became engaged to Eleanor Green, the sister of the novelist Julian Green, but in August the engagement was broken off. No more than this is known, but Eleanor Green later chose to describe the affair as a ridiculous misunderstanding on Bennett's part: this explanation was accepted by Bennett's biographers and repeated by Dorothy Cheston, who had her own reasons to present Bennett as a clumsy provincial, frightened of women, whose marriage to Marguerite Soulie was a reaction to his rejection by Eleanor Green. This story too hurt Bennett's reputation. He met Marguerite Soulie in January 1907 and married her in July. She was a tall, dark, striking woman who worked in a dressmaker's shop but had theatrical ambitions.

Despite implications that he was reacting to a broken heart, Bennett's marriage heralded a most inspired period of his life: in October of 1907 he began to write *The Old Wives' Tale* (1908), his most ambitious novel to that time; he interrupted work on it for a few weeks in early 1908 to write *Buried Alive* (1908), one of his most popular light novels, which has been adapted to the stage and the screen. In March 1908 for the weekly *New Age* he began his series "Books and Persons," a causerie which he signed Jacob Tonson. For the next three years he used this series to discuss books, painting, publishing, magazines, newspapers, travel, theater, censorship, ballet, and European news of cultural significance. These articles created a stir; through them Bennett became known as erudite and knowledgeable, a writer who had broken through the crust of rather smug insularity that surrounded most of his British colleagues. The year 1908 saw the publication of *The Old Wives' Tale,* the novel which he felt had to make his reputation—he was now past forty years old—and which succeeded to his complete satisfaction. In the same year he produced *How to Live on 24 Hours a Day,* the most successful of his "pocket philosophies," and began to see some success on the stage. The Stage Society produced his *Cupid and Commonsense,* a dramatization of *Anna of the Five Towns,* at the Shaftesbury Theatre in London.

In 1909 his work appeared in the prestigious *English Review:* "The Matador of the Five Towns" in April, and in July the script of his play

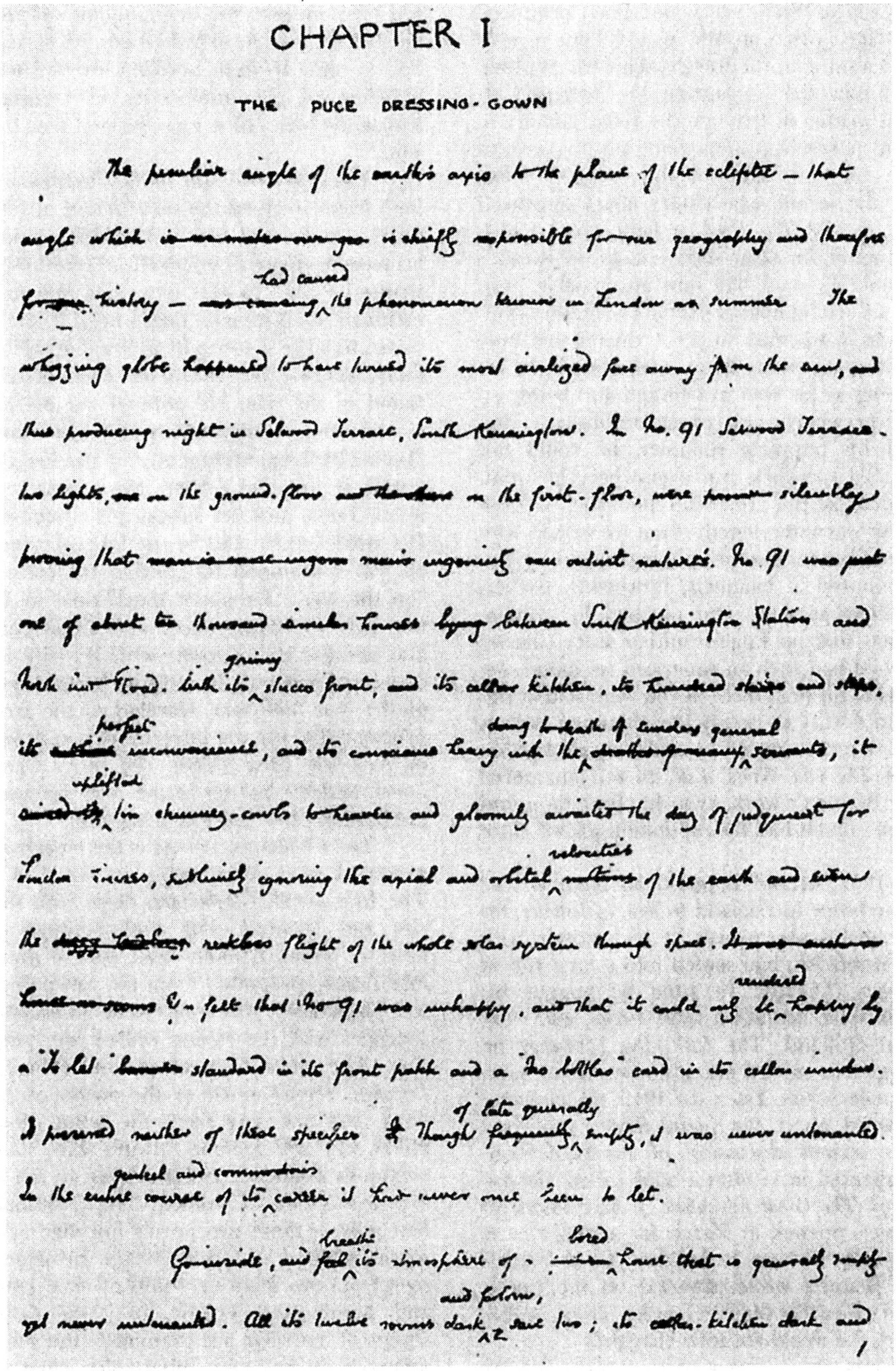

CHAPTER I

THE PUCE DRESSING-GOWN

The peculiar angle of the earth's axis to the plane of the ecliptic — that angle which is chiefly responsible for our geography and therefore history — had caused the phenomenon known in London as summer. The whizzing globe happened to have turned its most civilized face away from the sun, and thus producing night in Selwood Terrace, South Kensington. In No. 91 Selwood Terrace two lights, one on the ground-floor and on the first-floor, were silently proving that man's ingenuity can outwit nature's. No. 91 was just one of about ten thousand similar houses lying between South Kensington Station and North End Road. With its grimy stucco front, and its cellar kitchen, its hundred stairs and steps, its perfect inconvenience, and its conscious doing without the labour of general servants, it uplifted its twin chimney-cowls to heaven and gloomily awaited the day of judgment for London houses, sublimely ignoring the axial and orbital velocities of the earth and even the reckless flight of the whole solar system through space. One felt that No. 91 was unhappy, and that it could only be rendered happy by a "To let" standard in its front patch and a "No bottles" card in its cellar window. It possessed neither of these specifics, and though of late generally empty, it was never untenanted. In the entire course of its genteel and commodious career it had never once been to let.

Go inside, and breathe its atmosphere of a bored house that is generally empty yet never untenanted. All its twelve rooms dark and forlorn, save two; its cellar-kitchen dark and

Page from the manuscript for Buried Alive *(American Art Association/Anderson Galleries, sale 4253, 22-23 April 1936)*

What the Public Wants, which had been produced by the Stage Society in May to excellent reviews and was running at the Royalty Theatre. September 1910 saw the publication of *Clayhanger*. It had been written in five months, from January to June, and it received immediate, positive critical attention on both sides of the Atlantic; *Hilda Lessways*, the second Clayhanger novel, appeared in 1911, as did *The Card*, a light novel which achieved much the same success as *Buried Alive*.

Arnold Bennett had now an enviable position as a successful man of letters. His literary popularity was confirmed in 1911 during his only trip to America, where in six weeks he visited six cities, going as far west as Chicago and being received everywhere with eager enthusiasm. Because of his crippling stammer, he could not make public speeches. But everywhere he went, shepherded by the American publisher George Doran, he was interviewed, often by writers who were celebrities themselves; photographed; caricatured; honored at banquets, luncheons, parties, autographing sessions; and mobbed by women. Doran said that no English author since Charles Dickens had had such an American reception. Serial rights to his next three novels were sold at figures from twenty to twenty-five thousand dollars (Doran had not been able, immediately after publication of *The Old Wives' Tale*, to sell any serial rights to Bennett's work, even for four thousand dollars—so much had his reputation grown since 1908).

In 1912 Arnold Bennett, an assured success, came home to England to live. *Milestones*, his most successful play, which he had written with Edward Knoblock, had settled into a long run at the Royalty Theatre. In June he bought his yacht, the *Velsa*, actually a large barge, and went sailing in Holland. The following February he and Marguerite moved into a house, Comarques, at Thorpe-le-Soken, Essex. In 1913, the last year before World War I, the *English Review* published Bennett's serious discussion of his profession, which appeared in 1914 as a book called *The Author's Craft*. *The Great Adventure*, a play based on *Buried Alive*, opened in March for a long run at the Kingsway Theatre in London. Until the fall of 1914 Bennett wrote, traveled on the Continent, and sailed the Mediterranean. Then, in August 1914, the world abruptly changed.

He was not a flag-waving patriot, but he was an activist by nature, and he could not avoid being swept up in the war. At forty-seven he was too old for active service. He believed that the war was a mistake, but he thought it was an inevitable mistake; and he expected positive social revolution to come from it. Looking forward to the destruction of the autocracies of Germany and Russia, he believed it was essential that the Allies win.

The war cost him money immediately: the *Daily News* dropped the serialization of his newest novel, *The Price of Love* (1914); his receipts from his plays dropped dramatically. Nevertheless he instructed Pinker to give money to any writer less fortunate than he who might need it. He himself began to write a series of political articles for the *Daily News* that were to run more or less for the duration of the war. He pointed out inefficiencies in recruiting, mistreatment of soldiers and their families by the government, and attacked the mandarins at the War Office, the jingoistic Harmsworth Press, and the supporters of conscription. His articles were read by the Liberal cabinet, and he was summoned to London for consultations "on the war." He spent much time in London, not only for conferences and fund-raising but also because his relations with his wife were increasingly strained. In 1915 he became a director of the *New Statesman*, traveled to the front as a propagandist for the government, and published in America *These Twain*, the third Clayhanger novel, and his last set in the Five Towns. British publication came the following year.

The *Clayhanger* trilogy is the largely autobiographical story of a family in the Five Towns. The first novel, *Clayhanger*, deals with the rivalries and tensions that exist between generations—a theme Bennett dealt with in *Anna of the Five Towns*—presented from the viewpoint of Edwin Clayhanger, who longs to be an architect and struggles with the strong will of his father, Darius. The second novel in the trilogy, *Hilda Lessways*, retells much of the action of the first book, but this time from the point of view of Hilda, who will become Edwin's wife. This novel continues Bennett's strong interest in the psychological situation of women. The technique Bennett uses in these two novels foreshadows James Joyce's method in *Ulysses* (1922): the same events seen from two separate points of view gain depth and significance. Finally, in *These Twain*, the strains of marriage are examined, and the author struggles to maintain impartiality while he uses points of view of both husband and wife. *The Roll-Call* (1919), which continues the Clayhanger story with the son of Hilda and Edwin, is set in Lon-

Dorothy Cheston, with whom Bennett began living in 1922 (photograph by Sasha). Cheston, who took the name Bennett by deed poll, was the mother of Bennett's daughter, Virginia, born in 1926.

don and is not considered part of the *Clayhanger* series.

In 1918 Bennett was appointed first director of British propaganda in France and then director of propaganda for the Ministry of Information under Lord Beaverbrook. He also produced *The Pretty Lady,* his first novel since 1916. Set in London, it struck a new note for Bennett: its atmosphere is nightmarish; the characters appear to have been wrenched from their normal grooves of behavior by the horrors of the war. The leading female character is a French prostitute with a primitive faith in the Virgin Mary. An interesting aspect of the book is its dialogue: when the characters speak French, Bennett uses almost literal translation, a device later used by Ernest Hemingway. Although most reviewers praised the book, some were shocked at what they considered its cynicism; there were threats of legal action against it from the Catholic Federation of Westminister, but these came to nothing. Despite such distractions and the organization work he was required to do at the ministry, Bennett continued his journalism during the last year of the war, writing series not only for the *Daily News,* but for the *New Statesman, Nash's Pall Mall Magazine,* and *Lloyd's Sunday News,* as well. In addition, *The Roll-Call* ran from April to October in *Munsey's Magazine.*

During the next three years Bennett separated formally from Marguerite and occupied himself with theater matters and travel. He replaced the *Velsa,* which had been commandeered by the government, with a new yacht, the *Marie Marguerite.* The amount of journalism he produced fell off markedly, rising again in 1922, when he met Dorothy Cheston. At the end of 1922 Bennett began to write *Riceyman Steps,* arguably his most impressive work since *Clayhanger,* and moved with Dorothy Cheston into a house at 75 Cadogan Square in London. She eventually took the name Bennett by deed poll, but the two were never married.

When *Riceyman Steps* was published in 1923, response to it, both critical and popular, was gratifying. H. G. Wells, Joseph Conrad, and Thomas Hardy all praised the book highly, Wells maintaining that it was better than *The Old Wives' Tale.* Bennett was delighted, but annoyed that the character of the maid, Elsie, had attracted so much positive attention. The book, he felt, contained a good deal more than Elsie. And in fact *Riceyman Steps* differs from Bennett's other novels: it is a dark, Dostoyevskian tale; its symbolic framework is almost Freudian. Despite the absorbing charm of its realistic detail, it is not a realistic novel. Bennett intended far more than that and realized his intention, although readers were not accustomed to reading his work in that way.

Although he deplored the popular sentimental attitude toward his character Elsie, Bennett brought her to life again in a short story, "Elsie and the Child," which he liked well enough to make it the title story of his 1924 collection and to have it published in 1929 in a limited edition illustrated by McKnight Kauffer, whose work Bennett greatly admired.

Nineteen twenty-six was another year of importance: his daughter, Virginia, was born to Dorothy Cheston in April, *Lord Raingo* was published in October, and in November at Lord Beaverbrook's request he began his review column "Books and Persons" in the *Evening Stan-*

dard. Lord Raingo created a considerable stir, largely because it was based on real people in the war office; Bennett consulted closely with Beaverbrook for his working notes, and the novel has been called one of the great political novels in English. Like *The Pretty Lady* and *Riceyman Steps*, it is a dark book: the entire last third of it describes Raingo's lingering death from pneumonia—or from his own death wish. The novel deals not only with power, but with the relationship of a middle-aged man with his young mistress. Raingo himself is a rounded character, unlike Earlforward in *Riceyman Steps*. Frank Swinnerton has said that Raingo is Bennett himself.

Over the next three years, Bennett continued to travel and to write articles, fiction, and plays. Difficulties had arisen in his household, and the relationship with Dorothy Cheston was no longer pleasant. Toward the end of 1929, using the Savoy in London as his model, he began writing *Imperial Palace* (1930), his last completed novel, about the interior working of a great hotel. He wrote in his journal that he had been fighting against writing this long novel for years. Thirty years earlier, he said, he had been taken to the Savoy Hotel for tea and had gone home and written *The Grand Babylon Hotel* in three weeks of evenings. But *The Grand Babylon Hotel* was "a mere lark"; this novel was to be a serious study of "the big hotel de luxe." Some of the frustrations which had built in him over the critical reception of his work were expressed in this journal entry: "And when I have finished it [*Imperial Palace*] and corrected the manuscript and corrected the typescript and corrected the slipproofs and corrected the page-proofs, and it is published, half the assessors and appraisers in Britain and America will say: 'Why doesn't he give us another "Old Wives Tale" '? I have written between seventy and eighty books. But also I have written only four: 'The Old Wives Tale,' 'The Card,' 'Clayhanger' and 'Riceyman Steps.' All the others are made a reproach to me because they are neither 'The Old Wives Tale', nor 'The Card', nor 'Clayhanger', nor 'Riceyman Steps.' And 'Riceyman Steps' would have been made a reproach too, if the servant Elsie had not happened to be a very 'sympathetic' character. Elsie saved 'Riceyman Steps' from being called sordid and morbid and all sorts of bad adjectives. As if the 'niceness' of a character had anything to do with the quality of the novel in which it appears!"

Imperial Palace, a massive novel, sold well, but critical reactions to it were mixed. In the same year that it appeared, Vicki Baum's *Grand Hotel* was published. Also about the workings of a large luxury hotel and dealing with many characters, it was not as ambitious a novel as *Imperial Palace*, nor did it have the complexities of Bennett's novel; but *Grand Hotel* became an international best-seller, and *Imperial Palace* was to some extent swept aside by it.

Bennett's investments were hurt somewhat by the market crash of 1929. He fretted about money and about the amount of money which Dorothy Cheston insisted on investing in theatrical ventures (she had always had the ambition to become an actress). Despite these financial worries he became fascinated by new apartments at Chiltern Court, above the Baker Street Underground Station, where H. G. Wells had taken a flat. Part of his reason for giving up Cadogan Square was that he wished to cut down somewhat on his servant staff (Dorothy could not get along with them).

Two flats were converted into one; McKnight Kauffer was engaged as an interior designer; and Bennett eagerly looked forward to living in a modern Bauhaus-influenced interior (he had always surrounded himself with antique furniture, although he bought modern paintings). Miles of steel shelving were ordered for his seven thousand books. In her biography of Bennett, Dorothy Cheston gives the impression that this move to Chiltern Court was a reflection of a mind at the end of its tether. Certainly it reflected a desire for change, which was in fact characteristic of Bennett. Frank Swinnerton, who became one of the executors of Bennett's will, has said that his financial affairs were in relatively good order; and he was not squeezed for money. In January of 1931 Bennett and Dorothy Cheston went to France for a holiday, and she later wrote that there Bennett contracted the disease from which he was to die two months later.

After his death both Cheston and Marguerite Bennett wrote memoirs about him. Both women had axes to grind; both provided a picture of Arnold Bennett which each wished the world to remember. Reginald Pound, Bennett's first biographer, trod warily, since both women were still alive when he wrote his book. Although Pound's book is thus far the most reliable biography of Bennett, it is not in the last analysis an attempt at the whole truth; and the picture of Bennett's last years is heavily colored by Dorothy Cheston's narrative. When Pound's book appeared in 1952, Bennett's reputation rested on

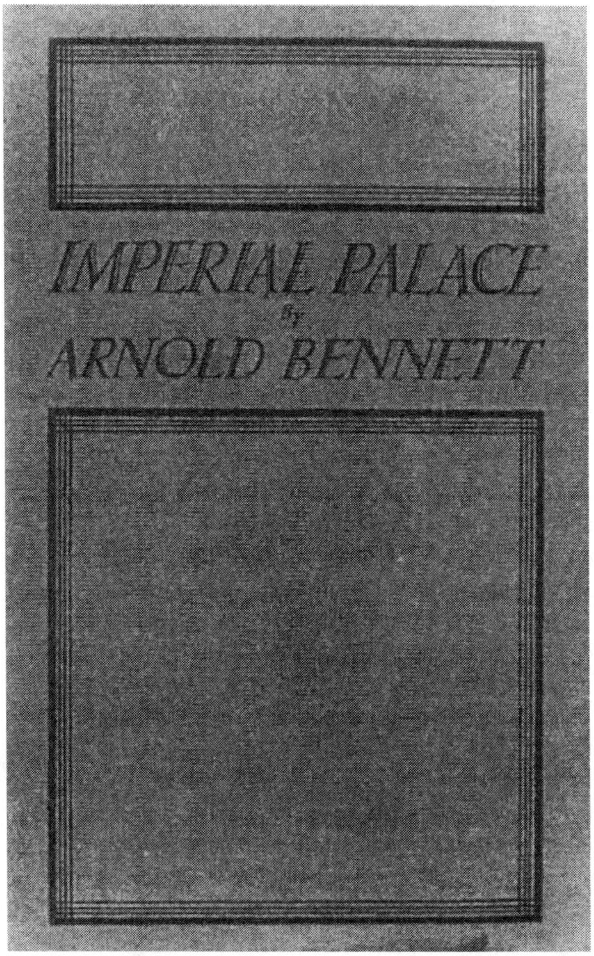

Dust jacket for Bennett's 1930 novel, which was overshadowed by Vicki Baum's Grand Hotel, *published the same year*

The Old Wives' Tale, the only book of his still in print in America.

The second biography appeared in 1966. Written by Dudley Barker, its title is *Writer by Trade,* which recalls the attitude of Bloomsbury toward Bennett. Called into being undoubtedly by the death of Marguerite Bennett, the book contains a good deal of information about the collapse of Bennett's marriage which until then had not been publishable. It also contains many errors, and the picture that emerges is the picture that Dorothy Cheston has carefully shaped: a good man but befuddled, talented but not of the first rank, and, in his last years, not quite responsible for his actions. The evaluation of the novels is, however, stronger than Pound's evaluation. Despite its slanted view of Bennett himself, Barker's book suggests that *Clayhanger, Riceyman Steps, Lord Raingo* and even *Imperial Palace,* a book Dorothy Cheston particularly disliked, are powerful novels. The third biography of Bennett, by Margaret Drabble, is heavily influenced by Dorothy Cheston and contains little that is new except fresh errors.

However, there has been some revision of the condescending attitude toward Bennett. The most important was the publication in 1963 of James Hepburn's *The Art of Arnold Bennett,* which attempted to examine seriously work that had been dismissed because of the peculiar attitude of critics toward Bennett as a man. Barker's most respectful approach to the work in 1963 reflects this revision of attitude. Of great importance was the publication of Bennett's letters in four volumes edited by Hepburn, from 1966 to 1986. Also of great importance, although as yet perhaps generally unappreciated, is Frank Swinnerton's *Arnold Bennett: A Last Word,* which was published in 1978, shortly after the death of Dorothy Cheston Bennett, and in which Swinnerton, the last of Bennett's friends, attempts to tell the truth at last about this writer and his unfortunate private life. A consensus seems to be growing, despite the mass of negative comment which grew during Bennett's last years and for three decades or so after his death, that he was in fact a great novelist, and that ignorance of his work impoverishes the body of English literature.

Letters:

Arnold Bennett's Letters to His Nephew, edited by Richard Bennett (New York & London: Harper, 1935; London & Toronto: Heinemann, 1936);

Dorothy Cheston Bennett, *Arnold Bennett: A Portrait Done at Home, together with 170 Letters from A. B.* (London: Jonathan Cape, 1935; New York: Kendall & Sharp, 1935);

Arnold Bennett and H. G. Wells: A Record of a Personal and a Literary Friendship, edited by Harris Wilson (London: Hart-Davis, 1960; Urbana: University of Illinois Press, 1960);

Correspondence André Gide-Arnold Bennett: Vingt Ans D'Amitié Littéraire (1911-1931), edited by Linette F. Brugmans (Geneva: Librarie Droz, 1964);

Letters of Arnold Bennett, 4 volumes, edited by James Hepburn (London & New York: Oxford University Press, 1966-1986);

Arnold Bennett in Love, edited and translated by George and Jean Beardmore (London: Bruce & Watson, 1972).

Bibliographies:

Norman Emery, *Arnold Bennett: A Bibliography*

(Stoke-on-Trent, U.K.: Central Library, Hanley, 1967);
Anita Miller, *Arnold Bennett: An Annotated Bibliography, 1887-1932* (New York: Garland, 1977).

Biographies:

Marguerite Bennett, *Arnold Bennett* (London: Philpot, 1925);
Bennett, *My Arnold Bennett* (New York: Dutton, 1932);
Dorothy Cheston Bennett, *Arnold Bennett, a Portrait Done at Home* (New York: Kendall & Sharp, 1935);
Margaret Locherbie-Goff, *La Jeunesse d'Arnold Bennett* (Avesne-sur-Helpe: Editions de l'Observateur, 1939);
Reginald Pound, *Arnold Bennett* (London: Heinemann, 1952; New York: Harcourt, Brace, 1953);
Dudley Barker, *Writer by Trade: A View of Arnold Bennett* (London: Allen & Unwin, 1966);
Margaret Drabble, *Arnold Bennett: A Biography* (London: Weidenfeld & Nicolson, 1974);
Frank Swinnerton, *Arnold Bennett: A Last Word* (London: Hamish Hamilton, 1978).

References:

Walter Allen, *Arnold Bennett* (Denver: Swallow, 1949);
William Bellamy, *The Novels of Wells, Bennett and Galsworthy, 1890-1910* (New York: Barnes & Noble, 1971);
F. J. Harvey Darton, *Arnold Bennett* (New York: Holt, 1915);
James Winford Hall, *Arnold Bennett: Primitivism and Taste* (Seattle: University of Washington, 1959);
James Hepburn, *The Art of Arnold Bennett* (Bloomington: Indiana University Press, 1963);
Hepburn, ed., *Arnold Bennett, the Critical Heritage* (London & Boston: Routledge, 1981);
L. G. Johnson, *Arnold Bennett of the Five Towns* (London: Daniel, 1924);
Georges Lafourcade, *Arnold Bennett: A Study* (London: Muller, 1939);
J. B. Simons, *Arnold Bennett and His Novels* (Oxford: Blackwell, 1936);
Patrick Swinden, *Unofficial Selves: Character in the Novel from Dickens to the Present Day* (London: Macmillan, 1972);
Frank Swinnerton, *Arnold Bennett* (London: Longmans, Green, 1950);
Louis Tillier, *Studies in the Sources of Arnold Bennett's Novels* (Paris: Didier, 1949);
Geoffrey West, *The Problem of Arnold Bennett* (London: Joiner & Steele, 1932);
Virginia Woolf, *Mr. Bennett and Mrs. Brown* (London: Leonard & Virginia Woolf, 1924);
Walter F. Wright, *Arnold Bennett: Romantic Realist* (Lincoln: University of Nebraska Press, 1971).

Papers:

Major collections of Bennett's papers are located at the University of Arkansas, Bibliothèque Littéraire Jacques Doucet in Paris, Cambridge University, University of Illinois at Urbana, Keele University, Berg Collection in the New York Public Library, City Museum of Stoke-on-Trent, University of Texas in Austin, and University College in London.

Robert Bridges

(23 October 1844 - 21 April 1930)

This entry was updated by Donald E. Stanford (Louisiana State University) from his entries in DLB 19: British Poets, 1880-1914 *and* DLB 98: Modern British Essayists: First Series.

Robert Bridges (photograph by Hollyer)

SELECTED BOOKS: *Poems* (London: Pickering, 1873);

The Growth of Love, anonymous (London: Bumpus, 1876; revised and enlarged edition, Oxford: Daniel, 1889);

An Account of the Casualty Department (London: St. Bartholomew's Hospital, 1878);

Poems (London: Bumpus, 1879);

Poems (London: Bumpus, 1880);

Prometheus the Firegiver (Oxford: Printed at the private press of H. Daniel, 1883);

Poems (Oxford: Printed at the private press of H. Daniel, 1884);

Nero Part I (London: Bell & Bumpus, 1885);

Eros & Psyche (London: Bell, 1885; revised, 1894);

On the Elements of Milton's Blank Verse in Paradise Lost (Oxford: Clarendon Press, 1887); revised and republished in *Milton's Prosody* (1893);

The Feast of Bacchus (Oxford: Privately printed by H. Daniel, 1889);

On the Prosody of Paradise Regained and Sampson Agonistes (Oxford: Blackwell / London: Simpkin, Marshall, 1889); revised and republished in *Milton's Prosody* (1893);

Palicio (London: Bumpus, 1890);

The Return of Ulysses (London: Bumpus, 1890);

The Christian Captives (London: Bumpus, 1890);

Achilles in Scyros (London: Bumpus, 1890);

The Shorter Poems (London: Bell, 1890);

Eden: An Oratorio, words by Bridges, music by C. V. Stanford (London: Bell / London & New York: Novello, Ewer, 1891);

The Humours of the Court (London: Bell & Bumpus, 1893; New York: Macmillan, 1893);

Shorter Poems Book V (Oxford: Printed by H. Daniel, 1893);

Milton's Prosody (Oxford: Clarendon Press, 1893); revised and enlarged edition, with an additional chapter by William Johnson Stone (Oxford: Oxford University Press, 1901; revised and enlarged again, 1921);

Nero Part 2 (London: Bell & Bumpus, 1894);

John Keats: A Critical Essay (Oxford: Privately printed, 1895);

Invocation to Music: An Ode (In Honour of Henry Purcell) (London: Novello, Ewer, 1895);

Poetical Works, 6 volumes (London: Smith, Elder, 1898-1905);

Now in Wintry Delights (Oxford: Daniel Press, 1903);

Demeter (Oxford: Clarendon Press, 1905);

Poetical Works (London, New York, Toronto & Melbourne: Oxford University Press, 1912);

An Address to the Swindon Branch of the Workers' Educational Association (Oxford: Clarendon Press, 1916);

The Necessity of Poetry (Oxford: Clarendon Press, 1918);
October and Other Poems (London: Heinemann, 1920; New York: Knopf, 1920);
The Tapestry (London: Privately printed, 1925);
New Verse (Oxford: Clarendon Press, 1925);
Henry Bradley (Oxford: Clarendon Press, 1926); republished in *Three Friends* (1932);
The Influence of the Audience: Considerations Preliminary to the Psychological Analysis of Shakespeare's Characters (Garden City, N.Y.: Doubleday, Page, 1926);
Collected Essays, Papers, &c., 10 volumes, volumes 4-10 edited by Monica Bridges (London: Oxford University Press, 1927-1936);
The Testament of Beauty (Oxford: Clarendon Press, 1929; New York: Oxford University Press, 1929);
Poetry (London: British Broadcasting Corporation, 1929);
Three Friends: Memoirs of Digby Mackworth Dolben, Richard Watson Dixon, Henry Bradley (London: Oxford University Press, 1932).

OTHER: *Hymns: The Yattendon Hymnal*, edited by Bridges and H. Ellis Wooldridge, four parts (Oxford: Oxford University Press, 1895-1899);
The Influence of the Audience, in *The Works of William Shakespeare*, volume 10 (Stratford-upon-Avon: Shakespeare Head Press, 1907);
Poems by the Late Rev. Dr. Richard Watson Dixon, edited, with a memoir, by Bridges (London: Smith, Elder, 1909);
The Poems of Digby Mackworth Dolben, edited, with a memoir, by Bridges (London, New York, Toronto & Melbourne: Oxford University Press, 1911);
Ibant Obscuri, an experiment in the classical hexameter, paraphrases of *Aeneid*, VI: 267-751, 893-898, and *Iliad*, XXIV: 339-660 (Oxford: Clarendon Press, 1916);
The Spirit of Man, edited by Bridges (London, New York, Bombay, Calcutta & Madras: Longmans, Green, 1916);
Gerard Manley Hopkins, *Poems*, edited, with a preface and notes, by Bridges (London: Milford, 1918).

One of the dominant figures of late-Victorian and early-twentieth-century British poetry, poet laureate of England from 1913 to 1930, Robert Bridges became best known in his day and is known in ours as a master of lyric verse and as author of the philosophical poem *The Testament of Beauty* (1929). Of his famous collection of lyric poetry, *The Shorter Poems* (1890), A. E. Housman said that all of it was so excellent that anthologists would have great difficulty in making their selections. Because of his early retirement from the medical profession in 1881, made possible by an inheritance from his father which left him financially independent, Bridges was able to devote the rest of his long life to the writing of poetry and to the cultivation of wide-ranging interests including prosody, music, hymnology, literary criticism, editing, and typography. His interest in typography began early. He designed almost all his books, and he was one of a group of very few men responsible for reestablishing the type collected in the seventeenth century by the bishop of Oxford, John Fell, with his publication of *Hymns: The Yattendon Hymnal* (1895-1899). He was one of the first in this century to employ the Arrighi type designed by Frederic Warde and Stanley Morison for his collection of poems *The Tapestry* (1925). As an editor he is best known for his wartime anthology, *The Spirit of Man* (1916), and for his compiling, editing, and annotating the first edition of Gerard Manley Hopkins's *Poems* (1918). Of his perceptive literary criticism, his essays on Keats (1895) and *The Influence of the Audience*, an essay on Shakespeare's characters (published in the 1907 Shakespeare Head edition of Shakespeare's works and in 1926 as a separate work), are the most important. The results of his learned investigations into Latin and English prosody are available in his essays on Milton's prosody, his essay "On the prosody of Accentual Verse" (all included in the final, 1921 edition of *Milton's Prosody*), and his article on Virgilian hexameters which is prefatory to the *Aeneid* section of *Ibant Obscuri* (1916), his experimental paraphrase of parts of the *Aeneid* and the *Iliad*.

Robert Seymour Bridges, whose yeomen ancestors had lived for centuries on the Isle of Thanet, was born on 23 October 1844 in Walmer, Kent, and spent his childhood in a house overlooking the anchoring ground of the British fleet there. Recollections of his birthplace and of the duke of Wellington, who was a friend and neighbor of his father's, are beautifully presented in his "Elegy: The Summer-House on the Mound" (1899). His father, John Thomas Bridges, died in 1853. His mother, Harriet Elizabeth Affleck Bridges, the next year married the Reverend J. E. N. Molesworth, and the family moved to Rochdale, where his stepfather was

Bridges, circa 1862

the vicar. Bridges frequently spent his vacations there. At Eton College from 1854 to 1863, he became associated with a High Church Anglican group which included the poet Digby Mackworth Dolben, whose brief life he memorialized in an introduction to his edition of Dolben's poems (1911). The memoir was effusively praised by Henry James. A close and long friendship with Lionel Muirhead (1845-1925) began at Eton. Almost four hundred letters from Bridges to Muirhead are extant and supply much-needed information about Bridges's life. (Bridges's wish that no biography be written of him has made even a short account of his life difficult.) Soon after he entered Corpus Christi College, Oxford, he became acquainted with the poet Gerard Manley Hopkins (1844-1889), who in effect made him his literary executor by entrusting to him the manuscripts of his poems. After his graduation from Oxford, Bridges spent more than a year traveling in Egypt and Syria with Muirhead and residing in Germany with his friend from Eton days, the Reverend William Sanday (1843-1920). In the fall of 1869 he entered St. Bartholomew's Hospital, London, as a medical student, having abandoned an earlier plan to take orders in the Church of England. The most notable literary result of his experience as a physician is the poem "On a Dead Child." After receiving his medical degree in 1874 he was appointed house physician and then casualty physician at St. Bartholomew's. Later he was assistant physician at the Hospital for Sick Children, Great Ormond Street, and then physician at the Great Northern Hospital, Holloway. In *An Account of the Casualty Department* (1878), Bridges criticizes the heavy work load imposed on the physicians there. He himself diagnosed and treated thirty-one thousand patients a year. In 1881, after a severe attack of pneumonia, he retired from the medical profession, traveled in Italy with Muirhead, and then moved with his mother into the Manor House at Yattendon, an attractive village in the county of Berkshire. There he met and married Monica, daughter of the famous architect Alfred A. Waterhouse. During the Yattendon years, from 1882 to 1904, which were certainly among the happiest of his life, he wrote most of his best-known lyrics as well as eight plays and two masques, all in verse.

Early in his career, in the mid-1870s, Bridges began experiments in what he called "stress prosody" and his friend Hopkins called "sprung rhythm." In recent years the term *sprung rhythm* is usually associated with Hopkins; but the two prosodies are actually the same in theory. In practice Hopkins pushed his experiments much further than Bridges. Nevertheless, Bridges for several years was seriously interested in the new prosody, and he considered it to be an important revolution in English poetry. He wrote many notable poems in stress meter. Those most widely admired (all published 1879-1880) are "The Downs," "A Passer-by," "On a Dead Child," and "London Snow." The frequently anthologized "Nightingales," published more than a decade later, also may be scanned in the new prosody. In "London Snow," one of his most popular poems, we see stress rhythm at its best:

When men were all asleep the snow came
  flying,
In large white flakes falling on the city brown,
Stealthily and perpetually settling and loosely
  lying,
Hushing the latest traffic of the drowsy town;
Deadening, muffling, stifling its murmurs
  failing;

> Lazily and incessantly floating down and
> down.

There is no straining here for the highly pitched emotional effects so often sought by Hopkins in his experiments in sprung rhythm. The rhythms have the naturalness of quiet speech. The soft airiness of the falling snow is suggested by the very texture of the verse, which is achieved by carefully modulated sound effects as well as by a slightly irregular rhythm—irregular, that is, when compared with the smoothness of most conventional accentual-syllabic verse. The subtle rhythms of "The Downs" are similarly successful in combining precision and naturalness:

> Where sweeping in phantom silence the cloudland
> flies;
> With lovely undulation of fall and rise;
> Entrenched with thickets thorned,
> by delicate miniature dainty flowers adorned!

Hopkins admired the first of these lines and commented somewhat ambiguously on the "accumulated epithets" of the last line, which seem to some readers to be a risky but rhetorically successful employment of three adjectives to modify a single noun.

As interesting as these poems are, the more numerous poems in conventional accentual syllabic verse have achieved the highest praise. In 1876, after calling in and destroying almost all copies of his first book, *Poems* (1873), Bridges had published anonymously a sequence of twenty-four sonnets entitled *The Growth of Love*, inspired by a lady who "died unwon / By death transfigured to the light of day." The sequence has a definite Platonic note in which the dead lady is praised for her "intelligence of heavenly things / Unsullied by man's mortal overthrow." The sequence was enlarged and revised for a second edition published in 1889 with ten sonnets omitted, the others revised, and sixty-five new sonnets added. In the third and final edition of 1898, which appeared in volume one of *Poetical Works*, ten of the sonnets were omitted. The theme of the two enlarged editions is the dominant theme of Bridges's entire career, the poet's response to both earthly and spiritual beauty wherever it may be found—in woman, in nature, and in the arts, as well as in heaven. In those sonnets addressed to a woman, the Platonic note is still dominant, but there are more expressions of earthly passion than in the first edition. Throughout, there are obvious influences of Shakespeare, Milton, and several Italian poets, but the poems are much more than mere pastiche. Bridges has mastered the English and the Italian sonnet forms. *The Growth of Love* is one of the few successful sonnet sequences of the late Victorian period.

In 1885 Bridges produced his narrative poem *Eros & Psyche*, using Apuleius's version of the well-known tale as it appears in *The Golden Ass*, but embellishing it considerably with descriptive passages such as his depiction of a sunset, inspired by the dramatic volcanic sunsets in England after the eruption of Mt. Krakatoa in 1883, and a stanza describing the swimming gull, greatly admired by Hopkins. The story is allegorized by Bridges far more than it is by Apuleius. It is a parable of the growth of love from the purely sensual to the spiritual, the growth occurring in the soul of Psyche, who in her patient, steadfast purpose to regain the love of Eros in spite of the obstinate malevolence of Venus becomes one of Bridges's most appealing heroines.

The publication in 1890 of the *Shorter Poems* (books 1-4), selected from the best of his short poems written up to that date, marked the climax of Bridges's growing fame as a lyric poet. Besides the poems in stress prosody, there were many lyrics in conventional meters. Among the finest are "Assemble, all ye maidens," "Elegy Among the Tombs," "Dejection," "I have loved flowers that fade," "Thou didst delight my eyes," "Joy, sweetest life born joy," "Awake, my heart," "The evening darkens over," "I love all beauteous things," "The birds that sing on autumn eves," and "The snow lies sprinkled on the beach." Book 5 of the *Shorter Poems*, first published in 1893 and included in subsequent editions of the *Shorter Poems*, includes two more excellent lyrics—"The Affliction of Richard" and "Nightingales," the latter in stress prosody. His powerful poem "Eros" and his important "Elegy: The Summer-House on the Mound" appeared in "New Poems," collected for the first time in volume two (1898) of his *Poetical Works*. "Low Barometer," perhaps the greatest of all Bridges's shorter poems, was first published in *New Verse* (1925).

The early "Assemble, all ye maidens" is a conventional elegy on a lady who died of grief after the death of her betrothed. The elaborate ornamental rhetoric (unusual in the poetry of Bridges) is handled with great skill:

> Cloke her in ermine, for the night is cold,
> And wrap her warmly, for the night is long,
> In pious hands the flaming torches hold,

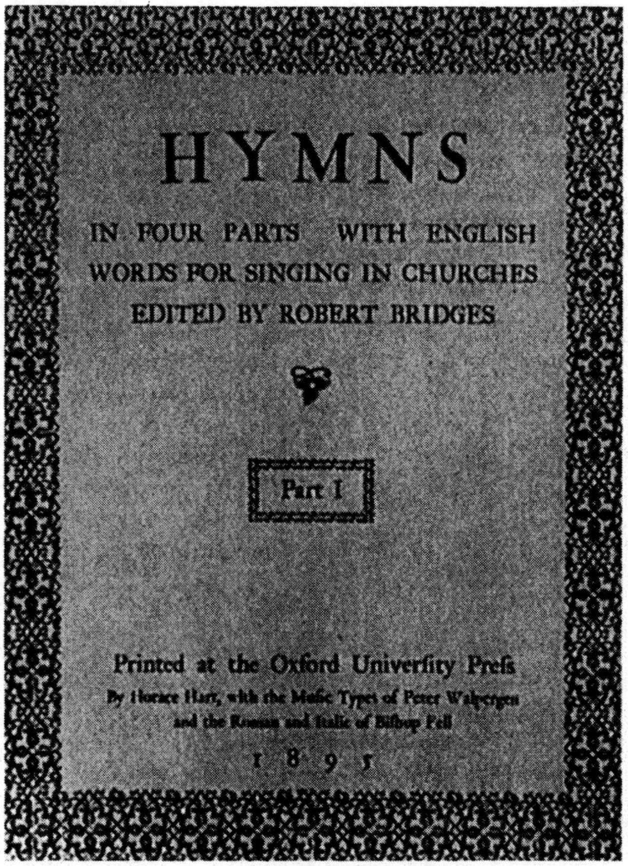
HYMNS

IN FOUR PARTS WITH ENGLISH WORDS FOR SINGING IN CHURCHES EDITED BY ROBERT BRIDGES

Part I

Printed at the Oxford Univerfity Prefs
By Horace Hart, with the Mufic Types of Peter Walpergen
and the Roman and Italic of Bifhop Fell

1 8 9 5

Title page for the first part of the Yattendon hymnal. It was printed in Fell type, an antique face collected at Oxford by Bishop Fell in the seventeenth century, rediscovered and reestablished by Bridges and the publisher H. Daniel in the 1870s.

While her attendants, chosen from among
Her faithful virgin throng,
May lay her in her cedar litter,
Decking her coverlet with sprigs of gold,
Roses, and lilies white that best befit her.

Mrs. Humphry Ward, in a prefatory note to her novel *Fenwick's Career* (1906), wrote: "Any lover of modern poetry will recognize the lines" which she quoted from the fifth stanza, describing a torchlit funeral procession. In the novel, the poem inspires a painting by the artist Fenwick. In contrast to the rhetoric of the elegy, "Dejection" reveals Bridges's plain, direct style at its best:

Wherefore to-night so full of care,
My soul, revolving hopeless strife,
Pointing at hindrance, and the bare
Painful escapes of fitful life?

Shaping the doom that may befall
By precedent of terror past.

Dejection, however, is not the dominant note in Bridges's poetic career, although there are other fine poems with tragic overtones. And even in "Dejection" the poet finds consolation in "Some strain of music to thy mind, / Some praise for skill not spent amiss." Bridges was never as boisterously optimistic as Robert Browning; nevertheless, joy and hope and a zest for living are prevalent in much of his verse. "Joy, sweetest life born joy" is characteristic. The poem opens with somber reflections on the plight of modern man in what appears to be a purposeless universe, but

Then comes the happy moment: not a stir
In any tree, no portent in the sky:
The morn doth neither hasten nor defer,
The morrow hath no name to call it by,
But life and joy are one,—we know not why,—
As though our very blood long breathless lain
Had tasted of the breath of God again.

The euphoric mystical moment in which the poet realizes "Divinity hath surely touched my heart" is the source of Bridges's prevailing optimism in this poem and in others. Even in the beautiful "Elegy Among the Tombs," while reflecting on

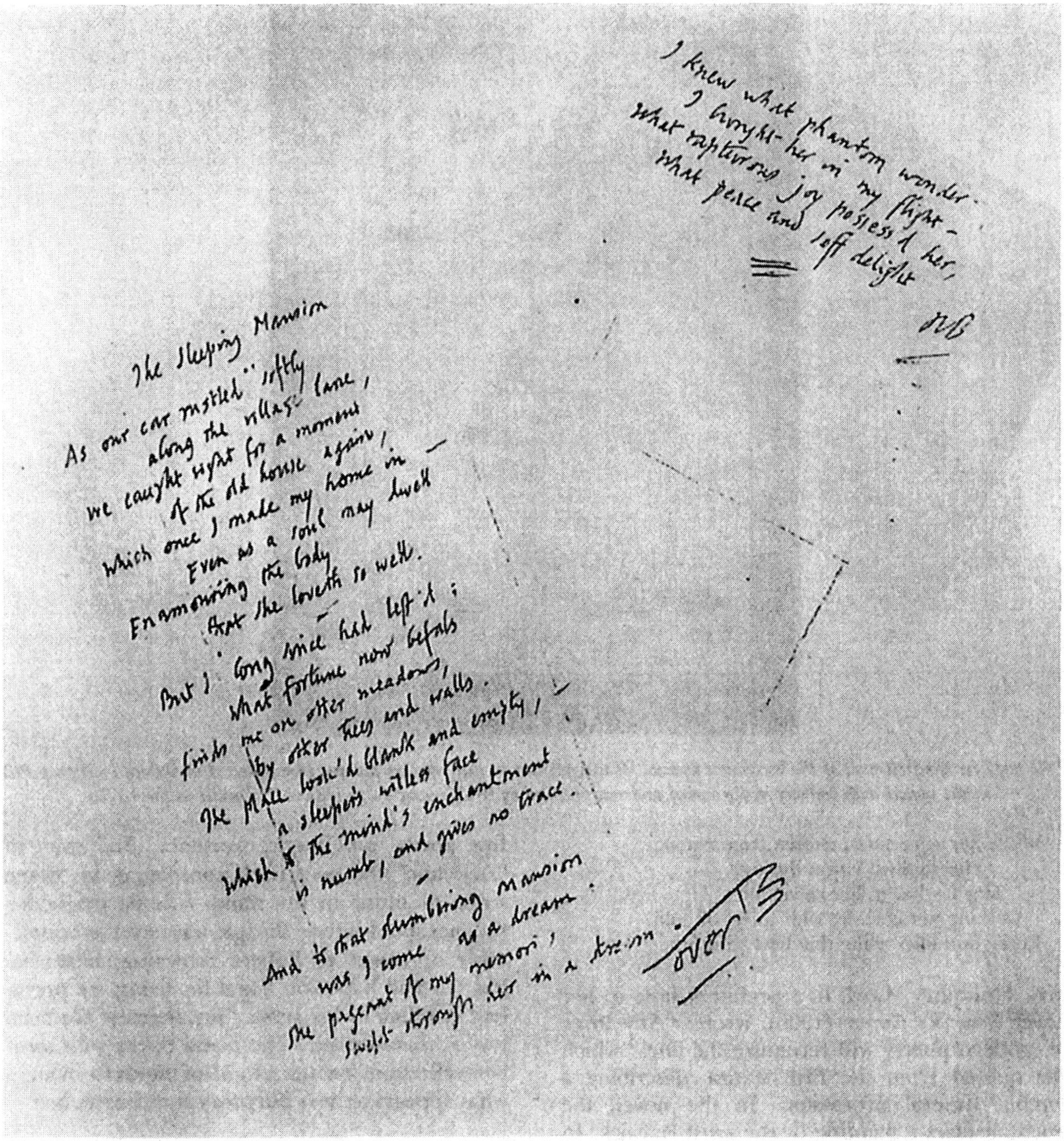
The Sleeping Mansion

As our car rustled softly
along the village lane,
we caught sight for a moment
of the old house again,
which once I made my home in —
Even as a soul may dwell
Enamouring the body
that she loveth so well.

But I, long since had left it;
what fortune now befals
finds me on other meadows,
by other trees and walls.
The place look'd blank and empty,
a sleeper's witless face
which of the mind's enchantment
is numb, and gives no trace.

And to that slumbring mansion
was I come as a dream:
the pageant of my memori's
swept through her in a dream.

OVER RB

I knew what phantom wonder
I brought her in my flight —
what rapturous joy possess'd her,
what peace and soft delight

RB

Manuscript of a 1921 poem sent by Bridges to his friend Lionel Muirhead in January 1925, as Muirhead lay on his deathbed. In the accompanying letter Bridges wrote: "The poem tells of a visit to Yattendon, and I think it describes feelings on the occasion of seeing an old home different from other poets' " (The Bodleian Library).

death and the ravages of time, he reminds himself that he is one of the many "who have once reined in their steeds at any shrine / And given them water from the well divine." "Awake, my heart," an ecstatic exercise in the aubade tradition, reveals another source of Bridges's optimism, the possibility of perfect or nearly perfect human love:

Awake, my heart, to be loved, awake, awake!
The darkness silvers away, the morn doth
  break,
It leaps in the sky: unrisen lustres shake
The o'ertaken moon. Awake, O heart, awake!

The poem was greatly admired by H. J. C. Grierson, who quoted it in his introduction to his

Chilswell, Boar's Hill, Oxford, Bridges's home from 1907 until his death in 1930. Bridges designed the house.

edition of the *Poems of John Donne* (1912) as an example of a modern love poem which surpassed the love poetry of Donne. In the little lyric with the major theme, "I love all beauteous things," we have yet another source of the poet's joy—the existence of beauty in all its forms and the capacity of the poet to respond to it. The response to beauty is the great dominant experience of the poet's life, and it finds poetic expression from his first book of poems in 1873 until his last poem, *The Testament of Beauty*, published in 1929.

Bridges was not immune to the religious difficulties which beset so many of the intellectuals of the late Victorian period. Like his friend Hopkins, he was a man of strong religious temperament, and (like Thomas Hardy) he wished when young to become a minister. But (like Hardy again) he could not wholly resist the impact of J. S. Mill, Charles Darwin, and modern science. In "The sea keeps not the Sabbath day" the scientific worldview is dominant:

> We talk of moons and cooling suns,
> Of geologic time and tide,
> The eternal sluggards that abide
> While our fair love so swiftly runs.

And man is "so fugitive a part / Of what so slowly must expire," but characteristically, Bridges finds final consolation in "human art, / Worthy of the Virgilian muse, / Fit for the gaiety of Mozart."

"The Affliction of Richard" is the most important poetic expression of Bridges's religious difficulties. Written in his plain style at its best, it defines his early loss of religious faith and his eventual recovery of it:

> Though thou, I know not why,
> Didst kill my childish trust,
> That breach with toil did I
> Repair, because I must:
> And spite of frighting schemes,
> With which the fiends of Hell
> Blaspheme thee in my dreams,
> So far I have hoped well.

The poem makes an interesting contrast in style and thought to the religious verse of Hopkins.

"Nightingales," first published in 1893, marks a return to the earlier experiments in stress prosody. It is one of Bridges's most beautiful poems as well as one of his most popular, and it is frequently anthologized. The poem begins with an address by the poet to the nightingales, who, says the poet, because of the beauty of their song, must live in beautiful surroundings. The answer of the nightingales suggests the theme of the poem: "Alone, aloud in the raptured ear of men / We pour our dark nocturnal se-

Bridges beside his Dolmetsch clavichord, a gift from friends on his eightieth birthday

cret." Their secret is that in fact their surroundings are dismal and dark and that their song is an attempt to transcend their barren mountains and "spent streams." Beauty which comes from suffering and suggests the darkness of tragedy is more moving than beauty which springs from the innumerable, cheerful birds of day. The nightingales "Dream, while the innumerable choir of day / Welcome the dawn."

The subject of "Eros" (first published in 1899 in volume two of the *Poetical Works* under the rubric of "New Poems") is naked, sensual, pagan ("unchristen'd") passion, an unusual subject for Bridges. One would expect to find it, rather, in Swinburne, but in Bridges's poem the experience is understood better, and it is communicated with greater precision and power than it is in any poem by Swinburne. Eros embodies "shameless will and power immense, / In secret sensuous innocence." This power is completely physical, without soul and without thought, yet for its victims it is completely sufficient in itself:

> O king of joy, what is thy thought?
> I dream thou knowest it is nought,
> And wouldst in darkness come, but thou
> Makest the light where'er thou go.

In May 1897, while vacationing with his family in Folkestone, Bridges took an excursion by bicycle to his birthplace in Walmer, Kent, "where," he wrote to his friend Lionel Muirhead, "it will delight me to see the old paths that I scrambled over when a small boy." From this trip came the fine poem (also first published in the "New Poems" of 1899) "Elegy: The Summer-House on the Mound," which begins "How well my eyes remember the dim path." Written in beautifully controlled heroic couplets, the poem is a vivid recollection of childhood days at Walmer with the focus of interest on the summerhouse:

And there 'tis ever noon, and glad suns bring
Alternate days of summer and of spring,
With childish thought, and childish faces bright,
And all unknown save but the hour's delight.

From the summerhouse he could see the anchoring ground of the British fleet. He recalls one occasion at the age of ten when he watched Gen. Charles Napier's fleet sail to the Baltic at the outbreak of the Crimean War:

One noon in March upon that anchoring ground
Came Napier's fleet unto the Baltic bound:
Cloudless the sky and calm and blue the sea,
As round Saint Margaret's cliff mysteriously,
Those murderous queens walking in Sabbath sleep
Glided in line upon the windless deep.

He remembers especially one ship for personal reasons:

But chief, her blue flag flying at the fore,
With fighting guns a hundred thirty and one,
The Admiral ship *The Duke of Wellington*,
Whereon sail'd George, who in her gig had flown
The silken ensign by our sisters sewn.

The references to his brother George and their sisters are followed by recollections of his father's friend Wellington, "the iron Duke himself." Bridges's care in authenticating details of his poem is evident in a letter he wrote to his friend the naval historian Sir Henry Newbolt in July 1899, shortly before the poem was published, asking him if his childhood memory was correct—was it indeed a *blue* flag that the admiral was flying? Newbolt investigated and replied that it was. Bridges also reinforced his memory before writing his description of the fleet by purchasing in April 1899 Vice-Admiral Napier's *The History of the Baltic Campaign of 1854* and R. E. Hughes's *Two Summer Cruises with the Baltic Fleet in 1854-5*.

During the Yattendon years Bridges wrote two masques and eight plays. All except his first play, *Nero Part I* (1885), were intended for the stage, but there were actually only a few performances of Bridges's dramatic works. His masque *Demeter* (1905) has been staged more frequently than any other of his dramatic works: at Somerville College, Oxford, 11 June and 22 June 1904; at the University of Liverpool three times in the summer of 1908; at Heath House School, Weybridge, 23 July 1920; at Frensham School in New South Wales in 1933; and again at Somerville College on 26 June 1954, the fiftieth anniversary of the first performance. His other masque, *Prometheus the Firegiver* (1883), was performed at a boys' grammar school near Newbury with Bridges in attendance. *Achilles in Scyros* (1890) was performed at the Cheltenham Ladies' College on 27 and 29 June 1912, with Bridges attending the first performance, and in two performances at the County Girls School in Cambridge, October 1923. *The Humours of the Court* (1893), the only play by Bridges to receive a professional performance, was acted by the Oxford Dramatic Society in London at the Arts Theatre on 5 and 7 January 1930. Edith Evans had the lead role. There may be a few amateur performances of Bridges's dramatic works that have been overlooked, but Bridges's sustained and heroic effort to restore verse drama to the stage must be considered a failure as far as the history of the theater goes. But as "closet drama" several of them, though never popular, have received high praise. Hopkins considered *Nero Part I* and *Prometheus the Firegiver* to be great achievements. Yvor Winters and Albert Guerard have written enthusiastically about *Nero Part I*, *Nero Part 2* (1894), and *The Christian Captives* (1890). Much of *Achilles in Scyros* has been praised for its poetic beauty.

Bridges's first and last plays (as distinct from his masques), *Nero Part I* and *Nero Part 2*, can be read as one long play and could be acted in a single performance. The action of the entire work takes place in the years A.D. 54-65, that is, from the first year of Nero's reign until the death of Seneca. The chief characters are Nero; Nero's mother, Agrippina; and Nero's tutor, the philosopher Seneca. Part one, taken up with the struggle between Nero and Agrippina for control of the empire, is dominated by the fierce and ruthless Agrippina, who achieves an almost heroic dig-

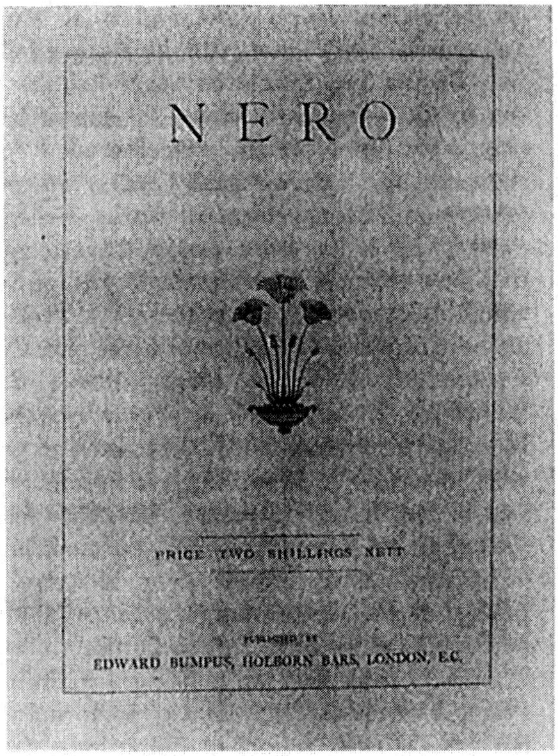

NERO

PRICE TWO SHILLINGS NETT

PUBLISHED BY
EDWARD BUMPUS, HOLBORN BARS, LONDON, E.C.

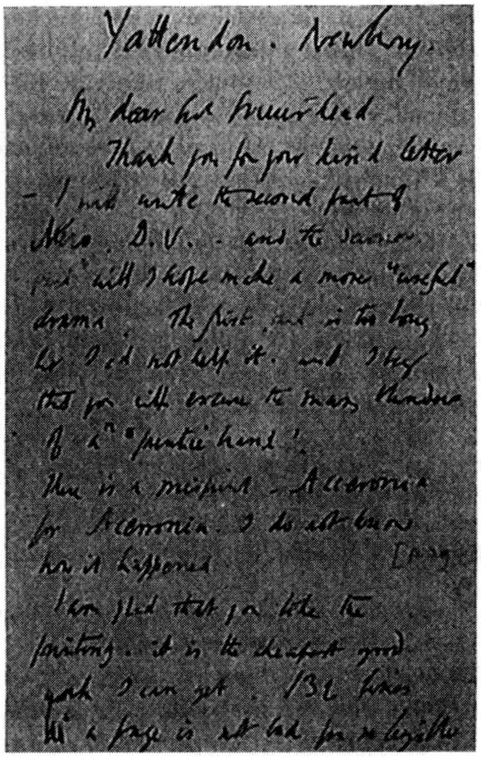

Yattendon. Newbury.

My dear Mr Muirhead
Thank you for your kind letter
– I will write the second part of
Nero. D.V. – and the second
part will I hope make a more "useful"
drama. The first part is too long
but I did not help it. and I hope
that you will excuse the many blunders
of a "prentice hand".
There is a misprint – Acceronia
for Acceronia. I do not know
how it happened. [p.t.o.]
I am glad that you like the
printing. It is the cheapest good
work I can get. 132 lines
to a page is not bad for so legible

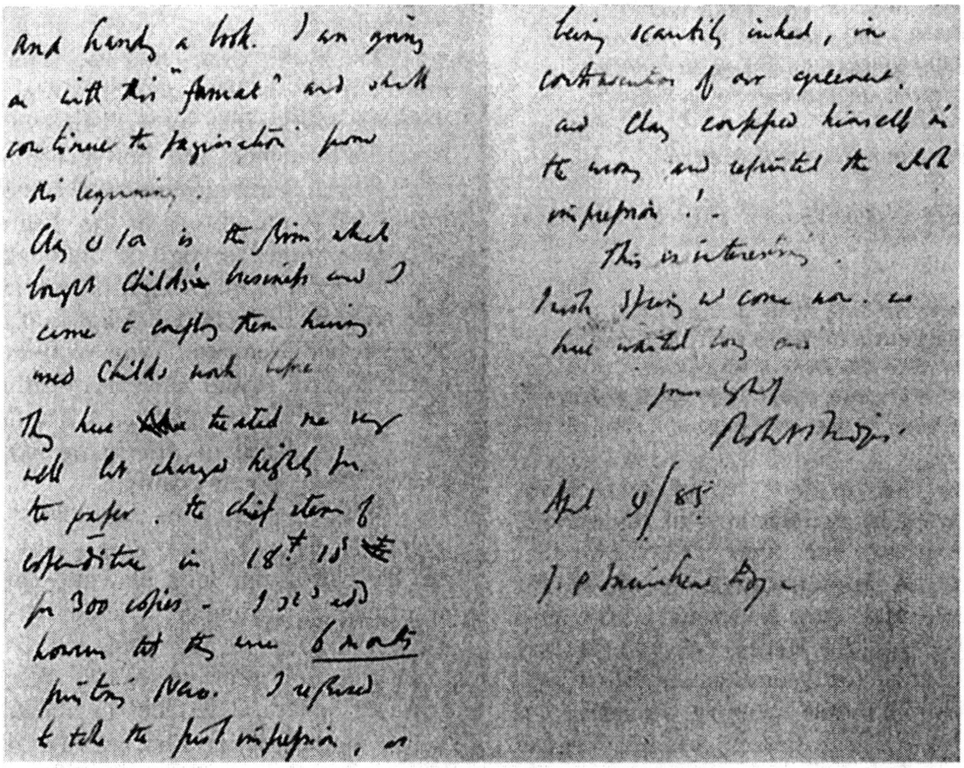

and handy a book. I am going
on with this "format" and shall
continue the pagination from
the beginning.
Clay & Son is the firm which
bought Childs's business and I
came to employ them having
used Childs's work before.
They have treated me very
well but charged highly for
the paper. the chief item of
expenditure is 18£ 10s
for 300 copies – I should add
however that they were 6 months
printing Nero. I refused
to take the first impression, as
being scantily inked, in
contravention of our agreement.
and Clay confessed himself in
the wrong and reprinted the whole
impression.
This is interesting.
Surely Spring will come now. we
have waited long enough
yours truly
Robert Bridges.

April 9/85

J. P. Muirhead Esq.

Front cover for J. P. Muirhead's copy of the first part of Nero *with Bridges's 9 April 1885 letter to Muirhead (Thomas Cooper Library, University of South Carolina)* nity at the end in her courageous defiance of the assassins sent by her son to murder her:

None answered, and awhile
Was such delay as makes the indivisible
And smallest point of time various and broad.
. . . .
Only she showed her spirit to the last,
and made some choice of death, offering her body,
"That bare the monster," crying with that curse,
"Strike here, strike here!"

In part 2, which presents the conspiracy of Piso and its failure, Seneca becomes the most interesting character. At times throughout both parts he appears to be the cautious timeserving politician and at times the heroic man of principle. His character is finally redeemed by the calm and stoic manner of his death by suicide at the command of Nero. In his portrayal of Agrippina and Seneca, Bridges demonstrated his ability to create credible, fully realized characters. His blank verse, the medium of all his dramatic works except *The Feast of Bacchus* (1889), is sophisticated and supple, capable of being employed for low-key realistic dialogue as in *The Humours of the Court*, for heroic speeches of considerable intensity and rhetorical power as in the Nero plays, and for descriptive passages of poetic beauty as in *Achilles in Scyros* and the two masques. His dramatic works deserved a better chance than they received to reach the professional stage.

The Return of Ulysses, *Achilles in Scyros*, and *The Christian Captives* (all 1890) may still be read with interest today. Bridges had high hopes for a theater production of *The Return of Ulysses*, and he drew up plans (which are still extant) for staging and directing the play, but his hopes were disappointed even though William Butler Yeats wrote a favorable critique of it in 1896 and on at least two occasions planned to stage it. When *Achilles in Scyros* was given its amateur production at Cheltenham Ladies' College in 1912, Bridges was disappointed in the performance. The young ladies did not make convincing Greek warriors. *The Christian Captives* is perhaps his most successful drama except for *Nero*, parts 1 and 2. The action, which takes place in Fez in the fifteenth century, centers on the Portuguese Prince Ferdinand's love for Almeh, the daughter of the king of Fez, and on his efforts (while a captive of the Moors) to retain the town of Ceuta for the Portuguese against the threats of the Moors to kill him if he does not yield. The play has dramatic power and, if staged, would appeal to a patriotic English audience because Ferdinand and his brother, Henry the Navigator, were grandchildren of John of Gaunt, son of England's King Edward III, and the British have been allies of Portugal for centuries.

Ever since his school days at Eton, Bridges had had a serious interest in Greek and Latin poetry and prosody. About the turn of the century he became involved in exploring the possibilities of composing English verse in the quantitative meters of the Greeks and Romans. A brief but important friendship with William Johnson Stone, son of a master of Eton, which began in 1898 and lasted until Stone's death in 1901, strengthened his resolve to write poems in classical prosody. Stone, who strongly believed in the viability of classical meters for English poetry, had a treatise on the subject published in 1898, and Bridges included it in his own 1901 edition of *Milton's Prosody*. After Stone's unexpected death at the age of twenty-nine, Bridges felt bound to carry out a promise to Stone to put Stone's ideas into poetic practice. The result was more than two thousand lines of quantitative verse. One of the best of these experiments is "Now in Wintry Delights," a verse epistle in hexameters modeled on Horace's *Epistles* and addressed to Bridges's friend Lionel Muirhead. It was first published in 1903. Another poem of this group, "Johannes Milton, Senex," has been frequently admired and anthologized. Also in classical prosody are an ode, "O that the earth," and a chorus, "Gay and lovely is earth," both written for his masque *Demeter,* and a few epigrammatic poems, the best of which are "Who goes there?" and "Askest thou of these graves?"

In 1902 Bridges's wife and his daughter Margaret became seriously ill, probably from tuberculosis. Bridges decided to move from the manor house at Yattendon with the hope of finding a healthier climate for his family. After residing in temporary homes in Gloucester County and on Boar's Hill and Foxcombe Hill near Oxford, Bridges took his family for an extended stay in Switzerland which lasted from July 1905 to March 1906. While in Switzerland he continued his writing in classical prosody. Much of *Ibant Obscuri* (first published in the *New Quarterly* in 1909), a paraphrase of part of book 6 of the *Aeneid* written in quantitative hexameters, was composed while Bridges was ice-skating at St. Moritz. Soon after returning to England in March 1906, Bridges began building Chilswell House on Boar's Hill overlooking Oxford University. The house, designed by Bridges, was completed in the summer of 1907. Bridges lived there for the remainder of his life.

A year after the one-volume edition of his *Poetical Works* (1912) was published, Bridges began to engage in another experiment, his "neo-Miltonic syllabics" as he called them. His first two poems in this new meter, "The Flowering Tree" and "Noel: Christmas Eve, 1913," were widely praised. Bridges had noted that Milton in his blank verse had frequently "freed" every foot of his line except the last foot. Bridges decided to free the last foot as well and to extend Milton's line from five to six feet. By freeing the feet Bridges meant that there was no place in the line in which a syllable was necessarily accented or unaccented. The result was a syllabic line of twelve syllables with a flexible pattern of accents. In short poems such as "The Flowering Tree" and "Noel" the line was divided into two hemistichs of six syllables each. The best-known poem in the prosody is "Noel," which was first published for the new poet laureate "by his Majesty's desire" in the London *Times* on 24 December 1913 (a few months before the outbreak of World War I) with the Latin epigraph *Pax hominibus bonae voluntatis.* It is a beautiful tone poem describing a clear and frosty Christmas Eve as observed by the poet from Boar's Hill as he listens to the church bells:

> The constellated sounds
> ran sprinkling on earth's floor
> As the dark vault above
> with stars was spangled o'er.

Bridges wrote twelve poems in neo-Miltonic syllabics, most of them in 1921. Eleven of these were published in *The Tapestry* (1925), beautifully printed in a new Arrighi type. The neo-Miltonic line of twelve syllables later became the "loose Alexandrine" of *The Testament of Beauty.*

When England declared war against Germany in August 1914, Bridges considered it his duty as poet laureate to contribute his poetic talents to the war effort. War poetry was a genre not congenial to his lyric muse, although he was fiercely patriotic, and his poems as well as his letters written early in the war are strongly militant in tone. But from 1917 on, as the horror of trench warfare became more apparent and anxiety about his son Edward (later the first Lord Bridges), who was seriously wounded on the western front, increased, his poetry took on a more somber note.

In 1915 the publisher Longman, who had lost a son in the trenches, asked Bridges to compile and edit a volume of poems and prose selections which would appeal to a nation at war. Much of that year was taken up with editing and seeing through the press *The Spirit of Man* (1916), which brought together 449 separate pieces of ancient, Oriental, and Western literature to illustrate what the editor considered to be permanent spiritual values of the human race that must be asserted in a time of widespread adversity and suffering. The volume had a popular success, second only to *The Testament of Beauty* in Bridges's career. A facsimile edition was reprinted in 1973 with an introduction by W. H. Auden.

The Spirit of Man contains six selections from the poetry of Gerard Manley Hopkins. Bridges had published Hopkins's poems in previous anthologies, but now, for the first time, Hopkins's poems received favorable critical notice by the reviewers. Bridges now felt that the

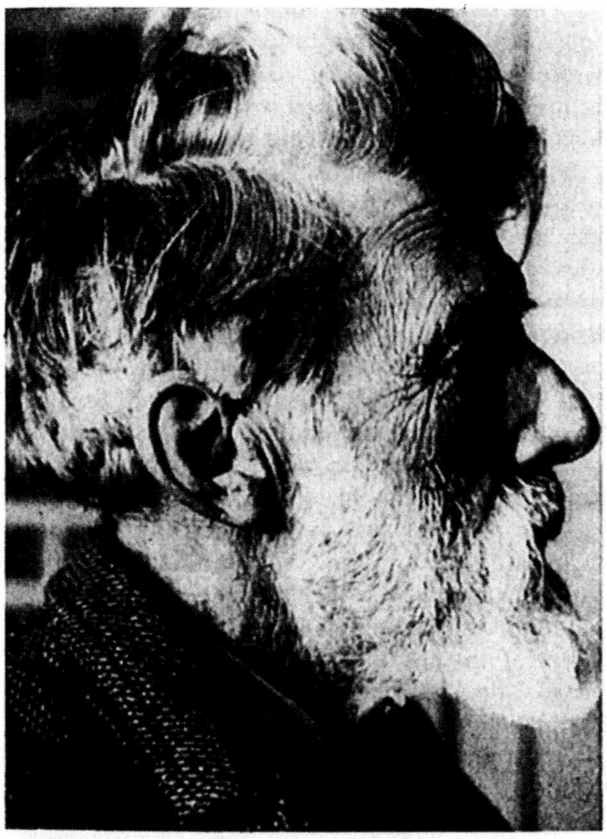

Robert Bridges, 1922 (photograph by Spicer-Simson)

time had come for an edition of Hopkins's poetry. Much of the year 1918 was spent in arranging and annotating the poems in consultation with Hopkins's mother and his sister Kate. The first edition appeared in December 1918.

Bridges's own war poems, most of them not successful from a literary point of view, were collected in *October and Other Poems* (1920). The best of these is probably "Gheluvelt," written in quantitative elegiacs, and a stirring naval ode, "The Chivalry of the Sea," dedicated to Charles Fisher, a student of Christ Church, Oxford, who was lost on the battleship *Invincible*. The ode was set to music by Sir Charles Parry. After the war, Bridges was a leader in the controversial Reconciliation Movement at Oxford, designed to promote a return to normal friendly relationships among the professors of Germany, Austria, and England. The Oxford Letter of Reconciliation, which appeared in the London *Times* on 18 October 1920 and which caused heated debates in Oxford and in the pages of the *Times*, was signed by Bridges as well as other Oxford professors and was probably composed by Bridges.

The Society for Pure English (S.P.E.) was founded in 1913 by Bridges, Henry Bradley, and Walter Raleigh to establish "a sounder ideal of the purity of our language." Within a year the society had almost a hundred members, but with the outbreak of World War I, the work of the society temporarily ceased. It was resumed again in 1919 and lasted until 1948. Bridges, until his death in 1930, was considered the founder and leading member. During his life the society published thirty-four tracts of which at least ten were wholly or partly by Bridges. Bridges also solicited many of the contributions and saw all the tracts through the press and contributed miscellaneous notes and comments. Work for the S.P.E. took up a considerable part of the poet laureate's time, and it was the primary reason for his first and only trip to America in the spring of 1924. He was a guest of the University of Michigan at Ann Arbor much of the time. During his stay in the United States he strengthened the interest of American scholars in the S.P.E.

New Verse (1925) republished seven of the poems in neo-Miltonic syllabics from *The Tapestry* and added others in accentual verse, in traditional rhythms, and in quantitative verse. The most important poem in the volume and, according to Yvor Winters, the best of all Bridges's short poems is "Low Barometer," written in February 1921 in accentual-syllabic tetrameter verse. The poem begins with a graphic description of a storm. The storm becomes symbolic of various forces in the soul of man which may overthrow reason:

And Reason kens he herits in
A haunted house. Tenants unknown
Assert their squalid lease of sin
With earlier title than his own.

Unbodied presences, the pack'd
Pollution and remorse of Time,
Slipped from oblivion reenact
The horrors of unhouseld crime.

According to Winters in *Forms of Discovery* (1967), "The poem deals with an attack on Reason by the 'unconscious' mind, which is seen as an inheritance from a remote and savage past. . . . The house is the mind of man; the 'tenants unknown' are the forces of what the Christian would call his lower nature, of what the psychologist would call his unconscious mind, of what the anthropologist would call his pre-human memory."

On Christmas Day 1924 Bridges wrote fourteen lines of syllabic verse, each twelve syllables long, similar to the verse of his neo-Miltonic experiments. He later referred to this form as his "loose Alexandrines." The first seven lines stand today as the opening lines of *The Testament of Beauty*:

> Mortal Prudence, handmaid of divine
>   Providence,
> hath inscrutable reckoning with Fate and
>   Fortune:
> We sail a changeful sea through halcyon days
>   and storm,
> and when the ship laboureth, our stedfast
>   purpose
> trembles like as the compass in a binnacle.
> Our stability is but balance, and conduct lies
> in masterful administration of the
>   unforeseen.

He set the fourteen lines aside until 1926. In April of that year his daughter Margaret died after a long illness. In July, at the suggestion of his wife, who thought that poetic composition might alleviate grief over the loss of their daughter, he resumed work on what was to become a long philosophical poem, at first called "De Hominum Natura" after Lucretius's *De Rerum Natura*. More than four thousand lines and divided into four books—"Introduction," "Selfhood," "Breed," and "Ethick"—the work is a kind of spiritual autobiography depicting the development of a poet's sense of beauty, his response to beauty wherever he finds it, for "Beauty is the prime motiv of all his excellence, / His aim and peaceful purpose," and it "wakeneth spiritual emotion in the mind of man." This spiritual elation, this response to beauty, according to Bridges is the highest experience possible for man, and Bridges's poem is a testament to the nature and quality of such an experience in his own life. The final title of the poem was probably suggested by Stanley Morison, who in a letter to Bridges commenting on book 1 said, "I read it as a testament." Morison's letter was one of many written to Bridges during the composition of the poem. Bridges welcomed the advice of his friends. As he completed each of the four books, he had them set up in his beloved Fell type and circulated to friends with the request that they criticize it. These readers included Stanley Morison, R. C. Trevelyan, Edward Thompson, Logan Pearsall Smith, and Kenneth Sisam.

In developing his main theme—the poet's sensitivity to and response to beauty—Bridges wrote many remarkable passages describing the beauties of rural England, especially its flowers, bird songs, landscapes, and skyscapes. The passage in book 1 on clouds beginning "The sky's unresting cloudland, that with varying play / sifteth the sunlight thru' its figured shades" has been widely admired. But there are other important themes, for the poem is a compendium of Bridges's opinions on such subjects as psychology, metaphysics, ethics, religion, the arts, history, war, and politics. His philosophy of idealism based on natural foundations and the possibility of man becoming one with God in the ring of Being owes something to Plato, but it owes more to George Santayana, as the poet himself stated in a letter to Santayana. He is indebted also to Santayana (as well as to Plato) for his psychological notion that happiness for man consists in a harmony of the instincts—especially the instinct of preservation of self (the subject of book 2) and the instinct of sex (the subject of book 3)—a harmony brought about and maintained by the faculty of reason. Bridges's political conservatism, his dislike of socialism and of all forms of tyranny, led to one of the finest passages in the poem, the description of his friend Sir Leonard Woolley's excavations at Kish and Ur in book 4, which reads in part:

>   his spirit, dazed awhile
> in wonder, suddenly was strick'n with great
>   horror;
> for either side the pole, where lay the
>   harness'd bones
> of the yoke-mated oxen, there beside their
>   bones
> lay the bones of the grooms, and slaughter'd
>   at their post
> all the king's body-guard, each liegeman
>   spear in hand,
> in sepulchred attention; and whereby lay the
>   harp
> the arm-bones of the player, as there she had
>   pluck'd her dirge,
> lay mingled with its fragments; and nearby
>   disposed,
> two rows of skeletons, her sisterly audience
> whose lavish ear-pendants and gold-filleted
>   hair,
> the uniform decoration of their young
>   service,
> mark'd them for women of the harem,
>   sacrificed
> to accompany their lord, the day when he set
>   forth

to enter into the presence of the scepter'd
shades
congregated with splendour in the mansions
of death.

The entire passage was intended as an attack on socialism, which, Bridges thought, would lead to a tyranny that would disregard the rights of the individual just as they were disregarded in the ancient kingdoms of Kish and Ur. But the passage transcends its narrow political intention and becomes a magnificent comtemplation on the passing of a civilization and the ravages of time.

The Testament of Beauty was published on 24 October 1929, one day after the poet's eighty-fifth birthday. The deluxe quarto edition was designed by Morison. The trade edition sold thousands of copies the first year. The poem was a commercial and a literary success, although there were a few dissenting opinions. Dean Inge was reported to have said that he hated "loose Alexandrines" worse than loose living, and Justice Holmes said that the poem depicted the cosmos arranged to suit polite English taste. But most reviewers were enthusiastic and hailed *The Testament of Beauty* as one of the most important poems of the century.

On 2 July 1927, the composer Gustav Holst and a group of his pupils came to Chilswell and put on a concert consisting of seven of Bridges's lyrics set to music by Holst. The occasion was a success, and it marked the culmination, late in life, of Bridges's long devotion to music, both religious and secular. A few years later Holst composed *A Choral Fantasia* using the words of Bridges's "Dirge." It was first performed in 1931 and was dedicated to the memory of the former poet laureate.

Bridges and his family frequently held "musicals" at Yattendon and Chilswell in which madrigals were often featured. The poet was also active in assisting the church choir at Yattendon, and he collected the words and music of one hundred hymns for his *Hymns: The Yattendon Hymnal* (1895-1899). *Eden: An Oratorio* (1891), with music by C. V. Stanford and words by Bridges, was performed at the Birmingham Festival of 1891. Four of Bridges's odes were set to music by Sir Charles Parry. One of these, *Invocation to Music* (1895), was performed at Leeds in October 1895. And on his eightieth birthday friends of the poet presented him with a clavichord made by Arnold Dolmetsch in recognition of his devotion to music of the fifteenth and sixteenth centuries.

In October 1927 Bridges's essay on the plays of Shakespeare, *The Influence of the Audience*, was reprinted as volume one of Bridges's *Collected Essays*. The series was continued after his death under the supervision of his widow and was completed in 1936. Morison designed the special type for the essays, a font which had new typefaces to indicate the pronunciation of diphthongs, ligatures, and vowels. Also a simplification of spelling was introduced, such as the dropping of the final *e* in the verb *have*. Bridges's interest in spelling reform, in spelling which would in a uniform manner indicate pronunciation, was of many years duration. By 1901 he and his wife were engaged in writing out various poems in phonetic script. By 1903 he had completed "Now in Wintry Delights" (438 lines) in script, and by 1908 Horace Hart of the Oxford Press was casting his phonetic type. The reform did not catch on, and the only results of Bridges's experiments available to the general public are to be found in the *Collected Essays* printed in Morison's type and in a few simplified spellings in *The Testament of Beauty*.

Bridges wrote to his brother-in-law Samuel Butler on 16 February 1900, "I should like you to read my 'Essay on Keats.' Art is what I most care for, and that tract expresses or at least implies my attitude toward it." Bridges's most substantial and important essay, "A Critical Introduction to Keats," was commissioned by A. H. Bullen in the spring of 1894 for the Muses Library edition of the poems of Keats (1896). It was first published separately (as *John Keats: A Critical Essay*) in Oxford in 1895 and republished as volume 3 of *Collected Essays, Papers, &c.* (1929). Because Bridges considered Keats "one of the highest gifted poets that was ever born into the world," he undertook his commission with care and deliberation. As was his custom when composing his most important works, Bridges asked for advice from friends whose literary judgment he respected. He sent drafts of his essay to the novelist and poet Margaret L. Woods, the poet Canon Richard Dixon, and the music historian Harry Ellis Wooldridge. In his letters to Woods he discussed in detail the major problems to be overcome in achieving his aim—a just evaluation of all the poetry of Keats. There were difficulties of interpretation and questions of style. Specifically, how could the argument in "Ode to a Nightingale" that the bird was immortal and man was not be maintained when

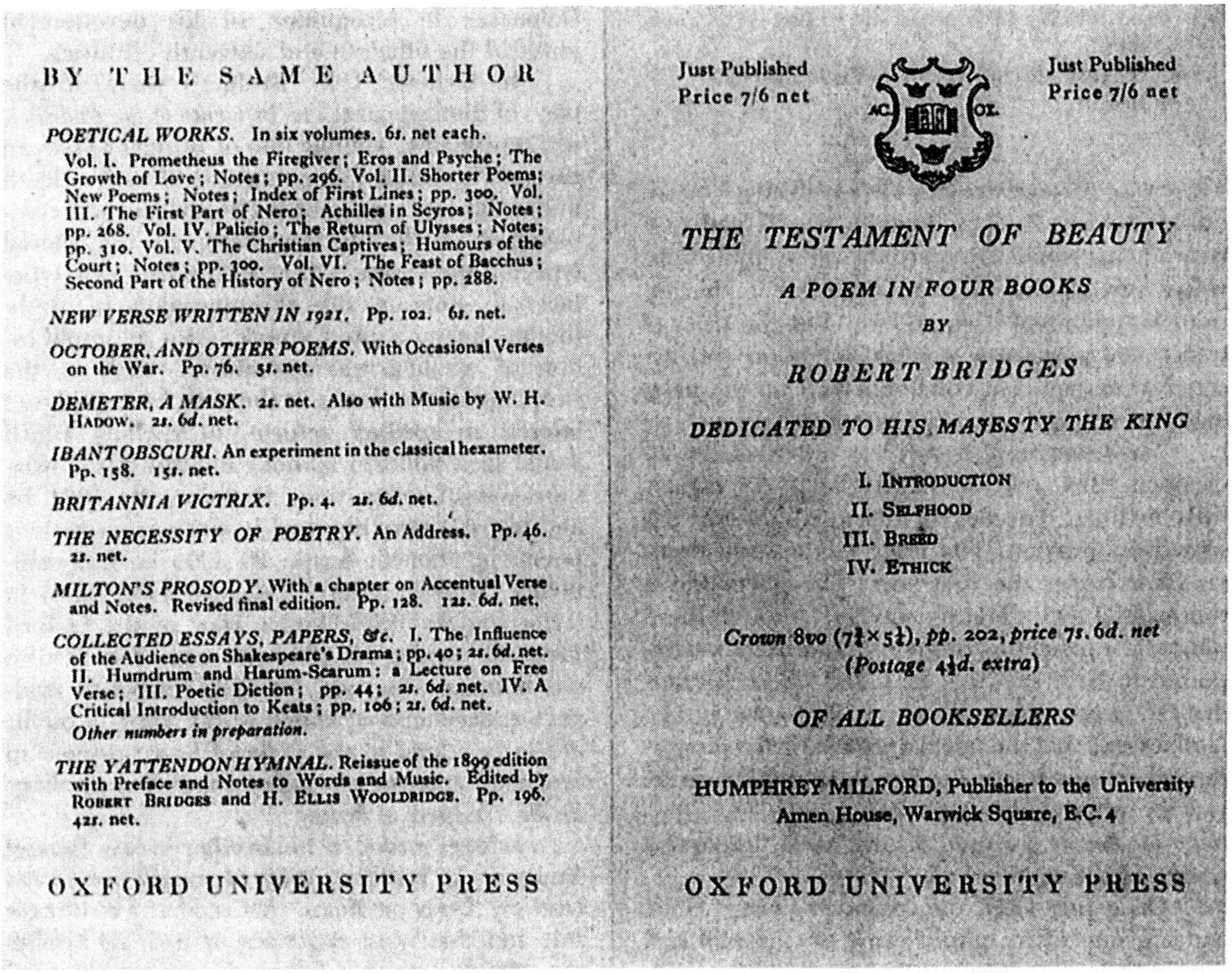

BY THE SAME AUTHOR

POETICAL WORKS. In six volumes. 6*s.* net each.
Vol. I. Prometheus the Firegiver; Eros and Psyche; The Growth of Love; Notes; pp. 296. Vol. II. Shorter Poems; New Poems; Notes; Index of First Lines; pp. 300. Vol. III. The First Part of Nero; Achilles in Scyros; Notes; pp. 268. Vol. IV. Palicio; The Return of Ulysses; Notes; pp. 310. Vol. V. The Christian Captives; Humours of the Court; Notes; pp. 300. Vol. VI. The Feast of Bacchus; Second Part of the History of Nero; Notes; pp. 288.

NEW VERSE WRITTEN IN 1921. Pp. 102. 6*s.* net.

OCTOBER, AND OTHER POEMS. With Occasional Verses on the War. Pp. 76. 5*s.* net.

DEMETER, A MASK. 2*s.* net. Also with Music by W. H. Hadow. 2*s.* 6*d.* net.

IBANT OBSCURI. An experiment in the classical hexameter. Pp. 158. 15*s.* net.

BRITANNIA VICTRIX. Pp. 4. 2*s.* 6*d.* net.

THE NECESSITY OF POETRY. An Address. Pp. 46. 2*s.* net.

MILTON'S PROSODY. With a chapter on Accentual Verse and Notes. Revised final edition. Pp. 128. 12*s.* 6*d.* net.

COLLECTED ESSAYS, PAPERS, &c. I. The Influence of the Audience on Shakespeare's Drama; pp. 40; 2*s.* 6*d.* net. II. Humdrum and Harum-Scarum: a Lecture on Free Verse; III. Poetic Diction; pp. 44; 2*s.* 6*d.* net. IV. A Critical Introduction to Keats; pp. 106; 2*s.* 6*d.* net.
Other numbers in preparation.

THE YATTENDON HYMNAL. Reissue of the 1899 edition with Preface and Notes to Words and Music. Edited by Robert Bridges and H. Ellis Wooldridge. Pp. 196. 42*s.* net.

OXFORD UNIVERSITY PRESS

Just Published
Price 7/6 net

Just Published
Price 7/6 net

THE TESTAMENT OF BEAUTY

A POEM IN FOUR BOOKS

BY

ROBERT BRIDGES

DEDICATED TO HIS MAJESTY THE KING

I. Introduction
II. Selfhood
III. Breed
IV. Ethick

Crown 8vo (7¾×5¼), pp. 202, price 7s. 6d. net
(Postage 4½d. extra)

OF ALL BOOKSELLERS

HUMPHREY MILFORD, Publisher to the University
Amen House, Warwick Square, E.C. 4

OXFORD UNIVERSITY PRESS

Publisher's brochure for Bridges's 1929 book

in fact both were equally mortal or "immortal" in the terms of the poem? And what were the proper explanations of the obscure allegorical matter in *Endymion* and *Hyperion*? As to style, Bridges mentioned blemishes in diction and imagery found in "Ode to Autumn," "Ode to Indolence," and "Bacchic Ode to Sorrow." All of these subjects discussed in the correspondence found their way into the final version of the essay, which was completed in October 1894. Bridges's overall judgment was positive; Keats had "the highest gift of all poetry . . . the power of concentrating all the far-reaching resources of language on one point, so that a single and apparently effortless expression rejoices the aesthetic imagination at the moment when it is most expectant and exacting and at the same time astonishes the intellect with a new aspect of truth."

In the summer of 1905 Bridges took his family to Switzerland for their health, and by winter he had begun writing an essay on Shakespeare's plays that had been commissioned by A. H. Bullen as an introduction to volume 10 of the Stratford Town edition of Shakespeare's works. He wrote to Bullen from St. Moritz on 15 January 1906, offering to withdraw the essay (not yet completed) for fear that Bullen and his readers would not like it. He said that his attempt to "solve the problem which his [Shakespeare's] extraordinary mixture of brutality with extreme, even celestial gentleness offers" would "be unpleasant to most readers." Bullen persisted and Bridges finished the article in time for publication in 1907. Entitled "The Influence of the Audience on Shakespeare's Drama," it soon became Bridges's most notorious essay. Bridges examines Shakespeare's offenses against propriety and common sense and explains the mixture of "brutality" and "celestial gentleness" by blaming Shakespeare's desire to please a heterogeneous theater audience that for the most part held aesthetic ideals far below Shakespeare's. Shakespeare's offenses indicate that the dramatist "had to reckon with an audience far blunter in feeling than he would find today." The chief offenses are unnecessary and irrelevant obscenities to please the pit; unmitigated horror such as the blinding of Gloucester; unnecessary rudeness of manners and speech; incredible changes in behavior such as the sudden repentance of Angelo in *Measure for Measure* followed by his pardoning; incredible actions such as Macbeth, a man of "magnificent qualities of mind," stooping to the murder of Duncan, and of Othello being so quickly and completely duped by Iago. According to Bridges, these last offenses reveal a weakness of motivation in many of Shakespeare's plots. That is, the characters, even the most noble, are made to act *surprisingly* without proper cause for the sake of dramatic effect, and indeed the effects are often so intense that even a modern audience will overlook them in the theater, but not if they read the plays deliberately and carefully as literature, as Bridges was doing when he wrote this essay.

The essay was controversial, as Bridges intended it to be, coming after a century of Shakespeare idolatry. It drew sharp responses from Alfred Harbage, who in his book *Shakespeare's Audience* (1941) called it a "frivolous assault"; from Augustus Ralli; and from other Shakespearean scholars. However, from the viewpoint of the literary critic (in contrast to the theatergoer) Bridges's objections to Shakespeare's improprieties are not wide of the mark.

When Bridges's friend Mary Elizabeth Coleridge, the great-grandniece of Samuel Taylor Coleridge, died unexpectedly in the summer of 1907, Bridges set to work immediately on a generous tribute to her that appeared in the *Cornhill Magazine* in November of that same year under the title "The Poems of Mary Coleridge" (republished in volume 5 of *Collected Essays*, 1931). Bridges praises Coleridge's verses for their intimacy, spontaneity, beauty, and originality, finding in them "Imagination of a very rare kind, conveyed by the identical expression of true feeling, and artistic insight." Her imagination, which Bridges describes as "intellectual" and "tyrannous," coexisted with "a wide, light hearted active enjoyment of life." From this tension came her best poetry. The obscurity of some of her imagery reminds him of her favorite poet, William Blake; the ethereal tone of her verse owes something to her good friend Richard Watson Dixon. Bridges concludes that she resembles the German poet Heinrich Heine in the masterful ease of her style, but she is more successful than he in approaching the Greek attainment (form) and the Christian Ideal (spirituality), for Heine's verse is not spiritual and is cheapened by cynicism.

An examination of Bridges's other favorite woman poet, "The Poems of Emily Brontë" was first published in the London *Times Literary Supplement*, 12 January 1911, as a review of *The Complete Poems of Emily Brontë*, edited by Clement Shorter. (It was republished in volume 7 of *Collected Essays*, 1932.) However, Bridges finds that Brontë is "not delicately conscious" of her rhythm or her rhyme, that her diction is sometimes stereotyped, her imagery sometimes ambiguous. She has not "a perfected style." On the other hand, her simplicity of diction is in her successful poems "the best means of verbal touch with felt reality." She has "a wide intellectual grasp" and "a concentrated fire of native passion." The essay is a judicious evaluation, with faults carefully weighed against virtues. Bridges reveals more enthusiasm for her work in his poem "Emily Brontë" (collected in *New Verse*, 1925), which begins, "Thou hadst all Passion's splendour."

There are several other essays on individual poets that deserve mention. In "Dryden on Milton" (*Speaker*, 24 October 1903; republished in volume 6 of *Collected Essays*) Bridges vents his lifelong contempt for John Dryden, whose verses in praise of Milton and other poets are quoted only to be attacked. Of Dryden's verse in general he says: "He sinks to dulness of metre, dulness of rhythm, dulness of rhyme (of which he was most proud), dulness of matter; a dulness as gross as his ruinous self conceit." Of Dryden's attempt to "improve" certain poems such as Geoffrey Chaucer's *The Knight's Tale*, he wrote: "How could Dryden imagine that he was 'improving' Chaucer when he was stuffing in all that stodgy padding?" And at the conclusion of the essays, Dryden's entire career is dismissed with "if all poetry had been like Dryden's, I should never have felt any inclination towards it."

In "Lord de Tabley's Poems" (*Speaker*, 12 December 1903; republished in volume 5 of *Collected Essays*, 1931) Bridges pays tribute to a well-liked friend whose social position he respected. Lord de Tabley was fairly well known in the Victorian period for his verse play *Philoctetes* (1866) and for several volumes of poems. Bridges, in reviewing in this essay a definitive selection of de Tabley's verse, finds much to praise, especially "Ode to Pan," written under the influence of Keats, and also those poems dealing with Lord de Tabley's favorite science, botany.

The essay "George Darley," published in 1930 in volume 4 of the *Collected Essays*, is a composite of an article published in the *Academy* (4 August 1906) and a review (*Times Literary Supplement*, 6 March 1908). Time has not dealt kindly with the reputation of the Romantic poet George Darley. Bridges criticized much of his poetry for weakness of sentiment and looseness of form, but he liked the blank verse of the historical play *Ethelstan* (1841) and the two completed cantos of the allegory *Nepenthe* (1835).

"Dante in English Literature" (*Times Literary Supplement*, 24 June 1909; republished in volume 6 of *Collected Essays*), a review of Paget Toynbee's *Dante in English Literature from Chaucer to Cary*, points to the Italian poet's influence on Chaucer, Milton, Thomas Gray, Percy Bysshe Shelley, Coleridge, William Wordsworth, Walter Savage Landor, and George Gordon, Lord Byron. In "The Springs of Helicon" (1909; republished in volume 7 of *Collected Essays*, 1933), a review of J. W. Mackail's book of the same title, Bridges discusses the faults and virtues of Chaucer, Edmund Spenser, and Milton. In "Wordsworth and Kipling" (1912; republished in volume 7 of *Collected Essays*) Bridges argues that in their use in poetry of the speech of the common man Wordsworth and Rudyard Kipling allow their styles to be flawed by the mannerisms resulting from the attempted "dialectic regeneration" of decaying speech forms. Bridges goes on to argue that the needed reforms in poetic style should be achieved by new prosodies but not necessarily by new poetic diction.

The most interesting passage in "The Glamour of Grammar" (1912; republished in volume 8 of *Collected Essays*, 1934), a review of Logan Pearsall Smith's *The English Language* and of Ernest Weekley's *The Romance of Words*, occurs when Bridges expresses his love of archaic locutions, those "exiled aristocrats," as he calls them, which, now banished, may eventually be welcomed, together with certain lowborn expressions, once again to the language: "there are many patiently awaiting their opportunity, like the democratic and oligarchical parties in the cities of ancient Greece; those whom one revolution drives out the next will bring back; and they have plenty of old friends at home ready to welcome them." Bridges not only welcomed them but frequently used them in his own poetry. Among the words he wants back are old vocalized inflections of plurals such as *frostës, postës*, and *flamës*, which he prefers to "the unpronounceable mono-syllables that, having taken their place, strew their cacophonies broadcast over our best literature."

In *An Address to the Swindon Branch of the Workers' Educational Association*, delivered on 28 October 1916 and published as a book by the Clarendon Press the same year (it was republished in volume 10 of *Collected Essays*, 1936), Bridges's topic is the "improvement of the educational condition of the working classes," which he says is important if democracy is to be preserved and stabilized after the war. Legislation necessary to give the workers leisure to educate themselves must be passed, but leisure alone is not enough, especially in the cities, where so many workers spend their free time in cheap, sensation-seeking amusements such as the cinema. "This trifling with the emotions is the most soul-destroying habit that can be indulged." The chief purpose of education is to awaken and train the inborn love of Beauty and Good. Proper environment for this would be provided if hostels and colleges could be established that would teach the workers to make proper use of the city's theaters, concert halls, and art galleries or to respond to the beauties of nature in the country. Thus the working man may escape "wrong-loving," which leads to "vulgarity . . . our national blemish and sin."

Bridges's famous critique of his friend Hopkins was written not as an independent essay but as a "Preface to Notes" for the *Poems of Gerard Manley Hopkins* (1918). Hopkins died on 8 June 1889, and by August of that year Bridges had written to Canon Dixon that he planned an edition of Hopkins's poems with a memoir. The following August, Bridges wrote to Hopkins's mother that the edition had not yet been completed and that it should contain a memoir or at least a preface that would "put the poems out of the reach of criticism." Bridges then decided that the time was not yet right for the publishing of his friend's highly experimental verse, and he delayed further work on the edition and preface until 1917. On 7 September of that year Bridges wrote to Hopkins's mother that the selection of her son's poems that he had published in *The Spirit of Man* the previous year had been well received and that the Oxford Press would probably be willing to publish a complete edition of the poems. By February 1918 Bridges was working up to seven or eight hours a day at his task. The edition was published in December 1918 with Bridges's preface.

In putting "the poems out of the reach of criticism" the editor attempted to foresee the faults that the critics might find in Hopkins's verse, to define them, and to point to the virtues of the poetry that he felt were in danger of being obscured by the faults. As to the faults—those of taste include affectation and exaggeration of metaphor. Bridges defined Hopkins's chief errors in style as those oddities deriving from his doctrine of inscapes, the frequent obscurities caused by the omission of the relative pronoun to make space for more "poetical" words, and the deliberate use of words (including homophones) that are ambiguous in meaning and in grammatical function. Clarity was always one of Bridges's criteria. Hopkins frequently preferred multiplicity of meaning to lucidity. Other faults are undue harshness in sound effect and freakish and repellent rhymes. The reader, warns Bridges, must learn to tolerate these flaws and not allow them to obscure the power of the "terrible posthumous sonnets" nor "the rare masterly beauties that distinguish Hopkins' work."

In "George Santayana" (*London Mercury*, August 1920; republished in volume 8 of the *Collected Essays*), a review of *Little Essays, Drawn from the Writings of George Santayana* (1920) by Logan Pearsall Smith, Bridges, in praising Santayana's style, achieved a beautifully written essay on Santayana, the man and his thought. Bridges was reading Santayana's work by the turn of the century, when he also began a correspondence with him. They met for the first time at Oxford during World War I and continued a friendly relationship until Bridges's death. In interpreting those concepts of Santayana's philosophy that had special meaning for him, Bridges wrote: "The philosophy as I understand it is very consonant with my own thought." A few years later when Bridges was writing *The Testament of Beauty* (1929), these ideas he shared with Santayana and which he discusses in this essay were very much in his mind, especially what he defines as the "building up of idealism—that is, the supremacy of the imagination—on a naturalistic or materialistic basis," and the function of reason, which "harmonizes the various instincts and impulses, and establishes an ideal good." He also agrees with Santayana about the importance of Beauty, which Santayana states "gives men the best hint of ultimate good which their experience as yet can offer," and of which Bridges writes in the *Testament of Beauty*:

> Beauty is the highest of all these occult influences,
> the quality of appearances that thru' the sense
> wakeneth spiritual emotion in the mind of man.

Furthermore, he shares Santayana's notion that "Morals ... requires only the harmony of each life," an idea which Bridges fully develops in book 4 ("Ethick") of the *Testament*. And by writing his long poem, Bridges put into practice Santayana's opinion that "it is the function of poetry to emotionalize philosophy." Bridges's essay is a valuable introduction to Santayana's work and also to *The Testament of Beauty*.

Milton's Prosody, published in its final version in 1921, was the culmination of a long interest in the intricacies of prosody, ancient and modern, a subject that Bridges approached from a theoretical as well as a practical point of view. The rules of prosody that he formulated were consistently applied in the composition of his own verse, which included two thousand lines of experimental poetry written according to the rules of classical (quantitative) prosody as laid down by his young friend William Johnson Stone in the tract "Classical Metres in English Verse," which was privately printed in 1898 and republished in the 1901 edition of Bridges's *Milton's Prosody*.

Bridges's first analysis of Milton's verse appeared as a pamphlet in 1887 entitled *On the Elements of Milton's Blank Verse in Paradise Lost*. Subsequent versions and expansions appeared in 1889, 1893, and 1901. Included in the 1921 edition is the final version of a tract entitled "On the Prosody of Accentual Verse." It has a history even longer than the work on Milton. Bridges's interest in accentual verse probably began about 1877 when Hopkins sent him a copy of "The Wreck of the Deutschland" (1875), written in what Hopkins called "sprung rhythm" and what Bridges usually referred to as accentual verse or the "new prosody." It was designed to invigorate poetic rhythms and bring them closer to speech rhythms. Bridges's formulation of the rules of accentual verse first appeared in 1901. There are elements of his system repeated in "A Letter to a Musician on English Prosody" (*Musical Antiquary*, October 1909), in which he examines the proposition that poetic rhythms derive their beauty from a conflict between metrical and speech rhythms.

In "Humdrum and Harum-Scarum: A Lecture on Free Verse," first published in the *London Mercury* (November 1922; republished in volume 2 of *Collected Essays*, 1928), Bridges confronts the free-verse movement begun by the French and continued in England by Ezra Pound and others. He sets out "to discover the meaning of the term Free Verse, and then to show some of the results that must follow from writing in the new or free manner." He comes to the conclusion that the poets of the future will find "a wide field for exploration in the metrical prosody." A complete rejection of all prosody will result in chaos.

Bridges's last comments on prosodic matters are in the form of a note rather than an essay. " 'New Verse:' Explanations of the Prosody of My Late Syllabic 'Free Verse' " was written in 1923 and first published in 1933 in volume 7 of the *Collected Essays*. The essays on prosody discussed above are written in a precise, analytical style appropriate for the subject and are not designed for easy or popular reading. To those who would object, Bridges, in his 1921 study of Milton, makes this statement: "people . . . think that prosody is pedantic rubbish, which can only hamper the natural expressions of free thought and so on. But in all arts the part that can be taught is the dry detail of the material which has to be conquered; and it is no honour to an art to despise its grammar."

In "Humdrum and Harum-Scarum" Bridges was concerned with revolt against prosody. In "Poetic Diction in English" (*Forum*, May 1923; republished in volume 2 of *Collected Essays*) he turned his attention to the simultaneous revolt against what he called "the old diction" as it appears in the "Poets of today," whom he does not name. He probably had in mind Pound and his fellow imagists who eschewed archaisms and poeticism (though Pound himself used many of them in his earliest poetry) and insisted on the vocabulary of common speech. He admits that the general attitude of these rebels is rational as was a similar movement the preceding century begun by Wordsworth and other Lake Poets. However, with quotations from Milton's "Lycidas," with its heightened and inspired poetic diction, from Shelley's "Adonais," with its extravagant yet beautiful expressions, and from Matthew Arnold's "Thyrsis," with its simplified diction, he attempts to demonstrate that Milton's and Shelley's poems are powerful and convincing whereas Arnold's poem is lacking in passion and is unconvincing. A diction elevated above the colloquial may be employed in our greatest poems and should not be rejected. He also defends the use of archaic language and poeticisms when they are appropriate for the texture of the verse, as he did in his essay "The Glamour of Grammar," discussed above.

Of Bridges's "capacity for friendship" R. K. R. Thornton has said that it "manifests itself in a variety of ways; and this is not the friendship which insists on the friend's perfections but a generous friendship which loves at the same time as perceiving faults." Nowhere is this capacity for loving friendship more evident than in the memoirs of Digby Mackworth Dolben, Richard Watson Dixon, and Henry Bradley. The first of these was published as an introduction to Bridges's edition of *The Poems of Digby Mackworth Dolben* (1911) and was republished after revisions in 1915 and again in *Three Friends* (1932). Bridges met Dolben at Eton in 1862 and quickly took the younger boy under his guidance. Dolben was always in delicate health, pale and sensitive with a strong interest in religion that became almost obsessive and that led him from High Church views toward Roman Catholicism. He was suspended from Eton in 1863 under suspicion of being a Catholic. Bridges describes their brief days at Eton and Dolben's religious and psychological problems there with tact and eloquence. In commenting on a picture of Dolben in the Eton Gallery he remarks, "You can see the saint, the soul rapt in contemplation, the habit of a stainless life, of devotion, of enthusiasm for high ideals." Henry James, on completing his reading of the volume sent him by Logan Pearsall Smith, was moved to write: "the disclosure and picture of the wondrous young Dolben have made the liveliest impression on me, and I find his personal report of him very beautifully and tenderly, in fact just perfectly, done. . . . Bridges seems to me right that no *equally* young case has ever given us ground for so much wonder (in the personal and aesthetic connection)."

Bridges's memoir includes a critique of Dolben's poetry that is chiefly about his religious experiences and that abounds in Pre-Raphaelite imagery and diction. Bridges's evaluation is generous, perhaps too generous. In the course of comparing Dolben's poetic methods with his own, Bridges makes a statement about personal and impersonal poetry that has become famous: "Our instinctive attitudes toward poetry were very dissimilar, he regarded it from the emotional, and I from the artistic side. . . . What had led me to poetry was the inexhaustible satisfaction of form, the magic of speech, lying as it seemed to me in the masterly control of the material.... Dolben imagined poetic forms to be the naive outcome of peculiar personal emotion."

The memoir of Richard Watson Dixon was published in 1909 as an introduction to a selection of Dixon's poems edited by Bridges, who had first heard about Dixon from Dixon's former student Hopkins in 1878. The next year he traveled to Hayton for a visit with the canon, who was rector there (they corresponded until Dixon's death in 1900), and when Dixon went to London to engage in research on his six-volume history of the Church of England, he stayed in Bridges's apartment. As with Dolben, the memoir is a tribute to the man as well as the poet. Bridges was much taken with the canon's personality. In the course of a long description he wrote, "his eyes did their angelic service to the soul without distraction." Bridges and Dixon liked to take long walks together in the woods, walks commemorated in Bridges's poem "Eclogue I: The Months." In his critique of Dixon's poetry Bridges commented on its mysticism, its medieval and Pre-Raphaelite sources, and on Dixon's response to the beauties of nature, especially as it appears in "The Feathers of the Willow," his finest poem according to Bridges.

In 1928, five years after the death of the philologist Henry Bradley, Bridges wrote to his widow in response to her praise of his memoir of Bradley that he was "among the few men with whom I have had full friendship without any intellectual or moral reserve." They met about the turn of the century at Oxford, and Bradley made his first visit to Bridges's home at Yattendon in September 1901. Their fast-developing friendship is described in Bridges' memoir, first published in 1926 and republished in *Three Friends*. Bradley's major contribution to scholarship was the part he played in the editing of the *Oxford English Dictionary*, to which he devoted forty years of his life. Beginning work on it in 1883, he became senior editor in 1915, a position he maintained until his death in 1923. Bridges loved the man and respected his learning and literary judgment. He consulted Bradley when he was compiling *The Spirit of Man* and when he was experimenting with his neo-Miltonic syllabics from about 1913 on, and also on such diverse matters as Chaucer's prosody and Bridges's own system of phonetic script. He chose Bradley in 1913 to be one of the founders of the Society for Pure English.

Two essays written a dozen years apart may be considered a defense of the importance of poetry in the scientifically oriented twentieth century. *The Necessity of Poetry* (1918; republished in volume 10 of *Collected Essays*) was delivered as an address to an audience of workingmen on 22 November 1917. It is an attempt to "justify the claim of poetry to that high place which is and always has been granted it." The poet, Bridges goes on to say, like the scientist, uses words, but he uses them as an artist, connotatively, with all their suggestive meanings, whereas the scientist uses them denotatively, in their single meanings. Yet the poet has truths to impart about the human condition just as important as those communicated by the scientist. Furthermore, the poet has the advantage of working in metered, that is, precisely rhythmic, language, which adds an extra emotional dimension to his compositions. This emotional power of poetry is identical with "those universal primary emotions of man's spirit which give rise also to morals and religion and which lead us naturally toward Beauty and Truth."

Bridges's final essay, *Poetry* (1929; republished in volume 10 of *Collected Essays*), was delivered as the first of the National Lectures on the BBC on 28 February 1929, when he was still at work on *The Testament of Beauty*. In his lecture as in his poem Bridges sees human life as a progression from material origins (the atom) to a vision of God, a vision motivated in some elect souls by a consciousness of Beauty to which the art of poetry contributes.

A few other essays deserve mention. The publication of volume 1 of *The Works of Sir Thomas Browne*, edited by Charles Sayle, gave Bridges the opportunity to attack this much-admired stylist of the seventeenth century. In his review-essay "Sir Thomas Browne" (*Speaker*, 14 May 1904; republished in volume 8 of *Collected Essays*) he argues that Browne "was a mass of superstition" and that his *Pseudodoxia Epidemica* (1646) contains "gems of fatuity." "I have never found it readable except piecemeal." Bridges is again on the attack in "Bunyan's *Pilgrim's Progress*" (*Speaker*, 8 April 1905; republished in volume 8 of *Collected Essays*), a review of a new edition of *Pilgrim's Progress* illustrated by George Cruikshank. It is a severe analysis of the aesthetic and ethical weaknesses of Bunyan's work. "The story being bad in itself, is not excused or sustained by the allegory." Bridges finds the style crude, the theology narrow, and Pilgrim's abandonment of wife and children morally inexcusable. "Studies in Poetry"

(1907; republished in volume 7 of *Collected Essays*), a review of Stopford Brooke's volume of the same name, praises Brooke for his "fine tastes" and "true instincts" but condemns him for faulty methods in evaluating and explaining poetry. Brooke overestimates the influence of such historical movements as the French Revolution on individual poets; he mistakenly thinks a poem can be explained by an account of its genesis; and he is not severe enough in his critical evaluations. Of Brooke's statement "When criticism seeks to find out faults, I never think it worth much," Bridges ironically observes, "It would have been delightful if Aristotle had said this when lecturing on Homer." Bridges also condemns Brooke's facile acceptance of the notion that the complicated structure of Shelley's "Ode to the West Wind" was the result of spontaneous, unconscious, unpremeditated inspiration; and of Brooke's statement that "there is a logic of emotion as well as of thought," Bridges observes that it would have been useful if Brooke had demonstrated "what some of the laws of this logic are."

In "Word-Books" (1910; republished in volume 7 of *Collected Essays*), a review of *A New Shakespearean Dictionary* by Richard John Cunliffe and a new edition of W. W. Skeat's *An Etymological Dictionary of the English Language*, Bridges argues the importance of sound dictionaries for the understanding, appreciation, and writing of literature; and to illustrate his point he mentions that Robert Browning "when he determined to devote himself to poetry . . . read the whole of Johnson's dictionary through." "The Bible" (first published in 1911; enlarged and republished the same year; enlarged version republished in volume 8 of *Collected Essays*) is one of the most positive essays that Bridges wrote. It gives high praise to the Miles Coverdale/William Tyndale Bible of the sixteenth century. It is "an early and inimitable masterpiece of abounding grace," and its coming into existence "we must recognize to be a piece of extravagant good fortune . . . it was Tyndale and Coverdale who raised the plant; the revisers of 1611 only pruned and trained it." An account of the composition of the Coverdale/Tyndale Bible and an analysis of the style are given to support Bridges's high estimate of its worth and of its influence on English-speaking peoples.

Of interest chiefly to specialists are "On the Musical Setting of Poetry" (1896), first published as a preface to Bridges's "ode" for the bicentenary of the death of Henry Purcell, which was set to music by Sir Hubert Parry and sung at the Leeds Festival and at the Purcell Commemoration in London in 1895, and three essays on church music: "A Practical Discourse on Some Principles of Hymn-Singing" (*Journal of Theological Studies*, October 1899), "English Chanting" (*Musical Antiquary*, April 1911), and "Anglican Chanting" (*Musical Antiquary*, January 1912). These four essays were republished in 1935 in volume 9 of *Collected Essays* (with some repetitious parts of "Anglican Chanting" omitted) together with a few separate notes on church music too brief to be considered essays. Bridges published two essays entitled "The Proper Pronunciation of Latin" (*Oxford Point of View*, May 1902 and November 1903), and later two more entitled "The Pronunciation of Latin" (*Speaker*, 30 July 1904; *Times Educational Supplement*, 1 October 1912), and he also wrote a brief letter in 1912 on the subject to the London *Times* (20 September). His essay "On the Pronunciation of English" appeared in the 23 July 1904 issue of the *Speaker*. To the tracts of the Society for Pure English from 1919 to 1928 he contributed the following essays: "On English Homophones," "On the Dialectical Words in Edmund Blunden's Poems," "What is Pure French?" (written under the pseudonym Matthew Barnes in collaboration with Monica Bridges), "On the Terms Briton, British, Britisher" (in collaboration with Henry Bradley), "Pictorial, Romantic, Grotesque, Classical," "Poetry in Schools," and "Words from the French, E—EE" (as Matthew Barnes in collaboration with Monica Bridges). Also, in 1927 he edited for S.P.E. *English Handwriting (Tract No. XXVIII)*, with thirty-one calligraphic plates and eleven pages by Bridges of "General Remarks."

As an essayist Bridges will be remembered chiefly for his critiques of the poetry of Keats and the plays of Shakespeare and his memoirs of Dolben, Dixon, and Bradley. His highly theoretical but valuable articles on prosody will not be forgotten by specialists in the field. However, Bridges's major contribution to English literature is in the short lyric poem on such traditional subjects as love, response to the beauties of nature, and grief for the death of the beloved, and in the short poem (not necessarily "lyric" in the usual sense) of substantial philosophic, psychological, or religious content such as "The Affliction of Richard," "Eros," and "Low Barometer." His poems show a technical skill deriving from a natural talent but also from his scholarly research into classical and modern prosody. Not mere personal expression but a mastery of poetic form was his abiding concern. "What had led me to poetry," he wrote in his memoir on Dolben, "was the inexhaustible satisfaction of form, the magic of speech, lying it seemed to me in the masterly control of the material." He was fairly conservative by nature, and his best poems are those in conventional accentual-syllabic meters. Yet he always believed that experimentation was necessary to keep poetry alive. He wrote successfully in accentual and quantitative meters, and he developed a new verse form, his "neo-Miltonic syllabics" and his "loose Alexandrines," which is itself an important contribution to the genre of the long philosophical poem. During the first three decades of this century he was considered one of England's most important poets. Within ten years of his death in 1930 his reputation had sharply declined as a result of the change in tastes brought on by the poetic revolution of the imagists and by the rise in the influence of such experimental writers as Ezra Pound and T. S. Eliot. In recent years there has been a return of interest to the traditional formalist poetry of which Bridges was a chief exemplar, and there are indications that Bridges's reputation as an important poet will be reestablished.

Letters:

The Correspondence of Robert Bridges and Henry Bradley 1900-1923 (Oxford: Clarendon Press, 1940);

Richard J. Finneran, ed., *The Correspondence of Robert Bridges and W. B. Yeats* (London: Macmillan, 1977);

Donald E. Stanford, *The Selected Letters of Robert Bridges with the Correspondence of Robert Bridges and Lionel Muirhead*, 2 volumes (Newark: University of Delaware Press, 1983-1984).

Bibliographies:

George L. McKay, *A Bibliography of Robert Bridges* (New York: Columbia University Press / London: Oxford University Press, 1932);

Lee Hamilton, *Robert Bridges: An Annotated Bibliography* (Newark: University of Delaware Press, 1991).

References:

Nicolas Barker, *The Printer and the Poet* (Cambridge: University Printing House, 1970);

Sister Mary Gretchen Berg, *The Prosodic Structure of Robert Bridges' "Neo-Miltonic Syllabics"* (Washington: Catholic University of America Press, 1962);

Roy Fuller, "The Case for Bridges," *Times Literary Supplement*, 30 November 1970, p. 54;

Fuller, "Untroubled Waters," *London Magazine*, 24 (December 1984 - January 1985): 133-137;

Albert Guerard, *Robert Bridges: A Study of Traditionalism in Poetry* (Cambridge, Mass.: Harvard University Press, 1942);

William G. Holzberger, "Remembering the Bard of Boar's Hill," *Michigan Quarterly Review*, 19 (Winter 1980): 117-127;

George L. Lensing, "Bridges Redivivus," *Hudson Review*, 32 (Summer 1979): 308-312;

Catherine Phillips, "Robert Bridges and the English Musical Renaissance," in *Order in Variety: Essays and Poems in Honor of Donald E. Stanford* (Newark: University of Delaware Press, 1991);

Jean-Georges Ritz, *Robert Bridges and Gerard Hopkins 1863-1889: A Literary Friendship* (London: Oxford University Press, 1960);

John Sparrow, *Robert Bridges* (London: Oxford University Press, 1955);

Lindon Stall, "Robert Bridges and the Laws of English Stressed Verse," *Agenda*, 2 (Spring-Summer 1973): 96-108;

Donald E. Stanford, *In the Classic Mode: The Achievement of Robert Bridges* (Newark: University of Delaware Press, 1978);

Stanford, "Robert Bridges and the Free Verse Rebellion," *Journal of Modern Literature*, 1 (September 1971): 19-31;

Edward Thompson, *Robert Bridges* (London: Oxford University Press, 1944);

R. K. R. Thornton, Review of *The Selected Letters of Robert Bridges*, *Hopkins Quarterly*, 11 (Spring-Summer 1984): 48-55;

Yvor Winters, "Robert Bridges and Elizabeth Daryush," *American Review*, 8 (January 1937): 353-367;

Winters, "The Shorter Poems of Robert Bridges," *Hound & Horn*, 5 (January-March 1932): 321-327;

Elizabeth Cox Wright, *Metaphor Sound and Meaning in Bridges' Testament of Beauty* (Philadelphia: University of Pennsylvania Press, 1951);

F. E. Brett Young, *Robert Bridges: A Critical Study* (London: Secker, 1914).

Papers:
Most of Bridges's papers are in the Bodleian Library, Oxford. There are letters in the British Library, London; the University of Reading Library; and in the archives of the Royal College of Physicians, London; and letters and manuscripts in the Thomas Cooper Library, University of South Carolina, Columbia, South Carolina.

Samuel Butler

(4 December 1835 - 18 June 1902)

This entry was updated by Lee E. Holt from his entry in DLB 18: Victorian Novelists After 1885.

See also the Butler entry in DLB 57: Victorian Prose Writers After 1867.

BOOKS: *A First Year in Canterbury Settlement* (London: Longmans, Green, 1863; New York: Dutton, 1915);

The Evidence for the Resurrection of Jesus Christ, as Given by the Four Evangelists, Critically Examined, anonymous (London: Williams & Norgate, 1865);

Erewhon; or, Over the Range, anonymous (London: Trübner, 1872; New York: Dutton, 1907);

The Fair Haven: A Work in Defence of the Miraculous Element in Our Lord's Ministry upon Earth, both as against Rationalistic Impugners and Certain Orthodox Defenders, by the Late J. P. Owen, Edited by W. B. Owen, with a Memoir of the Author, anonymous (London: Trübner, 1873; New York: Kennerly, 1914);

Life and Habit: An Essay after a Completer View of Evolution (London: Trübner, 1878; New York: Dutton, 1910);

Evolution, Old and New: or the Theories of Buffon, Dr. Erasmus Darwin, and Lamarck, as Compared with That of Mr. Charles Darwin (London: Hardwicke & Bogue, 1879; Salem, Mass.: Cassion, 1879);

Unconscious Memory: A Comparison between the Theory of Dr. Ewald Hering, Professor of Physiology at Prague, and the Philosophy of the Unconscious of Dr. Edward von Hartmann; with Translations from these Authors (London: Bogue, 1880; New York: Dutton, 1910);

Alps and Sanctuaries of Piedmont and the Canton Ticino (London: Bogue, 1882; New York: Dutton, 1913);

Selections from Previous Works, with Remarks on Mr. G. J. Romanes' "Mental Evolution in Animals," and a Psalm of Montreal (London: Trübner, 1884);

Gavottes, Minuets, Fugues, and Other Short Pieces for the Piano, by Butler and Henry Festing Jones (London: Novello, 1885);

Luck or Cunning as the Main Means of Organic Modification? An Attempt to Throw Additional Light upon the Late Mr. Charles Darwin's Theory of Natural Selection (London: Fifield, 1886);

Ex Voto: An Account of the Sacro Monte or New Jerusalem at Varallo-Sesia, with Some Notice of Tabachetti's Remaining Work at the Sanctuary of Crea (London: Trübner, 1888; London & New York: Longmans, Green, 1890);

Narcissus: A Cantata in the Handelian Form, by Butler and Jones (London: Weekes, 1888);

A Lecture on the Humour of Homer, January 30th 1892; Reprinted with a Preface and Additional Matter from the "Eagle" (Cambridge: Metcalfe, 1892);

On the Trapanese Origin of the "Odyssey" (Cambridge: Metcalfe, 1893);

The Life and Letters of Dr. Samuel Butler, Headmaster of Shrewsbury School 1798-1836, and Afterwards Bishop of Lichfield (2 volumes, London: Murray, 1896; 1 volume, New York: Dutton, 1924);

The Authoress of the "Odyssey," Where and When She Wrote, Who She Was, the Use She Made of the "Iliad," and How the Poem Grew under Her Hands (London: Longmans, Green, 1897; New York: Dutton, 1922);

Shakespeare's Sonnets Reconsidered, and in Part Rearranged; with Introductory Chapters, Notes, and a Reprint of the Original 1609 Edition (London: Longmans, Green, 1899);

Erewhon Revisited Twenty Years Later, both by the Original Discoverer of the Country and by His Son (London: Richards, 1901; New York: Dutton, 1910);

The Way of All Flesh, edited by R. A. Streatfeild (London: Richards, 1903; New York: Dutton, 1910);

Essays on Life, Art and Science, edited by Streatfeild (London: Richards, 1904);

Ulysses: An Oratorio, by Butler and Jones (London: Weekes, 1904);

God the Known and God the Unknown, edited by Streatfeild (London: Fifield, 1909; New Haven: Yale University Press, 1917);

The Note-Books of Samuel Butler: Selections, edited by Jones (London: Fifield, 1912; New York: Kennerly, 1913);

Butleriana, edited by A. T. Bartholomew (London: Nonesuch, 1932);

Further Extracts from the Note-Books of Samuel Butler, edited by Bartholomew (London: Cape, 1934);

Samuel Butler's Notebooks: Selections, edited by Geoffrey Keynes and Brian Hill (London: Cape, 1951; New York: Dutton, 1951).

Collection: *The Collected Works of Samuel Butler*, Definitive Edition, edited by Henry Festing Jones and A. T. Bartholomew, 20 volumes (London: Cape, 1923-1926; New York: Dutton, 1925).

OTHER: *The Iliad of Homer, Rendered into English Prose*, translated by Butler (London: Longmans, Green, 1898; New York: Dutton, 1921);

The Odyssey, Rendered into English Prose, translated by Butler (London: Longmans, Green, 1900; New York: Dutton, 1920).

SELECTED PERIODICAL PUBLICATIONS—UNCOLLECTED: "On English Composition," *Eagle*, 1, no. 1 (1858): 41-44;

"Our Tour," *Eagle*, 1, no. 5 (1859): 241-255;

"Our Emigrant," *Eagle*, 2 (1861): 101, 149; 3 (1862): 18;

"Darwin on the Origin of Species: A Dialogue," *Press* (New Zealand) (20 December 1862);

"Darwin Among the Machines," *Press* (New Zealand) (13 June 1863);

"The Mechanical Creation," *Reasoner* (1 July 1865);

"Lucubratio Ebria," *Press* (New Zealand) (29 July 1865);

"A Psalm of Montreal," *Spectator* (18 May 1875);

"A Clergyman's Doubts," *Examiner* (February-June 1879);

"God the Known and God the Unknown," *Examiner* (May-July 1879);

"Quis Desiderio . . . ?," *Universal Review* (July 1888): 411-424;

"A Medieval Girl School (Oropa)," *Universal Review* (December 1889);

"The Deadlock in Darwinism," *Universal Review* (April-June 1890);

"The Humour of Homer," *Eagle*, 17 (March 1892): 158-193;

"Not on Sad Stygian Shore," *Athenaeum* (4 January 1902): 18;

"The Note Books," *New Quarterly Review* (November 1907): 137-164; (March 1908): 295-324; (June 1908): 447-484; (October 1908): 613-632; (April 1909): 219-224; (February 1910): 109-128; (May 1910): 229-248.

Although Samuel Butler was largely overlooked by the general public in his own time—only one of his books, *Erewhon Revisited Twenty Years Later* (1901), was published without financial support from its author—Samuel Butler achieved fame soon after his death in 1902 and has ever since been recognized as a significant Victorian writer. The powerful and original critique of the family in the posthumously published *The Way of All Flesh* (1903) was acclaimed in 1906 by an enthusiastic George Bernard Shaw, whose comments together with those of others brought it wide attention. The insights into family life presented in this novel have aroused a strong response in many generations of readers, and countless writers have since carried them on. Butler's many-faceted appraisal of the whole human condition in his satire *Erewhon* (1872), in his books on evolution, and in his *Note-Books* (1912) still evokes a kind of shock of recognition, and his speculations concerning the unconscious give additional dimensions to the findings of psychoanalysis. The clear, direct prose, contrasting sharply with Victorian "fine writing"; the startling use of irony and ambiguity; and the iconoclastic attacks on the bigwigs of his time have continued to delight and stimulate thoughtful and imaginative people of the twentieth century.

Born on 4 December 1835 at Langar Rectory near Nottingham, England, Samuel Butler was the son of the Reverend Thomas Butler and the grandson of Dr. Samuel Butler, headmaster of Shrewsbury School and bishop of Lichfield, whose career and times his namesake later enthusiastically recorded in a two-volume biography. His mother was Fanny Worsley, the daughter of Philip John Worsley, a Bristol sugar refiner. Four children grew up in the Butler household: Samuel, the oldest, his two sisters, and a younger brother; a fifth child died in infancy. Butler was not related to the seventeenth-century Samuel Butler, author of *Hudibras* (1663, 1664, 1678), with whom he is sometimes confused. Butler attended a private school at Allesley near Coventry and Shrewsbury School, traveled to Italy twice as a youngster with his family and once as a university student with a friend; after 1872 he vacationed in Italy annually. He never married but remained by deep conviction a bachelor. In 1858 he took a first-class degree in classics at St. John's College, Cambridge.

Butler's career as a publishing author began tentatively with occasional pieces in his college journal, the *Eagle* of St. John's. These include some telling comments on how to write, praising the clear, direct style of two hundred years earlier which he emulated; an account of his Easter trip to France, Switzerland, and Italy; and two articles describing a voyage out to New Zealand and the life of a frontiersman. The voyage had come about as a result of a family quarrel. Because his family wished him to enter the ministry as his father had done before him, Butler, hoping to discover what he wanted to become, had worked for a time after his graduation from St. John's among the poor in London as an amateur lay assistant to a clergyman. Growing doubts about religion—from his own close reading of the Greek New Testament and from his observation that the boys in his evening class who had not been baptized were no worse than those who had been—and growing interest in art and music, especially the music of George Frideric Handel, led him to decide against entering the church. After much heated discussion, his angered father, who firmly refused to support him in the art studies he now wished to undertake, advanced money which eventually would have been his anyway, since his grandfather had designated him as "tenant in tail" to a considerable estate. This allowed him to emigrate from England and chart out a life of his own. On his initial night aboard the ship *Roman Emperor*, bound for New Zealand, Butler for the first time in his life failed to say his prayers, and he never said them again. During the three-month voyage he read Edward Gibbon's *History of the Decline and Fall of the Roman Empire* (1776-1788), a book regarded with abhorrence by many orthodox Victorians and surely reading that would have been frowned upon at the rectory.

From 1859 to 1864 Butler lived in New Zealand, managing his own eight thousand-acre sheep run and gradually building up a satisfactory mode of life, with new friends and plenty to do. He had a piano transported by bullock dray to the house he had built. (It was a two-day trip from the nearest town, Christchurch.) There in off hours he entertained himself and his infrequent visitors by playing Handel. In 1883, looking back on his life, Butler wrote: "Of all dead men Handel has had the largest place in my thoughts. In fact, I should say that he and his music have been the central fact in my life ever since I was old enough to know of the existence of either music or life. All day long—whether I am writing or painting or walking—but always—I have his music in my head."

Finally, when Butler's capital had been nearly doubled, he returned to London and took up residence at Fifteen Clifford's Inn, his home for the remainder of his life. While in New Zealand, in addition to the two articles for the *Eagle*, he had sent home letters of such interest that his father, now somewhat placated, combined the articles and the letters into a volume with the writer's approval and underwrote their publication. *A First Year in Canterbury Settlement* (1863) still makes interesting reading, although for reasons hard to fathom its author came to hate it and to wish it had never been published. Designed in part as a "how-to" manual to interest would-be emigrants, it vividly narrates the events of the three-month voyage from England, telling the reader how to equip himself for such a trip; describes the towns of Lyttleton and Christchurch; and, with considerable attention to financial details, explains how to go about acquiring a sheep run. It gives an account of explorations that eventually led Butler to the discovery of a mountain and a pass later named for him. Butler emphasizes the independence and self-reliance of frontier existence. He indeed remained a kind of intellectual "frontiersman" for the rest of his life.

More important for Butler's later career than *A First Year in Canterbury Settlement* were an indeterminate number of pieces he had published in the *Press*, the newspaper of Christchurch, under various pseudonyms, concerning the theory of evolution which Charles Darwin, a schoolfellow of Butler's father at Cambridge, had recently formulated. These pieces expressed views both for and against Darwinism and suggested, among many other ideas, that machines had their own evolution and might someday take over the world. Back in England, Darwin somehow came into possession of the first of these articles. He liked it so much that he sought to have it reprinted in England. Later, Butler sent his pamphlet *The Evidence for the Resurrection of Jesus Christ* (1865) to Darwin, who wrote him a cordial note of acknowledgment to which Butler replied, sending him his second *Press* article on evolution. In 1872 Butler spent a weekend at Down, Darwin's home, at Darwin's invitation, and he later visited there again. One of the real tragedies of Butler's life is that this friendly relationship soon degenerated into bitterness as a result of misunderstandings for which neither Darwin nor Butler was solely to blame.

After his return from New Zealand, Butler devoted himself assiduously for thirteen years to

Samuel Butler at Cambridge, mid 1850s

the study of painting; several of his pictures were exhibited at the Royal Academy. The best known of these, *Family Prayers*, is sometimes on view at the Tate Gallery in London. Butler continued writing in off-hours and on weekends, and published at his own expense the pamphlet on the conflicting accounts of the Crucifixion and Resurrection in the Gospels which he sent to Darwin. He then gradually completed a satirical fantasy called *Erewhon* based on his New Zealand experience, on his study of Darwin, and on his critical thoughts about religion and society. In this work as in much of his later writing, he was encouraged by Eliza Mary Ann Savage, a fellow art student with whom Butler developed a warm friendship. She read each of Butler's manuscripts with delight and helped him with her intelligent comments and unfailing enthusiasm until her death in 1885. (Her many sprightly letters to Butler and some of his replies were published in 1935.)

In search of new pastures and possible wealth, the unnamed hero of *Erewhon* travels through the realistic mountain landscape of New Zealand to an imaginary topsy-turvydom on the other side of the range. On the top of the pass into Erewhon he encounters ten hollow statues which howl so in the wind as to scare off all would-be passersby—these statues clearly stand for the ten commandments. The hero, after losing his guide, almost in spite of himself gets past the statues, down a frightening ravine, and across a river, nearly losing his life. Then he enters the country of Erewhon, is jailed, falls in love with the jail keeper's daughter Yram, is taken to the capital city where he is treated as a guest, and finds out about the looking-glass country where the hollowness of many of the "eternal verities" of Victorianism (and of today as well) is exposed.

On realizing that machines will take over the world, Erewhonians have banned them. Since they are convinced that being sick is a willful and wicked act, they impose long jail sentences for such things as the common cold and pneumonia; but people who lie or steal are commiserated with and placed in the care of a "straightener" for cure because they are thought not to be blamable for their deeds. The Erewhonians have two currencies: one, the hard cash of commerce; and the other, the money of the Musical Banks (churches), which is reputed to lead to salvation but has no value at all in the real world. Their colleges are institutions of "unreason," where "hypothetical languages" of no conceivable use to anyone are taught. After his experiences of these and other satirical transpositions of the European order, the hero escapes in a balloon to avoid punishment for his possession of a watch and returns to England.

This extravaganza has been criticized by some as too various in its scope, combining satire and utopianism in an inextricable mixture. But it is probably the most effective book of its kind in English literature since Jonathan Swift's *Gulliver's Travels* (1726), which it resembles and which certainly influenced Butler. As Swift had done, Butler also makes the reader aware of the new perspectives from which any culture can be seen when reflected and distorted in an alien setting. Among his many telling suggestions, perhaps the most prophetic is that crime can be viewed as disease and illness as malingering: now there are specialists in the psychology of the criminal and in psychosomatic medicine. *Erewhon*, rejected by several publishers and then printed anonymously at its author's expense, was the only one of Butler's books that made a profit during his lifetime. Butler put his name on the fifth edition of *Erewhon* (1873).

Perhaps encouraged by the initially promising sales of *Erewhon*, Butler wrote and published at his own expense another book, again with satiric intent, building it around the substance of the pamphlet on *The Evidence for the Resurrection of Jesus Christ*, which had gone almost unnoticed upon its publication eight years before. In response to Eliza Savage's urging that he write a novel, he dramatized his ideas in *The Fair Haven* (1873) by inventing an author, John Pickard Owen, who, before he dies insane, presents Butler's own analysis of the discrepancies in the Gospel accounts of Christ's death and resurrection; and he has the author's brother, William Bickersteth Owen, open the book with an extensive "Memoir" of John. This memoir, the most lively part of *The Fair Haven*, creates living pictures of Mr. and Mrs. Owen, culminating in a stream-of-consciousness daydream of the mother which ends with the martyrdom of her sons. In tone and detail it is a forerunner of *The Way of All Flesh*.

At the close of the memoir William gives passages from his brother's writings during the period when he had lost his faith. These passages are so convincing and effective that they tend to override the ostensible evangelizing of the body of the book. They sound like the notes Butler was writing for himself and kept on writing throughout the rest of his life, selections from which were later published as *The Note-Books of Samuel Butler*. John Pickard Owen's argument, which commences after the memoir is done, is developed in an absolutely exasperating form, presenting material which grows more and more damaging to a literal faith in the Bible, meanwhile repeating over and over that all of this is leading up to a greater argument yet to come which will contradict it. When that greater argument finally arrives, it is that one must believe in spite of logical inconsistencies and flat contradictions. No wonder John fell into a state of idiocy and religious melancholy, and then died.

Some readers and reviewers thought the book a genuine defense of Christian faith, perhaps proving thereby that Butler's wish to make it a satire had not been fully realized. But when, upon reading Butler's preface to the second printing (the book had appeared anonymously at first, with no preface), they discovered that it was indeed intended as a satire and that they had been taken in, their dislike of Butler knew no bounds, and from that time they never forgave him. Indeed, some readers even today find the book too clever, arguing that when he wrote it Butler himself was unsure of his position and thus could

Rendering of Butler's homestead in New Zealand by his friend and collaborator Henry Festing Jones (St. John's College, Cambridge University)

not adequately control what he was doing. Since in 1873 even more than today an author dared not play fast and loose with religious faith, Butler's difficulty in finding an audience was surely increased by *The Fair Haven.*

Undeterred by its lack of success, Butler began work on *The Way of All Flesh,* which grew gradually into the sort of novel Eliza Savage had hoped he would write. Since its composition had been so closely related to his affection for her, he set it aside after her death in 1885, never to work on it again. Many of its details had been drawn from his own family experience, and so he also felt that publication would hurt the feelings of his closest relatives. The one book that might have been a commercial triumph in his lifetime thus did not appear until a year after his death. By 1953 it had appeared in sixty-eight editions in England, America, France, Germany, Spain, and Italy; there have been many others since, including one in the Houghton Mifflin Riverside series that restores the text of the 1885 manuscript, removing much of R. A. Streatfeild's (Butler's literary executor) editorial work. It is probably the most successful English novel of its era, both in numbers of readers and in influence on other writers, among them Shaw, Arnold Bennett, Somerset Maugham, E. M. Forster, and James Joyce. Like Vincent van Gogh and so many others, Butler could have been a wealthy and much-praised man had his fame not been posthumous.

More successfully than *The Fair Haven, The Way of All Flesh* also uses multiple perspectives. The principal narrator, Overton, belongs to the generation of Ernest Pontifex's father, but unlike Theobald Pontifex, he is a relaxed, worldly, imaginative man, though a trifle stuffy; thus he can interpret and to some extent empathize with the tense and sometimes tragic events he narrates and can take Ernest's side. But the novel does not adhere meticulously to Overton's perspective. Many passages have an omniscient narrator who reports inner thoughts and daydreams and has a wider view and greater knowledge than the thoughtful but complacent Overton: the book's implications reach beyond the ken of its elderly narrator.

Since *The Way of All Flesh* is about the evolutionary development of a family and about the unconscious but devastating influence of unexamined thoughts, Butler proceeds most deliberately, sketching in the simple and happy life of Ernest's great-grandfather John Pontifex (the name means "builder of bridges"), carpenter, organ maker, and amateur artist, and the eighteenth-century world in which he lived; then describing the gradual decay of this pastoral mode of life in the "successful" career of the grandfather, George Pontifex, whose one aim in life is money and achievement, and who becomes a big-city man. In the feeble attempt of his son, Theobald, to defy George Pontifex and not become a clergyman, the reader sees what Ernest's life would have been had he not reincarnated some of his great-grandfather's strength. Since Theobald is weak, his incipient rebellion leads nowhere. His entrapment into marriage—Christina becomes his wife through her luck at a game of cards—and the miserable honeymoon as well as the miserable career as a clergyman, a life for which he had no inner calling or talent, all are etched with acid and are quite unforgettable.

Well into the novel the "hero" Ernest appears, ganged up against by mother and father, who, thinking they are doing their duty, make his existence wretched. Theobald beats Ernest constantly for failing to learn his lessons, for saying "tum" instead of "come," and indeed for each and every expression of natural childhood. "All was done in love, anxiety, timidity, stupidity, and impatience," Overton says. "They were stupid in little things; and he that is stupid in little will be stupid also in much." For a long time Ernest is sure that Theobald and Christina are right to blame him for everything, but another side of Ernest knows that he is surrounded by lies and must discover what he himself would be. Long before Sigmund Freud, Butler has the real Ernest say to Ernest: "The self of which you are conscious . . . will believe these lies. . . . This conscious self of yours, Ernest, is a prig. . . . Obey *me*, your true self, and things will go tolerably well with you. . . . I, Ernest, am the God who made you." But Ernest cannot hear.

To provide an outside force that will help Ernest discover his true self, Butler creates a sister of Theobald, Alethea (modeled on Eliza Savage), beloved by Overton (though they had too much good sense to marry), who befriends her nephew and for a time counteracts the misery of his life. Independently wealthy, she moves to the village where Ernest now attends prep school and quietly arranges for him to have lessons in carpentry so that he can learn to build an organ, as his great-grandfather had done before him (note the implication of sexual maturity in the term *organ*). She skillfully makes it seem that he does this because he wants to, not because he is told to. Having learned carpentry, he will have one thing he can do well because he loves it, and will begin to be proud of himself. Unfortunately, Alethea dies before her work is completed, but she leaves a large sum of money to come to Ernest when he is twenty-eight, though he is not to be told that this will happen. Theobald puts a quick end to the carpentry lessons, but Alethea's brief influence has given Ernest the strength to survive the deadly ordeals lying ahead.

In the next events of the novel, showing the unremitting tortures to which Christina and Theobald are eager to put their schoolboy son, all in the name of love, Butler dramatizes his conviction that each generation is ruined by too much conscious interference from the previous generation—by the demands of the superego, as Freud would say. Chapters thirty-eight through forty-four present such a string of disasters that some readers might think, "No parents could be so cruel!," while others might think, "This is the truth about parents!" Only Theobald's coachman, John, defends the browbeaten Ernest, declaring to Theobald, who is discharging him: "If you bear hardly on Master Ernest . . . I'll come back and break every bone in your skin." Unfortunately, he is unable to carry out this threat. Butler's uncanny ability to make the reader see the hidden, unconscious motives of both parents and child is the source of the power of this part of the novel.

Ernest survives the thumbscrews of parental inquisition, but just barely. At last he gets to Cambridge, where he has more freedom to grow. He takes an honors degree and, when he is twenty-two, comes into five thousand pounds left to him by his grandfather. Upon returning home a free and wealthy man, however, he still through habit defers to his father in all things and spends several hours a day studying the classics and his math, so wretchedly has he been molded. Back in Cambridge, he prepares for ordination. Unlike his father, who had felt his faith fading as this event approached, Ernest, upon hearing an evangelical preacher, suddenly becomes more passionately devoted to Christ than ever Christina or

Theobald had been. They are frightened by his sudden zeal and regard him as a fool.

The newly ordained Ernest takes up his duties in central London where he becomes acquainted with a High Church curate, Pryer, who moves him rapidly toward Rome. Pryer persuades Ernest to turn his money over to him to invest in order, he says, to found a School of Spiritual Pathology to regenerate the Church of England. Overton apologizes for his godson, using an argument from biology: "The vagaries which it will now be my duty to chronicle," he says, are the result of "the shock of change," and are not surprising "when his antecedents are remembered." Butler's hero is definitely not heroic in these rapid changes but is nonetheless fascinating: a new type of hero-loser in the world of the novel. To put his ideas into immediate practice, Ernest rents a room in the slums of London from a landlady who sizes him up quite well: "He don't know nothing at all, no more than a unborn babe." Meeting Towneley, a classmate from Cambridge, by chance, he explains that he finds poor people fascinating. "Don't you like poor people?" he asks. Towneley answers "No, no, no," and "It was all over with Ernest from that moment." Towneley,wealthy, handsome, courteous, is Butler's portrait of what a man can be if he is as lucky in his parents (they died when he was two) as Ernest is unlucky, and if he has mastered life sufficiently to act without introspection and self-consciousness.

Doubts about what he is doing now haunt Ernest. He attempts to convert an atheist tinker, but instead is converted by him; then, with sensual—not spiritual—thoughts in mind, he goes to see a prostitute, one of two girls who live in his rooming house. Finding that Towneley already has an appointment with her, he rushes off to the other girl, who unfortunately for him is not a prostitute; he is arrested for assault, and sentenced to six months in jail because, as the judge says, he did not have "the common sense to be able to distinguish between a respectable girl and a prostitute." On his way to tell Theobald and Christina about their son's disaster, Overton speculates that no one is really to blame: neither Theobald for his treatment of his son, considering how badly his father treated him, nor Ernest for his actions, considering how he has been brought up. He puts the matter in a biological framework, reflecting his creator's *Life and Habit* (1878) theory (Butler was concurrently working on his next book): "If a man is to enter into the Kingdom of Heaven, he must do so, not only as a little child, but as a little embryo, or rather as a little zoosperm—and not only this, but as one that has come of zoosperms which have entered into the Kingdom of Heaven before him for many generations."

In prison, Ernest has an attack of brain fever, like John Prickard Owen before him, though unlike Owen he does not die. Having recovered, he is informed that his fellow curate, Pryer, has absconded with his wealth. Ernest learns to be a tailor and on leaving prison sets up an old-clothes shop. He marries Ellen, a servant girl who had been expelled from Theobald's house when she became pregnant. (The marriage turns out to be illegal because she is already married.) For a while real happiness comes to him. As he looks back, he sees that his school and university careers were "a lie" and "a sickly debilitating debauch" compared with life in prison and as a shopkeeper.

Now Ernest is approaching the age when his aunt's money will be his, and Overton, again using his creator's *Life and Habit* theory and feeling that "poverty is very wearing; it is a quasi-embryonic condition through which a man had better pass if he is to hold his later developments securely," persuades Ernest—who has separated from Ellen because she is an incurable alcoholic—to give up his tailor shop and become his secretary and steward. The novel moves rapidly to a close. Whether the climax is effective or not depends on each reader's perspective: can he believe that human fulfillment does not have to mean conventional recognition, success, and marriage?

To free the two children born to him and Ellen from the dangers of parental abuse, Ernest insists that they be brought up by others and is pleased when his son becomes a boatman and his daughter marries one of her playfellows. Ernest and Overton travel abroad; then Ernest, wealthy again, revisits his home to say farewell to his mother, who is dying. Theobald is shocked to see him looking so robust and well groomed: "This was not what he had bargained for." At the reader's final glimpse of Ernest, he is a creative writer who insists on antagonizing people by his radical views concerning the family, evolution, and religion and will thus probably never win an audience.

Although many of the details in *The Way of All Flesh* closely parallel events in its author's life, it is nevertheless a genuine work of art, not

Family Prayers
"I did this in 1864 and if I had gone on doing
things out of my own head instead of making
Studies, I should have been all right." S.B.
Canvas 20 in. by 16 in.

Butler's best-known painting, now at the Tate Gallery, London

merely an autobiographical novel: it presents a generalized case for all parent-child relationships. For this reason, those who argue that Butler distorted what had happened in his own family life because he had a chip on his shoulder miss the point. All children are in a way Ernest, and Ernest is no more identical with the historical Samuel Butler than Tom Jones is with his creator, Henry Fielding.

The Way of All Flesh, Butler's greatest work, became famous soon after it appeared in 1903 because Victorian smugness and traditional family relationships were ripe for questioning as Butler questioned them. The constructive side of the book—the way it illustrates theories of evolutionary memory and the development of unconscious learning, and the way it exposes the unconscious motives of its characters (even beyond the comprehension of Overton)—is its most enduring quality. It has not yet been fully explored. Can one understand an author who, after justifiably crucifying Theobald for his cruelty toward Ernest and saying when he dies that he had never been more than half alive, acknowledges the wisdom of a kind of racial learning by remarking: "This, however, was not the general verdict concerning him, and the general verdict is often the truest"? Butler is suggesting that the common view may possess a deeper wisdom, inherited over the centuries, than the critical judgment of the intellectual modern man.

When Butler had left New Zealand, he had paid the expenses of a friend, Charles Paine Pauli, to return to England with him for medical treatment. Ever since that time, and up to Pauli's death in 1898, Butler generously gave him a monthly allowance on his repeated claim that he was nearly destitute. He did not learn until Pauli's funeral that he had been lied to all those years. In addition to this continuous drain on his modest capital, Butler failed to sell more than a few pictures or to make much money by writing and was soon perilously short of funds due to poor investments. In hope of higher dividends and on the advice of a banker friend, he had put his money into several new ventures, among them a Canadian tanning-extract company that soon showed signs of failure. In 1875 Butler traveled three times to Montreal to find out what was happening to this company (of which, because of his investment, he had been made a director) and to try to straighten out its affairs. From that time until his father's death in 1886, he had to worry continuously about money, so much so

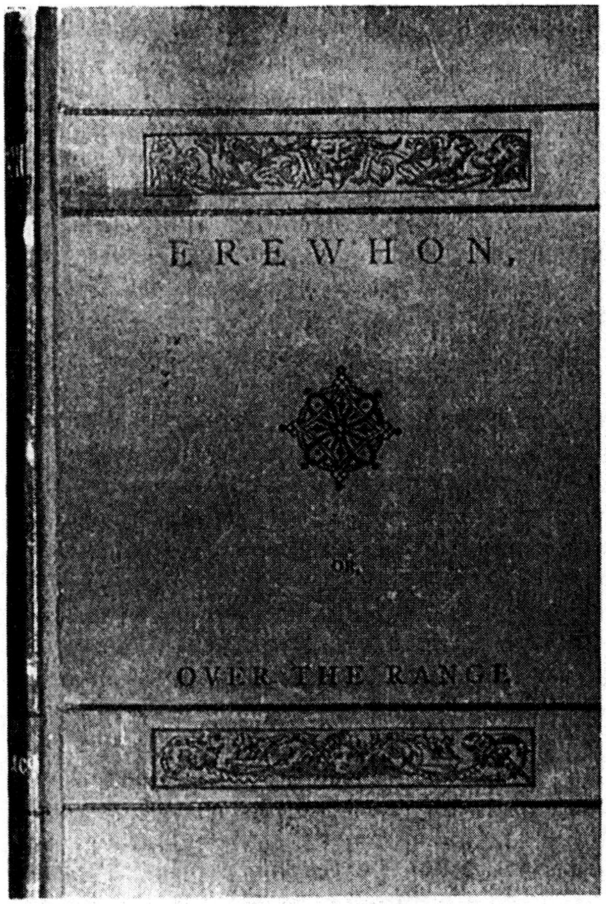

Front cover for the only book by Butler that made a profit during his lifetime. It was written anonymously and published at Butler's expense (Thomas Cooper Library, University of South Carolina).

that he was forced to ask his father for help; nevertheless, he went on writing and publishing. In 1877 he gave up his nearly fruitless attempt to become a successful painter. He later blamed his lack of success on the academic style of the art schools. On the canvas of his *Family Prayers* he wrote in pencil across the ceiling of the room: "If I had gone on doing things out of my own head instead of making copies I should have been all right."

While in Montreal, and on Montreal Mountain for the first time, Butler had heard the bells of Notre Dame. Their sound as they echoed over the city gave him the idea that they were like ancestral selves in each of us calling out their messages. A creature's "past selves," he wrote, "are living in unruly hordes within him at this moment and overmastering him. 'Do this, this, this, which we too have done, and found our profit in it,' cry the souls of his forefathers within him. Faint are the far ones, coming and going as the sound of the bells wafted on to a high mountain; loud and clear are the near ones, urgent as an alarm of fire. 'Withhold,' cry some. 'Go on boldly,' cry others. 'Me, me, me, revert hitherward, my descendant,' shouts one as it were from some high vantage-ground over the heads of the clamorous multitude. 'Nay, but me, me, me,' echoes another; and our former selves fight within us and wrangle for our possession."

This notion of ancestral voices became a key thought in his next book, *Life and Habit*, the most important of Butler's studies of evolution. In *Life and Habit* Butler examines the phenomenon of memory, relates it to heredity, and notes its paradoxical connection with consciousness and unconsciousness. What we really know, he observes, we cannot know that we know, just as a pianist must achieve unconscious command of all the infinite details of a passage if he is to play well. So the things we (that is, ourselves and our ancestors) have laboriously learned through eons of trial and error must now be performed without awareness—for example, digestion of food and the beating of the heart. This unconscious knowledge which has been handed on to us complete and perfect by our successful forefathers cannot be infringed upon by awareness without becoming problematical: "perfect knowledge and perfect ignorance" become "extremes that meet." Yet as we progress and acquire new abilities and knowledge we must go through an awkward stage before they can be perfected. "Beauty is but knowledge perfected and incarnate.... It is not knowledge, then, that is incompatible with beauty; there cannot be too much knowledge, but it must have passed through many people ... before beauty or grace will have anything to say to it."

In this book, one of the first to make extensive use of the concept of the unconscious and contemporary with his exploration of unconscious motives in *The Way of All Flesh*, Butler thus explains heredity as identical with memory—memory of practices so often repeated as to be unconscious. Life itself is also identical with memory: to say that a piece of matter lives is to say that it remembers, and what cannot remember is dead. Later, Butler came to believe that no hard line can be drawn between living and dead: "When people talk of atoms obeying fixed laws, they are either ascribing some kind of intelligence and free-will to atoms or they are talking nonsense," he writes. Some day, Butler thought, we will read and write as instinctively as we now circulate our blood.

But if human records should be lost, it would take another William Harvey to discover that we do so. Butler explores many of the implications of his ideas about memory and the unconscious, some full of humor, but none lacking seriousness as well. He indeed invented the term "unconscious humor" for people who give themselves away, as the unconscious unbeliever did who prayed to the Almighty "to change our rulers *as soon as possible*," or as Francis Bacon did when he remarked that "reading good books on morality is a little flat and dead." Indeed, if this humor becomes excessive it distresses a healthy person. "Truly, if there is one who cannot find himself in the same room with the Life and Letters of an earnest person without being made instantly unwell, the same is a just man and perfect in all his ways."

In *Life and Habit* Butler argues that all living beings (who, in terms of their cells and thus in terms of their deeper memories, are identical with their ancestors) must have worked so long and so hard at such complex matters as digesting, breathing, hearing, and seeing, as to have acquired the ability to do them without conscious attention. "Is there anything," Butler asks, "in digestion, or the oxygenization of the blood, different in kind to the rapid unconscious action of a man playing a difficult piece of music on the piano?" He answers that there is not. Although we use the word "heredity" to explain our possession of such talents, he adds, the word explains nothing; whereas the analogy with memory and practice casts much light on what goes on. For example, accomplishments which we have in common with our remotest ancestors, such as digestion, are in us most unconscious and most beyond our control; whereas more recent acquisitions such as speech, the arts and sciences, and the upright position are much more within our control.

So obvious does Butler's interesting theory become to him that he argues that the burden of proof that his analogy is meaningless rests on those who think him wrong: "Shall we say, then, that a baby of a day old sucks (which involves the whole principle of the pump, and hence a profound practical knowledge of the laws of pneumatics and hydrostatics), digests, oxygenizes its blood (millions of years before Sir Humphry Davy discovered Oxygen), sees and hears . . . shall we say that a baby can do all these things at once . . . and at the same time not know how to do them, and never have done them before?" In discussing the problem of personal identity in *Life and Habit* Butler is at his most brilliant, handling, with the skill of a trained dialectician, the problem of where the self begins and ends. His conclusion that there are no clear demarcations between the present ego and the primordial spark of life in the original ooze is defended with a brilliance that would warm the heart of the teacher of logic; yet all the time he is ready to acknowledge the practical value of the demarcations set up in ordinary speech. To acquire the immense skill it possesses, the egg must be the chicken, must be the egg, must be the chicken for thousands of generations without gap in personal identity except for lapses into the unconscious as learning becomes perfected. Butler's book delights the thoughtful mind; still, to one (like most modern readers) who thinks only in terms of laboratory experiments and things that can be proved not by argument but by the microscope, it may all seem useless. What, one wonders, may be the connection between Butler's unconscious memory and the latest findings concerning DNA?

Butler's early support for Darwin's theory was now rapidly disappearing. His *Life and Habit* theory, he was convinced, got behind the back of natural selection by actually explaining how it works: namely, through memory in the individual and in the race and by ascribing a purpose to each individual being. "A chicken . . . is never so full of consciousness, activity, reasoning faculty, and volition, as when it is an embryo in the egg-shell, making bones, and flesh, and feathers, and eyes, and claws, with nothing but a little warmth and white of egg to make them from . . . . Is it in the least agreeable to our experience that such elaborate machinery should be made without endeavour, failure, perseverance, intelligent contrivance, experience, and practice? . . . What is the discovery of the laws of gravitation as compared with the knowledge which sleeps in every hen's egg upon a kitchen shelf?" Butler now argued that the "natural selection" principle amounted to no more than saying that when variations arise, they will accumulate. He hoped that the Darwinians would respond to his theory. "Pitch into it and into me by all means" he wrote to Francis Darwin—but in vain. Although *Life and Habit* was fairly widely reviewed, no one confronted the thesis it set forth.

In the opening pages of *Life and Habit* Butler had warned his readers that he was not a scientist and had no wish to instruct, but rather to entertain and interest them. He also said, "Let no

Front cover for Butler's posthumously published autobiographical novel, widely regarded as his greatest work (Thomas Cooper Library, University of South Carolina)

unwary reader do me the injustice of believing in *me*. In that I write at all I am among the damned." Developing his idea that no sharp line can be drawn between the individual and his ancestors or between the whole body and its parts, Butler had suggested that it is just as well that our cells do not know the larger life in which they participate. If a blood corpuscle should discover that it was part of a larger animal which would not die with its death, it would be introspecting too much. "I should conceive he served me better," Butler writes, "by attending to my blood and making himself a successful corpuscle, than by speculating about my nature." In this way this curious writer condemns his own work, since he at least refuses to be a complacent cell minding his own business and not asking questions. However, he found his work forcing itself upon him. "I never make them [his books]; they grow," he wrote; "they come to me and insist on being written."

Owning few books himself, Butler now, like Karl Marx, adopted the habit of working daily in the British Museum reading room where he could have access to an enormous library, a habit he continued for the rest of his life. He generally worked from 10:30 in the morning until 1:00, and found that he was happier in the British Museum than he was anywhere else, except in Italy. His search for material for *Life and Habit* had led him to discover Jean-Baptiste Lamarck, Georges-Louis Buffon, Erasmus Darwin, and other pre-Darwinian evolutionary theorists whom Charles Darwin had dismissed in a "brief but imperfect sketch" of previous speculations added to later editions of *On the Origin of Species by Means of Natural Selection* (1859).

In order to set before the general reading public a more complete picture of evolutionary theory and to show how his *Life and Habit* speculations fitted into it, Butler wrote *Evolution, Old and New* (1879). He came to link his memory theory with the purposeful evolutionary development of living forms, believing that it showed how the strivings of one individual were connected with those of other individuals and thus of the race and became latent in becoming intense. Butler succeeded in demonstrating that many passages in *On the Origin of Species* imply the necessity of use and disuse in evolution, and also that Buffon, Erasmus Darwin, and Lamarck had all stated the survival-of-the-fittest principle for which Charles Darwin and Alfred Russel Wallace were given credit.

In November 1879 an English translation of a German study of Erasmus Darwin, printed before *Evolution, Old and New* had appeared, was published with a foreword by Charles Darwin. In this book Butler found an attack upon himself, without his name being mentioned, and some of the same passages from Buffon he had used, translated by exactly the same words he had used in making his translation from the French. On checking the original German text (after hastily learning that language), he discovered to his amazement that this material had been added by the translator, although Darwin's foreword made no mention of the text's having been altered, and thus it would appear to predate Butler's book. He thereupon wrote Darwin inquiring what had happened, and Darwin replied that alterations in translations were so common a practice that he had not thought the changes worth mentioning in his foreword. Naturally this answer did not satisfy Butler, who then aired the whole matter in a letter to the *Athenaeum*. Darwin now recalled that the printer had inadvertently omitted a statement that the text was a revision, not merely a translation, and wished to inform Butler of this fact, but Darwin's friend Thomas Henry Huxley advised him not to do so; and later, after Butler had attacked Darwin again in his next book, *Unconscious Memory* (1880), and Darwin once more wished to reply, Leslie Stephen also advised silence. Thus Butler was never to learn that the misrepresentation was an error, compounded on Darwin's part by timidity and the taking of bad advice, and not really the commonplace of scientific behavior he came to believe it was.

In *Unconscious Memory*, the most quarrelsome book he ever wrote, Butler uncovers verbal subterfuges in Darwin and Huxley in a way that is both cruel to his opponents, who are less skilled in the use of language than he is, and also very funny. He attempts to explain the paradoxical fact that people had by now become converted to Darwinism when actually "natural selection" accounts for neither the arising of variations nor for their being handed on: this remarkable triumph of conversion, he believes, was brought about by a conspiracy to hoodwink the public by treating the key problems ambiguously and vaguely. He delights in proving that Darwin continually lets purposive concepts slip into his explanations while always denying that he is doing so. He points out again that his own *Life and Habit* theory deals effectively with the key issues on which Darwin, Huxley, and the others have to hedge. To give an example of scientific honesty as a contrast to what he thought was Darwin's shabby treatment of previous evolutionists, Butler carefully discusses the work of a certain Ewald Hering, a German scientist who in 1870 had set forth a memory theory similar to his own, and also explains the difference between his theory of the unconscious and that of Eduard von Hartmann.

Butler's books on evolution aroused only moderate interest; they sold poorly and were discussed infrequently by reviewers and writers to the editors of various journals. Undaunted, Butler tried one more time, publishing *Luck or Cunning as the Main Means of Organic Modification?* (1886), in which he again stated the case for a revised Lamarckianism as opposed to what he regarded as the mindless mechanistic theory defended by the Darwinians. But now he is able to demonstrate by apt quotation that evolutionists such as Huxley, Grant Allen, and even Darwin himself are coming to link heredity and memory as he had done, though without giving him credit for the idea. He traces the shifting statements on instinct in the various editions of *The Origin of Species* to show that Darwin reversed himself again and again, and he explores similar shifts and obfuscations in the other champions of the day. In *Luck or Cunning?* more than in the three other books on evolution, Butler discusses the psychology of persuasion, pointing out how prone the mind is to reject extreme change and how bound we are by what we want to know and want to believe. All knowledge is compromise with extremes, he says, whether of life or death, luck or cunning, design or absence of design. Grant Allen, writing in the *Academy*, rightly said of *Luck or Cunning?*: "Here is a work of consummate ingenuity, rare literary skill, and a certain happy vein of sardonic humour a work pregnant with epigram, sparkling with wit, and instinct throughout with a powerful original fancy.... [Butler] stands by himself, a paradoxer of the first water, hopeless and friendless." But, typically, Allen considered none of the specific points Butler had raised. Perhaps some day there will be a reappraisal of Butler's strangely effective books on evolution.

While working on his books, Butler also carried out other literary projects, writing letters to magazines and newspapers, publishing book reviews and articles, and even, although he was really not fond of poetry except for Shakespeare and Homer, composing poems of his own. In "A Psalm of Montreal," which appeared in the *Spectator* in 1875, Butler humorously protests the failure of a Montreal museum to exhibit a plaster cast of the Discobolus because it had no clothes on, ending each stanza with the refrain "O God! O Montreal!" Later he wrote several sonnets, two moving ones about Eliza Savage and one about immortality which was printed in the *Athenaeum* in 1902. In this, the last of his sonnets, he wistfully denies the possibility of personal survival but celebrates instead the immortality of memory and fame: "Yet meet we shall, and part, and meet again, / Where dead men meet, on lips of living men."

In 1879 Butler published eight articles in the *Examiner* under the title "God the Known and God the Unknown," in which he speculates (as he had also done in *Life and Habit*) that as living cells make up our being, we and our ancestors and indeed all living forms, descended as we are from a common ancestor, may make up a larger being which we can call god, even though we are as unconscious of this being as our cells are of us. Henry Festing Jones says that Butler

Samuel Butler and Henry Festing Jones

wished some day to revise these articles to show that inorganic matter must be included in this god as well as organic. Butler spoke of his theory as "a modest Pantheism." During the same year, Butler entertained himself and readers of letter columns by writing to the *Examiner*, under different names a series of letters discussing the problems of an impoverished clergyman with a wife and five children who has come to doubt the literal truth of the Christian story he is paid to teach. In the opening letters he asks for help. Further letters in the series, purporting to be by other writers (and two or three of the sixteen actually were), propose different ways he might resolve his dilemma, either by dissembling his loss of faith or by courageously giving up his post and facing financial ruin and starvation for his family. Butler also occasionally lectured at the City of London College, the Working Men's College, and at the Somerville Club. Some of these lectures appeared in print at the time they were given; those for which manuscripts could be found are included in the Shrewsbury Edition of Butler's works. They explore Butler's biological theories, his Homeric speculations, and his general thoughts about life.

Even when his finances were at a low ebb, Butler had always insisted upon a summer vacation in Italy; in 1880 his publisher offered to pay him for an illustrated book about that country. He promptly wrote and made drawings for *Alps and Sanctuaries of Piedmont and the Canton Ticino* (1882), and when the publisher rejected it as not the sort of book he had had in mind, Butler published it at his own expense. Some of the drawings he included were by Henry Festing Jones, a close friend since 1876, who took many vacation trips with him. The two men were united by their mutual love for Italy and for music—for Handel especially—and from 1887 on, Jones, like Pauli, received financial aid from Butler, who was nothing if not generous. Together they composed music in the style of Handel and published *Gavottes, Minuets, Fugues, and Other Short Pieces for the Piano* (1885) and a cantata called *Narcissus* (1888). Later, to remove some of the amateurishness from their work, they took lessons in harmony from two professional musicians.

Alps and Sanctuaries opens with a paean to Handel, who "is as much above Shakespeare as Shakespeare is above all others," and to London, especially the view down Fleet Street. Then, in a mélange of biological philosophizing and general comment, following his ideas wherever they lead him, Butler describes his visits to Faido, San Michele, Lanzo, Varese, Locarno, and the other vil-

Clifford's Inn, London, where Butler lived the last thirty-eight years of his life

Butler's sitting room at 15 Clifford's Inn

lages and towns of northern Italy which he loved so well. He discusses lies, pointing out that "lying is so deeply rooted in nature that we may expel it with a fork, and yet it will always come back again"; the difference between Catholics and Protestants, Englishmen and Italians, priests and other men; and the radical changes in life to be expected from the advent of technology and advertising. Butler, who had a fluent command of Italian and could converse easily with many of the people he met, was able to fill the book with lively anecdotes and character sketches. In this work Butler reveals a mellow understanding of the paradoxes of life. He is especially kind to the Roman Catholicism of his Italian friends: the faith of the robust, beautiful, contented people of northern Italy must somehow be right since they themselves are so right. If Protestants understood Catholicism they "should find it to be in many respects as much in advance of us as it is behind us in others," he wrote.

Another expression of Butler's love for Italy appeared in 1888: *Ex Voto*, a study of the Sacro Monte at Varallo. But this time Butler was not so relaxed and casual as he had been in *Alps and Sanctuaries*. He had now developed an infatuation to match or even overtop his understandable devotion to Handel: this time it was for Tabachetti, who, he was convinced, had created in his *Journey to Calvary* "the most astonishing work that has ever been achieved in sculpture." Butler had acquired a camera; he illustrated this book with photographs he and Jones had taken. They do indeed show that the figures in the tableaux at Varallo are dramatic, full of motion and character, and surprisingly realistic, but they do not seem to justify Butler's fanatical enthusiasm. Was he longing to make the breakthrough as an art critic that the Victorian world had refused to admit that he had made in biological theory? In addition to *Ex Voto* he published several magazine articles on Tabachetti and on the Bellinis.

It is well to remember how completely Butler had come to trust intuitive insights. Having been so bitterly fooled as a young man by what he now regarded as pretensions, so that, for example, he had never questioned assumptions as diverse as religious literalism or the beauty of the St. Gothard Pass and had not learned to trust his conviction that Handel was the greatest composer, he now became at times a little ridiculous in championing private insights. He justifiably rejected any evaluation he found people making because it was "the right thing" and not because they really believed it. But he mercilessly extended this notion until he came to be convinced that all enthusiasms except his own were hollow and empty. His scorn for established "greats" can be withering and distressing to those with different insights from his, though often very funny in their hyperbole: for example, his attacks on Johann Wolfgang von Goethe, Francis Bacon, Wolfgang Amadeus Mozart, Johann Sebastian Bach, Ludwig van Beethoven, Raphael, George Eliot, and a host of others. Eventually, although enjoying the humor, one cannot help coming to question Butler's judgment. But then when one considers his often sly, skillful, thoughtful justifications of his idiosyncracies, one is in a way won back to him again.

Between 1888 and 1890 Butler contributed eight articles to the *Universal Review* on art, Darwinism, and other topics, some in the loose-knit tradition of the personal essay. He speculates in "Quis Desiderio . . . ?" that Wordsworth, in concert with Southey and Coleridge, probably murdered Lucy; with this thought in mind, he says, "there is not a syllable in the poem. . . . that is not alive with meaning." Quite unknowingly and in the spirit of fun, he is on the trail of the discovery made in 1922 of Wordsworth's love affair in France, which to some extent took him off the high moral pedestal he had occupied. In "A Medieval Girl School (Oropa)" he meditates on the unwillingness of the church to admit that it deals not with literal truth but with a kind of universal myth helpful to the well-being of mankind: "The cleric and the man of science (who is only the cleric in his latest development) are trying to develop a throat with two distinct passages—one that shall refuse to pass even the smallest gnat, and another that shall gracefully gulp even the largest camel; whereas we men of the street desire but one throat, and are content that this shall swallow nothing bigger than a pony."

In 1888 Butler was asked to prepare a memoir of his grandfather, Dr. Samuel Butler (1774-1839). When he looked into Dr. Butler's voluminous unpublished correspondence, the material so fascinated him by its clarity and directness that he decided to write a book-length portrait of the man and his age, not just a memoir, and to put before his readers as much of the original material as he could. The biography rapidly grew into two large volumes, *The Life and Letters of Dr. Samuel Butler* (1896), published at the author's expense. Butler felt at home in the world of his grandfather; people then were genuine and honest, he thought, understood the value of common sense, and possessed a conviction of order. Science had not yet frightened them, and they loved the classical learning which Butler had lampooned in *Erewhon* but which he now saw that he loved, too. This work received the most favorable press accorded any book by Butler during his lifetime, but even then it did not sell.

In 1891, when Butler and Jones were composing their oratorio, *Ulysses* (1904), Butler, who wrote most of the lyrics, looked into the Greek text of the *Odyssey* once more and found the poem so delightful that he could not put it down. He thereupon set himself to make a translation of it which would be as much at home in contemporary English as the poem itself no doubt had been in the classical Greek of Homer's day. Later he translated the *Iliad* with the same objective in mind. He then built up an elaborate case for two intuitive convictions that came to him about the *Odyssey*: that it was written by a woman, and that the setting was Trapani and Mount Eryx in Sicily. Once again Butler had high hopes. "Nothing," he wrote, "has ever interested me (except, of course, Handel) so much as this *Odyssey* business has done; it is far the finest piece of good fortune that ever happened to me." He traveled to Sicily and later to the Troad to see for himself the relationship between the descriptions in the two poems and what he thought to be the actual places. But once again the professional world turned a deaf ear. It seemed that the courageous Butler could make no breakthrough, no matter how hard he tried. Reviewers were kinder to him, however, than they had usually been in the past. The *Saturday Review* said of *The Authoress of the "Odyssey"* (1897): "We do not disdain Mr. Butler's book. It is written with great vivacity, and if it takes a number of readers to the pure and beautiful text of the *Odyssey* . . . its action will not have been in vain." Later Butler published his two translations. They are still among the easiest to read and clearest available, though lacking in beauty and not to be compared with the best translations of recent decades.

A final adventure into literary detective work was *Shakespeare's Sonnets Reconsidered* (1899). Butler had long loved the sonnets, and now he learned them by heart. He did his utmost to rearrange the 128 separate poems into a coherent sequence, assuming, as others had before him, that they ought to tell a story. Unfortunately, the story that he makes them tell is unconvincing, involving as it does an all-too-literal interpretation of some of the sonnets to imply a degrading homosexual affair with someone far less sensitive than Shakespeare and quite capable of playing demeaning practical jokes at his expense. Still, like his other books of this period, his study of the sonnets sets one thinking, and as a result, although rejecting Butler's annoying literalism, one may come to know these amazing poems better.

In 1901 Butler completed *Erewhon Revisited Twenty Years Later*, a sequel he had been thinking about and planning for some time, and, with help from G. B. Shaw, for the first time in his life found a publisher willing to underwrite one of his books. The hero of *Erewhon* returns twenty years later to the topsy-turvy land he had discovered to find that the Erewhonians have formed a new religion around his previous visit, based on his seemingly miraculous departure by balloon. In Hanky, Panky, and Downey, three leaders of the new religion, Butler attacks High Church and Jesuit and approves of Broad Church attitudes. The relationship of the hero with his son George, born after his departure from Erewhon as a result of his love affair with Yram, indicates Butler's realization that a good father-son relationship is possible, something he had not believed earlier in his life. George wants his father to announce that he and his balloon ascension were not miraculous, but his father takes a compromise course, telling the Erewhonians the truth about himself but urging them to change the new religion only gradually. If you wish, he says, you can "make me a peg on which to hang all your own best ethical and spiritual conceptions. . . . Better a corrupt church than none at all." Lacking the variety of the earlier *Erewhon*, this book is more unified and, some have thought, better than its predecessor, though *Erewhon* is certainly more often read and more original.

One more achievement remained for Butler, this time one that was able to win an enthusiastic readership. As long ago as during his years in New Zealand he had begun jotting down each day in little black books, one of which he afterward always carried in his pocket, the thoughts that came to him. For at least a decade toward the end of his life he had commenced each working day by "posting" these notes, that is, revising, rewriting, and editing them, entering them into large volumes, and eventually preparing an index for each volume. He did this not because he expected them to be published and read ("they are not meant for publication," he noted) but because he found the work excellent practice and felt that every writer should keep a notebook: "One's thoughts fly so fast that one must shoot them; it is no use trying to put salt on their tails." Also, editing them was a creative process. "My notes always grow longer if I shorten them. I mean the process of compression makes them more pregnant, and they breed new notes." After Butler's death, his friend Henry Festing Jones, judging that Butler had really hoped for readers in spite of his statement to the contrary, selected from these books, edited the selections again, and made a sizable volume which appeared in 1912, after some of the notes had already been published in *New Quarterly Review* from 1907 to 1910. Many readers immediately came to regard the *Note-Books* as Butler's masterpiece. Since the Jones volume, several additional collections have been published from the same source. In 1984 the first volume in a series that will include all the notes appeared. Volume one encompasses Butler's notes of 1874-1883.

The notes are indeed a harvest of ideas; they probe and challenge. Many of them attracted early readers by what was at that time their shocking unconventionality; they attract the modern reader because they make him think. They search for the meaning of life, of religion, of philosophy; they reach pragmatic, mediating positions, deriding all extremism, whether of honesty or dishonesty, virtue or immorality. "American dishonesty," Butler notes, "refer it to their Puritan ancestry." "Ultimate triumph of Good. When we say that we believe in this, we mean that we are cocksure of our own opinions." "God as now generally conceived of is only the last witch." "Reason—if you follow it far enough, it always leads to conclusions that are contrary to reason."

Butler celebrates life and makes sport of those too idealistic to see that it should be lived: "I have squandered my life," he reminisces, "as a schoolboy squanders a tip.... I do not squander it now, but I am not sorry that I have squandered a good deal of it.... Had I not better set about squandering what is left of it?" "A sense of humor," he observes, will keep a man from committing all sins "save those that are worth committing." "It is as immoral to be too good as to be too anything else." "To love God is to have good health, good looks, good sense, experience, a kindly nature, and a fair balance of cash in hand." From notes like these some readers came to think Butler a hedonist; surely that is an oversimplification, since his life obviously contained so much idealism.

"Man," Butler theorizes, "is but a perambulating tool-box and workshop, or office, fashioned for itself by a piece of very clever slime, as the result of long experience.... Hence we speak of man's body as his 'trunk,' " thus adumbrating in brief form much of *Life and Habit.* Again, he speculates that "all things are either of the nature of a piece of string or of a knife" for bringing things together or keeping them apart. But each kind contains its opposite; thus "in high philosophy one should never look at a knife without considering it also as a piece of string" and vice versa.

The *Note-Books* copiously illustrate Butler's unhappiness concerning what seemed to him the pretensions of science, literature, and religion. Like Walt Whitman, he boasts: "I am the *enfant terrible* of literature and science. If I cannot, and I know I cannot, get the literary and scientific bigwigs to give me a shilling, I can, and I know I can, heave bricks into the middle of them." "Intellectual overindulgence," he writes, "is the most gratuitous and disgraceful form which excess can take, nor is there any the consequences of which are more disastrous." He notes that someone claims that the chattering of monkeys conveys ideas. With equal justice, he observes, monkeys might conclude "that in our magazine articles, or literary and artistic criticisms, we are not chattering idly but are conveying ideas to one another." "All philosophies," he writes, "if you ride them home, are nonsense; but some are greater nonsense than others." "Faith and authority are as necessary for Euclid as for any one else. True, he does not want us to believe very much; his yoke is tolerably easy, and he will not call a man a fool until he will have public opinion generally on his side; but none the less does he begin with dogmatism and end with persecution."

In March 1902 Butler set out for a trip to Sicily but fell ill on his arrival there and had to hurry back to London. His doctor put him in a nursing home, where his condition did not improve. On 18 June he died of what was diagnosed as pernicious anemia. His last words were to his servant: "Have you brought the chequebook, Alfred?"

It is interesting to recall how this strangely stubborn writer, who published sixteen books in his lifetime, of which only slightly more than seven thousand copies had been sold up to 1899, appeared to people who met him. He "never talked as if he was coming down to one's level." "His talk was always charming and full of fun," but "if there was one thing beyond all others he could not stand it was pretense of any sort." His "modest courtliness and gentleness . . . . the complete absence of anything that could be considered alarming or formidable" were striking. But as a young man he had been hot-tempered, and "anything approaching to ridicule where he was concerned was a mortal insult." Shaw thought him "a shy old bird," but others, such as a lady who met him in Greece, found him "delightfully simple and childlike" and very ready to reach out to others.

Butler's rise to fame after the comparative obscurity in which he had lived out his life makes an interesting chapter in the history of criticism. Obituaries reveal that in 1902 his work was not regarded as important, and *The Way of All Flesh* was hardly noticed on its publication in 1903; the *Times Literary Supplement* did not review it until 1919, by which time the novel's fame had finally forced it to do so. But slowly critics and writers began to speak out. Through the years he was studied, emulated, and praised by Arnold Bennett, Desmond MacCarthy, Arthur Clutton-Brock, George Bernard Shaw, Marcus Hartog, Augustine Birrell, Edmund Gosse, Gilbert Cannan, W. Bateson, C. E. M. Joad, and E. M. Forster. Butler was recognized for his "incessantly alive and stimulating mind" (Clutton-Brock) and was called "perhaps the most versatile genius of the Victorian age" (Hartog). When Shaw referred to him in the preface to *Major Barbara* (1906) as "in his own department the greatest English writer of the latter half of the XIX century," the tide turned in Butler's favor. From then on, increasing critical attention was given all aspects of his work, both in England and America, and when the *Note-Books* appeared in 1912, they received wide attention and were highly praised. The *Times Literary Supplement* gave them a glowing front-page review, calling Butler "a born writer." The *Athenaeum* blamed the reading public for having ignored Butler for so many years. Other reviewers compared Butler to Socrates, called *The Way of All Flesh* "masterly" and the *Note-Books* "perfect," and said that *Erewhon* and *Life and Habit* would not be forgotten. Several book-length studies of Butler soon appeared by Gilbert Cannan, John Harris, and Clara Gruening Stillman. Academic studies followed in France, the Netherlands, Germany, and the United States. Henry Festing Jones's two-volume biography (1919) provided a wealth of detail concerning Butler's life but did little to interpret his ideas. Negative reactions to Butler from religiously oriented writers such as May Sinclair (in *A Defence of Idealism*, 1917) culminate in Malcolm Muggeridge's onslaught in 1936 (*Earnest Atheist*). These attacks revealed that Butler's influence was great enough to merit fire from enemies of his liberal point of view. The Shrewsbury Edition of all of Butler's work in twenty volumes appeared in 1923-1926. The basis for this wide recognition is aptly put in the 1916 edition of *The Cambridge History of English Literature*, which rightly says that Butler is "very far from being a mere indiscriminating wit; he has, in the end, a constructive intention, not mockery, but the liberation of the spirit." More recently there have been fewer references to Butler in the general press, but academic studies continue. Formalistic criticism finds Butler hard to appraise; one recent writer says "the greater part of his writing is a formal disaster," and there is much skepticism concerning his constructive theories. Ralf Norman in 1986 interpreted Butler entirely on the basis of his chiastic insistence through-

Samuel Butler, age sixty-five

out his adult life on reversing all normal order, suggesting that the repeated transformations in his work of the order AB into the order BA can be traced to his traumatic early years and eventually became nothing but a tiresome habit. In 1978 James A. Donovan, Jr., began issuing a *Samuel Butler Society Newsletter*, continued through 1986 by Wayne G. Hammond as the *Samuel Butler Newsletter* but now no longer published.

This apparently lonely and unsuccessful but dedicated writer, who had so much trouble getting a hearing during his lifetime and yet kept courageously forging ahead, has thus earned a significant position in the literature of the country and the age he so energetically criticized but so deeply believed in. The spirit in which he wrote all his books on such varied subjects is effectively expressed at the conclusion of *Life and Habit*: "I saw, as it were, a pebble upon the ground, with a sheen that pleased me; taking it up, I turned it over and over for my amusement, and found it always grow brighter and brighter the more I examined it. At length I became fascinated, and gave loose rein to self-illusion. The aspect of the world seemed changed; the trifle which I had picked up idly had proved to be a talisman of inestimable value, and had opened a door through which I caught glimpses of a strange and interesting transformation. . . . Will the reader bid me wake with him to a world of chance and blindness? Or can I persuade him to dream with me of a more living faith than either he or I had as yet conceived as possible?"

What readers think of him now, at the end of the twentieth century, is hard to ascertain. Many of his books do not circulate often in most libraries, except for *Erewhon* and *The Way of All Flesh*, but these two are available in mass-circulation reprints and are read by many others besides college students. Butler's work is surely less dated than that of most of his "successful" contemporaries. In the modern age of militant beliefs and ideologies, perhaps Butler's willingness to see life as a compromise rather than as a crusade alienates some readers, and they are not interested in his biological reasons for believing as he did. But his own crusade against the mindlessness of dogmatic science, against uncritical deferring to authority, and against the stultifying superego of his age, and his brilliant dialectical maneuvering and use of satire, should ensure that he will continue to live, as he hoped, "on lips of living men."

Letters:

Samuel Butler and E. M. A. Savage, Letters 1871-1885, edited by Geoffrey Keynes and Brian Hill (London: Cape, 1935);

The Family Letters of Samuel Butler (1841-1886), edited by Arnold Silver (Stanford, Cal.: Stanford University Press, 1962);

The Correspondence of Samuel Butler with His Sister May, edited by Daniel F. Howard (Berkeley: University of California Press, 1962).

Bibliographies:

Henry Festing Jones and A. T. Bartholomew, *The Samuel Butler Collection at Saint John's College Cambridge* (Cambridge: W. Heffer, 1921);

A. J. Hoppe, *A Bibliography of the Writings of Samuel Butler* (London: Bookman, 1925);

Carroll A. Wilson, *Catalogue of the Collection of Samuel Butler (of Erewhon) in the Chapin Library Williams College* (Portland, Maine: Southworth-Anthoensen, 1945);

Stanley B. Harkness, *The Career of Samuel Butler (1835-1902) A Bibliography* (New York: Burt Franklin, 1955);

Daniel F. Howard, "Samuel Butler," *Victorian Fiction: a Second Guide to Research* (New York: Modern Language Assocation, 1978);

Wayne G. Hammond, "Samuel Butler. A Checklist of Works and Criticism," *The Samuel Butler Newsletter*, 3, nos. 1 & 2 (1980); 4, no. 1 (1981);

Hans-Peter Breuer, "Samuel Butler in the United States: a Bibliographical Survey," *The Samuel Butler Newsletter*, 6, no. 1 (1986).

Biographies:

Henry Festing Jones, *Samuel Butler, a Memoir*, 2 volumes (London: Macmillan, 1919);

P. N. Furbank, *Samuel Butler (1835-1902)* (Cambridge: Cambridge University Press, 1948);

Philip Henderson, *Samuel Butler* (London: Cohen & West, 1953);

Lee E. Holt, *Samuel Butler*, revised edition (Boston: Twayne, 1989);

Peter Raby, *The Life of Samuel Butler* (London: Hogarth, 1990).

References:

Gilbert Cannan, *Samuel Butler: A Critical Study* (Folcroft, Pa.: Folcroft Library Editions, 1915);

Joseph Fort, *Samuel Butler, l'écrivain: Etude d'un style* (Bordeaux: J. Bière, 1935);

R. S. Garnett, *Samuel Butler and His Family Relations* (New York: Dutton, 1926);
Phyllis Greenacre, *The Quest for the Father* (New York: International Universities Press, 1963);
John F. Harris, *Samuel Butler, Author of "Erewhon": The Man and His Work* (Folcroft, Pa.: Folcroft Library Editions, 1973);
Thomas L. Jeffers, *Samuel Butler Revalued* (University Park: Pennsylvania State University Press, 1981);
C. E. M. Joad, *Samuel Butler* (London: Parsons, 1924; Boston: Small, Maynard, 1925);
Joseph Jones, *The Cradle of Erewhon* (Austin: University of Texas Press, 1959);
Paul Meissner, *Samuel Butler, der Jüngerer* (Leipzig: Tauchnitz, 1931);
Malcolm Muggeridge, *Earnest Atheist: A Study of Samuel Butler* (London: Putnam's, 1936);
Ralf Norrman, *Samuel Butler and the Meaning of Chiasmus* (London: Macmillan, 1986);
Gerold Pestalozzi, *Samuel Butler der Jüngerer, Versuch einer Darstellung seiner Gedankenwelt* (Zurich: Universität Zürich, 1914);
Robert F. Rattray, *A Chronicle and an Introduction: Samuel Butler* (London: Duckworth, 1935);
May Sinclair, *A Defence of Idealism* (London: Macmillan, 1917);
Clara G. Stillman, *Samuel Butler: A Mid-Victorian Modern* (New York: Viking, 1932; London: Martin Secker, 1932);
Rudolf Stoff, *Die Philosophie des Organischen bei Samuel Butler* (Vienna: Phaedon Verlag, 1929);
Basil Willey, *Darwin and Butler—Two Versions of Evolution* (London: Chatto & Windus, 1960).

Papers:

The Samuel Butler Collection at St. John's College, Cambridge, contains many Butler manuscripts, paintings, and books. The Carroll A. Wilson Collection of Butler manuscripts, including the notebooks and first editions of most of his works, is at the Chapin Library at Williams College, Williamstown, Massachusetts. Many other Butler manuscripts and letters are in the British Museum.

Sir Winston Churchill

(30 November 1874 - 24 January 1965)

This entry was updated by Laurence Kitzan (University of Saskatchewan) from his entry in DLB 100: Modern British Essayists: Second Series.

Sir Winston Churchill (Gale International Portrait Gallery)

SELECTED BOOKS: *The Story of the Malakand Field Force: An Episode of Frontier War* (London & New York: Longmans, Green, 1898);

The River War: An Historical Account of the Reconquest of the Soudan, 2 volumes, edited by Col. Francis William Rhodes (London & New York: Longmans, Green, 1899; revised, 1 volume, 1902);

Savrola: A Tale of the Revolution in Laurania (New York: Longmans, Green, 1900; London: Longmans, Green, 1900);

London to Ladysmith via Pretoria (London & New York: Longmans, Green, 1900);

Ian Hamilton's March: Together with Extracts from the Diary of Lieutenant H. Frankland, a Prisoner of War at Pretoria (London & New York: Longmans, Green, 1900);

Mr. Brodrick's Army (London: Humphreys, 1903; Sacramento, Cal.: Churchilliana Co., 1977);

Why I Am a Free Trader (London: Stead, 1905);

Lord Randolph Churchill, 2 volumes (London & New York: Macmillan, 1906);

For Free Trade: A Collection of Speeches Delivered at Manchester or in the House of Commons during the Fiscal Controversy Preceding the Late General Election (London: Humphreys, 1906; Sacramento, Cal.: Churchilliana Co., 1977);

My African Journey (London: Hodder & Stoughton, 1908; New York: Doubleday, Doran, 1909);

Liberalism and the Social Problem (London: Hodder & Stoughton, 1909; New York: Doubleday, Doran, 1910);

The People's Rights (London: Hodder & Stoughton, 1910; New York: Taplinger, 1971);

Prison and Prisoners: A Speech Delivered in the House of Commons, 20th July, 1910 (London & New York: Cassell, 1910);

The World Crisis, 6 volumes (London: Butterworth, 1923-1931; New York: Scribners, 1923-1931); abridged and revised edition, 1 volume (London: Butterworth, 1931; New York: Scribners, 1931);

Parliamentary Government and the Economic Problem: The Romanes Lecture Delivered in the Sheldonian Theatre, 19 June 1930 (Oxford: Clarendon Press, 1930);

My Early Life: A Roving Commission (London: Butterworth, 1930); republished as *A Roving Commission: My Early Life* (New York: Scribners, 1930);

India: Speeches and an Introduction (London: Butterworth, 1931);

Thoughts and Adventures (London: Butterworth, 1932); republished as *Amid These Storms: Thoughts and Adventures* (New York: Scribners, 1932);

Marlborough: His Life and Times, 4 volumes (London: Harrap, 1933-1938; New York: Scribners, 1933-1938);

Great Contemporaries (London: Butterworth, 1937; New York: Putnam's, 1937; revised and enlarged, London: Butterworth, 1938; revised, London: Macmillan, 1943; revised, London: Odhams, 1958);

Arms and the Covenant: Speeches, edited by Randolph S. Churchill (London: Harrap, 1938); republished as *While England Slept: A Survey of World Affairs* (New York: Putnam's, 1938);

Step by Step: 1936-1939 (London: Butterworth, 1939; New York: Putnam's, 1939);

Into Battle: Speeches, edited by Randolph S. Churchill (London: Cassell, 1941); republished as *Blood, Sweat and Tears* (New York: Putnam's, 1941);

The Unrelenting Struggle: War Speeches, edited by Charles Eade (London: Cassell, 1942; Boston: Little, Brown, 1942);

The End of the Beginning: War Speeches, edited by Eade (London: Cassell, 1943; Boston: Little, Brown, 1943);

Onwards to Victory: War Speeches, edited by Eade (London: Cassell, 1944; Boston: Little, Brown, 1944);

The Dawn of Liberation: War Speeches, edited by Eade (London: Cassell, 1945; Boston: Little, Brown, 1945);

Victory: War Speeches, edited by Eade (London: Cassell, 1946; Boston: Little, Brown, 1946);

War Speeches: 1940-1945 (London: Cassell, 1946);

Secret Session Speeches, edited by Eade (London: Cassell, 1946); republished as *Winston Churchill's Secret Session Speeches* (New York: Simon & Schuster, 1946);

The Sinews of Peace: Post-War Speeches, edited by Randolph S. Churchill (London: Cassell, 1948; Boston: Houghton Mifflin, 1949);

The Second World War, 6 volumes (Boston: Houghton Mifflin, 1948-1953; London: Cassell, 1948-1954)—comprises volume 1, *The Gathering Storm*; volume 2, *Their Finest Hour*; volume 3, *The Grand Alliance*; volume 4, *The Hinge of Fate*; volume 5, *Closing the Ring*; volume 6, *Triumph and Tragedy*;

Painting as a Pastime (London: Odham Press, Benn, 1948; New York: Whittlesey House, 1950);

Europe Unite: Speeches 1947 and 1948, edited by Randolph S. Churchill (London: Cassell, 1950; Boston: Houghton Mifflin, 1950);

Churchill in 1900, the year he was first elected to Parliament (Churchill Photograph Albums: Broadwater Collection)

In the Balance: Speeches 1949 and 1950, edited by Randolph S. Churchill (London: Cassell, 1951; Boston: Houghton Mifflin, 1952);

The War Speeches of the Rt. Hon. Winston S. Churchill, O.M., C.H., P.C., M.P., 3 volumes, edited by Eade (London: Cassell, 1952; Boston: Houghton Mifflin, 1953);

Stemming the Tide: Speeches 1951 and 1952, edited by Randolph S. Churchill (London: Cassell, 1953; Boston: Houghton Mifflin, 1954);

A History of the English-Speaking Peoples, 4 volumes (London: Cassell, 1956-1958; New York: Dodd, Mead, 1956-1958)—comprises volume 1, *The Birth of Britain*; volume 2, *The New World*; volume 3, *The Age of Revolution*; volume 4, *The Great Democracies*;

The Unwritten Alliance: Speeches 1953 to 1959, edited by Randolph S. Churchill (London: Cassell, 1961);

Young Winston's Wars: The Original Despatches of Winston S. Churchill, War Correspondent, 1897-1900, edited by Frederick Woods (London: Cooper, 1972; New York: Viking, 1973);

The Collected Works of Sir Winston Churchill: Centenary Limited Edition, 34 volumes (London: Library of Imperial History, 1973-1976);

Winston S. Churchill: His Complete Speeches, 1897-1963, 8 volumes, edited by Robert Rhodes James (New York: Chelsea House, 1974);

The Collected Essays of Sir Winston Churchill, 4 volumes, edited by Michael Wolff (London: Library of Imperial History, 1976).

Sir Winston Churchill has become one of the legends of the twentieth century. A major and then an outstanding political figure in British and world history between 1905 and 1965, he was also a writer of substantial reputation and enormous output. A bibliographer, Frederick Woods, estimated in 1963 that "the total sales of his books in the English language alone are in the region of four million." In speech and written prose he has been noted as a master of the memorable phrase—"blood, toil, tears and sweat" caught the imagination of a generation. Although interest in his essays has been immeasurably enhanced by Churchill's status as statesman and historical writer, they have merit in their own right.

Winston Leonard Spencer Churchill was born at Blenheim Palace, the home of his grandfather, the seventh duke of Marlborough, on 30 November 1874. His parents were Lord Randolph Churchill, who was just beginning his erratically brilliant career as a Conservative member of Parliament, and the former Jennie Jerome, a socially prominent American from a wealthy family. Educated at private schools and at Harrow, Winston Churchill did not shine when exposed to the standard curriculum based on classics and to examiners who, as he noted in *My Early Life* (1930), "almost invariably" set questions "to which I was unable to suggest a satisfactory answer." A sensitive boy, Churchill suffered from his inability to establish a close relationship with his parents, especially his remote and much admired father. His educational deficiencies and his youthful interest in his battalions of toy soldiers convinced Lord Randolph that his son was destined for a military career, and he was duly enrolled at the Royal Military Academy, Sandhurst. He was commissioned in a cavalry regiment, the Fourth Hussars, in February 1895, shortly after the death of his father.

The various elements of Churchill's background were to have strong influences on his lengthy career. In his twenties Churchill began to show the same intense interest in politics that had characterized his father, and until almost the end of his life politics remained the passionate focus of his existence. A good deal of Churchill's determination in politics appears to stem from a continuing attempt to win, even posthumously, his father's approval. He idealized and attempted to realize Lord Randolph's political principles and initiatives—Tory democracy, social reform, and the reduction of military expenditure in times of peace. His outlook was always an aristocratic one, and his undoubtedly genuine reformist sentiments retained a strong element of paternalism. His experience in the military gave him a background different from that of most politicians: his martial expertise and his enthusiasm for making war were the despair of many of his colleagues during World War I but provided the makings of the Churchill legend in World War II.

The fact that his parents habitually lived beyond their income, as Lady Churchill continued to do throughout her widowhood, put into jeopardy Churchill's career as a cavalry officer—always an expensive proposition—and eventually helped push the young subaltern into a journalistic career. He attached himself to a North-West frontier punishment expedition in India in 1897 and sent reports to two newspapers. He had made a small amount of money by this means while serving with the Spanish forces during the Cuban revolt in 1895, but the publication of his revised reports from India as *The Story of the Malakand Field Force* (1898) brought him considerable notice in England as well as critical and financial success. In *The River War* (1899) he recounted his experiences in the Sudan campaign of 1898. During the Boer War he served as a war correspondent and was paid handsomely for his dispatches, which he then collected into two books, *London to Ladysmith via Pretoria* (1900) and *Ian Hamilton's March* (1900). The publicity surrounding Churchill's capture by the Boers in 1899 and his successful escape from a Pretoria prisoner-of-war camp helped sell his books and secure his election to Parliament as a Conservative in 1900. The profits from his publications and from a lecture tour in England and the United States recounting his South African experiences gave him the capital to operate in politics for many years without financial concern.

Churchill's dissatisfaction with the Conservative leaders and their lack of commitment to social reform, as well as frustrated ambition, led him to use the Conservative split over Joseph

Secretary of State for War and Air Churchill inspecting the British army of occupation in Cologne, August 1919 (Churchill Photograph Albums: Broadwater Collection)

Chamberlain's tariff reform campaign in 1904 as the occasion to move to the Liberal party, which was still committed to free trade. From 1905 to 1915 Churchill was continuously in office, first as under secretary for the colonies and then in the cabinet as president of the Board of Trade in 1908, home secretary in 1910, first lord of the Admiralty in 1911, and chancellor of the Duchy of Lancaster in 1915. His dedication to politics was so deep that on his honeymoon with the former Clementine Ogilvy Hozier in 1908 he carried on an extensive political correspondence. In the Board of Trade and as home secretary he was intimately involved with the social legislation of David Lloyd George but was also noted for an overenthusiastic deployment of troops in the railway strike of 1911. This action was indicative of his ability to switch rapidly from reasoned and moderate positions in times of peace to decisive action in what he perceived to be times of crisis. It was a capacity that earned him a great deal of suspicion and hostility.

Churchill was one of the first cabinet ministers to be convinced of the necessity of British entry on the side of France in World War I; subsequently he made strong efforts to force upon the cabinet his ideas about methods for prosecuting the war. Despite this contribution—or perhaps because of it—Churchill, already naturally disliked by the Conservatives but also viewed with distrust by Liberals and Labour, was made the scapegoat for the Dardanelles fiasco and dropped from the Admiralty in 1915. He resigned from the cabinet a few months later, and for a brief period served as a field officer in the trenches of the western front. He then returned to politics and in June 1917 was appointed by Lloyd George as minister of munitions. He served as secretary of state for war and the air from 1918 to 1921 and as secretary of state for the colonies in 1921 and 1922. De-

Window display at Harrod's in London, January 1938, on the publication of Churchill's collection of biographical sketches

feated in the election of 1922, Churchill began a migration of allegiances through two more electoral defeats before he was elected as a Constitutionalist in 1924 and appointed to Stanley Baldwin's Conservative cabinet as chancellor of the exchequer, a position he held until the defeat of the government in 1929.

Despite long experience in office, a reputation as a brilliant speaker, and solid friendships in the political world, for the next ten years he was left out of Conservative-dominated governments. This fate reflected his isolation in politics and his reputation as a dangerous independent colleague; it also indicated a certain naïveté which belied his long political experience. During this period he vehemently attacked the leaders of the Conservative party for their stand on constitutional reform in India, which he believed was not ready for reform. With the emergence of Hitler he solemnly and often scathingly warned Conservative ministers of their lack of preparedness to meet a growing German military threat. Yet Churchill appeared surprised and hurt that neither Baldwin nor Neville Chamberlain felt his presence to be necessary in their cabinets of the 1930s.

Churchill's stand on the Nazi threat, though perhaps not as consistent as he later presented it in *The Gathering Storm* (1948), was sufficient to ensure his reintroduction to government as first lord of the Admiralty with the outbreak of war in 1939. He was evidently the man for a crisis situation, and when it became necessary to reorganize the government in 1940 Churchill succeeded almost by default to the position of prime minister. In the midst of military victory Churchill lost the prime ministry when the Conservatives were defeated in the election of 1945, but he regained the office in 1951. He was knighted by Queen Elizabeth on 24 April 1953. Plagued by the infirmities of age, including a series of strokes, he resigned as prime minister in 1955 and did not run for Parliament in the election of 1964. He died on 24 January 1965.

A survey of Churchill's career emphasizes the overwhelming preponderance of politics in his life. And yet throughout this period he had his living to make, a task he carried out successfully through his extensive writings. He made an have other than as he did? Lord Curzon, with all his great gifts, lacked an essential quality: "In the

Churchill meeting at Tehran with Soviet leader Joseph Stalin and President Franklin D. Roosevelt in 1943

excursion into melodramatic fiction with *Savrola* in 1900, but though the book sold well he did not choose to repeat the experiment. Instead he concentrated on historical works. Some of these works describe events in which he himself was a participant: *The Story of the Malakand Field Force, The River War, London to Ladysmith via Pretoria, Ian Hamilton's March, The World Crisis* (1923-1931), and *The Second World War* (1948-1954); others deal with his family: *Lord Randolph Churchill* (1906) and *Marlborough: His Life and Times* (1933-1938); in still others, such as *A History of the English-Speaking Peoples* (1956-1958), he filters history through his own political experiences and comes up with an unabashed Whig interpretation. As a historian he is at his best in describing events with which he had an intimate connection, even given his biases and personal self-serving. Books more remote from Churchill's personal presence have serious weaknesses and illuminate his personality more than the period of which he is writing. Early in his political career he began the practice of publishing collections of his speeches with *For Free Trade* (1906). Two of his books are strictly autobiographical: *My African Journey* (1908) and *My Early Life*.

With the early establishment of his reputation as a vivid writer and political figure, Churchill was in considerable demand as a contributor to newspapers. His political eclipse between 1929 and 1939 did nothing to diminish this demand or his ability to profit by it. A collection of the best of his newspaper and journal articles, plus his Romanes Lecture delivered in 1930, was published in 1932 as *Thoughts and Adventures*. Biographical articles published between 1929 and 1936 were collected in 1937 as *Great Contemporaries*, which was republished several times with additions and deletions. It is mainly on these two books that Churchill's position as an essayist rests—though strictly speaking, almost all of his books can be viewed as collections of essays. Although the biographies and histories obviously have an overall unity, individual chapters tend to have an autonomy which turns them into set-piece essays. To a large extent this is a function of Churchill's method of composition. From early days, in fact from his years at Harrow when he dictated English essays to an older boy in return for Latin constructions, Churchill fell into the habit of dictating his works. By the 1930s the system was standardized; Maurice Ashley, one of his historical researchers, describes it in the 1974 biography of Churchill by Henry Pelling: "He would walk up and down the room (when I worked for him it was usually his bedroom) puffing at a cigar while a secretary patiently took it all down as best she could in Pitman. Occasionally he would say, 'Scrub that and start again.' At times he would stop . . . at others he would be entirely swept on by the stimulus of his imagination." The creation of these works, consequently, was similar to the creation of his speeches. Articles and books were the speaking of ideas that he had mulled over in his mind, in the same way as were both the impromptu speeches he made to dinner guests and acquaintances and the formally prepared speeches he gave on election platforms or to Parliament. But speeches by their nature are limited and self-contained, like essays. By "speechifying" his books, Churchill turned his chapters into essays.

As might be expected in an individual as single-minded and self-centered as Churchill, most of the essays included in the two collections are fragments of his autobiography. *Great Contemporaries* could have been subtitled "Great Men I Have Known, and Their Impact upon Me." These essays provide interesting viewpoints on many historical events and people. Churchill's "thoughts" in *Thoughts and Adventures* are often an amusing combination of shrewdness and naïveté. His musings in "A Second Choice" on being given the chance to live his life over again lead him to reject the desirability or usefulness of such a gift: "Life is a whole, and good and ill must be accepted together. The journey has been enjoyable and well worth making—once." Through its constantly growing capacity for destruction, science has made life potentially terrible, he points out in "Shall We All Commit Suicide?" It is science, too, that has created conditions in which heroes (Churchill was an inveterate hero-worshiper) and leaders are no longer relevant or possible, he says in "Mass Effects in Modern Life"; and by solving life's physical problems, without touching man's basic nature, he notes in "Fifty Years Hence," science had created dangers "out of all proportion to the growth of man's intellect, to the strength of his character or to the efficacy of his institutions." The Romanes Lecture, *Parliamentary Government and the Economic Problem* (1930), suggests the establishment of a parallel parliament of economic experts to offer advice to the elected Parliament—a proposal which indicates why Churchill has not been considered one of the great chancellors of the exchequer: he lacked understanding of both economics and economists.

Life for Churchill was an adventure to be recounted with relish. In "My Spy Story" he vivifies a spy scare in the Highlands of Scotland; in "A Day with Clemenceau" he tells about being under fire on the western front; "In the Air" presents him as pioneer aviator and air passenger. Joyous satisfaction is coupled with a dash of self-justification in "Consistency in Politics" and "The Battle of Sidney Street" and with a strong sense of the hand of fate that preserved his life in "With the Grenadiers" and " 'Plugstreet.' " The same sense of fatedness pervades his recounting of his political career in "Election Memories." He even adopted his hobbies in a dramatic fashion. In "Painting as a Pastime" he describes his desperation when he was removed from the Admiralty in 1915: "Like a sea-beast fished up from the depths, or a diver too suddenly hoisted, my veins threatened to burst from the fall in pressure. I had great anxiety and no means of relieving it; I had vehement convictions and small power to give effect to them." From this crisis he was rescued by experiments with his children's paint boxes, which turned him to the hobby of painting; the passionate pursuit of this hobby could distract his mind for periods of time even from politics.

Great Contemporaries deals with political figures, such as Archibald Philip Primrose, Fifth Earl of Rosebery; Herbert Henry Asquith; Arthur James Balfour; and King George V, and military men, such as John French, Paul von Hindenburg, Ferdinand Foch, and Douglas Haig. The playwright George Bernard Shaw appears mainly as a writer of political ideas to which Churchill did not warm. In friend and foe he picks the qualities that he most admires; political and moral courage rank high, as do steadfast convictions, even when the principles upon which the convictions are based are wrong—herein lay Hitler's potential for both great good and great evil. Churchill admired intelligence, wit, and conversational sparkle, particularly as shown by his best friend, Lord Birkenhead. There is criticism in the essays but it is somewhat muted. Could anyone really expect the Kaiser, raised and existing in the florid atmosphere of the German Imperial Court, to behave other than as he did? Lord Curzon, with all his great gifts, lacked an essential quality: "In the House of Commons he met his match; and compared with the great Parliamentary figures of that time he was never regarded, even in his day, as an equal combatant or future rival." An ironic judgment, because without his great achievements as prime minister in World War II, the conclusion on Churchill might have been the same.

The enormous sales of Churchill's written works came after World War II and reflect the reputation that he won from that conflict. But even before the war he was a popular and well-read author. The essays help reveal why. They are simply written and easy to understand, with all the warm immediacy of a radio "chat." This style reflects Churchill's method of creation—the essays read as if they were spoken because they *were* spoken. Churchill appears to be constantly talking—to friends, to acquaintances, to cabinet colleagues, to Parliament, to the crowds at lectures and speeches. In his newspaper articles and essays he spoke to the people at large. From 1936 to 1939, for example, in a series of newspaper articles published in 1939 as *Step by Step,* he simply, directly, and confidentially took the British public into the heart of great matters. The result was that despite horrendous political errors, Churchill's political career was never destroyed. He was always near the front of the public and political mind. In 1940 he was not the politicians' first choice to succeed Chamberlain, nor that of the public—Anthony Eden ranked ahead of him in the polls. But he was in the running, and by a fortunate combination of circumstances he won the role that fulfilled his eagerly sought destiny.

Bibliography:

Frederick Woods, *A Bibliography of the Works of Sir Winston Churchill, KG, OM, CH* (London: Vane, 1963; revised edition, London: Kaye & Ward, 1969).

Biographies:

Randolph S. Churchill and Martin Gilbert, *Winston S. Churchill,* 15 volumes (London: Heinemann, 1966-1988; Boston: Houghton Mifflin, 1966-1988);

Henry Pelling, *Winston Churchill* (London: Macmillan, 1974);

William Manchester, *The Last Lion: Winston Spencer Churchill, Visions of Glory 1874-1932* (Boston & Toronto: Little, Brown, 1983).

References:

Raymond A. Callahan, *Churchill: Retreat from Empire* (Wilmington, Del.: Scholarly Resources, 1984);

John Freeman, "Mr. Winston Churchill as a Prose-Writer," *London Mercury* (April 1927): 626-634;

Martin Gilbert, *Churchill's Political Philosophy* (London: Oxford University Press, 1981);

Robert Rhodes James, *Churchill: A Study in Failure 1900-1939* (London: Weidenfeld & Nicolson, 1970);

Robin Prior, *Churchill's "World Crisis" as History* (London: Croom Helm, 1983);

A. J. P. Taylor and others, *Churchill Revised: A Critical Assessment* (New York: Dial, 1969);

Manfred Weidhorn, *Sir Winston Churchill* (Boston: Twayne, 1979).

Papers:

The private papers of Sir Winston Churchill are in the Chartwell Trust in the Public Records Office, London. They are presently reserved to the official biographer.

Joseph Conrad

(3 December 1857 - 3 August 1924)

This entry was updated by Kingsley Widmer (San Diego State University) from his entry in DLB 34: British Novelists, 1890-1929: Traditionalists.

See also the Conrad entries in DLB 10: Modern British Dramatists, 1900-1945: Part One *and* DLB 98: Modern British Essayists: First Series.

Joseph Conrad (Beinecke Library, Yale University)

BOOKS: *Almayer's Folly: A Story of an Eastern River* (London: Unwin, 1895; New York & London: Macmillan, 1895);

An Outcast of the Islands (London: Unwin, 1896; New York: Appleton, 1896);

The Children of the Sea: A Tale of the Forecastle (New York: Dodd, Mead, 1897); republished as *The Nigger of the "Narcissus": A Tale of the Sea* (London: Heinemann, 1898 [i.e., 1897]);

Tales of Unrest (London: Unwin, 1898; New York: Scribners, 1898);

Lord Jim (Edinburgh & London: Blackwood, 1900; New York: Doubleday & McClure, 1900);

The Inheritors: An Extravagant Story, by Conrad and Ford Madox Hueffer [Ford] (New York: McClure, Phillips, 1901; London: Heinemann, 1901);

Youth: A Narrative, and Two Other Stories (Edinburgh & London: Blackwood, 1902; New York: McClure, Phillips, 1903);

Typhoon (New York & London: Putnam's, 1902);

Typhoon and Other Stories (London: Heinemann, 1903); published without "Typhoon" as *Falk; Amy Foster; To-morrow: Three Stories* (New York: McClure, Phillips, 1903);

Romance: A Novel, by Conrad and Ford (London: Smith, Elder, 1903; New York: McClure, Phillips, 1904);

Nostromo: A Tale of the Seaboard (London & New York: Harper, 1904);

The Mirror of the Sea: Memories and Impressions (London: Methuen, 1906; New York & London: Harper, 1906);

The Secret Agent: A Simple Tale (London: Methuen, 1907; New York & London: Harper, 1907);

A Set of Six (London: Methuen, 1908; Garden City, N.Y.: Doubleday, Page, 1915);

Under Western Eyes (London: Methuen, 1911; New York: Harper, 1911);

Some Reminiscences (London: Nash, 1912); republished as *A Personal Record* (New York & London: Harper, 1912);

'Twixt Land and Sea (London: Dent, 1912; New York: Hodder & Stoughton/Doran, 1912);

Chance: A Tale in Two Parts (London: Methuen, 1913; Garden City, N.Y.: Doubleday, Page, 1913);

Within the Tides (London & Toronto: Dent, 1915; Garden City, N.Y.: Doubleday, Page, 1916);

Victory: An Island Tale (Garden City, N.Y.: Doubleday, Page, 1915; London: Methuen, 1915);

One Day More: A Play in One Act (London: Privately printed by C. Shorter, 1917; Garden City, N.Y.: Doubleday, Page, 1920);

The Shadow-Line: A Confession (London & Toronto: Dent, 1917; Garden City, N.Y.: Doubleday, Page, 1917);

The Arrow of Gold: A Story Between Two Notes (Garden City, N.Y.: Doubleday, Page, 1919; London: Unwin, 1919);

The Rescue: A Romance of the Shallows (Garden City, N.Y.: Doubleday, Page, 1920; London & Toronto: Dent, 1920);

Notes on My Books (Garden City, N.Y., & Toronto: Doubleday, Page, 1921; London: Heinemann, 1921); republished as *Conrad's Prefaces to His Works* (London: Dent, 1937);

Notes on Life and Letters (London & Toronto: Dent, 1921; Garden City, N.Y., & Toronto: Doubleday, Page, 1921);

The Secret Agent: Drama in Four Acts (Canterbury: Printed for the author by H. J. Goulden, 1921);

The Rover (Garden City, N.Y.: Doubleday, Page, 1923; London: Unwin, 1923);

Laughing Anne: A Play (London: Bookman's Journal, 1923);

The Nature of a Crime, by Conrad and Ford (London: Duckworth, 1924; Garden City, N.Y.: Doubleday, Page, 1924);

Suspense: A Napoleonic Novel (Garden City, N.Y.: Doubleday, Page, 1925; London & Toronto: Dent, 1925);

Tales of Hearsay (London: Unwin, 1925; Garden City, N.Y.: Doubleday, Page, 1925);

Last Essays, edited by Richard Curle (London & Toronto: Dent, 1926; Garden City, N.Y.: Doubleday, Page, 1926);

The Sisters (New York: Gaige, 1928);

Joseph Conrad on Fiction, edited by Walter F. Wright (Lincoln: University of Nebraska Press, 1964);

Congo Diary and Other Uncollected Pieces by Joseph Conrad, edited by Zdzislaw Najder (Garden City, N.Y.: Doubleday, 1978).

Collections: *The Works of Joseph Conrad,* Uniform Edition, 22 volumes (London: Dent, 1923-1928); reprinted and enlarged, 26 volumes (London: Dent, 1946-1955);

Complete Works, Canterbury Edition, 24 volumes (Garden City, N.Y.: Doubleday, Page, 1924);

The Complete Short Stories of Joseph Conrad (London: Hutchinson, 1933);

Konrad Korzeniowski, 1874 (photograph by W. Rzewuski; Beinecke Library, Yale University)

The Portable Conrad, edited by Morton Dauwen Zabel (New York: Viking, 1947).

Joseph Conrad is now widely accepted as one of the modernist masters of serious narrative fiction. Historically placed, he is a major figure in the transition from Victorian fiction to the more perplexed forms and values of twentieth-century literature. Now, unlike in his lifetime, he is one of the most read British novelists of his period. However, his twenty volumes of novels and stories vary greatly in quality and interest. Since he was primarily a commercial storyteller aiming at the popular market, only a limited part of his work will bear much serious response and intellectual consideration. A handful of fictions, such as "Heart of Darkness" (1899), *Nostromo* (1904), "The Secret Sharer" (1910), and *The Secret Agent* (1907), are generally acknowledged to be outstanding. But since there is disagreement about some of the others, and since the larger context of his works might be illuminating, it may be useful to survey most of his fiction.

Conrad's life, explored in a spate of biographies, is also distinctive for its drastic fracturing. Several times exiled, with major changes of scene, nationality, and language, he seems to have suffered from a powerful sense of loss and alienation. This may have encouraged his emphatic pessimistic skepticism. Though writing in a time and culture often characterized as optimistic and affirmative, Conrad displays senses of defeat shading into a cosmic malignancy and an anxiously heavy ideological conservativism. With his exilic sense of foreignness—including the English he wrote in, learned relatively late in life (after Polish, German, and French)—he inclined to elaborately self-conscious writing and tendentious moralizing. A pervasive sense of anxiety about his roles, and other psychological involutions relating to considerable physical illness and repeated periods of great depression, may have further encouraged this elaborateness of manner and a rather un-British ideological insistence. Yet seeking popular acceptance in a foreign land and language, Conrad yoked ornate narrative methods with sentimental tales, and lush descriptive rhetoric with harshly narrow moral reflections. The resulting ideological melodramas have had considerable influence on major later novelists, such as Graham Greene and William Faulkner. Conrad's exotic scenes, stereotyped romantic figures, heavily adjectival poetic rhetoric, and moralistic male codes appear to have greatly influenced many other writers. There is considerable disagreement about the value of Conrad's rhetorical exoticism and Pyrrhonist conservativism.

Born Józef Teodor Konrad Korzeniowski in Berdichev, Russia, on 3 December 1857, Conrad was the only child of ardent Polish nationalists in the mid-nineteenth-century Russian empire. His parents were of impoverished landed-gentry background and romantic outlook. Besides rather unsuccessfully managing other people's estates, his father was a literary man (a minor conventional poet and translator). Conrad's parents were harshly exiled to Northern Russia in May 1862 for rebellious political activities preliminary to the Polish nationalist uprising of 1863. His mother died when he was seven, his father when he was eleven. Exile and the related orphaning appear to have had traumatic effects on the young Conrad.

Supported and raised by various relatives (most important, by a maternal uncle, Tadeusz Bobrowski, a prosperous lawyer who nagged his nephew but also indulged him and continued to provide financial aid until Conrad was in his thirties), he had a sickly childhood and irregular schooling in Russian exile, then in Polish Russia, and then in the Polish area of Austria. Information on Conrad's childhood and youth is limited—unlike many authors he never wrote directly about his early years. He did report that, in spite of sporadic schooling, he was a voracious reader of romantic novels and adventure accounts. In mid adolescence he carried his traumatic legacy, which apparently included considerable sexual and other emotional repression as well as orphaning and other displacement, even further into self-chosen exile.

Conrad had early developed a romantic yearning to go to sea, though he had no first-hand knowledge of sea life. In September 1874, when he was sixteen, with his uncle's help he moved to Marseilles, France, which became his home for nearly four years. From there he gained work experience on sailing ships, including voyages to the West Indies as an apprentice and steward. He may also have engaged in smuggling operations, perhaps transporting weapons from France to Spain for the Spanish Carlists (an unsuccessful right-wing monarchical restoration conspiracy). He may also have become involved in a romance with an older woman in the Carlist movement. While the evidence is uncertain, he apparently failed in several of these affairs, desperately lost more of his uncle's money gambling at Monte Carlo, and attempted suicide. (Suicide was to become a recurrent crux in Conrad's fictions.)

Having soon recovered from the bullet wound in his chest and having been financially rescued by his uncle, Conrad started his maritime career over again, leaving France for England and shipping out in 1879 as an ordinary seaman on a British steamer. In the following years he acquired English (though he always retained a heavy accent), worked on various British sailing ships, especially in the Far East, and with considerable ambition but some difficulty passed various maritime officers' examinations, culminating in a Master's Certificate in the British Merchant Service in November 1886. He had become a naturalized British citizen the previous August. The romantic Polish exile appeared to have become, before the age of thirty, a solid Britisher with a settled traditional vocation.

But Captain Conrad was not really very successful in the merchant marine: he had only one small regular command (in 1888), spent periods without a berth and briefly tried his hand at river steamboat captaining in the Congo, continued to live beyond his salary (with his uncle's help), suffered repeated physical and tempera-

Konrad Korzeniowski in Marienbad, 1883 (photograph by Otto Bielefeldt; National Library, Warsaw)

mental difficulties in his vocation, and worked in a dying industry—sailing ships. While his sea experiences and his travels in exotic foreign scenes provided much of the material for his later writing and fame, and while the role of sea captain was partly appropriate for one identifying with exile and hierarchy, the life of a minor maritime officer was not steady enough, remunerative enough, gentlemanly enough. (Throughout his life, Conrad, from a proud gentry background, was rather snobbish, and in appearance and manner rather a dandy.) His later accounts of sailing ships make clear that in spite of his efforts at romantic and moral exaltation of a sea career it was a boring, lonely, fearful, and harsh way of life. After nearly twenty maritime years, when he was in his late thirties, he entered another career—as an English commercial writer of fiction.

Conrad's efforts to be a British novelist were arduous and anxious. He was writing in a language not learned until he was in his twenties. He chose not just to write of his experiences and concerns but to make a commercial career as an English storyteller. Vehemently not a bohemian, he saw the writing career as a settled and orderly way of life, in contrast to his maritime career. He married Jessie George, a pleasantly dull and submissive younger woman, in 1896 and settled into conventional British middle-class family life, eventually with two sons born in 1898 and 1906. For many years he was burdened with debts, with physical and psychological illnesses, and with considerable anguish over writing. But with the aid of several outstanding English editors, including Edward Garnett and Ford Madox Hueffer (Ford), he established himself not only as an exotic novelist and a moderately popular magazine storywriter but as a gentlemanly artist, friend of Henry James, R. B. Cunninghame-Graham, H. G. Wells, and other well-known contemporaries. In his last years (from 1913 until his death) he finally had a considerable commercial success and a worldwide reputation. After a Polish childhood and youth, partly in exile, then some years as a French sailor and adventurer, and then after spending the larger part of two decades as a British merchant mariner, Conrad had successfully achieved a career as a famous British writer. It may be viewed as a striking Victorian-Edwardian success story.

He started out by writing exotic romances, a highly commercial-popular form of late-nineteenth-century literature—many of his sources appear to be French—and at times brought rather more moral seriousness to it than Rudyard Kipling, Robert Louis Stevenson, and other romancers writing in English during the period. His three linked novels placed in Malaya—*Almayer's Folly* (1895), *An Outcast of the Islands* (1896), and *The Rescue* (1920; begun in 1896, partly written in later years)—fancifully expand upon some episodes and characters drawn from his maritime experiences, and stories he heard, around Malayan commercial outposts. The first was slowly started in the 1880s when Conrad was still a merchant-marine officer. The lushness of the exotic materials is heightened by an often ornate descriptive style, strong in portentous atmospheric detailing. This suggests a Westerner's anxieties with the threatening tropical jungles and the alien native psyches, as well as the moral ambiguities of colonialism.

Though Conrad's later writing became more disciplined and polished in manner, it continued some of the oddity of style, especially a high-flown rhetoric of considerable redundancy (and perhaps an underlying Polish and French syntax). The heightening provided a persisting tone of ominousness, mysteriousness, and ironic reflectiveness, which partly distinguishes some of Conrad's fiction from simpler commercial exoticism. There is usually an anxious moralist in his intense undergrowth.

The lush rhetoric seems appropriate to the broad theme of the Malayan fictions: the destructiveness of debased romantic idealism in weak colonialist characters in an alien environment. The background pattern for the three early novels includes the ambitious plans of a paternalistic European trader, Tom Lingard, who aims at the restoration of a native kingdom and great colonial wealth. The awkwardly ordered *Almayer's Folly* is the first novel finished, but it describes episodes late in the chronology of political manipulations and wars among the Malayans, Arab traders, jungle tribes, and European colonialists. The trading station that gives the novel its title belongs to Almayer, Lingard's ambitious, but weak and corrupt, protégé. Married to a native woman (who reverts to local allegiances), he sentimentally adores his grown daughter. His deceitful treatment of Lingard and others and his incompetent and ill-fated greed direct the melodramatic actions in which he loses his daughter to a native leader (the rhetorical erotic scenes show Conrad at his weakest), is defeated in the complicated maneuvers of political control and commercial exploitation, and finally loses his despairing life. Romantic fantasies such as Almayer's, ending in weakness, failure, and despair, are nuclear Conradian fictional experiences.

An Outcast of the Islands, somewhat more clearly ordered, concerns earlier periods of this colonial history. Willems, another vain and corrupted European weakling, betrays his patron Lingard, becomes an outcast, and finally is killed by his native mistress (proper reward in the nineteenth-century European perspective for having gone "native"). *The Rescue,* completed only after several decades and marked by the less energetic handling of the older Conrad, focuses on yet earlier episodes of the colonial history. The paternalistic Lingard, a figure of more gentlemanly stature than Almayer and Willems, goes down to defeat because of his idealistic megalomania for commercial-political power. He was the victim of a "fixed idea"—a favorite phrase of Conrad's—which results in the loss of reality and in pathetic retribution. Perhaps the main interest in these early fictions, besides the exoticism, rests in the curious combination of the conventions of popular romance and an antiromantic, pessimistic analysis of moral corruption, which was to characterize many of Conrad's novels.

As a writer with commercial ambitions, Conrad early on eagerly sought the publication of his stories in magazines which paid better proportionately than the publication of novels. Several of the first five of his shorter fictions, later collected as *Tales of Unrest* (1898), were simply variations on the Far East materials of the early novels. "The Lagoon" (1897) rather awkwardly and unbelievably has a Malayan tell a European of his stealing a beloved but forbidden woman with the loyal help of his brother. But while the three are being pursued, and for motives which are not altogether clear, he abandons his brother and makes his escape with the woman. His brother is killed. During the telling of this story to the European, the beloved woman is reportedly dying of an illness. The main thrust of the skittishly exotic tale seems to be that bitter guilt is the final dark product of romantic "illusions."

The longer "Karain: A Memory" (1897) more elaborately uses the distancing narrative frame characteristic of many of Conrad's tales. The story-within-a-story technique has been one of Conrad's most influential bequests to later writers. In having a narrator tell a tale at one or more removes from the action, a more complex view is often suggested. Besides the substance of the tale, the reader sees the narrator's view of, and reflections on, the events. Here a somewhat perplexed European attempts to explain the mysterious native actions. The evidence also suggests that Conrad saw multiple narration as a "distancing" device to help him avoid what would otherwise be painfully intense subjectivity and to provide ambivalent moral separation from the action. In "Karain: A Memory" a European trader retrospectively tells the story of a Malayan native ruler obsessed with his best friend's sister, who has violated native taboos and run away with a European. After Karain and his friend have vengefully pursued the couple for many months, Karain finally kills his friend instead of the lovers, apparently out of some obscure romanticism. Guiltily haunted for many years by the ghost of his friend, he becomes increasingly deranged until his burden is exorcised by a totem made up by some sympathetically condescending Englishmen. Yet the English narrator finally reflects that

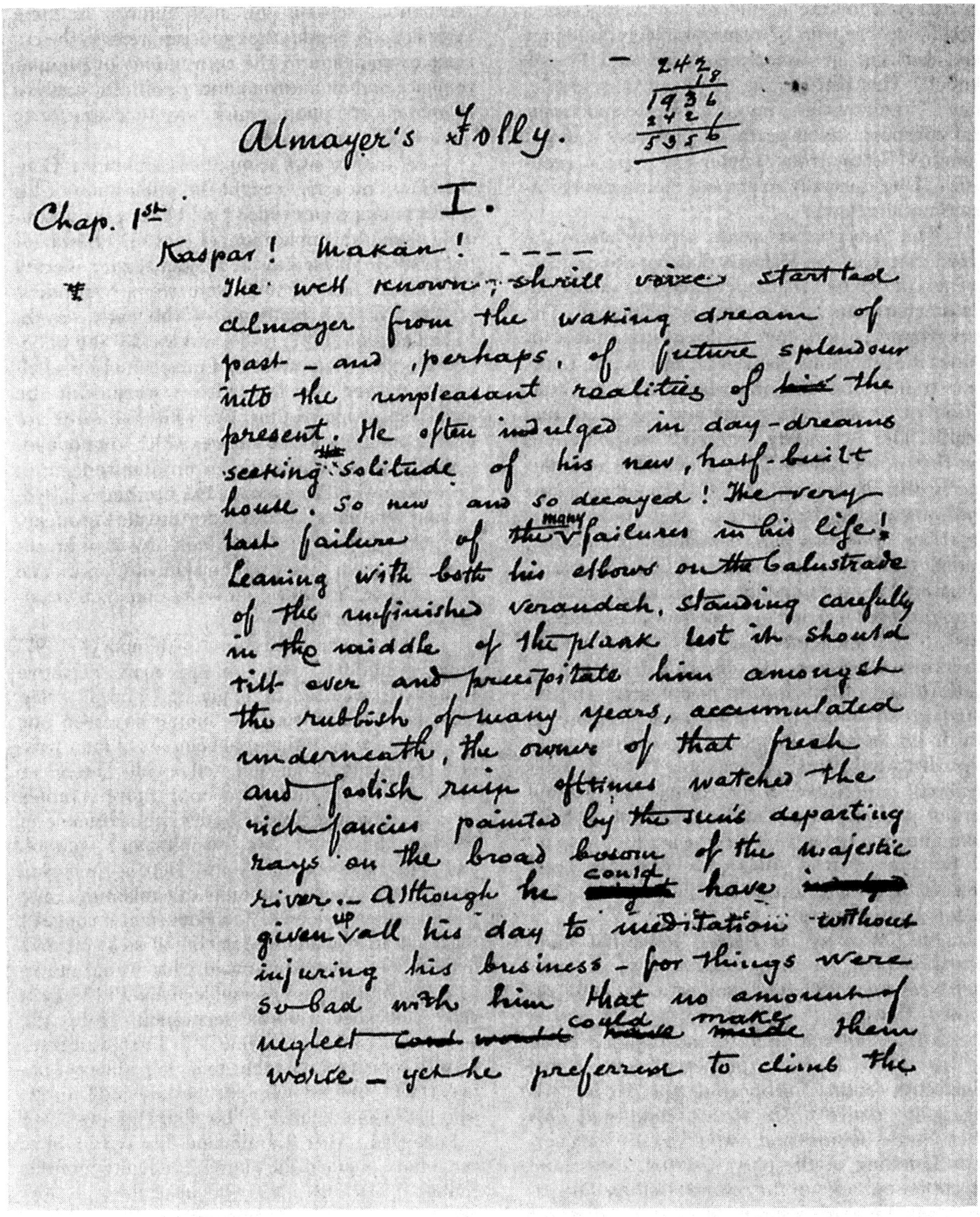

242
18
1936
242
5956

Almayer's Folly.

Chap. 1st I.

Kaspar! Makan! ---

The well known, shrill voice startled Almayer from the waking dream of past — and, perhaps, of future splendour into the unpleasant realities of ~~his~~ the present. He often indulged in day-dreams seeking the solitude of his new, half-built house. So new and so decayed! The very last failure of the many failures in his life! Leaning with both his elbows on the balustrade of the unfinished verandah, standing carefully in the middle of the plank lest it should tilt over and precipitate him amongst the rubbish of many years, accumulated underneath, the owner of that fresh and foolish ruin ofttimes watched the rich fancies painted by the sun's departing rays on the broad bosom of the majestic river. Although he ~~might~~ could have ~~indulg~~ given up all his day to meditation without injuring his business — for things were so bad with him that no amount of neglect ~~could would~~ could ~~have made~~ make them worse — yet he preferred to climb the

First page of the manuscript for Conrad's first book (Anderson Galleries, sale 1768, 12-14 November 1923)

the story, in spite of its oddity, has a deeper reality (a greater passion?) than the ordinary English scene he is now in. Such garrulous ambivalence in the antiromantic telling of romantic melodrama becomes essential Conradianism.

While the materials and narrative mode of Conrad seem set in these early fictions, he did experiment with some varying subject matter. The crudely overwritten "The Idiots" (1896), produced during his honeymoon in Brittany (biographers have psychologically made much of this), is a macabrely violent tale of a French peasant couple who have produced four idiots. In an action quite unprepared for in the story, the wife kills the husband during sex in order to stop producing yet more idiots. Then in a guilty frenzy she destroys herself. Polar in subject matter yet parallel in the theme of domestic hatred is the novella "The Return." The characters, unusual in Conrad, consist of a contemporary upper-class London husband and wife. The wife starts to run off with a literary man but quickly returns to her husband. Conrad's early analysis of that stolidly obtuse stock gentleman of English society shows sardonic perceptivity, emphasizing the insularity, rigidity, and smugness. But the story gets muddled midway with absurd domestic dialogue, erratic shifts in point of view, and Conrad's pervasive inability to present a believable woman. The final reversal has the husband leaving the wife, supposedly never to return. Essentially, the story argues that the upper class, of both sexes, lacks loving faithfulness. The hunger for "fidelity" persists through all of orphaned-and-exiled Conrad's writings, though usually in the maritime and colonial materials in which he seems to have felt greater assurance and in which he was rather entrapped by his commercial writing role.

Clearly the best, and best known, of the early stories is the satiric "An Outpost of Progress" (1897). Here Conrad makes his first fictional use of the brief period he spent in the Belgian Congo nearly a decade earlier. Perhaps because of his great anger at what he saw there, this story shows little moral ambivalence. With harsh irony, Conrad directly recounts the disintegration of two lower-middle-class European incompetents during a few months at an isolated jungle trading post. They let their native workers be enslaved in exchange for ivory, and they lose most connection with their surroundings. In a petty rage over precedence, culminating in a fight over some sugar when supplies run low, one murders the other and then, a bit improbably, guiltily commits suicide by hanging himself on the cross marker on the grave of the previous manager. The mocking tone savages not only the Great Civilizing Company's colonial exploitation and its hypocritical pretenses at progress but the representative weak fools of modern European mass society.

Joseph Conrad, 1896 (Beinecke Library, Yale University)

Committed to prolific writing, Conrad was extending the range of his subject matter. He drew on his job in 1884 as second mate on the British sailing ship *Narcissus*, and on some related experiences, for his third published novel, *The Nigger of the "Narcissus,"* first published as *The Children of the Sea* in 1897. This is the work that launched his reputation as a noted writer about the sea. Favorably commented upon by literary contemporaries, it also brought him some artistic recognition. While it is better written, more stylistically disciplined, than the Malayan novels, it is hardly the "masterpiece" that some later critics have called it, marred as it is by a confused narration and irascible bigotries. The telling gets muddled with a mixture of detached omniscience and reminiscence by an unidentified crew member, who grossly identifies with the officers and simplemindedly exalts them. Much of the treatment of the crew alternates between contempt for their overwhelmingly "childish" ways (and for any touches of dissidence), and sentimentalization of their endurance. Their stoicism is mystifyingly ennobled in Old Singleton, a seaman for fifty years, powerful, inchoate, and stupid, who stays at the helm for thirty hours during a devastating storm. His spare revelations consist of stock superstitions and, ultimately, a "chilling . . . resignation" to endless work, obedience, brutalization, and death. The narrative view insists that such are about all that ordinary humans can plausibly expect.

Fortunately for the narrative, the old royalist sea peasant plays only a small role, compared with the storm and other troublemakers. Nearly capsized in a gale on the run from Bombay to London, the *Narcissus* luckily survives in spite of apparently faulty design, an overconfident and rigid captain, and a terrified crew. The lengthily developed storm scene is often praised for its "realism" when what is really meant is its intensity. Some of the scene is quite powerful. The lavish visualization of the storm-wracked ship depends less on verisimilitude than on the nearly surreal play upon the grotesque. Comic-horrific scenes include the descriptions of the frenzied fraternal rescuing of the dying black man, which creates solidarity, and the lunatic preaching of the evangelical cook, which provides absurdity. The intense descriptions of the crew's suffering suggest a nearly hysterical vision of human misery. This vision achieves an absurdist poetry with the "acrid savor of existence" in a hostile universe.

The central totemic figure of the "nigger"—un-able-bodied seaman James Wait, a West Indian black man—is partly presented in a racist rhetoric which may now appear less nasty than quaint: his "pathetic and brutal" face has "the tragic, the mysterious, the repulsive mask of a nigger's soul." In Conrad's fascinated repulsion (he almost always presented alien ethnic types as ominously mysterious), the black man himself, as well as much of the crew, is uncertain if he is resentfully shamming illness or really dying. He serves as the love-hate image of the crew's own emotional "extremity." We are told that their identification with him becomes the "sentimental lie" which provides the maintaining "common bond" under extreme duress. This childish transcendentalism energizes their common endurance, producing what Conrad elsewhere describes as his ultimate simple value of "fidelity."

In one episode, responding to a miscalculated insult to Wait by the captain, the crew nearly mutinies, but their rebellion peters out under coolly harsh authority because, the reader is told, they have confused their political revolt against bad treatment with their symbolic revolt against death. In other episodes, the crew's sympathetic bond with the black man makes them, as one of Conrad's rhetorical flights has it, "highly humanized, tender, complex," which is also to be "excessively decadent." In Conrad's ideology, the miserable laborers in the world must remain miserable and laboring, aspiring only to a stupidly stoic manliness, like Old Singleton.

Jessie George, 1896 (Collection of Borys Conrad)

The unstoical black man finally dies and is buried at sea. Even his corpse seems to resist burial for a moment—an apt touch. The poignant but futile rebellion against death is also exploited by the tale's other troublemaker, Donkin, a complaining cockney slacker. Conrad disproportionately loads the descriptions of him with epithets: he is ugly, lazy, whining, dishonest, parasitic, violent, and mutinous. He even robs the black man as the latter is dying. Early on, he is also set up as an ideological strawman, defined (but not shown) as a representative "pet of philanthropists and self-seeking landlubbers." And in the penultimate paragraph he is described as one "who never did a decent day's work in his life" but now "no doubt earns his living by discoursing with filthy eloquence upon the right of labor to live." In this view, laborers, including those whom Conrad contemptuously called the "children of the sea," had the right to live, barely and submissively, but they should be quiet about it. "Pity," as we are told here (and elsewhere in Conrad), is socially dangerous. Joseph Conrad undoubtedly long held this view, though just possibly he is emphasizing it here to accord with the bigotries of the middle-class British readers of his time.

In spite of the contemptuously overloaded denigration of Donkin, which constitutes a crude, ad hominem political polemic of Conrad's, the character does stand for demands for decency and justice. At one point, for example, he incites one of the seamen to suggest that the crew should eat as well as the officers—a practice now widely accepted in Western maritime services. Conrad did seem to be somewhat aware of a moral dilemma: when the system is vicious, humanizing claims tend to undermine "the unspoken loyalty that knits together a ship's company" in the only solidarity that keeps a drastically arbitrary and exploitative system going in a malign cosmos. So false and precarious is the shipboard order that any complaint—such as the one about food—or any other dissidence must be treated as outrageous blasphemy. Conrad, a drastically pessimistic ideologue, seems to hold that misery for most is so inevitable that it can only be quietly endured, at its best achieving a heroic submission, and not much ameliorated or changed. Otherwise, the whole top-manipulated illusionary fidelity will collapse, sinking the storm-wracked ship and the cosmically ill-fated human community.

It is this insistent heightening of the issue, this surreal ideological pressuring of the rhetoric and the scene, which produces the enlarged anxiety and exceptional intensity of some of Conrad's sea writings. However, direct ideologizing is skittishly avoided in the next novella, "Youth" (1898), which was also based on Conrad's earlier maritime experience. Here Conrad first employed part of a perspective and narrative device for somewhat distancing the anxiety and pessimism, the garrulous retrospective narrator Captain Marlow, who was to be employed as a persona of the author in novel after novella for many years.

In "Youth" Captain Marlow gives, with nostalgic high spirits, a generation-later account of his first berth as a second mate while young. His ill-fated sailing bark, on a coal run from London to Bangkok, is rammed at the start. Although it is repaired, it repeatedly leaks and must be returned for more repairs. Then it is storm-beaten, then catches fire, and then explodes and sinks in the Indian Ocean. The young officer's first command is of a small lifeboat. In the story's odd disproportion, the fear, pain, frustration, and exhaustion of a multiply ill-fated voyage, ending with an unsympathetic shore society, are treated as a genial initiation rite. The disparity between the harsh events and Marlow's burbling tone in recounting them produces an emphasis upon the absurd. The far-distancing narration allows amoral bemusement at the futility and produces a work of grotesquerie.

To follow the sequence of sea tales is to see the varied uses Conrad made of the limited set of incongruities of his maritime experiences. He explored artistic variations on a few themes. The bumbling captain in "Youth" was earnestly foolish. The bumbler captain in the longish novella *Typhoon* (1902) comes out heroic, in spite of himself. Captain MacWhirr, master of a small steamship trading the China coast, is a totally dutiful creature of very limited intelligence, imagination, and responsiveness—"ignorant of life to the last, without ever having been made to see all it may contain of perfidy, of violence, and of terror." But his very lack of sympathy and insight, his very literalism, is also his virtue. Unlike his second mate, who goes out of his mind in the typhoon, and unlike his responsive first mate, whose imagination and despairing sensitivity make him ineffective in the storm, the captain stolidly endures the worst, which he perhaps could have avoided. His stupidity and literalism, and his vague "sense of the fitness of things," ironically work out to be a fundamental practicality and decency. The ship survives. Furthermore, the two hundred Chinese indentured workers, carried in the hold and brutally beaten around in

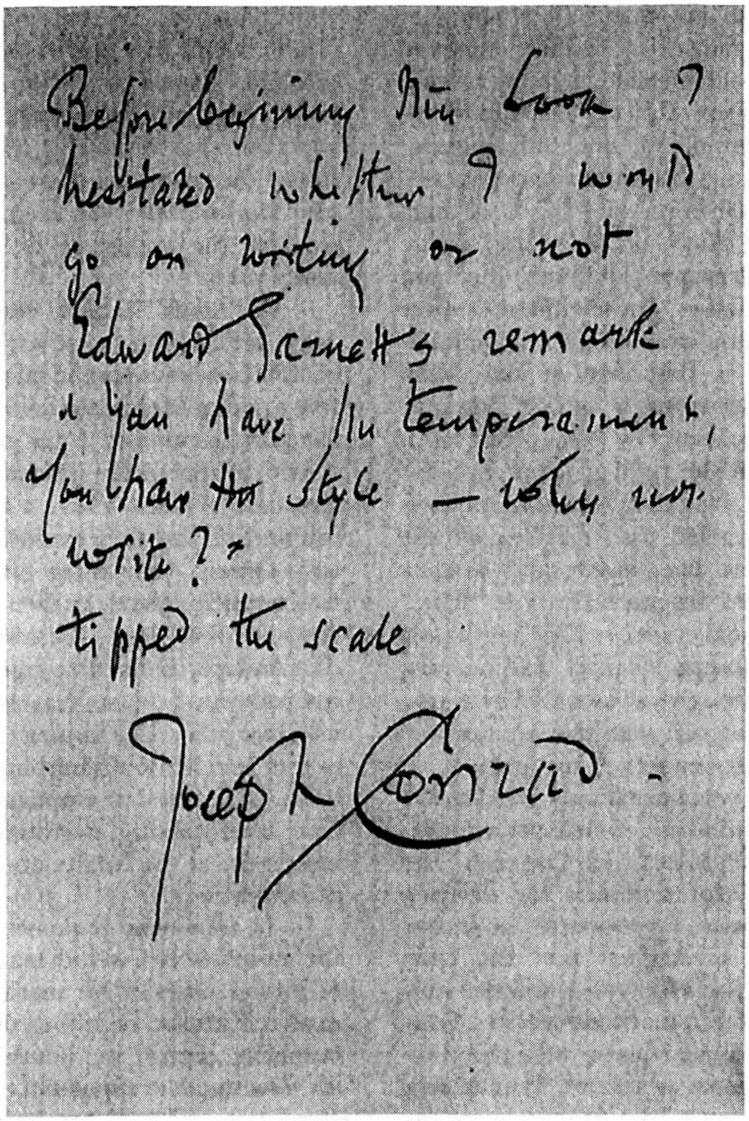
Before beginning this book I
hesitated whether I would
go on writing or not
Edward Garnett's remark
« You have the temperament,
You have the style — why not
write? »
tipped the scale.
Joseph Conrad -

Inscription in a copy of the first edition of An Outcast of the Islands *(American Art Association, 28 April 1927)*

the storm, are treated with a crude approximate justice in dividing up their jumbled possessions because of the captain's dutiful simplicity. Conrad, apparently to maintain his underplaying of the emotional intensity of the material, employs displaced descriptions (pieces of letters, logs, and comments by other people) in order to praise the captain's stupid literalism and hard Protestant virtues. By background and temperament, Conrad was not such a person, but he was making—not without some irony—a paean to the traditional unemotional English character.

In such an intriguing performance as *Typhoon* we might recognize Joseph Conrad as countering his own much more anxiously emotional responses, a self-reversal of his own romanticism, which in his life took the form of the romantic Polish exile's becoming an imitation English gentleman. The duality takes more subtle form in Conrad's most famous maritime tale, the later novella "The Secret Sharer" (1910). Drawing on his experience in the late 1880s of suddenly being given an emergency first command of a strange ship in a Far Eastern port, Conrad, in an unusual form for him, has his first-person narrator tell his own tale rather than musing over the actions and motivations of others in a story that is not preceded by a frame narrative. The emotional split within the young captain becomes the subject of the story by way of the doppelganger device and theme. The "secret self" takes form as the captain's double, a look-alike fugitive first mate the captain takes on board his first night, secretes with endless anxiety, and finally aids in flight. At the level of conventional characterization, the captain's immediate and full identification with the criminal mate—though they are of the same age and physique, social class, maritime school, and of similar experience—is inexplicable. And it remains so, leaving the story fundamentally ambiguous; for Leggatt, the mate with whom the earnest captain identifies to an extreme degree, is a murderer. In a rage, though with some provocation in a storm, Leggatt killed a seaman under his command. The murderer shows no remorse for his action, and weeks later he still thinks of his victim as a "snarling cur" who deserved to die. The captain immediately agrees with this attitude. Thus his aid to the murdering mate is neither justice nor charity but secret identification, which he does not fully understand. The captain's narration emphasizes his immediate anxieties but does not treat the deeper sources of his identification, his near mergence with the fugitive. Suggestively, the young captain rejects sea authority (the fugitive's captain) and law and order (the fugitive's return for trial) as responses for what is identified as the Cain-cursed dark side of the self.

The "secret self " of Conrad's account need not be allegorized as the Freudian id or the Christian demon—as some critics would have it—since the author maintains the surface verisimilitude of the fiction. To stay with Conrad's issue: for a young man to achieve his own identity—"that ideal conception of one's own personality every man sets up for himself secretly," as the captain announces early in the story—he must dispose of the dark secret self without either total repression or total mergence. Yet the anxious captain must avoid probing the deeper sources of his secret identification with the violent mate. What the captain does is aid the fugitive to escape by a dangerous testing of himself, drifting his becalmed sailing ship close to a desolate rocky island under the somewhat plausible guise of picking up the off-land breeze. The testing of his command, it should be noted, is made quite drastic: as the new captain, he knows little of the ship, the officers, the crew, and the place, and he outrageously risks the lives of all. Furthermore, on a dark night he goes much closer to the rocks than needed (the fugitive is an expert swimmer who did a greater distance originally to arrive at the captain's ship). By a mixture of daring and luck, the young captain succeeds in dropping the fugitive and getting the ship underway. The captain then feels he has achieved a sense of mastery, overcome some hidden "shadow" on himself, and arrived at "the perfect communion" of his first command, and his ideal fantasy of himself. But the final words of the story are his for his fugitive "second self," outcast "to take his punishment: a free man, a proud swimmer striking out for a new destiny." The curious mergence of freedom and punishment, and of new destiny as fugitive outcastness, may give the reader the deepest tropes for Conrad's perplexed views in this somewhat overwrought tale around obscure ambivalences about playing authority figure.

In the pattern of Conrad's fictions and ideology, the antimoral story "The Secret Sharer" is a breakthrough to the romanticism that Conrad usually attacks. He could not often maintain the artistry of the split psyche, the balancing of the violent fugitive and the young master making the desperate gamble. When in the late novel *The Shadow-Line* (1917) he attempts to repeat the initiatory "first command" experience, including some of the same metaphors, the same scene (the ship becalmed off Koh-ring in the Java Sea), and the same testing, it loses the narrative immediacy and precariously balanced doubleness in a mixture of the skittish and the sentimental. Introduced with an elaborately redundant jocularity, the story becomes another exercise in endurance in which the young captain must deal with a becalmed ship, and, this time, a sick crew as well. In a tale that is dialectically as well as stylistically flat, the only double for this captain consists of the dead master he has replaced, a man who went mad in his final days and disposed of the needed shipboard medicine. Conrad dallies a bit with the ex-captain—the sick mate is obsessed with the sense of a ghost—but supernaturalism is essentially uncongenial to Conrad and the motif is dropped. The only aid on the ship for the young captain is a heroically submissive invalid, Ransome, a sailor with a bad heart. He saves the ship. But since he is only mawkishly presented, that service is not very interesting. What strength the tale has is (as in *Typhoon*) the vivid description of the malignant weather, but the heavily jocular opening, the belabored theme of endurance, the sentimental handling of character, and a very paltry sense of what constitutes maritime maturity make the whole slight stuff.

Conrad several times commented that he felt entrapped in the public expectations of him as a producer of sea tales. His best work usually does lie elsewhere. To move back to chronologi-

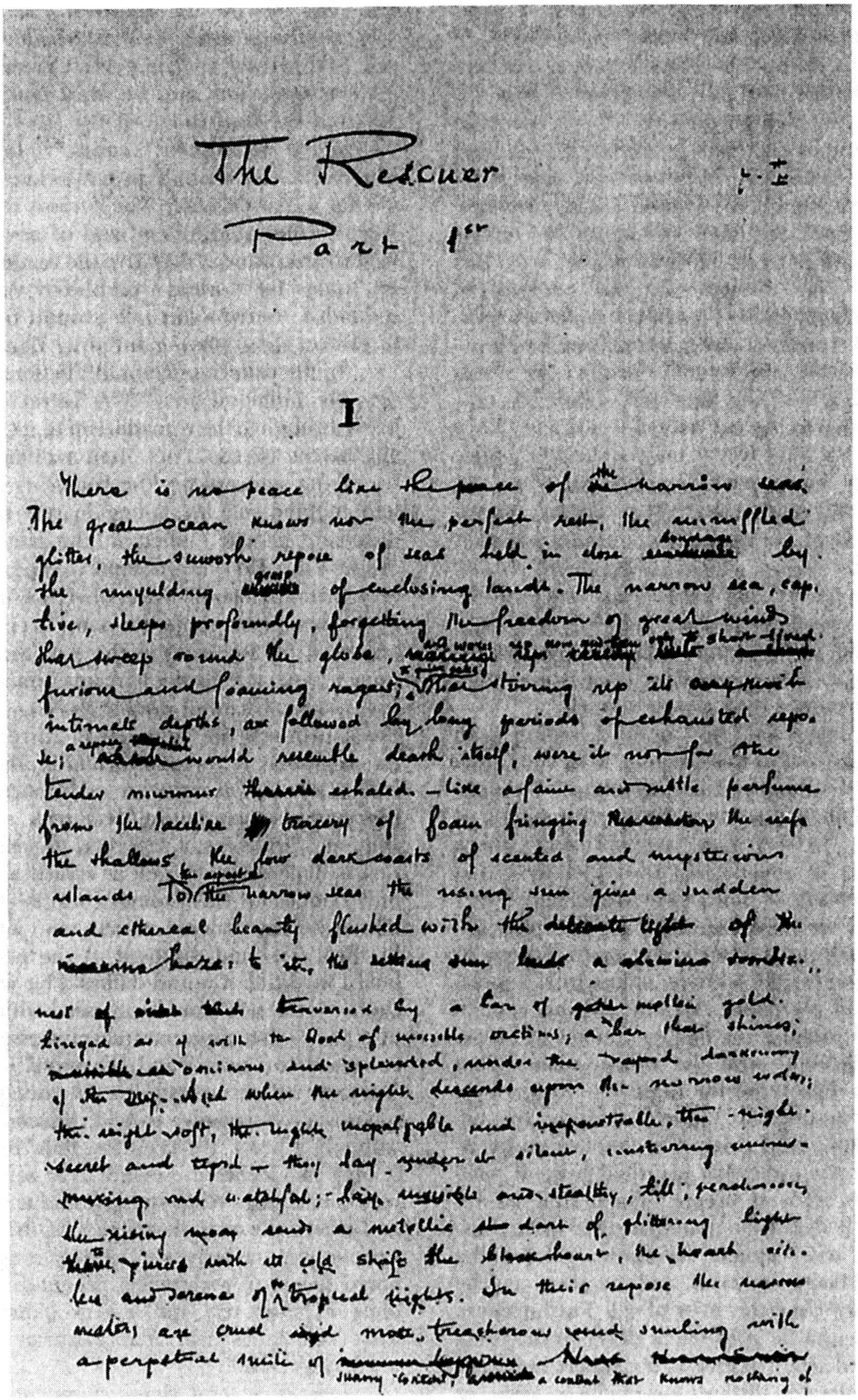
The Rescuer

Part 1st

I

First page of an early draft, with working title, for The Rescue *(Thomas J. Wise,* A Bibliography of the Writings of Joseph Conrad, *1921)* cal sequence: after "Youth" Conrad wrote what is now his most famous novella, "Heart of Darkness" (1899), which has become even more famous because of adaptation in the serio-popular movie *Apocalypse Now* (1979). In 1890 Conrad had spent a few months under contract to captain a river steamer in what was then the relatively new, and brutally exploited, Belgian colony of the Congo. He commanded one for only a few days, after lengthy travel in central Africa, and in serious illness and disgust invalided out and returned to Europe. He briefly drew on the materials in "An Outpost of Progress," then several years later made more complex use of the scene in "Heart of Darkness," with the retrospective narration of his recurrent persona Captain Marlow. It has been suggested that some of the special intensity of the story derives from Conrad's own near-death in the Congo, an experience given to Marlow. Certainly Conrad's moral rage at what he saw of colonialism in Africa also informs the novella.

But the thrust of the tale is yet wider. A shadowy narrator describes Captain Marlow's telling the story, some years after the events, to four solid citizens on a pleasure yawl in the Thames estuary one evening. As darkness closes in, multiple parallels are suggested: Congo and Thames, Belgian and British colonialism—indeed, European imperialistic history back to the time when Roman legions brutally conquered primitive Britain, which has, like "darkest Africa," also "been one of the dark places of the earth." There are further elliptical ironies in a damning account of imperialism being told to its representative London profiteers (a corporate director, etc.). Marlow grants partial exemption of the British colonial exploitation to the usual brutality because of British "devotion to efficiency." Otherwise colonialism is mostly "robbery with violence" of those "who have a different complexion or slightly flatter noses," and, says Marlow, the viciousness of colonization of other peoples can be redeemed only by an unselfish dedication to a larger "idea." However, the rest of the story undercuts that pious hope by shadowing forth a large darkness at the heart of things.

Throughout Marlow's account of his obtaining the Congo job through family connections in the "whited sepulchre" capital city where the company has its headquarters reverberates the hypocrisy of the "noble cause" and the ominousness of the "philanthropic pretense" disguising the exploitation. Conrad's play upon metaphoric and atmospheric effects in this scene are famous. The brutal absurdity—"the merry dance of death and trade"—also appears in striking images on Marlow's sea trip to Africa and then the journey inland, where not only crazy inefficiency but "rapacious and pitiless folly" get annotated with descriptions of chained, dying, and murdered natives. The colonialists, high and low, provide satiric images of callous exploiters and apathetically demoralized brutes. An odd partial exception is a company chief accountant, meticulously starched and turned out in the jungle like a "hairdresser's dummy." His books are in "apple-pie order." While he may maintain efficiency and a moral image of keeping up appearances, he is cruelly indifferent to sick whites as well as dying natives. But he is the first to inform Marlow of a larger possibility, of Kurtz, a "remarkable" man and unusually successful trader far up the river. Through gradual, though ambiguous, disclosures to Marlow, Kurtz comes to represent some larger conception of value, even "pity, and science, and progress," thus some positive purpose beyond brutal greed. A man "with moral ideas of some sort," sent out by a reforming group, Kurtz becomes the focus of Marlow's Congo quest, his hope for some redeeming "idea" in the moral darkness of what he sees as the colonial "nightmare."

The conception of Kurtz, the source evidence suggests, is largely a product of Conrad's moral imagination. Moral indignation certainly dominates the delineation of most of the other Europeans, who are sarcastically described as fraudulent "pilgrims" and "sordid buchaneers." To counter any sense of romantic adventurism, for example, Conrad epitomizes one typical enterprise, the Eldorado Exploring Expedition, as "reckless without hardihood, greedy without audacity, and cruel without courage." Marlow sardonically surveys such efforts while he is delayed by the broken-down steamboat, the general inefficiency, and the machinations of the jealously mediocre manager and the others plotting in "imbecile rapacity." Captain Marlow maintains some sense of values, Conrad insists, only by his work. The effort is presented as not just dutiful repair of the boat but as an article of larger faith in the personal redemption of disciplined labor. The only positively described Europeans are the few mechanics. Later, work is linked to a "deliberate belief" which commands reality and resists the reversion to savagery. Work becomes a larger dedication, as with the primitive native whom Marlow has trained to religious devotion to the steamboat's boiler. Another instance of the moral penumbra of "efficiency" cited in the early part of the story comes with Marlow's discovery of a carefully annotated handbook on seamanship, belonging to a romantic wandering trader. This book illustrates, Marlow says, "an honest concern for the right way of going to work" (regardless of however irrelevant in the middle of the jungle), and thus an implicit moral ordering "luminous with another than a professional light." Whether this exalted work ethic can adequately counter the overwhelming evil of the exploitative order must remain doubtful, but Conrad does make it the clearest moral affirmation of the tale.

In this context, Marlow's fascination with and affirmation of Kurtz must remain ambiguous. Kurtz, Marlow insists, has been corrupted by his solitude from "civilization" and has lost the absolutely essential "restraints" that keep one human, and which Marlow finds even in the cannibals. Kurtz's charismatic qualities, usually attributed to a powerful rhetoric (little heard by the reader, as many critics have noted), subordinate to his ruthlessness. Of course, much about Kurtz remains dark, enigmatic; what we know of him comes from the refractions of other consciousnesses (as is usually true when Conrad presents puzzling characters). Even one of the greatest admirers of Kurtz, the quixotically devoted romantic wanderer (owner of the redeeming sea manual), has been taken gross advantage of by Kurtz. But apparently representative of Kurtz's moral contradictions is the report, given to Marlow, that Kurtz wrote for a European committee on civilizing the natives. It is full of highfalutin benevolent rhetoric, but it ends with Kurtz's scrawled "Exterminate all the brutes!"

Though claiming the rhetoric of idealist and reformer, Kurtz is consumed with greed and power. He has accumulated vast quantities of ivory not by trade but by theft and warfare, made himself ruler (with a native queen—a subject for Victorian shivers) of a native tribe and army, and let himself be worshiped as a god. He has systematically engaged in conquest, terror, executions, and other undescribed "horrors." Confused about returning to the colonial order, in which he retains large ambitions, he has both ordered the steamboat attacked by his native army and boarded it, critically ill, to leave. He slips away in the night to be worshiped by the natives but is easily persuaded by Marlow to come back because of his European commercial-political ambitions, about which he continues to rant egomaniacally. He obviously lacks all character, which is later confirmed by Marlow in details about Kurtz's manipulative European past.

At the river scene, Marlow decides that Kurtz is morally "mad" and "hollow at the core." Just why Marlow takes Kurtz so seriously, other than as an exemplum of the "powers of darkness" unrestrained, may be puzzling to the reader. For Marlow sees Kurtz even on his ideal side as a devotee of "sham" fame and power and "childish" in his cult of himself. Yet Marlow still credits Kurtz with endless struggles of conscience and with being a "remarkable man." He is, of course, Marlow's chosen "nightmare" in a rather perverse defiance of the prevailing petty nightmares. Kurtz, then, is less morally real than a reflection of Marlow's moral needs. Thus Marlow elaborately rationalizes Kurtz's last dark words, "The horror! The horror!," taking them as an "affirmation, a moral victory paid for by innumerable defeats, by abominable horrors, by abominable satisfactions." Kurtz had the courage, Marlow fervently insists, to make a judgment on himself, to achieve moral insight. However vicious, then, Kurtz had the redeeming larger "idea" which Marlow has been looking for as a saving grace in the European colonial evil.

But the moral claim is entirely the good captain's, not the nasty colonialist's, though overlooked by many readers; considering the gross viciousness and futility of Kurtz, Marlow's entirely private affirming interpretation remains at best a Pyrrhonist value. The rest of the narrative skeptically suggests that value may be all there is, as in the often-noted Marlow statement of Conradian pessimism: "Droll thing life is—that mysterious arrangement of merciless logic for a futile purpose."

After recovering from his own near-fatal illness and returning to Europe, Marlow, still dedicated to his idea of Kurtz, learns that he was not only a megalomaniac colonialist but a rootless semi-intellectual, all manipulation and no value—the type now recognized as a demagogic seeker of power and celebrity. The hollow evil in the colonies is also the evil hollow at the heart of Western culture.

Marlow concludes his sense of obligation to his myth of Kurtz by visiting Kurtz's middle-class fiancée, who romantically continues to idealize Kurtz as a great man. Moralist Marlow decides it would be "too dark altogether" to disillusion the egotistical lady. Though he hates lies, he accedes

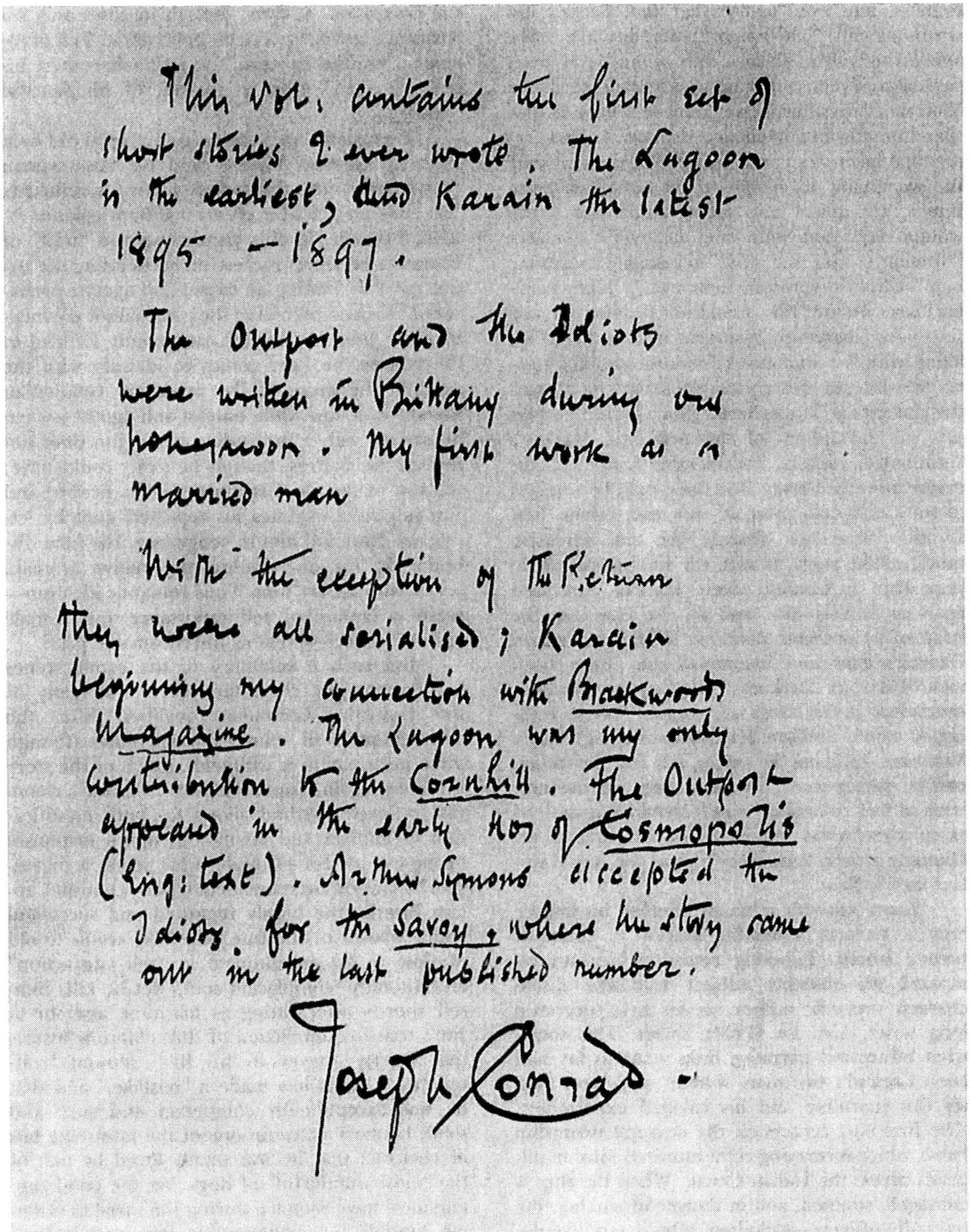

This vol. contains the first set of short stories I ever wrote. The Lagoon is the earliest, and Karain the latest 1895 – 1897.

The Outpost and the Idiots were written in Brittany during our honeymoon. My first work as a married man

With the exception of The Return they were all serialised; Karain beginning my connection with Blackwoods Magazine. The Lagoon was my only contribution to the Cornhill. The Outpost appeared in the early Nos of Cosmopolis (Eng: text). Arthur Symons accepted the Idiots for the Savoy, where the story came out in the last published number.

Joseph Conrad.

Inscription in a copy of the first edition of Tales of Unrest *(American Art Association, 28 April 1927)*

to hers, and even assures her that Kurtz's last words (actually "The horror!") were her name spoken lovingly. For Marlow, this saving lie is justified because he is speaking to a female idealist, a Victorian lady, that is, someone he views as less than humanly intelligent and responsive. This bigotry has been prepared for by Marlow's playing the sycophant to his powerful aunt (while he thinks, "It's queer how out of touch with truth women are") and with later chauvinist remarks ("women . . . are out of it," necessarily dreaming in a "beautiful world of their own"). Many readers have found this pseudoidealization of the pure lady (insistently recurrent in Conrad) to be, along with the sometimes footloose moral rhetoric (as with the description of Kurtz's end), and the portentous atmospherics (such as the endless play on metaphors of darkness and Marlow's Buddha-like wisdom), considerable flaws in an otherwise powerful story. But they may be integral to the Conradian point of view and values. Nor do they altogether obscure the real corrosive moral of the story, as with the final scenic metaphor back in London where Marlow, described again as Buddha-like, and all else flow into the heart of an immense darkness. Whatever Captain Conrad's conscious intentions may have been with "Heart of Darkness," his Captain Marlow's revelations in this harsh tale must be seen as verging on moral nihilism. Half camouflaging it for a Victorian audience by saving lies for the ladies, and by saving more involuted ones for the captains of this colonialist world, should not mislead as to where vivid impressionism of scene (a redeeming artistic "efficiency"?) and the moral ironies darkly flow.

Kurtz was only a "sham" idealist, his fiancée only a pathetic romantic, Marlow a romantic turned ironist. Exposing romantic idealism remained an obsessive subject with the disenchanted romantic author, as his first successful long novel, *Lord Jim* (1900), shows. This somewhat bifurcated narrative links what so far had been Conrad's two main sources of subject matter, his maritime and his colonial experiences. The first part centers on the decrepit steamship *Patna,* which is carrying eight hundred Muslim pilgrims across the Indian Ocean. When the ship is damaged, stopped, and in danger of sinking, the cowardly officers—including, after a sensitive delay, the young mate-protagonist Jim—abandon the ship, making no provision for the passengers. But the *Patna* survives and is safely towed to port by another ship. Jim is tried and convicted of patent dereliction of duty, though he loses only his mariner's certificate and his good name. Full of romantic "exalted egotism," he rationalizes away his cowardice and goes in pursuit of his fanciful "honor."

Eventually, with the help of several old men (fatherly Captain Marlow and his businessman friend Stein) who themselves yearn for romance, Jim ends up a trader on a far-distant colonial island, Patusan. In this parallel second "trial" of character he seems successful, befriending the native ruler by leading an expedition against predatory Arabs and becoming the paternalistic colonialist Lord Jim. But though supposedly faithful to the natives, he later comes to identify with the devil in the guise of the predatory Gentleman Brown—a fellow white outcast and egotist—when he arrives with a marauding gang. Jim does not protect the natives, though he easily could have; the son of the chief is murdered by Brown, and Jim suicidally expiates his repeated guilt by letting the chief kill him in vengeance. His final dishonor is his abandoning the native woman, Jewel, who adores him. Thus romantic idealism—really a fantasy of self-importance and a male code of honor—shows its unredeemable price.

But such a summary of the exotic scenes and stereotyped characters leaves out many of the distinctive Conradian qualities. After the early chapters of omniscient narration (though some information is withheld), much of the story is told by, again, Captain Marlow. Conrad's elaborate reflexive method allows for both mystification of motives and ambiguous moral responses to the events. For example, what seems a digression by Marlow becomes ideologically central: Captain Brierly, the highly regarded and successful young master of the fine ship *Ossa,* seems to old Marlow to be an ultimate in "self-satisfaction" and a totally "complacent soul," yet he kills himself shortly after sitting as maritime assessor at Jim's trial for dereliction of duty. Marlow asserts that Brierly "never in his life" showed "self-mistrust," much less made a "mistake," and that he was exceptionally competent and sure and solid; he even states (in one of the most trite bits of rhetoric) that he was totally loved by one of the "most wonderful" of dogs. Yet the good captain must have been led during Jim's trial to examine himself for contemptible fear and lack of decency—the issues with Jim—and his self-verdict "must have been of unmitigated guilt." To justify the character improbability, Marlow eliminates other motives (money, drink, age, incompetence, madness, women, and irrational impulse). Captain Brierly went to his death calmly, carefully providing for the future of his ship and his first mate, rechecking the navigation and even oiling the log, carefully saving his dog and gold watch (an award for brave dutifulness), and efficiently preparing himself to sink in the sea with four weights attached to his body. Since many suicides, probably including Conrad's own attempt as a young man, show ambivalent muddle, what the author typically does here is not pose probabilities of character but paradoxes of moral ideology.

Conrad's manner in presenting this story shows an ideological emphasis and not, contrary to some critics, psychological analysis and dramatization of probable character. Brierly had quite implausibly—given his character, success, and the circumstances—identified with romantic-loser Jim during Jim's trial. Conrad gives him a doctrinal conclusion, contrary to character and psychology, that the conventions of duty by which the captain lived did not work, and so concluded himself. Brierly had believed in "professional decency": the mariner's fidelity not to goodness or intelligence or people but to a role and routine (even if it be caring only for a shipload of old rags). Since "simple" officer Jim, from a proper background, also belonged within this convention—we are repeatedly told and then retold in the conclusion to the later "Author's Note" that Jim "was of the right sort; he was one of us"—his case should exemplify the adequacy of the mariner's convention of duty, "the sovereign power enthroned in a fixed standard of conduct." Conrad seemed to believe that a professional ethic was the only basis of what little modern moral community there is. Brierly is reported to have held that "the only thing that holds us together is just the name . . . for decency." But Jim's behavior, the trial, and Brierly's state of mind show this ethic as not only insufficient but irrelevant. The "name" of decency, the appearance of a code of values and its "sense of dignity" and all that is "supposed to be," have again been revealed as sham. The moral conventions do not really work, and so Conrad ideologically pushes Captain Brierly to a suicide which is improbable for the character and his role but that logically expresses the moral fear in Conrad's own extreme doubt.

Finding it unbearable that the inadequacy of conventional decency and dignity should be revealed, sternly righteous Brierly, we are told, even offered to bribe Jim to skip out on the rest of the trial and hide. When Jim, pursuing his romantic fantasy of honor, does not flee underground, Brierly puts himself under the sea. This Dostoyevski-like acting upon the logic of an idea is not, surely, the probable behavior of a young, confident, obtuse, successful British Master Mariner. Conrad imposes on his representative captain what he described elsewhere as the excesses of "reflection," leading to the terrors which come from the radical idea that all may be illegitimate. Marlow also gives what he calls the "last word of amazing profundity" on the suicide, Brierly's first mate's epitaph: "neither you nor I, sir, had ever thought so much of ourselves." Nor apparently so much of conventional appearances. Seasoned doubters, like the mate and Marlow—and Conrad—can live on, skeptically holding to the "name" of simple ideas and faiths in which they humbly do not believe. Without such life-lies (as Conrad's contemporary Henrik Ibsen called them), a self-respecting man (much less an ideal lady) can hardly live with the terrifying truth that claims to disciplined routines, civilized pretenses, finally amount to very little, though there is not, in Conrad's alien world and pessimistic view, much else.

In the ornate structure of *Lord Jim,* Captain Brierly's suicide provides an aslant parallel to Jim's self-sacrificial death for an egotistical fantasy of self-importance. Jim, too, repeatedly appears as the "simple" mariner who indeed thinks much of himself and his "shadowy ideal of conduct." Jim's case is complicated by his guilt over previous failure, by chauvinistic pretenses to masculine "honor," and by his ambivalent role as colonial autocrat arrogantly doing good for his natives while playing out a debilitating different role. In a much-quoted passage, philosophical Stein advises Jim to follow out his romantic dream, "in the destructive element immerse." True enough, the destructive dream allows the only possibility of heroic shape and meaning, however fatal to himself, and others.

Carried into the reflective depths, the Conradian sea-captain morality of simple ideas and fidelities will hardly do for humane purpose, though several die well by them. The sly moralizing of another, Marlow, must again be recognized as peculiarly ironical, as when he says: "For a moment I had a view of a world that seemed to wear a vast and dismal aspect of disorder, while, in truth, thanks to our unwearied efforts, it is as sunny an arrangement of small conveniences as

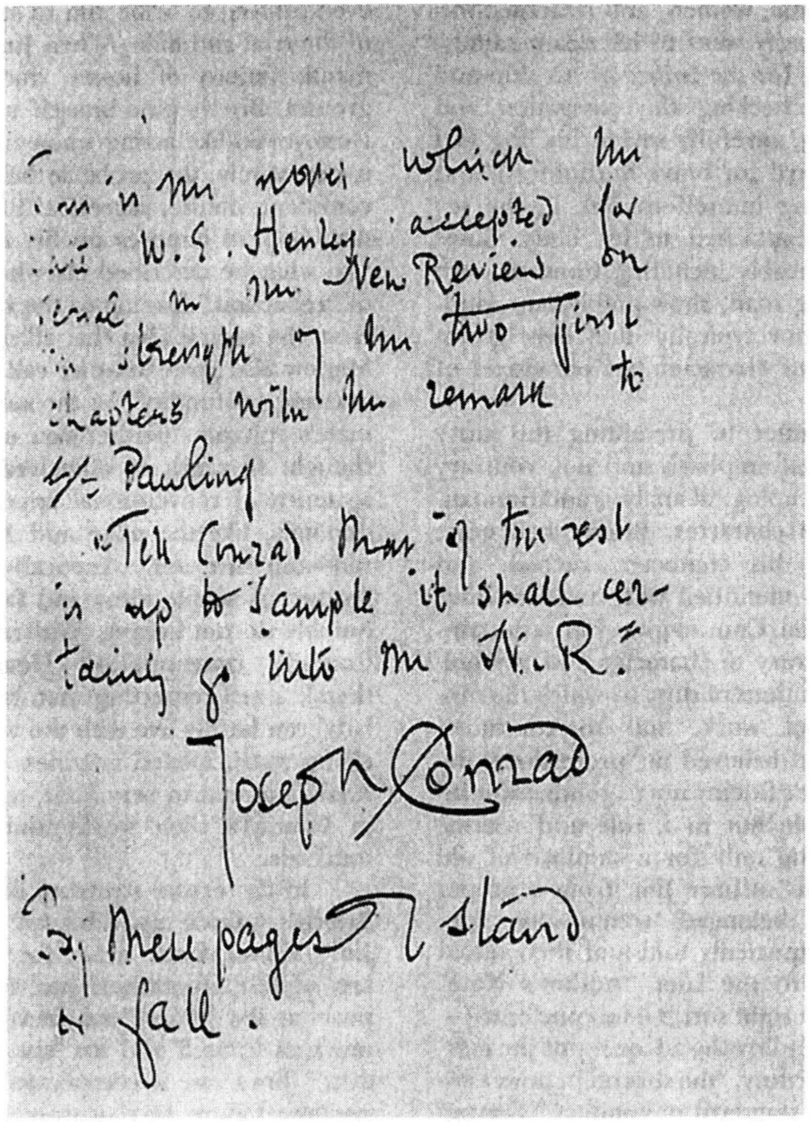

...in the novel which the
... W. E. Henley accepted for
serial in the New Review on
... strength of the two first
chapters with the remark to
Wm Pawling
"Tell Conrad that if the rest
is up to sample it shall certainly go into the N.R."
Joseph Conrad
By these pages I stand
or fall.

Inscription in a copy of the first English edition of The Nigger of the "Narcissus" *(American Art Association, 28 April 1927)*

the mind of man can conceive." Ah, yes, sunny indeed, and the next paragraph echoes "Heart of Darkness" again in that "it had grown pitch-dark where we were."

Conrad's writing in these most productive years was not confined to the dark moral riddling of exotic maritime and colonial scenes. For some years he attempted to collaborate on popular fictions with his younger close friend Ford Madox Hueffer (Ford). Probably Conrad's contribution was the smaller part of the artistically poor but still commercially unsuccessful collaborations, *The Inheritors* (1901), *Romance* (1903), and *The Nature of a Crime* (not published until 1924). Ford was almost surely a more general intellectual source for Conrad, and may have contributed to, as well as influenced, some of Conrad's other writings, including his best, such as *Nostromo* (1904).

Conrad also wrote more short fictions. "Amy Foster" (1901) is another attempt to deal with the more obscure land (rather than sea) peasants. Yanko, a poor Carpathian lad washed ashore from a wrecked emigrant ship on a rural English shore, is harshly mistreated because of his simplicity and inability to communicate to the cold English peasants. Though always the alien, eventually he marries a homely and dumb local girl, Amy Foster. But in fear and misunderstanding she abandons him when he is ill. Yanko dies, the story concludes, of "the supreme disaster of loneliness and despair." This moral, and the narration, come from an intelligent local doctor. What is he doing there? In a characteristic charge, Conrad says that the man's intellectuality, "like a corrosive fluid, had destroyed his ambition." Amy Foster, we are also told, though dull, has just enough "imagination" to fall in love, but not enough to go on loving the alien. These curious distinctions of Conrad's anti-intellectualism, which marks much of his work, serve here as ideological rivets for one of his most bathetic templates of loneliness and outcastness.

"To-Morrow" (1902) is an awkward and redundant effort at writing a pathetic comedy about a retired and lunatic coastal captain whose fantasy of what his son will be like when he returns denies the actual son when he does come back. (Freudian critics relate this to obsessive parent-child fantasies in the orphaned Conrad's work.) The novella "Falk" (1903) is an awkwardly rambling story around a mock-heroic Scandinavian tugboat captain in an Eastern port and his elaborate efforts to marry a German shipowner's niece. Curiously, Falk's sexual hunger is displaced into his digressive story of when he committed cannibalism in order to survive on a long-disabled ship. But Conrad's Victorian-shocker deployment of the primordial passions seems undercut by the skittish handling. Sheer will to endurance, quite beyond moral decorum, wins in hunger and in lust.

"The End of the Tether" (1902) is a sentimental short story inflated into near-novel length (apparently, as happened several times with Conrad, to meet the demands of a publishing contract). A once superior sailing captain, Whalley attempts in his late sixties to keep up the facade of a fastidiously proud gentleman and master, though actually impoverished and with a leeching married daughter. Whalley successfully connives for a petty steamboat command and pretends to captain, though really almost blind. A hysterically malicious owner (Conrad's suggestive portrait of a compulsive gambler) tricks the captain, and the ship ends up on a reef for the insurance money. Captain Whalley goes down with the ship. Though Conrad apparently meant to mock his old captain as an optimist who does not believe in "evil," and who with dangerous sentimentality went on too long, the maudlin repetition of his virtues and the crude melodrama undercut the pessimistic idea.

While these tales have implicitly powerful themes—obtuseness of the aging, voracious sexuality, egotistical fantasy, alienated loneliness—and touches of graphic rhetoric, they are poor. Some of the mawkishness and forced melodrama may, of course, be attributed to the popular magazine audience for which they were written.

But Conrad was doing partly more serious work as well. *Nostromo* is Conrad's largest novel in size, scope, and ambition. The first half engages the reader, by a back-and-forth movement in time and focus, in a broad nineteenth-century world of diverse characters and politics. While the mosaic is thin and stereotyped on subjective experience, it is rich on mythic history. In the central action, the town of Sulaco, Coastaguana (placed in South America), turns its province into a separate country, the Occidental Republic, in a conservative counterrevolution after a long period of misrule by a psychopathic tyrant, a weak traditional oligarchy, and a debased military-populist coup. Finally, in the Conradian disenchantment, the controlling politics "rest in the development of material interests," that is, standard colonial capitalism.

Specifically, the "material interests" are those almost "mystically" idealized by a local self-aggrandizing upper-class Englishman, Charles Gould (this stick figure certainly represents the traditional gentlemanly "solid English sense not to think too much"), whose San Tome silver mine is backed by a prudent and pious American millionaire. Lesser roles are played by a foreign railroad and a shipping company. While the machinations, bribery, and finally even the military power of the Gould Concession bring commercial modernization and an appearance of order, a choral character (Dr. Monygham) insists at a crucial point near the end that it is all based on "inhuman" expediency, not moral principle and continuity, and so will again result in "barbarism, cruelty, and misrule." Conrad shows considerable political intelligence.

But this intelligence does not extend to his handling of his already disenchanted idealists, such as Mrs. Gould, another high-minded Victorian lady devoted to charity who feels that the obsessive faith in "material interests" has alienated her from her husband and kinder purposes. Conrad's prescient and tough-minded reflections on historical change in exploited countries should not be misread as skeptical evenhandedness. There are bad and worse. The "better class" traditionalists, such as the sentimentalized Avellanos, appear as foolish, patriotic "constitutionalists" but individually are given bravery and other nobility. Fatuous, they nonetheless avoid "the somber imbecility of political fanaticism." In contrast, the "liberal" demagogues, such as the savagely caricatured Monteiros, come out only as greedy and brutal scoundrels leading the "scum" of the revolting populace. Only the cool opportunistic capitalists, and their devotedly obtuse servitors (Major Pépé, Captain Mitchell, the engineers) show effectiveness, with a redeeming efficiency but no faith in better values. Again Conrad combines an extreme conservativism with a drastic skepticism.

The novel's entitling figure, Nostromo, is also one of the servitors. An Italian ex-sailor become "captaz de cargadores" (port foreman—Conrad's shrewd conviction that the foreman, sergeants, and chiefs keep the institutions going) turns out to be a courageous man and a "prodigy of efficiency." But he is also consumed by vanity and a lust for fame and popularity. Another of Conrad's figures trapped in the romantic fantasy of himself, he is supposedly incorruptible but in the end is totally dominated by his obsession with a secreted load of silver. Conrad's slow exposure of this corrupted romantic overbalances the larger events. The last part of the novel is an ornately manipulated melodrama in which Nostromo pretends to love and becomes engaged to a lighthouse keeper's frigid daughter (he is actually in love with her more responsive sister) in order to retrieve his cache of silver. He is shot by the women's father, a man Nostromo has looked on as his own father, who does not know whom he is shooting. Thus the twentieth-century novel of political skepticism reverts to earlier popular romance and moralizing, with strange psychological undertones.

But more intriguing things appear. A late-introduced character, upper-class journalist Martin Decoud, poses some of the Conradian dilemmas of mind in an indifferent universe. As so often in Conrad, the intellectual is a suicide: "The brilliant Costaguanero of the boulevards had died from solitude and want of faith in himself and others." For this urbanely cultivated ex-Parisian and "the spoiled darling of the family, the lover of Antonia [stock highfalutin lady of the dominant upper-class family] and journalist of Sulaco, was not fit to grapple with himself single-handed." In three days of isolation, after spiriting to a desert island with Nostromo (who leaves) a crucial load of silver needed to maintain a coup, he reached a "state of soul in which the affectations of irony and skepticism have no place." Skeptical Conrad is punishing his skeptical alter ego, as several critics have noted.

Decoud (in an unusually direct narrative for Conrad) is described as being driven into an "exile of utter unbelief" so great that he started losing "his own individuality." This includes passively merging into "nature," which for sea-fearful Conrad seems horrible. Decoud has by chance been separated from the usual social conspiracy for active illusions against a destructive cosmos. By the seventh day of anxiously sleepless solitude in "waiting without faith," he "beheld the universe as a succession of incomprehensible images" and sank into despair.

Conrad argues that Decoud's values have been "intelligence" and "passion." But these are antithetical to saving illusions. By the tenth day the silence of his natural solitude has become "a still cord stretched to breaking-point, with his life, his vain life, suspended to it like a weight." He attempts to break this cord of despair with a pistol shot, at himself, yet never hears "the cord of silence snap aloud in the solitude" as, weighted down with four bars of silver (as Brierly in *Lord Jim* with four weights), he falls to his death in the sea, "swallowed up by the immense indifference of things." It is such intense images of precarious existence and lack of human meaning which give Conrad much of his modernity in his Victorian romances.

Conrad rather pushes his anti-intellectual ideological issue with the figure of Decoud. We are told he is a "victim of the disillusioned weariness which is the retribution meted out to intellectual audacity." Yet the hyper-simple Nostromo also reaches disillusion as "the reward of audacious action," and in a few hours of isolation is overwhelmed by a "sense of loneliness, abandonment, and failure," and so also finds himself in Decoud's state of "universal dissolution." If both the ironic intellectual and the vain man of action end up the same, temporarily, discrimination has been submerged in Conrad's ideological obsession with despair and his prose-poem on universal meaninglessness.

But the contrast between action and intellectuality did not really exist anyway, in spite of the assertions. While Decoud has been described as a Parisian *flaneur,* a striking "dandy," and a "cosmopolitan" ironist, he has also been dramatized as a man of action: he purchased and arranged for the improved rifles finally crucial to the defense of the new state; he was founder and editor of the local bombastic conservative newspaper; he was an energetic fighter against the populace in the Sulaco riots and activist organizer of the pro-

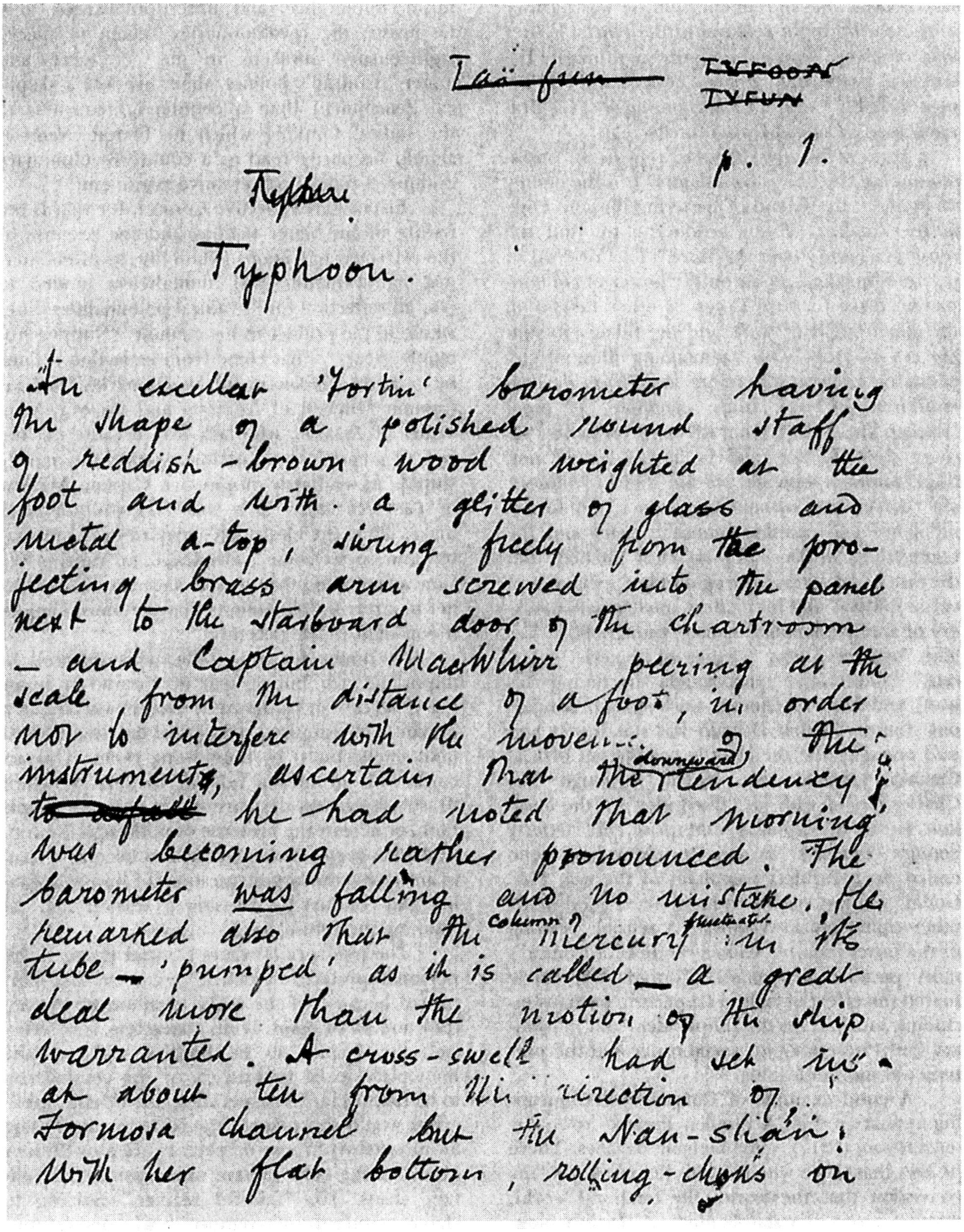

~~TYFOON~~
~~TYFUN~~
Taï-fun
p. 1.

~~Typhoon~~
Typhoon.

An excellent 'Fortin' barometer having the shape of a polished round staff of reddish-brown wood weighted at the foot and with a glitter of glass and metal a-top, swung freely from the projecting brass arm screwed into the panel next to the starboard door of the chartroom — and Captain MacWhirr peering at the scale from the distance of a foot, in order not to interfere with the movement of the instrument, ascertain that the downward tendency ~~to fall~~ he had noted that morning was becoming rather pronounced. The barometer <u>was</u> falling and no mistake. He remarked also that the column of mercury fluctuates in its tube — 'pumped' as it is called — a great deal more than the motion of the ship warranted. A cross-swell had set in at about ten from the direction of Formosa channel but the Nan-shan; with her flat bottom, rolling-chocks on

First page of the manuscript for Conrad's 1902 novella (Anderson Galleries, sale 1768, 12-14 November 1923)

vincial separatist movement; and he was partner in the daring night removal of the crucial lighter load of silver. To see this figure as primarily the skeptical intellectual, as some critics have, is to accept foolishly Conrad's assertions against his dramatizations. Conrad feared intellectuals.

Early in *Nostromo* Conrad repeats an obsessive moral: "Action is consolatory. It is the enemy of thought, the friend of flattering illusion. Only in the conduct of our action can we find the sense of mastery over the Fates." This reversal of the traditional emphasis on the power of contemplation takes form in Conrad's other fictions in the glorification of work and the fidelity to simple sea routines. Our maintaining illusions depends on keeping idle minds away from devilish awareness of our futile condition as men. (Women are exempt from the need for action because they do not, and he insists should not, think—women who do, we are told in *Nostromo,* are "barren and without importance.") A forced indolence and solitude ostensibly bring out the faithlessness of Decoud's skeptical intellect, but the case really seems to be against his "habit of universal raillery" and his modern intellectual's mockery of vanity, stupidity, sadism, usual politics, English hypocrisy, the "virtues of material interests," conservative propaganda (including his own), and vulgar patriotism. Such men are dangerous. Can it be that Decoud was not stupid and dull enough, like the blandly complacent official Captain Mitchell, not "insane" enough like Charles Gould with his "fixed idea" of the absolute virtue of capitalist enterprise, not bitterly enough "crushed" as was Dr. Monygham, who ended up a ruthless sycophant of the rich Mrs. Gould, and not vicious enough, like a good many other characters in *Nostromo?* A sensible reading of the novel requires some awareness of Conrad's most peculiar arguments. Conrad desperately feared the effect of radical skepticism, perhaps including his own, on the simple ideas and illusionary faiths necessary for social order and the pretenses at moral meaning.

A good example of Conrad's will-to-meaning appears in his "A Familiar Preface" to *A Personal Record* (1912), some memoir sketches. There he says that those who read his fictions know "my conviction that the world, the temporal world, rests on a very few simple ideas.... It rests notably ... on the idea of Fidelity." No casual statement, this is contrasted in the following paragraph with the ideas involved in the "revolutionary spirit," which he condemns for optimism, intolerance, and unscrupulousness; and, he insists, the revolutionaries' "claim to special righteousness awakens in me ... scorn and anger." Conrad's politics, then, are less a skeptical detachment than a counterrighteousness to the radical thinking which he feared. *Nostromo* should be partly read as a counterrevolutionary critique, a radical conservative argument.

Elaborately reflective Conrad, for that is the nature of his better fictions and the premise of the refracted narrations (when not, as often later, just moral mannerism), nonetheless tended to fear all reflection for its radical potentialities. Elsewhere in the preface to his memoir: "Nothing humanly great ... has come from reflection." Thus he presents his successful functionaries (such as Captain Mitchell of *Nostromo* and Captain MacWhirr of *Typhoon,* who lack fear because of "the lack of a certain kind of imagination") as mostly stupid. As endlessly ruminative Captain Marlow of *Lord Jim* says, "it is this very dullness that makes life to the incalculable majority so supportable and so welcome"; elsewhere he repeats the Conradian credo that what is necessary is the "belief in a few simple notions that you must cling to if you want to live decently."

No doubt this anti-intellectualism is itself an important idea, but we may do Conrad an injustice if we do not recognize it usually working as a defiant commonplace, a practical barring of ideas (and intellectuals) by disallowing them. This accords with an ancient fideistic method by which drastic skepticism despairingly encourages simple faith, or at least the pretense of it, though the contradiction seems obvious (and can become mean) in answering the largest questions of human meaning and conduct by refusing to answer and yet claiming the refusal as the answer.

The one specific value Conrad claims in his personal preface, "Fidelity," must remain perplexed because of the exilic situation of the author and of so many of his characters, who often lack the friends to be faithful with, or the homeplace to be faithful to, or the communion to be faithful in. In desperation, the fideistic modernist would short-circuit the issue by often using an unworthy purpose or petty routine or illusory honor as the cord to save one from darkly solitary chaos. His "faithful seamen" holding to "fixed standards of conduct" and "simple routines of the sea," or similar subserviences, can attempt to answer large perplexities with small loyalties. But even they often require rather special human limitations. As Conrad wrote of a storm-

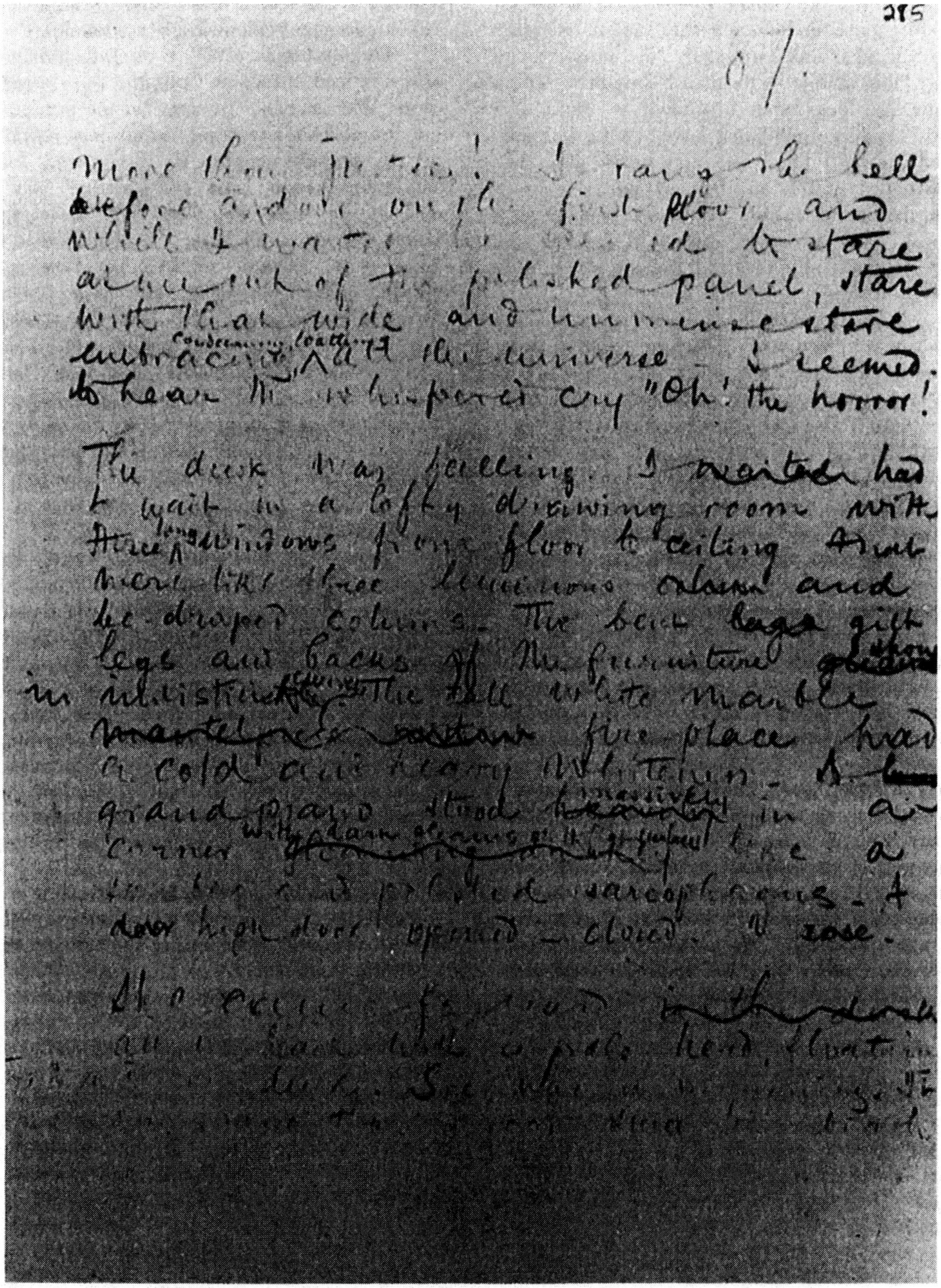
285

more than justice! I rang the bell
before a door on the first floor, and
while I waited he seemed to stare
at me out of the polished panel, stare
with that wide and immense stare
embracing, condemning, loathing all the universe. I seemed
to hear the whispered cry "Oh! the horror!"

The dusk was falling. I ~~waited~~ had
to wait in a lofty drawing room with
three long windows from floor to ceiling that
were like three luminous and
bedraped columns. The bent ~~legs~~ gilt
legs and backs of the furniture shone
in indistinct curves. The tall white marble
~~mantelpiece~~ fire place had
a cold and heavy whiteness. A
grand piano stood massively in a
corner with dark gleams on the flat surfaces like a
sombre and polished sarcophagus. A
~~door~~ high door opened — closed. I rose.

She came forward ~~in the dusk~~
all in black with a pale head, floating

Page from the manuscript for "Heart of Darkness" (Beinecke Library, Yale University) wracked, real-life captain in *The Mirror of the Sea* (1906), more memoir sketches, about seafaring life, the man was fortunately "too simple to go mad, too simple with manly simplicity which alone can bear man unscathed in mind and body" against annihilating forces. (What fear pursued Conrad!) Those not quite simple enough—Kurtz, Brierly, Jim, and Decoud, among others—are driven to suicide. Conrad's political and moral conservativism is unusual in claiming neither religious absolutes nor organic order, only fear and fragility.

A combination of ideological obsession and the romantic fictionist's desire for extreme situations led Conrad even in his crude commercial stories to touch on nineteenth-century radicalism, as in *A Set of Six* (1908). "Gaspar Ruiz" (1906) awkwardly tells of a simple strong-man South American guerrilla leader repeatedly switching from the republican to the Spanish royalist sides in the endless brutal confusions of the war of independence. He dies absurdly holding up a cannon. His coldly superior wife then commits suicide, apparently revealing her romanticism.

"An Anarchist" (1906) is pathetic but less maudlin. A simple French mechanic is convicted as an anarchist, mostly because of accidental circumstances, then sent off to a French penal colony in South America. He escapes but ends up as practically a slave on a colonial ranch. While the arch narration seems somewhat ambivalent in attitude, that being reached for is contempt for anarchists' wicked silliness. "The Informer" (1906) also utilizes contemptuously distant narration to tell of a London revolutionary group with an upper-class patroness (a role which repeatedly enraged Conrad). She is disillusioned when, through a tricky plot, her anarchist lover turns out to be a police informer. He commits suicide; she withdraws from life. The reader is provided little internal sense of the characters but is to realize from external evidence that such sad results must be inevitable to revolutionary posturing.

Other stories of the period include "The Brute" (1906), an elaborately empty pub anecdote about a repeatedly ill-fated ship. "The Duel" (1908) lengthily retells a legendary tale of two French officers of the Napoleonic period who repeatedly duel over minor points of honor in their juvenile homoerotic love. "Il Conde" (1908), a simpler but more ominous account of a Neapolitan aristocrat repeatedly held up by the same gentleman mugger, and caught in paranoid delicacy, is the best of these stories of implicit but unrecognized complicity in an irrational fate.

The Secret Agent (1907) is of quite a different order; indeed, it may be Conrad's most powerful novel. With criminal "mystery" in the purlieus of London political terrorism, he may have found especially suitable material for his harshly ironic melodramatization. The confirmation may be seen in the more disciplined and direct style, which achieves a heightened fusion of vivid description and sardonic reflectiveness. Gone is the garrulity and digressive lushness; only rarely (a bit in the final chapter, and a few other passages) does Conrad fall back on narrative indirection and redundant portentousness. Subtitled *A Simple Tale,* the novel is both infernally complicated in its neatly savage plotting and yet devastatingly simple in the fixed (obsessional) ideas of all the characters. With several of them, Conrad reaches a degree of intense subjectivity beyond that of his other fictions.

Perhaps this resulted from the negative political milieu. There is little place for romantic inflation and Victorian sentimentality, except mockingly, in this absurdist tale of a bumbling agent provocateur, grotesque marginal terrorists, conniving police officials, and the yellow journalism fears of the time. While Conrad's grimly conservative ideology permeates the fiction, the impassioned disdain also allows some acute impartiality (for example, "terrorist and policeman both come from the same basket"). The perspective demands law and order yet insists on its inadequacy.

The most ardent admirer of law and order is Adolf Verloc, a longtime petty secret agent of an east European government and an informer to British police who passes for a passive member of an ostensibly revolutionary group in London. In temperament and character, the double agent is a "highly respectable" petit bourgeois shopkeeper—prudent, regular, domestic, anxiously complacent—an occupation which is also his secret-agent cover. Driven by his diabolical foreign employer to carrying out a nihilistic provocation in order to bring repression down on the radicals, the bombing of a scientific symbol (the Greenwich Observatory), he anxiously messes it up—a shopkeeper with too big a deal. The disproportions come out macabre. Verloc's bomb-carrying dupe is his wife's mentally retarded brother, his surrogate son, who stumbles and blows himself to bits. Verloc is sorry about that.

Now he will have to sell his shop and make various other prudent domestic rearrangements.

With ponderous self-pathos, the put-upon murderer tries to explain the arrangements to his devoted wife, revealing his one "amiable weakness: the idealistic belief in being loved for himself." Conrad's cynical analysis cuts deep and wide. But Winnie Verloc, from a mean and abused childhood, has only one passion, her devotion to her retarded brother; indeed, she married fat, crude little Verloc solely in order to provide a protective family. When the obtuse agent of others' needs concludes his self-pitying display with a sexual demand, the outraged Winnie sticks the family carving knife in him. Fearfully fleeing, the desperately simpleminded woman latches on to comrade Ossipon, a compulsive womanizing radical who has been after her. He robs her of Verloc's savings and in his fright of the police deserts her. She throws herself over the railing of a channel boat, another of Conrad's suicides from solitude and thought. Ossipon, glib ex-medical student, is left to disintegrate in guilt. No wonder the story concludes with a savage description of yet another terrorist, the lunatic bomb-making "professor" with the "simplicity of his idea calling madness and despair to the regeneration of the world." Conrad, of course, has deployed madness and despair for the simplicity of his idea of *not* trying to change an impossible world.

Using political images popular at the turn of the century, the author calls his revolutionaries "anarchists." But they are not: the "professor," a resentful failure acknowledged to have talent, avows nihilism with an elitist neo-Nietzschean hatred of mediocrity and the masses; another revolutionary spouts the clichés of anti-anarchist Marxian economic determinism; the most noted caricature is a gentle, crippled ex-convict (police-protected and supported by an eccentric wealthy patroness) whom even the author views as a pathetically quaint religious utopian. Stevie, Winnie Verloc's witless brother, in his anguished sympathy for both a beaten horse and its miserably poor cab-driver, and his stuttering moral indignation that it is "bad world for poor people," appears to be the only libertarian, though unrecognized as such, in the story. Possibly Conrad thought he was exposing, as he claimed, the "criminal futility" of anarchists, but it is rather more an ideological psychodrama of simple crippled people carried into despair.

Not that Conrad does not play upon conservative bigotries. The radicals and double agent Verloc are repeatedly charged with "indolence" and self-indulgence, though mostly shown in frenzied efforts and puritanical asceticism. But such prejudices are submerged in the brilliantly heightened misconfrontation of Winnie and Adolf Verloc. Almost equally acute is the bureaucratic infighting of class-separated types, the callous Chief Inspector and the opportunistic Assistant Commissioner of Police, though Conrad skimps on completing the disillusioning action with the officials, a parallel to the radicals, perhaps in fear of too obviously exposing the establishment nihilism.

Conrad's denigration of political-moral ideas and his often astutely cynical ironies against all (including a "great" MP) make this ostensibly political novel quite antipolitical. All ideals—as with retarded Stevie's desperate and fatal fidelity to Verloc, the professor's "frenzied puritanism of ambition" soured to destructiveness, and Verloc's complacent respectable-husband misjudgment of his wife—get reduced to small, private desperations and illusions. Rightly enough, the shrewd police official-politician sees the main action of the story as less a political than a "domestic drama" (and further demonstrates his shrewd insight by partly subverting the investigation in ways to please his socially ambitious wife). No one can play a larger scene. Showing that all political theater quickly reduces to private needs and vanities and resentments, the nihilistic conservative author has dissolved politics into fatal charades.

Again, as with Decoud in *Nostromo,* the real terrorism is solitary thinking, though here the desert island is modern anomic urban life. Winnie Verloc "felt profoundly that things did not stand much looking into," and it was her "distant and uninquiring acceptance of facts which was her force and safe guide in life." She "did not allow herself to fall into the idleness of barren speculation" (intellectual "speculation" may be really what Conrad means by radical "indolence"). We might see Mrs. Verloc's failure as similar to Captain Brierly's in *Lord Jim.* Solid citizens driven to reflection—she by Stevie's death—end in despair at the bottom of the sea.

Granted, Conrad sometimes loads the analysis; for example, he gives Winnie a quite improbable association of ideas: three minutes after she kills her husband she starts obsessively to visualize herself dropping from the gallows (the conservative's dubious, and irrelevant, idea of the effi-

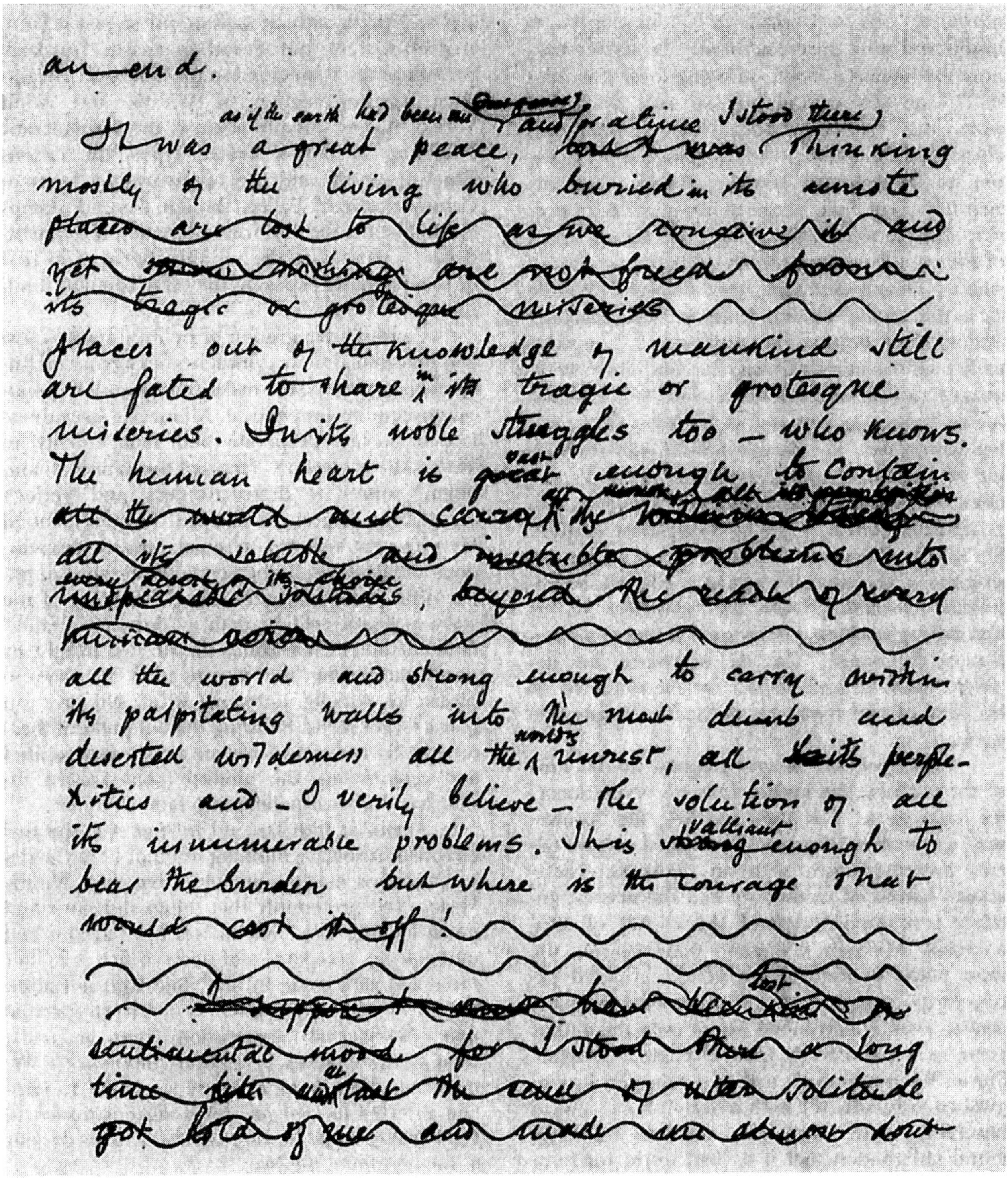
an end.

It was a great peace, as if the earth had been one grave, and for a time I stood there thinking mostly of the living who buried in remote places out of the knowledge of mankind still are fated to share in its tragic or grotesque miseries. In its noble struggles too — who knows. The human heart is vast enough to contain all the world and strong enough to carry within its palpitating walls into the most dumb and deserted wilderness all the world's unrest, all its perplexities and — I verily believe — the solution of all its innumerable problems. It is valiant enough to bear the burden but where is the courage that would cast it off!

Page from the manuscript for Lord Jim *(Thomas J. Wise,* A Bibliography of the Writings of Joseph Conrad, *1921)* cacy of capital punishment). But rather more interesting is the implicit authorial self-irony. Conrad has given simple Winnie a "singleness of purpose" and simple solidarity, the maternal devotion to her brother, as he has given Verloc his simple respectable faith in his wife's domestic love and as he has given simpleminded Stevie his unquestioned fidelity to Verloc and his bomb. Yet in all the cases the intellectual simpleness and virtue and fidelity become a "fixed idea" with an "insane logic." Conrad's own credo of "simple ideas" and ordinary virtues and "Fidelity" is devastatingly shown as fatal.

Some of Conrad's power of thought in *The Secret Agent* shows the distinctive modernist artistry of rendering ironic one's own values. The ostensible antinihilist nihilistically makes his most powerful case against himself. Intensely entering the minds of pathetically repulsive characters, yet maintaining the dialectics of the sardonically anti-intellectual fable, Conrad brings the reader to a conservativism totally radical in which there are no bedrock values (religion, tradition, community) and the examined life is not worth living. Even "The force of sympathy," Conrad cynically notes by way of a policeman, is a "form of fear." He has made the fear palpable as the "impenetrable mystery" of despair at the heart of human affairs.

Under Western Eyes (1911), Conrad's other and longer novel employing the materials of political revolutionism, seems a considerably lesser work than *The Secret Agent* in style, artful ordering, subjective intensity, and insightful paradoxes. Part of the difficulty is the use of a rather Jamesian narrator, an obtusely lofty-mannered teacher of languages and English literature. While the figure may have been psychologically desirable to Conrad for distancing himself from the painful revolutionism, which is almost as hopeless as that of his father, the narrative creaks badly and sometimes breaks down, as with the sentimental old Englishman who defensively provides the entitling perspective. This excuses Conrad from understanding or sympathetically presenting the revolutionaries.

Most of the story is set in Geneva—although the protagonist's absurdly improbable diary and some other two- or three-times removed reports give some St. Petersburg scenes—which allows further denigration of the whole Russian madness when contrasted to the bland Swiss order. Given such distanced scene and narration, the exiled revolutionaries come out mostly as pathetic grotesques. The English teacher, and apparently the author, naturally see them as ill-mannered, theatrical, badly dressed, extreme, bombastic, dangerous, and providing a most slovenly tea. The leading figure, an heroic escapee from Siberia, is caricatured as a pompous, mystic feminist and sycophant to a rich, hysterical, and ugly refugee woman. He in fact exploits women. But the women, from their adolescent fixations on, have been horrendously, even comically, self-exploited. The authorial contempt rests heavily. While Conrad despises the "lawless autocracy" of Czarist Russia, which exiled his parents and from which he was a refugee, the reactive ideological conservative insists that the equally lawless revolutionaries are utterly incompetent, false, and ugly, and provide no answer other than another form of mystic nastiness.

For the true answer, as with the seamen of the *Narcissus*, is suffering endurance. Its main, though not only, exemplification is protagonist Razumov, orphaned bastard of a Russian prince. A depressive, ambitious, conformist university student, Razumov is imposed upon by young revolutionary fellow student Victor Haldin. The romantic idealist, only son of a small-landowning widow of mildly liberal sentiments, Haldin has been the backup assassin in a plot against a repressive minister. (Conrad's details here obviously draw on the high-minded Russian nihilist movement of a generation earlier.) Fleeing the police, Haldin, inexplicably lacking an escape plan, somewhat fortuitously goes to the apartment of Razumov, whom he knows only slightly but has been romantically impressed by as a high-minded solitary. He asks Razumov to carry a message to a driver with a team, asking the driver to meet him that night for his flight. Fearful and resentful, Razumov finds the driver, but he is in a drunken stupor, and Razumov ragingly beats him without arousing him. Feeling trapped, Razumov goes to his putative father and then to the secret police, trying to prove his orphan self to authority by betraying his supposed friend and his own uncertain sentiments. Then he goes back to deceive Haldin, who is captured and secretly executed. A police official persuades Razumov to exploit for his own and the government's advantage his erroneous reputation as a revolutionary friend of Haldin's by going to Geneva to spy on the revolutionary refugees. Most of the narrative presents Razumov's anguish leading to his self-exposure as a police spy and the denouncer of Haldin, a version of the outcast's betrayal-and-repentance suicidal pat-

James Lingard, the Berau trader who was the inspiration for the character Lord Jim

tern earlier established in Conrad's fictions, as in *Lord Jim.*

Since assassin Haldin has been only slightly (and inadequately for the story) presented, and even then as mostly a phantom of guilt in Razumov's bad conscience, the idealistic opposite pole takes the form of Haldin's sister Nathalie (who, with her dying mother, is a refugee in Geneva). This totally virtuous and beautiful young lady believes in the eventual reign of love and concord but not in any lesser revolution. Blandly presented by the covertly lusting English teacher, Conrad's trite vaporings about the idealistic Victorian lady (effectively presented Winnie Verloc was no lady) further weaken the style.

Razumov's irritable relations with the despised revolutionaries reveal piecemeal his bad conscience. When he fortuitously establishes revolutionary credentials, his rage at acceptance drives him to confess his betrayal of Victor Haldin to Miss Haldin. Shortly later, he concludes "it was myself, after all, whom I have betrayed most basely." Just how remains unclear since he does not apparently change his fearful conformist and self-serving politics. In spite of Conrad's stiff elaboration of his protagonist, many readers have difficulty in sympathizing with him since his was an endless pathological betrayal, not simply the aberration of a single night. He has even meanly gotten a fellow student to gratuitously rob his own father. And the spying is part of an elaborate and long-term viciousness. But Razumov's intelligence is rather thin and fatuous, as in the political credo he writes emphasizing anti-intellectual patriotism and submissiveness.

Razumov also confesses to all at a party of revolutionists. A terrorist (later revealed as a secret police agent) vengefully breaks Razumov's eardrums—a rather small punishment belying the charges of extremism leveled against them but reinforcing those of ineffectiveness against the revolutionaries. Perhaps realizing this, Conrad later has the deaf Razumov fail to hear a tram bell so that he is run over and permanently crippled. Perhaps his further longing for punishment gets gratified by the Good Samaritan devotion of a revolutionary woman, heavily described as ugly and bedraggled and masochistic, who returns with Razumov to Russia as his caretaker as he slowly dies. These matters are all summarized by a twice-removed narrative that flattens their impact.

Miss Haldin also returns to Russia, we learn in a vague and roundabout way, to do loving charitable work. The police official who set Razumov to spying is reported as having been later purged for another offense—the extremist autocracy, like the extremist revolution, devouring its own. The revolutionaries remain as ineffective as ever. The great feminist revolutionary, financially betrayed by his rich patroness, has covertly returned to Russia and inspirationally "united himself to a peasant girl." The madness and viciousness go on as usual. Apparently only a fool or a scoundrel would be active for either side. Politics is impossible. One must go on lovingly enduring the inevitable suffering, without thinking about it.

Why this rather inferior imitation of Dostoyevski should be treated with high seriousness as a political fable is puzzling. Perhaps the lesser political moral, presented with deprecating, sententious asides by the old English teacher, that Russia failed in not having gentle, law-abiding, anti-intellectual, decently conservative English his-

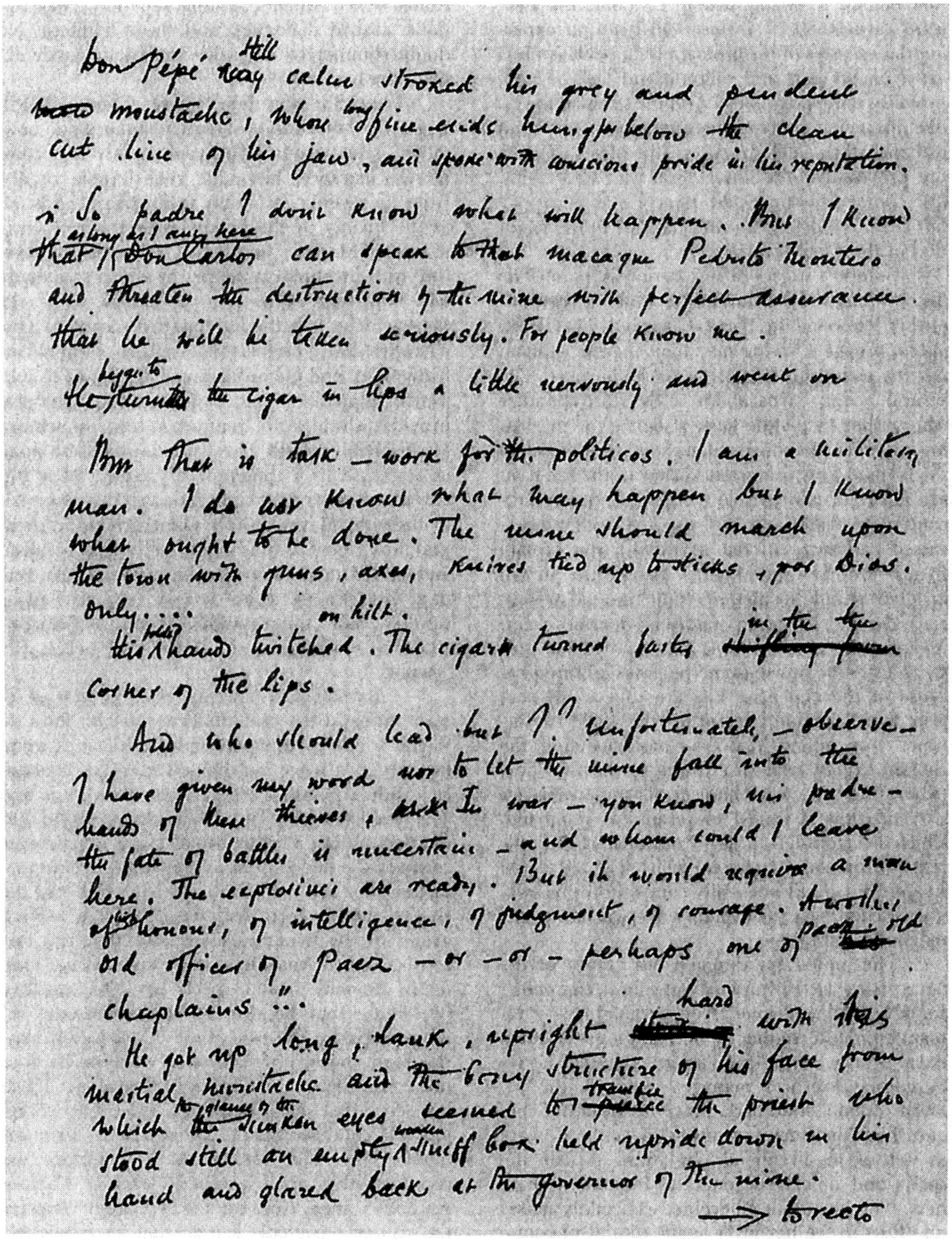
Don Pépé still calm stroked his grey and pendent moustache, whose very fine ends hung far below the clean cut line of his jaw, and spoke with conscious pride in his reputation.

"So padre I don't know what will happen. But I know that as long as I am here Don Carlos can speak to that macaque Pedrito Montero and threaten the destruction of the mine with perfect assurance that he will be taken seriously. For people know me."

He began to turn the cigar in lips a little nervously and went on

"But that is talk — work for the politicos. I am a military man. I do not know what may happen but I know what ought to be done. The mine should march upon the town with guns, axes, knives tied up to sticks — por Dios. Only.... on hilt."

His lean hands twitched. The cigar turned faster in the corner of the lips.

"And who should lead but I? Unfortunately — observe — I have given my word not to let the mine fall into the hands of these thieves. In war — you know, mi padre — the fate of battles is uncertain — and whom could I leave here. The explosives are ready. But it would require a man of high honour, of intelligence, of judgment, of courage. Another old officer of Paez — or — or — perhaps one of Paez' chaplains..."

He got up long, lank, upright hard with his martial moustache and the bony structure of his face from which the sunken eyes seemed to glance at the priest who stood still an empty wooden snuff box held upside down in his hand and glared back at the governor of the mine.

→ to recto

Page from the manuscript for Nostromo *(Thomas J. Wise,* A Bibliography of the Writings of Joseph Conrad, *1921)*

tory behind it, is comforting. Certainly the awkward earnestness of a conservative author exposing the excesses of his protagonist, a sickly conservative in his fear and solitude and lack of love, provides some poignancy. And the strained narrative distancing also suggests more ambiguity than the moralistic melodrama really offers. Unlike the provocative *The Secret Agent* with its Pyrrhonist conservativism, *Under Western Eyes* is a poor but curious work of an unusual cast in the tradition of the English novel.

Conrad's stories of this period include "The Secret Sharer." The novella "A Smile of Fortune" (1911), collected in *'Twixt Land and Sea* (1912), also concerns a young merchant marine captain, but the scene this time is set mostly in port. The central action turns about a sly ship chandler who wishes to peddle both potatoes for marketing and his illegitimate daughter, an outcast in the bigoted European caste society of the Far Eastern port. Sexually excited by the resentful and eccentrically mannered girl (treated with embarrassed caricature in the narration), the captain hangs around and finally kisses her in an aroused manner (something quite unusual in Conrad). Guiltily, he buys potatoes he does not want; inexplicably, he also turns cold toward the girl. By chance, the burdensome potatoes acquired because of the expensive kiss are sold at his next port for a substantial profit—"the smile of fortune." But, without reason or understanding, the captain cannot bear to go back to the first port (where the girl awaits him) as his shipowners insist and thus is forced to resign his command, which he considers a large misfortune. But the real misfortune, of course, which Conrad could suggest but could not really confront in this awkward fiction, was the captain's overwhelming sexual and social fear.

The intolerably dragged out "Freya of the Seven Isles" (1912) turns about suitors competing for a bumbling farmer's young daughter—a romantic English trading captain and a gross Dutch naval officer, in the Far Eastern islands. The rejected naval officer manages to wreck the beloved captain's fine bark. Since his beautiful ship gave him his romantic "power" over the woman, as well as his livelihood, the young captain despairs and quickly degenerates into sickly madness. The abandoned heroine, who oddly makes no effort to see her lover again, dies of pneumonia and love. Conrad's lovers oddly engage in the most ornate evasions. The obtuse father is one of the inconsistent narrators of this romantic melodrama which switches between repetitious descriptions, absurd dialogues, and sheer bombast. No doubt commercial magazine intentions partly explain the badness.

Conrad's next long novel, *Chance* (1913), was, after American serialization, a moderate best-seller. After years of financial anxiety and commercial hackery, he made considerable money from his writing, generally in inverse proportion to the quality of the fiction. Now the refracting narrator, Marlow, becomes a tiresome mannerism, with involuted strategies by which somebody tells somebody who tells somebody who tells Marlow, who tells the unidentified narrator. This narrative device furthers plot trickery (withheld information), and the unfortunate avoidance of subjective immediacy and understanding, and also provides a vehicle for redundant sententiousness. Much of the skittish moralizing seems to be done in response to a contemporary issue, the women's movement of the time. The aged sentimentalist bachelor Marlow offers numerous smug denigrations, often contradictory, of female idealism and lack of idealism, toughness and weakness. Perhaps his clearest point is that feminism turns women "into unscrupulous sexless nuisances," while true femininity is always and necessarily "passive."

A pathological passivity, male as well as female, informs the plot. Sixteen-year-old Flora de Barral is cruelly dumped by her governess when her father, a naive and fixated speculative financier with a pyramid scheme, goes bankrupt and gets seven years for fraud. Thus traumatized and unloved by her various brutal lower-middle-class relatives—in one of Conrad's few sharp social comments, they are petty and righteous with "all the civic virtues in their very meanest form"—Flora grows up self-denigrating, suicidal, "painfully forlorn." Captain Anthony, a merchant marine master in his mid thirties, meets her. Oversensitive (we know that because we are repeatedly reminded that he is the son of a poet), he legally marries Flora out of pity, but out of idealism he does not consummate the marriage. Out of need and her sense that she is unlovable, the twenty-three-year-old child accepts the arrangement. For many months she and her crazed and jealous ex-convict father live separately aboard Captain Anthony's ship. And for many skittish chapters the reader repeatedly learns what an impossible situation it is.

Amid the run of dully garrulous prose and tiresome narrative maneuvers, Conrad does make several serious points. The obvious one is about sexual repression: since pairing is natural, the denial of "the embrace" is unnatural and "a sin against life" which results in a "forcibly tortuous involution of feelings." But for Conrad this problem is less sexual-psychological than misguided moral idealism, again, though this time unegotistical. What Captain Anthony in his "delicacy" has stirred up are "the troubles of transcendental good intentions, which, though ethically valuable . . . cause often more unhappiness than the plots of the most evil tendency." But since all the main characters are stupidly passive, the transcending goodness remains obscure.

A concluding series of melodramatic chance happenings resolves the situation. The ex-convict father, apparently gone mad in incestuous paranoia, poisons Captain Anthony's brandy. The decent young second mate, who got his job by sheer chance and by even more farfetched chance happens to see the potion, rushes to save his master. But the captain despairingly gives up. That takes Flora a little out of her passivity, and she leans against him. Seeing this betrayal, the evil father takes the poisoned drink and dies, though this is hidden from the sensitive Flora. Apparently the marriage is then consummated. But sometime later the ship sinks and, after saving his wife and second mate, the captain goes down with it. After passively hanging around Flora-the-widow for four more years, the second mate (encouraged by Marlow, who has also encouraged Flora), acts finally as if he is going to have his turn with flowery, passive femininity.

Melodrama, of course, has been interestingly employed by some serious writers (Euripides, Honoré de Balzac, Dostoyevski, Jean-Paul Sartre), but Conrad's here is not only exceptionally mechanical, it mostly lacks compensatory social and psychological perceptions and ideas, except clichéd prejudices, such as antifeminism. His earlier melodramas at least had stronger ideological arguments and more exotic scenes to enliven them. Like the one-sided notion of "chance" in *Chance,* the whole novel is rather shoddy.

Chance marks Conrad's not-so-fortuitous financial success (pushed by friends, publishers, and the press, and his own eagerness) as well as a wider celebrity. So after a few more stories he gave up his hack magazine writing, though he continued with popular novels. The stories, collected in *Within the Tides* (1915), include "The Planter of Malta" (1914). The entitling figure is another of Conrad's solitaries, visiting in a Far Eastern port. Meeting a celebrated society beauty searching for her missing fiancé whom she had wronged, he develops an obsessive passion for her. Under false pretenses—her missing lover was his assistant, dead for some time—he lures her and her family to his island plantation. Eventually he reveals the death of the unworthy drug-addict lover and his own passion. The lengthy early sections concern plot manipulations and skittish comments on stereotyped figures (the manipulative and hypocritical philosopher-father, the pretentiously vain and empty woman, the irredeemably snobbish aunt, the pontificating newspaper editor, the superior protagonist suffering from vague despair and anxiety). The love scenes show such a gross self-parody of inflated language as to sink any story. Rejected by the woman who is unable to love, the solitary planter neatly commits suicide in the sea. This compulsively repeated pattern in Conrad of the superior solitary descending into despair and suicide in an artificial and false world can be taken as the author's nuclear trope. But the writing, as well as being sentimental melodrama, suggests obscured motives of anxious impotence, guilt, and self-hatred.

The shorter "The Partner" (1910) is better. In this simple story, a conniving businessman gets his partner to plant a crooked first mate on his brother's ship in order to help sink it for the insurance money, which they want to use for a patent medicine scheme. The connivance works, but chance complicates matters when the criminal mate robs and kills the captain who, in the necessary cover-up, must be treated as a suicide. Thus the partners do not get sufficient insurance money to carry out their scheme, and all end in failure. The ex-stevedore, who is the partner in the telling with the commercial writer-narrator, is treated denigratingly for his "raw" and ruffianly insistence on de-romanticizing the tale by placing it in the real world of cowardice, cupidity, and chance. While the story is not really probing of motives or other meanings with its stereotyped characters, its melodramatic action is presented well and with an appropriately cynical morality (perhaps traceable to Guy de Maupassant, a main influence on Conrad, along with Alphonse Daudet and less meritorious French fictionists). Defensively, the narrating commercial writer admits that he failed "to cook it for the consumption of magazine readers," that is, give it the ornate exoticism and inflated rhetoric that Conrad exploited in many of his fictions. That is its rare advantage.

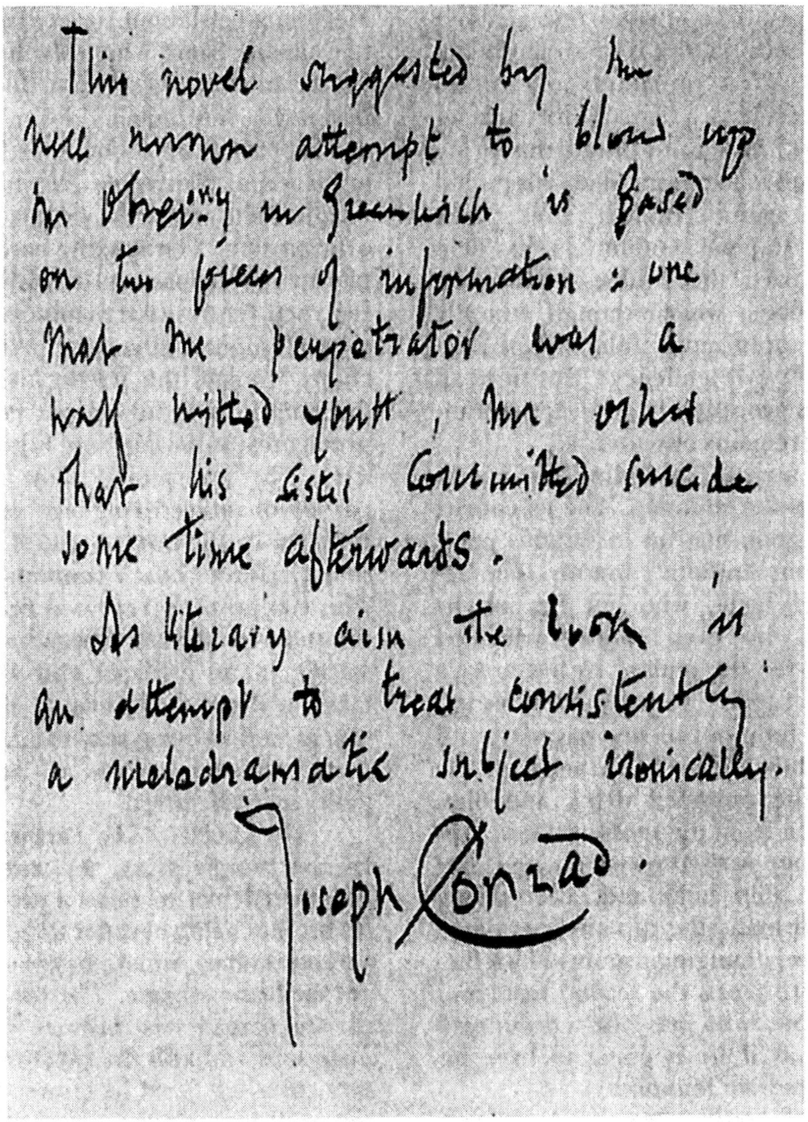

This novel suggested by the well known attempt to blow up the Observatory in Greenwich is based on two pieces of information: one that the perpetrator was a half witted youth, the other that his sister committed suicide some time afterwards.

As literary aim the book is an attempt to treat consistently a melodramatic subject ironically.

Joseph Conrad.

Inscription in a copy of the first edition of The Secret Agent *(American Art Association, 28 April 1927)*

The also short "The Inn of the Two Witches" (1913) has been all too cooked for commercial magazine readers. Drawing, as he frequently did in his later years, on his hobbyist's interest in the Napoleonic wars, Conrad places the scene a hundred years earlier in the Peninsula Campaign. A brave trusted seaman on a secret mission disappears at a Spanish country inn run by several old crones and a wicked Gypsy. About to undergo the same fate, a young English officer accidentally discovers the fatal device, a murderous mechanical bed. He escapes and a Spanish band punishes the witches and those related to them. The whole is an empty piece of heavily atmospheric costume flummery.

The shortly following story "Because of the Dollars" is a return to the romantic Far Eastern material. Captain Davidson, a "*really* good man" (the same benign figure appears later in *Victory*, 1915), is victim of a conspiracy to rob him of government dollars he is transporting on his trading route steamboat in the islands. Warned by a kindly prostitute he has platonically befriended, he successfully defends himself, but the woman is brutally killed. With a sense of decent obligation to the dead woman, he brings her young son to his wife to raise. She, a stupid and righteous petite bourgeoise with a "mean little soul," uses the questionable propriety of the situation as an excuse to leave the captain for good. His foster son trained by missionaries to become one of them,

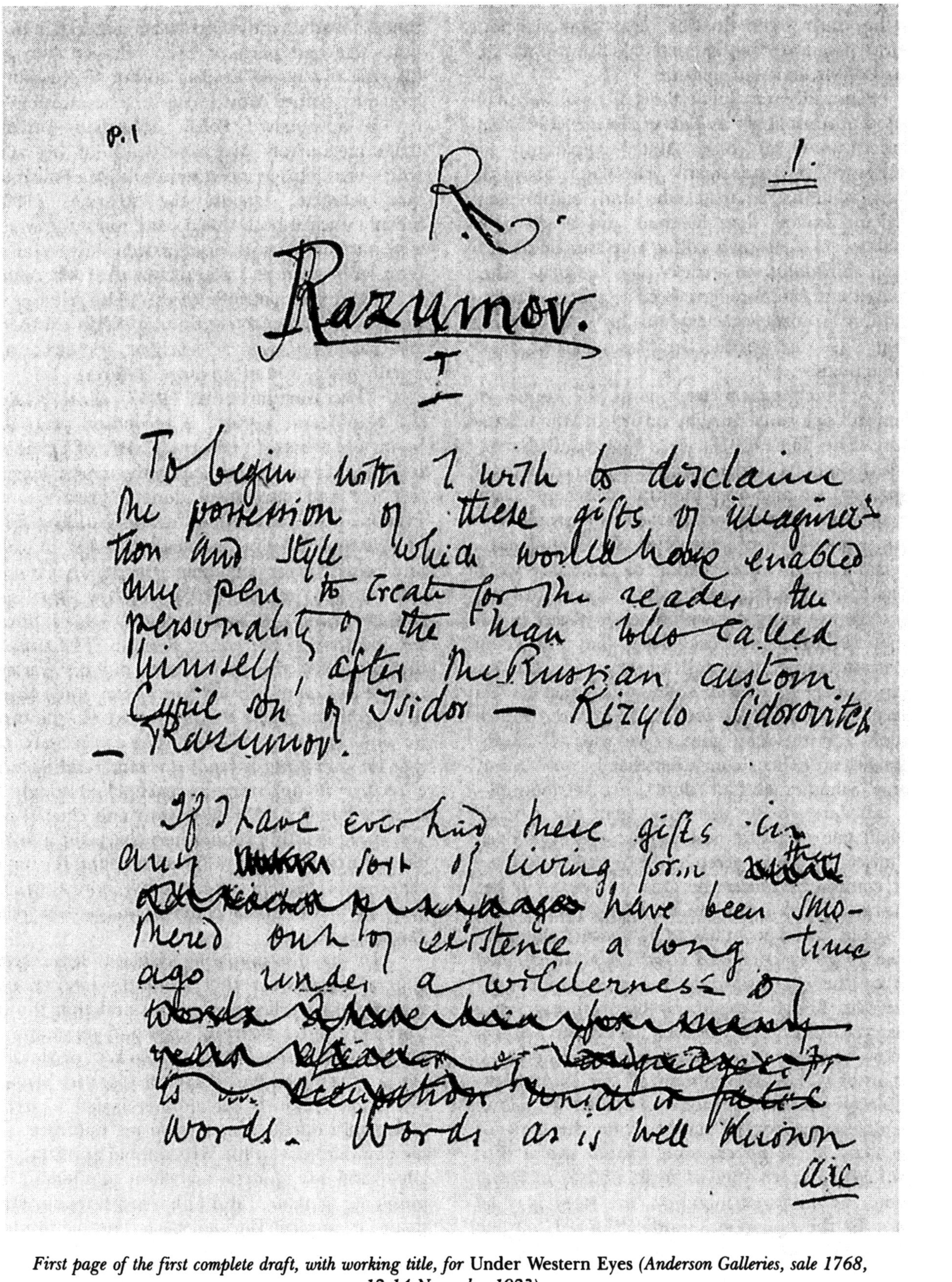

P. I

1.

R.

Razumov.

I

To begin with I wish to disclaim the possession of those gifts of imagination and style which would have enabled my pen to create for the reader the personality of the man who called himself, after the Russian custom, Cyril son of Isidor — Kirylo Sidorovitch — Razumov.

If I have ever had these gifts in any sort of living form, they have been smothered out of existence a long time ago under a wilderness of words. Words as is well known are

First page of the first complete draft, with working title, for Under Western Eyes *(Anderson Galleries, sale 1768, 12-14 November 1923)*

the good captain is left "without a single human affection near him." In this mean and malicious world, Conrad's sentimental tale insists, the reward of virtue is sad solitude.

Conrad's remaining short fictions were collected posthumously as *Tales of Hearsay* (1925). Included was "The Black Mate," apparently his first story, rewritten many years later, about an aging white-haired mate who finds employment difficult and so dyes his hair and beard deep black to get a job on a sailing ship captained by a mean spiritualist. In a tricky plot, the mate, after an accident, claims to have been attacked by an apparition in order to explain his hair turning white. This ruse works in this tiresome bit of magazine dalliance.

A much graver trick is at the center of Conrad's one story drawing on World War I materials, "The Tale" (1917). In a vague and portentous manner, a British naval captain recounts his boarding an anchored neutral merchant vessel on the suspicion that it had been supplying German submarines. In spite of careful examination, he can find no confirmation of neutrality violations by its Scandinavian master, who claims simply to be lost in the fog with no clear idea of his location. The British officer orders him to leave on a certain course; if he fails to do so, it means he knows where he is; if he follows the order he will smash on a reef in the fog. He follows the British order, and the ship goes down with all hands. The British officer concludes that he will "never know" whether he had "done stern retribution—or murder." While this may seem like a Conradian tale of moral ambivalence (and has been so misread), it is as given a tale of malicious murder committed under the guise of "duty." If the neutral captain had been supplying submarines, he would have known where he was and either refused to go or corrected course (suicide is ruled out by the characterization). Since he does neither, the British captain, by his own logic, is a mass murderer. His claim to uncertainty, not to "know," and his woman auditor's claim that he is a man of virtue and "humanity" (yet another example of feminine illusion?) are bitter ironies of self-deceit. Is Conrad muddled on the logic of the story, or is he exposing vicious moral illusion? While there appears to be no way of being certain of authorial intention, the story may be both. In the apparent muddle, Conrad may be claiming a conservative-moral gesture while simultaneously dramatizing its falsity—the essential self-illusory nature of most human values.

"Prince Roman" (1917) seems to be the only time Conrad directly used Polish material in his fictions. He had perhaps been released into it by his visit as a noted English author to Russian Poland just before World War I. The entitling figure is an exalted Polish nobleman—suffering from melancholy over the death of his young wife—who joins as a common soldier a Polish military rebellion against the Russians (1830s). Sternly dutiful both during and after the war, he is sent to Siberia and serves a twenty-five-year sentence. But even as a completely deaf old man he is noted for his patriotic charity. The tale is a simpleminded paean to continuing Polish aristocracy and patriotism, Conrad's origins, somewhat awkwardly done, and of no larger interest.

"The Warrior's Soul" (1917), another tale of the Napoleonic period, is recounted years later by an old Russian officer and tells of an adolescent Russian officer of supposedly tender sensitivities. He had once been done a great favor in Paris by a French officer, an outstanding figure of love and nobility, and had fervently promised any return favor any time. During the Napoleonic army's retreat from Moscow, the same French officer, ill and hopeless, makes himself the prisoner of the young Russian. The prisoner demands that the youth carry out his warrior's pledge of honor and kill him. After some pained hesitation, the young Russian carries out the promise and shoots the French officer. We are told that he later resigns from the army and becomes a recluse in apparent melancholy. Though the story is handled in an awkward and clichéd way, and there is little probing into character and psyche, we do sense again Conrad's feeling for impossible moral dilemma and the Pyrrhonist affirmations of a traditional code of honor—his Polish gentry legacy.

In the discriminating criticism there seems general agreement that Conrad's later fictions magnify the earlier weaknesses and that the late works are more weary in style and tendentiously sentimental. *Victory*, the most earnest of the later works, is a sometimes disputed case. Its protagonist, Axel Heyst, is yet another isolated intellectual whose defeat comes from his failure at simple commitment to life. His double appears as an allegorical Mr. Jones—diabolical gentleman, homosexual, gambler, and killer—with whom Heyst forms an implicit Faustian pact. The plenitude of evil is enhanced by the presence of Jones's two bestial assistants and a malicious hotel keeper. The minor moral virtues, as so often in Conrad, are em-

Joseph Conrad, 1912 (photograph by William Cadby; Collection of John Conrad)

bodied by several ship captains, one the delicate-prudent part-narrator Davidson. But Conrad attempts to go beyond their stoic virtues by providing a figure of transcendental goodness, Lena, a pathetic but exalted heroine reminiscent of some of Charles Dickens's heroines. It is a heavy morality play.

Conrad's allegory becomes more insistent here than in his earlier fictions while the background has become much thinner. Basic information about Heyst, thirty-five-year-old aristocratic wanderer in the Indies, is withheld through three-fourths of the narrative and then consists of a few summary paragraphs. Reportedly, he once believed in "progress" and seems "mysterious"—"Enchanted Heyst"—a romantic finally disenchanted by a predatory society. But Conrad also insists that Heyst's failure really goes back to his fixation at eighteen in a "profound mistrust of life" and a "pitilessly cold" intellectuality that denies human affirmation (a more absolute Decoud of *Nostromo*). Heyst's deficiencies are related to his father, a Schopenhauerian "romantic" philosopher who indoctrinated his son with a pessimistic skepticism and bequeathed the world a book "that claimed for mankind the right to absolute moral and intellectual liberty of which he no longer believed them worthy." By a logical rather than psychological deduction, Conrad has Heyst guiltily follow his father's spoiled romanticism and become an unemployed, disdainful intellectual with a private income. He neither works to change the world nor submits to it.

The two times Heyst ventures out of his romantic withdrawal, he gets into disproportionate trouble. The first time his "sceptical mind was dominated by the fullness of his heart," pity leads him to lend money to a desperate captain to save his brig. His charity results in his acquiescing to the insistently grateful captain's invitation to take part in an abortive coaling scheme, the captain's death on a business trip, and Heyst's guilty remorse and further withdrawal. A later chance departure from his abandoned coaling station on a deserted East Indian island, remains of the failed business, includes a chance visit to a malicious German's hotel. There Heyst makes his second fall into common humanity when, out of pity, he rescues Lena, a poor orphan girl, and takes her back to his island refuge. As with Lord Jim, Heyst's romantic act resulted from "undisciplined imagination." For Conrad, romantic love is but an extension of romantic skepticism. But the guilty pity produces impotence, and Heyst cannot love. Even when alone with Lena on his tropical island he treats the adoring woman as a stranger, and he continues to believe that "he who forms a tie is lost," continues to follow his father's nihilistic philosophy and "remain free from the absurdities of existence." But such avoidance results in the greatest absurdity of all. Conrad brings the grim outside world to the island retreat in the form of simple allegorical figures of evil. Misled by the malicious hotel keeper's fantasy (a Dickensian idée fixe of sexual jealousy), three crooks go to rob Heyst. Pedro, savage ape and unimaginative Caliban, serves as Conrad's metaphoric argument against positive natural law. The "feral" Ricardo serves as Conrad's image of the renegade, an ex-ship's officer reverting to the wild and thus exemplifying the danger of removing quasi-military restraints. Just as supposed anarchism belongs to cripples in *The Secret Agent,* and claims to equality and workman's rights to a liar, thief, and coward (Donkin) in *The Nigger of the "Narcissus,"* so avowals of "independence" and "freedom" belong to the predatory Ricardo in *Victory.* He lives by the rule of competitive egoism in which "man depended on himself as if the world were still one great, wild jungle without law." The leading third crook, Mr. Jones, is simply the devil himself. It is all unrelievedly tendentious.

After an animalistic attack on Lena, Ricardo falls adoringly in love with her. The simple Victorian girl uses this to embark on an elaborate deception to save Heyst. The combination of unmotivated reversals in Ricardo's adoration and Lena's sudden cleverness may be a low point in Conrad's characterization. The rhetoric follows. Because of Heyst's perseveration, Lena accidentally receives a bullet in the "sacred whiteness" of her breast and dies "with a divine radiance on her lips." We are told her meaning: "the great exaltation of love and self-sacrifice which is woman's sublime faculty."

And we also have Conrad's sublime facilitation of "symbolic readings." Conventional patterns of light-and-dark metaphors: blond Lena-Alma (both names), and the purity of sacrifice and love of day; the three black-hearted and black-haired villains and their nighttime gambling, plotting, corruption, and murder; the dark-light oxymorons of Heyst, with light and shadow, his enterprise of "black diamonds," the combined volcanic smoke and bright fire which marks his hermitage, and other adumbrations of his moral ambivalence between dark evil and light goodness. These patterns, and the bestiary of evil, metaphors of diabolism, and rhetoric about the isolated romantic skeptic are not balanced by the novelist's essential nonrecurrent imagery of tangible life in this self-parodying allegory.

The melodramatic plotting has literally dozens of absurdities which undermine the ostensible theme of willed choice as against romantic skepticism. But perhaps most portentous is the diabolism. Conrad clearly had no religious faith, yet Mr. Jones is patently supernatural. That "insolent spectre on leave from Hades," that "outlaw from the higher spheres," is a nineteenth-century villain, similar to the decayed gentleman who is Ivan Karamazov's devil and to Rigaud in Dickens's *Little Dorrit,* and he evokes the sexual inversion and intellectual ennui of late romanticism in French literature. He repeatedly provides standard echoes of Satanism. Apparently Heyst's reluctance to acknowledge his pact with the Jones-devil results also from skepticism; the "ill omened chaos of the sky" denies any "Christian virtue," any positive providence. But he has missed the Conradian point that while there may be no absolute good, there is absolute malignancy.

And certain kinds of good become malignant. The parallelism between gentle Heyst and murderous Jones, the romantic skeptic and the diabolical criminal, may be more extreme than Conrad's earlier doublings—Lord Jim and Gentleman Brown, fugitive Leggatt and the young captain, and the others—because both are here treated as intellectuals with "the privileged detachment of a cultivated mind, of an elevated personality." The ironists go in "spectral brothership" to confront the feared female, perfect shot Jones somehow shooting wild, and then, Heyst's demonism done, his devil (Jones) inexplicably drops dead.

Even when Heyst realizes Lena's true sacrifice for him, his too "fastidious soul" (like homosexual Jones's) "kept the true cry of love from his lips in its infernal mistrust of life." His demonic "despair" allows him to declare but not to show active faith in that famous last speech: "woe to the man whose heart has not learned while young to hope, to love—and to put its trust in life." But how could the intellectual, with his denuded consciousness? As Heyst once explained to Lena, "I don't think. Something in me thinks—something foreign to my nature." The self-alienated intellec-

Dust jacket for the British edition of Conrad's 1915 novel

tual, then, cannot be redeemed, only exorcised by Heyst's burning himself in his own house, Lena's funeral pyre, a suicide, yet again, because of self-consciousness.

Some sentimentalist readers of the novel try to see *Victory* as the protagonist's progressive redemption, but clearly his pattern runs from skepticism to demonism to despairing suicide. The only victory was sacrificial Lena's, as Conrad emphasized nine years after writing, when on his celebrity American tour he emotionally read to an American audience his favorite passage, Lena's death scene. Conrad was not about to trust those intellectuals (Heyst, Decoud, and the like) with posthumous life. For "Thinking is the enemy of perfection," wrote Conrad in the later "Author's Note" to *Victory*. But the obsessive anti-intellectualism suffers from excessive intellectualism, including some very bad styling and plotting around allegorical abstractions. Conrad's counterromanticism became a cerebral inversion of the cerebral inversion he set out to expose. The real Conradian irony is the victory of evil over evil, a homeopathic art in which the malady and the medicine have become identical.

It is hard to present *Victory* as other than a bad novel. Still, it has some suggestiveness. Few find even this true of the remaining fictions. One was the tired finishing of his Malayan saga, *The Rescue*. Two others were simply popular sentimental romances. *The Arrow of Gold* (1919) draws on the author's youthful experiences in Marseilles, though, as recent biographies suggest, with considerable defensive distortion. Covering about a year and a half (in the 1870s), it is the account of an ill-defined young man, M. George, in love with a beautiful and rich ex-courtesan (and ex-Basque goatgirl), Dona Rita, who is a conspirator for the Carlists, the supporters of the Spanish royalist pretender in southern France. George coordinates the smuggling of weapons to the Carlist gangs. But the cursory treatment of the gunrunning and politics leaves them vague and largely irrelevant.

The early sections of the novel disproportionately concern minor characters in a mannered account that seems to combine—badly—Henry James and popular fiction. The George-Rita love affair suffers rhetorical inflation and displacement (typically: "I had the time to lay my infinite adoration at her feet whose white insteps gleamed below the dark edge of the fur out of quilted blue silk bedroom slippers, embroidered with small pearls."). There are scorned lovers, treated with uncertain mock heroics, a piously rapacious sister, a knocked-off indecisive duel, arbitrary symbolic flourishes (the entitling gold hair decoration), the inexplicable decamping of the beloved lady, and other folderol. Embarrassed treatment of politics and sex makes it self-parodying. *The Arrow of Gold* would not make it in the current exploitative romance market because of its inferiority.

The Rover (1923), like several of the novellas discussed above, is a maudlin costume piece in clichéd rhetoric about the Napoleonic era. Peyrol, an ex-pirate and "disinherited soul," sacrifices himself in a fantastic plot for the great English navy, the righteous anti-Jacobins, and an old man's quaint "honor." It also helps unite two young isolated figures in the "unearthly experience" of love so to transcend the humbly wise rover's "disenchanted philosophy." The anxiety of the solitary, suicide, trite prejudices, conservative sentimentalities, and boats do link it to the rest of Conrad. At his death, Conrad was working on yet another Napoleonic period romance, the incomplete work published posthumously as *Suspense* (1925). Reasonably enough, no serious commentator has spent much time on these fictions, which would no longer be read at all if they were not by the author of "Heart of Darkness" and *The Secret Agent*. Fame and financial ease in his last decade rather confirmed Conrad's role as a commercial entertainer. He seems to have had little awareness of his literary decline.

Perhaps because of the burden of bad writing, Conrad's literary reputation declined markedly in the mid 1920s after his death. A generation later there was a critical-academic revival of interest in Conrad, largely centering on a limited body of works (mostly those written in the decade from 1898 to 1910), which somewhat uncertainly gave his works the status of modern classics. While literary reputations partly depend on extraneous matters (fashion, taste, mythological needs, markets, etc.), they can also sometimes become self-generating when taken up by noted followers. Though the interest in Conrad now may be somewhat less intense than in the 1950s, his centrality to modern fiction is widely accepted and results in a variety of editions, massive studies, cinematic adaptions, specialist journals, and other responses to his writings. His major transitional role between Victorian forms and sentiments and modernist ideologies and perplexities seems well established.

While much of Conrad's fiction is patently poor, even some of that, when compared to other contemporary commercial fiction, is sometimes suggestive and probably retains some historical interest. At a more important level, Conrad's sea stories also have a documentary fascination in their reports of dying nineteenth-century merchant marine sailing experience. Furthermore, some of the maritime accounts display an exceptional intensity, partly from the anxiously heightened style and partly from the unusually negative view of nature which provides a distinctive malignancy and a grotesqueness of human response. While the ideological insistence on exalting disciplined routines, arbitrary authority, and stupid captains (as in *The Nigger of the "Narcissus"* and "Typhoon") seems a moralistic burden, the peculiarity fascinates authority-yearning readers. The maritime initiation-maturation themes (as in "Youth," the *Patna* section of *Lord Jim,* and *The Shadow-Line*) artistically culminate in the anxious extreme identification with the dark double in "The Secret Sharer," which remains a classic of moral ambivalence.

But Conrad is reported several times as having been upset at being considered primarily a sea writer, though his sea writing accounted for much of his reputation in his lifetime. Certainly both his commercial-popular and artistic-intellectual ambitions went beyond that maritime role. Conrad's seriousness is displayed in his insistent concern with "romantic egoism," from the early Malayan saga through *Lord Jim* and *Nostromo*—those works in which moral ambivalence is exotically tested. In the period of his best writing, from "Heart of Darkness" through *The Secret Agent,* he achieved a distinctive moral resonance and rhetorical intensity. His antipolitical romances of politics sometimes succeeded in disciplining the exoticism and the rhetoric into the cathartic extremity of modernist intellectual probing. He achieved this kind of success in spite of being heavily burdened with some of the worst literary characteristics of his time—including gross sentimentality, shoddy melodrama, chauvinistic moralisms, and sickly repressed eroticism. He achieved some victories over Victorian pathology.

The modernism which Conrad's best work achieved, and upon which his authentic reputation rests, undercuts accepted social and other moral values. In modernism, inherited hierarchies and pieties lost their sanctity under extreme explorations and questions. Conrad, rather in spite of himself, also questioned the authority and legitimacy of most values. This may have been less his intention than the inevitable, double-edged outlook of the exilic orphan who did not really have the honor, the solidarity, the patriotism, the simple human faith that he desperately posited. Thus in Conrad we paradoxically see an intellectual anti-intellectualism, a radicalness of tone even when conservative in emphasis, an extremity of imagination which becomes a stern engagement, in spite of the sentimental camouflage, to subterranean denials.

Conrad was simultaneously one of the most nihilistic and most antinihilistic of fictionists in English, obsessed with finding, and exposing, meaninglessness. Even as he insisted on the negative process, he deplored it, homeopathically countering alienation, despair, and meaninglessness with doses of the same. A would-be sanctifier of conventionally traditional values, he was yet a drastic doubter—"like most men of little faith," as he described himself in one of his letters, and generally with "scepticism . . . the agent of truth," as he defensively insisted in another. His cosmic doubt often becomes cosmic malevolence, or as a striking phrase of Captain Marlow's in "Heart of Darkness" has it, our world is viewed as a "mysterious arrangement of merciless logic for a futile purpose."

The inverted melodrama of malignant fate in Conrad is not just a popular vice but, at his

Joseph Conrad, 1923 (photograph by T. R. Annan & Sons)

best, a sense of metaphysical extremity. Fended-off negation was central to his art, with its circling forms, labyrinthine narrative removals, peculiar exaltation of evil chance, mystifying rhetoric, and a defensive ideological insistence overriding human psychology, probability, and decency. He seems driven to the dark "heart of the matter" in which he insistently portrayed failing, suicidal, hollow heroes without sufficient heart. Simple goodness of behavior became the only defense against what he repeatedly called the "cosmic chaos." But as Marlow tells Jewel in *Lord Jim*, "Nobody, nobody, is good enough."

The "simple ideas" with which Conrad wanted to keep desperate faith turn out to be inadequate even when not gross illusions for his solitaries struggling with civilized absurdities as well as oppressive jungles and indifferently tormenting seas. Conrad wanted a "Fidelity" which he did not really possess. He insisted on conventional notions without real faith in them, made even more impossible by extreme situations; in dramatic and dialectical fact, he insisted on harsh skepticism and self-destructiveness. This is true in the best fictions, such as "Heart of Darkness," *Nostromo,* "The Secret Sharer," and *The Secret Agent,* as well as in the more grossly tendentious allegories such as *Under Western Eyes* and *Victory.* (His thin nonfiction is of little intrinsic interest: two volumes of reminiscent sketches—*The Mirror of the Sea* [1906] and *A Personal Record* [1912]—and two late collections of reviews and miscellaneous pieces—*Notes on Life and Letters* [1921] and *Last Essays* [1926].) For what Conrad often means by his credo of "simple ideas" that informs his fictions is a nihilist's defensive sticking with the limited duties and affirmations of ordinary illusions, in fear of destruction from a malignant world and self. His forced efforts at a positive morality by reversal of radical doubts, which he so obviously had, may remain unpersuasive, not least in their fictional and rhetorical arbitrariness, but may be nonetheless intriguing and significant. Conrad is truly read for his perplexity.

As with much of modern moral conservatism, which lacks any transcendent order and organic society, Conrad tried to form a precarious fideistic dialectic from his doubts and fears. His desire for simple virtues and fidelities, on the explicit assumption that "man is a desperately conservative creature," remains poignant. He profoundly recognized that, somehow, values have to be simple or most men will be excluded from them, and thus from purposive life. The unexamined life, Conrad deeply felt, must be worth living because the examined life is suicidally dangerous. Conrad was constitutionally incapable of considering more radically redemptive forms of simple ideas and human fidelities (except as maudlin assertions and tricks). We might therefore respect the unresolvable difficulties of Conrad's moral dilemma of conservative needs versus powerful denials, even when we see that they drove him to pyrrhonist, and sometimes incoherent and bad, art and ideologies which lacked sufficient humanity. In his best ideological melodramas it is often exemplary the way the nihilist triumphs over the ostensible antinihilist, the villainous intellectual over Conrad's conservative sentiments, the provocative modernist over the mere literary hack and conventional moralist.

Letters:

The Collected Letters of Joseph Conrad, 4 volumes, edited by Frederick R. Karl and Laurence Davies (Cambridge: Cambridge University Press, 1983-1990).

Bibliographies:

Theodore G. Ehrsam, *A Bibliography of Joseph Conrad* (Metuchen, N.J.: Scarecrow Press, 1969);

Bruce E. Teets and Helmut E. Gerber, *Joseph Conrad, An Annotated Bibliography of Writings About Him* [1895-1966] (DeKalb: Northern Illinois University Press, 1971);

Teets, *Joseph Conrad, An Annotated Bibliography* [1967-1975] (New York: Garland, 1990).

Biographies:

Ford Madox Ford, *Joseph Conrad: A Personal Remembrance* (Boston: Little, Brown, 1924);

Jessie Conrad, *Joseph Conrad and His Circle* (New York: Dutton, 1935);

Joselyn Baines, *Joseph Conrad* (London: Weidenfeld & Nicolson, 1960; New York: McGraw-Hill, 1960);

Bernard Meyer, *Joseph Conrad: A Psychoanalytic Biography* (Princeton: Princeton University Press, 1967);

Gustave Morf, *The Polish Shades and Ghosts of Joseph Conrad* (New York: Astra, 1976);

Frederick R. Karl, *Joseph Conrad, The Three Lives* (New York: Farrar, Straus & Giroux, 1979);

Zdzislaw Najder, *Joseph Conrad: A Chronicle*, translated by Halina Carroll-Najder (New Brunswick, N.J.: Rutgers University Press, 1983);

Jeffrey Meyers, *Joseph Conrad: A Biography* (New York: Scribners, 1991).

References:

John Batcheler, *The Edwardian Novelists* (London: Duckworth, 1982);

Jeffrey Berman, *Joseph Conrad: Writing as Rescue* (New York: Astra, 1977);

Ted Billy, ed., *Critical Essays on Joseph Conrad* (Boston: G. K. Hall, 1987);

M. C. Bradbrook, *Joseph Conrad: Poland's English Genius* (Cambridge: Cambridge University Press, 1941);

H. M. Daleski, *Joseph Conrad: The Way of Dispossession* (London: Faber & Faber, 1977);

Avrom Fleishman, *Conrad's Politics: Community and Anarchy in the Fictions of Joseph Conrad* (Baltimore: Johns Hopkins University Press, 1967);

Peter J. Glassman, *Language and Being: Joseph Conrad and the Literature of Personality* (New York: Columbia University Press, 1976);

John Dozier Gordon, *Joseph Conrad: The Making of a Novelist* (Cambridge, Mass.: Harvard University Press, 1940);

Lawrence Graver, *Conrad's Short Fiction* (Berkeley: University of California Press, 1969);

Albert Guerard, *Conrad the Novelist* (Cambridge, Mass: Harvard University Press, 1958);

Eloise Knapp Hay, *The Political Novels of Joseph Conrad* (Chicago: University of Chicago Press, 1963);

Douglas Hewitt, *Conrad: A Reassessment* (London: Bowes & Bowes, 1975);

Irving Howe, *Politics and the Novel* (New York: Horizon, 1957);

Bruce Johnson, *Conrad's Models of Mind* (Minneapolis: University of Minnesota Press, 1971);

F. R. Leavis, *The Great Tradition: George Eliot, Henry James, Joseph Conrad* (London: Chatto & Windus, 1948);

Elsa Nettels, *James and Conrad* (Athens: University of Georgia Press, 1977);

Royal Roussel, *The Metaphysics of Darkness* (Baltimore: Johns Hopkins University Press, 1971);

Norman Sherry, *Conrad's Eastern World* (Cambridge: Cambridge University Press, 1966);

Sherry, *Conrad's Western World* (Cambridge: Cambridge University Press, 1971);

Ian Watt, *Conrad in the Nineteenth Century* (Berkeley: University of California Press, 1979);

Kingsley Widmer, *Edges of Extremity: Some Problems of Literary Modernism* (Tulsa: University of Tulsa, 1980);

Morton D. Zabel, *Craft and Character: Text, Methods, and Vocation in Modern Fiction* (New York: Viking, 1971).

Papers:

Collections of Conrad's papers are located at the Beinecke Library, Yale University; New York Public Library; British Library; Brotherton Collection at Leeds University; Colgate University Library; Cornell University Library; Dartmouth College Library; Houghton Library at Harvard University; Harry Ransom Humanities Research Center at the University of Texas, Austin; Lilly Library at Indiana University; Pierpont Morgan Library; William T. Perkins Library at Duke University; Princeton University Library; Philip H. and A. S. Rosenbach Foundation; University of Birmingham Library; and University of Virginia Library.

Sir Arthur Conan Doyle

(22 May 1859 - 7 July 1930)

This entry was updated by J. Randolph Cox (St. Olaf College) from his entry in DLB 70: British Mystery Writers, 1860-1919.

See also the Conan Doyle entry in DLB 18: Victorian Novelists After 1885.

BOOKS: *A Study in Scarlet* (London: Ward, Lock, 1888; Philadelphia: Lippincott, 1890);

The Mystery of Cloomber (London: Ward & Downey, 1889; New York: Fenno, 1896);

Micah Clarke (London: Longmans, Green, 1889; New York: Harper, 1889);

Mysteries and Adventures (London: Scott, 1890); republished as *My Friend the Murderer and Other Mysteries and Adventures* (New York: Lovell, Coryell, 1893);

The Captain of the Polestar and Other Tales (London & New York: Longmans, Green, 1890);

The Firm of Girdlestone (London: Chatto & Windus, 1890; New York: Lovell, 1890);

The Sign of Four (London: Blackett, 1890; New York: Collier, 1891); republished as *The Sign of the Four* (Philadelphia: Lippincott, 1890);

The White Company (3 volumes, London: Smith, Elder, 1891; 1 volume, New York: Lovell, 1891);

The Doings of Raffles Haw (New York: Lovell, 1891; London: Cassell, 1892);

The Adventures of Sherlock Holmes (London: Newnes, 1892; New York: Harper, 1892);

The Great Shadow (Bristol: Arrowsmith, 1892; New York: Harper, 1893);

The Refugees (3 volumes, London: Longmans, Green, 1893; 1 volume, New York: Harper, 1893);

Jane Annie; or, The Good Conduct Prize: A New and Original English Comic Opera, by Conan Doyle and James M. Barrie (London: Chappell, 1893);

The Great Shadow and Beyond the City (Bristol: Arrowsmith, 1893);

The Memoirs of Sherlock Holmes (London: Newnes, 1894; New York: Harper, 1894);

An Actor's Duel and The Winning Shot (London: Dicks, 1894);

Round the Red Lamp: Being Facts and Fancies of Medical Life (London: Methuen, 1894; New York: Appleton, 1894);

The Parasite (London: Constable, 1894; New York: Harper, 1895);

The Stark Munro Letters (London: Longmans, Green, 1895; New York: Appleton, 1895);

The Exploits of Brigadier Gerard (London: Newnes, 1896; New York: Appleton, 1896);

Rodney Stone (London: Smith, Elder, 1896; New York: Appleton, 1896);

Uncle Bernac: A Memory of the Empire (London: Smith, Elder, 1897; New York: Appleton, 1897);

The Tragedy of the Korosko (London: Smith, Elder, 1898); republished as *A Desert Drama* (Philadelphia: Lippincott, 1898);

Songs of Action (London: Smith, Elder, 1898; New York: Doubleday & McClure, 1898);

A Duet with an Occasional Chorus (London: Richards, 1899; New York: Appleton, 1899);

Hilda Wade: A Woman with Tenacity of Purpose, by Conan Doyle and Grant Allen (London: Richards, 1900; New York & London: Putnam's, 1900);

The Green Flag and Other Stories of War and Sport (London: Smith, Elder, 1900; New York: McClure, Phillips, 1900);

The Great Boer War (London: Smith, Elder, 1900; New York: McClure, Phillips, 1900);

The Immortal Memory (Edinburgh: Mitchell, 1901);

The Hound of the Baskervilles (London: Newnes, 1902; New York: McClure, Phillips, 1902);

The War in South Africa: Its Cause and Conduct (London: Smith, Elder, 1902; New York: McClure, Phillips, 1902);

Adventures of Gerard (London: Newnes, 1903; New York: McClure, Phillips, 1903);

A Duet (A Duologue) (London: French, 1903);

The Return of Sherlock Holmes (London: Newnes, 1905; New York: McClure, Phillips, 1905);

The Fiscal Question: Treated in a Series of Three Speeches (Hawick: Henderson, 1905);

Arthur Conan Doyle, 1894, in his study at the house in South Norwood that he bought in 1891

An Incursion into Diplomacy (London: Smith, Elder, 1906);
Sir Nigel (London: Smith, Elder, 1906; New York: McClure, Phillips, 1906);
The Story of Mr. George Edalji (London: Roberts, 1907); republished as *The Case of Mr. George Edalji* (Putney: Blake, 1907);
Through the Magic Door (London: Smith, Elder, 1907; New York: Doubleday, Page, 1908);
The Croxley Master: A Great Tale of the Prize Ring (New York: McClure, Phillips, 1907);
Waterloo (London & New York: French, 1907);
Round the Fire Stories (London: Smith, Elder, 1908; New York: McClure, Phillips, 1908);
The Crime of the Congo (London: Hutchinson, 1909; New York: Doubleday, Page, 1909);
Divorce Law Reform: An Essay (London: Divorce Law Reform Union, 1909);
Why He Is Now in Favour of Home Rule (London: Liberal Publication, 1911);
Songs of the Road (London: Smith, Elder, 1911; Garden City, N.Y.: Doubleday, Page, 1911);
The Last Galley: Impressions and Tales (London: Smith, Elder, 1911; Garden City, N.Y.: Doubleday, Page, 1911);
The Speckled Band: An Adventure of Sherlock Holmes (New York & London: French, 1912);
The Case of Oscar Slater (London: Hodder & Stoughton, 1912; New York: Doran, 1913);
The Lost World (London: Hodder & Stoughton, 1912; New York: Doran, 1912);
The Poison Belt (London: Hodder & Stoughton, 1913; New York: Doran, 1913);
Great Britain and the Next War (Boston: Small, Maynard, 1914);
To Arms! (London: Hodder & Stoughton, 1914);
The German War (London: Hodder & Stoughton, 1914);
The Valley of Fear (London: Smith, Elder, 1915; New York: Doran, 1915);
A Visit to Three Fronts (London: Hodder & Stoughton, 1916; New York: Doran, 1916);
The British Campaign in France and Flanders, 6 volumes (London: Hodder & Stoughton, 1916-1919; New York: Doran, 1916-1920);
His Last Bow: Some Reminiscences of Sherlock Holmes (London: Murray, 1917); republished as *His Last Bow: A Reminiscence of Sherlock Holmes* (New York: Doran, 1917);

The New Revelation (London: Hodder & Stoughton, 1918; New York: Doran, 1918);
Danger! and Other Stories (London: Murray, 1918; New York: Doran, 1919);
The Vital Message (London: Hodder & Stoughton, 1919; New York: Doran, 1919);
Spiritualism and Rationalism (London: Hodder & Stoughton, 1920);
The Wanderings of a Spiritualist (London: Hodder & Stoughton, 1921; New York: Doran, 1921);
The Coming of the Fairies (London: Hodder & Stoughton, 1922; New York: Doran, 1922);
The Poems of Sir Arthur Conan Doyle: Collected Edition (London: Murray, 1922);
The Case for Spirit Photography (London: Hutchinson, 1922; New York: Doran, 1923);
Our American Adventure (London: Hodder & Stoughton, 1923; New York: Doran, 1923);
Three of Them: A Reminiscence (London: Murray, 1923);
Our Second American Adventure (London: Hodder & Stoughton, 1924; Boston: Little, Brown, 1924);
Memories and Adventures (London: Hodder & Stoughton, 1924; Boston: Little, Brown, 1924; revised edition, London: Hodder & Stoughton, 1930);
Psychic Experiences (London & New York: Putnam's, 1925);
The Land of Mist (London: Hutchinson, 1926; New York: Doran, 1926);
The History of Spiritualism, 2 volumes (London: Cassell, 1926; New York: Doran, 1926);
Pheneas Speaks (London: The Psychic Press and Bookshop, 1927; New York: Doran, 1927);
The Case-Book of Sherlock Holmes (London: Murray, 1927; New York: Doran, 1927);
The Maracot Deep and Other Stories (London: Murray, 1929; Garden City, N.Y.: Doubleday, Doran, 1929);
Our African Winter (London: Murray, 1929);
The Edge of the Unknown (London: Murray, 1930; New York: Putnam's, 1930);
The Field Bazaar (London: Athenaeum, 1934; Summit, N.J.: Pamphlet House, 1947);
The Professor Challenger Stories (London: Murray, 1952);
The Crown Diamond: An Evening with Sherlock Holmes, a Play in One Act (New York: Privately printed, 1958);
Strange Studies from Life: Containing Three Hitherto Uncollected Tales (New York & Copenhagen: Candlelight Press, 1963);
The Unknown Conan Doyle: Uncollected Stories, edited by John Michael Gibson and Richard Lancelyn Green (London: Secker & Warburg, 1982; Garden City, N.Y.: Doubleday, 1984);
The Unknown Conan Doyle: Essays on Photography, edited by Gibson and Green (London: Secker & Warburg, 1982; North Pomfret, Vt.: David & Charles, 1983).

PLAY PRODUCTIONS: *Jane Annie*, by Doyle and J. M. Barrie, London, Savoy Theatre, 13 May 1893;
Foreign Policy, London, Terry's Theatre, 3 June 1893;
A Story of Waterloo, Bristol, Princess's Theatre, 21 September 1894; London, Lyceum Theatre, 4 May 1895;
Halves, Aberdeen, Scotland, Haymarket Theatre, 10 April 1899; London, Garrick Theatre, 10 June 1899;
Brigadier Gerard, London, Imperial Theatre, 3 March 1906;
The Fires of Fate, London, Lyric Theatre, 15 June 1909;
The House of Temperley, London, Adelphi Theatre, 27 December 1909;
A Pot of Caviare, London, Adelphi Theatre, 19 April 1910;
The Speckled Band, London, Adelphi Theatre, 4 June 1910;
The Crown Diamond, London, London Coliseum, 16 May 1921.

It is difficult to imagine the shape which detective fiction might have taken had it not been for the creation by Arthur Conan Doyle of Sherlock Holmes. Conan Doyle took a form of fiction which had become popular through the works of his predecessors, Edgar Allan Poe and Emile Gaboriau, and reshaped it, adding elements which made his own contributions among the most popular fiction of all time. The stories themselves have been considered in several contexts, both serious and facetious.

The period within which the stories were set and against which they can be examined was one of social, economic, and political change. They came at a time when the growing degree of literacy was combined with an expanding amount of leisure time. Thus, the era was right for the particular type of story which they represent. The periodical was a significant channel of communication; fiction had a growing influence; and a new

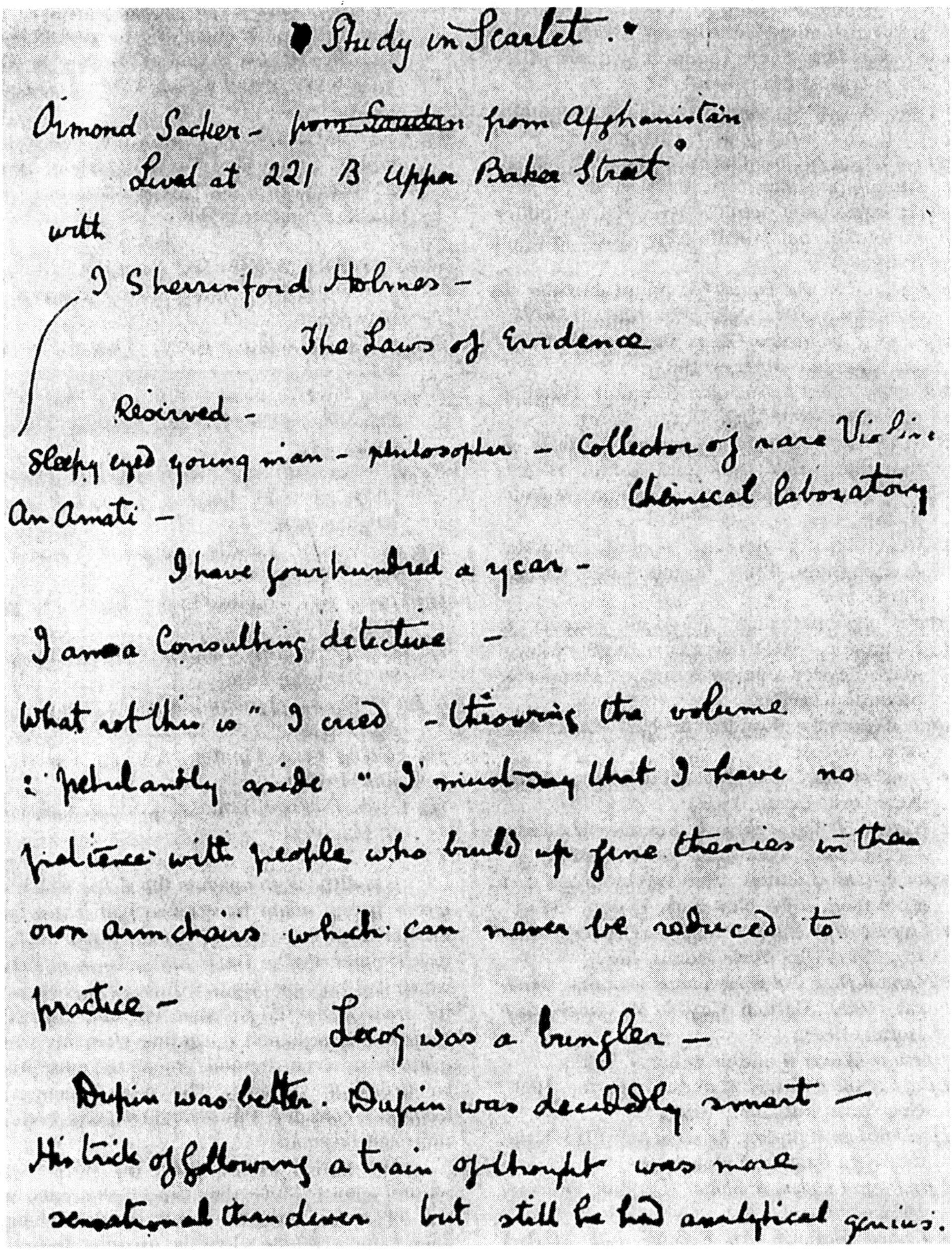

Study in Scarlet.

Ormond Sacker – ~~from Sowdan~~ from Afghanistan

Lived at 221 B Upper Baker Street

with

I Sherrinford Holmes –

The Laws of Evidence

Reserved –

Sleepy eyed young man – philosopher – Collector of rare Violins

Chemical laboratory

An Amati –

I have four hundred a year –

I am a Consulting detective –

What rot this is" I cried – throwing the volume

: petulantly aside " I must say that I have no

patience with people who build up fine theories in their

own armchairs which can never be reduced to

practice –

Lecoq was a bungler –

Dupin was better. Dupin was decidedly smart –

His trick of following a train of thought was more

sensational than clever but still he had analytical genius.

Notes for Conan Doyle's first novel, demonstrating how his initial conceptions of Sherlock Holmes and John Watson were modified (Stanley Mackenzie Collection) concept, the best-seller, was developing. There was a literature not for the elite, but for the people.

The Gothic novel, the Newgate novel, even the so-called penny dreadful contained elements of mystery, suspense, and horror which set the stage for what Poe called the tale of ratiocination. A few years later, the French writer Gaboriau used some of these same elements in his novels, collectively referred to as his "romans policiers," but which the growing number of followers of the form came to call the mystery or detective story. In *A Study in Scarlet* (1888) Sherlock Holmes disparages both of these writers, but only because his creator wished to add personality to his character. In reality, the author was among the greatest admirers of both Poe and Gaboriau.

Arthur Conan Doyle was born in Edinburgh, Scotland, on 22 May 1859. "Art in the blood is liable to take the strangest forms," Sherlock Holmes once said about his own family. He might have been speaking of his creator. Conan Doyle's grandfather John Doyle was an artist and political cartoonist of the Georgian and early Victorian era. Conan Doyle's father, Charles Doyle, made a precarious living at the Scottish Office of Works, but he was also an artist, supplementing his income with book illustrations. Charles's older brother, Richard (Dickie) Doyle, drew pictures for *Punch* and designed the famous cover which appeared on each issue for one hundred years.

Conan Doyle's mother, Mary Foley Doyle, was well read and a great storyteller, both characteristics clearly responsible for leading his interests toward literature. Less obvious, but also significant, was her passion for genealogy. On her mother's side she could trace her roots to the Plantagenets, and she projected a fierce pride in his family to her son. To her family, Mary Foley Doyle was always referred to as "the Ma'am."

For Arthur Conan Doyle, art would mean literature and not illustration or painting. He was named for an uncle, Michael Conan, and King Arthur. Later he came to prefer Conan Doyle (unhyphenated), rather than Doyle, as a surname.

As a boy he read Sir Walter Scott's historical novels, especially *Ivanhoe*. This book by the father of the historical novel helped to implant the spirit of chivalry in young Arthur's character. It also led him to emulate Scott in writing his own historical novels. In Conan Doyle's personality, as well as in his writing, there are the same traits of courage, nobility, fairness, courtesy, respect for women, protection of the poor, and all the rest of the attributes of knighthood. And though Sherlock Holmes professes a dislike for and distrust of women and says in *The Sign of Four*: "I assure you that the most winning woman I ever knew was hanged for poisoning three little children for their insurance money," he remains courteous and considerate toward the women in the stories.

Conan Doyle had other favorite authors besides Scott. Among them was Mayne Reid, a writer of popular adventure fiction, whose best-known work was *The Scalp-Hunters* (1851), a tale of marauding Indians in northern Mexico.

The Conan Doyle family was Roman Catholic, so young Arthur was sent to Hodder, the preparatory school for Stonyhurst, a Jesuit public school in Lancashire. At Stonyhurst life was Spartan, and one was toughened in both body and spirit by frequent applications of a length of India rubber called a "Tolley."

It was at Stonyhurst that young Arthur became a distinguished amateur at sports, something he remained all his life. He excelled in the use of the singlestick (a sort of wooden swordstick with a guard, used in fencing) as well as in boxing, cricket, and football. Some of these abilities (especially singlestick and boxing) were shared by Sherlock Holmes.

At the same time that his intellectual and physical horizons were being broadened, his spiritual life was changing. He spent a year in Austria at Feldkirch College, another Jesuit school, when he was sixteen, but he began to draw away from the church and organized religion. He never became an atheist, however. Atheism was something he found incomprehensible. This attitude may help to explain his later belief in spiritualism.

In 1876, at the age of seventeen, Conan Doyle entered the medical school at the University of Edinburgh. It was here that he seems to have first become interested in spiritualism, and it was here that he met Dr. Joseph Bell, who was to serve as the prototype for Sherlock Holmes.

In his autobiography, *Memories and Adventures* (1924), he recalls his experience in Dr. Bell's classes. Bell was a skillful surgeon, but his specialty was diagnosis, not only of disease but also of character and occupation. Although he was sometimes incorrect, usually the results were dramatic and accurate. He could look at a former soldier, not long discharged, and tell him what regiment he had served in and where he had been stationed. Conan Doyle was able to use the

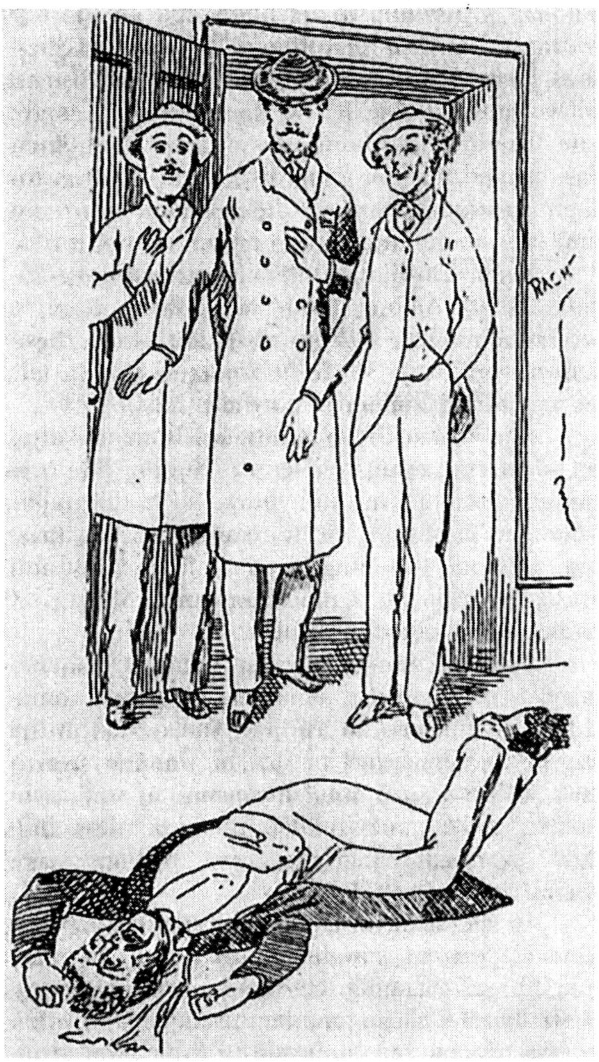

Illustration by Charles Doyle, the author's father, for the first edition of A Study in Scarlet

method of medical diagnosis in explaining the working of Holmes's method of "scientific deduction." When Holmes says to Dr. Watson, "You know my methods," he is speaking the literal truth. The methods Holmes applies are also those of Dr. Watson, but in a different context.

While in medical school, Conan Doyle had begun to write fiction and sold his first short story, "The Mystery of Sasassa Valley," to *Chambers's Journal* in 1879. This story of the search for diamonds in Africa gives little evidence that its author would ever make his living from anything except medicine. Even medicine was anything but a certain path. Newcomers to the profession found little work and less money.

While still a student he signed to go as a surgeon aboard the steam whaler *Hope,* bound for the Arctic. After this adventure he was graduated in 1881 with the degrees of bachelor of medicine and master of surgery and returned to the sea on a passenger liner to West Africa.

Conan Doyle returned from Africa in 1882 to take up a partnership with a former fellow student, Dr. George Budd. An account of the partnership may be found in the semi-autobiographical novel *The Stark Munro Letters* (1895). A flamboyant character, half genius and half quack, Dr. Budd was distrusted by Conan Doyle's mother, who did not hesitate to speak her mind in her letters to her son. Dr. Budd and his wife contrived to extract these letters from Conan Doyle's pocket when he hung up his coat. Told that his services in the partnership would no longer be needed, Dr. Conan Doyle removed his brass nameplate from the door and moved his office to No. 1, Bush Villas, Elm Grove, Southsea, a suburb of Portsmouth.

Patients were few and far between and so were the number of stories he wrote which were accepted for publication. In 1883 he sold "Habakuk Jephson's Statement," a story about the mystery ship the *Mary Celeste,* to James Payn's *Cornhill,* one of the most respected of the journals. (It was in that same journal that Dr. Watson would read Sherlock Holmes's article "The Book of Life," in *A Study in Scarlet* [1888].)

In 1885 Conan Doyle received his M.D. from Edinburgh and did what many an impoverished young man had done before: he added to his living expenses by getting married. His bride, Louise Hawkins, was the sister of one of his patients. His writing continued, and he added a novel, "Girdlestone & Co.," to the manuscripts which went the rounds of the publishers and were returned. It would take him years to find a publisher for it under its new title of *The Firm of Girdlestone* (1890). A novel of business life, it is scarcely read today.

In 1886 he began to jot down ideas, names, and bits of dialogue and description for a story he intended to call "A Tangled Skein." All that appears to remain of the manuscript of what became the first Sherlock Holmes story are those fragmentary notes. He apparently planned to have the story narrated by a man named Ormond Sacker, who had once lived in Afghanistan and now had rooms at 221B Upper Baker Street. Sacker's friend's name was I. Sherrinford Holmes. (In Conan Doyle's handwritten notes there is no period after the letter "I" in "I Sherrinford Holmes." Did he forget to include it

A 1904 "portrait" of Sherlock Holmes by Sidney Paget, illustrator of the first editions of The Adventures of Sherlock Holmes, The Memoirs of Sherlock Holmes, The Hound of the Baskervilles, *and* The Return of Sherlock Holmes

or did he intend the letter to stand for the personal pronoun? The question remains unanswered and his intention ambiguous.) As Conan Doyle was to remark later in reconstructing his creation, he was preparing the way for a new kind of detective, one who would be an improvement on Poe's Dupin and Gaboriau's Lecoq: where those detectives achieved their results largely by chance, Holmes was to achieve his by scientific reasoning.

Today, a writer of detective literature can turn to many textbooks on police methods to keep the stories reasonably accurate. In 1886 there was no such textbook. Hans Gross's pioneering work, *Criminal Investigation*, was not published until 1891. Conan Doyle had to rely primarily on his imagination, his encyclopedic knowledge, his eye and memory for detail, his faculty for relating facts to causes, his ability to reconstruct the past from the present, plus some knowledge of human nature—in short, some of the methods of Sherlock Holmes himself. The anecdotes which support the suggestion that the stories had some influence on real-life crime detection are probably apocryphal. Neither the claim that the French police, the Sureté, once named its crime laboratories at Lyons after the detective nor the story that the Egyptian police used the stories themselves as a textbook in crime detection are supported by concrete evidence. Conan Doyle soon abandoned the names Ormond Sacker and Sherrinford Holmes for the ones by which the characters are known today. Those discarded names were replaced by John H. Watson (a name borrowed, perhaps, from a friend at Southsea, Dr. *James* Watson) and Sherlock Holmes (*Holmes*, perhaps, after the American author Oliver Wendell Holmes, and *Sherlock* for a cricketer against whom Conan Doyle once bowled). "A Tangled Skein" became *A Study in Scarlet* from the comments Holmes makes at the end of the fourth chapter: that there is a scarlet thread of murder running through this skein of life and that it is his and Watson's duty to unravel and expose it.

Conan Doyle began writing the story in March 1886 and completed it the following month. It was not until December 1887 that it finally appeared, after having been rejected by several other publishers, in the pages of *Beeton's Christmas Annual*. The publishers Ward, Lock offered the author twenty-five pounds for the complete rights, and Conan Doyle, not being in a position to argue, accepted.

While awaiting the publication of his first novel, the author began the research into seventeenth-century history which resulted in the first of his historical novels, *Micah Clarke*. When the novel was published in 1889 it was an immediate success, both critically and commercially.

A first-person narrative, it is an episodic work, more chronicle than novel. The story covers Micah Clarke's childhood, during which he hears the accounts of Oliver Cromwell and the Puritans; his adventures in the company of a soldier of fortune, Decimus Saxon, who sides with the Duke of Monmouth against King James; his diplomatic mission for Monmouth and the military operations which end with the battle of Sedgemoor and Monmouth's defeat; and his escape to seek his fortune as a soldier in Europe.

There has been some difference of opinion regarding the reception of *A Study in Scarlet*. Some histories of the genre have indicated that it was an immediate success, but the truth is somewhat different. While not generating wild enthusiasm, sales were sufficient for Ward, Lock to publish it as a hardcover book in 1888. By 1892 it had gone through six printings, but three of those appeared after the success of the first series of short stories about Sherlock Holmes in the *Strand Magazine*.

A Study in Scarlet is historically important for more reasons than that it was its author's first novel and that it was the story which introduced Holmes and Watson. It follows the pattern of Gaboriau's novels in that there are really two stories: in the first the reader follows the investigation of a murder by the detective; in the second there is a detailed explanation of the entire family history and situation which lead up to the murder. Gaboriau had presented this structure in the form of two separate volumes; Conan Doyle dealt with the same situation in a single volume divided into two parts. (The final chapter is a return to the style and content of part 1.) *A Study in Scarlet* can, therefore, be viewed as a transitional work in the genre; it is a transition to the detective novel in which the murderer's motivation is integrated into the main plot.

While Gaboriau had used the third-person point of view in his novels, Poe had employed a first-person narrator in the Dupin short stories. Conan Doyle applied the latter method but replaced Poe's nameless friend of the detective with John Watson, a fully developed character in his own right. In so doing he added a dimension to the detective story which had been lacking in the works of his predecessors: the human element. But like most strokes of genius, this one was not fully grasped by the author at the time. Doyle abandoned Sherlock Holmes for other endeavors. In 1889 he wrote and published a novel which is decidedly among his minor works and deservedly obscure. Only those interested in tracing his development as a writer are likely to derive much pleasure from *The Mystery of Cloomber*, a somewhat confusing and unconvincing story of the retribution visited upon Maj. Gen. J. B. Heatherstone forty years after his murder of a holy man in India. The novel does gain some significance in its author's biography from its early evidence of his interest in spiritualism, as well as for some of the elements in it which he used with greater success the following year in *The Sign of Four*. The mysterious Indians; Cpl. Rufus Smith, an ague-ridden old India hand with a lame foot; the pursuit by dog across the countryside; the love story; and the fateful Hole of Cree, which swallows up the object of the antagonists' quest, all have their parallels in the second Sherlock Holmes novel: Jonathan Small and his wooden leg; the pursuit by dog across London; Dr. Watson's love for Mary Morstan; and the Thames, which swallows up the Great Agra Treasure.

"The Sign of the Four"—the original magazine story title and the phrase used in the text itself—was first published in *Lippincott's Magazine* for February 1890. It was retitled *The Sign of Four* when published in book form in London that year, but the American edition, also published in 1890, restores the second *the*.

The year 1890 also saw the first official collection of Conan Doyle's short fiction (there had been an earlier, unauthorized collection), *The Captain of the Polestar and Other Tales*. In April Chatto and Windus published *The Firm of Girdlestone*, with its subtitle *A Romance of the Unromantic*. Few of Conan Doyle's biographers pay much attention to this novel; one of them dismisses it as being of interest only for its portrait of medical life, while another claims that it contains all of its author's merits and faults. The book is padded with descriptions of extraneous things, and the reader may wonder whether it is intended to be a guidebook to the University of Edinburgh or a thriller. The work is primarily important for what it reveals of its author's development as a writer.

It was also in 1890 that Conan Doyle completed one of his best historical novels, *The White Company*. Having steeped himself in the seventeenth century for *Micah Clarke*, which is set against a background of Monmouth's Rebellion, he now turned to the world of chivalry. The earlier novel had been compared to R. D. Blackmore's *Lorna Doone* (1869); but where Blackmore's novel used the historical setting as a pretext for its romantic plot, *Micah Clarke* consists of episodes strung together on the thread of its historic narrative. The same is true of *The White Company*.

Alleyne Edricson, on a year's leave from Beaulieu Abbey, takes up service with Sir Nigel Loring of Whitechurch. The White Company, a group of English bowmen, persuades Sir Nigel to lead its forces against Spain, and he and his new squire are joined by Hordle John (lately thrown out of the abbey for conduct unbecoming a monk) and bowman Samkin Aylward. The requisite romantic subplot is provided by Alleyne's relationship with Sir Nigel's daughter, Maude, but is overshadowed by the exciting adventures of the characters as they go into battle.

Robert Barr; Conan Doyle's sister Lottie; Conan Doyle; Louise Conan Doyle; and Robert McClure, circa 1894

The result of months of study of books on the Middle Ages in England, *The White Company* became a celebration of chivalry and a personal code for Conan Doyle's life and career. It is also a good adventure story. When he completed the manuscript in July 1890, he was so elated that he threw his pen across the room, splashing the wall with ink, as he shouted, "That's done it!" The novel was serialized in the *Cornhill Magazine* in 1891 and published as a book the same year.

While Conan Doyle could write that he was as fond of Hordle John, Samkin Aylward, and Sir Nigel Loring—all characters in *The White Company*—as though he knew them in the flesh, he could have had no idea that another publication of 1891 would place him in the realm of the immortals. The first Sherlock Holmes short story, "A Scandal in Bohemia," appeared that year in the *Strand Magazine*.

Today it is difficult to imagine the impact that a general-interest magazine could have on the reading public in 1891. The passing of the Education Act of 1870 had made it possible for more people to learn to read and thus made it almost necessary that there be something for them to read. The mass reading public demanded something lighter in tone than the periodicals available at the time, and thus the popular magazine came into being. From today's perspective the formula that developed seems simple: a price of sixpence or less an issue, plenty of light fiction and amusing nonfiction, and a multitude of illustrations. But such a formula would not have worked had there not been editors who could judge the demands of the great mass of new readers. H. Greenhough Smith, who launched the monthly *Strand* in January 1891, was such an editor.

In his autobiography Conan Doyle explained how the idea of writing a series of short stories about Sherlock Holmes came to him. The current periodicals had disconnected short stories; a series with a single character running through it should serve to attract the reader of those stories to a particular magazine. Furthermore, using a series of short stories rather than a serialized novel would remove the risk of a reader missing one number of the magazine and losing interest. As far as anyone has been able to determine, Conan Doyle was the first person to hit upon this idea, and the *Strand* was the first magazine to put it into practice.

According to the author's diary, the first half-dozen of the Sherlock Holmes stories were written in a remarkably short period of time. He mailed in "A Scandal in Bohemia," received the encouragement of the editor to submit more, and followed with five more within two months. Only the flu prevented him from mailing "The Five Orange Pips," the fifth story, until the middle of May. He was paid more for each story than he had received for the entire rights to the first Sherlock Holmes novel, but in spite of this handsome remuneration, he returned to the historical genre for his next novel, *The Refugees* (1893), set in Canada in the seventeenth century. Begun as a sequel to *Micah Clarke, The Refugees* became more of a companion volume to the earlier work. In a letter to his mother in 1892, Conan Doyle explained how he was going to introduce his young American hero, Amos Green, a shrewd woodsman, to the court of Louis XIV, and provide a foil to him in a New England Puritan seaman, Epharim Savage. The final version concludes with an account of adventures in the Canadian wilderness in the tradition of James Fenimore Cooper.

Conan Doyle had no intention of writing more than those first six Holmes stories. He had to plan each as carefully as though it were a novel and he felt that he might just as well be writing a novel. But when the first story appeared in the July 1891 *Strand*, the publishers knew they had something new, unique, and successful.

To illustrate the stories (one of the reasons the *Strand* was itself so popular was its lavish use of illustrations) a young artist named Sidney Paget was commissioned; the editor thought he had hired Paget's older and better-known brother Walter and had confused the names. Sidney used his brother as a model for the detective, and his illustrations became for many the definitive visual image of Sherlock Holmes. It was in the fourth story, "The Boscombe Valley Mystery," that Holmes was seen for the first time in what has become in the popular mind his standard uniform: the deerstalker cap and inverness coat. Paget drew this outfit based on what Dr. Watson described as a "long grey travelling-cloak and close-fitting cloth cap."

As public acceptance of Sherlock Holmes grew, the supply of stories which remained to be published dwindled, and Smith asked Conan Doyle for more. Impatient to get on with *The Refugees*, Conan Doyle said he would write more Holmes stories only if he received more money for them; he named what he considered an outrageous figure of fifty pounds per story. To his surprise, the editor agreed; so he set aside *The Refugees* in order to write six more stories, beginning with "The Adventure of the Blue Carbuncle." Once he had supplied those six, he was asked to write even more. He raised his price drastically and asked for one thousand pounds for the next dozen stories. Again the editor accepted. Conan Doyle set to work, although he warned Smith that he could not be expected to deliver these twelve stories as quickly as he had the previous ones.

By November 1891 he had the idea that in order to be quit of this assignment he would have to kill off his detective. He would have preferred to do so in "The Adventure of the Copper Beeches," but when he reported his intention to his mother she was horrified. "You won't!" she said. "You can't! You *mustn't*!" Holmes's life was spared for the time being.

The new cycle of Sherlock Holmes stories began in the December 1892 issue of the *Strand* and continued until December 1893. The twelve stories actually appeared in thirteen issues, for "The Adventure of the Naval Treaty" was sufficiently long to be divided into two parts for publication in October and November. Before that December 1893 issue, the author had written three minor works, *The Doings of Raffles Haw* (1891), *The Great Shadow* (1892), and "Beyond the City" (1893). *The Doings of Raffles Haw* concerns a chemist who learns to transmute base metals into gold, upsetting the economy and society. *The Great Shadow* is the first in a series of historical works set in Napoleonic times; it was to be overshadowed by the Brigadier Gerard stories. "Beyond the City" is one of several stories set in the London suburb of South Norwood, where the author and his family made their home.

The success of the Sherlock Holmes short stories has been the subject of much speculation. Certainly the unique factor of having a single character running through the series explains part of their appeal. What Conan Doyle did with the character and his vision for the series also account for much of it. In addition, there are many touches from the pen of a gifted storyteller and so many felicitous turns of phrase that the stories continue to please even on repeated readings.

The first of the series, "A Scandal in Bohemia" has often been held up as a model for the

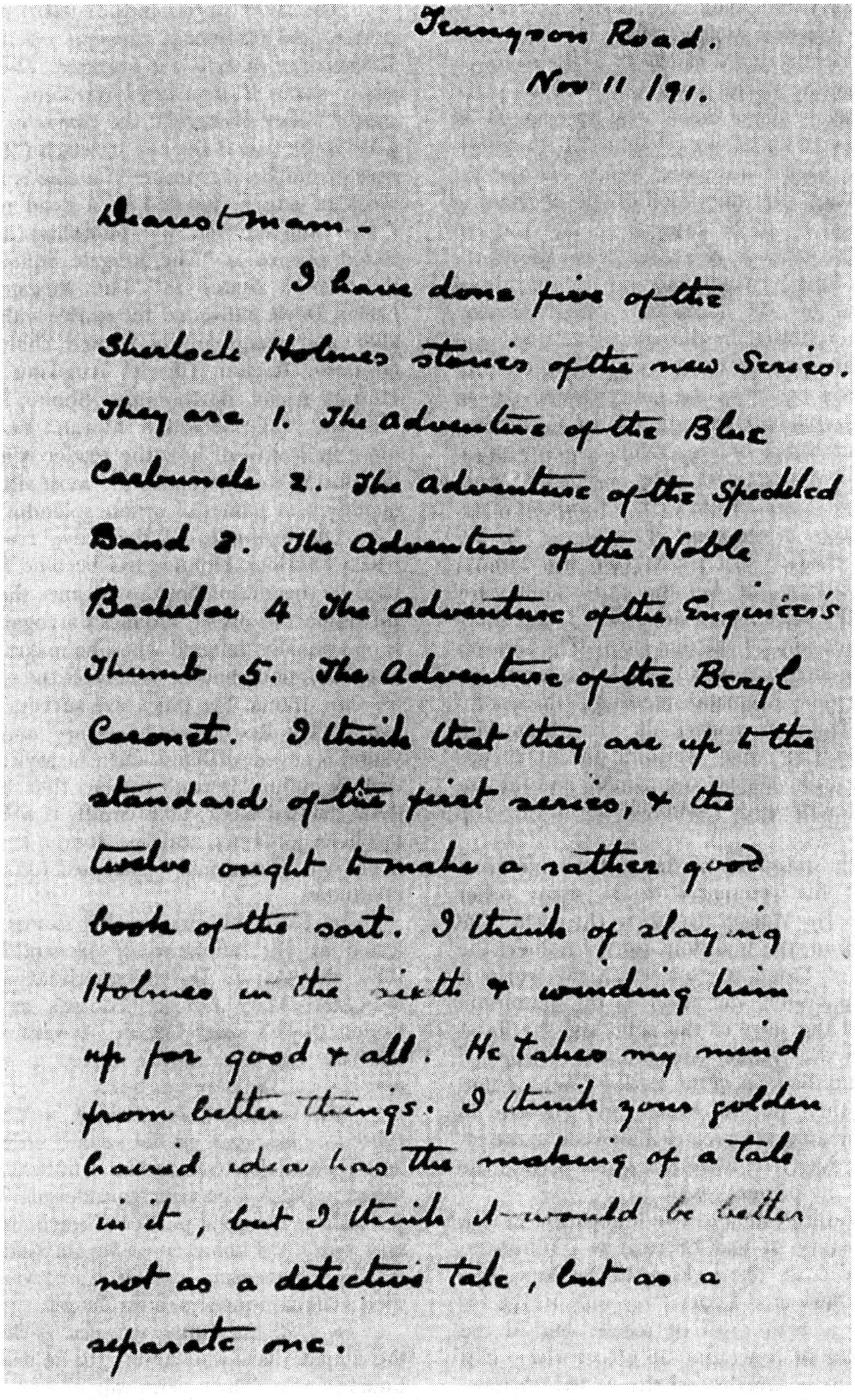

Tennyson Road.
Nov 11 /91.

Dearest Mam —

I have done five of the Sherlock Holmes stories of the new Series. They are 1. The Adventure of the Blue Carbuncle 2. The Adventure of the Speckled Band 3. The Adventure of the Noble Bachelor 4 The Adventure of the Engineer's Thumb 5. The Adventure of the Beryl Coronet. I think that they are up to the standard of the first series, & the twelve ought to make a rather good book of the sort. I think of slaying Holmes in the sixth & winding him up for good & all. He takes my mind from better things. I think your golden haired idea has the making of a tale in it, but I think it would be better not as a detective tale, but as a separate one.

Letter in which Conan Doyle told his mother that he was thinking of "slaying" his famous detective at the end of his second series of Sherlock Holmes stories, so that he could go on to writing "better things" (John Dickson Carr, The Life of Sir Arthur Conan Doyle, *1949)* rest. It is the prototypical Holmes tale. In *The Private Life of Sherlock Holmes* (1933), Vincent Starrett says that it contains nearly all of the elements which made the stories so enjoyable. There is the prologue set in Baker Street with an example of Holmes's use of his science of deduction, the reference to an earlier adventure which has not yet been recorded, the discussion of the problem at hand (or about to be presented), and the entrance of the client (in this instance the illustrious hereditary king of Bohemia) with an additional elaboration of the problem. These preliminaries are followed by the adventure itself and the solution and explanation of the mystery. This structure was based on the conventional pattern of tragic drama: the introduction or exposition, rising action, climax or crisis, falling action, and catastrophe or denouement. The Sherlock Holmes stories are well plotted and well told without material extraneous to the point of the story. The author once claimed that Dr. Watson was without humor as a narrator, but the opportunities for humor in the stories were not avoided, and there are examples which belie that claim. The series is overflowing in humorous concepts: a league of redheaded men, a romantic meeting at the gas fitters' ball, Holmes's remark (in "The Man with the Twisted Lip") that Watson's gift of silence makes him an invaluable companion, and the entire quest for the Blue Carbuncle lost in the crop of a goose.

Equally indicative of the author's intended humor are the references to the many other cases which Dr. Watson has yet to chronicle. The case of Wilson, the notorious canary trainer; the Giant Rat of Sumatra ("for which the world is not yet prepared"); the affair of the aluminum crutch; and the story of the politician, the lighthouse, and the trained cormorant are dropped teasingly into the texts of the stories. They are tantalizing in their puckish humor and effective in the way they suggest a greater dimension to the career of the detective; there is a world beyond the confines of the present case.

The author's debt to Poe is apparent in that first short story. It may be read as a tribute to the best and most "Sherlockian" of the Dupin trilogy, "The Purloined Letter," not only in the involvement in both cases of royalty but in the basic premise of concealing an object where it is most likely to be overlooked due to the obviousness of its hiding place. In both stories the place of concealment is revealed after a smoke bomb is thrown by a confederate of the detective.

The short stories include many of the basic devices and traditional concepts upon which the literature of detection is founded. The seemingly guilty party is invariably innocent ("The Boscombe Valley Mystery"); the character who is too good to be true is the one to watch ("The Adventure of the Beryl Coronet"); a clue is found on a scrap of paper clutched in a dead man's hand ("The Reigate Squire"—published in the collected edition as "The Reigate Squires" and in the United States as "The Reigate Puzzle"). Conan Doyle enlivened his stories with appropriately and imaginatively named characters: Dr. Grimesby Roylott, Charles Augustus Milverton, Hosmer Angel, Bartholomew Sholto, Prof. James Moriarty, Col. Sebastian Moran. The name is often indicative of how the reader is intended to respond to the character; the most villainous frequently bear names of ornate splendor.

The examples of deductive reasoning for which Sherlock Holmes has become famous are used by the author both to advance the story and for humorous effect. Holmes's arrogant certainty is occasionally deflated when he makes the wrong diagnosis, but when he is correct the scene crackles with drama. His quick eye surveys Jabez Wilson in "The Red-Headed League," and his observation is almost offhand when he says that he can deduce nothing beyond the fact that the man has done manual labor, takes snuff, is a Freemason, has been to China, and has done a lot of writing lately. Mr. Wilson may be excused for seeming incredulous.

In 1892 the first twelve stories were collected as *The Adventures of Sherlock Holmes*. By then the Conan Doyle household included a daughter, Mary Louise; Louise's mother; and Conan Doyle's sister Connie. Toward the end of the year his sister Lottie moved in with them, and his son Kingsley was born.

The historical novel which had been interrupted by his work on the second series of Sherlock Holmes short stories was completed and published in 1893. One critic considered *The Refugees* to combine the worst parts of French historical fiction with a bad imitation of Mayne Reid, but Robert Louis Stevenson enjoyed it and wrote the author what amounted to a fan letter.

In 1893 the family traveled to Switzerland; the climate there was thought to be beneficial for Louise Conan Doyle, who was ill with tuberculosis. It was there that the author first saw the Reichenbach Falls and realized how he could dispose of Sherlock Holmes. He was finding the requests for more of the detective's adventures irksome; he felt that he had more arrows in his quiver than those aimed at the market for detective fiction. And so, in the last of the new series, the world's greatest consulting detective met his "Final Problem" locked in mortal combat with his old enemy, Prof. James Moriarty. Dr. Watson closed his casebook on "him whom I shall ever regard as the best and wisest man whom I have ever known," paraphrasing Plato's description of the death of Socrates.

London and the rest of the world went into mourning when "The Final Problem" appeared in the *Strand* in 1893. Conan Doyle could not understand the public reaction. The death of his father and the illness of his wife were real-life tragedies with which the one of his imagination could not compare.

The second series of Sherlock Holmes stories was collected in 1894 under the title *The Memoirs of Sherlock Holmes*. In addition to "The Final Problem" it contained "Silver Blaze," with its famous cryptic remark about the significance of the actions of the dog in the nightmare. In keeping with the "memoirs" theme the author revealed something of the detective's earlier life in "The *Gloria Scott*" and "The Musgrave Ritual" and in "The Greek Interpreter" introduced Sherlock Holmes's older brother Mycroft. By expanding the stage on which the dramas were enacted, Conan Doyle added to the verisimilitude of the stories. The great detective did have a life beyond what had been preserved in book form to date.

In the meantime, the author had much to occupy his time and mind. As his wife's health improved, he found new interests to fill the hours when he was not writing. The snow-covered mountains of Switzerland were a perfect place to try out an activity he had discovered on a visit to Norway—skiing. He sent for a pair of skis and astonished the Swiss, to whom the sport was something new. He predicted that someday visitors would come to Switzerland as much for the skiing as for health reasons.

He continued his writing, creating new characters who would appear in a series of stories designed to bind readers to the *Strand*. One was Brig. Etienne Gerard, whose adventures partially filled the gap left by the death of Sherlock Holmes. He also published *Round the Red Lamp* (1894), a collection of stories about doctors.

His growing interest in spiritualism led him to write a novel about it. *The Parasite* (1894), however, is a strange novel in many ways. He later disowned it and hoped it would be forgotten. It concerns a doctor who is converted to belief in spiritualism by an unattractive female mesmerist who turns on him when she learns what he really thinks of her. Under her spell he commits acts he considers to be criminal, and she makes him speak nonsense at his lectures. When he refuses to retract his statements about her, she forces him to break into a bank and to attempt to disfigure his girlfriend with acid. The novel is out of character for the creator of Sherlock Holmes, the master of logic.

In 1895 he published *The Stark Munro Letters*, the story of his experience with Dr. Budd of the previous decade. The requests for more Sherlock Holmes stories continued. But readers had to be content with the two novels and the two collections of short stories which remained in print. There seemed to be no diminution in the popularity of the four books.

The first eight Brigadier Gerard stories were collected as *The Exploits of Brigadier Gerard* (1896). Its success was matched by Conan Doyle's Regency novel of prizefighting, *Rodney Stone* (1896), which was serialized in the *Strand* with illustrations by Sidney Paget. In 1897 another Napoleonic novel, *Uncle Bernac*, appeared. An uneven work, it has its moments of interest but seems to lose momentum when its hero joins the army of the emperor. Included in its cast of characters is a young officer named Etienne Gerard. Other minor works followed: *The Tragedy of the Korosko* (1898), about the reconquest of the Sudan and its restoration to Anglo-Egyptian control; a collection of verse, *Songs of Action* (1898); and a new collection of short fiction, *The Green Flag and Other Stories of War and Sport* (1900).

Among these works, the adventures of the boastful Gascon, Etienne Gerard, stand out. For many readers they have a special place, and the account of his career from Zurich to Waterloo (1799-1815) is a capsule history of the Napoleonic Wars. There are seventeen short stories about Gerard (a second collection, *Adventures of Gerard*, appeared in 1903). Narrated in the first person by the Brigadier, they present him as he saw himself: "gay-riding, plume-tossing, debonair, the darling of the six brigades of light cavalry" and indispensable aide to Napoleon in his campaign. The fun that Conan Doyle had in writing the stories becomes apparent to the reader.

When the Boer War began, Conan Doyle attempted to enlist in the Middlesex Yeomanry but

Crayon sketch by G. K. Chesterton of Holmes and Moriarty struggling at the top of Reichenbach Falls (The Lilly Library, Indiana University)

was rejected due to his age, for he was nearly forty. He joined a hospital unit and went to South Africa in 1900. The Boers had captured the water supply at Bloemfontein, and before long the hospital was filled with men dying of enteric fever; one quarter of the forty-eight members of the hospital staff, including Conan Doyle, were stricken. At one point during the epidemic, a London journalist asked Conan Doyle which of the Sherlock Holmes stories was his favorite. The answer given by the weary senior physician has not been recorded for posterity.

His experiences in the war resulted in *The Great Boer War* (1900), which was known for years as the standard history of that segment of the story of British imperialism. His description of the people against whom the British fought between 1899 and 1902 was both objective and compassionate. Napoleon and his veterans had never treated the British as roughly as those fierce farmers of Dutch extraction.

In 1901, inspired by conversations with the journalist Fletcher Robinson (1871-1907), Conan Doyle dreamed up a ghost story with a rational explanation. *The Hound of the Baskervilles* (1902) was not originally intended as a Sherlock Holmes story; but, needing a hero, Conan Doyle used Holmes, who fit the part admirably. He made it clear, however, that this was an adventure from before May 1891—that is, before the events at the Reichenbach Falls described in "The Final Problem." Holmes had not been revived except in a historical sense.

The Hound of the Baskervilles, serialized in the *Strand* between August 1901 and April 1902, was an instant success. It is considered by many to be the finest of the entire canon and certainly the finest of the four novels. As a ghost story it belongs more to the literature of skepticism than to the literature of belief, as the ghostly hound is integrated into a story of scientific materialism. It is interesting to contrast it with another terror tale of two decades earlier, Stevenson's *Strange Case of Dr. Jekyll and Mr. Hyde* (1886), in which reality is redefined.

Readers have often complained that for a Sherlock Holmes story, the detective spends far too much time offstage, leaving Dr. Watson to carry on the bulk of the investigation. A close reading of the novel reveals this to be a necessity and even a strength of the story. The opening chapters are devoted to setting up the tale of the spectral hound and then demolishing the legend. There are repeated references to the men of science who have to deal with this supernatural situation, men whose logic refuses to believe in the hound or the curse visited upon the Baskervilles. The phrase "man of science" is used repeatedly to refer to Sherlock Holmes, to Dr. James Mortimer, to men of precise minds. The theme of the novel clearly is that of science versus superstition.

The legend of the Baskerville family is presented in the classic manner which is traditional in ghost stories: an ancient document is produced by Dr. Mortimer and read aloud. Its authenticity is attested to in the first of a series of reassurances that we are dealing with fact and not fancy. The passage in which Hugo Baskerville swears to sell his soul to the devil also belongs to the tradition.

When Dr. Mortimer has finished reading the document from the past, he turns to one from the present—the 1880s, when the events of the novel are supposed to occur. A newspaper account of the facts surrounding the death of Sir Charles Baskerville emphasizes the cause of death as having been natural, in spite of the circumstances which were suspiciously unusual. As Dr. Mortimer says, putting away the folded newspaper clipping, these are the *public* facts. He then goes into the *private* facts, based on his own observations, and ends his account with one of the most memorably chilling lines in all of literature, ranking with Robinson Crusoe's discovery of a footprint on an otherwise uninhabited island. He had seen traces around the body of Sir Charles, traces that no one else had observed: "Mr. Holmes, they were the footprints of a gigantic hound."

Having taken pains to establish the scientific background and training of the characters in his novel, Conan Doyle continues to emphasize these qualities when he describes Dr. Mortimer's observant nature. He is not one to jump to conclusions or make hasty judgments. Readers are as certain that he has seen the footprints as if they had been there and seen them.

All of the mysterious occurrences in these opening chapters—the message made up of words clipped from a newspaper, the man who seems to be following Dr. Mortimer and Sir Henry Baskerville on the street—can be explained by rational means. The case against this being a true tale of the supernatural has been set up so concretely that the ghost seems to have been exorcised. The only way for the author to restore the superstition theme is to arrange for Sherlock Holmes to be absent from most of the rest

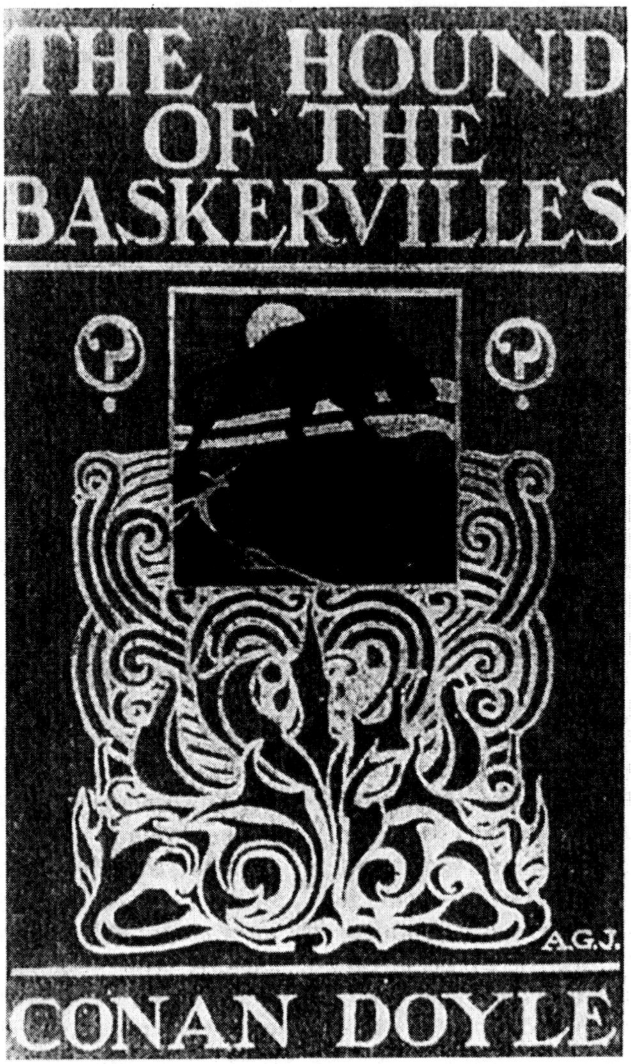

Cover for Conan Doyle's 1902 Sherlock Holmes novel, written after "The Final Problem," the 1893 short story in which he killed his fictional detective, but set before Holmes's plunge over Reichenbach Falls

of the story, and so Dr. Watson is sent to accompany Sir Henry to Baskerville Hall.

Once Dr. Watson is on center stage, the tone of the novel changes. On the journey to Baskerville Hall, the author is able to use his powers of description to restore the eerie quality to the story. It is autumn, when things are dying. Baskerville Hall is described in terms that emphasize its ancient Gothic architecture. The only hint of science to dispel the gloom is Sir Henry's desire to install electric lights in front of the main entrance.

Every event from that point up to the reappearance of Sherlock Holmes is there for the purpose of emphasizing the supernatural and the power of superstition. Mystery is added to mystery until Holmes returns as a deus ex machina to set things right, and the powers of light and science triumph. The denouement is handled with fitting dramatic effect. The explanation of the spectral hound is made back at Baker Street when the tension of the final chase over the moor has been relieved and there is a period for objective analysis.

From this temporary return of Sherlock Holmes the author turned to some of his other concerns. He published a sixty-thousand-word pamphlet, *The War in South Africa: Its Cause and Conduct* (1902), in which he defended the British soldier's role in the war and refuted the charges of barbarism, rape, and murder which were appearing in newspapers both abroad and at home. Shortly thereafter he received a knighthood from King Edward VII for his services to his country.

The new Sir Arthur, like the former Dr. Conan Doyle, was besieged by requests for more Holmes stories. Finally, offered five thousand dollars per story by the editors of *Collier's Weekly,* an American popular periodical, and about half that sum per story for the English rights by the editor of the *Strand,* Conan Doyle agreed. And so, in the fall of 1903, readers on both continents learned that Holmes had really survived the battle with Professor Moriarty: it was Moriarty alone who went over the cliff and into the dreadful abyss at the Reichenbach Falls. As luck would have it, Conan Doyle had written "The Final Problem" in such a way that he had never really described Holmes's death. He was able to come up with an exotic explanation for what had happened to account for the detective's being absent from London for three years. During the period, which has become known to students of the detective's career as the Great Hiatus, he had been traveling incognito through the Middle East and Europe as a Norwegian explorer named Sigerson.

People lined up for blocks to buy the magazines containing the new story, "The Empty House." The stories appeared on a monthly schedule for the next year before being collected into book form as *The Return of Sherlock Holmes* in 1905.

There are those who maintain that the stories which appeared after Holmes's return are not as good as the earlier ones. Certainly there is not quite the same level of imagination and inspired genius, or the same touches of humor in the later years. Many of the later stories repeat ideas and situations found in the early ones, but there are many which are the equal of anything in *The Adventures of Sherlock Holmes* or *The Memoirs of Sherlock Holmes,* just as there are weak efforts among the early gems.

The novelty of those early years of the 1890s had worn off, and the host of imitators and detractors in the fictional detectives who followed Holmes through the pages of the popular magazines tended to take some of the glory away from the original. By the time that *The Return of Sherlock Holmes* had been published the leading character and his creator were household names. Some of this fame was due to the appearance of the detective on the stage in a play written by and starring the American actor William Gillette, which premiered in New York in November 1899. The stories in *Collier's* were illustrated by the American artist Frederic Dorr Steele, who based his image of Holmes on the rugged-

Jean Leckie shortly before her marriage to Conan Doyle on 18 September 1907

looking Gillette. It was this licensing of his character for use in other media which helped to preserve the persona of Sherlock Holmes and make of him a sort of folk hero. Conan Doyle himself had written a play about Sherlock Holmes, the text of which has been lost; Gillette received permission to rewrite this play, and what survives is more Gillette than Conan Doyle. Conan Doyle did have some success with the Sherlock Holmes drama *The Speckled Band* (1912), which premiered in 1910.

The return of Sherlock Holmes and his perpetuation on the stage having added to his financial security, Conan Doyle continued gathering material for more historical novels. He also purchased two motor cars and a motorcycle for use at his country home, Undershaw, at Hindhead in Surrey. In his *Life of Sir Arthur Conan Doyle* (1949), John Dickson Carr tells the story of the time the author was driving his mother in one of the cars, a Wolseley, and collided with two farm wagons loaded with turnips. The horses bolted, overturning the wagons and covering the old lady with the vegetables. Her son sprang out of the car, rushed to see if his mother was injured, and found that she was not even disturbed. She took out her knitting and worked away while the celebrated author and the farmer debated their driving abilities in voices that could be heard for miles around. News of the acquisition of a motorcycle by the author having reached the ears of a reporter for a magazine, Conan Doyle was asked whether Sherlock Holmes would soon begin pursuing villains, accompanied by the faithful Watson, both riding the latest model of that vehicle. Conan Doyle replied in all seriousness that the detective had retired from active duty and that the motorcycle was something he would not care to utilize.

The historical novel *Sir Nigel* (1906) was planned as a companion volume to *The White Company*. Like that work it is set in medieval England, but at an earlier day, and tells the story of the boyhood and early manhood of the knight Nigel Loring. (Rather than a sequel to *The White Company*, it is what is now termed a "prequel.") The author hoped that it would be considered his masterpiece, a bit of living history which reproduced the Middle Ages in all their Gothic splendor, but the critics only pronounced it a rousing adventure yarn. Nigel Loring, a poor boy of noble ancestry, borrows his father's armor, which fits him badly, and sets out to become a knight by the classic tradition of performing three deeds. It is best not to look too closely at its connections with *The White Company*, but to consider it as a companion volume.

The only time Conan Doyle addressed himself directly to a discussion of literature was in 1906, in a series of twelve articles for *Cassell's Magazine* collected in 1907 as *Through the Magic Door*. The essays take the form of appreciations or "book chats" that were popular at the time. In the articles he discusses his favorite authors from earlier days: Sir Walter Scott, James Boswell, Edward Gibbon, Samuel Pepys, George Borrow, Poe, and Stevenson. He considers Poe the supreme writer of short fiction; all subsequent writers of short stories, and especially detective stories, owe a monumental debt to Poe. His two masterpieces, which could not have been bettered, are "The Gold Bug" (1843) and "The Murders in the Rue Morgue" (1841); the proportion and perspective lacking in his other works are definitely present in those two. The horror and weirdness are intensified by the coolness of the protagonists, Le Grand in the first story and Dupin in the second.

In the year in which these articles appeared in *Cassell's* and *Sir Nigel* saw publication as a book, Conan Doyle's wife Louise died. On 18 September of the following year he married Jean Leckie, a friend of several years' standing. He had been in love with Jean for nearly as long as he had known her, but he had refused to treat their relationship as anything but platonic until after his wife's death. Just before the marriage he had bought a modest country house, Windlesham, in Sussex. Enlarged and improved by the time they moved in, it remained his home for the rest of his life.

It was there, in his study on the second floor, that he wrote the rest of the Sherlock Holmes stories, consisting of a final novel and twenty short stories. He also wrote letters and articles pleading the cause of justice for individuals who had been unjustly imprisoned, playing Sherlock Holmes himself on behalf of George Edalji and Oscar Slater. His articles to the press were instrumental in reopening the cases of the accused sufficiently for them to receive their freedom if not a just recompense.

While not remembered for his contributions to the dramatic art, he did compose plays based on his own stories, including one about his favorite creation, Brigadier Gerard. In 1912 he wrote the first of several stories about Professor George Edward Challenger, *The Lost World*. The story of a lost race of dinosaurs existing in the twentieth century on a plateau in South America, it has served as inspiration for many writers of science fiction and producers of films and has itself been filmed several times. The claims that George Challenger has found a world inhabited by prehistoric animals are met with disbelief by the scientific world. An expedition in quest of the truth is mounted, led by the professor and made up of his most active opponent, a renowned explorer, and a journalist. Their encounter with savages as well as dinosaurs had led some critics to make favorable comparisons between Conan Doyle's novel and *Robinson Crusoe*. The conclusion in which the pterodactyl, brought back alive by Challenger as proof of his discoveries, escapes from the Queen's Hall and flies out to sea, once read, is difficult to forget.

He was so excited about his creation of the brusque and memorable scientist with the great black beard that he sold the *Strand* on the idea of illustrating the serial with photos of himself made up as Challenger. The editor acquiesced but was afraid that readers would think that the magazine was trying to perpetrate a hoax to convince them that the story was factual. Conan Doyle was so proud of his disguise that he drove thirty miles to try it out on E. W. Hornung, who was the husband of his sister Connie and the creator of the "gentleman burglar" Raffles. Calling at Hornung's house, he kept in character as Challenger, and it was several minutes before Hornung realized he was the butt of a joke. Conan Doyle's brother-in-law swore that he would never forgive him. This taste for dressing up and mimicry backfired on another occasion when he dressed up as a sort of Jabberwocky figure, frightening his children so severely that they took a long time to be comforted. He followed up *The Lost World* with another Challenger novel, *The Poison Belt* (1913), which deals with the supposed destruction of the entire planet when a belt of deadly gas drifts across the earth.

World War I gave Conan Doyle an opportunity to contribute to the growing number of writings and commentaries on the conflict, along with propaganda articles and pamphlets. In a prophetic vein he wrote about the possibility of digging a tunnel under the English Channel and the advisability of using steel helmets and tanks. His belief that he had actually heard from his wife's brother after the latter's death in the war was the final incident which made him a convert to spiritualism in 1916. For the remainder of his life he lectured, wrote, and lived this philosophy of communication with the dead. The deaths of his son Kingsley, a victim of influenza in 1918 after he was wounded in the war, and his brother Brig. Gen. Innes Doyle in 1919 only strengthened his convictions.

There had been no hint of his impending change in philosophy in 1914 when he wrote *The Valley of Fear* (1915). This fourth and final novel about Sherlock Holmes is a return to the structure established by Gaboriau. Like *A Study in Scarlet*, it was constructed in two parts with an epilogue, the first part describing the aftermath of the murder of John Douglas and the solution to the mystery provided by Sherlock Holmes, the second telling what led up to the murder. As in the earlier novel, the solution lies in the American background of the murdered man.

Although the author had disposed of Holmes's archenemy, Professor Moriarty, more than twenty years earlier in "The Final Problem," there are suggestions here that he may have regretted such hasty action. The professor, though offstage, is very much alive in *The Valley of Fear*, giving rise to the inference that this story, like *The Hound of the Baskervilles*, predates the events at Reichenbach Falls. In the two decades since "The Final Problem" was written, the author had evidently forgotten that Dr. Watson had never heard of Professor Moriarty before the flight to Switzerland. Since Conan Doyle's death, this type of inconsistency has fueled much debate among those aficionados of the stories—called "Sherlockians" in the United States and "Holmesians" in Great Britain—who study the tales as though they represent factual accounts.

Sir Arthur Conan Doyle, 1921

The problem in *The Valley of Fear* concerns not only the identity of the murderer but also that of the victim. The physical and psychological clues are distributed fairly enough so that the reader should have some idea of the significance of the events surrounding the murder; thus, there is an even chance that the reader can predict the ending before arriving at it. While not as dramatic as those in *The Hound of the Baskervilles*, the deductions made by the detective are as interesting as any in the canon, and the puckish humor of the author is in evidence. In addition, the passing years seem to have made Holmes less arrogant and more quietly self-confident.

So much of the mystery has been dispelled by the final chapter of the first section that only an epilogue should have been required to complete the tale. Instead, the author has one of the characters hand a bundle of papers to Dr. Watson ("You are the historian of this bunch"), who dutifully inserts it in the text. There is a seven-chapter flashback to events two decades earlier involving Jack McMurdo and the Scowrers, a secret society in the Vermissa Valley in the Pennsylvania coalfields, before the narrative returns to Baker Street for the real epilogue.

The double-plot structure of *The Valley of Fear* demonstrates the weakness of most Sherlock Holmes novels and suggests the real strength of the short stories. When Holmes is not present with a startling display of his science of deduction there is a diminution of the tension and a resulting lack of interest on the part of the reader. While the story of the Scowrers has its moments, most readers are in the habit of skimming quickly the second half of the novel in order to get back to basics and the "wonderful happenings" (in Dr. Watson's words) of the rooms at Baker Street.

The events of World War I seem to have increased Conan Doyle's sense of social consciousness. Like many of his contemporaries in popular letters (John Buchan, William Le Queux, and Edgar Wallace among them), he wrote a multivolume history of some aspects of the war while it was still being waged, *The British Campaign in France and Flanders* (1916-1919). He also wrote a prophetic story, "Danger!" (1918), in which he warned of the threat from submarine torpedoes before they were ever in wide use.

He continued to write Sherlock Holmes stories, but no longer at the rate of one every month. The eight stories in the penultimate collection, *His Last Bow* (1917), represent a span of nearly a decade in their original periodical publications, the earliest having appeared in 1908. One story, "The Adventure of the Cardboard Box," actually dates from 1893, when it was omitted from all collections but the first American edition of *The Memoirs* because its story of an illicit love affair was thought to be too scandalous for a Victorian audience. The title story of the collection serves both as an account of the war service of the great detective and as an epilogue to his career. "His Last Bow," with its third-person narration to preserve the secret until the end, depicts an older Holmes come out of retirement to serve his country.

The majority of his publications for the next decade concerned spiritualism or were accounts of his travels. His mother died in 1921, still unconvinced by those matters he found so convincing. He debated the subject of spiritualism with the American magician Harry Houdini, an avowed skeptic who gained an incredible amount of publicity from his regular challenges to mediums.

In 1925 Conan Doyle resurrected Professor Challenger for a novel published the following year, *The Land of Mist.* The semiautobiographical book presents its author's years as a spiritualist in narrative form and provides an accurate picture of the spiritualist movement in the 1920s. The third novel in the Challenger series presents a considerable change in that character: Professor George Edward Challenger, man of science, is a convert to spiritualism following the death of his wife, "that little bird of a woman [who] had made her nest in the big man's heart." The novel was not the most successful in the series, either artistically or commercially, and has survived only in an omnibus edition with its companions, *The Professor Challenger Stories* (1952).

While Conan Doyle had intended "His Last Bow" to be the final Sherlock Holmes story, he was persuaded to continue writing them by the success of a series of filmed versions starring Eille Norwood. He wrote a one-act play, *The Crown Diamond,* with Holmes in it, and then turned it into a short story, "The Adventure of the Mazarin Stone," which was published in the *Strand* in September 1921. After the editor of the magazine supplied him with the idea for the plot, he wrote "The Problem of Thor Bridge," which appeared early in 1922. The remaining ten stories were completed, by all accounts, by 1925. The last of them, "Shoscombe Old Place," was published early in 1927, and all twelve were collected in *The Case-Book of Sherlock Holmes* that same year.

The author's final years were spent in the cause of spiritualism, although he published a short science-fiction collection, *The Maracot Deep and Other Stories* (1929), which included two short stories about Professor Challenger, "The Disintegration Machine" and "When the World Screamed." The last two stories indicate that their author's puckish humor was still intact. Stricken with angina pectoris in the fall of 1929, he maintained his working schedule to the best of his ability. He died on the morning of 7 July

1930 and was buried on his estate at Windlesham. The inscription on his headstone reads "Steel True, Blade Straight."

Arthur Conan Doyle is an author whose major creation has long outlived him. Sherlock Holmes has taken on a life beyond anything his creator intended or could have predicted. Unlike many writers of detective stories who use a recurring character, Conan Doyle had a vision for his series which did not allow him to write an infinite number of stories about an ageless figure. While it is not described in detail, Sherlock Holmes has a chronological life, with a period of young manhood, ancestors referred to briefly, a year when he definitely retired, and a brief emergence from that retirement. It is easy to believe in him as a real person.

Among the works that have given readers pleasure over the years, Conan Doyle's diverse short stories should not be overlooked. Apart from those featuring Sherlock Holmes, he wrote nearly one hundred other stories drawn from activities and interests that he enjoyed: sports, army life, piracy and the high seas, terror and mystery, fantasy, medicine, and historical tales.

Before Doyle wrote his historical novels he steeped himself in the periods treated in them. He was justifiably proud of his work in that field and hoped to be remembered for it. Ironically, he is remembered chiefly for his stories of Sherlock Holmes—which, after *The Hound of the Baskervilles,* were just as much historical fiction as *Micah Clarke* or *The White Company.* By keeping them set in Victorian or early Edwardian times he was writing of the recent past, his own past.

A few years after Conan Doyle's death, his creation took on an immortality which has been granted to few literary figures. The American writer Christopher Morley proposed in his column, "The Bowling Green," in the *Saturday Review of Literature,* an organization of followers of Sherlock Holmes to be called the Baker Street Irregulars. The purpose of the society was the study of what came to be called the Sacred Writings, the sixty stories about Sherlock Holmes. In emulation of other learned societies and in a spirit of fun, the members began to exchange notes and write "scholarly" papers concerning the minutiae of the stories. Eventually these "scholarly" activities came to form a sort of satire on the world of academic research.

At about the same time, in 1933, the Chicago critic, novelist, and short-story writer Vincent Starrett published a loving tribute to Conan Doyle and his work called *The Private Life of Sherlock Holmes.* Apart from a reading of the stories themselves, it may be the best explanation of their continued appeal. It fueled the growing interest in having fun with the character of the great detective.

The movement might have foundered as a sort of elaborate joke of its day but for the arrival on the scene in 1938 of a General Motors executive, Edgar W. Smith, who collected the better of the Sherlockian studies in *Profile by Gaslight* (1944). More important, he founded and edited a quarterly journal devoted to the study of Holmes and his times called the *Baker Street Journal.* First published in 1946, it continues publication, having had five editors since Smith. In 1975 the publication and subscription offices were transferred to Fordham University Press in the Bronx.

Since 1934 there has been an annual dinner in New York City, on or near 6 January, which Morley had established as the birthday of the Master, as Holmes has come to be called. Since a handful of scholarly papers are presented at this function it serves as the parallel to the annual conference of scholars in any discipline. The major Sherlockian periodicals as of 1988 are the *Baker Street Journal* and the *Baker Street Miscellanea* in the United States and the *Sherlock Holmes Journal* in Great Britain. A European periodical with a strong claim to be included for its longevity alone is *Sherlockiana,* the publication of the Danish Baker Street Irregulars.

In the half century since Conan Doyle's death, most critical attention paid to his work has been about Sherlock Holmes. With rare exceptions, such as Alvin E. Rodin and Jack D. Key's *The Medical Casebook of Dr. Arthur Conan Doyle* (1984), only the biographies touch on his other writings at all. And of the multitude of publications about Sherlock Holmes, the emphasis until recently has been on the internal world of the stories, examinations of those inconsistencies of which the author was well aware, but which did not matter because of the story he wanted to tell.

In 1912, when Ronald Knox wrote his satire on the higher criticism as applied to the Bible, "Studies in the Literature of Sherlock Holmes," he had to invent titles and authors for the "learned publications" which he cited. Today, so many of the same topics have been the subject of real publications that no writer need invent sources to cite. The vast literature of Sherlock Holmes has achieved its own bibliographical control in two publications by Ronald De Waal (1974, 1980).

Arthur Conan Doyle is a minor but significant figure in English literature. Since 1980, biographies do not merely repeat the platitudes of the past but examine his relationship to his times and the people with whom he came in contact. Even the publications of the various Sherlockian societies acknowledge him as more than the "literary agent" for John H. Watson. His position in the history of the literature of detection remains secure. No other figure, with the possible exception of G. K. Chesterton, represents the detective story of the early twentieth century so well as Conan Doyle. His accomplishment was in creating two characters who are recognizable even to those who have never read the stories. For the real readers the recognition is much the same. Long after the details of their adventures have receded from memory, the readers remember those two good comrades.

How did he do it? The answer is a complex formula: take two well-drawn central characters. Surround them with a story which is not so remarkable for its incidents as for the manner in which it is told. Use a setting which seems familiar but is not mundane. Filter it through a mesh made from the strings of your own inner being, finely tuned to that of a majority of your readers. The result may well be a kind of immortality.

Letters:

Letters to the Press, edited by John Michael Gibson and Richard Lancelyn Green (London: Secker & Warburg, 1986; Iowa City: University of Iowa Press, 1986).

Interviews:

R. Blathwayt, "Talk with Dr. Conan Doyle," *Bookman* (London), 2 (May 1892): 50-51;

Harry How, "A Day with Dr. Conan Doyle," *Strand Magazine,* 4 (August 1892): 182-188;

Robert Barr, "A Chat with Conan Doyle," *Idler,* 6 (October 1894): 340-349; republished in *McClure's Magazine,* 3 (November 1894): 503-513.

Bibliographies:

Harold Locke, *A Bibliographical Catalogue of the Writings of Sir Arthur Conan Doyle, M.D., LL.D., 1879-1928* (Tunbridge Wells: Webster, 1928);

Edgar W. Smith, *Baker Street Inventory: A Sherlockian Bibliography* (Summit, N.J., 1945);

Jay Finley Christ, *The Fiction of Sir Arthur Conan Doyle* (N.p.: Privately printed, 1959);

Ronald Burt De Waal, *The World Bibliography of Sherlock Holmes and Dr. Watson* (Boston: New York Graphic Society, 1974);

Donald A. Redmond, *A Checklist of the Arthur Conan Doyle Collection in the Metropolitan Toronto Library* (Toronto: Metropolitan Toronto Library Board, 1977);

De Waal, *The International Sherlock Holmes: A Companion Volume to the World Bibliography of Sherlock Holmes and Dr. Watson* (Hamden, Conn.: Archon, 1980; London: Mansell, 1980);

Richard Lancelyn Green and John Michael Gibson, *A Bibliography of A. Conan Doyle* (Oxford: Clarendon Press, 1983).

Biographies:

John Lamond, *Arthur Conan Doyle: a Memoir* (London: Murray, 1931; Port Washington, N.Y.: Kennikat Press, 1972);

Hesketh Pearson, *Conan Doyle: His Life and Art* (London: Methuen, 1943; New York: Walker, 1961);

Adrian Conan Doyle, *The True Conan Doyle* (London: Murray, 1945; New York: Coward McCann, 1946);

John Dickson Carr, *The Life of Sir Arthur Conan Doyle* (London: Murray, 1949; New York: Harper, 1949);

Sir Arthur Conan Doyle Centenary, 1859-1959 (London: Murray, 1959; Garden City, N.Y.: Doubleday, 1959);

Michael and Mollie Hardwick, *The Man Who Was Sherlock Holmes* (London: Murray, 1964; Garden City, N.Y.: Doubleday, 1964);

Pierre Nordon, *Sir Arthur Conan Doyle: L'Homme et L'Oeuvre* (Paris: Didier, 1964); translated as *Conan Doyle: A Biography* (London: Murray, 1966; New York: Holt, Rinehart & Winston, 1967);

Ivor Brown, *Conan Doyle, a Biography of the Creator of Sherlock Holmes* (London: Hamish Hamilton, 1972);

Charles Higham, *The Adventures of Conan Doyle: The Life of the Creator of Sherlock Holmes* (New York: Norton, 1976; London: Hamish Hamilton, 1976);

Ronald Pearsall, *Conan Doyle: a Biographical Solution* (London: Weidenfeld & Nicolson, 1977; New York: St. Martin's Press, 1977);

Julian Symons, *Portrait of an Artist—Conan Doyle* (London: Whizzard Press, 1979; New York: Mysterious Press, 1987);

Owen Dudley Edwards, *The Quest for Sherlock Holmes: A Biographical Study of Arthur Conan Doyle* (Edinburgh: Mainstream, 1983);

Howard Lachtman, *Sherlock Slept Here, Being a Brief History of the Singular Adventures of Sir Arthur Conan Doyle in America* . . . (Santa Barbara: Capra Press, 1985);

Jacqueline A. Jaffe, *Arthur Conan Doyle* (Boston: Twayne, 1987);

Jon L. Lellenberg, ed., *The Quest for Sir Arthur Conan Doyle: Thirteen Biographies in Search of a Life* (Carbondale: Southern Illinois University Press, 1987);

Christopher Redmond, *Welcome to America, Mr. Sherlock Holmes, Victorian America Meets Arthur Conan Doyle* (Toronto: Simon & Pierre, 1987);

Geoffrey Stavert, *A Study in Southsea, The Unrevealed Life of Doctor Arthur Conan Doyle* (Portsmouth, Hants: Milestone, 1987).

References:

William S. Baring-Gould, *Sherlock Holmes of Baker Street: A Life of the World's First Consulting Detective* (New York: Potter, 1962; London: Hart-Davis, 1962);

Baring-Gould, ed., *The Annotated Sherlock Holmes*, 2 volumes (New York: Clarkson N. Potter, 1967);

H. W. Bell, *Sherlock Holmes and Dr. Watson: A Chronology of Their Adventures* (London: Constable, 1932; Morristown, N.J.: Baker Street Irregulars, 1953);

Bell, ed., *Baker Street Studies* (London: Constable, 1934; Morristown, N.J.: Baker Street Irregulars, 1955);

T. S. Blakeney, *Sherlock Holmes: Fact or Fiction?* (London: Murray, 1932; Morristown, N.J.: Baker Street Irregulars, 1954);

Gavin Brend, *My Dear Holmes: A Study in Sherlock* (London: Allen & Unwin, 1951);

Bryce L. Crawford, Jr., and Joseph B. Connors, eds., *Cultivating Sherlock Holmes* (LaCrosse, Wis.: Sumac Press, 1978);

William D. Goodrich, *Good Old Index* (Dubuque, Iowa: Gasogene Press, 1987);

Richard Lancelyn Green, ed., *The Further Adventures of Sherlock Holmes, After Sir Arthur Conan Doyle* (Harmondsworth, U.K.: Penguin Books, 1985);

Green, ed., *The Sherlock Holmes Letters* (Iowa City: University of Iowa Press, 1986);

Michael Hardwick, *The Complete Guide to Sherlock Holmes* (London: Weidenfeld & Nicolson, 1986; New York: St. Martin's Press, 1986);

Michael and Mollie Hardwick, *The Sherlock Holmes Companion* (London: John Murray, 1962; Garden City, N.Y.: Doubleday, 1963);

Michael Harrison, *In the Footsteps of Sherlock Holmes* (London: Cassell, 1958; New York: Fell, 1960);

Harrison, *The London of Sherlock Holmes* (Newton Abbot: David & Charles, 1972; New York: Drake, 1976);

Harrison, *A Study in Surmise: The Making of Sherlock Holmes* (Bloomington, Ind.: Gaslight Publications, 1984);

Harrison, ed., *Beyond Baker Street: A Sherlockian Anthology* (Indianapolis & New York: Bobbs-Merrill, 1976);

Irving Kamil, "In the Beginning," *Baker Street Journal*, (new series) 33 (December 1983): 217-224;

H. R. F. Keating, *Sherlock Holmes: The Man and His World* (New York: Scribners, 1979);

Walter Klinefelter, *Sherlock Holmes in Portrait and Profile* (Syracuse, N.Y.: Syracuse University Press, 1963);

Ronald A. Knox, "Studies in the Literature of Sherlock Holmes," *Blue Book* (Oxford), 1 (July 1912): 111-132;

Tsukasa Kobayashi, Akane Higashiyama, and Masaharu Uemura, *Sherlock Holmes's London* (San Francisco: Chronicle Books, 1986);

Jon L. Lellenberg, *Nova 57 Minor, The Waxing and Waning of the Sixty-First Adventure of Sherlock Holmes* (Bloomington, Ind.: Gaslight Publications, 1990);

Ely M. Liebow, *Dr. Joe Bell: Model for Sherlock Holmes* (Bowling Green, Ohio: Bowling Green University Popular Press, 1982);

E. W. McDiarmid and Theodore C. Blegen, eds., *Sherlock Holmes: Master Detective* (LaCrosse, Wis.: Sumac Press, 1952);

Janice McNabb, *The Curious Incident of the Hound on Dartmoor: A Reconsideration of the Origins of the Hound of the Baskervilles* (Toronto: Bootmakers, 1984);

Sam Moskowitz, "Arthur Conan Doyle: A Study in Science Fiction," in his *Explorers of the Infinite* (Cleveland: World, 1963), pp. 157-171;

John Nieminski and Jon L. Lellenberg, eds., *"Dear Starrett—"/"Dear Briggs—"* (New York: Baker Street Irregulars, 1989);

Ian Ousby, *The Bloodhounds of Heaven* (Cambridge: Harvard University Press, 1976), pp. 140-175;

Michael Pointer, *The Public Life of Sherlock Holmes* (Newton Abbot: David & Charles, 1975; New York: Drake, 1975);

Donald A. Redmond, *Sherlock Holmes: A Study in Sources* (Downsview, Ontario: McGill-Queen's University Press, 1982);

S. C. Roberts, *Holmes and Watson: A Miscellany* (London: Oxford University Press, 1953);

Alvin E. Rodin and Jack D. Key, *Lost Worlds in Time, Space and Medicine: The Science Fiction of Arthur Conan Doyle* (Beavercreek, Ohio: KeyRod Literary Enterprises, 1988);

Rodin and Key, *The Medical Casebook of Dr. Arthur Conan Doyle: from Practitioner to Sherlock Holmes and Beyond* (Malabar, Fla.: Krieger, 1984);

Samuel Rosenberg, *Naked is the Best Disguise: The Death and Resurrection of Sherlock Holmes* (Indianapolis & New York: Bobbs-Merrill, 1974);

Dorothy L. Sayers, *Unpopular Opinions* (London: Gollancz, 1946);

Philip A. Shreffler, ed., *The Baker Street Reader: Cornerstone Writings about Sherlock Holmes* (Westport, Conn. & London: Greenwood Press, 1984);

Shreffler, ed., *Sherlock Holmes by Gas-Lamp: Highlights from the First Four Decades of The Baker Street Journal* (New York: Fordham University Press, 1989);

Edgar W. Smith, ed., *The Incunabular Sherlock Holmes* (Morristown, N.J.: Baker Street Irregulars, 1958);

Smith, ed., *Profile by Gaslight: An Irregular Reader about the Private Life of Sherlock Holmes* (New York: Simon & Schuster, 1944);

Vincent Starrett, *The Private Life of Sherlock Holmes* (New York: Macmillan, 1933; London: Nicholson & Watson, 1934; revised edition, Chicago: University of Chicago Press, 1960; revised and expanded edition, New York: Pinnacle, 1975);

Starrett, ed., *221B: Studies in Sherlock Holmes* (New York: Macmillan, 1940);

Chris Steinbunner and Norman Michaels, *The Films of Sherlock Holmes* (Secaucus, N.J.: Citadel Press, 1978);

Jack Tracy, *The Encyclopaedia Sherlockiana* (Garden City, N.Y.: Doubleday, 1977);

Tracy, ed., *Sherlock Holmes: The Published Apocrypha* (Boston: Houghton Mifflin, 1980);

Charles Viney, *Sherlock Holmes in London: A Photographic Record of Conan Doyle's Stories* (Wellingborough, U.K.: Equation Books, 1989; New York: Viking Penguin, 1989);

Guy Warrack, *Sherlock Holmes and Music* (London: Faber & Faber, 1947).

Papers:

Manuscript material by Conan Doyle is housed in the Berg Collection, New York Public Library; the Lilly Library, Indiana University, Bloomington; and the Harry Ransom Humanities Research Center, University of Texas, Austin. The largest collection of Conan Doyle material, including correspondence, is in the Arthur Conan Doyle Collection, Metropolitan Toronto Library, Toronto, Ontario; the largest collection of Sherlockiana in a public institution is the Philip S. and Mary Kahler Hench Collection, O. Meredith Wilson Library, University of Minnesota, Minneapolis; the largest private collection of Sherlockiana belongs to John Bennett Shaw, Santa Fe, New Mexico, and is designated for deposit at the University of Minnesota.

John Galsworthy

(14 August 1867 - 31 January 1933)

This entry was updated by Brian Murray (Loyola College in Maryland) from his entry in DLB 34: British Novelists, 1890-1929: Traditionalists.

See also the Galsworthy entries in DLB 10: Modern British Dramatists, 1900-1945: Part One *and* DLB 98: Modern British Essayists: First Series.

photograph by Pearl Freeman

BOOKS: *From the Four Winds*, as John Sinjohn (London: Unwin, 1897);

Jocelyn, as Sinjohn (London: Duckworth, 1898); as Galsworthy (St. Clair Shores, Mich.: Scholarly Press, 1972);

Villa Rubein: A Novel, as Sinjohn (London: Duckworth, 1900; New York & London: Putnam's, 1908);

A Man of Devon, as Sinjohn (Edinburgh & London: Blackwood, 1901);

The Island Pharisees (London: Heinemann, 1904; New York: Putnam's, 1904; revised edition, London: Heinemann, 1908);

The Man of Property (London: Heinemann, 1906; New York & London: Putnam's, 1906);

The Country House (London: Heinemann, 1907; New York & London: Putnam's, 1907);

A Commentary (London: Richards, 1908; New York & London: Putnam's, 1908);

Fraternity (London: Heinemann, 1909; New York & London: Putnam's, 1909);

Plays: The Silver Box; Joy; Strife (London: Duckworth, 1909; New York & London: Putnam's, 1909);

Justice: A Tragedy in Four Acts (London: Duckworth, 1910; New York: Scribners, 1910);

A Motley (London: Heinemann, 1910; New York: Scribners, 1910);

The Patrician (London: Heinemann, 1911; New York: Scribners, 1911);

The Little Dream: An Allegory in Six Scenes (London: Duckworth, 1911; New York: Scribners, 1911);

The Pigeon: A Fantasy in Three Acts (London: Duckworth, 1912; New York: Scribners, 1912);

Moods, Songs, and Doggerels (New York: Scribners, 1912; London: Heinemann, 1912);

The Inn of Tranquillity: Studies and Essays (London: Heinemann, 1912; New York: Scribners, 1912);

The Eldest Son: A Domestic Drama in Three Acts (London: Duckworth, 1912; New York: Scribners, 1912);

The Fugitive: A Play in Four Acts (London: Duckworth, 1913; New York: Scribners, 1914);

The Dark Flower (London: Heinemann, 1913;

New York: Scribners, 1913);

The Mob: A Play in Four Acts (London: Duckworth, 1914; New York: Scribners, 1914);

The Little Man and Other Satires (New York: Scribners, 1915; London: Heinemann, 1915);

A Bit o' Love: A Play in Three Acts (London: Duckworth, 1915; New York: Scribners, 1915); also published as *The Full Moon: A Play in Three Acts* (London: Duckworth, 1915);

The Freelands (London: Heinemann, 1915; New York: Scribners, 1915);

A Sheaf (New York: Scribners, 1916; London: Heinemann, 1916);

Beyond (New York: Scribners, 1917; London: Heinemann, 1917);

Five Tales (New York: Scribners, 1918; London: Heinemann, 1918);

Another Sheaf (London: Heinemann, 1919; New York: Scribners, 1919);

The Burning Spear, Being the Experiences of Mr. John Lavender in Time of War, as A. R. P-M (London: Chatto & Windus, 1919); as Galsworthy (New York: Scribners, 1923);

Addresses in America (New York: Scribners, 1919; London: Heinemann, 1919);

Saint's Progress (New York: Scribners, 1919; London: Heinemann, 1919);

Tatterdemalion (London: Heinemann, 1920; New York: Scribners, 1920);

The Foundations: An Extravagant Play in Three Acts (London: Duckworth, 1920; New York: Scribners, 1920);

The Skin Game: A Tragi-comedy in Three Acts (London: Duckworth, 1920; New York: Scribners, 1920);

In Chancery (London: Heinemann, 1920; New York: Scribners, 1920);

Awakening (New York: Scribners, 1920; London: Heinemann, 1920);

The First and the Last (London: Heinemann, 1920; enlarged edition, New York: Scribners, 1925);

To Let (New York: Scribners, 1921; London: Heinemann, 1921);

Six Short Plays (London: Duckworth, 1921; New York: Scribners, 1921);

The Forsyte Saga (New York: Scribners, 1922; London: Heinemann, 1922);

A Family Man, in Three Acts (London: Duckworth, 1922; New York: Scribners, 1922);

Loyalties: A Drama in Three Acts (London: Duckworth, 1922; New York: Scribners, 1923);

Windows: A Comedy in Three Acts for Idealists and Others (London: Duckworth, 1922; New York: Scribners, 1923);

Captures (London: Heinemann, 1923; New York: Scribners, 1923);

The Forest: A Drama in Four Acts (London: Duckworth, 1924; New York: Scribners, 1924);

The White Monkey (New York: Scribners, 1924; London: Heinemann, 1924);

Abracadabra & Other Satires (London: Heinemann, 1924);

Old English: A Play in Three Acts (London: Duckworth, 1924; New York: Scribners, 1925);

Caravan: The Assembled Tales of John Galsworthy (London: Heinemann, 1925; New York: Scribners, 1925);

The Show: A Drama in Three Acts (London: Duckworth, 1925; New York: Scribners, 1925);

The Silver Spoon (London: Heinemann, 1926; New York: Scribners, 1926);

Escape: An Episodic Play in a Prologue and Two Parts (London: Duckworth, 1926; New York: Scribners, 1927);

Verses New and Old (London: Heinemann, 1926; New York: Scribners, 1926);

Castles in Spain, & Other Screeds (London: Heinemann, 1927; New York: Scribners, 1927);

Two Forsyte Interludes: A Silent Wooing; Passers By (London: Heinemann, 1927; New York: Scribners, 1928);

Swan Song (New York: Scribners, 1928; London: Heinemann, 1928);

Exiled: An Evolutionary Comedy (London: Duckworth, 1929; New York: Scribners, 1930);

Four Forsyte Stories (New York: Fountain / London: Heinemann, 1929);

A Modern Comedy (London: Heinemann, 1929; New York: Scribners, 1929);

The Roof: A Play in Seven Scenes (London: Duckworth, 1929; New York: Scribners, 1931);

On Forsyte 'Change (London: Heinemann, 1930; New York: Scribners, 1930);

Soames and The Flag (London: Heinemann, 1930; New York: Scribners, 1930);

The Creation of Character in Literature (Oxford: Clarendon Press, 1931);

Maid in Waiting (London: Heinemann, 1931; New York: Scribners, 1931);

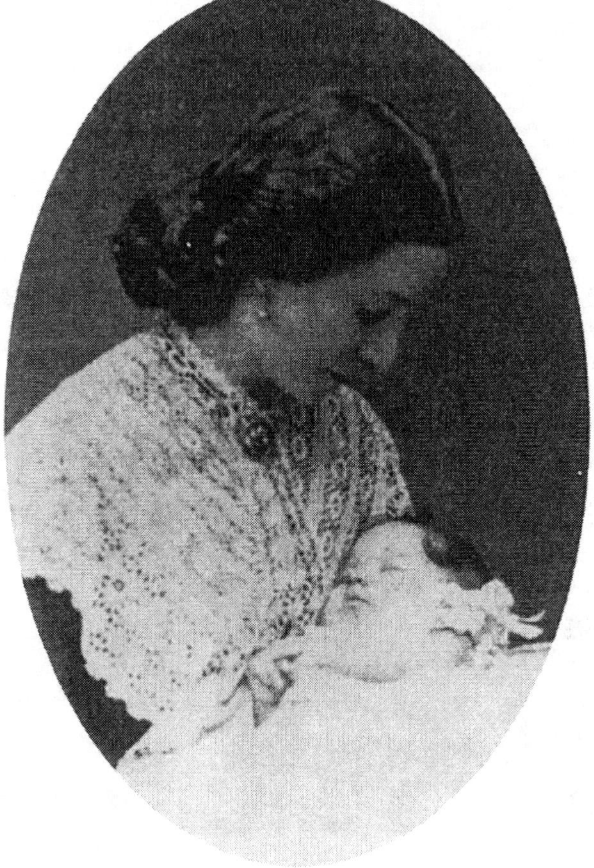

Galsworthy's parents: John Galsworthy, Sr., and Blanche Bartleet Galsworthy (holding the infant John)
(Collection of Mr. Rudolf Sauter)

Flowering Wilderness (London: Heinemann, 1932; New York: Scribners, 1932);
Author and Critic (New York: House of Books, 1933);
Over the River (London: Heinemann, 1933); republished as *One More River* (New York: Scribners, 1933);
End of the Chapter (New York: Scribners, 1934; London & Toronto: Heinemann, 1935);
The Collected Poems of John Galsworthy (New York: Scribners, 1934; London: Heinemann, 1934);
Forsytes, Pendyces, and Others (London: Heinemann, 1935; New York: Scribners, 1935);
The Winter Garden: Four Dramatic Pieces (London: Duckworth, 1935);
Glimpses and Reflections (London & Toronto: Heinemann, 1937).

Collections: *The Works of John Galsworthy*, 18 volumes (London: Heinemann, 1921-1925 [i.e., 1923-1924]);
The Works of John Galsworthy, Manaton Edition, 25 volumes (New York: Scribners, 1922-1929; London: Heinemann, 1923-1929);
The Novels, Tales and Plays of John Galsworthy, Devon Edition, 22 volumes (New York: Scribners, 1926-1929);
Plays, by John Galsworthy (New York & London: Scribners, 1928);
The Plays of John Galsworthy (London: Duckworth, 1929);
Candelabra: Selected Essays and Addresses (London: Heinemann, 1932; New York: Scribners, 1933);
Ex Libris John Galsworthy [quotations from his writings], compiled by John and Ada Galsworthy (London: Heinemann, 1933);
Galsworthy in His Humour (London: Duckworth, 1935).

During the first decade of the twentieth century, John Galsworthy was widely regarded as one of England's leading writers. As a novelist

Coombe Warren, the first of three houses Galsworthy's father built on adjoining sites on his twenty-four-acre estate in the London suburbs

and a playwright, he was commercially successful and critically esteemed. After World War I and until his death in 1933, Galsworthy remained one of Britain's most widely read and widely translated authors, even as younger, more experimental writers proclaimed his fiction obsolete. In November 1932 he was awarded the Nobel Prize for Literature. By 1950, however, Galsworthy's reputation had widely and radically declined, especially among academic critics who followed the lead of his earlier detractors—such as Virginia Woolf and D. H. Lawrence—and pointed to his not infrequent lapses into sentimentality and his tendency to "over-write." But as an increasing number of commentators are pointing out, Galsworthy was much more than an earnest "middlebrow" entertainer. Aside from his impressive accomplishments as a playwright, Galsworthy was the author of novels of considerable literary merit as well as historical worth. As Anthony West put it: "In the context of his time, he was, for his class, a master storyteller."

John Galsworthy's roots, on his father's side, were in Devon. His grandfather, a prosperous Plymstock merchant, came to London in 1833 and quickly increased his wealth by investing shrewdly in local real estate. John Galsworthy III, the novelist's father, was not only a practicing solicitor but a skilled businessman in his own right. "Old John" Galsworthy served as a director of several firms and also bought, sold, and managed a good deal of property in and around London. When he died in 1904 at the age of eighty-seven, he left an estate valued in the six figures, a generous portion of which provided each of his four children with a handsome legacy and a lifelong annuity. Galsworthy was devoted to his father, whose relentless business sense was paralleled by the unfailing gentleness he showed his children. In an autobiographical sketch written in 1919, Galsworthy observed that "my father really predominated in me from the start, and ruled my life. I was so truly and deeply fond of him that I seemed not to have a fair share of love left to give my mother (Blanche Bartleet Galsworthy)."

Galsworthy in his football uniform at Harrow

Galsworthy at Oxford

As Alec Fréchet points out, Galsworthy "admitted his mother's charm, elegance, taste, distinction, goodness: in short her nobility of character"; but his novels implicitly show that he could not tolerate her "lack of critical spirit, her dreadful conventionalism in every way, her maternalism." Indirectly, then, says Fréchet, Mrs. Galsworthy exerted a "major influence" by eventually arousing in her son "a reaction against the type of family life she had imposed on him."

With his younger brother and two sisters as his constant companions, Galsworthy's boyhood was happily spent in a series of three spacious homes built by his father on a twenty-four-acre estate near Epsom in suburban London. In his 1919 story "Awakening," Galsworthy sentimentally re-creates the well-upholstered leather and mahogany world of his childhood, casting himself as little Jon Forsyte—a hearty boy of eight whose "fancy" is "cooked" by the sea yarns and adventure tales he constantly devours.

In 1876 Galsworthy was sent to Saugeen, a small, family-run prep school in the scenic village of Bournemouth. He participated enthusiastically in many school activities even as he impressed his masters with the wide range of his reading. In 1891 Galsworthy entered Harrow, where he became a gymnastics champion, a football (soccer) captain, and a monitor. In 1886—the same year his parents moved to the Kensington district of London—he went up to New College, Oxford, to study jurisprudence in accord with his father's wishes. Galsworthy was better known at Oxford for the nattiness of his dress—which by this time included lavender gloves and a monocle—than for the brilliance of his mind or for his creativity. Although he took part in, and wrote, some amateur theatricals, Galsworthy spent considerable time socializing and gambling. He was, then, what he would much later call one of his own fictional creations—"a dyed in the wool Whyte-Melville type." Indeed, as an undergraduate, Galsworthy was quite fond of the writings of George

Whyte-Melville (1821-1878), a popular novelist best known for his frothy depictions of England's glib aristocrats at play.

After graduating with a second-class degree in 1889, Galsworthy returned to London and—soon afterward—began practicing law at Lincoln's Inn. Galsworthy had little interest in achieving distinction in the legal field; in fact, he still showed little evidence of possessing great ambition of any kind. In the summer of 1891, Galsworthy undertook the first of several long trips that would enable him to inspect some of the family's far-flung investments while sharpening his understanding of maritime law. Over the next two years he sailed to Canada, Russia, and South Africa, among other places. Galsworthy was eventually joined by his friend Ted Sanderson, whose doctor had prescribed sea air as a cure for fatigue and bad nerves.

In November 1892 Galsworthy and Sanderson sailed to Australia, and managed to visit several exotic spots along the way. They spent nearly a month on the Fiji Islands, going deep into the bush and gradually forging friendships with many native inhabitants. For the voyage back to Britain, Galsworthy and Sanderson boarded the clipper *Torrens,* whose first mate was an as-yet unpublished Polish author who called himself Joseph Conrad. After spending many evenings together on the poop deck of the *Torrens* talking of literature and life, Galsworthy and Conrad formed a friendship that deepened considerably over the next three decades. It was Conrad who eventually brought Galsworthy into a literary circle that included such figures as Ford Madox Ford and Edward Garnett, the eccentric and extraordinarily influential editor whom Ford once described as "London's literary—if Nonconformist—Pope."

Soon after returning from his Far Eastern cruise, Galsworthy established his own modest legal chambers at 3 Paper Buildings, Temple. But the law continued to bore him. Indeed, by the spring of 1895 he was devoting most of his energy not to the scrutiny of legal briefs and the acquisition of clients but to the secret study of the fictional techniques of best-selling authors and to the cultivation of his own writing skills. Galsworthy's literary ambitions finally became known to his family and friends when, in the spring of 1897, he paid for the publication of *From the Four Winds,* a collection of short stories written in heavy-handed imitation of Rudyard Kipling and Bret Harte. In later years, Galsworthy himself called this little volume "vile" and "dreadful" but admitted that the experience of seeing it through print made him "more proud" than did the publication "of any of its successors."

Galsworthy's decision to choose literature over the law was strongly supported—in fact, largely inspired—by Ada Cooper Galsworthy, the young wife of his first cousin Arthur, a military man. In turn, Galsworthy consoled Ada, who thought Arthur a bore and a brute and her marriage of convenience to him a hopeless mistake. Galsworthy and Ada had become lovers in September 1895. From the start, Galsworthy's sisters and a few of his closest friends knew of this affair, which at any rate became conspicuous—to everyone except, perhaps, Galsworthy's parents—during Arthur's two-year tour of duty in the Boer War. Galsworthy and Ada finally married on 23 September 1905, ten months after the death of Galsworthy's father and six months after Ada's divorce.

Ada's role in assisting Galsworthy's career was profound. She was his muse, his amanuensis, and—along with Garnett—his most trusted editor. In 1922 Galsworthy dedicated *The Forsyte Saga* in its entirety to Ada, noting that without her "encouragement, sympathy and criticism, I could never have become such a writer as I am."

Of equal importance was the fact that Ada functioned as the model for many of Galsworthy's heroines and helped him to formulate one of his principal themes. As Anthony West observes, Galsworthy—through his affair with Ada—"became an active participant in the sexual revolution that was transforming the patterns of middle class life in England." By frequently depicting characters who suffer guilt, disrepute, and often destruction as a result of breaking Victorian conventions of sexual behavior, Galsworthy—notes West—"gave expression to the secret fears and anxieties that revolution aroused in the members of his class."

Galsworthy's first novel, *Jocelyn* (1898), signals his interest in dealing with illicit sexual passion and its consequences. Its "unheroic hero"—as one reviewer called him—is the world-weary Englishman Giles Legard, who for ten years has been living on the Italian Riviera with his tedious wife Irma, a "confirmed invalid" addicted to morphine. When Giles falls in love with Jocelyn Ley—a moody, Ada-like young woman of twenty-two—he finds himself frighteningly alive, and so strongly "under the pressure of the throbbing passion which possessed him" that "conventional mo-

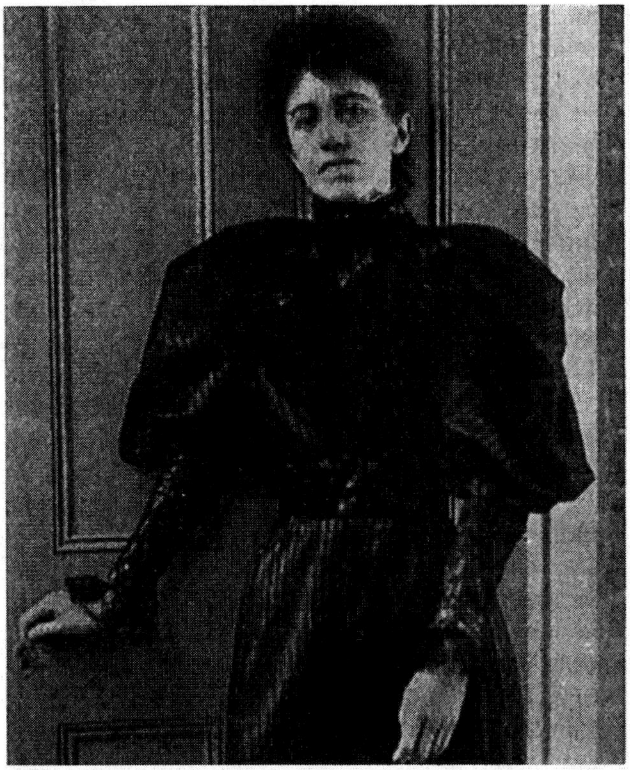

Galsworthy's sister Lilian and her husband, Georg Sauter. Their relationship, and Galsworthy's parents' opposition to it, inspired the plot of Villa Rubein.

rality ceased to be anything to him but a dim, murky shadow falling at times across the path of his longing." Giles is so determined to sate his longing that when he discovers Irma in a drug-induced coma, he does nothing to save her; instead, he spends the day making love to Jocelyn on a picturesque bluff overlooking an appropriately "angry white" sea. Of course, when Irma dies, Giles and Jocelyn are overwhelmed by guilt, and they separate. But soon they realize that their passion inextricably links them, and—at the novel's close—they rendezvous once more and vow that they will start anew, wiping out the past.

In later years, Galsworthy thought *Jocelyn* badly written and too emotionally explicit, and he refused to allow its republication. But when the novel first appeared, it drew some encouraging praise. The *Saturday Review* thought it rather too full of "tiresome psychological subtleties" but appraised it as being "above the common run of fiction." Conrad, in one of his avuncular letters to Galsworthy, described *Jocelyn* as "*desperately* convincing" and "inspiring."

Galsworthy's second novel, *Villa Rubein* (1900), tells of the love between Christian, a sensitive but sheltered English girl, and Harz, a German painter interested in radical politics and wholly devoted to his art. Critics have often suggested that *Villa Rubein* was at least partly inspired by the character of Galsworthy's sister Lilian and her marriage to the artist Georg Sauter, who—like Harz—worked hard to succeed after beginning life in a poor Bavarian family. But as Galsworthy biographer James Gindin has more recently pointed out, Sauter himself was not particularly political, and there is no firm evidence to suggest that his marriage into the Galsworthy family brought forth anything like the kind of hostility displayed by Christian's guardian in *Villa Rubein.* "Rather," writes Gindin, "the novel, in its rebellions against English insularity and its endorsements of the commitments to art and love, is another version of the story of Galsworthy himself." *Villa Rubein,* writes Gindin, "the first novel written during the years in which the 'critical' side of Galsworthy's nature was beginning to dominate the 'emotional,' is the process of his own learning and assimilation of new ideas—ideas about art, class, politics, and the influence of the Continent—that qualify the axioms of

Ada Cooper, who married Galsworthy's cousin, and later Galsworthy (Collection of Mr. Rudolf Sauter)

the commercial English middle-class bred and trained into him."

Villa Rubein was not widely noticed, but fared well with Galsworthy's new literary friends. H. G. Wells noted that its characters were "finely modelled and drawn." Ford wrote Galsworthy to say that the novel's prose was "lucid and excellent" and quite beyond the ordinary, but that "you are too kind, too deferential to your characters; you haven't enough contempt, enough of the *saeva indignatio.*" Ford prescribed more "vinegar."

There is plenty of vinegar in Galsworthy's third novel, *The Island Pharisees* (1904), the first of his books to bear his own name instead of the pseudonym John Sinjohn. Its hero, Richard Shelton, is a young Oxford-educated Englishman who finds his awareness of the world much broadened after a chance encounter with one Ferrand, a Belgian tramp. Ferrand, full of rage, tells Shelton of the harshness of life for the unwanted and the unmoneyed on London's meanest streets; Shelton grows uneasy as he considers more fully the utter apathy of the socially privileged. Indeed, like Shelton, Galsworthy was acutely aware that he could no longer share the sense of social complacency common among members of Britain's middle class. In the mid 1890s, at about the time he was starting his literary career, he had frequently left his flat on Victoria Street and taken his own excursions through the slums, amazed and angered by what he saw. A few years later, while "among the sparrows in the Champs-Elysées," he had struck up a friendship with a Belgian vagabond with whom he corresponded for years and upon whom he modeled Ferrand. Through this man, Galsworthy explained in 1932, "the world of failures, of the rolling stones, the underworld became disclosed to me."

Galsworthy worked closely with Edward Garnett on the writing of *The Island Pharisees*; in fact, because of Garnett's proddings, Galsworthy utterly recast the book three times before submitting it for publication to Garnett's employer, Gerald Duckworth. In his reader's report, Garnett urged Duckworth to accept *The Island Pharisees,* calling it "a really clever criticism of modern society—a criticism that nobody has yet made so ably." But Duckworth, pointing to the poor sales of *Jocelyn* and *Villa Rubein,* rejected the manuscript, which Joseph Conrad then successfully recommended to his own publisher, William Heinemann. The *Athenaeum* proclaimed *The Island Pharisees* an honest, subtle, and sometimes funny satire, but the *Nation* thought it nothing but a harangue full of "cheap cynicism" and "unconvincing psychology." Other reviews described the novel as too moralistic and too full of boring, predictable characters.

Still, with Garnett's encouragement, Galsworthy pressed on with another novel that would not only blast the upper middle class for its materialism and social apathy but would once again dramatize the agony of lovers who risk the execration of that bourgeois world by breaking social conventions to achieve romantic fulfillment. This was *The Man of Property* (1906), which is set in London and its suburbs in 1886.

Galsworthy spent more than two years revising and restructuring *The Man of Property,* often in order to accommodate Garnett's suggestions—or, more frequently, those of Ada. As Dudley Barker notes, Ada virtually stood at her husband's side as he completed *The Man of Property,* "discussing with him every word, every incident, every motive of character; and necessarily, discussing it

Galsworthy (second from left) with fellow playwrights J. M. Barrie (left) and Bernard Shaw (third from left), and producer Harley Granville Barker (photograph by E. O. Hoppé)

from the point of view of the woman who knew she was the model for Irene, and whose life was, obliquely, being argued."

Irene is the wife of "flat-shouldered, clean-shaven, flat-cheeked, flat-waisted" Soames Forsyte, a solicitor and prolific investor—"the man of property." Like most of the members of his large, nouveau riche London family, the thirty-one-year-old Soames is opportunistic, arrogant, and militantly unsentimental. Soames is unable fully to appreciate Irene, who exudes warmth, sweetness, and sensuality; he loves her, but tends to think of her as another piece of property—a portable, highly coveted work of art. Irene loathes Soames and eventually leaves him for Philip Bosinney, the gifted but impecunious architect who has been overseeing the construction of Soames's country mansion. In due course, Soames succeeds in financially ruining Bosinney, who later, in a distracted state after hearing that Soames has asserted his claim to Irene by raping her, is run over in London traffic. Soames also succeeds in breaking Irene, who, after Bosinney's death, is chillingly depicted as "huddled" into the sofa. With nowhere to go, she is pathetically "caged" once again with Soames.

The correlative plot in *The Man of Property* focuses on Old Jolyon Forsyte and his poignant attempts to reestablish intimacy with his son, Young Jolyon, Soames's cousin. Some years earlier, Young Jolyon had horrified the cold-blooded Forsytes by surrendering to honest passion and marrying a mere governess. Unlike the other Forsytes, the two Jolyons are for the most part sympathetically drawn. Young Jolyon, an amateur watercolorist, is blessed with what Galsworthy says is that rarest of all Forsyte traits—the ability to appreciate beauty. Old Jolyon (who is modeled in part on Galsworthy's father) is capable of "tenderness" and "gaiety."

The Man of Property is, on the whole, the most acidic of all Galsworthy's novels: he skewers the Forsytes and displays them pinned and wriggling on the wall. At one point, Soames is described as "carrying his nose with that aforesaid appearance of 'sniff,' as though despising an egg which he could not digest." Elsewhere, soon after Galsworthy describes the Forsytes' greed and usuriousness, he points out that of course they are all members of the Church of England, and even "paid for their pews, thus expressing in the most practical form their sympathy with the teachings of Christ."

Some reviewers were troubled not only by the causticity of *The Man of Property* but by its frank treatment of marital warfare; the *Spectator* said that the novel's "repellent details" rendered it "unacceptable for general reading." But its sales proved steady and brisk, particularly among university students, who, throughout the first de-

Galsworthy on his horse, Peggy, at Wingstone, his home in the Devon village of Manaton

cade of the twentieth century, proved receptive to many books which savaged the fixations of their parents' generation—books such as Samuel Butler's *The Way of All Flesh* (1903) and Edmund Gosse's *Father and Son* (1907). Thus, wrote Galsworthy in 1924, with *The Man of Property* "my name was made; my literary independence assumed; and my income steadily swollen."

Galsworthy added to his reputation and income when his first completed play, *The Silver Box* (1909), triumphantly debuted at London's Court Theatre on 25 September 1906, just six months after the publication of *The Man of Property*. Produced by Harley Granville Barker, *The Silver Box* aims to expose a cynical judicial process that inevitably accommodates the rich and the powerful. An unemployed workman is sentenced to a month's hard labor so that the debauched son of a wealthy member of Parliament can escape punishment and the besmirching of the family name. In subsequent plays, Galsworthy again focused on the injustices of the British legal system—perhaps most notably in *Justice* (1910), which dramatizes the horrors that befall a pathetic office clerk sentenced to solitary confinement for doctoring a check. *Justice* proved so potent and so popular that it prompted Home Secretary Winston Churchill to initiate a series of prison reforms.

Over the next twenty-five years Galsworthy wrote at least twenty-five plays, many of which were successfully produced. Indeed, it is probably safe to say that until the publication of *The Forsyte Saga* in the early 1920s, his fame owed more to his drama than his fiction. Galsworthy was generally perceived to be a practitioner of the Ibsen-inspired "new drama," his name often linked with such figures as Granville Barker and George Bernard Shaw. Like them, Galsworthy placed a premium on realistic characters and situations, and did not hesitate to confront controversial social issues. Thus, in *Strife* (1909), Galsworthy focuses on a long, bitter labor dispute at a tin mine in Cornwall. In *The Eldest Son* (1912), he sympathetically portrays a character who becomes pregnant out of wedlock—an artistic gesture still considered somewhat shocking to many theatergoers in Britain. Of these, *Strife* was a particular success, perhaps because its portrayal of the plight of workers was not burdened by an overtly didactic tone. "Although a few critics responded to the play as propaganda," notes biographer James Gindin, "one or two complaining because it was too socialistic, one because it was not socialistic enough, many, like Max Beerbohm, thought that the 'ardent socialism' of the play did not injure Galsworthy's estimable 'dramatic balance.' "

By 1907 Galsworthy had grown uneasy with his reputation as a "revolutionary" and had begun not only to adopt a less acerbic tone in his fiction but to depict more scrupulously upper-class virtue as well as upper-class vice. In *The Country House* (1907), he depicts the tradition-drunk Horace Pendyce as the very symbol of social reaction. Like his spaniel John, "a dog of conservative instincts," Pendyce begins "barking and showing his teeth" at "the approach of any strange thing." But Pendyce's wife, Margery, is a bastion of compassion and common sense.

In *Fraternity* (1909), Galsworthy continued his fictional analysis of the British class system, this time by overtly intermingling characters from the upper class with characters from the slums. Basically, *Fraternity* focuses on the liberal-minded, middle-aged novelist Hilary Dallison

Grove Lodge, Galsworthy's home in Hampstead

and his involvement with Ivy Barton, a slum girl who once modeled for his wife Bianca, a painter. Dallison has not felt a twinge of erotic desire for Bianca for years, but at the mere sound of Ivy's voice he can experience "a sensation as if his bones had been turned to butter." Dallison woos Ivy and wins her love; but in the end, he is unable to commit himself to "the little model" because his attraction to her electric sexuality is checked by his squeamishness in the face of her "traditions, customs, life." Dallison, then, is for Galsworthy typical of his class: he is paralytically self-conscious and terrified of deviating from propriety. But he is not an entirely unsympathetic figure. Unlike the Soames Forsyte depicted in *A Man of Property,* he does have a social conscience of sorts, and he is at least somewhat sensitive to beauty. One reviewer suggested that *Fraternity* proved that Galsworthy's "class hatred had gone mad." In fact, as a more perceptive critic noted with surprise, there is throughout the book "a leaven of humanitarianism."

In his 1923 preface to the Manaton Edition of *The Country House,* Galsworthy explains his belief that "birth, property, position" result from "luck," and that to assume otherwise is simply "ridiculous." "If those who had luck behaved as if they knew it," he argues, "the chances of revolution would sink to zero." These hardly radical notions are at the center of Galsworthy's political philosophy and inform such works as *The Country House* and *Fraternity.* Galsworthy admitted to "a temperamental dislike, not to say horror, of complacency." But like many nineteenth-century gentleman liberals before him, he backed social evolution, not revolution. As he put it elsewhere, "If my work has any mission, it is only a plea for proportion, and for sympathy and understanding between man and man."

Galsworthy himself was remarkably generous and for years donated huge sums to charities designed to help the poor and to numerous groups devoted to such causes as slaughterhouse reform and the abolition of vivisection. Of course, he was wealthy enough to be heroically philanthropic and still live quite comfortably. For years he and Ada kept a residence in London—most notably, from 1918 on, at Grove Lodge in the London suburb of Hampstead—as well as one in the Devon village of Manaton. They also spent a good deal of time traveling on the Continent and elsewhere. They journeyed to the United States on several occasions, once going as far west as Santa Barbara; they also toured South Africa and Brazil.

Yet every morning, wherever he was, Galsworthy religiously picked up his J-nib and wrote. Between 1910 and 1915 he completed six plays, three novels, and a book of reminiscences. The best of these undistinguished novels is perhaps *The Dark Flower* (1913), which Galsworthy described as an attempt to render the "psychology and the atmosphere of passion." To do so, he follows the sculptor Mark Lennan from young adulthood through middle age, focusing on his love life. At one point, Lennan finds himself desperately in love with his tutor's wife; at another, with Olive Cramier, a woman who—like Ada in her relationship with Arthur Galsworthy—feels imprisoned by her marriage. Later, when Lennan is forty-seven and contentedly married, he finds himself enamored of Nell Dromore, the lissome, "fiery" eighteen-year-old daughter of an old college friend. Finally, Lennan realizes that his faithful and devoted wife—not Nell—deserves his allegiance, and—more painfully—that he has reached the stage in life at which he must say "good-bye" to "the wild, the passionate, the new," to that "aching" which "never quite dies in a man's heart."

Many reviewers praised *The Dark Flower* for its lyricism, its gusto; but others thought it morbid, mawkish, or plainly immoral. When Sir Arthur Quiller-Couch, writing for the *Daily Mail*, called *The Dark Flower* "fatuous" and "sordid," Galsworthy answered him in a letter which reveals that, eight years after his marriage, he was still quite touchy about the subjects of adultery and divorce: "You can never have looked first hand into the eyes of an unhappy marriage, of a marriage whose soul has gone or never was there, of a marriage that lives on the meanest of all diets, the sense of property, and the sense of convention. . . . My gorge rises within me when I encounter that false glib view that the vow is everything, that people do better to go on living together (for nothing else *is* marriage) when one of them, or both, sicken at the other."

It has long been assumed that in describing Lennan's affair with Olive Cramier, Galsworthy gave one of his most exact accounts of his affair with Ada. It is now also known that Nell owed a great deal to Margaret Morris, a beautiful young dancer with whom Galsworthy had an intense but apparently platonic affair in 1911. In her 1967 memoir, Morris wrote of being "startled" by the accuracy with which Galsworthy, in *The Dark Flower*, "quoted almost word for word whole passages of dialogue that actually took place between us." As Galsworthy informed Quiller-Couch, "passion" is "that blind force which sweeps upon us out of the dark and turns us pretty well as it will."

Upon the outbreak of the First World War, Galsworthy began to donate all of his literary earnings directly to the war effort; his diary reveals that he had already contributed more than a thousand pounds to various relief agencies by early August 1914. Indeed, his novel *Beyond*, a monotonous work describing another Ada-like heroine's miseries and ecstasies, was cranked out simply for the healthy sum it yielded in American serial rights—a sum immediately turned over to a soldiers' fund. Galsworthy gave of his time as well as his money to help with the war effort. From the start of the war to its end, he turned out countless "appeal" letters that were run in the popular press: letters, as Ada later remembered, "for refugees, for camp libraries, for vegetables for the fleet, for cigarettes to soldiers, for London horses to be better fed, for Belgians to have a good Christmas dinner. . . ." He spent several months during the winter of 1916-1917 at a military hospital in France providing Swedish massage to bedridden soldiers. In April 1918 he assumed editorship of *Reveille*, a journal devoted largely to providing disabled soldiers with information about retraining and rehabilitation. With Galsworthy at its helm, *Reveille* had no trouble attracting pieces from such writers as Conrad, Thomas Hardy, J. M. Barrie, and Ralph Mottram.

Margaret Morris, the dancer with whom Galsworthy had an apparently platonic relationship in 1911 (Collection of Mr. Rudolf Sauter)

The war utterly absorbed Galsworthy and, as his diary shows, depressed him continually. In 1918, in what he called "a revenge of the nerves," he dashed off *The Burning Spear* (1919)—a "comedic satire" and the most curious of all his books. Published under the pseudonym A. R. P-M, *The Burning Spear* features a quixotic hero, John Lavender, who is normally a middle-aged suburbanite of "gentle disposition." But Lavender's wits become "somewhat addled from reading the writings and speeches of public men." As a result, he turns into a Hun-baiting jingoist who stumps the country for the Ministry of Propagation, retching forth the political and journalistic clichés he has fed upon for the past five years. In his preface to a 1923 edition of *The Burning Spear,* Galsworthy underlines his moral: "Was it not bad enough to have to bear the dreads and strains and griefs of the war without having to read day by day the venomous or nonsensical stuff which began pouring from tongues and pens soon after the war began and never ceased till months after the war stopped?" No doubt because his brother-in-law Georg Sauter had been interned throughout the war, Galsworthy found the constant, gleeful "insult to the enemy" especially hard to take.

The second of Galsworthy's books to be completed in the year of the Armistice was *Saint's Progress* (1919), a "legitimate" novel. It evokes the atmosphere of both the battlefield and the home front, and its tone is rather dark. But because *Saint's Progress* is free of the overwrought, perfumed prose style that characterizes much of Galsworthy's work published between 1910 and 1920, it is—like the rest of his later fiction—eminently readable. Its central character is a fifty-year-old Anglican priest, Edward Pierson, whose equanimity is repeatedly tested by Noel, his passionate and eager daughter of eighteen. The earnest Pierson is in some ways a sympathetic figure; but, as Galsworthy makes clear, he has spent too many years suppressing his own "devil of wild feeling" in order to adhere to dogma, and as a result is pathetically prone to misunderstand the sexually impulsive but noble-hearted Noel.

In a later preface to *Saint's Progress,* Galsworthy pointed out that Pierson was a "symbol of the English Church left somewhat high and dry by the receding waters of orthodox faith." The "ebbing" of faith in "orthodox religion" did not pain Galsworthy, who insisted that, like Pierson, the church had for too long "tried to command instead of being content to serve." He thought Christianity true only in "essence," not in fact. He hints at his own religious philosophy near the end of *Saint's Progress* in a scene which shows Pierson, now an army chaplain during the Great War, trying to comfort a dying young soldier. Pierson reminds the boy that he is going to God, and the boy responds with nothing more than "a smile of doubt, of stoic acquiescence." Pierson interprets that smile to mean "Waste no breath on me—you cannot help. Who knows—who knows? I have no hope, no faith; but I am adventuring." And Pierson is horrified. Was it possible, he wonders, to go through life and to confront death "uncertain, yet undaunted"? "Was that, then," he asks himself, "the uttermost truth, was faith a smaller thing?" For Galsworthy, a humanist and agnostic, the answer to both questions was yes.

During the summer of 1918, Galsworthy first conceived of what he hoped would become "the most sustained and considerable piece of fiction of our generation at least": a trilogy based on *The Man of Property* that would follow Soames and certain other Forsytes through the opening decades of the twentieth century. He immediately began work on "The Indian Summer of a Forsyte," the short story which links *The Man of Property* to its sequels, *In Chancery* (1920) and *To Let* (1921). In the beautifully shaped "Indian Summer," the dying Old Jolyon Forsyte strikes up a curious friendship with Irene, whose ill-treatment by Soames has moved him to pity and—as is revealed in *In Chancery*—to provide her with an annuity upon which she can live in France, beyond Soames's reach.

The Soames depicted in *In Chancery* is well into his forties and obsessed with producing an heir. To this end, he divorces Irene and marries Annette Lamotte, the daughter of a Soho restaurant proprietress. But to Soames's disappointment, Annette presents him with a daughter, Fleur. Irene, meanwhile, marries Young Jolyon, by whom she has a son, Jon—the heir Soames will never have.

To Let, which picks up in 1920, is basically the story of how Fleur and Jon fall in love and thus complicate the lives of Soames and Irene, who remain bitterly estranged. Eventually, Soames agrees to sanction Fleur's marriage to Jon. But Jolyon reluctantly writes Jon a letter explaining why Irene would be "utterly destroyed" by Jon's marriage to the daughter of a man who had, twenty years earlier, caused her immeasurable pain. Marry Fleur, writes Jolyon to Jon, and "your children . . . would be the grandchildren of Soames, as much as of your mother, of a man who once owned your mother as a man might own a slave." Jon withdraws his proposal, and a depressed Fleur, "on the rebound," marries Michael Mont, a member of an old-line, landowning family and a future baronet.

When it appeared in one volume in May 1925, the acclaim that greeted *The Forsyte Saga* convinced Galsworthy that he had finally produced his "passport" to "the shores of permanence." Crit-

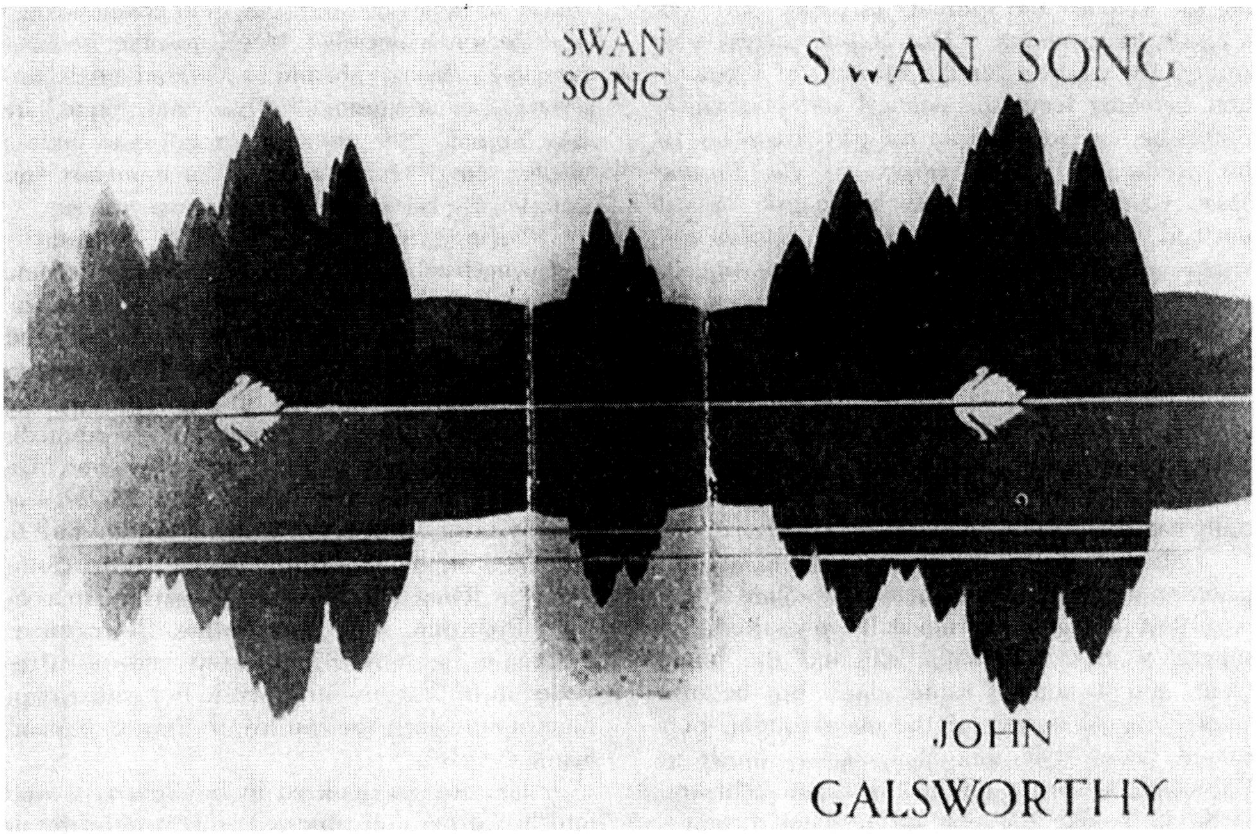

Dust jacket for Galsworthy's novel in which Soames Forsyte meets his end

ics praised the trilogy for its sweep and control and proclaimed Galsworthy a modern Thackeray. The book also brought Galsworthy a fortune in royalties. Within months of its publication, more than two million copies of *The Forsyte Saga* were sold in Britain and America. Forty-two years later, after being adapted for a television serial by the British Broadcasting Company, *The Forsyte Saga* was back on the British best-seller lists. In late 1969 *The Forsyte Saga* was broadcast in the United States by the National Educational Television network and became the first successful dramatic series ever broadcast on what was soon to be renamed the Public Broadcasting System. As a result of the N.E.T. series, paperback sales of *The Forsyte Saga* soared throughout North America.

Undoubtedly, much of the popularity of *The Forsyte Saga* has stemmed from the public's fascination with Soames, whose role in *The Man of Property* had assured him an exalted place among modern literature's most unsavory characters. In his first incarnation, Soames was basically an easy-to-hate caricature—perhaps the "classical embodiment of the Freudian anal-erotic type, complete with hoarding instinct," as the critic Bernard Bergonzi described him. But as *The Forsyte Saga* progresses, Soames becomes a more intricate, surprising character, even if taxes and interest rates still worry him greatly. By the middle of *To Let,* it is apparent that Soames's self-absorption has lessened as a result of his love for Fleur—that, in the wake of his many disappointments, he has mellowed.

The favorable treatment of Soames continues throughout *A Modern Comedy* (1929), another trilogy of Forsyte novels linked together by a pair of short stories, "A Silent Wooing" and "Passers By." In *The White Monkey* (1924), Soames emerges as a businessman of unusual integrity when he abjures the shady practices of a London insurance company whose board he has joined. In *The Silver Spoon* (1926), Soames dramatically expels from a party at Fleur's house the heiress Marjorie Ferrar after hearing her call Fleur a "born little snob." Ferrar takes Soames to court, where he is vindicated. In *Swan Song* (1928), Soames sacrifices his own life rescuing Fleur from a house fire she has accidentally caused. Quite literally, the villain becomes a hero.

Galsworthy leaving St. James's Palace after receiving the Order of Merit in 1929

Throughout the episodic *A Modern Comedy*, Soames is allowed interior monologues which reveal him to be disarmingly sensitive—even vulnerable. In "Passers By," the seventy-year-old Soames sees Irene for the first time in years and finds himself neither bitter nor angry but sad and full of regret. Automatically, he begins replaying long-buried images of Irene and of "her body crumpled and crushed into the sofa in the dark" on the night of Bosinney's death. "There sits a woman," he realizes, "that I have never known."

Soames is often visited by crystalline recollections of his youth—when his mother called him "Summy"—and by thoughts of his inevitable demise. In *Swan Song*, Soames's meditations on death closely parallel those of Old Jolyon Forsyte in "An Indian Summer of a Forsyte." Like Old Jolyon, Soames becomes aware that he has been a bit too compulsive in his pursuit of money and property. One afternoon, as he sits in a postprandial glow, smoking a cigar and staring out the window, it occurs to him that, as an adult, he has utterly forgotten about the natural world. "With age," he realizes, "one suffered from the feeling that one might have enjoyed things more. Cows for instance, and rooks, and good smells."

In *The Silver Spoon*, in one of the most affecting passages in all of Galsworthy's fiction, Soames—the man who once "elbowed" his way everywhere—stops along the roadside to tend to a pig struck by his car. The sight of the dying pig, snorting and grunting in a ditch, stirs "a sort of fellow feeling" in Soames and moves him to meditate once more upon death. He resolves to make plans that will insure his burial in some unmarked corner, in the shade of "an apple-tree or something." "The less people remembered him," Soames decides, "the better."

In fact, however, when it was revealed with the July 1928 publication of *Swan Song* that Soames had been killed off, his death was front-page news in several London newspapers. With this kind of publicity, it is not surprising that *Swan Song* quickly went through several editions and that *A Modern Comedy* was a prodigious success when it appeared as an omnibus volume a year later.

The change in Soames's character reflects the change in Galsworthy's own attitude toward English society. He was in his mid-fifties when he began *A Modern Comedy* and had come through the Great War with his sense of citizenship strengthened. He was happily married and had long since become successful enough to settle scores with those among his friends and relatives who once thought him dotty for thinking that he could write novels. Indeed, throughout the 1920s Galsworthy was easily England's most honored author. In 1921 he was elected the first president of the P.E.N. Club, the writers' society that sought world harmony through communication. Between 1920 and 1931 he was awarded honorary Litt.D. degrees by Manchester, Dublin, Sheffield, Cambridge, Oxford, and Princeton universities. In June 1929 he was entered into the Order of Merit.

The authorial voice that informs Galsworthy's later works is often that of the humane but pragmatic public figure: the ex-angry young man turned elder statesman who is eager to offer the breadth of his knowledge. In *A Modern Age*, for example, Michael Mont's parliamentary career—which intersects with the "General Strike" of 1926—enabled Galsworthy to call atten-

Galsworthy at work on Maid in Waiting

tion to certain political schemes he favored, including those of Sir James Foggart, who argued that a policy of setting up underemployed young Englishmen in the dominions would reduce the number of British slums while increasing the number of staunch Britons around the world. In *Maid in Waiting* (1931), the first volume of his final trilogy, *End of the Chapter* (1934), Galsworthy again allows Mr. and Mrs. Hilary Cherrell—Michael Mont's aunt and uncle—to champion, as they did in *Swan Song*, the utilization of the unemployed in a "National Slum Clearance Scheme" that would, as Mrs. Cherrell puts it, "kill the two birds with one stone."

End of the Chapter, which focuses on various members of the Cherrell family, was written largely at Bury House—a fifteen-bedroom Sussex mansion which Galsworthy purchased in 1926 as a residence for his nephew Rudolf Sauter and his wife, and as a country retreat for himself. Galsworthy employed a cook, several maids, and a squad of gardeners at Bury. Predictably, Squire Galsworthy was consistently kind to his employees. He gave them all lifetime security with higher-than-scale wages and for some he built homes in the nearby village.

No doubt Bury House, with its formal gardens and surrounding acreage, provided Galsworthy with an especially conducive atmosphere in which to construct the elegant and civilized world of the Cherrells, to whom Fleur is related through her marriage to Michael Mont. "Seated" since 1217 at Condaford Grange at Oxfordshire, the Cherrells represent—as Galsworthy himself discreetly put it—"the older type of family with more tradition and sense of service than the Forsytes." According to Galsworthy, this type of family, "much neglected" in modern fiction, deserved scrutiny precisely because it was "dying out."

Galsworthy does not apotheosize the Cherrells, but his treatment of them and of their vanishing world is a good deal less than hostile. James Gindin, one of Galsworthy's most eloquent critics, has suggested that by inventing the Cherrells, Galsworthy "wrote the family he wished he had had, one of gentle anthropologists and radical churchmen who could change and care, one in which aristocracy was not a matter of striving or class superiority, but one of calm responsibility and socialistic concern."

Dust jacket for separate publication of the first volume of Galsworthy's End of the Chapter *trilogy*

Dinny Cherrell, the central character throughout the trilogy, is certainly sympathetically drawn: she is perhaps, as Catherine Dupré has suggested, "Galsworthy's final portrait of an ideal woman, combining the proud dignity of Ada with the youthful vitality and optimism he had met with in Margaret Morris." In *Maid in Waiting,* Dinny saves her brother Hubert from extradition to Bolivia on a trumped-up murder charge. In *Flowering Wilderness* (1932), she comforts her lover, Wilfred Desert, a well-known agnostic poet. Desert is greatly disliked by some in Dinny's circle because years earlier, while stationed in the Middle East, he had refused to die "for a gesture that I don't believe in." At the point of a pistol, he had renounced Christianity and had pretended to admit to the truth of the Islamic faith. In *One More River* (1933), Dinny supports her sister Clare, who is regularly abused by her husband, a horsewhip-wielding sadist.

Flowering Wilderness is probably the best of these novels—and is certainly one of the better novels in the Galsworthy canon. The "burning tension" and the "classic rigour" that Alec Fréchet finds displayed in *Flowering Wilderness* derive in part from the fact that the novel is refreshingly free of long stretches of ornate prose and contains no meandering subplots. Desert is especially convincing as the intense young veteran whose experience in the war left him, as Dinny puts it, "bitter about the way lives are thrown away, simply spilled out like water at the orders of people who don't know what they're about"; who has both "contempt for convention" and yet enough residual respect for the customs of his class to be wounded deeply when the press and his former comrades accuse him of cowardice and betrayal.

In the *New York Times* of 13 November 1932, Lionel Stevenson proclaimed *Flowering Wilderness* a finer book than *The Man of Property,* but Stevenson was by then a well-known Galsworthy supporter. Most English and American reviewers regarded *Flowering Wilderness* politely—sometimes warmly—but without real empressement. By the early 1930s Galsworthy's standing within Anglo-American literary circles had become a bit shaky, even though—or perhaps because—his popularity among the reading public had soared. After Galsworthy died of a brain tumor in January 1933, just two months after winning the Nobel Prize, foreign critics hailed his work with a reverence that probably embarrassed many of their English colleagues. One Argentine reviewer favorably compared Galsworthy to Jane Austen and Henry James; an Italian eulogist called him another Marcel Proust.

In England, Galsworthy's reputation had been dealt its first truly damaging jolt by Virginia Woolf in her witty 1924 monograph, *Mr. Bennett and Mrs. Brown.* Like Arnold Bennett and H. G. Wells, Galsworthy—argued Woolf—was a well-meaning but superficial writer whose novels were full of predictable, stereotypical characters. Four years later, in an equally influential essay, D. H. Lawrence described Galsworthy as a cynical vulgarian who poured "a sauce of sentimental savouriness" over everything he wrote, including *The Man of Property.* The "sentimentalising of Old Jolyon Forsyte," complained Lawrence, "fatally blemished" *The Man of Property,* which otherwise "has the element of a very great novel, a very great satire."

But as Galsworthy's career was being reexamined in the 1920s and early 1930s, other British and American critics, while admitting to his weaknesses, called attention to some of his strengths

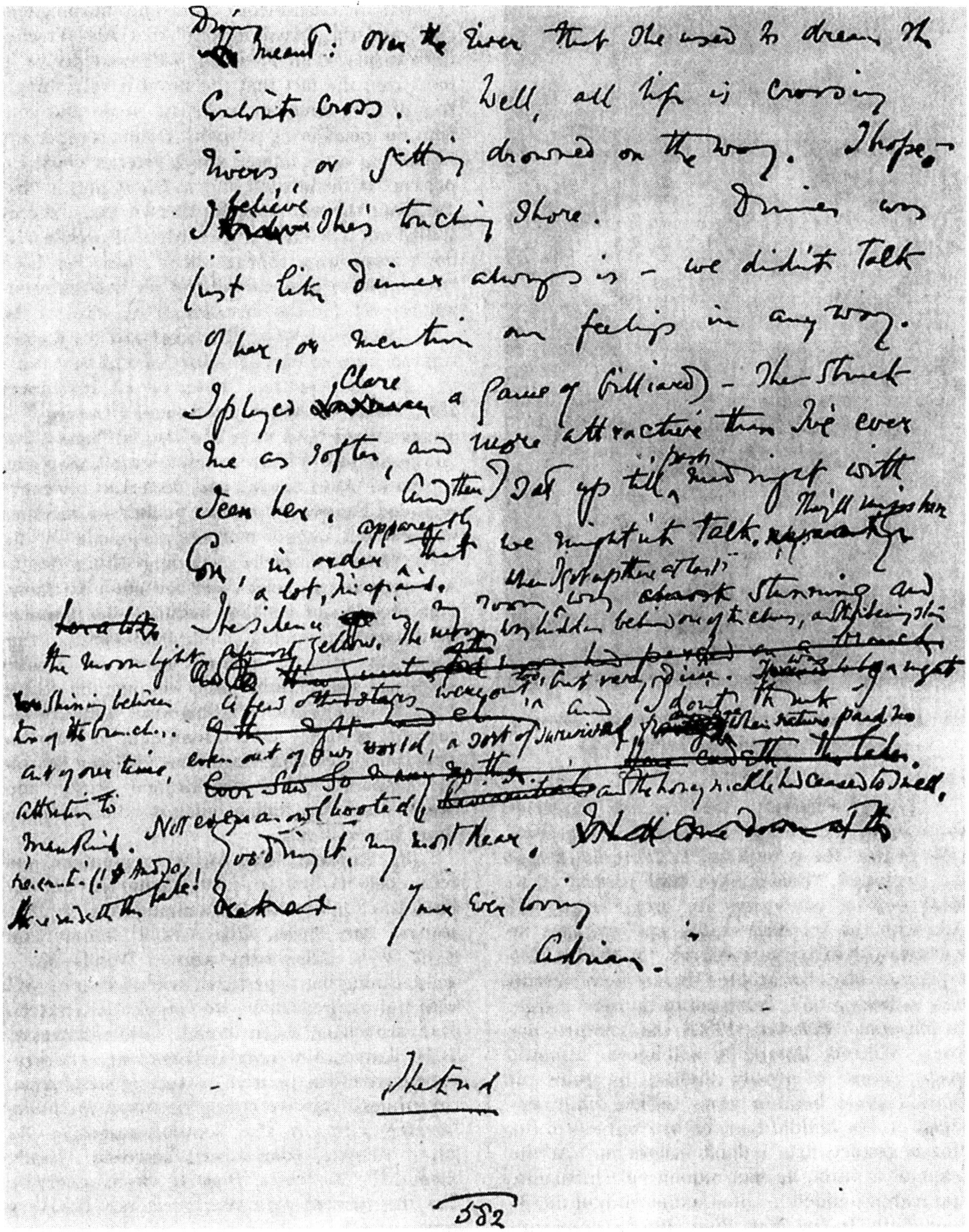

Dinny meant: Over the River that she used to dream of
... Cross. Well, all life is crossing
rivers or getting drowned on the way. I hope –
I believe she's touching shore. Dinner was
just like dinner always is – we didn't talk
of her, or mention our feelings in any way.
I played Clare a game of billiards – she struck
me as softer, and more attractive than I've ever
seen her. And then I sat up till past midnight with
Con, in order, apparently, that we mightn't talk.

Good night, my dearest.
Your ever loving
Adrian.

The End

582

Last page of the manuscript for Over the River

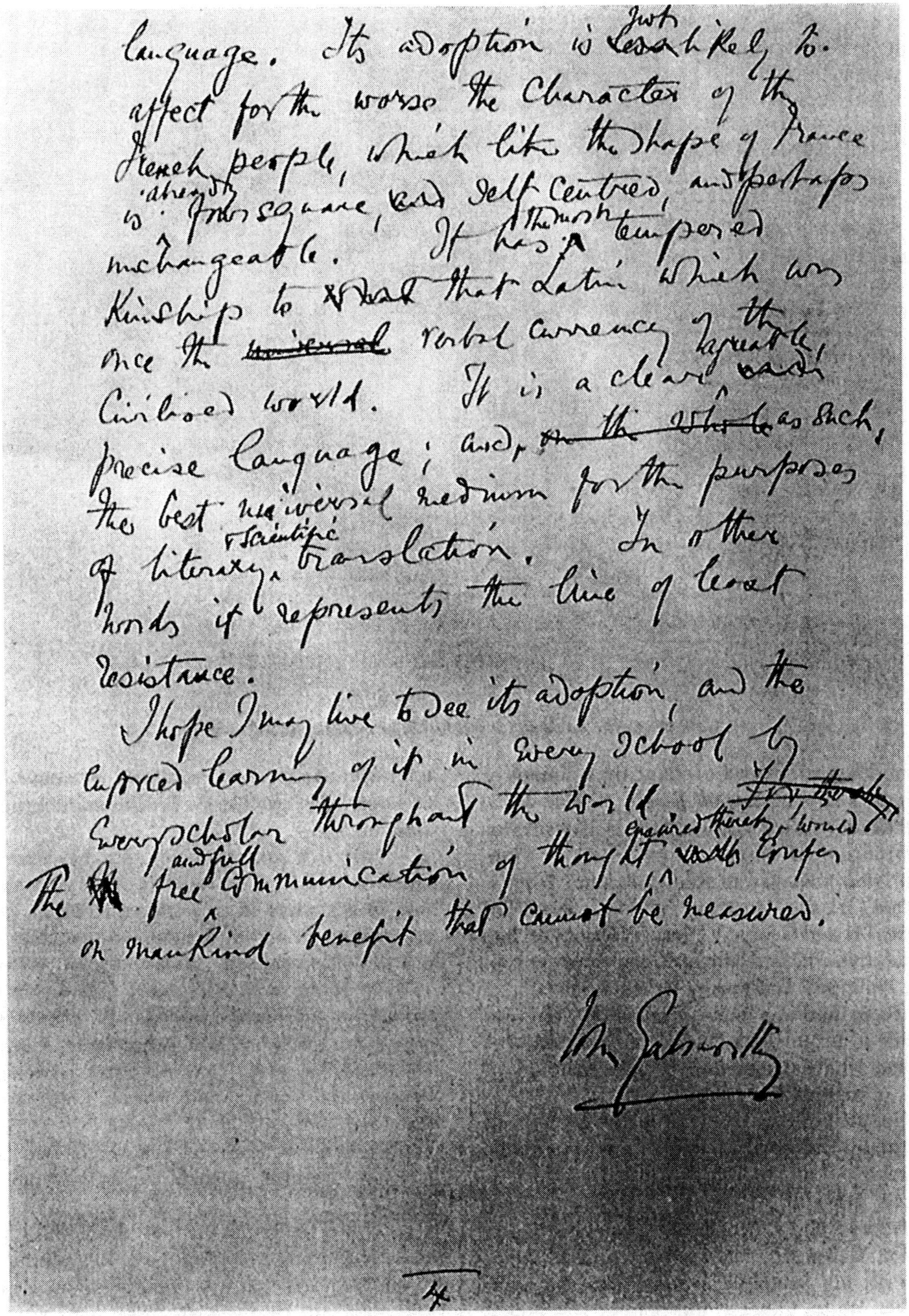

language. Its adoption is just likely to affect for the worse the character of the French people, which like the shape of France is already foursquare, and self centred, and perhaps unchangeable. It has the most tempered kinship to that Latin which was once the verbal currency of the civilised world. It is a clear, agreeable, precise language; and, as such, the best universal medium for the purposes of literary & scientific translation. In other words it represents the line of least resistance.

I hope I may live to see its adoption, and the enforced learning of it in every school by every scholar throughout the world. The free and full communication of thought engendered thereby would confer on mankind benefit that cannot be measured.

John Galsworthy

4

Last page of the manuscript for Galsworthy's essay "For a Better Understanding" (Collection of R. H. Sauter)

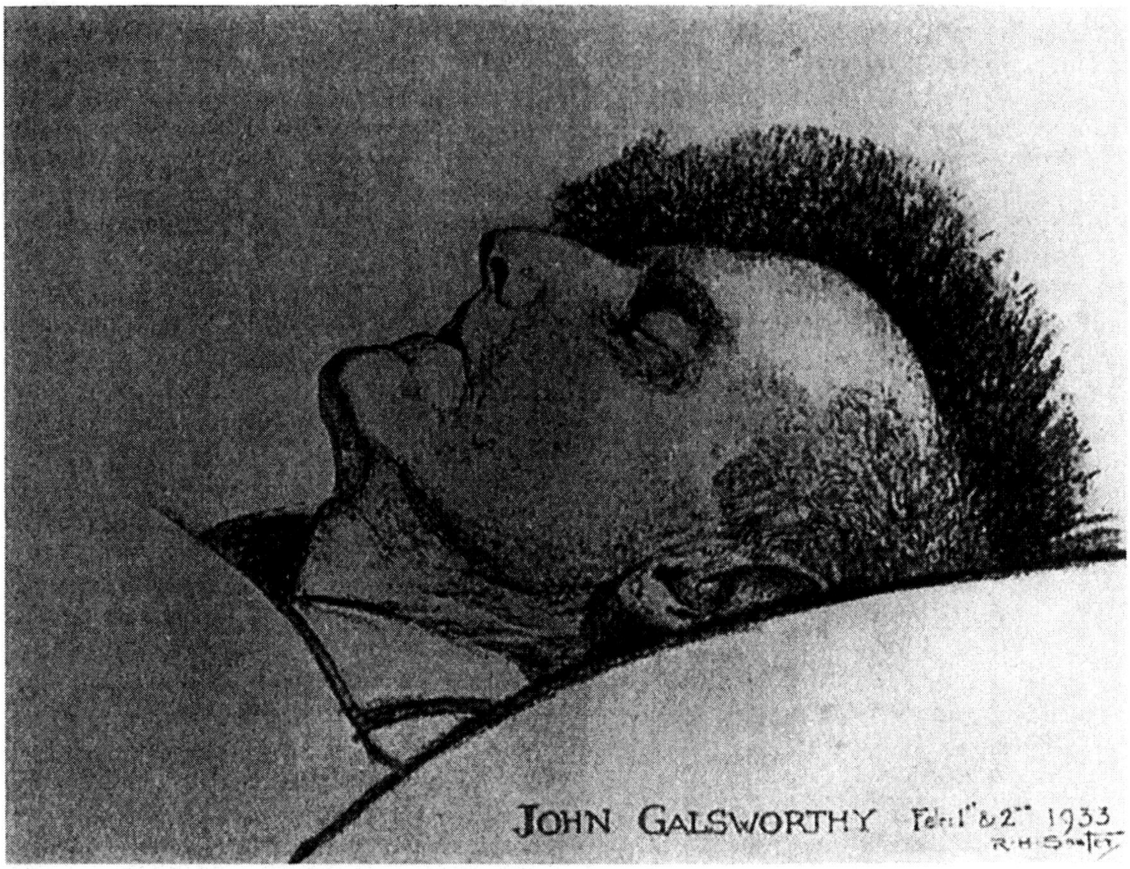

Galsworthy after his death, as sketched by his nephew, Rudolf Sauter

and, in doing so, helped to shape the opinions of later critics. In the *English Journal* of May 1925, J. B. Priestley called Galsworthy a brilliant "critic and historian of contemporary social developments" who managed to forever capture "the established if not decaying middle classes of Edward VII and George V," just as Honoré de Balzac had immortalized "the insurgent bourgeois of Louis Philippe." Galsworthy lacked Balzac's "creative force and demonic imagination" but was still able to produce his "lively" representation of a period while maintaining "a high standard of sanity, of dignity, and of wit."

Joseph J. Reilly observed in the *Bookman* in 1932 that Galsworthy's mind was essentially "feminine"—a quality which revealed itself in his "smooth, graceful, supple" style. With a "quicker sensitiveness" and a "deeper pity" than his contemporaries, Galsworthy "saw poverty and its attendant evils not primarily as superscientific questions like Wells . . . not as things to be triumphed over by an imagination, a fairy godmother, or a happy turn of fortune like Barrie, but first of all as objects of human sympathy and after that as intolerable effects of a social and economic situation over which well-to-do Britons must be answerable."

Still, it is not surprising that Lawrence and Woolf should have so roundly thrashed Galsworthy. To advocates of an artistic revolution, he was an antique: an artistic Forsyte unashamedly sticking to "old-fashioned" literary forms. When, in 1920, a young man had asked Galsworthy what writers an ambitious novelist-to-be should read, he was not told to consult James Joyce, Katherine Mansfield, or even Conrad; read Dickens, instructed Galsworthy, and Robert Louis Stevenson, "and above all, *W. H. Hudson.*" In 1915, in a preface to *Green Mansions,* Galsworthy had called Hudson "the most valuable [writer] our age possesses."

In *John Galsworthy's Life and Art* (1987)—a particularly thorough biography—James Gindin persuasively argues that it is "very much an oversimplification" to continue to insist that, after *The Man of Property,* Galsworthy the writer steadily declines. "The bulk of Galsworthy's work," Gindin insists, "comprises a considerable achievement."

Much of that work, he writes, "and especially the fiction written after the First World War, reveals considerable quality and complexity, particularly as the creation of a man who sometimes found polite smiling silence comfortable and self-expression sometimes difficult." Still, as Gindin notes, Galsworthy "was self-critically dissatisfied with some of his work and he knew that he was not as good a writer as he wanted to be."

Moreover, as John Batchelor notes, Galsworthy's "real strength" was for the sort of "social comedy" he demonstrated in *The Man of Property* and in the plays *The Silver Box, Strife,* and *Justice.* These works make their points cleanly, confidently, "without resorting to Shavian 'arias.' " But unfortunately, Galsworthy "did not know his own talent, and was determined to be, like Wells and Shaw, a polymath and prophet, a critic of the age." The result was that he created too many humorless, propagandistic works populated by flat characters who stand too baldly for good or for bad.

As Galsworthy bibliographers Earl and H. Ray Stevens suggest, one can perhaps better assess Galsworthy's stature once one is willing to view him as "the last major Victorian writer." Like many of the very best Victorian novelists, Galsworthy was sometimes facile, prolix, and didactic; but like them, he was also repeatedly able to construct well-built narratives and to invent characters—such as Soames Forsyte and Wilfred Desert—who are subtle and complex enough to intrigue modern readers.

Letters:

Letters from John Galsworthy, 1900-1932, edited by Edward Garnett (London: Cape, 1934; New York: Scribners, 1934);

Margaret Morris, *My Galsworthy Story Including 67 Hitherto Unpublished Letters* (London: Owen, 1967);

John Galsworthy's Letters to Leon Lion, edited by Asher Boldon Wilson (The Hague: Mouton, 1968).

Bibliographies:

H. V. Marrot, *A Bibliography of the Works of John Galsworthy* (London: Mathews & Marrot / New York: Scribners, 1928);

Earl E. Stevens and H. Ray Stevens, *John Galsworthy: An Annotated Bibliography of Writings about Him* (De Kalb: Northern Illinois University Press, 1980).

Biographies:

H. V. Marrot, *The Life and Letters of John Galsworthy* (London: Heinemann, 1935; New York: Scribners, 1936);

M. E. Reynolds, *Memories of John Galsworthy by His Sister* (London: Hale, 1936; New York: Stokes, 1937);

R. H. Mottram, *For Some We Loved: An Intimate Portrait of John and Ada Galsworthy* (London: Hutchinson, 1956);

Dudley Barker, *The Man of Principle: A View of John Galsworthy* (London: Heinemann, 1963; New York: Stein & Day, 1963);

Rudolf Sauter, *Galsworthy the Man: An Intimate Portrait* (London: Owen, 1967);

Catherine Dupré, *John Galsworthy: A Biography* (London: Collins, 1976; New York: Coward, McCann & Geoghegan, 1976);

James Gindin, *The English Climate: An Excursion into a Biography of John Galsworthy* (Ann Arbor: University of Michigan Press, 1979);

Gindin, *John Galsworthy's Life and Art: An Alien's Fortress* (Ann Arbor: University of Michigan Press, 1987).

References:

John Batchelor, *The Edwardian Novelists* (London: Duckworth, 1982), pp. 183-202;

William Bellamy, *The Novels of Wells, Bennett and Galsworthy: 1890-1910* (London: Routledge & Kegan Paul, 1971; Totowa, N.J.: Barnes & Noble, 1971);

R. H. V. Bloor, *The English Novel from Chaucer to Galsworthy* (London: Nicholson & Watson, 1935);

Henry Seidel Canby, "Galsworthy: An Estimate," *Saturday Review of Literature,* 9 (18 March 1933): 485-487;

Ford Madox Ford, "Galsworthy," *American Mercury,* 37 (April 1936): 448-459;

Alec Fréchet, *John Galsworthy: A Reassessment* (Totowa, N.J.: Barnes & Noble, 1982);

Richard Gill, *Happy Rural Seat: The English Country House and the Literary Imagination* (New Haven & London: Yale University Press, 1972);

David Leon Higdon, "John Galsworthy's *The Man of Property:* 'now in the natural order of things,' " *English Literature in Transition,* 21 (1978): 149-157;

David Holloway, *John Galsworthy* (London: Morgan-Grampion, 1968);

Jefferson Hunter, *Edwardian Fiction* (Cambridge, Mass.: Harvard University Press, 1982);

Richard M. Kain, "Galsworthy, the Last Victorian Liberal," *Madison Quarterly,* 4 (1944): 84-94;

Sheila Kaye-Smith, *John Galsworthy* (New York: Holt, 1916);

Frank Kermode, "The English Novel, circa 1907," in *Twentieth Century Literature in Retrospect,* edited by Reuben A. Brower (Cambridge, Mass.: Harvard University Press, 1971), pp. 45-64;

D. H. Lawrence, "John Galsworthy," in *Scrutinies by Various Writers,* edited by Edgell Rickword (London: Wishart, 1928);

J. D. Leavis, *Fiction and the Reading Public* (London: Chatto & Windus, 1932);

Kathryne S. McDorman, "Imperialism Debit and Credit—Some Edwardian Authors' Views," *Illinois Quarterly,* 43 (Summer 1981): 41-50;

Peter McQuitty, "The Forsyte Chronicles: A Nineteenth Century Liberal View of History," *English Literature in Transition,* 23 (1980): 99-114;

R. H. Mottram, *John Galsworthy* (London: Longmans, Green, 1953);

Herman Ould, *John Galsworthy* (London: Chapman & Hall, 1934);

Joseph John Reilly, "John Galsworthy—An Appraisal," *Bookman,* 74 (January-February 1932): 483-493;

William J. Scheick, "Chance and Impartiality: A Study Based on the Manuscript of Galsworthy's *Loyalties,*" *Texas Studies in Language and Literature,* 17 (1975): 653-672;

Leon Schlit, *John Galsworthy: A Survey* (New York: Scribners, 1928; London: Heinemann, 1929);

Sanford Sternlicht, *John Galsworthy* (Boston: Twayne, 1987);

Earl E. Stevens, "John Galsworthy," in *British Winners of the Nobel Prize,* edited by Walter Kidd (Norman: University of Oklahoma Press, 1973), pp. 130-167;

Harold Ray Stevens, "Galsworthy's *Fraternity:* The Closed Door and the Paralyzed Society," *English Literature in Transition,* 19 (1976): 283-298;

Walter H. R. Trumbauer, *Gerhart Hauptmann and John Galsworthy: A Parallel* (Philadelphia: University of Pennsylvania Press, 1917);

Anthony West, Introduction to *The Galsworthy Reader* (New York: Scribners, 1967);

Virginia Woolf, *Mr. Bennett and Mrs. Brown* (London: Hogarth, 1924).

Papers:

Some of John Galsworthy's manuscripts and letters are held by the Bodleian Library, Oxford University; Houghton Library, Harvard University; and Firestone Library, Princeton University.

Thomas Hardy

(2 June 1840 - 11 January 1928)

This entry was updated by Norman Page (University of Nottingham) from his entry in DLB 18: Victorian Novelists After 1885.

See also the Hardy entry in DLB 19: British Poets, 1880-1914.

Thomas Hardy

BOOKS: *Desperate Remedies: A Novel,* anonymous (3 volumes, London: Tinsley, 1871; 1 volume, New York: Holt, 1874);

Under the Greenwood Tree: A Rural Painting of the Dutch School, anonymous (2 volumes, London: Tinsley, 1872; 1 volume, New York: Holt & Williams, 1873);

A Pair of Blue Eyes: A Novel (3 volumes, London: Tinsley, 1873; 1 volume, New York: Holt & Williams, 1873);

Far from the Madding Crowd (2 volumes, London: Smith, Elder, 1874; 1 volume, New York: Holt, 1874);

The Hand of Ethelberta: A Comedy in Chapters (2 volumes, London: Smith, Elder, 1876; 1 volume, New York: Holt, 1876);

The Return of the Native (3 volumes, London: Smith, Elder, 1878; 1 volume, New York: Holt, 1878);

The Trumpet-Major: A Tale (3 volumes, London: Smith, Elder, 1880; 1 volume, New York: Holt, 1880);

A Laodicean: A Novel (New York: Harper, 1881; 3 volumes, London: Low, Marston, Searle & Rivington, 1881);

Two on a Tower: A Romance (3 volumes, London: Low, Marston, Searle & Rivington, 1882; 1 volume, New York: Holt, 1882);

The Mayor of Casterbridge: The Life and Death of a Man of Character (2 volumes, London: Smith, Elder, 1886; 1 volume, New York: Holt, 1886);

The Woodlanders (3 volumes, London & New York: Macmillan, 1887; 1 volume, New York: Harper, 1887);

Wessex Tales: Strange, Lively, and Commonplace (2 volumes, London & New York: Macmillan, 1888; 1 volume, New York: Harper, 1888);

A Group of Noble Dames (London: Osgood, McIlvaine, 1891; New York: Harper, 1891);

Tess of the d'Urbervilles: A Pure Woman Faithfully Presented (3 volumes, London: Osgood, McIlvaine, 1891; 1 volume, New York: Harper, 1892);

Life's Little Ironies: A Set of Tales with Some Colloquial Sketches Entitled "A Few Crusted Characters" (London: Osgood, McIlvaine, 1894; New York: Harper, 1894);

Jude the Obscure (London: Osgood, McIlvaine, 1895; New York: Harper, 1895);

The Well-Beloved: A Sketch of a Temperament (London: Osgood, McIlvaine, 1897; New York: Harper, 1897);

Wessex Poems and Other Verses, with Thirty Illustrations by the Author (London: Harper, 1898; New York: Harper, 1899);
Poems of the Past and the Present (London: Harper, 1901; New York: Harper, 1901);
The Dynasts, Part First (London: Macmillan, 1904; New York: Macmillan, 1904);
The Dynasts, Part Second (London: Macmillan, 1906; New York: Macmillan, 1906);
The Dynasts, Part Third (London: Macmillan, 1908; New York: Macmillan, 1908);
Time's Laughingstocks and Other Verses (London: Macmillan, 1909);
A Changed Man, The Waiting Super, and Other Tales (London: Macmillan, 1913; New York: Harper, 1913);
Satires of Circumstance: Lyrics and Reveries with Miscellaneous Pieces (London: Macmillan, 1914);
Selected Poems (London: Macmillan, 1916);
Moments of Vision and Miscellaneous Verses (London: Macmillan, 1917);
Collected Poems (London: Macmillan, 1919; enlarged, 1923, 1928, 1930);
Late Lyrics and Earlier with Many Other Verses (London: Macmillan, 1922);
The Famous Tragedy of the Queen of Cornwall (London: Macmillan, 1923; New York: Macmillan, 1923);
Human Shows, Far Phantasies, Songs and Trifles (London: Macmillan, 1925; New York: Macmillan, 1925);
Winter Words in Various Moods and Metres (London: Macmillan, 1928; New York: Macmillan, 1928);
Chosen Poems (London: Macmillan, 1929; New York: Macmillan, 1929);
Thomas Hardy's Personal Writings: Prefaces, Literary Opinions, Reminiscences, edited by Harold Orel (Lawrence: University of Kansas Press, 1966);
The Complete Poems, edited by James Gibson (London: Macmillan, 1976; New York: Macmillan, 1978);
The Personal Notebooks of Thomas Hardy, edited by Richard H. Taylor (London: Macmillan, 1978; New York: Columbia University Press, 1979);
The Variorum Edition of the Complete Poems of Thomas Hardy, edited by Gibson (London: Macmillan, 1979; New York: Macmillan, 1979).

Collections: *The Wessex Novels* (18 volumes, London: Osgood, McIlvaine, 1895-1913);

Hardy's drawing of his birthplace at Higher Bockhampton

The Works of Thomas Hardy in Prose and Verse, with Prefaces and Notes, Wessex Edition (24 volumes, London: Macmillan, 1912-1931);
The Complete Poetical Works of Thomas Hardy, 3 volumes, edited by Samuel Hynes (Oxford: Clarendon Press, 1982-1985);
The Literary Notebooks of Thomas Hardy, 2 volumes, edited by Lennart A. Bjork (London: Macmillan, 1985).

OTHER: Florence Emily Hardy, *The Early Years of Thomas Hardy, 1840-1891,* and *The Later Years of Thomas Hardy, 1892-1928,* ghostwritten by Hardy (London: Macmillan, 1928, 1930; New York: Macmillan, 1928, 1930); modern edition published as *The Life and Work of Thomas Hardy, by Thomas Hardy,* edited by Michael Millgate (London: Macmillan, 1984).

In the later years of his long life, Thomas Hardy was probably the most famous English man of letters of his time, his reputation extending throughout the world. He is now generally regarded as both a major late-Victorian novelist and a major twentieth-century poet, and is the subject of more intense scholarly, critical, editorial, and biographical attention than ever before; as a result, knowledge and understanding of his life, personality, and literary achievement are continually increasing and deepening. Nor is his appeal restricted to academics or students: he has long been one of the most widely read of English novelists; ten thousand people tramp every year through the modest cottage that was his birthplace; and he now reaches a mass audience through film and television adaptations of his books.

The time and place of his birth determined the early experiences on which he was to draw so heavily as a writer. In 1840 the county of Dorset was still relatively little touched by the sweeping changes that were transforming the rest of England: the railway, for instance, which had spread its network across the country in the 1820s and 1830s, did not reach Dorset until seven years after Hardy's birth, and the folk traditions of a small and scattered population thus survived longer there than in most other places. Higher Bockhampton, though within walking distance of the county town of Dorchester, was no more than a hamlet; Dorchester itself, though an ancient town dating back to Roman times and an important center for the surrounding agricultural region, was small. During his early years Hardy was to witness the hand of change at work on landscape and rural community at the same time that his own intellectual and emotional development was leading him in directions for which family history offered no precedent. Intensely individual, he was also in many respects a representative member of his generation.

His father and grandfather, alike named Thomas Hardy, were builders; the family was long settled in the district and, while certainly not affluent, lived comfortably enough at a time when Dorset was something of a byword for poverty and wretchedness. Thomas Hardy III, not a physically robust child, stayed at home until he was eight and then enjoyed only eight years of schooling, first in a nearby village and then in Dorchester. But he was zealous in pursuing a course of self-education after he left school at the age of sixteen and throughout his life retained a wide-ranging intellectual curiosity. As a young man, his interests were mainly literary, philosophical, and theological; and, like so many of his contemporaries, he underwent a crisis of faith—he was nineteen when Charles Darwin's *Origin of Species* appeared, twenty in the year of the controversial theological symposium *Essays and Reviews*—that led him to abandon the Christianity in which he had been brought up. He retained for the rest of his life, however, his close knowledge of the Bible, his interest in church architecture, and his sense that something was missing in a godless world.

He had been apprenticed at sixteen to a Dorchester architect. During this period he came to know William Barnes, a Dorchester schoolmaster who was also a dialect poet of great distinction. Eventually the successful pursuit of his profession (to which he was to devote sixteen years of his life) took Hardy to London. During his years there (1862-1867) he read at the British Museum in his leisure hours, studied the pictures at the National Gallery, and began—with a total lack of success—to submit poems to the magazines. Back in Dorset as a result of ill health, he wrote his first novel, "The Poor Man and the Lady." The turning to fiction fairly early clearly represented an acceptance of the realities of the contemporary publishing situation. The novelist's profession had by this time become lucrative and well-regarded: in 1863, for instance, George Eliot had been paid ten thousand pounds for *Romola;* and Charles Dickens had made a fortune as well as becoming a household name. Hardy accepted the fact that, whatever his poetic aspirations, he must turn to the novel if he were to succeed as an author.

Hardy at age sixteen, about the time he began his architectural training (Hermann Lea Collection)

His early novels show him attempting a variety of kinds of fiction without any very strong conviction as to where his true gifts lay, and to some extent this lack of confidence persisted almost to the end of his career as a novelist. As late as 30 June 1891, for instance, he wrote in a letter that "much of my work hitherto has been of a tentative kind, and it is but latterly that I have felt any sureness of method." "The Poor Man and the Lady," unpublished and later destroyed, was evidently a social satire and episodic in structure; its title summarizes neatly a continuing preoccupation of his fiction and seems to reflect the social self-consciousness that continued to haunt him for the rest of his days. This early attempt was followed by *Desperate Remedies* (1871), a conscientious and still readable exercise in the "sensation novel" form that Wilkie Collins and others had made immensely popular during the previous decade. Hardy wrote it in the later months of 1869 and the opening months of 1870, having been advised by George Meredith (who, as a reader for Chapman and Hall, had rejected "The Poor Man and the Lady") to write a novel with a strong element of plot. Although it contains some melodramatic absurdities, there are also touches that can be recognized as characteristic—for example, in the sharply visualized quality of certain episodes—and that show Hardy in the process of devising an idiosyncratic technique of narration and description to convey a highly individual vision and sensibility.

Desperate Remedies was published anonymously in the conventional and expensive three-volume form, and its reception was unenthusiastic, though not actually as hostile as Hardy seems to have believed. The *Athenaeum* (1 April 1871) described it as "an unpleasant story . . . [but] undoubtedly a very powerful one"; the *Spectator* (22 April 1871) judged it "disagreeable, and not striking in any way," but praised the unknown author's "very happy facility in catching and fixing phases of peasant life"—approval that was to be echoed by critics of some subsequent novels. In his biography, *The Life of Thomas Hardy* (two volumes, 1928, 1930; one volume, 1984)—actually an autobiography, since it was largely ghostwritten by Hardy, though attributed to his second wife, Florence—Hardy describes his anguish at reading the *Spectator* review: "He remembered, for long years after, how he had read this review as he sat on a stile leading to the eweleaze he had to cross on his way home to Bockhampton. The bitterness of that moment was never forgotten; at the time he wished that he were dead." Commercially, the book was not a success; Hardy, who had contributed seventy-five pounds of his modest savings toward the expenses of publication, recovered only part of his money, and within three months the book was remaindered.

By this time, however, he was at work on another novel of an entirely different kind. *Under the Greenwood Tree* is the shortest of Hardy's novels and arguably the least flawed—a minor classic, but assuredly a classic. It was written rapidly and incorporates material salvaged from "The Poor Man and the Lady." After a discouraging response from Alexander Macmillan, to whom he had first offered it, Hardy sent his manuscript in April 1872 to William Tinsley, who had published *Desperate Remedies.* Tinsley accepted it, and it was published, anonymously and in two volumes, in June. It was more favorably reviewed than its predecessor, and Hardy's friend Horace Moule praised it warmly in the influential *Saturday Review* (28 September 1872): "This novel is the best prose idyl that we have seen for a long while past . . . the book is one of unusual merit in its own special line, full of humour and keen observation, and with the genuine air of the country breathing throughout it." The small edition was slow to sell, however, and it was more than a year before another edition was called for. At about the same time, it was published (June 1873) in New York by Holt and Williams—the first of Hardy's novels to be published in America, and the small beginning of what was eventually to become a considerable American readership. It could not be said, though, that Hardy, then in his thirties, had made a spectacular beginning as a novelist.

Moule's review of *Under the Greenwood Tree* makes a significant reference to *Silas Marner* (1861), and indeed the influence of George Eliot's early stories of rural life is apparent. Hardy's subtitle is *A Rural Painting of the Dutch School,* a phrase that recalls the famous defense of realistic portraits of peasant life and the analogy with seventeenth-century Dutch art in chapter 17 of *Adam Bede* (1859). Hardy can only have felt flattered at comparisons with a novelist who was not only a best-selling author but was venerated as an intellectual and a sage. At the same time, the influence of George Eliot on his work was not altogether happy and was not quickly to be shaken off; it probably helps to account for a habit of ponderous moralizing and a somewhat ostentatious display of learning (or at least information) that mar even Hardy's finest novels.

In *Under the Greenwood Tree,* however, his aims were far from grandiose. For the first time he was drawing on his own intimate knowledge of rural life, and the social world of this novel is presented with an authority that is impressive with-

The fictional county created by Hardy

out being assertive. The novel is a love story that ends with the marriage of the heroine, Fancy Day, to the unassuming Dick Dewy. The course of true love has not run altogether smooth, however, for Fancy (whose name is significant) has been tempted by a rival suitor, Maybold, before finally returning to the faithful and unsuspecting Dick. Social distinctions are crucial in this situation: Fancy is a schoolteacher, Dick a countryman, Maybold a parson and thus the superior of them both in the local hierarchy. As it so often does in Hardy's subsequent fiction, the drama arises partly from social inequalities and social aspirations. Another theme of the novel is indicated by Hardy's original title, "The Mellstock Quire." The traditional church band (Hardy's father had played in a real-life counterpart) is in the process of being superseded by an organ: change has come to the village; the old is giving way to the new, the human to the mechanical. Here, again, is a theme which was to recur throughout Hardy's career as a novelist, and nowhere more potently than in his final works.

During the same busy summer of 1871, Hardy had conceived the idea of another novel, originally titled "A Winning Tongue Had He" and eventually known as *A Pair of Blue Eyes*. The favorable reviews of *Under the Greenwood Tree* led Tinsley to ask Hardy for a story to be published in the monthly magazine that was one of his enterprises; and in the summer of 1872. Hardy took up the outline of the novel he had sketched a year earlier and set to work on it. It was the first of his books to be serialized—a mode in which all his subsequent novels were to make their initial appearance. Tinsley's offer of two hundred pounds was an impressive advance on the terms he had offered for *Desperate Remedies* and *Under the Greenwood Tree*. (Hardy had accepted thirty pounds for the copyright of the latter.) Serialization began in September 1872 and continued until July 1873; publication in three volumes at the end of May 1873 was no doubt timed to anticipate the final installments and to tempt impatient readers into purchasing the book, which is the first of Hardy's novels to bear his name as author. Its critical reception was generally favorable: the *Saturday Review* (2 August 1873) again invoked the name of George Eliot ("Mr. Hardy has . . . developed, with something of the ruthlessness of George Eliot, what may be called the tragedy of circumstance") and concluded that, although the author had "much to learn, and many faults yet to avoid," he was "a writer who to a singular purity of thought and intention unites great power of imagination."

Social differences, and their impact on love relationships, are again prominent in *A Pair of Blue Eyes.* The heroine, Elfride Swancourt, is loved by two men: Stephen Smith, "a rural builder's son" and architect engaged in church restoration, bears a strong resemblance to Hardy; Henry Knight, a metropolitan intellectual who contributes to the reviews, has something in common with Horace Moule. The plot makes a somewhat excessive use of coincidence, but there is one famous and impressive scene which, for all its contrivance, possesses a haunting, imaginative power. When Knight, hanging from a cliff and apparently about to plunge to his death, looks at the cliff face a few inches from his eyes, he sees "an imbedded fossil, standing forth in low relief from the rock. It was one of the early crustaceans called Trilobites. Separated by millions of years in their lives, Knight and this underling seemed to have met in their place of death." The awed Victorian awareness of the immensity of geological time and the corresponding insignificance of human life is dramatized in a vivid fictional moment.

Horace Moule, a Dorchester friend and a Cambridge man, had acted as a tutor or mentor to Hardy during Hardy's slow process of self-education; and his suicide on 21 September 1873 was a great blow to Hardy, whose biographer, Robert Gittings, has suggested that the influence of Moule's death was both profound and far-reaching: "we can date the emergence of Hardy as a fully tragic artist, an expounder of man's true miseries, from the suicide of his friend, and the appalling revealed ironies of that personal history."

The autobiographical element in *A Pair of Blue Eyes* owes much to experiences of a happier kind. In 1870 Hardy had traveled down to St. Juliot on the coast of Cornwall on architectural business; there he had met Emma Lavinia Gifford, sister-in-law of the local clergyman. It was only after a lengthy courtship, and in the face of opposition from both families, that they were able to marry (17 September 1874), for Hardy's earning capacity was limited. The success of his next novel, *Far from the Madding Crowd* (1874), enabled him to marry as well as to quit architecture for the precarious—but, in the event, highly successful—profession of full-time writer.

Emma Lavinia Gifford, who became Hardy's first wife (Dorset Natural History and Archeological Society)

Leslie Stephen, distinguished critic and editor, had been impressed by *Under the Greenwood Tree* and wrote to Hardy in November 1872 to invite him to contribute a novel to the *Cornhill* magazine, a prestigious monthly that had published the work of such established authors as Anthony Trollope and Mrs. Gaskell. Hardy replied that he was busy with *A Pair of Blue Eyes,* which was already promised to Tinsley, but that "the next should be at Mr. Stephen's disposal." He added that "the chief characters would probably be a young woman-farmer, a shepherd, and a sergeant of cavalry." The title had already been settled on. Stephen responded enthusiastically, and in June 1873 Hardy sent him "a few chapters . . . with some succeeding ones in outline"; more followed in September, Stephen accepted the work, and publication began in January 1874, continuing for the rest of that year. Hardy finished writing the novel in July 1874, and it appeared in volume form in November.

It was widely reviewed in England and also marked an important stage in the growth of Hardy's international reputation: the famous Paris journal *Revue des deux mondes,* for example, made it the occasion for a long survey-article on Hardy's work to date. After the appearance (anonymously) of the first installment, the *Spectator* observed that "If *Far from the Madding Crowd* is not written by George Eliot, then there is a new light among novelists." The portrayal of rustic life received especial praise, though one can well imagine that the feelings of the socially ambitious Hardy, painfully aware of his modest origins, were distinctly mixed when he read Henry James's comment in the *Nation* (24 December 1874): "Mr. Hardy describes nature with a great deal of felicity, and is evidently very much at home among rural phenomena. The most genuine thing in his book, to our sense, is a certain aroma of the meadows and lanes—a natural relish for harvesting and sheep-washings." Although he had achieved success on a scale unprecedented in his short career, Hardy was to show no enthusiasm to be typecast as a chronicler of rural life.

The outline of the novel as originally submitted to Stephen makes no mention of Boldwood; his introduction was presumably an afterthought. In its final version the story is constructed around a quartet of characters: the attractive young woman-farmer Bathsheba Everdene and the three men who, in their quite different ways, all love her. The story is thus, among other things, a study in the various faces and aspects of love. Bathsheba is vivacious and independent, even headstrong, like so many of Hardy's heroines, from Fancy Day in *Under the Greenwood Tree* to Sue Bridehead in *Jude the Obscure* (1895) more than twenty years later. Gabriel Oak, the shepherd, is the faithful, noble, deep-feeling, and long-suffering type of hero that Hardy was to present again in Giles Winterborne in *The Woodlanders* (1887); his surname suggests something of his unpretentious dependability, and his work identifies him with all the timeless world of the countryside, with its traditional skills and values. Sergeant Troy is his opposite: an outsider, rootless and restless, a striking and colorful figure in his scarlet uniform, a Victorian version of the soldier-seducer to be found in many popular ballads and folk songs. Boldwood is a farmer whose passion for Bathsheba, stimulated by an irresponsible joke, turns into an obsession and leads to madness and death. At this stage in his career Hardy is still prepared to bring about a happy ending, and the faithful Gabriel is eventually rewarded by marriage with Bathsheba; but this is only attained by a route which involves much suffering and sorrow and three deaths. A subplot deals with the innocent maiden Fanny Robin, who has been seduced by Troy and dies bearing his child. Rural life is invaded by violence and tragedy; and the title, taken from Gray's *Elegy Written in a Country Churchyard* (1751), is obviously intended ironically.

In writing *Far from the Madding Crowd,* Hardy encountered a problem that was to become much more acute as his career continued. His desire to write novels about the relations of the sexes and the problems of love and marriage brought him into head-on collision with the watchful forces of propriety and with the censorship that was exercised, in fact if not in name, by readers, circulating libraries, and editors and publishers. Study of Hardy's manuscript has shown that he had to make extensive alterations in the portions of the novel referring to Fanny Robin and her illegitimate child. In a revealing letter, Stephen wrote to him that he thought that "the cause of Fanny's death is unnecessarily emphasized" and added that he would "somehow be glad to omit the baby"—pointing out also, however, that "I object as editor, not as critic, i.e. in the interest of a stupid public, not from my own taste." In the event, the serial version omitted virtually all references to the baby. Not for the last time Hardy was forced to effect a compromise between the kind of novel that he wanted to write and what his editor, acting on behalf of a conservative public, was prepared to tolerate. As one who hoped to make a living by his pen, he could not afford to sacrifice the additional profits that accrued from serialization.

During these early years, however, Hardy may not have found the censorship of his work particularly irksome: he was still seeking to establish himself as an author and seems to have been prepared to listen patiently to an experienced editor and to abide by his suggestions. A few years later (12 April 1877) he was to write to the pub-

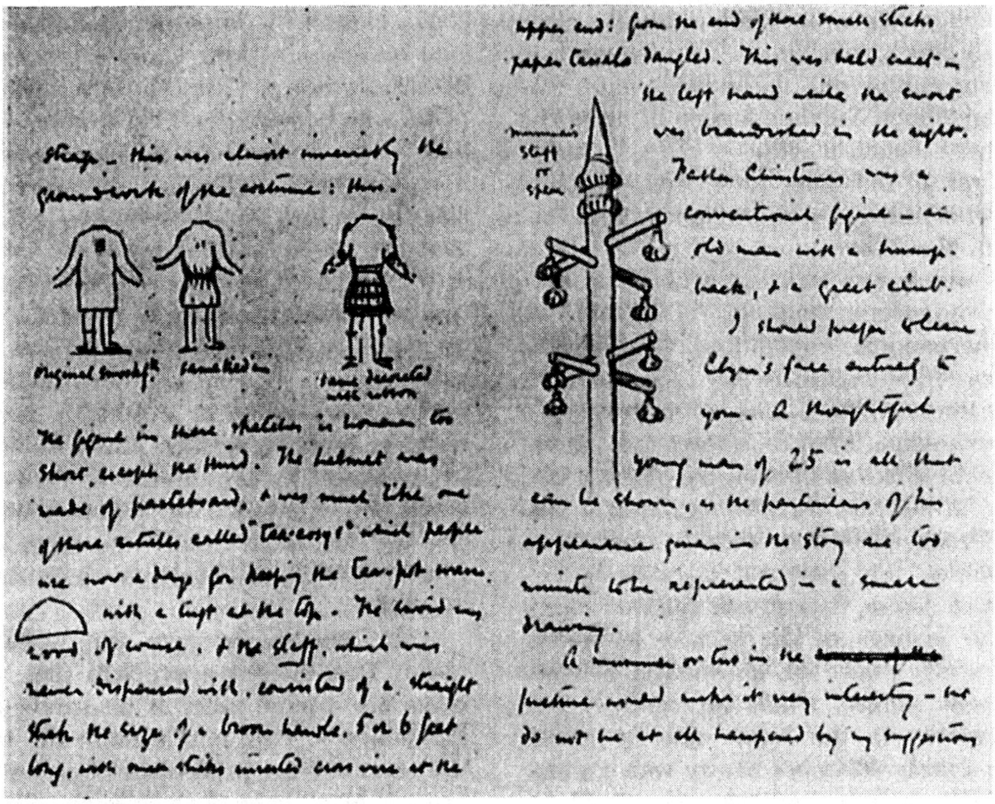

Smock – this was almost invariably the groundwork of the costume: thus.

Original smockfrock — same tucked in — same decorated with ribbons

The figures in these sketches are rather too short, except the third. The helmet was made of pasteboard, & was much like one of those articles called "tea-cosy" which people use now a days for keeping the tea-pot warm, with a tuft at the top. The sword was wood of course, & the staff, which was never dispensed with, consisted of a straight stick the size of a broom handle, 5 or 6 feet long, with small sticks inserted crosswise at the upper end: from the ends of these small sticks paper tassels dangled. This was held erect in the left hand while the sword was brandished in the right.

mummer's staff or spear

Father Christmas was a conventional figure – an old man with a hump-back, & a great club.

I should prefer to leave Clym's face entirely to you. A thoughtful young man of 25 is all that can be shown, as the particulars of his appearance given in the story are too minute to be represented in a small drawing.

A mummer or two in the [struck out] picture would make it very interesting – but do not be at all hampered by my suggestions

Part of a letter from Hardy suggesting illustrations for the serialization of The Return of the Native

lisher John Blackwood, in sending him part of the manuscript of *The Return of the Native* (1878), that "should there accidentally occur any word or reflection not in harmony with the general tone of the magazine, you would be quite at liberty to strike it out if you chose. I always mention this to my editors, as it simplifies matters." Later in his career, however, as the divergence between the kind of novel Hardy wanted to write and the kind his editors and publishers would tolerate became wider, and the required bowdlerization damaged the fabric of his work more extensively, Hardy became less easygoing and chafed more bitterly at the burden of censorship.

What renders the suppression of such details as the dead baby doubly absurd is that in chapter 28 of *Far from the Madding Crowd* ("The Hollow amid the Ferns"), Hardy wrote one of the most erotic scenes in the whole of his fiction. Both the physical setting and the vivid account of Sergeant Troy's swordplay are fraught with sexual symbolism; but because the eroticism is symbolic and not explicit, its effectiveness belonging to the whole scene and situation rather than being located in any specific word or detail that might be deemed overtly offensive, it seems to have aroused less excitement than a reference to a dead child lying in a coffin.

In a preface he wrote when *Far from the Madding Crowd* was republished in a collected edition of his works (1895), Hardy recalled that it was in that novel that he first used the term *Wessex* to delineate a fictional region that nevertheless bore a close resemblance to actuality: "I first ventured to adopt the word 'Wessex' from the pages of early English history, and give it a fictitious significance as the existing name of the district once included in that extinct kingdom. The series of novels I projected being mainly of a kind called local, they seemed to require a territorial definition of some sort to lend unity to their scene." At the same time, Hardy drew a map to illustrate his fictional territory. Wessex extends well beyond the bounds of his native Dorset, east into Hampshire and north into Somerset and Wiltshire. In the novels, he usually modifies placenames, so that (for instance) Salisbury becomes Melchester, Dorchester becomes Casterbridge, and Bournemouth becomes Sandbourne. In this way he can create a fictional world that is authentic without being bound by a slavish realism. Today thousands of enthusiasts explore "the

Hardy country" in quest of places made interesting for them by incidents in the novels; but it is important to remember that the world of the novels is, after all, a *fictional* world, however closely at times it may resemble that on the map or in a book of photographs.

Hardy's wedding, which took place in London while *Far from the Madding Crowd* was appearing in the *Cornhill,* was attended by no member of his own family. He was conscious that he had married above the social level into which he had been born; for Emma came of a middle-class family and had an uncle who was an archdeacon. The marriage that was later to cause such heartache and bitterness began brightly; and for the first ten years or so, the couple lived in a series of rented houses and furnished lodgings in Dorset and London. Hardy had at that point given up the practice of architecture and depended on his writings for a livelihood. His next novel, *The Hand of Ethelberta,* also appeared in the *Cornhill* but did not repeat the success of its predecessor. The new novel, subtitled *A Comedy in Chapters,* resolutely turns its back on the pastoral world of *Far from the Madding Crowd*—somewhat perversely, indeed, for Hardy must have been aware of the grounds of that book's success. At this stage in his career, Hardy seems to have had aspirations to write an entirely different kind of fiction, dealing with fashionable life rather than rustics and with ideas rather than homely incidents. Perhaps he was also feeling some discontent at being launched on a career as a novelist when his real desire was to succeed as a poet; such seems to be the implication of the remark in *The Life of Thomas Hardy: "finding himself committed to prose,* he renewed his consideration of a prose style" (italics added).

Hardy wrote the early chapters of *The Hand of Ethelberta* at the beginning of 1875 in prompt response to Leslie Stephen's request for another serial, and publication began in July. Composition was completed in January 1876, serialization the following May, and volume-publication was in April. Reviewers were lukewarm; R. H. Hutton, for instance, one of the most perceptive of Victorian critics, found the characters unconvincing. The novel contains ingredients that were becoming familiar in Hardy's fiction. The heroine is a girl of spirit and energy seeking to make her way in the world in spite of her modest background; for her father is a butler, and on one occasion she undergoes the painful experience of being served by him when she dines at the fashionable house where he is employed. The suitors between whom she must choose (after she comes to accept that marriage is a woman's only road to security) include Christopher Julian, a faithful and self-effacing musician, and Lord Mountclere, a dissipated aristocrat old enough to be her grandfather. She marries the latter, and the novel limps to a somewhat unconvincing conclusion. Comparison with *Far from the Madding Crowd* suggests that what is missing is a social and physical world presented with confidence and authority: Hardy is dealing with themes close to his heart but attempts to present scenes and characters that for the most part he knows only as an outsider.

Hardy about the time of the publication of The Trumpet-Major *(1880)*

His last two novels having been of entirely different kinds, Hardy seems to have been uncertain in which direction to move after completing *The Hand of Ethelberta;* and in a letter dated 5 March 1876, he wrote to a publisher that "I do not wish to attempt any more original writing of any length for a few months, until I can learn the best line to take for the future." His next novel, *The Return of the Native,* returns to a Wessex setting.

The title of *The Return of the Native* suggests a theme that recurs in his fiction and also reflects the fact that during this period of his life Hardy spent a good deal of time away from Dorset. Much of the novel was written at Sturminster Newton, where he and Emma seem to have been happier than they ever were again; but it was finished in London. It was probably started in the summer of 1877, and serialization in the monthly magazine *Belgravia* began in January 1878, continuing until the end of the year. Hardy had first offered it to Leslie Stephen for the *Cornhill,* but Stephen had been dismayed by the potentially explosive situation involving Eustacia, Wildeve, and Thomasin, and had prudently declined the offer. It was published in three volumes in November 1878, and its reception was mixed. Some reviewers praised the graphic descriptions, but others found Hardy's writing strained and pretentious and objected that his peasants talked more like Shakespearean clowns than nineteenth-century Englishmen.

From the portentous and celebrated opening description of Egdon Heath to the drowning (whether accidental or suicidal) of Eustacia Vye and Damon Wildeve, this was Hardy's most somber and tragic novel to date. Its structure has been compared to the five acts of a Shakespearean tragedy (the sixth book is in effect an epilogue, the deaths of Eustacia and Wildeve occurring at the end of the fifth book). Hardy's preoccupation with time—geological as well as historical—and his vision of human life against a backdrop of millennia are clear from the outset; equally apparent is his anxious awareness of the unprecedentedly difficult lot of contemporary man, faced with the intellectual and spiritual upheavals of the nineteenth century: "to know that everything around and underneath had been from prehistoric times as unaltered as the stars overhead, gave ballast to *the mind adrift on change, and harassed by the irrepressible New*" (italics added). The story is based on character contrasts of a kind by then familiar in Hardy's fiction. The gentle, undemanding Thomasin Yeobright is the antithesis of the restless, egotistical, and ambitious Eustacia; Diggory Venn, the "reddleman" (itinerant dealer in dye), loyal and undemanding, contrasts with the dashing and heartless Damon Wildeve (as so often in Hardy, the names carry symbolic implications, though not always of the most obvious kind). Eustacia's passionate nature finds no satisfaction in a marriage to Clym Yeobright, the returned native; she resumes her premarital affair with Wildeve, flees with him, and—at the same time accomplishing a tragic destiny and satisfying the moral expectations of the reader—they die together. Eustacia has been compared to Emma Bovary, though Hardy claimed that he had not read Gustave Flaubert's 1856 novel at this time.

The setting of the story possesses a unity that may derive from a conscious attempt to follow the Aristotelian prescription for tragic drama. Hardy made this point in suggesting, in a letter to the publisher of the book version (1 October 1878), that a map might be provided (a suggestion that was taken up): "Unity of place is so seldom preserved in novels that a map of the scene of action is as a rule impracticable: but since the present story affords an opportunity of doing so I am of opinion that it would be a desirable novelty, likely to increase a reader's interest." The sense of place is intensified by the numerous references to local folk customs (for example, the mummers' play, and the scene in which a peasant woman, regarding Eustacia as a witch, makes a wax effigy of her). Such allusions also emphasize the contrast between two worlds—the traditional way of life (represented by the reddleman) and "the irrepressible New," manifested by Eustacia's cravings for independence. Clym Yeobright's rejection of the city (he has worked for a jeweler in Paris) and his return to Wessex to embrace successively the occupations of schoolmaster, furze cutter, and itinerant preacher, represent an impulsive turning back from the new to the old.

The shaping of the novel gave Hardy a certain amount of trouble. Thomasin seems originally to have been intended to play a fuller role than she does in the final version; but, some way into the task of writing the novel, Hardy changed his mind and made Eustacia the tragic heroine. The happy ending, with Thomasin united at last to Diggory Venn, was a concession to the readers of the serial: Hardy's original intention had been to make Venn disappear and to leave Thomasin in her widowhood.

The Return of the Native was followed by three minor novels. *The Trumpet-Major* (1880) represents Hardy's attempt at historical fiction; it is set in the Napoleonic period, which always held a great fascination for him and a generation later became the setting for his grandiose epic-drama *The Dynasts* (1904, 1906, 1908). A notebook in which he recorded material for use in the novel has been recently published and provides the fullest surviving evidence of Hardy's preparations

Hardy's sketch from memory of the Three Mariners Inn, Dorchester, the model for the inn of the same name in The Mayor of Casterbridge *(Dorset County Museum)*

for writing fiction: his painstaking research in the British Museum reveals his concern for authenticity, not only of historical events but of details of costume and manners. The novel seems to have been written in 1879-1880, when Hardy was living in London, and was serialized in the magazine *Good Words* during the twelve months of 1880; publication in three volumes was in October 1880.

The Trumpet-Major is set against a background of public events and, like Tolstoy's *War and Peace* (1864-1869), introduces into the fiction historical characters, such as King George III and that Admiral Hardy (as he later became) with whom Thomas Hardy claimed kinship. But the heart of the novel is concerned with private experience in times of crisis and uncertainty, and the love story has similarities to that of *Far from the Madding Crowd.* The heroine, Anne Garland, is loved by three men: the modest and self-sacrificing John Loveday (the trumpet-major of the title), his insensitive and shallow sailor-brother Bob, and the loutish Festus Derriman, a cruder version of Sergeant Troy. The novel has charm but lacks the solidity, the suggestiveness, and the power of Hardy's major fiction; the texture is thin and the writing lacks resonance; but a good word must be said for the poignancy of the conclusion. The modesty of Hardy's aims in *The Trumpet-Major* is suggested by his statement in a letter dated 9 June 1879 that the novel he was engaged on would be "above all things a cheerful story, without views or opinions, and . . . intended to wind up happily"—a promise that was not entirely kept.

During this period, Hardy's fame was growing steadily. He had established himself in a London suburb so as to be near the literary circles of the metropolis; he joined a club, dined out regularly, and met celebrities. He also formed friendships which lasted for the rest of his life—for example, with the critic Edmund Gosse. Hardy and his wife took occasional holidays on the Continent; as yet, they had no permanent home. Toward the end of 1880, while Hardy was at work on his next novel, *A Laodicean,* a serious blow fell; he became seriously ill with an internal hemorrhage and spent months in bed. He continued work on the novel, dictating it to Emma, though his pain and anxiety must have been considerable. Soon after his recovery in the spring of 1881, they set about looking for a house in Dorset. They eventually made a temporary home at Wimborne Minster—the first stage in what was to turn out to be a permanent return to Hardy's native county.

The circumstances of its composition make it unsurprising that *A Laodicean* is one of Hardy's least successful books, labored and unconvincing. Nevertheless, like everything he wrote, even the shortest poem, it is stamped with his individuality. It appeared in monthly installments from December 1880 to December 1881 and was serialized almost simultaneously in America. Book publication in both countries was toward the end of 1881. That Hardy, who usually preserved his manuscripts, should have destroyed that of *A Laodicean* suggests that he was not satisfied with the novel.

The hero is an architect, the heroine an heiress: in other words, the reader is offered yet another version of "the poor man and the lady."

There is a certain desperation about the plotting of the latter half of the book, and many of the conventional trappings of Victorian fiction and melodrama are resorted to—a bastard son and other guilty secrets, overheard conversations, coincidental meetings, and blackmail. The painful circumstances of its production, with Hardy anxious to complete what he must at times have thought of as meager financial provision for his widow, account for its weakness. But there remains the larger problem of why the period of about five years from 1879 should be so barren of major creative achievement. At about forty, Hardy might have been expected to be at the height of his powers; but the greatest works still lay ahead. He always insisted that he was a late developer, and a happy corollary of this was that he retained his creative powers into extreme old age. Perhaps the fact that he was still, in middle life, without a settled home or a place in any community caused a deep discontent. Certainly, the flowering of his genius that followed the decision to settle permanently in Dorchester is very striking.

Meanwhile, the third of the minor novels of this period came in rapid succession to *A Laodicean*. In September 1881, while that novel was still running its course, the editor of the *Atlantic Monthly* invited Hardy to write a serial for his magazine. The result was *Two on a Tower*, serialized from May to December 1882 and published in book form at the end of October 1882. The dates of composition are unclear, but Hardy admitted in a letter to Gosse (21 January 1883) that "though the plan of the story was carefully thought out, the actual writing was lamentably hurried—having been produced month by month. . . . " It looks as though Hardy was conscious of paying a heavy artistic price for the insatiable demands of serialization.

The universe that had opened up so disconcertingly for the Victorians required a radical readjustment to new concepts of space as well as time: not only had the earth been shown to be immensely more ancient than had usually been believed, but the discoveries of nineteenth-century astronomy revealed a universe of boundless space. Hardy said in another letter (4 December 1882) that his aim in his new novel had been "to make science, not the mere padding of a romance, but the actual vehicle of romance." The hero of *Two on a Tower* is a young astronomer; his romantic entanglement with a high-born lady (yet again the theme of social inequality is prominent) takes place against a background of what

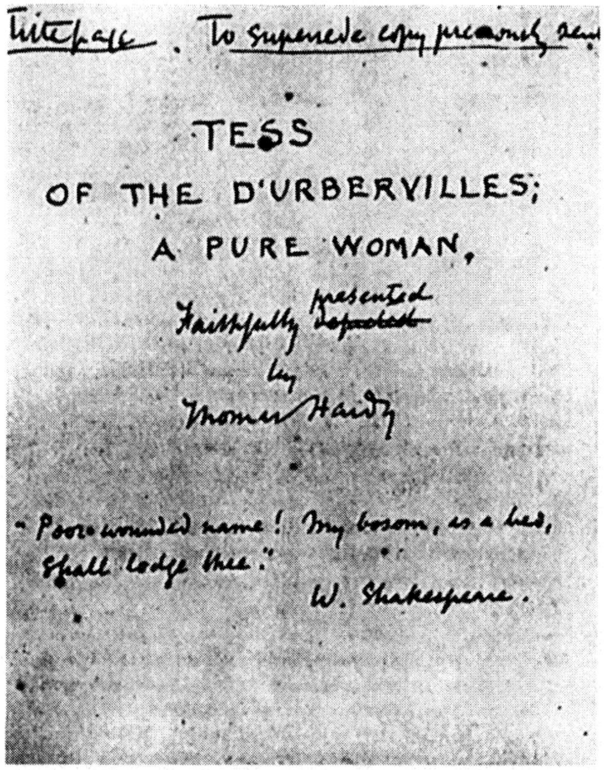
TESS
OF THE D'URBERVILLES;
A PURE WOMAN,
Faithfully presented
by
Thomas Hardy

"Poor wounded name! My bosom, as a bed,
Shall lodge thee."
W. Shakespeare.

Hardy's revised draft of the title page of his controversial 1891 novel, with subtitle and quotation from The Two Gentlemen of Verona *added (Dorset County Museum)*

Hardy calls "the stellar universe." Lady Constantine is ten years older than Swithin St. Cleeve—a drop in the ocean of astronomical time, but woefully significant in human lives. She is also married; but an erroneous report of her husband's death enables her to love and marry Swithin without moral turpitude but with complex consequences. Again, the latter part of the novel resorts to a huddle of melodramatic incidents. But the initial conception has genuine imaginative power—an idea of strength and originality that, in working out, falls victim to the demand for strong plotting generated by the serial mode, as well as (perhaps) to the haste imposed on the serious novelist catering to an eager public.

It would have been surprising if reviewers had been wildly enthusiastic about these three minor novels. But Hardy was by then an established author, and his work sold steadily. The first edition of *Two on a Tower*—one thousand copies—sold quite quickly, and a reprinting was called for. His royalties on volume sales were, of course, in addition to the fees he received from the magazines that serialized his work; and this double profit was no doubt what kept him at work as a serial novelist even though the task was often irksome and in violation of his artistic conscience.

After settling at Wimborne Minster in 1881, Hardy seems to have attempted to put down some roots in Dorset: for instance, he joined the Dorset Natural History and Antiquarian Field Club. But he still spent considerable periods in London during the social "season," mixing freely with other literary personalities in clubs and salons and at dinner tables. The urge to settle was strong, however; and by this time his financial position justified him in taking a major step—building a house, to his own designs. He considered various sites and eventually selected a piece of land just outside Dorchester. From the upstairs windows of the house he built, his old home could be seen across the fields; and the homecoming—the return of the native—seems to have been in a sense a symbolic act. In June 1883 Hardy and his wife moved into temporary accommodations in Dorchester so as to be on hand to supervise the building of the house, which he decided to call Max Gate (after Henry Mack, a former toll-gate keeper of the neighborhood). The move into Max Gate was made in June 1885, and apart from visits to London and elsewhere, Hardy remained there for the rest of his life.

The move to Dorchester initiated a major period of Hardy's creative life as a novelist, and it is surely significant that the first novel he wrote after returning to Dorchester is set in "Casterbridge," the fictional equivalent of that ancient borough. *The Mayor of Casterbridge* seems to have been begun early in 1884 and, in spite of numerous interruptions, was finished in April 1885. Unusually, composition was complete before serialization began, for it was not until 2 January 1886 that its first installment appeared in the weekly *Graphic,* where it continued until 15 May. Volume publication was only a few days in advance of the completion of serialization. In America, the novel appeared simultaneously in *Harper's Weekly.*

Weekly serialization no doubt helps to account for the high proportion of dramatic and sensational incidents in this novel, some of them contrived and inessential; but unity is ensured by the dominant presence of the hero, Michael Henchard. His impulsive and ultimately self-destructive nature is evident in the opening incident, the bizarre but historically authentic wife-selling (scholars have unearthed comparable cases reported in nineteenth-century newspapers); it is also emphasized by being set in contrast with the cautious, rational character of Farfrae, the outsider ("from far," as his name indicates) and new man whose scientific methods render outdated the traditional, largely intuitive business methods of Henchard. As with *The Return of the Native,* the novel invites comparison with Shakespearean tragedy, especially *King Lear;* a parallel with the Old Testament story of Saul and David has also been suggested.

The dating of the action remains rather obscure, and manuscript evidence suggests that Hardy may have changed his mind on this point. It has been suggested that the *Mayor of Casterbridge,* like *Tess of the d'Urbervilles* (1891), is concerned with the plight of English agriculture and the agricultural laborer during the crisis years toward the end of the nineteenth century. Another interpretation holds that Hardy had an earlier period in mind. The reference to a royal visitor may allude to Prince Albert's visit to Dorchester in 1849, but not all the other incidents and allusions are chronologically consistent with this. What is fairly clear is that the bulk of the action takes place around the mid century, and that, like so many Victorian novelists, Hardy is therefore going back a generation before the date of composition, to the period of his own youth. The first two chapters of the novel form a prologue, with a gap of eighteen years between the second and third chapters. The work, like so much elsewhere in his prose and verse, is permeated by an aching sense of loss: Hardy is aware of the irrevocable destruction of a way of life which involves both an epoch of history and a precious part of his own early memories.

A note of discontent with the constraints of serialization makes itself heard from Hardy at this time—a discontent that was to be exacerbated rather than relieved as time went on. Hardy later wrote in *The Life of Thomas Hardy* that *The Mayor of Casterbridge* was "a story which [he] fancied he had damaged more recklessly as an artistic whole, in the interest of the newspaper in which it appeared serially, than perhaps any other of his novels, his aiming to get an incident into almost every week's part causing him in his own judgment to add events to the narrative somewhat too freely." Consideration of the fight in the loft and the encounter with the bull is likely to lead the reader to endorse this view. Before volume publication, Hardy took pains to tone down some of the more sensational incidents; and his subtitle, *The Life and Death of a Man of Character,* insists that the stress must fall on what Henchard is

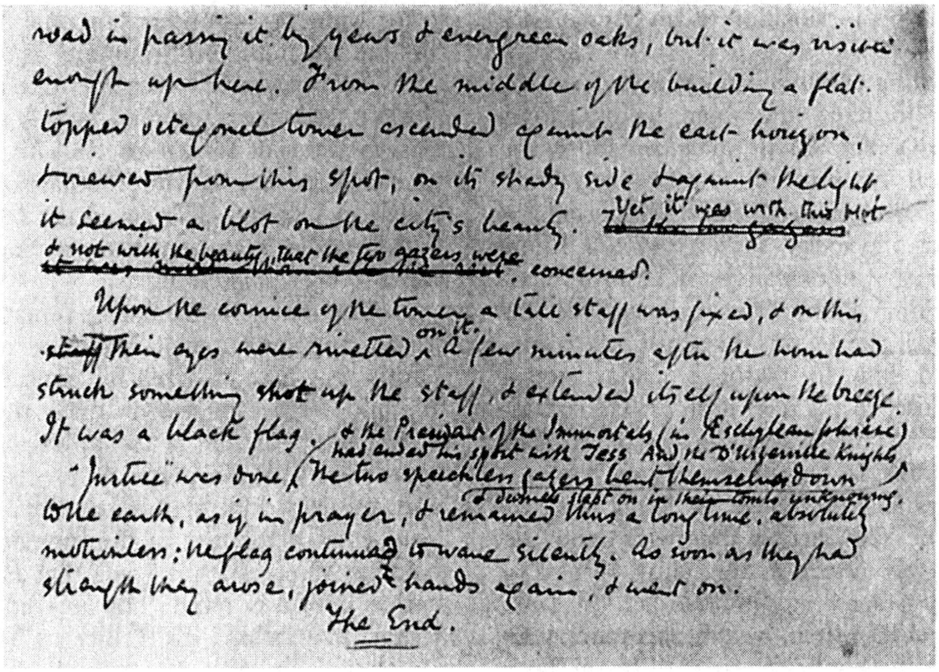
road in passing it by yews & evergreen oaks, but it was visible
enough up here. From the middle of the building a flat-
topped octagonal tower ascended against the east horizon,
& viewed from this spot, on its shady side & against the light
it seemed a blot on the city's beauty. Yet it was with this blot
& not with the beauty, that the two gazers were concerned.
Upon the cornice of the tower a tall staff was fixed, & on this
Their eyes were riveted on it. A few minutes after the hour had
struck something shot up the staff, & extended itself upon the breeze.
It was a black flag. & the President of the Immortals (in Aeschylean phrase)
had ended his sport with Tess. And the D'Urberville knights
"Justice" was done, & the two speechless gazers bent themselves down
& dames slept on in their tombs unknowing.
to the earth, as if in prayer, & remained thus a long time, absolutely
motionless: the flag continued to wave silently. As soon as they had
strength they arose, joined hands again, & went on.
The End.

The end of the manuscript for Tess of the d'Urbervilles *(Dorset County Museum)*

rather than what he does or suffers. (The pathetic incident in which Henchard returns to Elizabeth-Jane with his wedding present, a caged goldfinch, was omitted but subsequently restored to the text.) Though flawed, it remains one of the great tragic novels of the nineteenth century and Henchard one of Hardy's finest characters. The professional reviewers were disappointingly unappreciative of *The Mayor of Casterbridge,* though its reputation now stands high among Hardy's major fiction. Three writers, however, all praised it privately—George Gissing and Robert Louis Stevenson in letters to Hardy, and Gerard Manley Hopkins in a letter to Robert Bridges praising the wife sale.

In the new burst of creativity that followed the return to Dorchester, Hardy was at work on his next novel even before *The Mayor of Casterbridge* began to appear. He started *The Woodlanders* in November 1885, having undertaken to provide a serial in twelve installments for *Macmillan's Magazine;* serialization began in May 1886, but composition proceeded rather slowly, and the book was not completed until February 1887. Volume publication followed in March. Once again, there was editorial interference with Hardy's creative intentions: Mowbray Morris, the editor of the magazine, suggested that Fitzpier's sexual escapade with Suke Damson needed tactful handling.

In the 1895 preface to *The Woodlanders,* Hardy notes that what he rather pedantically calls "the question of matrimonial divergence" was raised in the novel but not pursued with any thoroughness or boldness. It is, however, a topic that was to constitute one of the major themes of his later fiction; and his portrayal of Grace Melbury's unhappy marriage to Fitzpiers is followed by other and more searching studies of failed marriages. A 1912 postscript to the preface touches on another matter, that of the location of Little Hintock. Hardy declares that "I do not know myself where that hamlet is more precisely than as explained above and in the pages of the narrative," adding ironically that "tourists assure me positively that they have found it without trouble." The reminder that Hardy's landscapes are partly real and partly fictional—that he laid a map of the imagination over the map of Dorset and the surrounding areas, and that "Wessex" exists fully only within the novels—is one that is still often disregarded.

The opening of this novel is highly characteristic: the reader is shown an empty road, then an unidentified and solitary figure, joined by other figures, their identities and purposes emerging only gradually from the account given by a narrator who is watchful and perceptive but certainly not omniscient. It is one of the most striking of Hardy's openings and displays a narrative technique both assured and original. The anticipation by Hardy of what later came to be thought of as cinematic techniques is well illustrated: one has the sense of a camera moving and registering the scene and its visual peculiarities. The first chapter ends with another characteristic motif: an outsider looks through the window of a cottage and observes the scene within. Hardy's novels are full of such moments of multiple spying: the reader watches the narrator watching a character who watches another. The scene inside the cottage—Barber Percomb's purchase of Marty South's hair, to be used to adorn the head of Mrs. Charmond—hints at one of the themes of the novel: naturalness versus artificiality. After her marriage, Grace is to feel this contrast very poignantly when she sees Giles Winterborne, "Autumn's very brother," and contrasts him with her effete husband.

The relationships of the characters are mainly on familiar lines. Grace is caught between two impulses: her long-standing commitment to her childhood friend, the faithful Giles, and her fascination with the elegant doctor, Edred Fitzpiers. As usual, the choice is between one belonging to the rural community and in harmony with its traditions, and one who is an exotic outsider unattached to the rural world by any ties of affection or loyalty; and, inevitably, social differences underscore the problem of a choice of husband, for Fitzpiers promises to lift her into another social sphere, whereas Giles can offer to share with her only the life of a working man. Hardy also introduces the theme of education: Grace's well-meaning and ambitious father has sent her away to school, with the result that she has lost touch with her old home (in Hardy's phrase, "fallen from the good old Hintock ways"). For one who had himself made such heroic—and successful—efforts at self-education and self-improvement as a path to social advancement, Hardy had a curiously ambiguous attitude toward education and was conscious of the losses as well as the gains it brings.

This outline suggests that the plot of the novel has much in common with *Far from the Madding Crowd* a dozen years earlier, and even with *Under the Greenwood Tree* earlier still. But there are differences: Fitzpier's sexual immorality is dealt with more fully and involves not only a country girl, Suke Damson, whose frank carnality contrasts strikingly with the sentimental pathos attached to Fanny Robin, but the wealthy Mrs. Charmond—another outsider and exotic. Moreover, this time there is no question of a happy ending: Gabriel's patience and long-suffering had been rewarded, but Giles dies miserably, a quixotic victim of the proprieties. As for Grace, Hardy later pointed out to a correspondent (19 July 1889) that "the *ending* of the story, as hinted rather than stated, is that the heroine is doomed to an unhappy life with an inconstant husband. I could not accent this strongly in the book; by reason of the conventions of the libraries &c." A subplot concerns the unrequited love for Giles of the simple country girl Marty South, and one of the finest scenes in the novel shows them working side by side planting young trees: an occupation both traditional and creative, involving a communion between them that requires no words and contrasts strikingly with the middle-class world into which Grace is so unhappily drawn.

The Victorian reviewers were troubled by certain aspects of *The Woodlanders*. Richard Holt Hutton, in the *Spectator* (26 March 1887), announced that "this is a very powerful book, and as disagreeable as it is powerful"—and "disagreeable" was one of the favorite epithets used of Hardy by contemporary critics. Hutton found the strength of the novel to consist in its pictures of rural life, but was disturbed by the moral implications of the story ("written with an indifference to the moral effect it conveys"). Like many others, he would obviously have been happier if Hardy had been content to remain a chronicler of quaint country ways; Hardy's determination to tackle highly controversial moral and social issues in his later fiction must be seen as going willfully against the tide of critical approval. It is only fair to add, however, that some critics were genuinely appreciative: the *Athenaeum* (26 March 1887), for instance, found the construction of the story "simply perfect," and urged "all who can tell masterly work in fiction when they see it" to read the book—though at the same time adding significantly that "the novel is distinctly not one for the young person of whom we have lately heard." Much earlier in his career, Hardy had been warned by Leslie Stephen to "remember the country clergyman's daughters"; and during the next few years his refusal to conform to the "young person" standard was to involve him in greater difficulties, and to lay him open to more severe attack, than ever before.

The Woodlanders had followed very quickly on the heels of *The Mayor of Casterbridge;* but there was to be a considerable interval before the appearance of his next novel, *Tess of the*

Hardy's study at Max Gate

d'Urbervilles. This is to some extent accounted for by the fact that Hardy was busy writing short stories based on the history of various Dorset families (published in various magazines and collected in 1891 as *A Group of Noble Dames*). But it is also true that *Tess of the d'Urbervilles* occupied him for a long time, partly because of the difficulties he underwent in finding a publisher and the necessity he eventually accepted of radical revisions to render the novel acceptable as a serial. *Tess of the d'Urbervilles* was begun in the autumn of 1888 and was intended for Tillotson and Son, a Lancashire newspaper syndicate with strongly Christian associations. At that time its title was "Too Late, Beloved!" In September 1889 Hardy sent portions of his manuscript (probably about one-half of the completed novel) to Tillotson's, who were considerably dismayed by such scenes as the seduction of Tess and the improvised baptism of her dying baby. Hardy refused to agree to their suggestion that certain scenes should be omitted, and the contract between them was canceled by mutual consent. The novel, still incomplete, was offered to *Murray's Magazine* and then to *Macmillan's Magazine;* both turned it down. Hardy thereupon set to work to "dismember" the story (his own vivid word) and produced a version that would not cause offense. This was accepted by the *Graphic,* and Harper accepted it for publication in America. There was still much work to be done, however, and the novel was not completed until the latter part of 1890. Serialization began in the weekly *Graphic* on 4 July 1891 and continued until 26 December. Two passages removed from the novel were published as separate sketches in other periodicals: "Saturday Night in Arcady," dealing with the seduction of Tess, and "The Midnight Baptism, A Study in Christianity."

Hardy's story was severely mangled for serialization: for example, he was obliged to introduce a mock marriage, staged by Alec to make Tess believe that she was his wife, and to omit the illegitimate baby. For volume publication (November 1891) Hardy carefully restored his original text, omitting the interpolations and restoring most of the omissions.

While he was engaged in the protracted attempts to find a publisher for *Tess of the d'Urbervilles,* Hardy wrote an essay published in the *New Review* in January 1890 as "Candour in English Fiction." The essay exposes the "fearful price" that a self-respecting artist has to pay for "the privilege of writing in the English language": thanks to the pressures imposed upon contemporary fiction by editors and librarians, and the prevalence of the "young person" standard, the literature of the day is largely "a literature of quackery," and it has become impossible to depict life as it really is. "Life being a physiological fact," writes Hardy, "its honest portrayal must be largely concerned with, for one thing, the relations of the sexes"; but to the frank treatment of this subject "English society imposes a well-nigh insuperable bar."

Tess of the d'Urbervilles received more attention than any of Hardy's previous books, though much of the discussion was of a moral rather than a critical kind. On the literary side, approval and disapproval were mixed in various proportions. The *Athenaeum* (9 January 1892) found the book "not only good, but great"; the *Academy* (6 February 1892) called it "a tragic masterpiece"; and in America the *Atlantic Monthly* gave it a long review, praising it as Hardy's greatest achievement. The *Saturday Review* (16 January 1892), on the other hand, spoke of "the terrible dreariness of this tale"; some critics objected to Alec as melodramatic and Angel as priggish; and the *Quarterly Review* (April 1892), in familiar terms, declared that "Mr. Hardy has told an extremely disagreeable story in an extremely disagreeable manner." Hardy, always much more affected by criticism than by praise, was so hurt by this last review that he declared: "Well, if this sort of thing continues no more novel-writing for me. A man must be a fool to deliberately stand up to be shot at."

One result of the controversy surrounding *Tess of the d'Urbervilles* was that it sold better than any of Hardy's previous novels. It comes as a surprise to find that, when Hardy's novels appeared in volume form, usually only 1,000 copies of the first edition were printed; but it is important to remember that the three-volume novel was an expensive luxury. In the case of *Tess of the d'Urbervilles,* the 1,000 copies were soon sold, and another 1,000 were printed within a few months; when a cheap reprint in one volume appeared in September 1892, it quickly ran into five impressions and sold 17,000 copies. The novel was also widely translated.

For many readers *Tess of the d'Urbervilles* is Hardy's greatest novel, and part of its richness derives from the different layers of interest that in-

Hardy's second wife, the former Florence Emily Dugdale

terpretation can uncover. It includes some of the archetypal situations of old ballads and folk songs—for instance, the ruined maid who murders her seducer—and at many points in the story Hardy invites the reader to see it as folk tale or morality play (Alec, for instance, is repeatedly identified with Satan). Yet it is also a novel of nineteenth-century life and is rooted in a highly specific landscape. When, in chapter 30, Tess stands at the railway station beside the "gleaming cranks and wheels," or when later in the novel she is obliged to work according to the mechanical rhythms of the steam-driven harvester, she belongs unmistakably to a rural world invaded by the results of the Industrial Revolution. The schooling she has received, insufficient to make her a really educated person, is enough to cut her off from the world to which her mother belongs; so that the "generation gap" is measurable in centuries rather than years. (Again, Hardy shows a distrust of the effects of popular education.) Tess speaks two languages, the dialect of her home and a standard form of speech acquired from her London-trained teacher; the result is a discontent with the sphere of life into which she has been born, and when, in the second chapter, Angel Clare has briefly passed into her life and (for the time being) out again, she has no time for the village lads, who "did not speak so nicely as the strange young man had done." Part of the social background of the novel is that depopulation of the countryside and breakdown of the old stable communities of which Hardy had written in an essay, "The Dorsetshire Labourer," printed in *Longman's Magazine* in July 1883; Hardy drew on his essay for certain passages in *Tess of the d'Urbervilles,* such as the account of the Lady-Day moving in chapters 51 and 52.

The various settings of the action to a large extent reflect the structure of the novel. Tess begins in her symbolically named native village of Marlott (her lot or destiny is from the outset marred or spoiled); she moves to the Durberville home at Trantridge; works successively at Talbothays and Flintcomb-Ash; and eventually murders Alec at Sandbourne, is arrested at Stonehenge, and is executed at Wintoncester (this list of her wanderings is selective). Although the geographical range of her experiences is not extensive, Hardy skillfully uses settings to contrast with each other and to symbolize her mood at various phases of her existence. The lush fertility of Talbothays is associated with the period of her growing love for Angel; the harsh life of Flintcomb-Ash (another significant name) harmonizes with her mood of despair after Angel has left her; the middle-class seaside resort of Sandbourne is the apt setting for her reunion with the shallow, pleasure-loving Alec; and, arrested at Stonehenge, she becomes a sacrifice to conventional morality and the victim of a barbaric system of justice. Tess's wanderings are also assigned to particular seasons of the year: she is at Talbothays in summertime, but Flintcomb-Ash is associated with winter and death. In many ways this is Hardy's most poetic novel, and his evocation of the natural world and of his heroine, in all their concrete, detailed, and often sensuous physicality, recalls the odes of John Keats.

Tess possesses an intensely physical presence and an unconsciously radiated sexuality that make her almost unique in Victorian fiction. (For somewhat later parallels, one may turn to the work of D. H. Lawrence, who studied Hardy's novels carefully, wrote about them, and probably owed them a good deal.) Her physical attractiveness is, however, a curse: when, in chapter 46, she asks Alec, "What have I done!," he tells her, "Nothing intentionally. But you have been the means—the innocent means—of my backsliding. . . . " It is true that Tess does "nothing intentionally," and this passivity or unconsciousness is a limitation of her character: there are numerous comparisons of her to a shy animal, she moves through scenes and experiences as if in a dream, and the reader is given virtually no sense of an inner life; when she finds herself involved in moral action or moral debate, as in the scene after her marriage to Angel, she is shown as naively and almost childishly lacking in worldly wisdom or even peasant common sense. The highly self-conscious and ironically named Angel is her antithesis in this respect: he reflects too much and obeys his instincts too little. As for Alec, he is both a figure out of Victorian melodrama and the occasion for satire on the rapid social advancement of the urban middle classes. Alec's father has made a fortune in the North of England, and in one generation the family has attempted to obtain gentility by purchase, not only moving into Wessex and buying land there but actually adopting the name of one of the old local families—that ancient name of which Tess's is itself a corruption. Hardy was much preoccupied by the decline of old families; then in his fifties, he probably felt deeply his own childlessness (in the event, none of his generation producing any issue, the family line died out). Tess's misfortunes begin on the day that her father, John Durbeyfield, learns that he is a descendant of the once-great family of d'Urbervilles; from that point—the thoughtless imparting of a piece of antiquarian information by a character who then disappears from the story—subsequent events move forward with a relentless logic, as her father's foolish notions of gentility drive Tess into service with Alec's family and eventually into Alec's arms.

Tess of the d'Urbervilles contains some of Hardy's best writing—surprisingly, when one recalls the frustrating and exasperating circumstances in which much of the novel was written. The recurrent imagery (one pattern throughout the novel associated with the color red, for instance, and another with the sun and the moon) gives it great density of texture; there is correspondingly less of the generalizing and moralizing that are among Hardy's defects as a prose writer and that must in part, at least, be laid at the door of the serial novel with its requirement of a specified length, and its consequent encouragement of padding. Certain passages (chapter 20, for example) have a poetic intensity rare in the late-nineteenth-century novel.

Hardy's next novel was to be poetic in conception but curiously schematic in structure and as thin in texture as *Tess of the d'Urbervilles* is rich. Hardy himself seems to have felt no great enthusiasm for *The Well-Beloved:* he described it in a let-

Thomas and Florence Hardy at Max Gate with their dog, Wessex, in 1914

ter to his American publishers as "short and slight, and written entirely with a view to serial publication," and he seems to have been in no hurry to see it appear in volume form. It is the product of an interlude of much less intense creative activity between the two major novels, *Tess of the d'Urbervilles* and *Jude the Obscure*. Begun toward the end of 1891, as the serialization of *Tess of the d'Urbervilles* drew to a close, it was serialized in the weekly *Illustrated London News* from 1 October to 17 December 1892. In view of the trouble that *Tess of the d'Urbervilles* had caused him, it is interesting to find Hardy assuring his publishers that in this new novel "There is not a word or scene . . . which can offend the most fastidious taste; and it is equally suited for the reading of young people, and for that of persons of maturer years." After serialization, Hardy put the novel aside for nearly four years; in 1896 he revised it and changed the ending, and it appeared in volume form in March 1897.

The Well-Beloved (originally titled "The Pursuit of the Well-Beloved") is subtitled *A Sketch of a Temperament* and bears on the title page a quotation from Percy Bysshe Shelley ("One shape of many names"). The story blends Shelleyan idealism with preoccupations that a knowledge of Hardy's temperament suggests may be autobiographical. His hero is an artist: Pierston is a sculptor who seeks perfection both in art and in life. The implausible plot shows him falling in love successively with three women belonging to three generations of the same family: time passes, he grows older, but his desire for the ideal remains as fresh as ever. None of his loves brings happiness. The tone of the novel is light, but the underlying conception is wistful and even melancholy. This short novel shows Hardy as haunted by the idea of time and growing old—"a time-torn man," as he describes himself in one of his poems. Although so much in the book is fanciful and insubstantial, the setting (on Portland Bill, referred to in the book as the "Isle of Slingers") has an admirable solidity.

Between the serialization and the volume publication of *The Well-Beloved,* Hardy wrote and published his last novel, *Jude the Obscure.* This work seems to have occupied him for longer than any other of his novels. As early as 1887, before *Tess of the d'Urbervilles* was even begun, he had begun making notes for the novel that was to become *Jude the Obscure;* in 1890 he "jotted down" its "scheme"—presumably a plot outline; in 1892-1893 he visited the village of Great Fawley in Berkshire (formerly the home of his grandmother and the prototype of Marygreen in the novel, as well as the source of the hero's surname), and also spent some time in Oxford (the Christminster of the novel); during the same period he wrote the story "in outline"; and in 1893-1894 he wrote it in full. It was serialized in *Harper's New Monthly Magazine* from December 1894 to November 1895 and published in volume form in November 1895.

Once again Hardy found himself forced to make extensive compromises with his original intentions in order to win acceptance for his novel as a serial. His early assurance to his editor that the story "could not offend the most fastidious maiden" was not justified by events and suggests that, in the course of composition, the novel underwent a radical shift of direction. The germ of the novel may be contained in a note Hardy made in his diary on 28 April 1888: "A short story of a young man—'who could not go to Oxford'—His struggles and ultimate failure. Suicide. There is something [in this] the world ought to be shown, and I am the one to show it to them. . . ." The theme, that is, was to be a poor man's quest for an education and the tragic outcome of his failure to storm the bastions of educational privilege. This theme survives in the completed novel, but it has become subordinate to the central discussion of marriage. Jude's tragedy is only partly caused by his unsuccessful struggles to gain admission to the university: his entanglements, first with the country girl Arabella and then with the intellectual Sue, occupy a dominant position in the novel. It is true that "the marriage question" was topical in the 1890s, and *Jude the Obscure* is not the only novel in which it is debated; but the state of Hardy's own childless marriage surely influenced his attitude toward the subject. His relationship with the snobbish, foolish, but not unlikable Emma Hardy deteriorated as they grew older; and by this time, although they continued to live under the same roof, the couple were leading virtually separate lives.

The effects of change and the breakdown of a traditional order had always been a major theme of Hardy's fiction; and in *Jude the Obscure* the note is sounded in the opening sentence: "The schoolmaster was leaving the village. . . ." Jude, an orphan, feels rootless and unwanted: Hardy presents a hero who is from the outset deprived of a place in the community. The short opening chapter moves ahead with great economy and assurance; its final paragraph briefly evokes the destruction of the past that is changing the face of rural England—thatched cottages have been pulled down, and the medieval church has been "restored" by some such well-meaning architect as Hardy himself had been a generation earlier.

Hardy declared that there was no autobiography in the novel, but the claim is transparently false. Like the young Hardy, Jude works painfully but patiently to educate himself, concentrating (as Hardy had done) on the traditional academic disciplines of the classics and theology. Since he must earn a living, he becomes a stonemason (recalling the occupation of Hardy's father and grandfather). His ambition takes him to Christminster, the great university town whose colleges are monopolized by the sons of the well-to-do rather than by the poor scholars for whom they were originally founded, and Hardy moves his hero outside the familiar Wessex world. Jude is the most restless of Hardy's protagonists, and his wanderings mirror the unsatisfied longings of his heart.

Hardy at Max Gate with the Prince of Wales in 1923

Jude's slow progress toward his distant goal is interrupted, and eventually frustrated, by his encounters with two women of contrasting types. Arabella, first seen washing a pig's innards and repeatedly associated with pigs, recalls the sorceress Circe, who turned Odysseus's companions into swine. She seduces Jude, traps him to begin his life afresh. In Christminster he meets his cousin Sue Bridehead, a study in the "new woman"—a boyish or androgynous figure, intellectual and skeptical, and a representative of the demand for female emancipation and equality of the sexes. Sue marries Phillotson, Jude's old schoolmaster—another disastrous marriage—even though she and Jude are in love; later Sue and Jude live together, but their children die tragically, they part, and Jude dies within a stone's throw of the colleges to which he has, to the very end, been denied admission. Hardy's treatment of marriage is bleakly uncompromising, and on one level *Jude the Obscure* is a propaganda novel, eloquently pleading a case—or, more precisely, two cases: one holding that marriage can only be binding for life at the expense of considerable human misery, the other advocating opportunities of higher education for the workingman. But it is also a work of poetic resonance that uses recurring symbols and allusions to unify the episodic narrative and shifting scenes. Jude, who dies at thirty, is a Christ-figure; and the novel contains numerous biblical allusions, including the association of Jude and Arabella with Samson and Delilah. Hardy makes much use of contrast: Christian and pagan beliefs, Gothic and classical styles of architecture, scholarship and manual labor, sexuality and frigidity. The patterning of the plot involves some fairly complex interrelationships between the four principal characters; Hardy remarked on this connection (in a letter dated 4 January 1896) that "the rectangular lines of the story were not premeditated, but came by chance." The tasks of mangling the original novel for serialization and subsequently restoring it to its original form seem to have wearied him, and he wrote in 1895 that "I have lost energy for revising and improving the original as I meant to do." Nevertheless, though there are unsatisfactory passages—the dialogues between Jude and Sue and the murder of their children by Jude and Arabella's son, who then commits suicide, have come in for frequent criticism—the novel is deeply impressive.

Hardy declared that he felt sure that the book "makes for morality," but this was not the opinion of many of its reviewers; and *Jude the Obscure* was more savagely attacked than any of its predecessors. One reviewer said that it was "almost the worst book I have ever read"; another described it as "steeped in sex"; and Hardy was accused of "wallowing in the mire" and "attacking the fundamental institutions of society." It was nicknamed "*Jude the Obscene,*" a bishop attacked it in the press, and a leading library withdrew it from circulation. Some, however, were not too blinded by prejudice to perceive its merits; and before Hardy's death it had been widely translated and was recognized as a masterpiece.

Though Hardy lived for another thirty-two years after the publication of *Jude the Obscure,* he never wrote another novel; and this silence has given rise to varied explanations. The traditional belief that he was so disgusted by the reception of *Jude the Obscure* that he declined to expose himself again to the same kind of treatment is hard to accept; there is evidence in his letters that he had thoughts of writing another novel several years later, though he never did so. The end of his novel-writing career was not abrupt or dramatic, and it can have dawned on the reading public only gradually that they were to have no more novels from his pen. From the last years of the nineteenth century, his energies went into the writing and publication of verse; although he had devoted a quarter of a century to fiction, his sense of a poetic vocation had never left him, and he had gone on writing poems (though not publishing them). In 1898 there appeared the first volume of his verse, *Wessex Poems,* and for the rest of his life he published poems frequently and in large quantities. He had long been impatient with the constraints of serialized fiction; in any case, the success of *Tess of the d'Urbervilles* and *Jude the Obscure* brought him financial security, and he died a rich man. But it would be wrong to suppose that he lost all interest in his novels: the first collected edition (*The Wessex Novels,* 1895-1913) was followed by the *Wessex Edition* (1912-1931), for which Hardy not only wrote a "General Preface" (1911) but meticulously revised his text.

Apart from his fourteen novels, Hardy was a prolific writer of short stories, most of which were collected in four volumes. They were written for magazine publication and are of uneven quality; the best, however, are not mere potboilers but are excellent specimens of their kind. Comparison of the balladlike "The Three Strangers" with the realistic stories of modern life such as "The Son's Veto" or "On the Western Circuit" will illustrate the range of Hardy's art in this genre.

Hardy's nonfictional prose also calls for mention. At various times he wrote nearly forty prefaces for his volumes of fiction and verse; and although these cannot be said to present any fully articulated aesthetic, they include interesting comments on specific novels and sometimes raise questions of general import. Among Hardy's essays, "The Dorsetshire Labourer" and "Candour in English Fiction" have already been mentioned; others of interest include "The Profitable Reading of Fiction" (1888) and "Memories of Church Restoration" (1906). Hardy's notebooks and commonplace books have been published and offer many insights into his reading and his intellectual interests. He was a prolific, though not a self-revealing, letter writer, but most of the surviving letters belong to his later years.

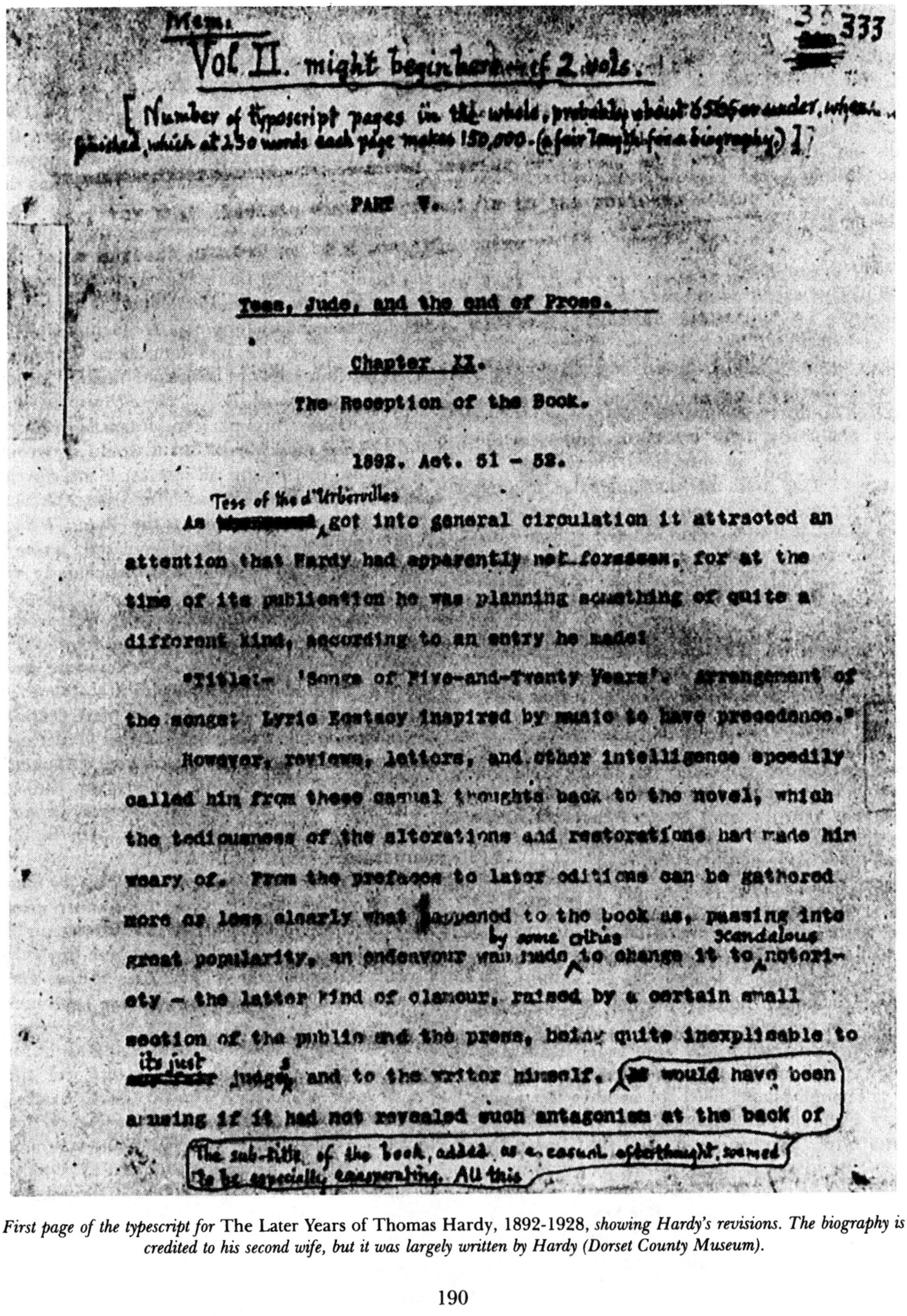

Mem.

Vol II. might begin here if 2 vols.

3[redacted] 333

[Number of typescript pages in the whole, probably about 650 or under, when finished, which at 230 words each page makes 150,000 - (a fair length for a biography)]

PART V.

Tess, Jude, and the end of Prose.

Chapter XI.

The Reception of the Book.

1892. Aet. 51 - 52.

As [redacted] Tess of the d'Urbervilles got into general circulation it attracted an attention that Hardy had apparently not foreseen, for at the time of its publication he was planning something of quite a different kind, according to an entry he made:

"Title:- 'Songs of Five-and-Twenty Years'. Arrangement of the songs: Lyric Ecstasy inspired by music to have precedence."

However, reviews, letters, and other intelligence speedily called him from these casual thoughts back to the novel, which the tediousness of the alterations and restorations had made him weary of. From the prefaces to later editions can be gathered more or less clearly what happened to the book as, passing into great popularity, an endeavour was made by some critics to change it to scandalous notoriety - the latter kind of clamour, raised by a certain small section of the public and the press, being quite inexplicable to [redacted] its just judges, and to the writer himself. [redacted] would have been amusing if it had not revealed such antagonism at the back of

The sub-title of the book, added as a casual afterthought, seemed to be especially exasperating. All this

First page of the typescript for The Later Years of Thomas Hardy, 1892-1928, *showing Hardy's revisions. The biography is credited to his second wife, but it was largely written by Hardy (Dorset County Museum).*

Hardy's fame increased steadily in his later years; and although he remained more and more at Max Gate, he received there a stream of distinguished visitors, including the Prince of Wales, who came to pay homage to the most famous English writer of his age. After declining the offer of a knighthood, he accepted the Order of Merit—bestowed by the sovereign and the highest honor that can be accorded to an English author—in 1910. Fifteen months after the death of Emma Hardy on 27 November 1912, Hardy married Florence Emily Dugdale, who was some forty years his junior. The volume of criticism devoted to his work increased steadily, and he was the subject of several full-length studies during his lifetime. He died at Max Gate on 11 January 1928 at the age of eighty-seven.

Letters:

The Collected Letters of Thomas Hardy, 7 volumes, edited by Richard Little Purdy and Michael Millgate (Oxford: Clarendon Press, 1978-1988).

Bibliographies:

Richard Little Purdy, *Thomas Hardy: A Bibliographical Study* (Oxford: Clarendon Press, 1954);

Ronald P. Draper and Martin Ray, *An Annotated Critical Bibliography of Thomas Hardy* (New York: Harvester Wheatsheaf, 1989).

Biographies:

Robert Gittings, *Young Thomas Hardy* (London: Heinemann, 1975);

Gittings, *The Older Hardy* (London: Heinemann, 1978);

Gittings, *The Second Mrs. Hardy* (London: Oxford University Press, 1980);

Michael Millgate, *Thomas Hardy: A Biography* (New York: Random House, 1982);

Simon Gatrell, *Hardy the Creator: A Textual Biography* (Oxford: Clarendon Press, 1988);

Timothy Hands, *Thomas Hardy: Distracted Preacher?* (London: Macmillan, 1989).

References:

John Bayley, *An Essay on Hardy* (Cambridge: Cambridge University Press, 1978);

Douglas Brown, *Thomas Hardy* (London: Longmans, Green, 1954);

R. G. Cox, ed., *Thomas Hardy: The Critical Heritage* (London: Routledge & Kegan Paul, 1970);

A. J. Guerard, *Thomas Hardy: The Novels and Stories* (Cambridge, Mass.: Harvard University Press, 1949);

Irving Howe, *Thomas Hardy* (New York: Macmillan, 1967);

J. T. Laird, *The Shaping of "Tess of the d'Urbervilles"* (Oxford: Clarendon Press, 1975);

J. Hillis Miller, *Thomas Hardy: Distance and Desire* (Cambridge: Belknap Press, 1970);

Michael Millgate, *Thomas Hardy: His Career as a Novelist* (London: Bodley Head, 1971);

Millgate, "Thomas Hardy," in *Victorian Fiction: A Second Guide to Research,* edited by George H. Ford (New York: Modern Language Association of America, 1978), pp. 308-332;

Rosemarie Morgan, *Women and Sexuality in the Novels of Thomas Hardy* (London: Routledge, 1988);

Norman Page, *Thomas Hardy* (London: Routledge & Kegan Paul, 1977);

Page, ed., *Thomas Hardy Annual,* nos. 1-5 (London: Macmillan, 1982-1987);

Page, ed., *Thomas Hardy: The Writer and His Background* (London: Bell & Hyman, 1980);

F. B. Pinion, *A Hardy Companion* (London: Macmillan, 1968);

Dennis Taylor, *Hardy's Poetry, 1860-1928* (London: Macmillan, 1981);

Taylor, *Hardy's Metres and Victorian Prosody* (Oxford: Clarendon Press, 1988);

George Wing, *Hardy* (Edinburgh: Oliver & Boyd, 1963).

Papers:

The manuscripts of many of Hardy's novels survive, complete or in part, and provide interesting evidence of his methods of composition and revision. *Jude the Obscure* is in the Fitzwilliam Museum, Cambridge; *The Mayor of Casterbridge, The Woodlanders,* and *Under the Greenwood Tree* in Dorset County Museum; *The Return of the Native* at University College, Dublin; *Tess of the d'Urbervilles* in the British Library; *The Trumpet-Major* at Windsor Castle; *Two on a Tower* in the Houghton Library at Harvard; and a portion of *A Pair of Blue Eyes* in the Berg Collection at New York Public Library. *Far from the Madding Crowd* is in private hands.

Gerard Manley Hopkins

(28 July 1844 - 8 June 1889)

This entry was updated by Jerome Bump (University of Texas at Austin) from his entry in DLB 35: Victorian Poets After 1850.

See also the Hopkins entry in DLB 57: Victorian Prose Writers After 1867.

SELECTED BOOKS: *Poems of Gerard Manley Hopkins,* edited by Robert Bridges (London: Milford, 1918); enlarged, edited by Bridges and Charles Williams (London: Oxford University Press, 1930); enlarged again, edited by W. H. Gardner (London & New York: Oxford University Press, 1948); revised, edited by Gardner (London & New York: Oxford University Press, 1956); enlarged again, edited by Gardner and N. H. MacKenzie (London & New York: Oxford University Press, 1967); corrected, edited by Gardner and MacKenzie (London & New York: Oxford University Press, 1970);

The Notebooks and Papers of Gerard Manley Hopkins, edited by Humphry House (London & New York: Oxford University Press, 1937); enlarged as *The Journals and Papers of Gerard Manley Hopkins,* edited by House and Graham Storey (London & New York: Oxford University Press, 1959);

The Sermons and Devotional Writings of Gerard Manley Hopkins, edited by Christopher Devlin (London & New York: Oxford University Press, 1959).

SELECTED PERIODICAL PUBLICATIONS—UNCOLLECTED: "Winter with the Gulf Stream," *Once a Week,* 8 (February 1863): 210;

"Barnfloor and Winepress," *Union Review,* 3 (1865): 579-580.

Gerard Manley Hopkins is one of the three or four greatest poets of the Victorian era and one of its most original prose writers. He is regarded by different readers as the greatest Victorian poet of religion, of nature, or of melancholy. However, because his style was so radically different from that of his contemporaries, his

Gerard Manley Hopkins

best poems were not accepted for publication during his lifetime, and his achievement was not fully recognized until after World War I. Eventually most of his essays, notes, sermons, literary criticism, and letters also appeared in print, and his accomplishments in prose began to attract attention as well.

Born in Stratford, Essex, on 28 July 1844, Hopkins's idiosyncratic creativity was the result of interactions with others, beginning with the members of his family. Hopkins's extended family constituted a social environment that made the commitment of an eldest son to religion, language, and art not only possible but highly probable. His mother, Kate Smith Hopkins (1821-1900), was a devout High Church Anglican who brought up her children to be religious. Hopkins read from the New Testament daily at school to fulfill a promise he made to her. The daughter of a London physician, she was better educated than most Victorian women and particularly fond of music and of reading, especially German philosophy and literature, the novels of Charles Dickens, and eventually her eldest son's poetry.

Her sister Maria Smith Giberne taught Hopkins to sketch. The drawings originally executed as headings on letters from her home, Blunt House, Croydon, to Hopkins's mother and father reveal the kind of precise, detailed drawing that Hopkins was taught. The influence of Maria Smith Giberne on her nephew can be seen by comparing these letter headings with Hopkins's sketch *Dandelion, Hemlock, and Ivy,* which he made at Blunt House. Hopkins's interest in the visual arts was also sustained by his maternal uncle, Edward Smith, who began as a lawyer but soon made painting his profession; by Richard James Lane, his maternal great-uncle, an engraver and lithographer who frequently exhibited at the Royal Academy; and by Lane's daughters, Clara and Eliza (or Emily), who exhibited at the Society of Female Artists and elsewhere. Another maternal uncle, John Simm Smith, Jr., reinforced the religious tradition which Hopkins's mother passed on to him; Smith was churchwarden at St. Peter's, Croydon.

These artistic and religious traditions were also supported by Hopkins's paternal relations. His aunt Anne Eleanor Hopkins tutored her nephew in sketching, painting, and music. His uncle Thomas Marsland Hopkins was perpetual curate at St. Saviour's, Paddington, and coauthor with Hopkins's father of the 1849 volume *Pietas Metrica Or, Nature Suggestive of God and Godliness,* "by the Brothers Theophilus and Theophylact." He was married to Katherine Beechey, who, with her cousin Catherine Lloyd, maintained close contacts with the High Church Tractarian movement which deeply affected Hopkins at Oxford. Her sister, Frances Ann Beechey, was a good painter, famous in North America for her documentary paintings of the Canadian voyageurs. In 1865 she was in London, where Hopkins met her, and after 1870 she exhibited at the Royal Academy. Charles Gordon Hopkins, Hopkins's uncle, developed the family interest in languages as well as religion. He moved to Hawaii, where he learned Hawaiian and helped establish an Anglican bishopric in Honolulu. In 1856 he helped Manley Hopkins, the poet's father, become consul-general for Hawaii in London.

Manley Hopkins was the founder of a marine insurance firm. It is no accident that shipwreck, one of the firm's primary concerns, was the subject of Hopkins's most ambitious poem, *The Wreck of the Deutschland* (1875). Nor can the emphasis on religion in that poem be attributed solely to the mother's influence. Manley Hopkins was a devout High Church Anglican who taught Sunday School at St. John's in Hampstead, where he was churchwarden. He loved music and literature, passing on his fondness for puns and wordplay to his sons Gerard and Lionel and his love for poetry to Gerard especially. His publications include *A Philosopher's Stone and Other Poems* (1843) and *Spicelegium Poeticum, A Gathering of Verses by Manley Hopkins* (1892). He also reviewed poetry for the *London Times* and wrote one novel and an essay on Henry Wadsworth Longfellow, which were never published.

This concern for art, language, and religion in Hopkins's extended family had a direct effect on the Hopkins children. Hopkins's sister Milicent (1849-1946) was originally interested in music but eventually became an "out-sister" of All Saints' Home, an Anglican sisterhood founded in London in 1851. She took the sister's habit in 1878. Hopkins's sister Kate (1856-1933) shared her brother's love of languages, humor, and sketching. She helped Robert Bridges publish the first edition of Hopkins's poems. Hopkins's youngest sister, Grace (1857-1945), set some of his poems to music and composed accompaniments for Hopkins's melodies for poems by Richard Watson Dixon and Bridges.

Hopkins's brother Lionel (1854-1952) sustained the family interest in languages. He was top of the senior division of Modern School at Winchester, with a reputation for thoughtful and thorough work in French and German. He became a world-famous expert on archaic and colloquial Chinese. He loved puns, jokes, parodies, and all kinds of wordplay as much as his father and his brother Gerard. Hopkins's brother Arthur (1847-1930) continued the family interest in the visual arts. He was an excellent sketcher and became a professional illustrator and artist. He illustrated Thomas Hardy's *Return of the Native* in 1878, was a member of the Royal Watercolour Society, and exhibited at the Royal Academy. The youngest brother, Everard (1860-1928), followed in Arthur's footsteps. He too became a professional illustrator and cartoonist for newspapers and periodicals, and he exhibited his watercolors and pastels in London. Both Everard and Arthur

Dandelion, Hemlock, and Ivy, *an early sketch by Hopkins showing the influence of Maria Smith Giberne's teaching*

were regular contributors to *Punch* and shared Hopkins's admiration for the paintings of John Everett Millais.

The relationship between Hopkins and his father reveals important early instances of creative collaboration and competition within the family. Hopkins copied eleven of the poems from his father's volume *A Philosopher's Stone* into his Oxford notebooks. In those poems his father expressed a Keatsian dismay over science's threat to a magical or imaginative response to nature. Manley Hopkins's desire to preserve a Wordsworthian love of nature in his children is evident in his "To a Beautiful Child":

> . . . *thy* book
> Is cliff, and wood, and foaming waterfall;
> Thy playmates—the wild sheep and birds that call
> Hoarse to the storm;—thy sport is with the storm
> To wrestle;—and thy piety to stand
> Musing on things create, and their Creator's hand!

This was a remarkably prophetic poem for Manley Hopkins's first "beautiful child," Gerard, born only a year after this poem was published. The phrase "and birds that call / Hoarse to the storm" invites comparison with the son's images of the windhover rebuffing the big wind in "The Windhover" (1877) and with the image of the great stormfowl at the conclusion of "Henry Purcell" (1879). The father's prophecy, "thy sport is with the storm / To wrestle," is fulfilled in Gerard's *The Wreck of the Deutschland* and "The Loss of the *Eurydice*" (1878). These two shipwreck poems, replete with spiritual instruction for those in doubt and danger, were the son's poetic and religious counterparts to his father's 1873 volume, *The Port of Refuge, or advice and instructions to the Master-Mariner in situations of doubt, difficulty, and danger.*

Gerard's response to nature was also influenced by a poem such as "A Bird Singing in a Narrow Street," one of the eleven poems from *A Philosopher's Stone* he copied into his notebook. This theme of the bird confined recurs most obviously in Gerard's "The Caged Skylark" (1877) but may be detected even in comments on the imprisoning narrowness of urban civilization in his letters. In addition, the son answered the father's representation of a bird filling the "throbbing air" with sound and "making our bosoms to thy cadence thrill" in "The Nightingale" (1866):

For he began at once and shook
My head to hear. He might have strung
A row of ripples in the brook,
    So forcibly he sung,
The mist upon the leaves have strewed,
And danced the balls of dew that stood
In acres all above the wood.

This particular motif of the singing bird appears again in Gerard's "Spring" (1877): "and thrush / Through the echoing timber does so rinse and wring / The ear, it strikes like lightnings to hear him sing." The father's attempt to represent what it is like to live in a bird's environment, moreover, to experience daily the "fields, the open sky, / The rising sun, the moon's pale majesty; / The leafy bower, where the airy nest is hung" was also one of the inspirations of the son's lengthy account of a lark's gliding beneath clouds, its aerial view of the fields below, and its proximity to a rainbow in "Il Mystico" (1862), as well as the son's attempt to enter into a lark's existence and express its essence mimically in "The Woodlark" (1876). A related motif, Manley's feeling for clouds, evident in his poem "Clouds," encouraged his son's representation of them in "Hurrahing in Harvest" (1877) and "That Nature is a Heraclitean Fire" (1888).

Competition and collaboration between father and son continued even long after Hopkins left home to take his place in the world. In 1879, for instance, Gerard Manley Hopkins wrote to Bridges, "I enclose some lines by my father called forth by the proposal to fell the trees in Well Walk (where John Keats and other interesting people lived) and printed in some local paper." Two months later Hopkins composed "Binsey Poplars" to commemorate the felling of a grove of trees near Oxford. Clearly, competition with his father was an important creative stimulus.

In addition to specific inspirations such as these, the father communicated to his son a sense of nature as a book written by God which leads its readers to a thoughtful contemplation of Him, a theme particularly evident in Manley and Thomas Marsland Hopkins's book of poems, *Pietas Metrica.* Consequently, Gerard went on to write poems which were some of the best expressions not only of the Romantic approach to nature but also the older tradition of explicitly religious nature poetry.

Pietas Metrica was devoted explicitly to that marriage of nature and religion which became characteristic of Gerard's poetry. This book is also valuable as a model of the norm of contemporary religious nature poetry which Hopkins was trying both to sustain and surpass. The aims of the authors of *Pietas Metrica* became Hopkins's own. As noted in the preface, "It was the design of the writers of this volume to blend together two of Man's best things, Religion and Poetry. They aimed at binding with another tie the feeling of piety with external nature and our daily thoughts. The books of Nature and Revelation have been laid side by side and read together."

The most joyous synchronic reading of the Bible and the Book of Nature was the hymn of creation, a traditional genre inspired by Psalm 148 to which such poems of Gerard's as "God's Grandeur" (1877), "Pied Beauty" (1877), "Hurrahing in Harvest," and "Easter" (1866) belong. A line such as "Flowers do ope their heavenward eyes" in Hopkins's "Easter," for instance, would normally be ascribed to the influence of George Herbert, but the representation of a flower "breathing up to heaven / The incense of her prayer" like a "natural altar" in "The Fraxinella" in *Pietas Metrica* reveals that it is just as appropriate to look to contemporary poetry for a context for Hopkins's poems as it is to look back to Metaphysical poets such as Herbert. Indeed, in some cases it may be more appropriate to seek contemporary models. Though Herbert's "The Flower" is a famous example of a flower straining toward heaven, he employs no satellite imagery of opening eyes; indeed he only twice uses the word *ope* in all of his poems, neither time referring to flowers, and he never uses the adjective *heavenward.*

The personification of Earth in Hopkins's "Easter"—"Earth throws Winter's robes away. / Decks herself for Easter Day"—also recalls the personification of Nature in "Catholic Truth" from *Pietas Metrica.* A reader of Hopkins's poetry familiar with contemporary creation hymns such as "Catholic Truth" would also expect the song rhythm which Hopkins employs in the third stanza of "Easter," because in this genre nature, rather than mankind, is usually represented as more faithfully singing God's praise:

Gather gladness from the skies;
Take a lesson from the ground;

Flowers do ope their heavenward eyes
And a Spring-time joy have found;
Earth throws Winter's robes away,
Decks herself for Easter Day.

Ultimately, mankind joins in the song in related hymns in this genre, including Christina Rossetti's "And there was no more Sea," in which all possible voices are united "In oneness of contentment offering praise." Hence Hopkins extends the rhythm to include man in the fourth stanza of "Easter":

Beauty now for ashes wear,
Perfumes for the garb of woe.
Chaplets for dishevelled hair,
Dances for sad footsteps slow;
Open wide your hearts that they
Let in joy this Easter Day.

Although man and nature are ultimately bound by love in one hymn of creation, contemporary readers of poems such as "Easter" know that nature is traditionally represented not only as more consistently heeding the commandment to song which concludes Hopkins's "Easter" but also as best fulfilling the demand of his first stanza for a plenitude of offerings:

Break the box and shed the nard;
Stop not now to count the cost;
Hither bring pearl, opal, sard;
Reck not what the poor have lost;
Upon Christ throw all away:
Know ye, this is Easter Day.

"Where are the Nine?" in *Pietas Metrica* develops this concept of nature's unstinted offering and points to the traditional contrast between man and nature implicit in the first stanza of "Easter": "And is it so that Nature stints her praise, / With niggard thanks makes offering to her God?" The answer of Hopkins's father and uncle is clear:

No, Nature is not backward, she declares
Each blessing as it comes, and owns her Lord,
She is no miser of her thanks, she spares
No praise, due to Heaven, beloved adored.

Hopkins agreed with his father and uncle that man seemed "backward" in comparison with nature, especially in "God's Grandeur," "Spring," "In the Valley of the Elwy" (1877), "The Sea and the Skylark" (1877), "Binsey Poplars," "Duns Scotus's Oxford" (1879), and "Ribblesdale" (1882). Hopkins also discovered to his despair the truth of the final complaint of "Where are the Nine?":

Alas for man! day after day may rise,
Night may shade his thankless head,
He sees no God in the bright, morning skies
He sings no praises from his guarded bed.

This apparent disappearance of God from nature in the nineteenth century inspired some of the didacticism which pervades Hopkins's later nature poetry. Unlike the Romantics, many Victorians thought of nature as another Book of Revelation to be used for the same practical ends as the Bible: to inculcate lessons in the religious life. As the statement in the Hopkins brothers' preface about placing the books of Nature and Revelation side by side suggests, *Pietas Metrica* is an excellent illustration of this tradition. While the Wordsworthian influence in the volume is occasionally implicit in poems such as "Love," the sermonical aim is almost always explicit, as in the title "Autumnal Lessons."

Flowers were especially popular for purposes of instruction, their function in Hopkins's "Easter." The flowers in "Catholic Truth," for example, are "All telling the same truth; their simple creed," and the author of "The Fraxinella" sighs, with the exclamation mark so characteristic of Hopkins, "Ah! could our hearts / Read thoughtful lessons from thy modest leaves." When we place Hopkins's nature poetry in this tradition we not only perceive the contemporary precedents for the homilies which conclude so many of his nature poems, we also begin to discern some of the distinguishing features of his didacticism. Hopkins's commands strike us as more direct and imperative, and we discover that his religious poetry was unusually proselytical before he became a Catholic and long before he became a Jesuit.

Nature poetry was not the only area in which father and son were rivals. Romantic love of childhood as well as nature is evident in Manley Hopkins's "To a Beautiful Child" and "The Nursery Window," and this theme of childhood innocence is also stressed by his son in "Spring," "The Handsome Heart" (1879), and "The Bugler's First Communion" (1879). The father also composed straightforward religious poems such as his long poem on John the Baptist in *A Philosopher's Stone,* and the son soon surpassed his father in this category as well. Gerard's many poems about martyrs recall his fa-

Manor Farm, Shanklin, *one of Hopkins's Ruskinesque sketches showing an obsession for minute detail (Harry Ransom Humanities Research Center, University of Texas at Austin)*

ther's preoccupation with physical suffering in poems such as "The Grave-Digger" and "The Child's Dream" from *A Philosopher's Stone.*

The son's melancholy, evident in poems such as the undated "Spring and Death," "Spring and Fall" (1880), and "The Leaden Echo" (1882), can also be traced to poems such as his father's sonnet "All things grow old—grow old, decay and change" and "A Philosopher's Stone," which warns that "The withered crown will soon slide down / A skull all bleached and blent" and concludes in that didactic mode typical of several of his son's religious poems:

"The Alchymists rare, are they who prepare
For death ere life be done;
And by study hard WITHIN THE CHURCHYARD
IS FOUND THE PHILOSOPHER'S STONE."

Gerard also wrote a poem about an alchemist, "The Alchemist in the City," but the poem of his which captures this didactic tone best is perhaps *The Wreck of the Deutschland,* especially the eleventh stanza:

'Some find me a sword; some
The flange and the rail; flame,
Fang, or flood' goes Death on drum,
And storms bugle his fame.
But we dream we are rooted in earth—Dust!
Flesh falls within sight of us, we, though our flower the same,
Wave with the meadow, forget that there must
The sour scythe cringe, and the blear share come.

The son clearly surpassed the father in many ways. For instance, the son resisted the temptation to become morbid better than the father's example might lead one to expect. Compare Gerard Manley Hopkins's version of an attempted rescue with the account in the *London Times,* one of the sources he used for *The Wreck of the Deutschland.* According to the *Times,* "One brave sailor, who was safe in the rigging went down to try to save a child or woman who was drowning on deck. He was secured by a rope to the rigging, but a wave dashed him against the bulwark, and when daylight dawned his headless body, detained by the rope, was swinging to and fro with the waves." Hopkins wrote:

> One stirred from the rigging to save
> The wild woman-kind below,
> With a rope's end round the man, handy and brave—
> He was pitched to his death at a blow,
> For all his dreadnought breast and braids of thew:
> They could tell him for hours, dandled the to and the fro
> Through the cobbled foam-fleece.

Hopkins transformed the prose into song, but he deleted the morbid details of the decapitation.

It was no doubt partly to escape contemplation of such details connected with his marine-insurance business that Manley Hopkins cultivated a Wordsworthian love of nature. The example of William Wordsworth's youth in nature and the contrasting example of Samuel Taylor Coleridge's youth in the city, "Debarr'd from Nature's living images, / Compelled to be a life unto itself" (*The Prelude*, VI: 313-314), encouraged Manley Hopkins to live in Hampstead rather than in London proper where he worked. He moved his family to Hampstead in 1852, and Gerard and his brother Cyril (1846-1932), who later rejoined his father's firm, were sent to live with relatives in the Hainault Forest, where they spent the summer exploring and studying nature. When he returned to his family, Gerard found himself living near groves of lime and elm, many fine views, the garden where Keats composed his "Ode to a Nightingale" under a mulberry tree, and the Heath celebrated in painting after painting by John Constable. Hopkins obviously enjoyed living there: Cyril recalls that he was a fearless climber of trees, especially the lofty elm which stood in their garden.

At the age of ten, Hopkins left the garden and his family home for Robert Cholmondley's boarding school at Highgate, a northern height of London less populous and more forested than Hampstead. Like Hampstead, it commanded a good view of the surrounding area and was associated with the memories of such artists as Andrew Marvell, Charles Lamb, Keats, and Thomas De Quincey; the tomb, even the coffin, of Coleridge could be seen in Highgate when Hopkins was there. One of Hopkins's friends at Highgate was Coleridge's grandson E. H. Coleridge, who became a biographer of George Gordon, Lord Byron and named one of his sons after his friend Hopkins. While at Highgate, Hopkins composed "The Escorial" (1860), his earliest poem extant. The description of the destruction of the Escorial by the sweeping rain and sobbing wind recalls Byron, but the allusions to painters Raphael, Titian, Velázquez, and Rubens, as well as to various styles of architecture, reveal Hopkins's desire to unite in some way his love of the visual arts and his love of poetry.

The sketches of Bavarian peasants Hopkins produced when his father took him to southern Germany in 1860 reveal his growing interest in being a painter as well as a poet. The only drawing manual in the Hopkins family library, as far as is known, was the Reverend John Eagles's *The Sketcher* (1856). Eagles, who was Manley Hopkins's maternal uncle, recommends the classical idealism of Gaspard Poussin and an elegant, expressive mode of pastoral. However, the fourth volume of John Ruskin's *Modern Painters* was published the same year as *The Sketcher*, and it promulgated important modifications of Eagles's ideal of amateur drawing. Ruskin's emphasis on objective, detailed representation of nature soon became evident in the sketches of Hopkins and other members of his family.

Hopkins's Ruskinian sketches are significant because although Hopkins is remembered as a poet, he wanted to be a painter, deciding against it finally because he thought it was too "passionate" an exercise for one with a religious vocation. Nevertheless, even after he became a Jesuit he continued to cultivate an acquaintance with the visual arts through drawing and attendance at exhibitions, and this lifelong attraction to the visual arts affected the verbal art for which he is remembered. In his early poetry and in his journals word painting is pervasive, and there is a recurrent Keatsian straining after the stasis of the plastic arts.

Hopkins's finely detailed black-and-white sketches were primarily important to him as special exercises of the mind, the eye, and the hand which could alter the sketcher's consciousness of the outside world. The typical Hopkins drawing is what Ruskin called the "outline drawing"; as Ruskin put it, "without any wash of colour, such an outline is the most valuable of all means for obtaining such memoranda of any scene as may explain to another person, or record for yourself, what is most important in its features." Many such practical purposes for drawing were advanced by Ruskin, but his ultimate purpose was to unite science, art, and religion. As Humphry House put it, "Because the Romantic tradition said that Nature was somehow the source of important spiritual experience, and because the habit of mind of the following generation (with an empiric scientific philosophy) was to dwell lovingly on factual detail, a suspicion came about that perhaps the cause of the spiritual experience lay in detail."

This is part of the motivation for the obsession with minute detail seen in Hopkins's *Manor Farm, Shanklin Sept. 21, 1863* and in his *May 12 n.r. Oxford.* According to Ruskin, those who sketched in this way possessed the further advantage of cultivating certain special powers of the eye and the mind: "By drawing they actually obtained a power of the eye and a power of the mind wholly different from that known to any other discipline, and which could only be known by the experienced student—he only could know how the eye gained physical power by the attention to details, and that was one reason why delicate drawings had, above all others, been most prized; and that nicety of study made the eye see things and causes which it could not otherwise trace." *Manor Farm* uses fairly heavy shading but combines it with fine detail for a more delicate effect. An effect of lighter delicacy is achieved in *May 12 n.r. Oxford,* a sketch of a convolvulus, by restricting the heavy shading to the shadows and by using fairly delicate gradations.

The powers of the mind which such study granted included the cultivation of patience, discipline, earnestness, and a love of work for its own sake, but perhaps the most important power developed was the ability to concentrate. Ruskin stressed the importance of concentration to perceptions of the unity of things: "No human capacity ever yet saw the whole of a thing; but we may see more and more of it the longer we look." By concentrating on the whole of a thing Hopkins was able to discover the "inscape," the distinctively unifying pattern of, say, "a white shire of cloud. I looked long up at it till the tall height and the beauty of the scaping—regularly curled knots springing up if I remember from fine stems, like foliage on wood or stone—had strongly grown on me. . . . Unless you refresh the mind from time to time you cannot always remember or believe how deep the inscape in things is . . . if you look well at big pack-clouds overhead you will soon find a strong large quaining and squaring in them which makes each pack impressive and whole." By concentrating in this way also on the formal aspects of running water he was able to discover some of the deeper, recurrent formations of "scaping" even in a tumultuous river: "by watching hard the banks began to sail upstream, the scaping unfolded." This kind of concentration was clearly aided by drawing exercises such as *July 18. At the Baths of Rosenlaui.*

A search for recurring regularity and distinctively unifying forms was one of the primary motivations of an outline drawing of a tree such as *June 26, '68.* Many of Hopkins's sketches of trees seem to be attempts to discover what Ruskin called the "fountain-like impulse" of trees in which "each terminates all its minor branches at its outer extremity, so as to form a great outer curve, whose character and proportion are peculiar for each species"; ultimately both Ruskin and Hopkins were seeking "organic unity; the law, whether of radiation or parallelism, or concurrent action, which rules the masses of herbs and trees."

One of Hopkins's journal entries makes this motivation clear and serves as an effective summary of his typically Victorian union of science and aesthetics: "Oaks: the organization of this tree is difficult. Speaking generally no doubt the determining planes are concentric, a system of brief contiguous and continuous tangents, whereas those of the cedar would roughly be called horizontals and those of the beech radiating but modified by droop and by a screw-set towards jutting points. But beyond this since the normal growth of the boughs is radiating and the leaves grow some way in there is of course a system of spoke-wise clubs of green-sleeve-pieces. . . . I have seen also the pieces in profile with chiselled outlines, the blocks thus made detached and lessening towards the end. . . . Oaks differ much, and much turns on the broadness of the leaves, the narrower giving the crisped and starring and Catherine-wheel forms, the broader the flat-pieced or shard-covered ones, in which it is possible to see composition in dips etc on wider bases than the single knot or cluster." Hopkins discovered that his genius lay in such translations of visual perceptions into words.

His drawings were often remarkably similar to the early sketches of his brother Arthur, although Arthur's drawings are often more fully detailed and unified. Hence it is difficult to accept the belief of critics that Gerard had more talent than his brother. On the contrary, the differences between Gerard's sketches and Arthur's suggest a need to revise the accepted opinion that Gerard could have been a professional painter if he had wanted to. Rather, it would appear that just

Hopkins's May 12 n.r. Oxford *(Harry Ransom Humanities Research Center, University of Texas at Austin)*

as Lope de Vega's success in Spanish drama induced Cervantes to develop an alternative genre, Arthur Hopkins's superior sketching abilities encouraged his older brother to concentrate his energies on literary and religious creativity instead.

This sibling rivalry between Hopkins and his brother Arthur reveals how crucial adaptive compromise can be in the development of a genius's creative potential. Although some of Hopkins's drawings suggest that he could have achieved more detail if he had tried, it is apparent that, while he shared the motivations of his family for drawing, he soon developed specific aims and interests which often differed significantly from theirs. His letter of 10 July 1863 to his friend A. W. M. Baillie confirms that he had developed special interests and did not find any member of his own family a congenial thinker in these matters: "I venture to hope you will approve of some of the sketches in a Ruskinese point of view:—if you do not, who will, my sole congenial thinker on art?"

Some of the differences between Hopkins's aims and those of his brother Arthur are most obvious in the results of their sketching from the cliff in Freshwater Bay on the Isle of Wight in 1863. Arthur, focusing on an unusual bridgelike rock formation in the sea, produced a memorable subject for a picturesque travel record: *Arched Rock. Freshwater Bay. (from the cliff) July 23. 1863.* Gerard, on the other hand, tried to reproduce the pattern made by the waves below and wrote: "Note: The curves of the returning wave overlap, the angular space between is smooth but covered with a network of foam. The advancing wave, already broken, and now only a mass of foam, upon the point of encountering the reflux of the former. Study from the cliff above. Freshwater Gate. July 23." Gerard's aims clearly diverged from Arthur's in at least two important ways: he became more interested in drawing as a means of visual research and more willing to supplement this visual art with verbal art.

In addition, these two sketches illustrate the meaning of "inscape," that conundrum of Hopkins's readers. A common misconception of the word is that it signifies simply a love of the unique particular, the unusual feature, the singular appearance, but that meaning fits *Arched Rock* better than it does Gerard's note on waves. Gerard lost interest in what was merely unique; as in the wave study he usually sought the distinctively unifying design, the "returning" or recurrent pattern, the internal "network" of structural relationships which clearly and unmistakably integrates or *scapes* an object or set of objects and thus reveals the presence of integrating laws throughout nature and a divine unifying force or "stress" in this world. The suggestion of metaphysical significance is obvious in an 1874 note by Hopkins on waves: "The laps of running foam striking the sea-wall double on themselves and return in nearly the same order and shape in which they came. This is mechanical reflection and is the same as optical: indeed all nature is mechanical, but then it is not seen that mechanics contain that which is beyond mechanics."

Arthur was also fascinated by waves and produced some excellent sketches of them, especially *1st September, '75, Breaking Waves, Whitby,* and *Study of the back of a breaking wave seen from above and behind. Whitby. 30 Aug. '75.* These sketches are clearly superior to any of Gerard's drawings of waves in detail, finish, delicacy of shading,

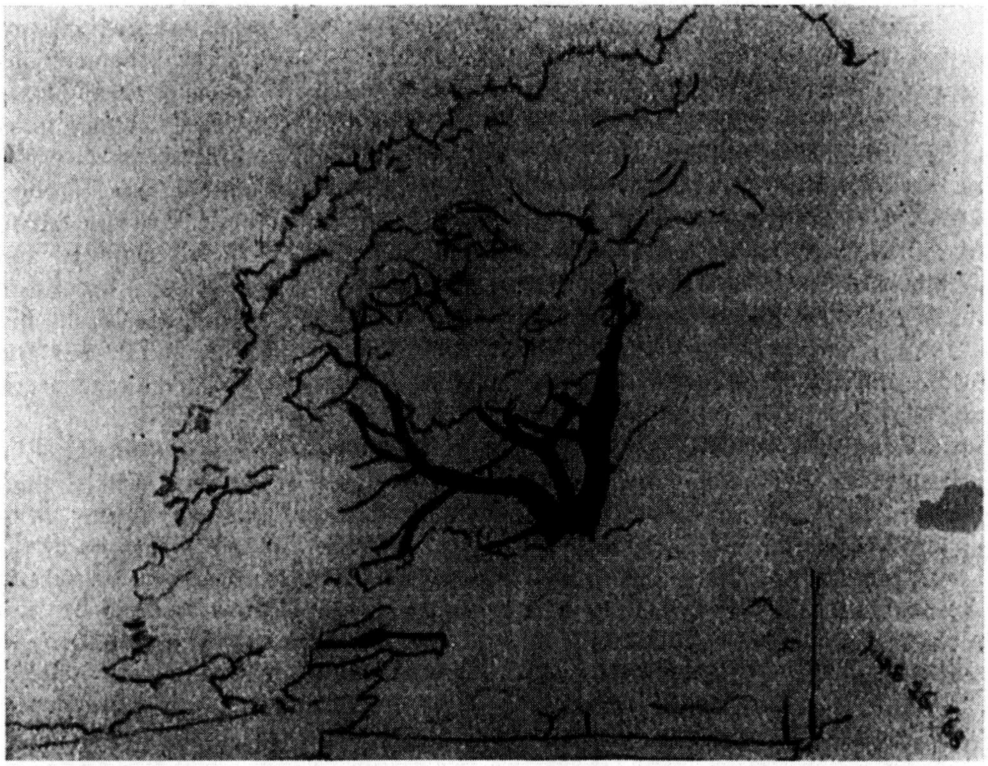

June 26, '68, *one of Hopkins's attempts to discover what Ruskin called the "fountain-like impulse" of trees*

July 18. At the Baths of Rosenlaui, *drawn by Hopkins in 1868 (Harry Ransom Humanities Research Center, University of Texas at Austin)*

and illusion of motion. Likewise, Arthur's *Study of 'The Armed Knight', a reef at the Land's End. 4 Sept. '79* easily surpasses Gerard's 1863 sketches of rock formations, both in truth of detail and aesthetic development, and his *At Whitnash. Warwickshire 8 Sept. '77* reproduces more subtle and delicate effects of light and shade than Gerard achieved in his studies of groups of trees.

Gerard did not even try to sketch the majesty and sublimity of an ocean wave as Arthur did, however. Characteristically, in his *Study from the cliff above*, Gerard conveyed the motion of the waves with words. Phrases such as "the advancing wave already broken, and now only a mass of foam" supply a scenario, a succession of events in time to complement the spatial representation. Eagles recommended not only sea pieces such as this but also shipwrecks, and eventually this advice, along with similar recommendations from Ruskin and the family preoccupation with danger at sea due to the father's insurance business, inspired Gerard's attempt to represent a shipwreck. Besides his father's publication of *Port of Refuge* another factor that motivated Gerard may well have been Arthur's wave studies of 30 August and 1 September 1875.

Only a few months after Arthur executed these studies, Gerard began his own response to the sea in the genre which was to make him famous: not painting, but poetry. If he had insisted on competing directly with his brother, he might well have gone on to become a draughtsman less well known than Arthur. However, his response to the sea, *The Wreck of the Deutschland,* was in some ways an even better fulfillment of the suggestion of his great-uncle, John Eagles, that those who appreciate the sublime acquire "greater notions of the power and majesty of Him who maketh the clouds his chariot, and walketh upon the wings of the wind."

It has been argued that the visual image, the painter's vision, is predominant in Hopkins's journal, but the essence of his creativity was verbal rather than visual, as this description of a glacier reveals: "There are round one of the heights of the Jungfrau two ends or falls of a glacier. If you took the skin of a white tiger or the deep fell of some other animal and swung it tossing high in the air and then cast it out before you it would fall and so clasp and lap round anything in this way just as this glacier does and the fleece would part in the same rifts: you must suppose a lazuli under-flix to appear. The spraying out of one end I tried to catch but it would have taken hours: it is this which first made me think of a tiger-skin, and it ends in tongues and points like the tail and claws: indeed the ends of the glaciers are knotted or knuckled like talons." Hopkins had tried to "catch" the spraying out of one end of the glacier in three sketches inscribed *July 15, '68; July 15;* and *July 15, Little Scheidegg,* but he realized that he had relatively little talent for sketching. He could have "taken hours" and persisted, but instead he let his visual impression stimulate his linguistic creativity, specifically his extraordinary capacity for metaphor. His frustration in one genre only stimulated him to be creative in another.

A similar shift from the visual to the verbal is suggested by his "A Vision of the Mermaids" (1862), a pen-and-ink drawing followed by a poem, both apparently inspired by the poetic vision of the mermaids in *The Sketcher.* Eagles's comment, "How difficult it would be, by any sketch, to convey the subject!," explains why Hopkins followed his drawing with words such as the following:

Plum-purple was the west; but spikes of light
Spear'd open lustrous gashes, crimson-white;
(Where the eye fix'd, fled the encrimsoning spot,
And gathering, floated where the gaze was not;)
And thro' their parting lids there came and went
Keen glimpses of the inner firmament:
Fair beds they seem'd of water-lily flakes
Clustering entrancingly in beryl lakes.

This kind of poetic diction reflects the influence of one of Hopkins's teachers at Highgate, Richard Watson Dixon. Dixon had been involved in the vanguard of much that seemed exciting in the art of the time. Dante Gabriel Rossetti had taught him painting and had praised his poems. Dixon's *Christ's Company and Other Poems* (1861) featured Rossetti's decorative, sensuous beauty and remote dream worlds and a typically Victorian love of word painting.

Yet Dixon's title emphasizes the fact that his longer poems are High Church hagiographical verses, and the Incarnation is a pervasive theme in the poems in this volume. Dixon had been attracted to the Oxford Pre-Raphaelites who followed Rossetti because of their Ruskinian stress on Christian art and because of the original pietism of the group itself. Almost every member of the group had initially intended to take Holy Orders, but most of them were deflected from their purpose by their desire to be artists. Dixon also at one point had given up his religious com-

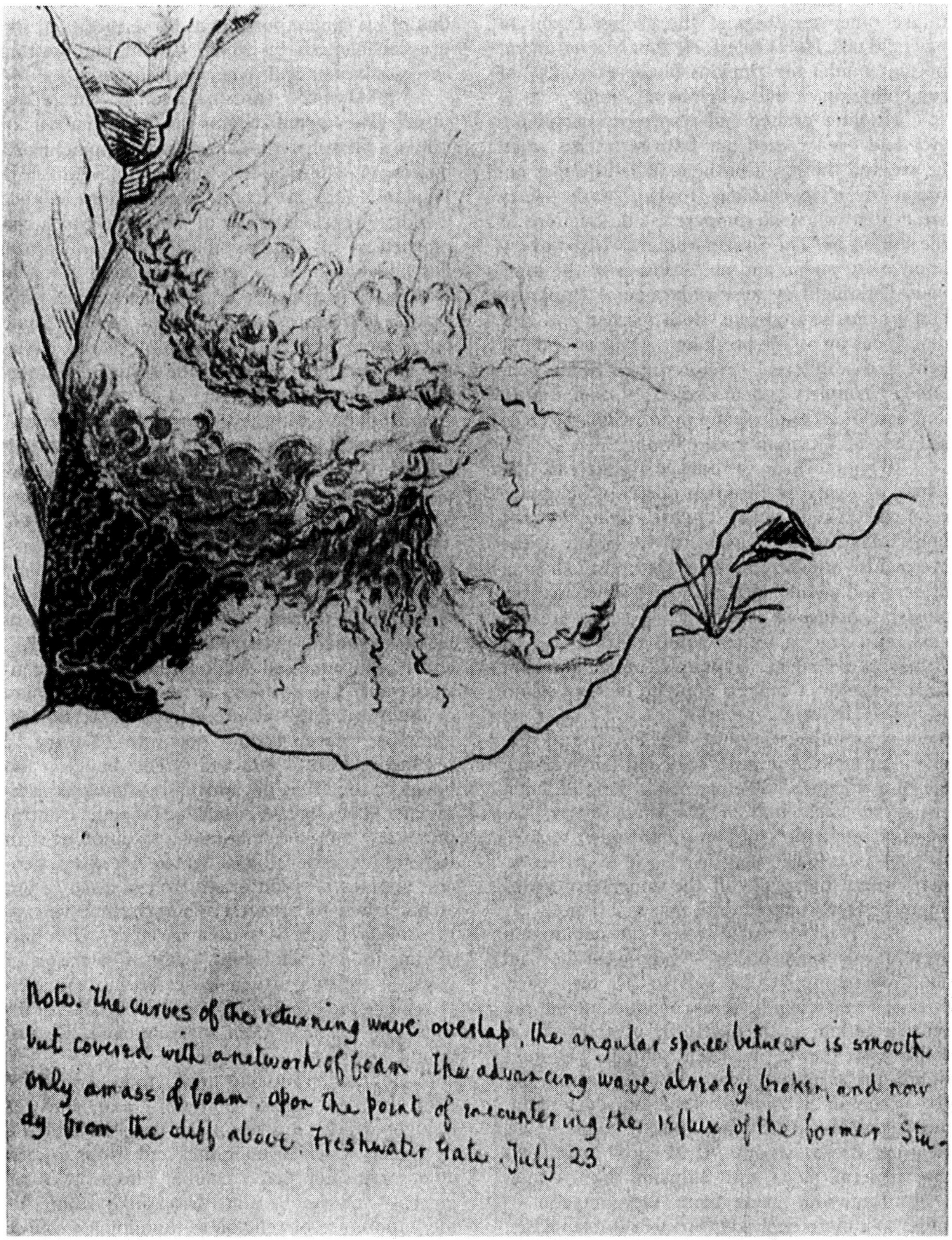

1863 study by Hopkins of wave patterns along the coast of the Isle of Wight

mitment to become a Pre-Raphaelite painter, but, unlike other members of the group, Dixon finally did take Holy Orders. He thus became an important model for Hopkins of the possibility of combining poetic and religious vocations.

Hopkins praised and respected Dixon's poetry and even copied out favorite stanzas when he entered the Jesuit novitiate. The affinities between Dixon's poems and Hopkins's early poetry are evident when we compare the descriptions of the sunsets in "The Sicilian Vespers," Dixon's boyhood prize poem, and in "A Vision of the Mermaids," thought by some to be one of Hopkins's best poems at Highgate. Both teacher and student focus on an isle breaking the sunset's tide of light; and both reveal a preference for iambic pentameter couplets and the adjectival compounds, long sentences, and colorful pictorial images characteristic of Victorian word painting.

In short, Dixon introduced Hopkins to "the school of Keats" in Victorian poetry. As Hopkins recalled, Dixon would "praise Keats by the hour." The result is obvious in "A Vision of the Mermaids," which reproduces the archaic diction, literary and mythological allusiveness, precious neologisms, luxurious sensuality, subjective dreaminess, and amoral, otherworldly aestheticism of Keats's early poems. Hopkins's comments about Keats's choice of subjects apply to his own poem as well: "His contemporaries . . . still concerned themselves with great causes / as liberty and religion, but he lived in mythology and fairyland the life of a dreamer." The mermaids' song of "piteous siren sweetness" in Hopkins's poem, the Keatsian temptation for him and the other Victorian poets, was to live alone in a world of private visions where the reality of the impersonal world might be freely altered to fit personal desire.

Yet Hopkins could resist the temptation even in his early poetry. Again what he said about Keats applies as well to his own early poems: "even when he is misconstructing one can remark certain instinctive turns of construction in his style, shewing his latent power." The most significant "instinctive turn" in Hopkins's early poetry occurs in "Il Mystico" (1862), in which older, more traditional religious ideals replace his Keatsian dream visions. "Il Mystico" anticipates that general move that Hopkins, like Alfred, Lord Tennyson, made from the imitation of Keats to a more explicitly Christian Romanticism, a conversion which enabled him to fulfill his own prophecy for Keats: "what he did not want to live by would have asserted itself presently and perhaps have been as much more powerful than that of his contemporaries as his sensibility or impressionableness, by which he did not want to live, was keener and richer than theirs."

"Il Mystico" contains another "instinctive turn." The poem begins as an imitation of Milton's "Il Penseroso," but its development embodies in embryo the general movement in Hopkins's early art from representations of ideal worlds to representations of this world which culminated in his famous 1877 poems on nature. His initial attempt to attain a spiritual vision in "Il Mystico" is fragmented until the speaker finds that his best expression of his aspiration for some other, more perfect realm is an objective correlative in nature, the ascent of the lark, which translates that desire into action.

Hopkins cultivated this "instinctive turn," and the result was his first published poem, "Winter with the Gulf Stream," which appeared in the popular periodical *Once a Week* on 14 February 1863, when Hopkins was only nineteen years old. This poem reveals the beginning of Hopkins's movement away from a pseudo-Keatsian dreamy subjectivity toward imitation of those traits of Keats's most valuable to Hopkins at this stage of his development: mastery of objective correlatives and evocative natural detail. Rather than being introduced to the speaker, as we are in "A Vision of the Mermaids," we are introduced to the object. The poem begins not with "Rowing, *I* reached a rock," but with "The boughs, the boughs"; the "I" is not introduced until six stanzas later. The objects to which we are initially introduced are, moreover, more closely observed than those of his earlier poems. We are not shown general features of a landscape from a distance but an immediate foreground of branches and vines—"Frost furred our ivies are and rough / With bills of rime the brambles shew." Instead of masses of trees we are shown their leaves hissing and scuttling along the ground and the clammy coats of foliage they become when the rain-blasts are unbound.

Hopkins eventually began to be critical of mere love of detail, however—"that kind of thought which runs upon the concrete and the particular, which disintegrates and drops toward atomism in some shape or other," he wrote in his journal—and he became increasingly aware of the importance of religion as the ultimate source of unity.

His religious consciousness increased dramatically when he entered Oxford, the city of spires.

From April of 1863, when he first arrived with some of his journals, drawings, and early Keatsian poems in hand, until June of 1867, when he graduated, Hopkins felt the charm of Oxford, "steeped in sentiment as she lies," as Matthew Arnold had said, "spreading her gardens to the moonlight and whispering from her towers the last enchantments of the Middle Ages." Here be became more fully aware of the religious implications of the medievalism of Ruskin, Dixon, and the Pre-Raphaelites. Inspired also by Christina Rossetti, the Catholic doctrine of the Real Presence of God in the Eucharist, and by the Victorian preoccupation with the fifteenth-century Italian religious reformer Girolamo Savonarola, he soon embraced Ruskin's definition of "Medievalism" as a "confession of Christ" opposed to both "Classicalism" ("Pagan Faith") and "Modernism" (the "denial of Christ").

At Oxford, Hopkins's consciousness of competition with contemporaries increased, apparently partly as a result of the tradition of oral contests which persisted at Oxford and also because of Hopkins's decision to focus on classical studies which tended to be highly agonistic and rhetorically oriented. At Highgate, Hopkins was encouraged to begin his literary career as a student of Keats by his teacher, Dixon, who also showed Hopkins how to resist Keats's dominance, partly by sublimating it in devotional poetry. While the initiation and direction of Hopkins's creativity in the relationship with Dixon was positive, Hopkins's relationship with a more famous teacher at Oxford, Walter Pater, was fiercely dialectical, with Hopkins defining his position in opposition to Pater's. Yet there was also a curious symbiotic quality in their relationship; they remained friends and shared related interests in Dante, Savonarola, medievalism, and the Pre-Raphaelites.

Among the Pre-Raphaelites the most important figure for Hopkins was Christina Rossetti. She benefited from the emphasis on the feminine in the Pre-Raphaelite focus on Marian figures such as Dante's Beatrice. When Hopkins met her in 1864 he met an icon, the model for the Virgin in the paintings of her brother Dante Gabriel Rossetti. She influenced Hopkins more than any other contemporary at this point in his career and was particularly important in Hopkins's replacement of Keats with Dante as the dominant paradigm in his poetic imagination.

Christina Rossetti became for Hopkins the embodiment of the medievalism of the Pre-Raphaelites, the Oxford Movement, and Victorian religious poetry generally. In the 1860s Hopkins was profoundly influenced by her example and succeeded, unbeknownst to her and to the critics of his time, in becoming a rival far greater than any of her contemporaries.

Their rivalry began with Hopkins's response to her poem "The Convent Threshold." Geoffrey Hartman suggests in the introduction to *Hopkins: A Collection of Critical Essays* (1966) that "Hopkins seems to develop his lyric structures out of the Pre-Raphaelite dream vision. In his early 'A Vision of the Mermaids' and 'St. Dorothea' he may be struggling with such poems as Christina Rossetti's 'Convent Threshold' and Dante Gabriel Rossetti's 'The Blessed Damozel,' poems in which the poet stands at a lower level than the vision, or is irrevocably, pathetically distanced." Such poems were the essence of medievalism in poetry, according to William Morris, who felt that Keats's "La Belle Dame Sans Merci" was the germ from which all Pre-Raphaelite poetry sprang. Standing beyond Keats, however, the primary source was Dante, as Christina Rossetti made clear.

She clearly alludes to Beatrice's appeal to Dante in "The Convent Threshold":

> I choose the stairs that mount above,
> Stair after golden skyward stair,
>
> . . . .
>
> Lo, stairs are meant to lift us higher:
> Mount with me, mount the kindled stair.
> Your eyes look earthward, mine look up.
>
> . . . .
>
> How should I rest in Paradise,
> Or sit on steps of heaven alone?
>
> . . . .
>
> Oh save me from a pang in heaven,
> By all the gifts we took and gave,
> Repent, repent, and be forgiven.

Hopkins read this appeal at a crucial moment in his career, when he was actually considering renouncing his own powerful attraction to this world for a life beyond the cloister threshold. He translated portions of Rossetti's poem into Latin elegiacs and devoted much of his poetic creativity in 1864 to his own response to it, which he called at first "A Voice from the World" (later "Beyond the Cloister") and subtitled "An Answer to Miss Rossetti's *Convent Threshold.*" The surviving fragments express the speaker's sense of spiritual inferiority and his admiration for the decision of Christina Rossetti's heroine to join the convent.

A Vision of the Mermaids *(1862), pen-and-ink heading by Hopkins for his poem of the same title*

Hopkins's first title identifies his persona as the one whose eyes "look earthward" but he is willing to lift up his gaze:

At last I hear the voice well known;
. . . .
You see but with a holier mind—
You hear and, alter'd, do not hear
Being a stoled apparel'd star.
. . . .
Teach me the paces that you went
I can send up an Esau's cry;
Tune it to words of good intent.
This ice, this lead, this steel, this stone,
This heart is warm to you alone;
Make it to God. I am not spent
. . . .
Steel may be melted and rock rent.
Penance shall clothe me to the bone.
Teach me the way: I will repent.

Hopkins was clearly oriented to the Pre-Raphaelite dream vision in which the poet is represented on a lower plane than the vision. By taking the part of Rossetti's heroine's earthly lover in his poem, moreover, Hopkins invites a comparison between his persona and Christina's erstwhile lover, James Collinson, who also became a follower of the Pre-Raphaelites and a convert to Catholicism and, for a while, a Jesuit. Eventually, by converting to Catholicism himself and joining the Society of Jesus, Hopkins exchanged the inferior position articulated in "A Voice from the World" for a superior one, superior at least in the sense that Christina Rossetti apparently felt that her sister Maria, who actually did cross the convent threshold and become a religious, had achieved a higher stage of religious development than she herself did.

Both Hopkins and Christina Rossetti believed that religion was more important than art. The outline of Hopkins's career follows that of Christina Rossetti's: an outwardly drab, plodding life of submission quietly bursting into splendor in holiness and poetry. Both felt that religious inspiration was more important than artistic inspiration. Whenever religious renunciation and self-expression were felt to be at odds, as they often were, self-expression had to be sacrificed. Poetry had to be subordinated to religion.

No doubt partly as a result of this attitude, both Hopkins and Rossetti were subject to intermittent creativity. Both thought of poetry as a gift which could not be summoned at will, and each turned to prose between bursts of poetic inspiration. In fact each went through a stage of about seven years in which writing prose almost entirely replaced composing poetry. Hopkins's prose period stretched from 1868 to 1875, when his literary energies were devoted primarily to his journal. In addition to passing through periods of writing prose, both poets concluded their literary careers with devotional commentaries: in Hopkins's case, his unfinished "Commentary on the Spiritual Exercises of St. Ignatius."

The attitudes of Christina Rossetti and Hopkins toward art and religion have destined them to share much the same fate at the hands of twentieth-century readers: criticism for deliberately narrowing their subjects to a range too limited for modern palates, for expressing religious convictions with which it is now difficult to sympathize, for allowing religion to take precedence over poetry, or for actually impairing the creative gift itself. On the other hand, both are often praised by twentieth-century readers for the same feature: the expression of counterpoised forces generating dramatic tensions.

One of the most dramatic tensions was that between their attraction to this world and their determination to transcend it. Like Hopkins, Christina Rossetti often reveals a Keatsian attraction to the life of sensations, especially to nature. Hopkins's wide variety of responses to nature, especially in the 1860s and 1880s, ranging from strong attraction to its beauty to belief that this beauty must be denied on religious grounds, is congruent with the range of Christina Rossetti's responses. Ultimately, however, she believed that God was not in nature but above and therefore that one must ascend the heavenly stair invoked in "The Convent Threshold," "A Shadow of Dorothea," and other poems. Hopkins's version of the legend of Saint Dorothea, "For a Picture of St. Dorothea" (1864), and his "Heaven-Haven" reveal a similar transition from the natural to the supernatural in his early poetry.

Hopkins's "For a Picture of St. Dorothea" originated in that section of his journal devoted primarily to the representation of nature. However, the flowers in his poem are not rooted in the earth but in legend. Hopkins's aim was not truth to nature primarily in this poem but the revival of medieval legend by defamiliarizing it, putting it in a new context and thereby restoring its original impact in the service of religion.

In "Heaven-Haven" Hopkins again responded to the transcendental, otherworldly aspiration so evident in the Dorothea legend and in Christina Rossetti's "A Shadow of Dorothea." As "Heaven-Haven" suggests, Hopkins's sense of the unreliability and instability of this world led him to a desire to transcend this world in order to discover some other, better world less subject to the triumph of time. Of the two paths to holiness, the outward or the inward—contemplation of God's presence in this world or contemplation of His presence within the self—by far the most common is the one Christina Rossetti usually followed: withdrawal from the external world in order to plumb the secret depths of one's own soul. Hopkins is perhaps more famous for his 1877 nature sonnets which focus on God in nature, but his sonnets of desolation of the 1880s turn inward, returning to the impulse already apparent in "Heaven-Haven," subtitled "A Nun Takes the Veil":

I have desired to go
    Where springs not fail,
To fields where flies no sharp and sided hail
    And a few lilies blow.

And I have asked to be
    Where no storms come,
Where the green swell is in the havens dumb,
    And out of the swing of the sea.

Hopkins's "A Soliloquy of One of the Spies Left in the Wilderness" (1864) is also a response to the recurrent call of desert Christianity. It appears to be based directly on one of the biblical interpretations of the great reformer Savonarola, the famous burner of profane art in Renaissance Italy. As Hopkins commented in a letter, Savonarola was "the only person in history (except perhaps Origen) about whom" he had "real feeling," because for Hopkins, Savonarola was "the prophet of Christian art." Savonarola's example reinforced Christina Rossetti's and at first encouraged Hopkins to move beyond not only his Greek studies but also the imitation of nature that had characterized his early art. Ultimately, Savonarola's example inspired Hopkins to give up nature, beauty, and art altogether.

The sequence of events is clear. On 18 January 1866 Hopkins composed his most ascetic poem, "The Habit of Perfection." On 23 January he included poetry in the list of things to be given up for Lent. In July he decided to become a Catholic, and he traveled to Birmingham in September to consult the leader of the Oxford converts, John Henry Newman. Newman received him into the Church in October. On 5 May 1868 Hopkins firmly "resolved to be a religious." Less than a week later, apparently still inspired by Savonarola, he made a bonfire of his poems and gave up poetry almost entirely for seven years. Finally, in the fall of 1868 Hopkins joined a "serged fellowship" like Savonarola's and like the one he admired in "Eastern Communion" (1865), a commitment foreshadowed by the emphasis on vows of silence and poverty in "The Habit of Perfection."

Hopkins had been attracted to asceticism since childhood. At Highgate, for instance, he argued that nearly everyone consumed more liquids than the body needed, and, to prove it, he wagered that he could go without liquids for at least a week. He persisted until his tongue was black and he collapsed at drill. He won not only his wager but also the undying enmity of the headmaster, Dr. John Bradley Dyne. On another occasion, he abstained from salt for a week. His continuing insistence on extremes of self-denial later in life struck some of his fellow Jesuits as more appropriate to a Victorian Puritan than to a Catholic.

Thus it is important to realize that he converted to Catholicism not to be more ascetic, for asceticism was as Protestant as it was Catholic, but to be able to embrace the Catholic doctrine of the Real Presence. This explanation was not enough to satisfy his family, however. Hopkins's letter informing them of his conversion came as a great shock. He wrote to Newman: "I have been up at Oxford just long enough to have heard fr. my father and mother in return for my letter announcing my conversion. Their answers are terrible: I cannot read them twice." Meanwhile, Manley Hopkins was writing to Gerard's Anglican confessor, H. P. Liddon: "The blow is so deadly and great that we have not yet recovered from the first shock of it. We had observed a growing love for asceticism and high ritual, and ... we believed he had lately resolved on taking orders in the English Church ... save him from throwing a pure life and a somewhat unusual intellect away in the cold limbo which Rome assigns to her English converts. The deepness of our distress, the shattering of our hopes and the foreseen estrangement which must happen, are my excuse for writing to you so freely." After receiving Liddon's reply, Manley Hopkins wrote to Liddon again, accusing Gerard of speaking "with perfect coldness of any possible estrangement from us, who have loved him with an unchanging love. His mother's heart is almost broken by this, and by his desertion from our Church, her belief in, and devotion to, which are woven in with her very being." Manley used similar terms in his letter to Gerard: "The manner in which you seem to repel and throw us off cuts us to the heart.... O Gerard my darling boy are you indeed gone from me?"

As these words suggest, when Hopkins converted to Catholicism he felt he had actually forfeited his rightful place in the family home; he did not even know if his father would let him in the house again. A letter from Hopkins reveals that his father consented to his presence there on one condition: "You are so kind as not to forbid me your house, to which I have no claim, on condition, if I understand, that I promise not to try to convert my brothers and sisters." This was not an easy condition for him to accept, however; "Before I can promise this I must get permission, wh. I have no doubt will be given. Of course this promise will not apply after they come of age. Whether after my reception you will still speak as you do now I cannot tell." Despite these differences Hopkins did spend his Christmas holidays with his family in 1866 and 1867, but what his father called "the foreseen estrangement which must happen" necessarily increased when Hopkins began his novitiate in the Society of Jesus at Manresa House, Roehampton, in September 1868 and later moved to St. Mary's Hall, Stonyhurst, for his philosophical studies in 1870. He spent Christmas away from his family from 1868 to 1871. He returned to the family hearth for the holiday in subsequent years, but in 1885 his Dublin poems still testify to the lonely isolation and anticipation of death characteristic of many Victorian orphans:

To seem the stranger lies my lot, my life
Among strangers. Father and mother dear,
Brothers and sisters are in Christ not near

. . . .

I am in Ireland now; now I am at a third
Remove. Not but in all removes I can
Kind love both give and get.

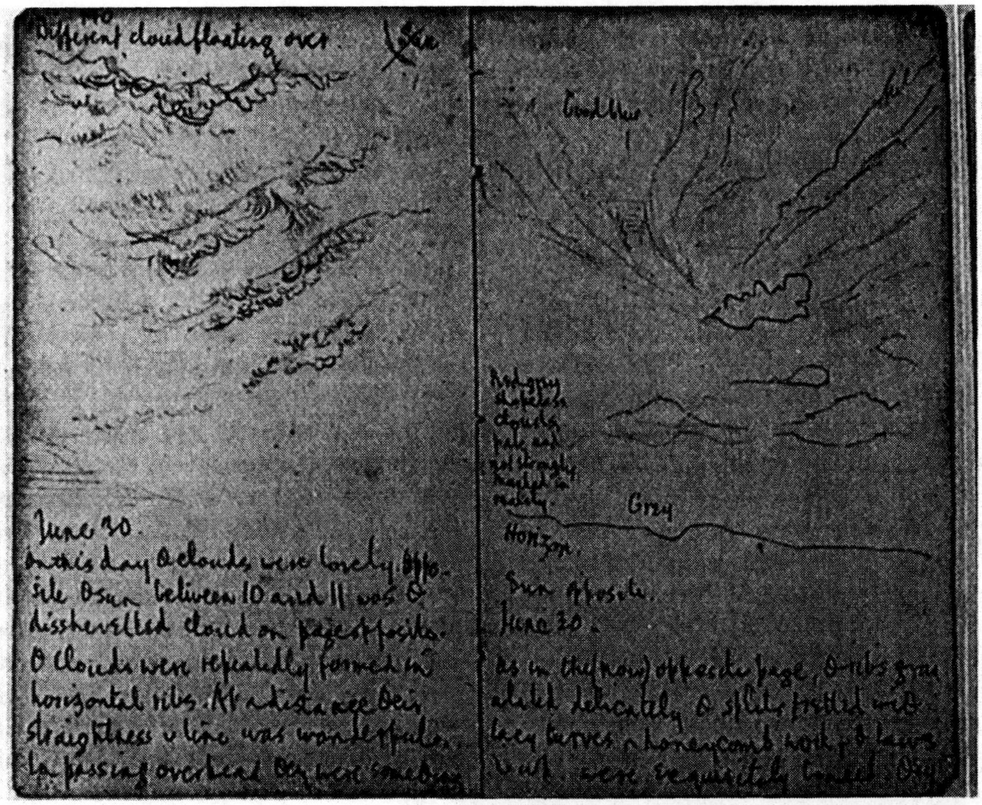

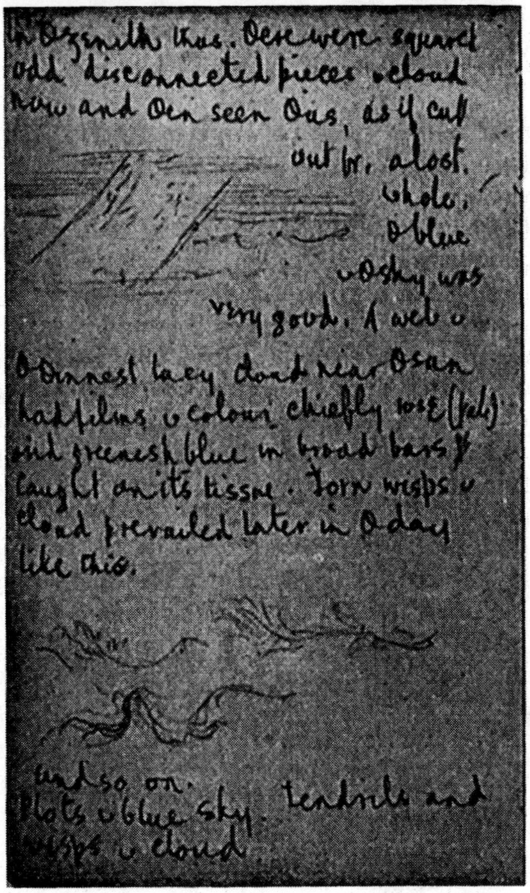

Pages from Hopkins's diary for 1864

When, aged only forty-four, he was finally close to the farthest remove, death, another reconciliation was attempted, but it was too late. His was a painful and poignant tragedy all too typical of Victorian families.

His father had written "by study hard WITHIN THE CHURCHYARD / IS FOUND THE PHILOSOPHER'S STONE." Ironically, it was by following this advice that father and son became estranged. The son did study hard within the churchyard, and he found that the Catholic concept of the Real Presence was his philosopher's stone. The Catholic doctrine of Transubstantiation became for him the mystical catalyst which could transmute into gold, redeem, and regenerate all that is base—what Hopkins called "the triviality of this life," "the *sordidness* of things." Contrary to his father's assertions, this was not a last-minute discovery. As early as June of 1864 Hopkins wrote to E. H. Coleridge: "The great aid to belief and object of belief is the doctrine of the Real Presence in the Blessed Sacrament of the Altar. Religion without that is sombre, dangerous, illogical, with that it is—not to speak of its grand consistency and certainty—loveable. Hold that and you will gain all Catholic truth." Ironically, as we have seen, "Catholic Truth" was the title of one of the poems in *Pietas Metrica*.

The next month Hopkins wrote to Baillie, "I have written three religious poems which however you would not at all enter into, they being of a very Catholic character." The first of these poems was apparently "Barnfloor and Winepress," published the next year in the *Union Review*. This poem adumbrates the poetic as well as religious importance of Hopkins's belief in the Real Presence of God in the Eucharist, the "Half-Way House" of God in this world as Hopkins called the sacrament in a poem of that name in 1864. "Barnfloor and Winepress" in some respects foreshadows the poetry of nature Hopkins was to compose in the late 1870s.

Though primarily a celebration of the Real Presence, this poem reveals how Hopkins could in his imagination extend the idea of the mystical Body of Christ in the communion bread and wine to the rest of nature. In this poem the wheat and grapes are not mere raw materials for Transubstantiation but are represented metaphorically as if they were already participating in the Being of God. One of the attractions of the doctrine of the Real Presence for Hopkins was that it was, as depicted in "Barnfloor and Winepress," the central instance of a metaphor participating in the reality it represents, an archetype for a sacramental poetry of nature.

This potential for a new sacramental poetry was first realized by Hopkins in *The Wreck of the Deutschland*. Hopkins recalled that when he read about the wreck of the German ship *Deutschland* off the coast of England it "made a deep impression on me, more than any other wreck or accident I ever read of," a statement made all the more impressive when we consider the number of shipwrecks he must have discussed with his father. Hopkins wrote about this particular disaster at the suggestion of Fr. James Jones, Rector of St. Beuno's College, where Hopkins studied theology from 1874 to 1877. Hopkins recalled that "What I had written I burnt before I became a Jesuit and resolved to write no more, as not belonging to my profession, unless it were by the wish of my superiors; so for seven years I wrote nothing but two or three little presentation pieces which occasion called for [presumably 'Rosa Mystica' and 'Ad Mariam']. But when in the winter of '75 the Deutschland was wrecked in the mouth of the Thames and five Franciscan nuns, exiles from Germany by the Falck Laws, aboard of her were drowned I was affected by the account and happening to say so to my rector he said that he wished someone would write a poem on the subject. On this hint I set to work and, though my hand was out at first, produced one. I had long had haunting my ear the echo of a new rhythm which now I realized on paper."

The result is an ode of thirty-five eight-line stanzas, divided into two parts. The first part, consisting of ten stanzas, is autobiographical, recalling how God touched the speaker in his own life. The second begins with seven stanzas dramatizing newspaper accounts of the wreck. Then fourteen stanzas narrow the focus to a single passenger, the tallest of the five nuns who drowned. She was heard to call on Christ before her death. The last four stanzas address God directly and culminate in a call for the conversion of England.

The Wreck of the Deutschland became the occasion for Hopkins's incarnation as a poet in his own right. He broke with the Keatsian word painting style with which he began, replacing his initial prolixity, stasis, and lack of construction with a concise, dramatic unity. He rejected his original attraction to Keats's sensual aestheticism for a clearly moral, indeed a didactic, rhetoric. He saw nature not only as a pleasant spectacle as Keats had; he also confronted its seemingly infinite destructiveness as few before or after him have done. In this shipwreck he perceived the possibility of a theodicy, a vindication of God's justice which would counter the growing sense of the disappearance of God among the Victorians. For Hopkins, therefore, seeing more clearly than ever before the proselytic possibilities of art, his rector's suggestion that someone write a poem about the wreck became the theological sanction he needed to begin reconciling his religious and poetic vocations.

Nevertheless, although *The Wreck of the Deutschland* was a great breakthrough to the vision of God immanent in nature and thus to the sacramentalism that was to be the basis of the great nature poems of the following years, when Hopkins sent the poem to his friend Robert Bridges, Bridges refused to reread it despite Hopkins's pleas. The poem was also rejected by the Jesuit magazine the *Month,* primarily because of its new "sprung" rhythm, and many subsequent readers have had difficulty with it as well.

Hopkins's readers have more easily understood the sonnets he wrote about the landscape he actually saw around him near St. Beuno's College, Wales. It was in an earlier poem, "Half-Way House," that Hopkins most clearly recorded his need to approach God in this world: "I must o'ertake Thee at once and under heaven / If I shall overtake Thee at last above." As "The Windhover," "God's Grandeur," and Hopkins's other sonnets of 1877 reveal, Hopkins found such a halfway house not only in the communion bread and wine but also in the Vale of Clwyd and the rest of the countryside around St. Beuno's. Wales clearly provided the occasion for his greatest experience of nature, as it had for Wordsworth (on Mt. Snowdon and near Tintern Abbey), John Dyer (on Grongar Hill), and Henry Vaughan.

Some of the most luminous symbols of the presence of God in Hopkins's Welsh poems are the sunrises and the "sea-sunsets which give such splendour to the vale of Clwyd," as Wordsworth put it in the preface to his own *Descriptive Sketches.* Such sights were prized and distilled in Hopkins's nature poetry in his imagery of sunlight which "sidled like dewdrops, like dandled diamonds" ("The furl of fresh-leaved dogrose down," 1879). Everything from ploughed furrows to clouds to their reflections in pools is shining and gleaming. Even night reveals a world of strangely translucent moonshine or of stars that gleam like "bright boroughs" or "diamond delves" or "quickgold" in gray lawns; all of nature was perceived as a "piece-bright paling" that was Christ's "home" ("The Starlight Night," 1877).

Hopkins's most famous Welsh sonnet, "The Windhover," reveals that for him this Book of Nature, like the Bible, demanded a moral application to the self. Hopkins wrote in his notes on St. Ignatius: "This world is word, expression, news of God"; "it is a book he has written . . . a poem of beauty: what is it about? His praise, the reverence due to him, the way to serve him. . . . Do I then do it? Never mind others now nor the race of man: DO I DO IT?" One of Hopkins's attempts to answer that question is "The Windhover."

The initial "I" focuses attention on the speaker, but the explicit application of the lesson of the Book of Nature to him does not begin until the line "My heart in hiding / stirred for a bird" at the conclusion of the octet. One biographical interpretation of this line is that he was hiding from fulfilling his ambitions to be a great painter and poet. Instead of ostentatiously pursuing fame in that way, wearing his heart on his sleeve, he had chosen to be the "hidden man of the heart" (1 Peter 3:4), quietly pursuing the imitation of Christ. As Hopkins put it, Christ's "hidden life at Nazareth is the great help to faith for us who must live more or less an obscure, constrained, and unsuccessful life."

Hopkins did live such a life, but the windhover reminded him of Jesus' great achievements after Nazareth. The windhover "stirred" his desire to become a great knight of faith, one of those who imitate not only the constraint but also the "achieve of, the mastery of " this great chevalier. The "ecstasy" of the windhover recalls Hopkins's initial desire in "Il Mystico" to be lifted up on "Spirit's wings" so "that I may drink that ecstasy / Which to pure souls alone may be." Ultimately, Hopkins became aware that he had been hiding from the emotional risks of total commitment to becoming a "pure" soul. The phrase "hiding" thus suggests not only hiding from the world or from worldly ambition but also hiding from God.

The words "here / Buckle" which open the sestet mean "here in my heart," therefore, as well as here in the bird and here in Jesus. Hopkins's heart-in-hiding, Christ's prey, sensed Him diving down to seize it for his own. Just as the bird buckled its wings together and thereby buckled its "brute beauty" and "valour" and capacity to "act," so the speaker responds by buckling together all his considerable talents and renewing his commitment to the imitation of Christ in order to buckle down, buckle to, in serious preparation for the combat, the grappling, the buckling with the enemy. As Paul said, "Put on the whole armour of God, that ye may be able to stand against the wiles of the Devil."

Hopkins wrote "The Windhover" only a few months before his ordination as a Jesuit priest, the ultimate commitment to sacrifice his worldly ambitions. Just as Jesus' paradoxical triumph was his buckling under, his apparent collapse, so Hopkins felt that the knight of faith must be prepared for the same buckling under or collapse of his pride, for a life of "sheer plod" and "blue-bleak" self-sacrifice, if need be. Nevertheless, the imagery of "The Windhover" promises that the knight of faith will have a fire break from his heart then—galled, gashed, and crucified in imitation of Christ. The fire will be "a billion times told lovelier" than that of his "heart in hiding," and far more "dangerous," both to his old self (for the fire is all-consuming) and to his enemy, Evil.

In Hopkins's case, the fire also became far more "dangerous" to his worldly poetic ambitions. Among other things, "The Windhover" represents Hopkins's Pegasus, the flying steed of classical myth. The collapse of his old poetic self is implied in the imagery, for Bellerophon was thrown off Pegasus because of his pride. Fearing his pride in his own poetry, Hopkins burned his poems upon entering the Society of Jesus: he believed that poetry always had to give way, buckle under, to the "greater cause" of religion. As a result there was a very real danger that his poems would never reach the public they deserved, that he would have to sacrifice all the worldly fame promised him as "the star of Balliol" for a life of "sheer plod."

Yet the "plod" makes the plough "shine" in "The Windhover." The plough scratching the field was in fact a common medieval metaphor for the writer's pen scratching across the paper, the furrows corresponding to the rows of letters. Hopkins's paradoxical triumph as a poet is that although his poems were created out of that life of sheer plod and remained as obscure as "blue-bleak embers" to most of his contemporaries, now that they have found an audience to appreciate them, they have burst into fire.

They remained unknown to most of his contemporaries, however, for whom nature existed only to be exploited. As Hopkins put it in "God's Grandeur," the shod feet of modern men "have trod, have trod, have trod; / And all is seared with trade; bleared, smeared with toil; / And wears man's smudge and shares man's smell." It was both the immediate loss of the landscape and the fact that the "After-comers cannot guess the beauty been" ("Binsey Poplars") that led Hopkins to plead, "What would the world be, once bereft / Of wet and wildness? Let them be left, wildness and wet; / Long live the weeds and the wilderness yet" ("Inversnaid," 1881).

Industrialization continued to consume the wilderness as it still does, however; whole landscapes like those around Oxford were destroyed by what Hopkins called "base and brickish" suburbs ("Duns Scotus's Oxford," 1879). Finally, in 1882 Hopkins concluded the octet of "Ribblesdale" by replacing the image of God brooding protectively over nature ("God's Grandeur") with a new image of God giving all of nature over to "rack or wrong." According to Hopkins the chief cause of that "self-bent" of man that made him "thriftless reave our rich round world bare / And none reck of world after" (Ribblesdale") was increasing urbanization.

Hence it was in Hopkins's first extended comparison of the city and the country, "The Sea and the Skylark" (1877), that he first fully expressed his tragic vision of environmental degradation. For Hopkins the sounds of the sea and the skylark ushered out like bells at the end of the year his own "sordid turbid time." His representation of his "sordid turbid time" breaking down to man's last "dust," draining fast toward man's first "slime," recalls similar accounts of dust, slime, and pollution in the works of Tennyson, Dickens, Ruskin, and other Victorian writers.

In October of 1877, not long after he completed "The Sea and the Skylark" and only a month after he had been ordained as a priest, Hopkins took up his duties as subminister and teacher at Mount St. Mary's College, Chesterfield. From this time until his death the pollution of the industrial cities to which he was assigned took a mounting toll on his energies and his spirit. Of his life in Chesterfield in 1878 he wrote to Bridges, "Life here is as dank as ditch-water. . . . My muse turned utterly sullen in the Sheffield smoke-ridden air." In July of that year he became curate at the Jesuit church in Mount Street, London. In December he became curate at St. Aloysius's Church, Oxford. While at Oxford he composed "Binsey Poplars" and "Duns

Scotus's Oxford," but in October 1879 he was put on the temporary staff as curate at St. Joseph's, Bedford Leigh, near Manchester, which he described to Dixon and Bridges as "very gloomy . . . there are a dozen mills or so, and coalpits also; the air charged with smoke as well as damp." In December 1879 he began as select preacher at St. Xavier's, Liverpool; there, he wrote Bridges, "the river was coated with dirty yellow ice from shore to shore." In September 1881 Hopkins was put on the temporary staff at St. Joseph's, Glasgow, and he wrote to Dixon, "My Liverpool and Glasgow experience laid upon my mind a conviction, a truly crushing conviction, of the misery of town life . . . of the degradation even of our race, of the hollowness of this century's civilisation: it made even life a burden to me to have daily thrust upon me the things I saw." After his third-year novitiate at Roehampton and two years as a teacher of classics at Stonyhurst College, in 1884 Hopkins took up his post as fellow in classics at the Royal University of Ireland and professor of Greek at University College, Dublin, which he described to Bridges as "a joyless place and I think in my heart as smoky as London is." In 1889 Hopkins died in Dublin of typhoid fever, apparently caused by the polluted urban water supply, and was buried in Glasnevin cemetery.

Although from the time of his departure from Wales in 1877 until his death Hopkins composed nature poems, his assignments in Victorian cities forced him to change the focus of his life and art from nature to man, and finally to one man—himself. No longer able to identify as completely with nature, an orphan in the surrounding world, Hopkins's speaker in "Spelt from Sibyl's Leaves" (1884) becomes "sheathe- and shelterless." Shifting from the outward way to God back to the inward, he decides to strip down to the essential self to concentrate on the generation of a "new self and nobler me," as he puts it in "The Blessed Virgin compared to the Air we Breathe."

Shifting his energies from admiration of nature to attempts to bring love and grace to urban man, Hopkins often succeeded, as "Felix Randal" (1880) so eloquently testifies, but he also frequently experienced frustration and the increased sense of social degeneration lamented in "Tom's Garland" (1887) and in the undated "The Times are nightfall." In the last Hopkins can find only one alternative: "Or what is else? There is your world within. / There rid the dragons, root out there the sin. / Your will is law in that small commonweal." "Rooting out sin" in the "world within" had been the subject of previous poems such as "The Candle Indoors" (1879) and his religious poems at Oxford, but it soon became the preoccupation of most of the poems of Hopkins's final years. Most of these poems focus on *acedia,* the fourth deadly sin, the sin of "spiritual sloth" or "desolation." These sonnets of desolation consist of the six original "terrible sonnets" of 1885—"Carrion Comfort," "No worst, there is none," "To seem the stranger," "I wake and feel," "Patience," and "My own heart"—and three sonnets of 1889—"Thou art indeed just," "The Shepherd's Brow," and "To R. B."

According to his own testimony Hopkins was subject to melancholy all his life, but his "terrible pathos," as Dixon called it, is most obvious in these late sonnets. Following Saint Ignatius, Hopkins defined "spiritual sloth" or "desolation" as "darkness and confusion of soul . . . diffidence without hope and without love, so that / the soul finds itself altogether slothful, tepid, sad, and as it were separated from its Creator and Lord." Called *acedia* in Latin, this sin is differentiated from physical sloth by the fact that the victim realizes his predicament, worries about it, and tries to overcome it.

The sense of coldness, impotence, and wastefulness evident in Hopkins's religious poetry of the 1860s is an important feature of *acedia,* but by far the most important is "world sorrow," the predicament lamented in Hopkins's "No worst, there is none" (1885). A great range of emotions are "herded and huddled" together in this "main" or "chief" woe as Hopkins calls it in the poem. Besides impotence and world sorrow per se, the *acedia* syndrome includes feelings of exile and estrangement, darkness, the disappearance of God, despair, the death wish, and attraction to suicide—all emotions which recur throughout Hopkins's life and art but become particularly evident toward the end.

While Hopkins's sonnets of desolation are generally considered his most modern poems, they are virtually a recapitulation of the medieval treatises on *acedia.* Even the kind of estrangement from one's family described in Hopkins's "To seem the stranger" is an important feature of *acedia* in Saint John Chrysostom's fourth-century *Exhortations to Stagirius,* for instance. John, whose homily on Eutropius Hopkins translated, begins with a summary of the *tristitia* or world-sorrow syndrome in Stagirius which bears a remarkable resemblance to Hopkins's situation. A man converts, gives up his family and his position in society, and then struggles manfully against, yet often succumbs to, *tristitia.*

Just as in Hopkins's "To seem the stranger," Stagirius's problem is exacerbated by the fact that he is exiled from his family. As in Hopkins's "Carrion Comfort," Stagirius also feels that he is both a passive victim of various tortures and one who battles with God Himself in nightmares. Like Hopkins's "No worst," moreover, John's final exhortation implies that *tristitia* is a universal phenomenon, that the whole "terrestrial kingdom" is full of causes for *acedia,* and John also uses the imagery of mountains and cliffs to represent the lure of insanity and suicide. Thus, although pride is usually regarded as the deadliest of the seven sins, John concluded that excessive sorrow was the most ruinous diabolic obsession.

One of the results of *acedia* is a feeling of the disappearance or withdrawal of God. This is most obvious in Hopkins's "Nondum" (1866) and in his phrase "dearest him that lives alas! away" in "I wake and feel," but is also implied in "Comforter, where, where is your comforting?" in "No worst." We think of this feeling as a modern phenomenon, but it is a common experience of the absence of spiritual consolation, and darkness is its traditional imagery, especially in Saint Bernard, Dante, Milton, and Saint John of the Cross, as it is in Hopkins's "Nondum," "Spelt from Sibyl's Leaves," "Carrion Comfort," and "My own heart." The darkness and confusion of soul represented in the first quatrain of Hopkins's "I wake and feel" recall specifically the opening of Dante's *Divine Comedy:* "In the middle of the journey of my life I awoke to mystery in a dark wood where the straight way was lost."

The ultimate result of God's withdrawal from the soul and the consequent darkness is often the temptation to despair, that loss of all hope which is the state of the damned in Dante's *Inferno.* This despair, the temptation resisted in the opening of Hopkins's "Carrion Comfort," was the natural culmination of *acedia* according to John Chrysostom and others. Despair in turn often leads to the death wish, as implied in the conclusion of Hopkins's "No worst," in his "The Times are nightfall," and in his lament in "To seem the stranger": "Not but in all removes I can / Kind love both give and get."

However, the conclusion of Hopkins's "I wake and feel"—"The lost are like this, and their scourge to be / As I am mine, their sweating selves; but worse"—is an allusion to Dante which clearly distinguishes the speaker of Hopkins's terrible sonnets from the damned who are continually referred to in the *Inferno* as "the lost" and the "sorrowful" who have lost all hope, even hope of death. Like Dante, Hopkins faced the "lost" and that which was most like them in his own soul, but his speaker also remains separated from the lost in that he is a living soul still addressing God in his prayers, still purging himself of his sins, and still living by hope in grace.

The ultimate context of Hopkins's purgation, therefore, as of Dante's, was the Bible. One of the biblical incidents echoed in the imagery and phraseology of "No worst," for instance, is that of Jesus' exorcism of the demons of Gadara. Like the imagery of Dante's *Purgatorio,* this exorcism imagery obviously provides a significant counterpoint of meaning. The suggestion is that the speaker is attempting to herd and huddle all the demons of ennui together in one category, "world-sorrow," and "heave" them out of himself. Hopkins's sonnets of desolation are especially suited to this cathartic, purging function because they are prayers as well as poems. Like Jesus' cry on the cross, Hopkins's sonnets of desolation are addressed to God and are themselves consolations.

Eventually, Hopkins, like Dante, was granted a glimpse of Paradise. Hopkins's sonnet of 1888, "That Nature is a Heraclitean Fire and of the comfort of the Resurrection," is apparently a direct reply to "No worst, there is none": the question in the earlier poem, "Comforter, where, where is your comforting?" is answered in the title of the later poem. *Acedia* has been conquered: "Enough! the Resurrection, / A heart's clarion! Away grief 's gasping, joyless days, dejection." As Dante put it, "The inborn and perpetual thirst for the godlike kingdom bore us away. . . . It seemed to me that a cloud covered us, shining, dense, solid and smooth; like a diamond smit by the sun." Hopkins concludes this poem with similar imagery: "I am all at once what Christ is, since he was what I am, and / This Jack, joke, poor potsherd, patch, matchwood, immortal diamond, / Is immortal diamond."

Letters:

The Letters of Gerard Manley Hopkins to Robert Bridges, edited by Claude Colleer Abbott (London: Oxford University Press, 1935; revised and enlarged, 1955);

Correspondence of Gerard Manley Hopkins and Richard Watson Dixon, edited by Abbott (London: Oxford University Press, 1935; revised and enlarged, 1955);

Further Letters of Gerard Manley Hopkins, edited by Abbott (London: Oxford University Press, 1938; revised and enlarged, London: Oxford University Press, 1955).

Bibliographies:

Tom Dunne, *Gerard Manley Hopkins, A Comprehensive Bibliography* (Oxford: Clarendon Press, 1969);

Susan I. Schultz, "A Chronological Bibliography of Hopkins Criticism: 1967-1974," *Hopkins Quarterly,* 3 (January 1977): 157-183;

Richard F. Giles, "A Hopkins Bibliography: 1974-1977," *Hopkins Quarterly,* 5 (Fall 1978): 87-122;

Ruth Seelhammer, "A Hopkins Bibliography: 1978," *Hopkins Quarterly,* 6 (Fall 1979): 95-106;

Seelhammer, "A Hopkins Bibliography: 1979," *Hopkins Quarterly,* 7 (Winter 1981): 135-142;

Seelhammer, "A Hopkins Bibliography: 1980," *Hopkins Quarterly,* 9 (Summer 1982): 43-50;

Pamela Palmer, "A Hopkins Bibliography: 1981-1986," *Hopkins Quarterly,* 16 (April-July 1989): 5-38.

Biographies:

G. F. Lahey, *Gerard Manley Hopkins* (London: Oxford University Press, 1930);

Eleanor Ruggles, *Gerard Manley Hopkins: A Life* (New York: Norton, 1944);

Alfred Thomas, *Hopkins the Jesuit: The Years of Training* (London: Oxford University Press, 1969);

Paddy Kitchen, *Gerard Manley Hopkins* (New York: Atheneum, 1979).

References:

Michael Allsopp and Michael Sundermeier, eds., *Gerard Manley Hopkins (1844-1889): New Essays on His Life, Writing, and Place in English Literature* (Lewiston, N.Y.: Edwin Mellen, 1989);

Bernard Bergonzi, *Gerard Manley Hopkins* (New York: Macmillan, 1977);

Jerome Bump, *Gerard Manley Hopkins* (Boston: G. K. Hall, 1982);

Bump, ed., "Gerard Manley Hopkins: A Centenary Celebration," *Texas Studies in Language and Literature,* 31 (Spring 1989);

Robert J. Dilligan and Todd K. Bender, *A Concordance to the English Poetry of Gerard Manley Hopkins* (Madison: University of Wisconsin Press, 1970);

W. H. Gardner, *Gerard Manley Hopkins (1844-1889), A Study of Poetic Idiosyncrasy in Relation to Poetic Tradition,* 2 volumes (London: Secker & Warburg, 1944, 1949);

Gerard Manley Hopkins, by the Kenyon Critics (New York: New Directions, 1945);

Geoffrey H. Hartman, ed., *Hopkins: A Collection of Critical Essays* (Englewood Cliffs, N.J.: Prentice-Hall, 1966);

Alan Heuser, *The Shaping Vision of Gerard Manley Hopkins* (London: Oxford University Press, 1958);

Eugene Hollahan, ed., "Centenary Revaluation of Gerard Manley Hopkins," *Studies in the Literary Imagination,* 21 (Spring 1988);

Wendell Stacy Johnson, *Gerard Manley Hopkins, the Poet as Victorian* (Ithaca, N.Y.: Cornell University Press, 1968);

F. R. Leavis, "The Letters of Gerard Manley Hopkins," in his *The Common Pursuit* (London: Chatto & Windus, 1952);

Maria R. Lichtmann, *The Contemplative Poetry of Gerard Manley Hopkins* (Princeton: Princeton University Press, 1989);

Jeffrey Loomis, *Dayspring in Darkness: Sacrament in Hopkins* (Lewisburg, Pa.: Bucknell University Press, 1988);

Norman MacKenzie, *A Reader's Guide to Gerard Manley Hopkins* (Ithaca, N.Y.: Cornell University Press, 1981);

MacKenzie, ed., *The Early Poetic Manuscripts and Note-Books of Gerard Manley Hopkins in Facsimile* (New York: Garland, 1989);

Paul L. Mariani, *A Commentary on the Complete Poems of Gerard Manley Hopkins* (Ithaca, N.Y.: Cornell University Press, 1970);

J. Hillis Miller, "Gerard Manley Hopkins," in his *The Disappearance of God: Five Nineteenth-Century Writers* (Cambridge, Mass.: Harvard University Press, 1963);

Marylou Motto, *'Mined with a Motion': The Poetry of Gerard Manley Hopkins* (New Brunswick, N.J.: Rutgers University Press, 1984);

Walter Ong, *Hopkins, the Self, and God* (Toronto: University of Toronto Press, 1986);

John Pick, *Gerard Manley Hopkins: Priest and Poet* (London: Oxford University Press, 1942);

Gerald Roberts, ed., *Gerard Manley Hopkins: the Critical Heritage* (London: Routledge/Kegan Paul, 1987);

Joseph Schwartz, ed., "Gerard Manley Hopkins, 1889-1989," *Renascence,* 42 (Fall 1989 - Winter 1990);

Alison G. Sulloway, *Gerard Manley Hopkins and the Victorian Temper* (London: Routledge, 1972);

Sulloway, ed., *Critical Essays on Gerard Manley Hopkins* (Boston: G. K. Hall, 1990);

R. K. R. Thornton, ed., *All My Eyes See: The Visual World of Gerard Manley Hopkins* (Sunderland, U.K.: Coelfrith Press, 1975).

Papers:

The most extensive collections of Hopkins's papers are at the Bodleian Library and Campion Hall, Oxford, and the Harry Ransom Humanities Research Center, University of Texas, Austin.

A. E. Housman

(26 March 1859 - 30 April 1936)

This entry was updated by William G. Holzberger (Bucknell University) from his entry in DLB 19: British Poets, 1880-1914.

SELECTED BOOKS: *Introductory Lecture Delivered in University College, London* (Cambridge: Cambridge University Press, 1892);

A Shropshire Lad (London: Kegan Paul, Trench, Trübner, 1896; New York: John Lane/Bodley Head, 1897);

Last Poems (London: Richards, 1922; New York: Holt, 1922);

The Name and Nature of Poetry (Cambridge: Cambridge University Press, 1933);

More Poems, edited by Laurence Housman (London: Cape, 1936; New York: Knopf, 1936);

The Collected Poems of A. E. Housman, edited by John Carter (London: Cape, 1939; New York: Holt, 1940);

The Manuscript Poems of A. E. Housman, edited by Tom Burns Haber (Minneapolis: University of Minnesota Press, 1955; London: Oxford University Press, 1955);

The Complete Poems of A. E. Housman, Centennial Edition, edited by Haber (New York: Holt, 1959);

Selected Prose, edited by Carter (London: Cambridge University Press, 1961);

The Making of a Shropshire Lad: A Manuscript Variorum, edited by Haber (Seattle & London: University of Washington Press, 1966).

OTHER: *Manilii Astronomica,* 5 volumes, edited by Housman (London: Richards, 1903-1930);

Iuvenalis Saturae, edited by Housman (London: Richards, 1905);

Lucani Bellum Civile, edited by Housman (Oxford: Blackwell, 1926).

Alfred Edward Housman was the greatest English classical scholar of his time and a poet of great ability and mastery within the limitations of his chosen themes and form. *A Shropshire Lad,* published in 1896 at the author's expense, became one of the most popular and best-selling books of verse in the English language, rivaling Edward FitzGerald's *Rubáiyát of Omar Khayyám,* with which it shares a conception of the briefness of youth and life, a disbelief in human immortality or the existence of God, and a carpe diem philosophy emphasizing the necessity of capitalizing on life's opportunities while one may.

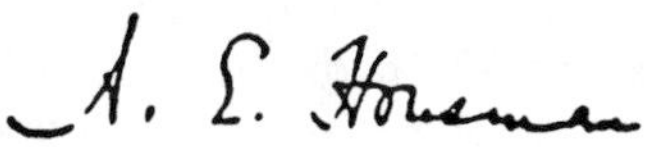

A. E. Housman was the first of the seven children of Sarah Jane and Edward Housman, a solicitor. He was born in Fockbury, Worcestershire, on 26 March 1859; the following year, the family moved to Bromsgrove, near Birmingham. From Perry Hall, the Housman family home in Bromsgrove, in the valley of the Severn River, the boy Housman could see in the distance the hills of Shropshire, a place that he would later, in his poems, imbue with mythical significance, although his firsthand experience with the actual Shropshire remained slight. Housman's birth occurred at the height of the Victorian period and was concomitant with the publication of George Eliot's *Adam Bede*, Fitzgerald's *Rubáiyát of Omar Khayyám*, Alfred, Lord Tennyson's *Idylls of the King*, and Charles Darwin's *On the Origin of Species*, all of which appeared in 1859.

Housman's childhood was not happy. He was small and frail and at a disadvantage in the rough and tumble of boyish games. His devotion to his mother, and the sympathetic confidences they shared, served to alienate his father, a bluff and sporting man, with a disastrous inclination to play the country squire in a manner well beyond his means. Thus, the death of Sarah Jane Housman, when Alfred Housman was only twelve, was the first of a series of personal catastrophes that would poison the young man's chances for happiness and a normal life.

Housman attended Bromsgrove School, an old and reputable, if not well-known, public school. Beginning there at age eleven, as a day boy on a scholarship, he distinguished himself by diligence in his studies. Unathletic, he was head-boy in his class, and in his last year at Bromsgrove School, won several prizes, including a coveted scholarship to St. John's College, Oxford University. Another prize was awarded for his poem "The Death of Socrates," published in the local newspaper, the *Bromsgrove Messenger*, on 8 August 1874. This poem, like other of his juvenile effusions, was completely conventional in form and artificially expressive of religious sentiments that, in fact, Housman had already left behind, because at the age of twelve he had declared himself a deist and by the time he was an Oxford undergraduate had given up religious belief entirely. The intensity of his application to his school studies, combined with the absence of congenial boyhood friendships—he was happiest and most comfortable among mature women relatives and family friends—and temperamental differences between him and his father, resulted in an emotional strain that expressed itself in a grotesque facial tic that first appeared at about age eleven and that Housman never completely overcame.

At Oxford, Housman was at first happy and successful. He matriculated at the university in the autumn of 1877, when he was eighteen. His letters home, to his kind and congenial stepmother, Lucy Housman, express his youthful criticisms of his teachers, among whom were John Ruskin and Benjamin Jowett. His favorite subjects at Bromsgrove had been Latin and Greek, and at Oxford he concentrated on these classical languages. For a specialty, he chose—over the officially preferred Plato—the Roman erotic poet Propertius. He was also entertaining himself in his leisure hours by reading contemporary English writers, among whom he liked best Matthew Arnold, whose poem "Empedocles on Aetna" was his favorite, and Thomas Hardy, whose themes and senti-

Housman, circa 1877

ments would later figure prominently in Housman's poetry.

Among his classmates at St. John's were two other young men who shared Housman's middle-class background and were also scholarship students: A. W. Pollard and Moses Jackson. Both were intelligent and studious. The three of them lived modest undergraduate lives and eventually shared lodgings together. Jackson was interested in earning a degree in science rather than in classics, and he was unlike his friend Housman in most other ways as well. Tall, good-looking, confident, and well-built, Jackson was a fine athlete who rowed with the St. John's crew. He was thoroughgoing and able in his scientific studies and good-naturedly condescending about Housman's preoccupation with dead languages. Self-consciously shy about his own physical ordinariness, Housman idolized his husky and brilliant friend, whom he later characterized as the ever-elusive and charming Mercury in his poem "The Merry Guide":

With mien to match the morning
  And gay delightful guise
And friendly brows and laughter
  He looked me in the eyes.
. . . .
With gay regards of promise
  And sure unslackened stride
And smiles and nothing spoken
  Led on my merry guide.
. . . .
With lips that brim with laughter
  But never once respond
And feet that fly on feathers,
  And serpent-circled wand.

Housman fell hopelessly and permanently in love with this paragon of manly grace and virtue. Jackson, although obviously fond of Housman, was apparently different from him in his sexual preferences. He evidently rebuffed Housman's proffered affections—whether gently or roughly is a matter of conjecture—with consequences that were for Housman disastrous; his spirit was left permanently warped and his emotions paralyzed. A more propitious consequence of this emotional trauma was the production, more than ten years afterward, of the poems that constitute *A Shropshire Lad*, the first and finest collection of Housman's verses.

Students of Housman's work agree that, except for the premature death of his beloved mother, this rejection was the most determinative event of Housman's life. Several of the poems of *A Shropshire Lad*, including "When I was one-and-twenty," represent the pain of unrequited and unfulfilled passion:

When I was one-and-twenty
  I heard a wise man say,
"Give crowns and pounds and guineas
  But not your heart away;
. . . .

"The heart out of the bosom
  Was never given in vain;
'Tis paid with sighs a plenty
  And sold for endless rue."
And I am two-and-twenty,
  And oh, 'tis true, 'tis true.

The most revealing of the poems dealing with Housman's love for Moses Jackson, however, were published posthumously in the collection edited by the poet's brother Laurence Housman in 1936, entitled *More Poems*, from which the following excerpts are taken:

truth and singleness of heart
Are mortal even as is man.
* * *
But this unlucky love should last
  When answered passions thin to air;
Eternal fate so deep has cast
  Its sure foundation of despair.

In another poem from *More Poems*, indignation is mingled with despair:

Crossing alone the nighted ferry
  With the one coin for fee,
Whom, on the wharf of Lethe waiting,
  Count you to find? Not me.

Despite his "unlucky" love for Jackson, Housman at first succeeded thoroughly in his work at Oxford, earning first-class honors in his first public examination in 1879. However, when two years later he sat for the final examination in "Greats," at which his tutors expected him to perform brilliantly, not only did he fail to take a first but to the consternation and disappointment of everyone he failed completely, turning in for parts of the examination, booklets which, except for some scribbled numerals or letters, were completely blank. Some sort of mental breakdown had evidently occurred, but what precisely had caused it is unknown. His other roommate at Oxford, A. W. Pollard, later averred that Housman spent too many evenings chatting with Jackson, who was assured of earning a first in his science examinations and did so. Others have said that Housman was overconfident and impractical in his preparations for the examination, indulging his interests and studying his favorite writers but neglecting study for the philosophical part of the examination and other parts in which he was not particularly interested. Another reason offered is his dismay over his father's failing health and fortunes and his consequent worry over the financial security of the family. Still another theory is that Housman deliberately, if not consciously, failed himself on the examination as a sort of alternative to actual suicide. The mystery of this exceptional student's failure, however, remains unresolved. Housman received neither honors nor even a pass degree, and he left Oxford in the summer of 1881 to return home to Bromsgrove in disgrace. At Bromsgrove he faced the disappointment and tacit accusation of his family, who had counted upon his success and subsequent assistance in helping his younger brothers through college. To add to his embarrassment, a relative who had been giving him a small annual stipend promptly withdrew this beneficence. The next fall, however, Housman was able to return to Oxford and qualify for the humble pass degree. But his failure in "Greats" the previous spring had shut the door to immediate opportunity for a financially and intellectually rewarding academic career, and Housman had to think of earning a living in some other way. Thus, he again returned home to Bromsgrove, where he stayed from May 1881 to December 1882. There he studied for the civil service examination, which he took and passed in the autumn of 1882.

Moses Jackson

During this time at home, Housman worked occasionally at Bromsgrove School, tutoring in Greek and Latin. Hostile relations continued between him and his father, whom he always considered inadequate. Now his father was ill, on the verge of mental and physical collapse. There is no record of Housman's having written any verse at this time. He was however continuing the classical studies in textual scholarship that he had begun during his Oxford undergraduate days, and an article that he submitted to the *Journal of Philology* was accepted and published in 1882. Thus, at twenty-three Housman began a career in classical scholarship that would eventually carry him to the top of the profession; but first a full decade in a very different occupation intervened.

Upon successfully passing the civil service examination, Housman qualified for a higher division clerkship in Her Majesty's Patent Office in London. The position was menial and the salary small. Arriving in London in December 1882, he took rooms in the West End with his friend Moses Jackson, who was also employed in the patent office, and Jackson's younger brother, Adalbert. This job left the evenings free, and Housman spent them at the British Museum library, reading Greek and Latin and working on the problems of conjectural emendation of Roman and Greek authors. These labors resulted in the learned articles that would later determine the course of his life. Indeed, the ten years from 1882 to 1892 that he spent at the patent office were years of unremitting labor for Housman. He was determined to redeem the hopes for a fulfilling career that had been dashed by his failure in "Greats"; and he was equally determined to escape the monotony of his work in the patent office, an occupation far from his real interests. During this period he had very little diversion and few friends; he remained aloof from his family, refusing their requests to visit him, and wrote them only occasionally. He was an efficient public servant during these years and was politically conservative, a Tory opposed to Gladstonian liberalism.

Although he was fond of both Moses and Adalbert Jackson, in 1886 Housman moved from the lodgings that he shared with the brothers to new quarters in Highgate. Now twenty-seven, a bachelor living alone, Housman adopted the habit of monkish seclusion that would characterize the rest of his life. His free time was devoted exclusively to his classical studies, working on emendations to the texts of Propertius for a *Journal of Philology* article, and continuing his studies of Aeschylus and Sophocles.

There is no indication that Housman's removal to his own separate quarters constituted a breach in his friendship with the Jackson brothers. However, in the following year, 1887, Moses Jackson resigned from the civil service to accept a position on the faculty of Sindh College, a small institution established for the education of the natives in Karachi, India. At this time, Jackson planned to marry a young widow, Mrs. Rosa Chambers, and he hoped that the position at Karachi would provide the financial and vocational opportunities to make this marriage possible. Jackson's departure for Karachi in 1888 was a loss from which Housman never really recovered. He retreated more completely into solitude and taciturnity. Jackson's departure is the subject of some of Housman's most powerful and revealing poems, published only after his and Jackson's deaths. It seems clear that the relationship to Jackson was the one profound emotional attachment of Housman's adult life, a compulsion and obsession which he never fully exorcized. It was simultaneously a source of bitter frustration and a wellspring of poetic inspiration. One poem in particular from *More Poems* expresses the anguish Housman experienced at Jackson's departure:

Because I liked you better
  Than suits a man to say,
It irked you, and I promised
  To throw the thought away.

To put the world between us
  We parted, stiff and dry;
"Good-bye," said you, "forget me."
  "I will, no fear," said I.

The rest of the poem (two more stanzas) conjectures the return of the departing one, who is admonished, in the event that his friend is now dead, to

Halt by the headstone naming
  The heart no longer stirred,
And say the lad that loved you
  Was one that kept his word.

Two other poems, first published in *A. E. H.: Some Poems, Some Letters, and A Personal Memoir* (1937), by Laurence Housman, express Housman's grief at Jackson's departure and his perpetual devotion. The final stanza of one reads:

If death and time are stronger,
  A love may yet be strong;
The world will last for longer,
  But this will last for long.

After Jackson's departure, Housman withdrew into the tight compass of his scholarly pursuits. In 1888, at the age of twenty-nine, Housman had learned articles published in the *Classical Review* and in the *Journal of Philology*: essays on Isocrates, Aeschylus, Propertius, and the *Agamemnon* of Aeschylus. These brilliant critiques, characteristic of Housman's meticulous scholarly writing, were distinguished by their lucidity of thought, range of knowledge, depth of insight, precision of method, and irritability in dealing with critics whom he regarded as careless or incompetent. His scholarly articles began to earn for him the respect of distinguished scholars throughout Europe and the fear and hatred of those classicists who were, despite the traditional restraints of scholarly decorum, openly identified and bluntly denounced by Housman in his essays.

Thus, by 1889, at the age of thirty, Housman had established a substantial reputation as a classical scholar, although still employed in his humble clerkship in the patent office. At this time, Moses Jackson, now principal of Sindh College in Karachi, returned to England to marry Mrs. Chambers. Housman attended the wedding and in the following year began a poem in commemoration of the event, his "Epithalamium," or wedding hymn, in which he records his second and perhaps even more permanent loss of the mercurial Jackson. Hymen, god of marriage, he says, has come "to join and part"—"Friend and comrade yield you o'er / To her that hardly loves you more." "Folly spurned and danger past," the wedding libation, he says, may be poured to the god at last.

In 1892 the Chair of Greek and Latin at University College, London, became available through the death of the incumbent professor. Housman, now ten years at the patent office, decided to apply for the position. Characteristic of his almost neurotic preoccupation with honesty and accuracy, he included in his application the information that he had at Oxford "failed to obtain honours in the Final School of Litterae Humaniores." This confession, however, was offset by the inclusion of testimonials to the brilliance and importance of Housman's scholarly articles by seventeen of England's foremost classical scholars. He got the appointment.

Although he had previously worked both with Greek and Latin authors, Housman, from the date of his appointment to the professorship at University College, limited his studies to Latin authors only. He felt that to achieve the sort of authoritative results that he wished for his scholarship he had to limit the field of his endeavors, and he felt that he would be more competent and successful in Latin studies. He delivered his *Introductory Lecture* before the faculty on 3 October 1892. His rigidly imposed and unremitting self-discipline had paid off: he left the obscurity of the patent office to become a leader of the faculty of University College and a textual critic of international reputation.

Housman's teaching duties at University College were numerous and demanding of time and energy. The students were ordinary undergraduates unable for the most part to share the intricacies of Housman's scholarly interests, but he took his teaching duties very seriously and was meticulous in the preparation of his lectures. As a teacher, however, Housman was always professorial, remote, and impersonal. He was not much liked by either the students or his professional colleagues because personally he was dry, humorless, and cold; but he was respected for his intelligence, mastery of his subject, and devotion to truth and accuracy.

Housman, 1896

During the ten years at the patent office Housman had confined his literary efforts to technical scholarship in the classical languages. He was not tempted by the prospects of a purely literary career because those prospects were too vague and uncertain. Rather he worked at something that promised more practical results, and his prudence and effort had been rewarded at last by his appointment to the professorship of Latin at University College. His capacity for poetic creativity, therefore, had evidently lain dormant all those years and needed only the combination of adequate leisure and an event of sufficient emotional power to summon it forth. This event occurred in the death of Adalbert Jackson, of typhoid, on 12 November 1892. Housman had liked Adalbert from the start, and when Moses Jackson had left for India four years earlier, Housman had transferred some of the tremendous fund of affection that he had for him to his younger brother. During these years Adalbert was probably Housman's closest friend. The intense grief and sense of loss caused by the young man's death was the immediate cause of the emotional explosion and great creative reaction that resulted directly in the production of the poems in *A Shropshire Lad*.

By February of 1893 Housman's poetry notebooks contained drafts of about one-sixth of the sixty-three poems that would constitute *A Shropshire Lad*. The early months of that year were a period of fervid creativity. These creative "spells," for that is really what they were, might last for several hours or for several days. During these times new poems would come to Housman, and he would revise and refine others. Then several months would pass during which he would do almost nothing on the poems. Autumn 1893 to early 1894 was the next period of intense creativity, and from August to December 1894 Housman filled his notebooks with drafts of poems. Concentration on the poetry was, however, interrupted by the death of his father on 27 November 1894; the poet traveled to Bromsgrove for the funeral. The first three months of 1895 were the period of greatest continuous creativity, and Housman described them as a time of "continuous excitement." Late summer 1895 was yet another time of great creative energy. In the autumn of that year, Housman confined himself to the composition of ballads and military poems, and virtually completed the text of *A Shropshire Lad*. No one knew that he had been writing poems or was thinking of having a volume of verse published, not even his brother Laurence Housman, who had the same idea and whose poems Housman had been reading and criticizing.

According to Housman's description, the process by which his poems were composed was essentially automatic. During the periods of creative intensity, the verses came to him, he said, while walking after luncheon, at which he had drunk a pint of beer. In this peculiar state of intensified emotion, the lines came crowding into his mind, welling up spontaneously from the depths of his subconscious, where they evidently had been forming. When he returned to his lodgings, he would quickly write down what had come to him, sometimes whole poems; other times only parts of poems would have come forth automatically, and he would, he recounted, have to labor consciously for hours or days to complete them. The composition of these poems was evidently a reaction of Housman's subconscious, instinctual self against the suppression of his emotions that had become a customary defensive characteristic of the prim, correct, Victorian gentleman that Housman had made of himself. The composition of these poems was, therefore, a form of necessary emotional release; they expressed the spiritual anguish that had characterized Housman's life from the disastrous final year at Oxford in 1882 to the pathetic death and painful loss of his friend Adalbert Jackson ten years later. He dreaded the social opprobrium associated with homosexuality. The intensity of this opprobrium had been demonstrated in 1895 in the public persecution and imprisonment of Oscar Wilde, which inspired Housman to write a poem (number eighteen of "Additional Poems," in the *Collected Poems*, 1939) about a man who was hated and condemned for having red hair, a quality no less intrinsic and beyond conscious determination than one's sexual nature. Indeed, the extremely reserved and proper Housman dreaded the personal revelations of whatever sort that publication of his poetry would entail, but despite this dread of public exposure, he wished to see his poems in print.

Housman's efforts to publish his first book of poems were not very successful. The manuscript was rejected by Macmillan and several other prominent London publishers. The original title of the poetry manuscript was "The Poems of Terence Hearsay," reflecting one of the literary personae Housman employs in the poems. It was his Oxford friend A. W. Pollard who suggested the substitute title *A Shropshire Lad*; he also suggested that Housman take the manuscript to Pollard's own publisher, Kegan Paul, Trench, Trübner and Company, who agreed to publish the book of poems on one condition: that Housman would himself pay the cost of publication, cash in advance.

Thus, the original edition of this famous book was published at the poet's own expense, and it was slow selling at first: not quite five hundred copies had been sold by the end of 1896. Two years later, a second edition was brought out by a different publisher, Grant Richards, who was impressed with the book and believed that it would eventually be successful. In signing with Richards, Housman refused any royalties, requesting instead that his share of any profits be used to keep down the purchase price of individ-

J. W. N. Sullivan, Grant Richards, and Housman

ual copies. Housman wanted his book of poems in the hands of the people. Richards brought out another edition of *A Shropshire Lad* in 1900, but still the public remained apathetic.

With his book of poems off his hands and conscience, Housman once again concentrated his attention on his scholarly enterprises, not neglecting, of course, his lectures and other University College duties and obligations. He was now in his early forties and comfortably well off. At this time he began spending the long summer holiday traveling on the Continent and indulging his interest and pleasure in food and fine wines. It was during one of these sojourns in Venice in 1900 that Housman met the young one-eyed gondolier, Andrea, whom he befriended and continued to assist financially over the years, actually making a special trip to Venice in 1926, when he was sixty-seven, in answer to a summons from Andrea for assistance. His friendship with the gondolier is commemorated in the last part of number forty-four of the posthumous *More Poems*: "Andrea, fare you well; / Venice, farewell to thee."

The Boer War broke out in 1899 and with it a fervid English patriotism which found stimulus and expression in the military poems that make up a substantial part of *A Shropshire Lad*; sales of the book increased dramatically. The poet's younger brother Herbert was killed fighting in South Africa, and Housman records this loss in his poem "Astronomy," written in 1901 (number seventeen of *Last Poems*, 1922). At this time Housman was completing work on the first volume of his edition of the writings of the Roman poet, astronomer, and mathematician Marcus Manilius. He published his first volume of Manilius's *Astronomica* at his own expense, with Grant Richards in 1903. The four subsequent volumes of Housman's edition of Manilius were published in 1912, 1916, 1920, and 1930.

Except for his single volume edition of the works of Lucan in 1926 and the earlier volume of Juvenal's *Saturae* that he had published in 1905, Housman devoted his scholarly life to the production of a meticulously researched and scrupulously prepared comprehensive edition of a Roman author he knew was second- or third-rate. Why had he not continued his work on Propertius, the delight and preoccupation of his Oxford days? The answer is simple but disconcerting, and it is profoundly revelatory of Housman's character. Propertius was by general acknowledgment and Housman's own opinion vastly superior in every way to Manilius, but the problems involved in successfully emending the

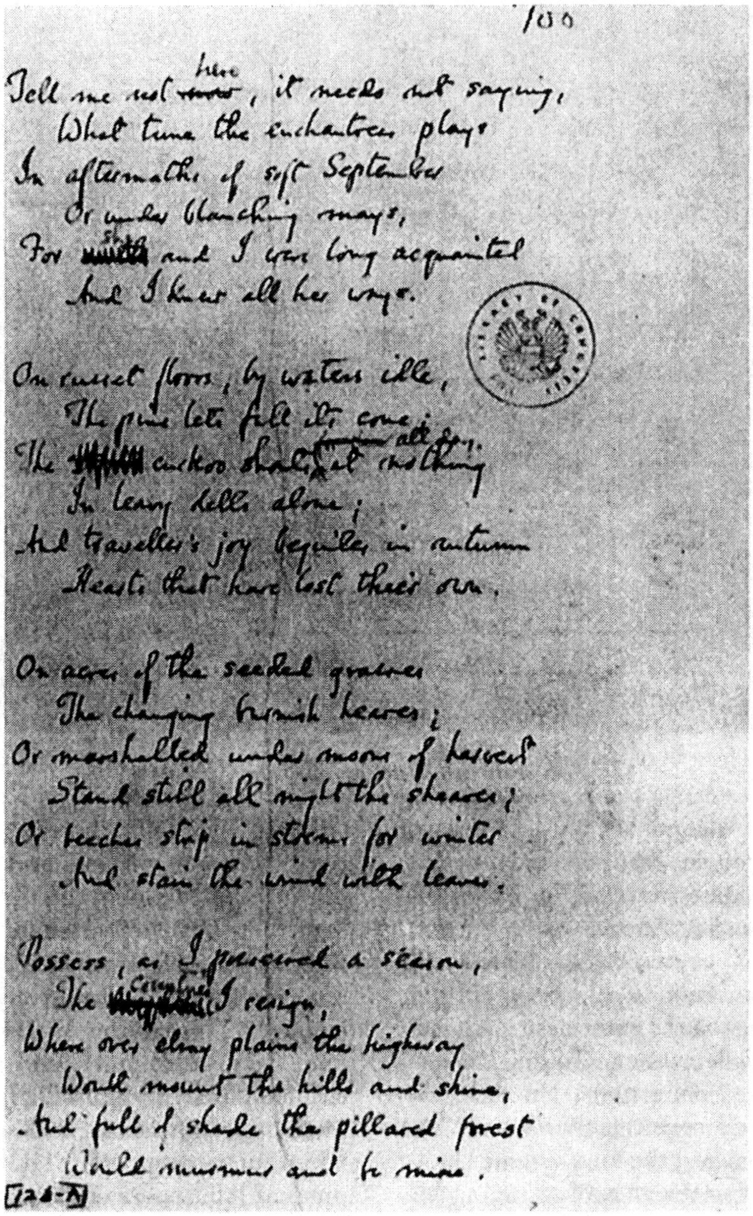

Page from the notebook version of poem number forty in Last Poems *(The Library of Congress)*

texts of Propertius were insuperable. On the other hand, those of editing the works of the dull Manilius were of such an order as to invite the attention of Housman's extraordinary critical gifts. By deliberately choosing an author whose texts, though inferior, would respond to his editorial ingenuity and show it off to advantage, Housman would achieve professional distinction and make a scholarly perfection of a task that was hardly worth doing at all. Even given the pedantry of nineteenth- and early-twentieth-century philology, surely this deliberate decision by Housman to abandon the Latin author in whom he had a deep and abiding interest to devote most of his professional life to a nonentity on whom he could do a brilliant job is perversely significant. Also significant is the fact that the first volume of Manilius carries a twenty-eight-line Latin inscription to Moses Jackson, absent but certainly not forgotten.

The publication in 1905 of Housman's edition of Juvenal's brilliant *Saturae* must have given the now modestly affluent professor satisfaction, particularly perhaps when he recalled lines from Juvenal that must earlier have had for him painful significance: "*Nil habet infelix paupertas durius in se, quamquod ridiculos homines facit*" ("Poverty has no more bitter sting than that it makes a man ridiculous"). Though he could now afford to, Housman belonged to no club at this time, but rather entertained his few intimate friends at dinner in the smart Cafe Royal, a leading London restaurant. When his landlady moved to the London suburb of Pinner, Housman went with her and spent the quiet and uneventful evenings reading detective stories, including those of Sir Arthur Conan Doyle, which were then all the rage. With affluence came also celebrity, for *A Shropshire Lad* had by this time gone through many cheap editions and had become a best-seller. Composers requested permission to set Housman's ballads to music; among those who did so were Vaughan Williams, John Ireland, and Charles Butterworth.

All of Housman's poetry is of a kind. There are no thematic or formal differences between the poems of *A Shropshire Lad* and those of his later collection, *Last Poems*, or those of *More Poems* and other pieces published posthumously. Indeed, one of the chief criticisms of his verse has been the lack of development. As Edmund Wilson remarked, Housman came "the same painful cropper over and over again." He shares with Thomas Hardy a preoccupation with the graveyard and a Greek sense of an inexorable fate or destiny. The celebrated German philologist Wilamowitz, who was Housman's only rival for the distinction of being the greatest classical scholar of the era, once said of the final words of Socrates in Plato's dialogue the *Phaedo* ("Remember, Crito, we owe a cock to Asklepios. . . .") that these words were not to be misinterpreted to mean that Socrates wished his friend to discharge for him the duty of sacrificing to the god of medicine a cock in payment for curing Socrates of the sickness of life. "Das Leben ist keine Krankheit, und Asklepios heilt kein Ubel der Seele" ("Life is no illness and Asklepios cures no sickness of the soul"), said Wilamowitz. The very opposite might be said of Housman's poems, in many of which life is depicted as a lingering illness, curable only by death. Housman never outgrew this attitude, and it is for this lack of development in either theme or technique, coupled with the fact that his poetic corpus is comparatively small, that he is generally regarded as a minor poet.

If Housman's voice is limited, however, it is, within the limits of its range, superb. Someone has said that Housman is "supremely, if narrowly, gifted." With the ballad and elegy, Housman achieves exquisite effects. Writing in the pastoral tradition, his language is simple, making frequent use of the idioms of the English provincial dialect. The characters of his poems are Shropshire agricultural laborers. The men have names such as Tom, Dick, Ned, Fred, a rather atypical Maurice, and Terence, Housman's literary persona in the poems. His girls are country wenches—Nancy, Fan, and Rose Harland. In addition to these farm lads and lasses, we also find in Housman's poems soldiers (dead and alive; heroes and deserters), craftsmen (a carpenter's son, who is hanged between thieves), culprits awaiting execution or fresh from the gibbet, and in two separate poems of *A Shropshire Lad*, Mercury and a talking Greek statue. The recurrent themes of Housman's verses are the celebration of the beauties of country life, the oblivion of death, early death, suicide, unrequited love, military life, and the celebration of the courage and patriotism of the common soldier. He makes effective use of the dramatic monologue in his poetry, adapting the complex techniques of Robert Browning to his own simpler pastoral mode. His poems benefit greatly from the sense of place they acquire from the inclusion of names of actual Shropshire towns, buildings, and rivers, such as Ludlow and Wenlock towns, Abdon and Clee, Hughley Steeple, and the Severn River. Like other English poets, Housman understood the special magic of place names and used them effectively in his art.

Housman's poetry is unique for his time. Certainly, it is very different in theme, language, and tone from the late-nineteenth-century phase of English romanticism that included the work of William Butler Yeats, Lionel Johnson, Ernest Dowson, and Algernon Charles Swinburne. Housman's poems are short, precise lyrics, most of which occupy only a single page. The forms are classical in their symmetry, many making use of the four-line ballad stanza, with rhyming alternate lines. The diction is straightforward and simple; most words are of Anglo-Saxon origin and of one or two syllables only. When a polysyllabic Latinism is used (showing the influence of Housman's unsurpassed mastery of the Latin language and literature), it appears with great effect. Another characteristic of Housman's poetic style is its great verbal economy: not a word too many. This characteristic again is the result of his mastery of Latin, one of the most economical of languages. The reader of Housman's poems is repeatedly inspired to admiration by the terse, memorable, and extremely well-put epigrams, pungent one-, two-, or three-line statements that arrest the attention:

> Breath's a ware that will not keep.
>
> * * *
>
> What flowers to-day may flower to-morrow,
> But never as good as new.
>
> * * *
>
> The troubles of our proud and angry dust
> Are from eternity, and shall not fail.
> Bear them we can, and if we can we must.
>
> * * *
>
> Ten thousand times I've done my best
> And all's to do again.
>
> * * *
>
> There's this to say for blood and breath,
> They give a man a taste for death.

Housman's poems contrast sharply with those of many twentieth-century modernists in that Housman sought perfect clarity. He despised obscurity and prized lucidity above everything. The straightforwardness of his style has caused some critics to dismiss his poetry as merely superficial. Such a judgment is not only unfair but overlooks the verbal richness, the musical effects, the dramatic power, and the psychological insight of Housman's verse. Housman said that he considered meaning not particularly significant to poetry, which, he believed, should be felt rather than understood intellectually: a matter of emotion rather than reason. He therefore relies for his effects upon rhythm, meter, rhyme, alliteration, and other traditional auditory devices, coupled with the beauty of images presented in carefully chosen and delicately weighted words. His successes are everywhere apparent in the poems but particularly so in a brilliant piece such as number two of *A Shropshire Lad*, whose first stanza paints an exquisite portrait of spring:

> Loveliest of trees, the cherry now
> Is hung with bloom along the bough,
> And stands about the woodland ride
> Wearing white for Eastertide.

Nature is magnificently evoked as a compelling but fickle mistress in the fortieth poem of *Last Poems*:

> Tell me not here, it needs not saying,
> What tune the enchantress plays
> In aftermaths of soft September
> Or under blanching Mays,
> For she and I were long acquainted
> And I knew all her ways.
> . . . .
> Possess, as I possessed a season,
> The countries I resign,
> Where over elmy plains the highway
> Would mount the hills and shine,
> And full of shade the pillared forest
> Would murmur and be mine.

Housman's treatment of nature is basically romantic, as are many of his poetic sentiments; yet he stops short of a romantic worship of nature. Thus, Housman's poetry might be described as classical in terms of conciseness and economy of language, precision of form, and in the Epicurean stoicism and materialism that provide the philosophical foundation for his conception of human life and the universe. But the extremism of temperament, the bitter rebelliousness against one's lot and against fate in Housman's poems are unclassical and typically romantic. At the same time, Housman's rejection of the elaborate rhetoric of the Victorian poets, the abundant irony in his poems, the absence of belief in love's immortality or any other sort of immortality, and the absence of nineteenth-century optimism ally him more with the moderns than with the romantic Victorians. Although invariably described as ultimately romantic, Housman really escapes categorization as either classical or romantic, and his poetry combines, in very interesting ways, characteristics of both schools.

Several specific influences may be identified in Housman's poetry. Those that he himself acknowledged directly are the songs of Shakespeare, the Scottish border ballads (whose melodramatic stories, realism, and violence characterize so many of Housman's pieces), and the poems of Heinrich Heine. Many of the German poet's characteristics are found in Housman, including the use of a double self-identity in some poems, farewells to untrue love, fratricides, lovers returned from the grave to inquire about their sweethearts, youthful criminals and suicides, and the transitoriness of human affection. It has been noted that some of Housman's lyrics are virtual translations of poems by Heine.

There are also other profound influences at work. Certainly the Bible, both Old and New Testaments, is significant, particularly for the language. It has been shown that many of the words and phrases of the poems are taken from the Bible, either directly or with slight adaptations. Lucretius, the Roman philosophical poet whose *De Rerum Natura* sets forth in verse the philosophy of Epicurus, is a potent source of Housman's own ideas. In Lucretius we find disbelief in the immortality of the soul, the indifference of the gods and nature to human enterprise or well-being, the frailty and corruptibility of all things, distrust of love between the sexes and a dislike for women generally, a preference for the country over the city, and a brooding sense of personal disaster, all of which are also characteristic of Housman's poems. Other influences on Housman's poetry are Shakespeare's plays, Dante, Milton, and Robert Browning. Housman's genius, of course, did not slavishly imitate these models; rather it borrowed from them, as it did from the conventional effects of classical poetry, to create verses that are fresh and original. Housman's voice is distinctive and unmistakable.

If Housman the poet was ultimately rewarded by the success of his *A Shropshire Lad* verses and the celebrity they brought him, Housman the scholar was rewarded in 1911 with the Kennedy Professorship of Latin at Cambridge University. He was also made a Fellow of renowned Trinity College. At the age of fifty-two, he had reached the summit of academic eminence. His professional life at Cambridge was different from what it had been at University College, London. His teaching duties were few, requiring him merely to give a certain number of lectures to the university annually, a duty that he fulfilled scrupulously up to the time of his death. He continued to be a grim lecturer, coolly detached and aloof from the students and most of the faculty. He at once established at Cambridge the same reputation for cold, even surly, manners that had characterized his deportment in London. He once told a visitor, who had come to Cambridge to meet him, that being a friend of Laurence Housman's was no introduction to *him*!

Despite his interest in architecture, the rooms that Housman chose at Trinity were utterly undistinguished, and he did nothing to make them comfortable or attractive. The sole decoration was a large tortoise shell; there was not even a comfortable lounge chair. Housman spent the rest of his life in these cheerless rooms at Trinity, producing the scholarly articles and editions of classical texts that made him preeminent in his field. He imperiously disdained the numerous honors and awards that were offered him over the years, including the royal Order of Merit; he would be condescended to by no one, not even by the king.

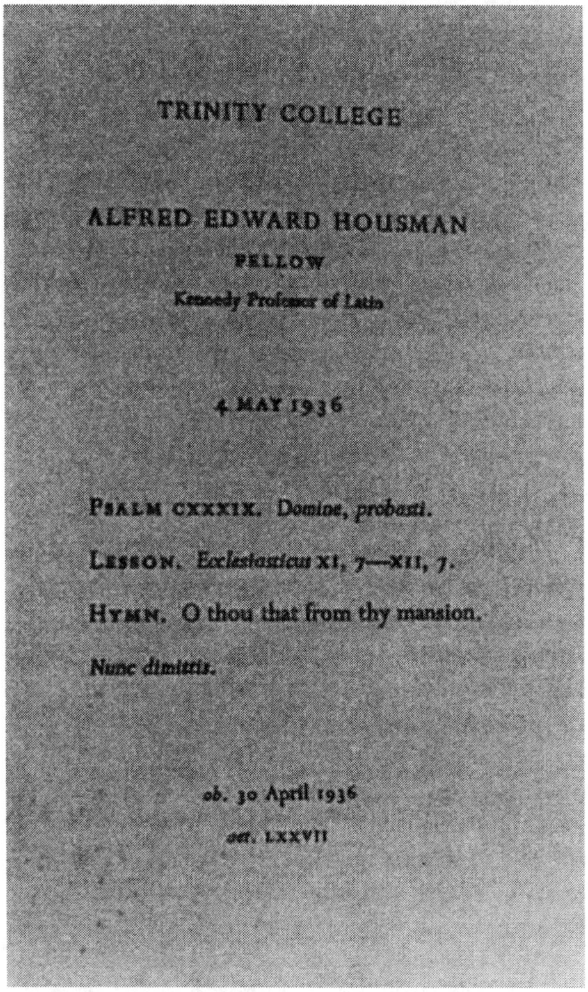
TRINITY COLLEGE

ALFRED EDWARD HOUSMAN

FELLOW

Kennedy Professor of Latin

4 MAY 1936

PSALM CXXXIX. *Domine, probasti.*

LESSON. *Ecclesiasticus* XI, 7—XII, 7.

HYMN. O thou that from thy mansion.

Nunc dimittis.

ob. 30 April 1936

aet. LXXVII

Program for Housman's funeral service

Housman had written no new poetry since 1903, and the advent of World War I did not inspire him to new creative efforts. *A Shropshire Lad*, with its poems extolling the virtues of the British soldier, continued to be popular and was several times reprinted. Housman continued to apply himself to his scholarly labors, and in 1930 the fifth volume of the Manilius was published, completing his life's work.

Much to everyone's surprise, Housman, in his sixty-second year, put together a collection of poems that his publisher, Grant Richards, was delighted to bring out the following year. *Last Poems* appeared in 1922. It contains forty-one numbered pieces, plus a short introductory poem. Only a few of these poems were new; the rest had simply been taken from the previously unpublished pieces in the poetry notebooks. Consequently, these poems are indistinguishable in theme and form and diction from those of *A Shropshire Lad*, published twenty-six years earlier. The same high degree of poetic discipline and quality of craftsmanship are, however, apparent in *Last*

Poems. The collection contains some splendid verses, among the most outstanding of which are "Eight O'Clock" (number fifteen, one of Housman's "bell" poems, which are among his best), "Epithalamium" (number twenty-four, the poem that commemorates the wedding of Moses Jackson), "The First of May" (number thirty-four), and number forty, in which Nature is personified as a fickle mistress. *Last Poems* also contains the bizarre "Hell Gate," an imaginary descent into the underworld, where the speaker meets a lost comrade with whom he makes a successful rebellion against the forces of darkness and death. The stalwart comrade is doubtless the perennial companion of Housman's imaginary poetic adventures, the young Moses Jackson.

Of course, the real Moses Jackson had not remained young and was at the publication of *Last Poems* dying of stomach cancer in a hospital in Vancouver, British Columbia, where he had gone with his family some years before to take up farming, after his retirement as principal of Sindh College. Housman sent his old friend a copy of *Last Poems* with an inscription saying that Jackson was "largely responsible" for them. Jackson died at the age of sixty-three, on 14 January 1923. The death of Moses Jackson coincided with the end of Housman's composition of poetry, with the exception of a few lines that he would write in 1925.

On 9 May 1933, when he was almost seventy-five, Housman gave the Leslie Stephen Lecture at the Senate House, Cambridge. In this well-known address, entitled *The Name and Nature of Poetry*, Housman discoursed on English verse generally and on the processes by which his own poetry was created, a poetry of intuition whose sources were inexplicable. The theory of poetry that Housman articulated in this lecture was extremely conservative and clashed with the modern theories of contemporary Cambridge critics such as I. A. Richards, who rejected such mysterious explanations of poetic creativity.

The last few years of Housman's life were characterized by the shortness of breath, fatigue, discomfort, and recurrent pain that accompany heart disease. Nevertheless, he continued to meet his professorial obligations virtually up to the time of his death, at seventy-seven, on 30 April 1936.

Letters:

Thirty Housman Letters to Witter Bynner, edited by Tom Burns Haber (New York: Knopf, 1957);

The Letters of A. E. Housman, edited by Henry Mass (Cambridge, Mass.: Harvard University Press, 1971).

Bibliographies:

Theodore G. Ehrsam, *A Bibliography of Alfred Edward Housman* (Boston: Faxon, 1941);

Robert W. Stallman, "Annotated Bibliography of A. E. Housman: A Critical Study," *Publications of the Modern Language Association of America*, 60 (1945): 463-502;

John Carter and John Sparrow, *A. E. Housman, An Annotated Hand-List* (London: Hart-Davis, 1952).

Biographies:

A. S. F. Gow, *A. E. Housman: A Sketch* (London: Cambridge University Press, 1936);

Laurence Housman, *A. E. H.: Some Poems, Some Letters, and A Personal Memoir* (London: Cape, 1937);

Housman, *The Unexpected Years* (London: Cape, 1937);

Housman, *My Brother, A. E. Housman* (New York: Scribners, 1938);

Percy Withers, *A Buried Life* (London: Cape, 1940);

Grant Richards, *Housman 1897-1936* (New York: Oxford University Press, 1942);

Ian Scott-Kilvert, *A. E. Housman* (London: Longmans, Green, 1955);

George L. Watson, *A. E. Housman: A Divided Life* (London: Hart-Davis, 1957; Boston: Beacon Press, 1958).

References:

A. F. Allison, "The Poetry of Housman," *Review of English Studies*, 19 (1943): 276-284;

John Peale Bishop, "The Poetry of A. E. Housman," *Poetry*, 56 (June 1940): 144-153;

R. P. Blackmur, "The Composition in Nine Poets: 1937," in his *The Expense of Greatness* (New York: Arrow Editions, 1940), pp. 202-205;

J. Bronowski, "A. E. Housman," in his *The Poet's Defence* (London: Cambridge University Press, 1939), pp. 209-228;

Cleanth Brooks, "The Whole of Housman," *Kenyon Review*, 3 (1941): 105-109;

Cyril Connolly, "A. E. Housman: A Controversy," in his *The Condemned Playground* (London: Routledge, 1945), pp. 47-52;

T. S. Eliot, Review of *The Name and Nature of Poetry*, *Criterion*, 13 (1933): 151-154;

William Empson, "Rhythm and Imagery in English Poetry," *British Journal of Aesthetics*, 2 (1962): 36-54;

Empson, *Seven Types of Ambiguity* (London: Chatto & Windus, 1935);

Empson, *Some Versions of Pastoral* (London: Chatto & Windus, 1935), pp. 57-58;

Empson, *The Structure of Complex Words* (London: Chatto & Windus, 1951), pp. 11-13;

H. W. Garrod, "Mr. A. E. Housman," in his *The Profession of Poetry* (London: Oxford University Press, 1929), pp. 211-224;

Tom Burns Haber, *A. E. Housman* (New York: Twayne, 1967);

Robert Hamilton, *Housman the Poet* (Folcroft, Pa.: Folcroft Press, 1953);

Maude M. Hawkins, *A. E. Housman: Man Behind A Mask* (Chicago: Regnery, 1958);

F. R. Leavis, "Imagery and Movement: Notes in the Analysis of Poetry," *Scrutiny*, 13 (1945): 119-134;

B. J. Leggett, *The Poetic Art of A. E. Housman: Theory and Practice* (Lincoln & London: University of Nebraska Press, 1978);

Norman Marlow, *A. E. Housman, Scholar and Poet* (London: Routledge & Kegan Paul, 1958);

George Orwell, "Inside the Whale," in his *Inside the Whale* (London: Gollancz, 1940), pp. 146-154;

John Crowe Ransom, "Honey and Gall," *Southern Review*, 6 (Summer 1940): 6-11;

Christopher Ricks, ed., *A. E. Housman: A Collection of Critical Essays* (Englewood Cliffs, N.J.: Prentice-Hall, 1968);

John Sparrow, "A Shropshire Lad at Fifty," in his *Independent Essays* (London: Faber & Faber, 1963), pp. 124-145;

Stephen Spender, "The Essential Housman," *Horizon*, 1 (1940): 295-301.

Papers:

Fair copies in Housman's handwriting of *A Shropshire Lad* and of *Last Poems* are at Cambridge University in the Library of Trinity College and the Fitzwilliam Museum, respectively. Substantial remains of the four poetry notebooks are in the Library of Congress, Washington, D.C.

Rudyard Kipling

(30 December 1865 - 18 January 1936)

This essay was written by Charles Cantalupo (Pennsylvania State University, Schuylkill Campus) for DLB 19: British Poets, 1880-1914.

See also the Kipling entry in DLB 34: British Novelists, 1890-1929: Traditionalists.

Rudyard Kipling

SELECTED BOOKS: *Schoolboy Lyrics* (Lahore: Privately printed, 1881);

Echoes, by Kipling and Alice Kipling (Lahore: Privately printed, 1884);

Departmental Ditties and Other Verses (Lahore: Privately printed, 1886; enlarged edition, Calcutta: Thacker, Spink, 1886; enlarged again, Calcutta: Thacker, Spink / London & Bombay: Thacker, 1890);

Plain Tales from the Hills (Calcutta: Thacker, Spink / London: Thacker, 1888; New York: Lovell, 1890; London & New York: Macmillan, 1890);

Soldiers Three (Allahabad: Wheeler, 1888; London: Low, Marston, Searle & Rivington, 1890);

The Story of the Gadsbys (Allahabad: Wheeler, 1888; Allahabad: Wheeler / London: Low, Marston, Searle & Rivington, 1890; New York: Lovell, 1890);

In Black & White (Allahabad: Wheeler, 1888; Allahabad: Wheeler / London: Low, Marston, Searle & Rivington, 1890);

Under the Deodars (Allahabad: Wheeler, 1888; Allahabad: Wheeler / London: Low, Marston, Searle & Rivington, 1890; New York: Lovell, 1890);

The Phantom 'Rickshaw and Other Tales (Allahabad: Wheeler, 1888; Allahabad: Wheeler / London: Low, Marston, Searle & Rivington, 1890);

Wee Willie Winkie and Other Child Stories (Allahabad: Wheeler, 1888; Allahabad: Wheeler / London: Low, Marston, Searle & Rivington, 1890);

Soldiers Three [and *In Black & White*] (New York: Lovell, 1890);

Indian Tales III (New York: Lovell, 1890)—includes *The Phantom 'Rickshaw and Other Tales* and *Wee Willie Winkie and Other Child Tales*;

The Courting of Dinah Shadd and Other Stories (New York: Harper, 1890);

Departmental Ditties, Barrack-Room Ballads, and Other Verses (New York: United States Book Company, 1890);

The Light That Failed (London: Lippincott, 1890; revised edition, New York: United States Book Company, 1890; revised again, London & New York: Macmillan, 1891; New York: Doubleday & McClure, 1899);

The City of Dreadful Night and Other Places (Allahabad: Wheeler, 1891; Allahabad: Wheeler / London: Low, Marston, 1891);

Letters of Marque (Allahabad: Wheeler, 1891; republished in part, London: Low, Marston, 1891);

American Notes (New York: Ivers, 1891);

Mine Own People (New York: United States Book Company, 1891);

Life's Handicap (New York: Macmillan, 1891; London: Macmillan, 1891);

The Naulahka: A Story of West and East, by Kipling and Wolcott Balestier (London: Heinemann, 1892; New York & London: Macmillan, 1892);

Barrack-Room Ballads and Other Verses (London: Methuen, 1892); republished as *Ballads and Barrack-Room Ballads* (New York & London: Macmillan, 1892);

Many Inventions (London & New York: Macmillan, 1893; New York: Appleton, 1893);

The Jungle Book (London & New York: Macmillan, 1894; New York: Century, 1894);

The Second Jungle Book (London & New York: Macmillan, 1895; New York: Century, 1895);

Out of India (New York: Dillingham, 1895)—includes *The City of Dreadful Night and Other Places* and *Letters of Marque*;

The Seven Seas (New York: Appleton, 1896; London: Methuen, 1896);

'Captains Courageous' (London & New York: Macmillan, 1897; New York: Century, 1897);

An Almanac of Twelve Sports, text by Kipling and illustrations by William Nicholson (London: Heinemann, 1898; New York: Russell, 1898);

The Day's Work (New York: Doubleday & McClure, 1898; London: Macmillan, 1898);

A Fleet in Being (London & New York: Macmillan, 1898);

Kipling's Poems, edited by Wallace Rice (Chicago: Star Publishing, 1899);

Stalky & Co. (London: Macmillan, 1899; New York: Doubleday & McClure, 1899);

Departmental Ditties and Ballads and Barrack-Room Ballads (New York: Doubleday & McClure, 1899);

From Sea to Sea and Other Sketches, 2 volumes (New York: Doubleday & McClure, 1899; London: Macmillan, 1900);

The Kipling Reader (London: Macmillan, 1900; revised, 1901);

Kim (New York: Doubleday, Page, 1901; London: Macmillan, 1901);

Just So Stories (London: Macmillan, 1902; New York: Doubleday, Page, 1902);

The Five Nations (London: Methuen, 1903; New York: Doubleday, Page, 1903);

Traffics and Discoveries (London: Macmillan, 1904; New York: Doubleday, Page, 1904);

Puck of Pook's Hill (London: Macmillan, 1906; New York: Doubleday, Page, 1906);

Collected Verse (New York: Doubleday, Page, 1907; London: Hodder & Stoughton, 1912);

Letters to the Family (Toronto: Macmillan, 1908);

Actions and Reactions (London: Macmillan, 1909; New York: Doubleday, Page, 1909);

Rewards and Fairies (London: Macmillan, 1910; Garden City, N.Y.: Doubleday, Page, 1910);

A History of England, by Kipling and C. R. L. Fletcher (Oxford: Clarendon Press / London: Frowde / London: Hodder & Stoughton, 1911; Garden City, N.Y.: Doubleday, Page, 1911);

Songs from Books (Garden City, N.Y.: Doubleday, Page, 1912; London: Macmillan, 1913);

The New Army, 6 pamphlets (Garden City, N.Y.: Doubleday, Page, 1914); republished as *The New Army in Training*, 1 volume (London: Macmillan, 1915);

France at War (London: Macmillan, 1915; Garden City, N.Y.: Doubleday, Page, 1915);

The Fringes of the Fleet (London: Macmillan, 1915; Garden City, N.Y.: Doubleday, Page, 1915);

Sea Warfare (London: Macmillan, 1916; Garden City, N.Y.: Doubleday, Page, 1917);

A Diversity of Creatures (London: Macmillan, 1917; Garden City, N.Y.: Doubleday, Page, 1917);

The Eyes of Asia (Garden City, N.Y.: Doubleday, Page, 1918);

Twenty Poems (London: Methuen, 1918);

The Graves of the Fallen (London: Imperial War Graves Commission, 1919);

The Years Between (London: Methuen, 1919; Garden City, N.Y.: Doubleday, Page, 1919);

Rudyard Kipling's Verse, Inclusive Edition, 1885-1918 (3 volumes, London: Hodder & Stoughton, 1919; 1 volume, Garden City, N.Y.: Doubleday, Page, 1919);

Letters of Travel (1892-1913) (London: Macmillan, 1920; Garden City, N.Y.: Doubleday, Page, 1920);

Selected Stories From Kipling, edited by William Lyon Phelps (Garden City, N.Y. & Toronto: Doubleday, Page, 1921);

A Kipling Anthology: Verse (London: Methuen, 1922; Garden City, N.Y.: Doubleday, Page, 1922);

A Kipling Anthology: Prose (London: Macmillan, 1922; Garden City, N.Y.: Doubleday, Page, 1922);
Kipling Calendar (London: Hodder & Stoughton, 1923; Garden City, N.Y.: Doubleday, Page, 1923);
Land and Sea Tales (London: Macmillan, 1923; Garden City, N.Y.: Doubleday, Page, 1923);
Songs for Youth (London: Hodder & Stoughton, 1924; Garden City, N.Y.: Doubleday, Page, 1925);
A Choice of Songs (London: Methuen, 1925);
Debits and Credits (London: Macmillan, 1926; Garden City, N.Y.: Doubleday, Page, 1926);
Sea and Sussex (London: Macmillan, 1926; Garden City, N.Y.: Doubleday, Page, 1926);
Songs of the Sea (London: Macmillan, 1927; Garden City, N.Y.: Doubleday, Page, 1927);
Rudyard Kipling's Verse, Inclusive Edition, 1885-1926 (London: Hodder & Stoughton, 1927; Garden City, N.Y.: Doubleday, Page, 1927);
A Book of Words: Selections from Speeches and Addresses Delivered Between 1906 and 1927 (London: Macmillan, 1928; Garden City, N.Y.: Doubleday, Doran, 1928);
The Complete Stalky & Co. (London: Macmillan, 1929; Garden City, N.Y.: Doubleday, Doran, 1930);
Poems 1886-1929, 3 volumes (London: Macmillan, 1929; Garden City, N.Y.: Doubleday, Doran, 1930);
Limits and Renewals (London: Macmillan, 1932; Garden City, N.Y.: Doubleday, Doran, 1932);
Souvenirs of France (London: Macmillan, 1933);
Rudyard Kipling's Verse, Inclusive Edition, 1885-1932 (London: Hodder & Stoughton, 1933; Garden City, N.Y.: Doubleday, Doran, 1934);
Something of Myself for My Friends Known and Unknown (London: Macmillan, 1937; Garden City, N.Y.: Doubleday, Doran, 1937);
Rudyard Kipling's Verse, Definitive Edition (London: Hodder & Stoughton, 1940; New York: Doubleday, Doran, 1940);
The Harbour Watch (Battle, U.K.: Spearman, 1990).

Collection: *The Sussex Edition of the Complete Works of Rudyard Kipling*, 35 volumes (London: Macmillan, 1937-1939); republished as *The Collected Works of Rudyard Kipling, The Burwash Edition*, 28 volumes (Garden City, N.Y.: Doubleday, Doran, 1941).

OTHER: *The Irish Guards in the Great War, Edited and Compiled from Their Diaries by Rudyard Kipling*, 2 volumes (London: Macmillan, 1923; Garden City, N.Y.: Doubleday, Page, 1923).

The years 1890-1932, during which Joseph Rudyard Kipling was having his books published in London and New York, coincided with the development of modernism and its establishment as the dominant literary style of the twentieth century. Kipling's immense body of writing—5 novels, roughly 250 short stories, more than 800 pages of verse, and many nonfiction pieces—seems to have little obvious relationship to modernism. Yet his books were extremely popular; 15 million volumes of his collected stories alone were sold. Kipling's work, particularly his poetry, has received far less scholarly and critical attention than the efforts of major modernist writers, and he has not had as great an influence as writers such as William Butler Yeats, T. S. Eliot, Ezra Pound, or Wallace Stevens on generations of successive writers. Kipling's inability to inspire the most intense kinds of critical interest and literary imitation seems due equally to his literary style and his subject matter. Increasingly readers since World War I have neither enjoyed nor felt instructed by poetry which often is, quite blatantly, politically imperialist and socially reactionary—sounding like and appealing to, in George Orwell's words, a "gutter patriot." Also contrary to most twentieth-century taste—which has, of course, been primarily formed by modernism—are Kipling's characteristically rhyming, rhythmically regular, formal stanzas. He was also intent on writing clear, matter-of-fact statements expressed by a voice certain about a particular point of view: again, rather the antithesis of a modernist persona. Nevertheless, such a characterization of Kipling's poetry, although justified and clearly recognized by most of its admirers, is superficial; for in his verse one can also find many of the great qualities of the best modernist poetry: plainness, concision, passionate utterance instead of worn-out poetic diction, conviction, sharp images, a revitalized sense of history, great artistic craft, originality.

In 1941 T. S. Eliot—who has written the most enlightening, evaluative essay on Kipling's work—resuscitated interest in the verse by editing and writing an introduction for *A Choice of Kipling's Verse*. Eliot saw three periods in Kipling's career: his living in India, his worldwide travel and residence in America, his final years in Sussex, England. Before he left India at age twenty-four, Kipling's stories and poems had achieved considerable fame, and 1890 had been a literary annus mirabilis for him in London. Moreover, upon returning to England in 1896, Kipling became an "unofficial laureate" of the British Empire and its people. From a not at all high-minded viewpoint, he wrote in verse of imperialist triumphs and defeats, illusions of peace, realities of war (particularly the conflict with the Boers of South Africa), local yet ancient history, and finally of World War I and its legacy.

Kipling was born on 30 December 1865 in Bombay, India, when it was a relatively secure colonial possession of Victorian England. His father was an architect and artisan who had gone to India purposefully to encourage, support, and restore native Indian art against the incursions of British business interests. Much like William Morris in England, John Lockwood Kipling sought in India to preserve, at least in part, and to copy styles of art and architecture which, representing a rich and continuous tradition of thousands of years, were suddenly threatened with extinction by an influx of new capital bent solely on immediate, commercial profit. Rudyard Kipling's mother, Alice Macdonald Kipling, also had more than an amateur's familiarity with the world of art. Her older sister had married the Victorian painter Sir Edward Burne-Jones. And attending the John Lockwood Kiplings' wedding, in March 1865, were many Pre-Raphaelite painters and writers including Algernon Charles Swinburne, both Christina and Dante Gabriel Rossetti, and Ford Madox Brown. In his autobiography, *Something of Myself for My Friends Known and Unknown* (1937), Kipling happily recalls his visits to the household of Burne-Jones (or Uncle Ned as he was called), his being told stories there by William Morris, and hearing the conversation of Robert Browning. A balance, perhaps, for Kipling's rather exotic childhood in India and his contact with some of the major influences on Victorian aesthetic sensibility is that his grandfathers on both sides were Methodist ministers. According to Angus Wilson, Kipling's later emphasis on the values of work, discipline, and earnestness flowed directly from this source of dissenting religion. According to the custom of the English in India, Kipling's parents returned him and his sister to England in 1871 so that the children could begin school there. His parents left them at Lorne Lodge in the Southsea suburbs, with a man and a woman who treated the children cruelly. In his autobiography Kipling described one childhood incident, typical of many others. Having given an incomplete account of his actions to his guardians, "I was well-beaten and sent to school through the streets of Southsea with the placard 'liar' between my shoulders." It is no wonder that Kipling vividly remembered this place as the "House of Desolation." Kipling's parents returned to England in 1877, however, and he was once again restored to his family's more enlightened atmosphere. He recalled that while visiting a museum with his mother, "I understood . . . that books and pictures were among the most important affairs in the world; that I could read as much as I chose and ask the meaning of things from anyone I met. I had found out, too, that one could take pen and set down what one thought, and that nobody accused one of 'showing off' by doing so." In 1878 Kipling went on to a school called Westward-Ho, quite recently established by a person connected with the Victorian artists, writers, and intellectuals, whom the Kipling family had met through Burne-Jones. The education was not particularly distinctive, though marked by a fairly wide exposure to literature and, just as important, a tolerant attitude by the school's authorities. Furthermore, Kipling wrote some verse at Westward-Ho, where he remained until 1882, and his mother, who had returned to India with her husband, had it printed, in 1881 in Lahore, as *Schoolboy Lyrics*.

The next stage of Kipling's life is, perhaps, most crucial. His parents could not afford to send him to Oxford, and instead he returned to India in 1882 to be "educated," that is, to begin practice as a newspaper writer for the *Civil and Military Gazette* in Bombay. For the next seven years, Kipling worked on this Indian newspaper for English-speaking people while he wrote short stories and poems. In his autobiography Kipling recalls that as a young journalist he worked ten to fifteen hours a day. He also dared to explore the exotic yet economically deprived conditions of a native Indian culture that he saw as a palimpsest through which "the dead of all times were about" him. Simultaneously, he seemed to consider his own writing, at least his journalism, as negligible: "I was a hireling, paid to do what I was paid to do . . . ," and he soon "learned that . . . statements of . . . facts are not well seen by responsible official authorities."

At least in part to serve as filler for empty columns, the *Gazette* began to publish Kipling's verse under the heading of "Bungalow Ballads." He

Page from a 17 November 1882 letter from Kipling to one of his former masters at Westward-Ho (The Anderson Galleries, sale 4283, 9-10 December 1936)

was also working on the short stories that were collected in *Plain Tales from the Hills* in 1888. Before this book was published, however, a collection of his verses from various Indian newspapers, *Departmental Ditties*, was anonymously published in 1886. First, 350 copies were privately printed, but then in the same year a Calcutta publishing house published an enlarged edition in Calcutta. They published a further enlarged edition in Calcutta and London in 1890. In India these books, especially *Plain Tales from the Hills*, became popular. Although both works were at least scrutinized by London critics, neither book sold very well in England.

"Prelude," which was added to the 1890 edition of Kipling's *Departmental Ditties* and which was later placed first in *Rudyard Kipling's Verse, Definitive Edition* (1940), strikes keynotes that clearly echo again and again throughout the forty-seven years and more than five hundred poems to follow. It is probably no accident that Kipling, who was quite aware that he was "The Man Who Could Write" (the title of another poem in the collection), struck such a prelude. As Eliot recognized, the technique of his early verse exhibited "perfect competence." For that matter, there is no particularly significant change or development in Kipling's poetic style; nor did Kipling show much need to change his personal values throughout his life of writing. "Prelude" begins:

I have eaten your bread and salt.
    I have drunk your water and wine,
The deaths ye have died I have watched beside,
    And the lives ye led were mine.

For Kipling the poet had the same plain yet essential needs and means—neither higher, nor particularly lower (art of the decadence was becoming more popular at the time)—as the people whom he wrote about. Charles Eliot Norton early recognized that Kipling in his own way fit Wordsworth's ideal that the poet is "a man speaking to men" who "binds together by passions and knowledge the vast empire of human society." At the same time Kipling seems to exemplify, in his own distinctive manner, Ben Jonson's dictum that poetry should exhibit the manners and language which people actually use. In his autobiography Kipling advises other writers, "never play down to your public, not because some of them do not deserve it, but because it is bad for your hand. All your material is drawn from the lives of men." The common "bread," "salt," "water," "wine," "deaths and lives" of human beings are a kind of initiation in which the writer must participate before he may portray it. Furthermore, for Kipling the poet was selfless. He often reiterated this ideal of the impersonality of the poet (an ideal that Eliot shared with him). Kipling contended that "The magic of literature lies in the words, and not in any man." Moreover, the identity of the poet exists solely through the society which he represents. In a much later poem, Kipling presents a fascinating portrait of St. Paul "At his Execution" claiming, much as Kipling did in "Prelude," that "I am made all things to all men": an exact quote from one of Paul's letters, yet further developed by Kipling:

Since I was overcome
    By that great Light and Word,
I have forgot or forgone
The self men call their own.

Kipling's Paul concludes that knowledge of himself is possible only through seeing "those I have drawn to the Lord." Kipling, of course, was aware that people are interested in a writer's personal life, and as someone who became famous at an early age he suffered badly at the hands of such interest. In the definitive edition of his verse, which Kipling himself carefully arranged, the final poem, "The Appeal," shows his expectation that someone who has read such a substantial volume might naturally want to know the biography of its author. Still, he asks the reader:

FOR THE LITTLE, LITTLE, SPAN
THE DEAD ARE BORNE IN MIND,
SEEK NOT TO QUESTION OTHER THAN
THE BOOKS I LEAVE BEHIND.

Along with the idea that the writer's only identity should be what he has in common with other people (most of whom are not writers) and what he or she manages to state plainly in the work itself is Kipling's appeal—a kind of *caveat lector* stated in the second stanza of "Prelude"—not to consider mere art as overly important:

I have written the tale of our life
    For a sheltered people's mirth,
In jesting guise—but ye are wise,
    And ye know what the jest is worth.

Kipling established himself as a writer when the phrase "art for art's sake" was a revolutionary fashion: uttered both "For a sheltered people's

Kipling's inscription and drawing in a copy of Echoes *presented to the United Services College (Parke-Bernet, sale 665, 24-25 April 1945)*

mirth" and to shock the overly earnest. Kipling, however, while he wrote many poems about art did not write "for art's sake," nor, for that matter, for artists. In "Prelude" Kipling rather modestly claims that his own art too is merely "jest" and "For a sheltered people's mirth." Yet he leaves the actual "worth" of his art finally unsaid; he expects that the wisdom of common humanity, more than the ultimately "jesting guise" of those who understood "art for art's sake," has the capacity to evaluate it.

Another kind of obvious appeal in "Prelude," echoing throughout *Departmental Ditties* and indeed throughout Kipling's subsequent poetry, is its sound. He wrote many of his poems to be read aloud. For Kipling this criterion required consistent use of regular rhythm, rhymes of all kinds, formal stanzas, the ballad, and forms of popular song. By the same measure, Kipling would avoid using free verse, which he likened to "fishing with barbless hooks." In his autobiography Kipling remembers how, when writing his poems in India, "I made my own experiments in the weights, colours, perfumes, and attributes of words in relation to other words, either as read aloud so that they may hold the ear or, scattered over the page, draw the eye. There is no line of my verse or prose which has not been mouthed till the tongue has made all smooth, and memory, after many recitals, has mechanically skipped the grosser superfluities."

Departmental Ditties contains other leitmotivs which continue throughout Kipling's verse and which together indicate the virtuosity of this volume of first poems. For example, "A General Summary" states the classical notion that human nature is unchanging regardless of geographical place or historical period:

We are very slightly changed
From the semi-apes who ranged
    India's prehistoric clay;
He that drew the longest bow
Ran his brother down, you know,
    As we run men down to-day.

Again adopting the rhetorical ploy of denigrating mere art, Kipling makes a plain assertion about his "artless songs":

Do not deal with anything
    New or never said before.
As it was in the beginning
Is to-day official sinning,
    And shall be for evermore.

The emphasis on "official sinning" as opposed to the more private abuses people manage to keep private is, perhaps, more typical of Kipling's early work. Yet this theme too indicates an even greater one running throughout Kipling's poetry: the value and ethic of work. For instance, Kipling also writes in "A General Summary":

Who shall doubt "the secrets hid
Under Cheops' pyramid"
Was that the contractor did
    Cheops out of several millions?

Samuel Johnson attacked the idea of building pyramids because they merely signified the vanity of the pharaohs, but Kipling attacks the work itself as fraud. "Official sinning" is also attacked in "Pagett, M.P.," a later poem about a government official who breaks down under the strain of the primitive conditions he finds on a "fact-finding" mission to the eastern British Empire—all to the delight of the local British official whom he is checking on. Satirizing "official sinning" is also the aim of a later dramatic monologue, clearly in

Kipling during his years as a writer in India (Bateman's, Burwash, Sussex)

the manner of Robert Browning, by a resigning English viceroy of India ("One Viceroy Resigns"). Another satiric poem in *Departmental Ditties* is "The Rupaiyat of Omar Kal'vin," a spoof on the popular poem and its pseudo-oriental translation by Edward FitzGerald. Boldly, he even wrote on the occasion of Queen Victoria's first jubilee in a poem added to the 1890 edition of *Departmental Ditties*, "What the People Said": "the wheat and the cattle are all my care, / And the rest is the will of God." Also in *Departmental Ditties*, to demonstrate further his talents and mastery of a variety of different poetic tones and genres, the young Kipling wrote distinctively of India itself:

Dim dawn behind the tamarisks—the sky is saffron-yellow—
 And the women in the village grind the corn,
And the parrots seek the river-side, each calling to his fellow
That the Day, the staring Eastern Day, is born.

His impressions of India's cultural institutions are not very positive and anticipate an attitude of Eliot's *The Waste Land*:

The smoke upon your Altar dies,
 The flowers decay,
The Goddess of your sacrifice
 Has flown away.

The lines also indicate that by 1887 Kipling had had enough of Indian culture and could no longer tolerate the extreme heat:

I am sick of endless sunshine, sick of blossom-burdened bough.
Give me back the leafless woodlands where the winds of Springtime range—
Give me back one day in England, for it's Spring in England now!

In 1888 occurred, according to C. E. Carrington, "the first Kipling boom." It was due to the publication of six volumes of his stories in an inexpensive series aimed particularly at railway travelers. Not only did Kipling's writing suddenly become more popular and, for the first time, profitable, but his books were also circulating throughout much of the British Empire. Furthermore, seeming to follow the path blazed by his literary works, Kipling himself left India.

In March 1889 he departed Calcutta on what was to be a seven-month journey to London. He traveled east, passing through Southeast Asia, China, Japan, and then arriving in San Francisco. The tour continued apace, with Kipling traveling up the Pacific Coast, through the western Rockies to Chicago, and then finally slowing down a bit through the East, which he seemed to like best. Although, unlike most English writers touring the United States, Kipling first traveled through America from West to East, on this first visit his impressions were typical—that is, mixed: delight in the landscapes and, generally, opprobrium for their inhabitants. When he returned, roughly two and a half years later, to remain in Vermont for more than four years, both his delight and disgust in America would be sharpened.

Absent for seven years, Kipling finally arrived in London in October 1889. In December one of Kipling's most famous poems, "The Ballad of East and West," was published in *Macmillan's Magazine*. Its couplets of fourteen syllables—the "fourteener" which Kipling would successfully employ again and again in subsequent verse, and which he favorably considered "a craft that will almost sail herself"—were immediately popular with the public and acclaimed by more scholarly writers such as Edmund Gosse and George Saintsbury. According to Kipling's criterion "to put things in a form in which people would not only read but remember them," the ballad's beginning and refrain—"Oh, East is East, and West is West, and never the twain shall meet"—was suddenly a common phrase in the English language. Worth remembering, however, is that while out of context the line seems to imply the opposite, Kipling's famous ballad clearly states that superseding the apparent, even dramatic, differences between Eastern and Western peoples is a universal yet divine element in human nature which knows no natural or racial boundaries.

Kipling had yet another world to travel through: the literary life of London. He was not favorably impressed and never would be, although he avoided the common reaction of merely trying to offend. Kipling is indeed remarkable as a writer for having early reached a decision scrupulously to avoid specifically commenting on fellow living writers. Nevertheless, he understood that "There is no provincialism like the provincialism of London" or of any place made out to be a kind of literary capital. Kipling had established himself as a writer, most important, in his own mind yet commercially too, long before his London success. He recalls in his autobiography that although he was pretty much accepted and appreciated by the literary establishment, "I was struck by the slenderness of some of the writer's equipment. I could not see how they got along with so casual a knowledge of French work, and, apparently, of much English grounding that I had supposed indispensable. Their stuff seemed to be a day to day traffic in generalities, hedged by trade considerations.... Had they been newspaper men in a hurry, I should have understood; but the gentlemen were presented to me as Priests and Pontiffs." Kipling also realized about most of his newly found, sophisticated, and wealthy admirers that "Unless it happened that I was the fashion for the moment, you'd let me die of want on your doorstep." Still, the fashion of Kipling had hardly begun.

Kipling's official biographer, Carrington, calls 1890 "Rudyard Kipling's year. There had been nothing like his sudden rise to fame since Byron.... He had no difficulty disposing of his wares. Eighteen-ninety saw the publication or republication, in England and America, of more than eighty short stories ... many ballads, and ... a novel. The market was flooded with his work in verse and prose...." Many of Kipling's poems of 1890 first appeared in the *Scots Observer* (which during that year became the *National Observer*), at the time an influential magazine edited by W. E. Henley. These verses along with others were collected in 1892 under the title *Barrack-Room Ballads* (later republished in an expanded form). Thirteen of these ballads were first published in New York in 1890. Kipling's topic was the British soldier: "arms and the man," expressed to the thumping rhythm of popular song and employing the low diction of cockney dialect. The individual soldier was the hero or, at least, the antihero in a society, an armed forces, and an empire which regarded him at best as an intolerable yet necessary evil. As several critics but not enough modern readers have recognized, Kipling does not idealize or glorify the life and death of common soldiers. Rather, Kipling's poems express, as George Orwell pointed out, "anxiety" that the soldier "shall get a fair deal" from a society which, liberal or conservative, through its essentially mean treatment of him is merely "makin' mock o' uniforms that guard you while you sleep ... " ("Tommy"). The poems are not about militarism as much as about men whom, for good and bad reasons, a nation compels to defend it abroad. Crude in form and subject, the poems are a blend of melody and horror unprecedented and unmatched in English. Poems such as "The Grave of the Hundred Head" and "Arithmetic on the Frontier," which first appeared in *Departmental Ditties*, presented a macabre combination of content and style: brutalities of war expressed in the manner of musical comedy. And the poet who sung in his early twenties, "The flying bullet down the Pass / That whistles clear: 'All flesh is grass,' " would go on to compose some of the most powerful epitaphs for the soldiers of World War I. Moreover, the success of the *Barrack-Room Ballads* was immediate and widespread. There were three reprints in the first year of its publication, and the next thirty years saw no fewer than fifty more editions with varying contents. Their technique, fresh and impressive then, might also seem extraordinary in light of later poetry. Not only were they conversational, factual, and not impressionistic, but they made statements to be understood as definite and not ambiguous. The poems themselves are about the harsh circumstances of enlisted life. "Danny Deever" presents the effect upon the regiment of Danny's swift execution for having "shot a comrade sleepin' ...":

> they're done with Danny Deever, you can 'ear
> the quickstep play,

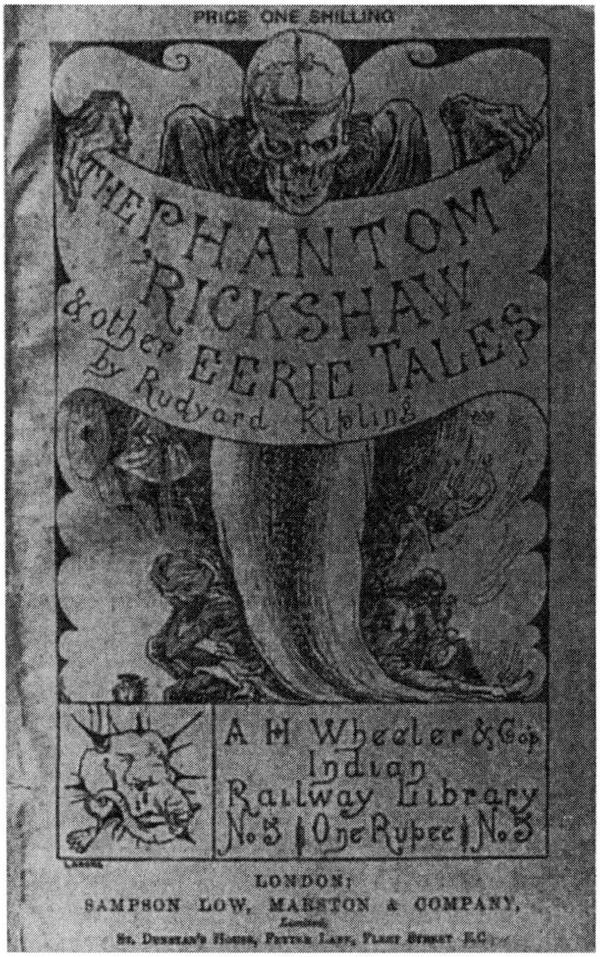

Front covers for two of the inexpensive Indian Railway Library editions which brought Kipling's writings to the attention of the English public and caused the "Kipling boom" of 1888

The Regiment's in column, an' they're marchin' us
away;
Ho! the young recruits are shakin', an' they'll want
their beer today,
After hangin' Danny Deever in the mornin'!

One week after publishing "Danny Deever" in its 22 February 1890 issue, the *Scots Observer* published "Tommy," another ballad, which also directly follows "Danny Deever" in the definitive edition of Kipling's verse. The last quatrain of "Tommy" typifies what Kipling recognized as the pathological love-hate relationship a society can maintain with its soldiers. The antithesis between war and peace, undoing relations between political states, has a perhaps even more debilitating effect upon the affinity between the defended and their defender:

For it's Tommy this, an' Tommy that, an' "Chuck
him out, the brute!"
But it's "Saviour of 'is country" when the guns
begin to shoot;
An' it's Tommy this, an' Tommy that, an' anything
you please;
An' Tommy ain't a bloomin' fool—you bet that
Tommy sees.

Seeing justice at its most unmerciful and nationalism at its most selfish, Kipling's soldier also sees the worst in himself: his rapine in "Loot," his uncontrollable drunkenness in "Cells," his racism in "Gunga Din." At the same time, in "Mandalay" he sees an alien world he is made to patrol yet which seems more friendly, exotic, and beautiful than his homeland:

When the mist was on the rice-fields an' the sun
was droppin' slow,
She'd git 'er little banjo and she'd sing "Kulla-lo-lo!"
With 'er arm upon my shoulder an' 'er cheek again
my cheek

We useteter watch the steamers an' the *hathis* pilin'
teak.
. . . .
In the sludgy, squdgy creek,
Where the silence 'ung that 'eavy you was 'arf
afraid to speak!
On the road to Mandalay . . .

Furthermore, in poems such as "That Day" Kipling's soldier also sees his penultimate enemy rout and retreat:

An' there ain't no chorus 'ere to give,
Nor there ain't no band to play;
But I wish I was dead 'fore I done what I did,
Or seen what I seed that day!

After the great success of Kipling's new ballads—so great that magazines began pirating his work and many unauthorized editions of Kipling's works were published—he was exhausted and already also surfeited with living in England. Therefore, he traveled a great deal for the next year, making brief visits to Italy and America and taking a more than four-month-long voyage to South Africa, Australia, New Zealand, and, for the last time, to India. Before and during this time he was writing poems on subjects other than the military. They cover a wide range of topics and employ a variety of forms, although the Kipling trademark of oral readability, rhythm-enforced memorability, and expository clarity is fully apparent. There is also plenty of storytelling throughout his verse. One of his greatest ballads, "The Gift of the Sea" (first published in *English Illustrated Magazine* in 1890), recites a tale as fatalistic and eerie as something out of Thomas Hardy. A young widow, living with her mother on the coast of northern England, tries to sing "The Passing Song" for her dead child beside her. Although "The gale in the teeth of the tide" rages around her, she thinks she hears another baby crying outside. Her mother with common sense dissuades her until finally the childless daughter can no longer resist:

"For the peace of my soul I must go," she said.
. . . .
In the heel of the wind-bit pier,
Where the twisted weed was piled,
She came to the life she had missed by an hour,
For she came to a little child.

Still she tries to revive the second child, and even gives it "her own child's name," but to no avail:

the dead child dripped on her breast,
And her own in the shroud lay stark;
And "God forgive us, mother," she said,
"We let it die in the dark!"

While Kipling was almost always telling stories, in prose or verse, he was at the same time as concerned with and highly critical of the course of contemporary politics. For instance, around the dawn of Queen Victoria's empire Alfred, Lord Tennyson had heroically memorialized the Light Brigade; but on a more practical, political level Kipling wrote about the same veterans thirty-seven years later in "The Last of the Light Brigade":

O thirty million English that babble of England's
might,
Behold there are twenty heroes who lack their food
tonight;
Our children's children are lisping to "honour the
charge they made—"
And we leave to the streets and the workhouse the
charge of the Light Brigade!

Kipling was undoubtedly and demonstratively a patriot; he knew, and was socially accepted by, the most powerful political leaders of his country. Nevertheless, as Orwell said of him, "Few people who have criticized England from the inside had bitterer things to say about her. . . ." His bitter criticism is implicit in *Barrack-Room Ballads*, and it derives substantially from what he considered the pride, ignorance, and parochialism of native British people, who, enjoying a worldwide empire, still regarded its inhabitants with contempt. To Kipling, whose mind had been formed in India and nurtured by his travels throughout the empire, such an attitude was irresponsible: it would lead inevitably to the loss of whatever empire had been gained and the worsening of whatever conditions had existed in places such as India before they were taken over by the British. As Eliot recognized, "For Kipling the empire was not merely an idea, a good idea or a bad one; it was something the reality of which he felt." While Kipling was the British Empire's most lyrical supporter, he at the same time tried to be its conscience by urging the British to stop being xenophobic and to start regarding the other parts of the empire as Britain's equals. The opening lines of Kipling's most positively imperialistic hymn, "The English Flag" (first published in the *National Observer* in 1891), precisely phrase his challenge: "Winds of the World, give answer! They

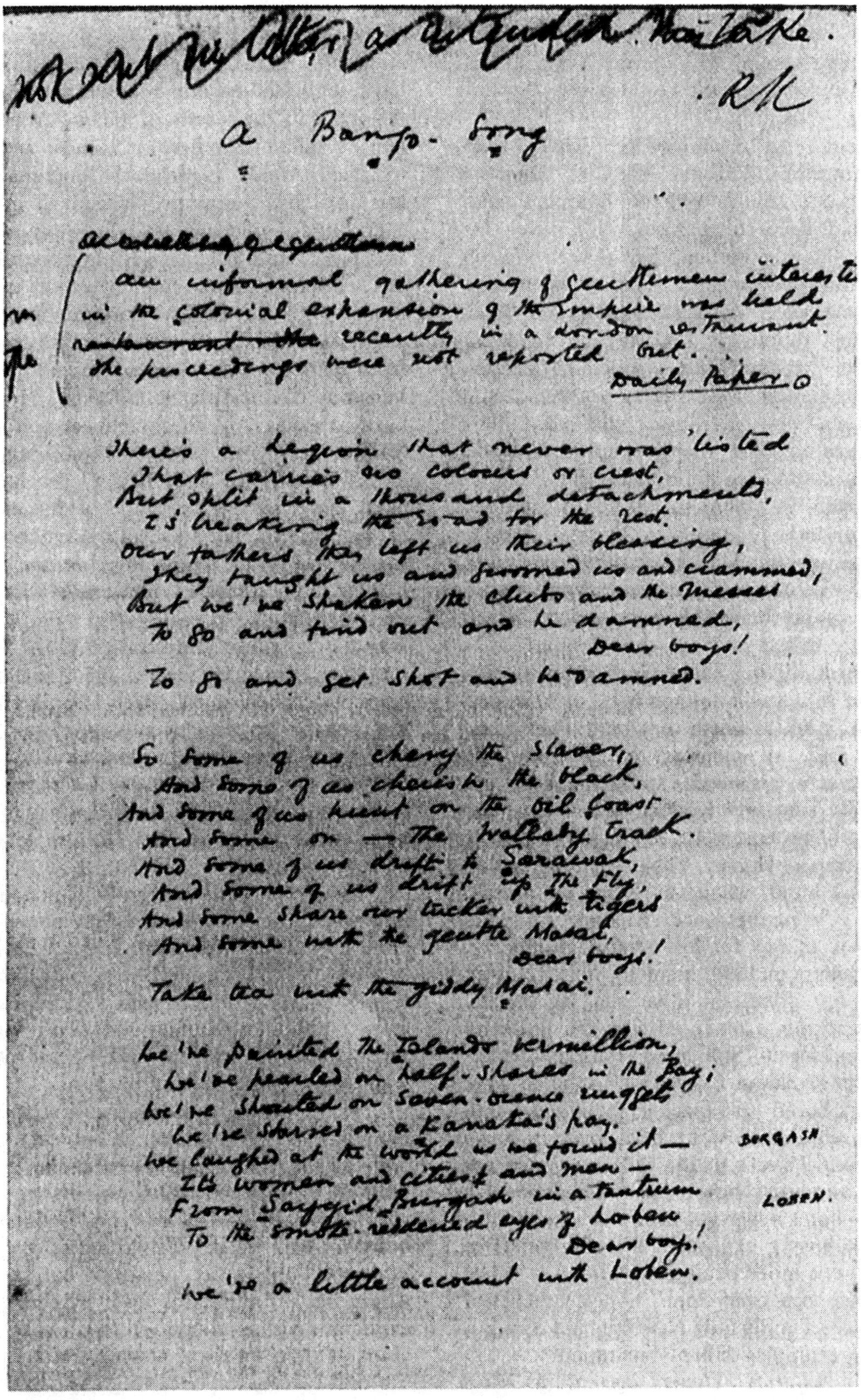

Page from the manuscript for an early version of "The Lost Legion." This version was sent to William Ernest Henley, who published it in the 13 May 1893 issue of the National Observer *(Sotheby Parke Bernet, 15 December 1982).*

are whimpering to and fro— / And what should they know of England who only England know?—." One should add, perhaps, that no empire has ever accepted the responsibility Kipling claimed for the British.

In London on 18 January 1892 Kipling married an American, Caroline Balestier, sister of Kipling's good friend Wolcott Balestier, with whom he had been collaborating on a novel, *The Naulahka: A Story of West and East* (1892). Wolcott Balestier's unexpected death seems to have precipitated the marriage, although Kipling and Caroline Balestier reportedly had already been engaged. The wedding was small and private, although attending were Edmund Gosse and Henry James, who gave away the bride. The Kiplings were married, happily it seems, until his death on their forty-fourth anniversary.

With his wife Kipling was happy to leave England again, and they sailed to America, eventually to settle on the Balestier family property in Brattleboro, Vermont. First they embarked on a proposed round-the-world honeymoon, which was abruptly halted in Japan due to failure of a bank in which Kipling had deposited his money. For a while in a small cottage back in Vermont, and then in a house which they built and named Naulakha [*sic*] in memory of Wolcott, the Kiplings were, in his words, "extraordinarily and self-centredly content." Kipling was in love and doing some of his best work. He had, as he wrote to William Ernest Henley, "The real earth within reach of my hand, whenever I tire of messing with ink. . . ." Furthermore, Kipling was soon earning good money for his writing—twenty-five thousand dollars in 1894, including five hundred dollars for one poem—and, as usual, he was becoming personally acquainted with the powerful in politics and society. Still, he was critical of America: from its President Grover Cleveland to what he saw as its bored yet rapacious materialism and its moral pretensions. As he later wrote in *Something of Myself*: "Every nation, like every individual, walks in a vain show—else it could not live with itself—but I never got over the wonder of a people who having extirpated the aboriginals of their continent more completely than any other modern race has ever done, honestly believed that they were a godly little New England community, setting examples to brutal mankind."

As for America's literary pretensions, Kipling claimed to have found in New York the "same old names cropping up week after week at the same old parties, same old gags; same old dish-water as it might be in any city we could name—allowing for local colour, and the necessity of creating the great American Literature." Critics have suggested several reasons why Kipling and America, in the words of Henry Adams, "could not be glued together. . . ."; most persuasive is Kingsley Amis's suggestion: loneliness. Kipling was isolated in Vermont, particularly by its harsh, cold winters, of which he was never fond in the first place. In Brattleboro, Kipling found less positive, endemic culture than he could in far-flung corners of the British Empire. Eventually he would be inspired to write superb verses derived from living in rural Sussex, England; but in the Vermont countryside he believed, "It would be hard to exaggerate the loneliness and sterility of life on the farms. The land was denuding itself of its inhabitants, and their places had not yet been taken by the wreckage of Eastern Europe or the wealthy city folk who later bought 'pleasure farms.' What might have become characters, powers and attributes perverted themselves in that desolation as cankered trees throw out branches akimbo, and strange faiths and cruelties, born of solitude to the edge of insanity, flourished like lichen on sick bark." Kipling's vision of poor, rural America eventually came to include his own pleasure farm, Naulakha, when a quarrel with his brother-in-law grew into a physical confrontation, a lawsuit, and then a storm of bad publicity from which he fled late in August 1896 back to England.

Regardless of his personal discontents, Kipling wrote many of his greatest poems while in America. Along with more *Barrack-Room Ballads*, he wrote several remarkably fresh dramatic monologues, some of his strongest verse about art and artists (although Kipling wrote on this subject throughout his career), and poems covering a wide yet original range of interests.

G. K. Chesterton was the first to point out Kipling's strong attraction to the theme of work and the discipline which it requires. Perhaps the greatest example of this theme is Kipling's writing particularly and extensively about the work—more so than the art—of writing poetry. Not that he wrote about his personal habits: for that would be too mundane, even irrelevant, neither exotic nor historical enough to provoke any more reaction than quizzical teasing. Back in 1890, in the midst of his early experiments in writing the first *Barrack-Room Ballads*, Kipling wrote in "The Conundrum of the Workshops" about the silliness and vanity in an artist's overweening attraction to speculating critically about what he is doing:

When the flush of a new-born sun fell first on
 Eden's green and gold,
Our father Adam sat under the Tree and scratched
 with a stick in the mould;
And the first rude sketch that the world had seen
 was joy to his mighty heart,
Till the Devil whispered behind the leaves, "It's
 pretty, but is it Art?"

In a poem written around the same time, Kipling was also able to conceive of the ideal lack of self-consciousness, and the proper confidence, understanding of the imagined audience, decisiveness, need, necessity, and joy which the greatest workers of art require in themselves and other artists; in a gently apocalyptic vein, Kipling imagined this scenario in "When Earth's Last Picture Is Painted":

only The Master shall praise us, and only The
 Master shall blame;
And no one shall work for money, and no one shall
 work for fame,
But each for the joy of working, and each, in his
 separate star,
Shall draw the Thing as he sees It for the God of
 Things as They are!

Such "joy," its vigor too, distinguishes Kipling's writing about art in the 1890s and subsequently from much other contemporary writing on the subject. In his autobiography he makes the claim—and it may be ingenuous, for he wrote almost constantly throughout his life—"Mercifully, the mere act of writing was, and always has been, a physical pleasure to me." (Of course, physical pleasure usually requires significant exertion.)

Kipling's verse about the artist's mind or art mostly emphasizes its limitations, affective powers, and sources. The artist's limitations are due primarily to his or her ego or his or her obsession with himself or herself. To present this thesis, Kipling often imagined primitive or prehistoric "makers." The pride of the egotistical artist is mocked in "Evarra and His Gods": an artist who makes, merely out of an image of himself, what is supposed to be the image of his tribe's god. Unfortunately, regardless of whether Evarra's image of God is praised or rejected, he must himself still die and, when finally God meets him, reject as absurd his pretensions. "The Story of Ung" presents an artist too obsessed with the challenge to teach and not merely to delight his audience. His being overly enamored of the truth and beauty, or reality, of his work makes him complain to his father about the ignorance of those who consider it. His father gently but firmly warns him: "If they could see as thou seest they would do as thou hast done, / And each man would make him a picture, and—what would become of my son?" Another limitation of the artist is his or her intolerance of other artists. "In the Neolithic Age" presents a poet who strips and then scalps whoever disagrees with him, until one day his "Totem" god makes him ashamed for his intolerance. The Neolithic poet concludes:

Here's my wisdom for your use, as I learned it
 when the moose
 And the reindeer roamed where Paris roars
 to-night:—
"There are nine and sixty ways of constructing tribal lays,
And—every—single—one—of—them—is—right!"

Nevertheless, these "*nine and sixty ways*" for Kipling should each affect the listener roughly the same way, whether that listener is a king or a common soldier. In "The Last Rhyme of True Thomas," the pain of which the medieval poet sings makes the king weep:

"Oh, I see the love that I lost long syne,
 I touch the hope that I may not see,
And all that I did of hidden shame,
 Like little snakes they hiss at me.

The sun is lost at noon—at noon!
 The dread of doom has grippit me.
True Thomas, hide me under your cloak,
 God wot, I'm little fit to dee!"

When True Thomas plays the different tune of pleasure on his harp, the king is as strongly affected, yet now exhilarated. Restored to strength he cries:

"Oh, I hear the tread o' the fighting-men,
 I see the sun on splent and spear.
I mark the arrow outen the fern
 That flies so low and sings so clear!"

The emotional effect of good poetry, whether it is sophisticated or crude, for Kipling can be similarly strong. He expresses his ideal in the "Song of the Banjo":

And the tunes that mean so much to you alone—
 Common tunes that make you choke and blow
 your nose—

Vulgar tunes that bring the laugh that brings the groan—
I can rip your very heartstrings out with those;
With the feasting, and the folly, and the fun—
And the lying, and the lusting, and the drink,
And the merry play that drops you, when you're done,
To the thoughts that burn like irons if you think.

For Kipling either *King Lear* or *King Kong* or any art that is good should have this strong emotional effect on either a professor or a pipe fitter. That art cause a significantly strong emotional reaction is Kipling's criterion. No doubt there are other standards for art: but this one makes it universal, transcending racial, social, intellectual, and economic obstacles. If for Kipling the final effect of great art on all kinds of people is ideally similar, then so is its source. To emphasize further this affective, egalitarian, undoubtedly challengeable ideal, Kipling wrote in cockney dialect, in "When 'Omer Smote 'Is Bloomin' Lyre," that working people—"The market-girls an' fishermen, / The shepherds an' the sailors, too . . ."—gave, and knew they gave, Homer his epic themes:

When 'Omer smote 'is bloomin' lyre,
He'd 'eard men sing by land an' sea;
An' what he thought 'e might require,
'E went an' took—the same as me!

In this poem, the "me," who would imitate vulgar dialect and manners in his writing, sounds like Kipling himself giving his own aesthetic principles, especially as exemplified in *Barrack-Room Ballads*. A more subtle, defensible, and persuasive exposition of the same contention about the necessarily extensive mimesis required of great art is expressed by Kipling in a later poem, "The Craftsman" (first published in 1910). Here, speaking with Ben Jonson, Shakespeare admits, after consuming some "Blessed . . . vintage":

at an alehouse under Cotswold,
He had made sure of his very Cleopatra
Drunk with enormous, salvation contemning
Love for a tinker.

The most unrefined kind of nature is the source of Shakespeare's most fearful, tragic effects:

How at Bankside, a boy drowning kittens
Winced at the business; whereupon his sister—
Lady Macbeth aged seven—thrust 'em under,
Sombrely scornful.

A perhaps logical consequence of Kipling's writing verse apparently inspired by extensive, creative mimicking is his mastery of the dramatic monologue. He wrote at least three such poems in America. The most famous is "McAndrew's Hymn": a vigorous meditation by the Calvinist "Scots Engineer" of a steamship on his engines and his soul:

Lord, Thou has made this world below the shadow of a dream,
An', taught by time, I tak' it so—exceptin' always Steam.
From coupler-flange to spindle-guide I see Thy Hand, O God—
Predistination in the stride o' yon connectin'-rod.
John Calvin might ha' forged the same—enormous, certain, slow—
Ay, wrought it in the furnace-flame—*my* "Institutio."

When the poem was first published, in *Scribner's Magazine* (December 1894), it was prefaced by a fictional letter which suggested that someone actually went down to an engine room and in fact heard such an engineer speak in such a way. Yet verisimilitude is mainly enforced through Kipling's use of vernacular and technical language (something else that appears in much of his poetry). At the same time, as Chesterton wrote, "Kipling has perceived the significance and philosophy of steam." Blatantly antiromantic (although the poem still contains some magnificent description of the natural beauty of the tropics tempting McAndrew), Kipling has McAndrew derive fundamental Christianity from his engines. "McAndrew's Hymn," although its tone is spontaneous, also echoes passages from Matthew's Gospel, Ecclesiastes, the Book of Job, the Psalms, and Genesis: the use of Scripture too is typical of much of Kipling's verse. Finally, McAndrew—with nearly all of Kipling's distinct poetic rhetoric building up its own steam—attacks the steamship's privileged passengers whose beliefs amount to romantic clichés:

That minds me of our Viscount loon—Sir Kenneth's kin—the chap
Wi' Russia-leather tennis-shoon an' spar-decked yachtin' cap.
I showed him round last week, o'er all—an' at the last says he:

"Mister McAndrew, don't you think steam spoils romance at sea?"
Damned Ijjit! I'd been doon that morn to see what ailed the throws,
Manholin', on my back—the cranks three inches off my nose.
Romance! These first-class passengers they like it very well,
Printed an' bound in little books; but why don't poets tell?
I'm sick of all their quirks an' turns—the loves an' doves they dream—
Lord, send a man like Robbie Burns to sing the Song o' Steam!

The "Song o' Steam," and also of machines in general, is analogous to the song of the human soul and employs the popular-song techniques of a contemporary "Robbie Burns": this distinctive combination also vitalizes two of Kipling's other great monologues written at this time, "Mulholland's Contract" and "The 'Mary Gloster.' " "Mulholland's Contract," with the fourteener couplets now amplified to triplets, records the conversion during a storm and the eventual ministry of a strong, heavy-drinking, and swearing sailor who tends the livestock pens on a steamship. "The 'Mary Gloster' "—according to Henry James, "triumphant" in its "coarseness"—presents a self-made steel baron on his deathbed, who is harshly dictating how he wants to be buried—his corpse placed in a steamship to be sunk at the specific spot in the South Pacific where his first wife died—to his aesthete son (who is leisurely unemployed and in his thirties). Simultaneously, the engaging rant of "The 'Mary Gloster' " subtly exemplifies, as Ralph Durand has pointed out, the history of modern shipbuilding. Each of the strongest messages of these monologues, of the meaning of Scripture and of machines to human beings, later recurs more and more in Kipling's verse.

Kipling's religious views, perhaps rightly so, are far more difficult to represent generally than his faith in the power of machines. His residence in so many different parts of the British Empire might have contributed to the formation in him of a kind of ecumenical spirit, as is suggested in "The Prayer" (first published in 1901 as "Kabir" in *Kim*):

My brother kneels, so saith Kabir,
To stone and brass in heathen wise
But in my brother's voice I hear
My own unanswered agonies.
His God is as his fates assign,
His prayer is all the world's—and mine.

His beliefs obviously far from the Calvinist statements of McAndrew, Kipling also did not attend very closely to the formal rites of Anglicanism, although officially that might be considered his denomination. As he tried, at least, to keep his personal life to himself and his family, so did he keep the details of his religion private. Nevertheless, that he had some sophistication in understanding religious thought is apparent in a poem such as "Natural Theology" (first published in 1914), which shows, at times humorously, how this form of belief might inevitably embitter the person who maintains it, whether he or she be, as the poem says, "Primitive," "Pagan," "Medieval," or "Progressive." A more subtle, explicit, positive, perhaps personal statement of faith occurs in the 1892 poem, "The Answer." Here a rose, broken and "in tatters on the garden path" appeals to God that it has been unjustly destroyed. The traditional yet no less difficult reply, "By Allah's Will," is distinctly developed: for the rose, and the reader, are told that a person who has seen the ruined rose has asked the same Job-like question: why? This human "why" becomes the key to faith; for the inevitable pain of creation, which leads, according to Kipling, natural theology away from God, draws true faith ever closer to him:

Whereat the withered flower, all content,
Died as they die whose days are innocent;
While he who questioned why the flower fell
Caught hold of God and saved his soul from Hell.

Kipling is undoubtedly heterodox in most of his beliefs, but probably no English poet since him has more extensively employed Scripture in his verse.

Not as difficult to decipher, Kipling's fascination with and faith in machines could not be clearer or more emphatic. In this, McAndrew spoke for him. In Kipling's time, machines and engines were not considered proper or interesting subjects for poetry, and perhaps are not still. Kipling, however, as adamantly as the futurists and some modernists (although from a different ideological perspective), hymned the dawn of modern technology. To him machines revealed their secret: "Our touch can alter all created things, / We are everything on earth—except The Gods" ("The Secret of the Machines"). These lines, signifying something intensely positive for Kipling, have become inadvertently ambiguous, at best, for the modern reader and could even be recognized as predicting ecological disaster. However, such was not the case for Kipling, who heard the machines sing:

> Though our smoke may hide the Heavens from
> your eyes,
> It will vanish and the stars will shine again,
> Because, for all our power and weight and size,
> We are nothing more than children of your brain!

Here machines are seen to be the natural extension of man's brain. Perhaps tempting fate even more, Kipling's "Song of the Dynamo" offers a total inversion of romantic, yet now perhaps justified, pessimism about just how much machines can help people without also harming them. Kipling sees human beings, not machines, as alienated from nature's greatest powers. The dynamo sings, again positively for Kipling, although like a machine gone mad in a science fiction for the modern reader:

> I only know that I am one with those
> True Powers which rend the firmament about
> me,
> And, harrying earth, would save me at the last—
> But that your coward foresight holds me fast.

A major characteristic of many of the poems which Kipling wrote while living in America, besides of much of his verse in general, is its concern with common, prosaic things of the world. As Chesterton said, Kipling recognized that few things, no matter how mundane, are not poetical. Thus a not always dependable seed salesman, who in early spring travels through the mud from farm to farm, is recognized as "Pan in Vermont." Observing the brutal practices of seal hunters, the reader may wince, but Kipling wrote in "Angutivaun Taina":

> Our gloves are glued with the frozen blood,
> Our eyes with the drifting snow;
> But we come back to our wives again,
> Back from the edge of the floe!

More and more, Kipling would consider the world's meanest or commonest things, "The Bell Buoy," for instance, and hear them sing their mysteries:

> There was never a priest to pray,
> There was never a hand to toll,
> When they made me guard of the bay,
> And moored me over the shoal.
> . . . .
> I dip and I surge and I swing
> In the rip of the racing tide,
> By the gates of doom I sing,
> On the horns of death I ride.

Perhaps the last poem Kipling wrote before fleeing from the frustration of his life in Vermont was the famous "Sestina of the Tramp-Royal." The poem's voice is familiar from the earlier *Barrack-Room Ballads*, and Kipling makes this highly difficult form of English poetry seem effortlessly to accommodate a natural rhythm and a conversational tone:

> It's like a book, I think, this bloomin' world,
> Which you can read and care for just so long,
> But presently you feel that you will die
> Unless you get the page you're readin' done,
> An' turn another—likely not so good;
> But what you're after is to turn 'em all.

With his wife and now two daughters, Josephine about four years old and Elsie only seven months, Kipling was back in England by September 1896. The family was generally unhappy and felt uprooted in a cold damp house in Maidencombe, near Torquay, until, toward the end of spring in 1897, they moved again: to a village near Brighton in Sussex, Rottingdean, where Burne-Jones, Kipling's longtime favorite uncle, had a summer house. Here the family settled for five years, a third child, John, being born in August of 1897, and Kipling produced, along with his usual rich and plentiful variety, some political poems. Kipling was becoming still more famous, and his fame increased as his poems began regularly to appear in the *Times* of London. At the same time, however, Kipling was always traveling out of England: to South Africa in January 1898, to America in February 1899 (a disastrous trip during which his eldest daughter died and he too nearly succumbed), and from 1900 to 1908 to South Africa again for most of every winter. Kipling's frequent voyaging to and from England led him to writing poems about his native country and the parts of its empire he visited, but by 1904 he was writing more and more about his now permanent home in Sussex, where he had settled in 1902. However, a poem of 1898, "The Explorer," seems to typify a need to discover new surroundings. The poem presents someone persevering and then discovering a new frontier, as in America or Australia. Nevertheless, the poem is easily seen as allegory, like many of Kipling's poems. In this case a human spirit is struggling alone to find new places, new conceptions, and fresh, original perspectives about which a tired culture can no longer even dream: " 'There's no sense in going further—it's the edge of cultivation,' / So they said, and I believed it—broke my land and sowed my crop. . . ." Still, Kipling's quatrains of fourteeners present his ideal explorer hearing "a voice as bad as Conscience" that whispers "day and night . . . / 'Something hidden. Go and find it. Go and look behind the Ranges. . . .' " The explorer follows this voice—there are scriptural echoes in the poem, too:

Till the snow ran out in flowers, and the flowers turned to aloes,
And the aloes sprung to thickets and a brimming stream ran by;
But the thickets dwined to thorn-scrub, and the water drained to shallows,
And I dropped again on desert—blasted earth, and blasting sky. . . .

Subject equally to beauty and near-despair, the explorer ultimately does find a promised land of "Rolling grass and open timber," "virgin ore-" beds, "unimagined rivers," and "illimitable plains" to nourish a new culture, which will never suffer, as he did, the "desert-fears." Yet if the explorer would himself accept the credit for having discovered and offered new territories to revive a feeble civilization, he is rebuked by the same conscience which bade him in the first place to cross "the range to see": "God forgive me! No, *I* didn't. It's God's present to our nation. / Anybody might have found it, but—His whisper came to Me!"

While "The Explorer" may be construed as an allegorical piece about ideas and the imagination, Kipling nevertheless specifically considered Britain's empire of imperial possessions to be one of God's most tangible "presents to His nation." Returning to England from America, Kipling resumed the role of being "a voice as bad as Conscience" for England, and even for America. Kipling's most famous political poetry is—although this is no doubt true of many artists' and writers' political viewpoints—one of the greatest obstacles, as Eliot recognized too, in appreciating his work. In general, one might admit with Orwell, who nevertheless admired Kipling's work, that Kipling was indeed "a jingo imperialist" and "morally insensitive." Eliot compares Kipling's political poetry favorably with John Dryden's. In dealing, for example, with seventeenth-century political poets, such as Dryden, Andrew Marvell, and John Milton, the political issues which they were disputing often become mere background because they seem remote. Yet, if their political points of view are considered, these poets at times might appear at least as jingoistic, "morally insensitive," and eager to build and sustain an empire as Kipling. No poet since the seventeenth century has written on popular political issues as considerably, coherently, and comprehensibly as Kipling. His efforts were not, furthermore, self-serving; he would take no payment for the political poems which appeared in the *Times* and, in 1899, refused the Conservative prime minister's offer of knighthood. Kipling was a member of no political party, and his explosive self-independence and extremism—he called himself "a political Calvinist"—as well as his occasional lack of reverence could at times embarrass anyone who claimed his allegiance. In his political writing Kipling somewhat resembled, although his observations obviously were neither as comprehensive nor astute, Niccolò Machiavelli or Thomas Hobbes in being, as Eric Stokes has said, "obsessed with the moral and political disease that seized men once they were secured from the omnipresence of death."

"Recessional," one of Kipling's best-known poems, was first published in July 1897, to commemorate Queen Victoria's second jubilee. For her first jubilee in 1887, Kipling had written the Barrack-Room ballad "The Widow at Windsor," which, as Carrington points out, could not be perceived as overly complimentary, either then or now:

'Ave you 'eard o' the Widow at Windsor
With a hairy gold crown on 'er 'ead?
She 'as ships on the foam—she 'as millions at 'ome,
An' she pays us poor beggars in red.

Kipling's attitude toward Queen Victoria seems at best ambivalent, and he wrote nothing on her death in 1901. "Recessional," however, is hardly ambivalent, although it is not, perhaps unexpectedly, merely sanguine about the empire. Amid pomp and celebration, which gathered armed forces and officials from all over the empire, Kipling wrote:

If, drunk with sight of power, we loose
Wild tongues that have not Thee in awe,
Such boastings as the Gentiles use,
Or lesser breeds without the Law—

Lord God of Hosts, be with us yet,
Lest we forget—lest we forget!

The "Wild tongues" and "boastings" of "Gentiles" and "lesser breeds" refer not necessarily, as some have thought, to those natives of countries who would resist the foreign domination of the British, but rather to, as Orwell indicated, the practice of mere "power politics." In his autobiography Kipling recalled that he wrote the verses because "the Great Queen's Diamond Jubilee" fostered "a certain optimism that scared me." In a later, perhaps less solemn poem, "The Peace of Dives" (first published in 1903), Kipling reiterates more explicitly his denunciation of the use of great political power, according to the needs of commerce, only to incite or suppress armed conflict. In this Orwell felt that Kipling failed "to realize, any more than the average soldier or colonial administrator, that an empire is primarily a money-making concern.... He could not foresee, therefore, that the same motives which brought the Empire into existence would end by destroying it." However true Orwell's statement, the reception of "Recessional" was overwhelmingly positive, and it immediately achieved the status of a popular, patriotic hymn to be sung at many kinds of official occasions.

In the coming years Kipling would continue to question and seek positively to correct the course of British and, as it was growing, American imperialism. He focused on two wars, neither very ennobling: the Spanish-American War of 1898 and the conflict, escalated to outright war in 1899, between the Dutch Boers and British in South Africa.

The Spanish-American War provoked Kipling to write for Vice-President Theodore Roosevelt (who, when he died, Kipling memorialized with the Bunyanesque appellation "Great-Heart") a poem with the now offensive title "The White Man's Burden." Its message was typical for Kipling. Seeing that America suddenly had acquired vast new colonial possessions from its defeat of Spain, Kipling argued that it was the responsibility of the United States to care for its new subjects liberally and humanely, if also proprietarily. (Roosevelt reportedly responded, though not to Kipling, "Rather poor poetry, but good sense from the expansionist viewpoint.")

The Boer War attracted Kipling even more to South Africa. Unquestionably he sided with the British and championed, in both his verse and his dispatches as a war correspondent, Cecil Rhodes and his unflagging plans for strengthening British imperialism. Kipling's best poems reacting to the war are of two sorts: those in which he assumes the sympathetic persona of the working soldier and those that in general condemn the lackadaisical, at best lukewarm, support for the war by the British at home. The poems are undoubtedly more depressed, gloomier, and less boisterous than Kipling's earlier works about the military. Stationed abroad in the empire, soldiers are now represented as desolate, bored, resigned. They are "Few, forgotten and lonely," and "take . . . appointed stations" while "the endless night begins" ("Bridge-Guard in the Karroo"). No better is the world in "The Broken Men":

Day long the diamond weather,
The high, unaltered blue—
. . . .
Day long the warder ocean
That keeps us from our kin.

The only solace is "once a month . . . When the English mail comes in." "Once a month," like British support for the war in general, was not enough. In the simplest terms, Kipling did not see England living up to the challenge he expressed in "Recessional." Instead, as he wrote in 1902 in "The Islanders," he saw a selfish, tiny, leisure-loving country bored with its empire, whose citizens preferred to play "With nets and hoops and mallets, with rackets and bats and rods" and believed in nothing more than "Idols of greasy altars built for the body's ease." Kipling considered the British war effort in South Africa a failure; yet, the "fault . . . and very great fault" ("The Lesson") was the British upper class's indifference and hedonism. As might be expected, he would not even tolerate those who criticized the war as an unnecessary waste; he called that political faction "The Hyaenas":

After the burial-parties leave
And the baffled kites have fled;
The wise hyaenas come out at eve
To take account of our dead.

Kipling's hope was that the defeat still could be "an Imperial lesson" and make Britain "an Empire yet" ("The Lesson"). Two poems of 1902, however, seem to state his realization that for the British Empire the sun had indeed set. Both poems too are easily detachable from their topicality and are allegories more timeless than

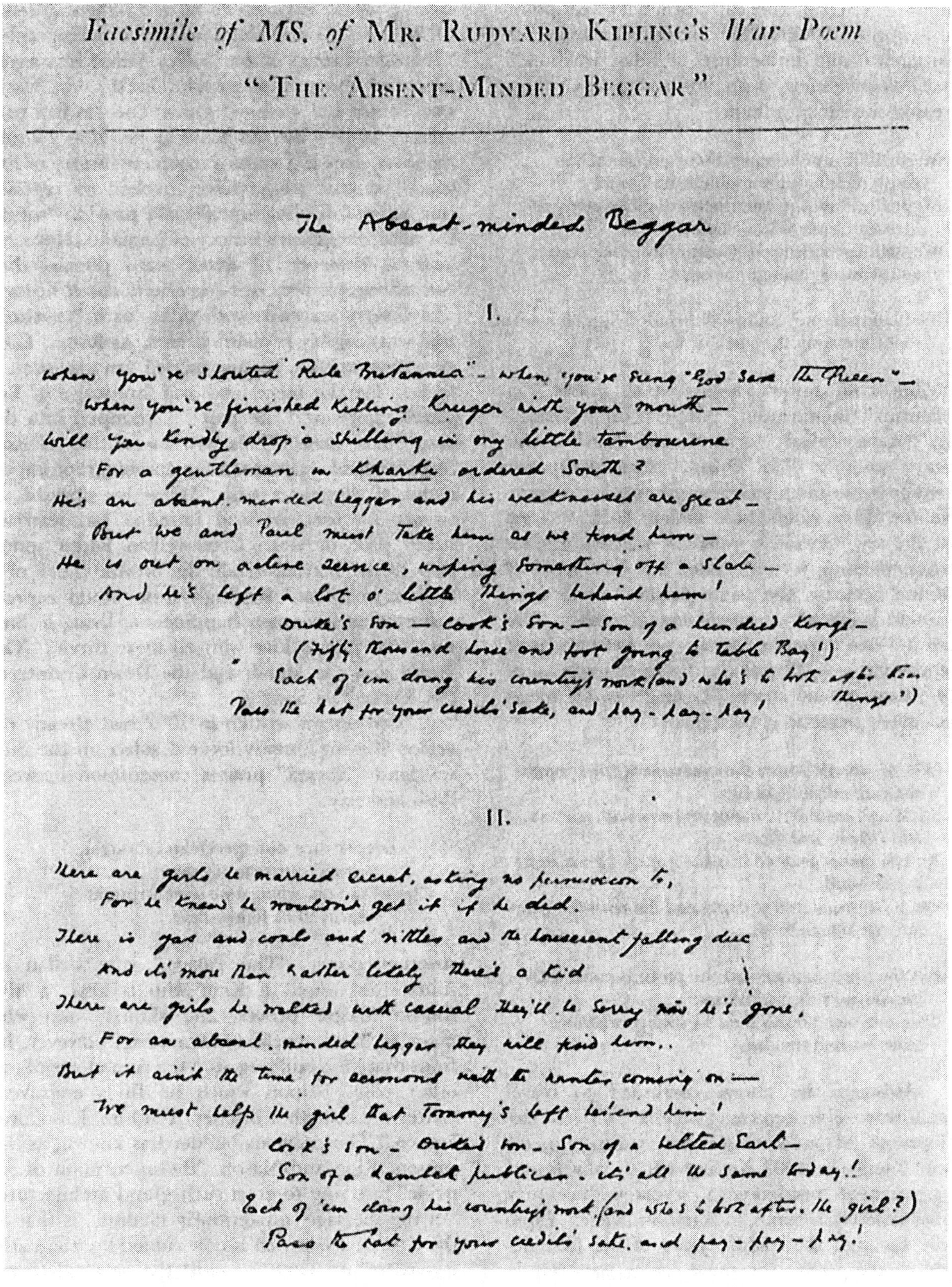

Facsimile of MS. of MR. RUDYARD KIPLING'S *War Poem*
"THE ABSENT-MINDED BEGGAR"

The Absent-minded Beggar

I.

When you've shouted "Rule Britannia" – when you've sung "God Save the Queen" –
When you've finished killing Kruger with your mouth –
Will you kindly drop a shilling in my little tambourine
For a gentleman in Kharki ordered South?
He's an absent-minded beggar and his weaknesses are great –
But we and Paul must take him as we find him –
He is out on active service, wiping something off a slate –
And he's left a lot o' little things behind him!
Duke's son – Cook's son – Son of a hundred Kings –
(Fifty thousand horse and foot going to Table Bay!)
Each of 'em doing his country's work (and who's to look after their things?)
Pass the hat for your credit's sake, and pay – pay – pay!

II.

There are girls he married secret, asking no permission to,
For he knew he wouldn't get it if he did.
There is gas and coals and vittles and the houserent falling due
And it's more than rather likely there's a kid.
There are girls he walked with casual. They'll be sorry now he's gone,
For an absent-minded beggar they will find him..
But it ain't the time for sermons with the winter coming on –
We must help the girl that Tommy's left behind him!
Cook's son – Duke's son – Son of a belted Earl –
Son of a Lambeth publican – it's all the same today!
Each of 'em doing his country's work (and who's to look after the girl?)
Pass the hat for your credit's sake and pay – pay – pay!

Page from the manuscript facsimile for "The Absent-minded Beggar," a poem Kipling used to generate funds for families of men fighting in the Boer War timely—a criterion, perhaps, of much great political poetry. "The Old Men" bitterly attacks the intransigence and intolerance of those who make what was once new, fresh, and strong into an oppressive, loveless tradition:

> We shall lift up the ropes that constrained our youth, to bind on our children's hands;
> We shall call to the water below the bridges to return and replenish our lands;
> We shall harness horses (Death's own pale horses) and scholarly plough the sands
> . . . .
> The Lamp of our Youth will be utterly out, but we shall subsist on the smell of it.

The lines could apply to anyone who upholds "Victorianism," "modernism," "imperialism," "liberalism," "conservatism," or any other "ism." A far greater poem is "The Dykes." Allegorically, the poem presents people who have forgotten to maintain the dikes which their fathers built to keep out the sea. Obviously political, warning against an overweening yet unjustified and false sense of national security, the poem partakes of an even broader, spiritual or psychological reality: "We have no heart for the fishing—we have no hand for the oar— / All that our fathers taught us of old pleases us no more." Kipling's mood seems even more pessimistic than Hardy's:

> O'er the marsh where the homesteads cower apart the harried sunlight flies,
> Shifts and considers, wanes and recovers, scatters and sickens and dies—
> An evil ember bedded in ash—a spark blown west by the wind . . .
> We are surrendered to night and the sea—the gale and the tide behind!
> . . . .
> But the peace is gone and the profit is gone, with the old sure days withdrawn . . .
> That our own houses show as strange when we come back in the dawn.

Although he always continued to travel extensively—even becoming obsessed with the development of automobiles and writing poems about them—in 1902 Kipling had finally found a permanent residence, a seventeenth-century house called Bateman's, in Burwash, Sussex. Especially through the middle years of the first decade of the 1900s, the move looms importantly for Kipling's poetry. Bucolic life in Sussex mitigated his gloom over the worsening fortunes of the empire and supplemented a pinched and narrowing vision of politics with a broadening sense of history. As he wrote in his autobiography, "The Old Things of our Valley glided into every aspect of our outdoor works. Earth, Air, Water and People had been—I saw at last—in full conspiracy to give me ten times as much as I could compass, even if I wrote a complete history of England, as that might have touched or reached our Valley." Kipling actually did provide "songs" for another author's history of England. More important, however, he wrote many poems—they are among his very best—precisely about history, and history leavened with myth, as it "touched" and was tangibly revealed to him. As Robert Conquest has written, Kipling gained "an atavistic . . . feeling for the mere land and landscape of England" and saw "The past . . . stamped into the very countryside." This new fascination of Kipling's is plainly apparent in an autobiographical account of digging a well: "When we stopped, at twenty-five feet, we had found a Jacobean tobacco pipe, a worn Cromwellian latten spoon and, at the bottom of all, the bronze cheek of a Roman horse-bit." Kipling's verse would express a simple, spontaneous happiness at living in Sussex: "I'm just in love with all these three. / The Weald and the Marsh and the Down Countree" ("A Three-Part Song").

Two poems written in 1902 had already revealed Kipling's newly located solace in the Sussex land. "Sussex" praises communion between flesh and clay:

> deeper than our speech and thought,
> Beyond our reason's sway,
> Clay of the pit, whence we were wrought
> Yearns to its fellow-clay.

Another poem, "The Palace," is a ballad of fourteeners about a King who is also "a Mason—a Master proven and skilled" and who plans to build a palace. Excavating, however, he finds that he is building atop the ruined site of another palace, upon which he finds engraved, "After me cometh a Builder. Tell him, I too have known." The previous builder has known, as the present King and Mason, "the open noon of . . . pride" in trying to erect such grand architecture. Yet the message, mysteriously fatalistic, is that as the first palace buried is now ruined by "the faithless years" of Time, so must the new palace remain unfinished: as a testimony to the necessary "spoil of a King who shall build." Kipling's own poetic spirit, blighted by the inevitable decay of cur-

Bateman's in Burwash, Sussex, Kipling's home from 1902 until his death (National Trust)

rent political events, would be restored by the idea, classically expressed by Sir Thomas Browne, that "Men are lived over again; the world is now as it were in ages past; there was none then but there hath been some one since that parallels him, and is, as it were, his revived self." No coincidence, perhaps, is that Kipling's new source of inspiration is further conceived in architectural imagery; for as he writes in his autobiography, "I visualized . . . ideas . . . in the shape of a semicircle of buildings and temples projecting into a sea—of dreams."

Kipling's "dreams" of history dominate the verses he set amid the prose of *Puck of Pook's Hill* (1906) and *Rewards and Fairies* (1910). Poem after poem has a startling yet gentle beauty, as in this poem named by its first line:

Cities and Thrones and Powers
    Stand in Time's eye,
Almost as long as flowers,
    Which daily die:
But as new buds put forth
    To glad new men,
Out of the spent and unconsidered Earth
    The Cities rise again.

Plain and biblical tones of hope make empire and "This season's Daffodil," "Shadow to shadow, well persuaded," say "See how our works endure!" Another lyric, "Puck's Song," asks the reader to look through nature's veil and see human history:

    see you marks that show and fade
Like shadows on the Downs?
O they are the lines the Flint Men made,
To guard their wondrous towns.

Nature would quickly and effortlessly take back what it has given and keep the transaction a secret if there were not lonely, human memory, as expressed hauntingly in "The Way Through the Woods":

They shut the road through the woods
Seventy years ago.
Weather and rain have undone it again,
And now you would never know
There was once a road through the woods. . . .

Such memory is so lonely, and so rare, that where "the badgers roll at ease" and "the night air cools on the trout-ringed pools" there in fact

Kipling's study at Bateman's (National Trust)

may be "no road through the woods." Kipling might have believed that machines and new technology would grandly and innocently solve many of civilization's worst problems. Nevertheless, he also foresaw that factories, industrial places, and even modern cities could one day too be buried "underneath the coppice and heath / And the thin anemones."

Imagining the past while situated in the present, Kipling's poems of this period also dream themselves to be actually in the past. His personae are exotic too. Plaintively, there is the "Harp Song of the Dane Women" who wonder why "when the signs of summer thicken, / And the ice breaks and the birch buds thicken" their Viking husbands turn from love "and sicken," that is, they want to go to sea:

> What is a woman that you forsake her,
> And the hearth-fire and the home-acre,
> To go with the old grey Widow-maker?

In "The Land" Kipling humorously presents a character named Hobden who, like each of his ancestors since Roman times, has worked although never purchased the same single piece of land. Nevertheless, it is Hobden who advises how the land should be managed and "whoever pays the taxes old Mus' Hobden owns the land." Kipling's dreams of ancient British history become mysterious when he imagines "The Runes on Weland's Sword." The lyric also uses stressed syllables, alliteration, and lack of rhyme typical of Old English poetry: "A smith makes me / To betray my Man / In my first fight."

Kipling's best poems written before the outbreak of World War I also contain some of his strongest moral and philosophical statements. "The Sons of Martha" (1907) is often considered the clearest representation of the value Kipling placed on work. Developing the biblical dichotomy between Mary and Martha—whom Christ gently reprimanded for criticizing Mary's listening to him, when she might have been helping Martha work in the kitchen for their guest—Kipling wrote that the "Sons of Mary" may "smile," be "blessed," and "cast their burden upon the Lord," but "the Lord He lays it on Martha's Sons." Kipling is willingly of their party: those whose ideal is "Not . . . a ladder from earth to Heaven, not as a witness to any creed, / But simple service simply given to his own kind in their common need." Kipling's obvious moralism is perhaps not so idiosyncratic in the poem which Kipling, probably more than anyone, considered "anthologized to weariness," "If—." In his autobiography Kipling deals humorously with the popularity "the mechanisation of the age" lent this poem. It was printed on cards to be hung up "in offices and bedrooms," and it became a supposedly constructive punishment for schoolboys to write it two times on a blackboard after class.

Kipling was for the most part uneasy about official honors and refused many. He rejected invitations to join the British Academy and the American Academy of Arts and Sciences and turned down all explicitly political honors. He twice rejected the Order of Merit. Nevertheless, he did accept honorary degrees from various universities and the 1907 Nobel Prize for literature.

Kipling is better known as a poet and short-story writer than as a novelist. He wrote only three novels and collaborated with Balestier on *The Naulahka: A Story of West and East.* The shorter forms were his métier, and after the publication of *Kim* in 1901, Kipling never attempted another novel.

Kipling's first novel, *The Light That Failed* (1890), is partly autobiographical, especially in its depiction of the "house of desolation," where the orphan Dick Heldar has been sent to be raised by the widow Mrs. Jennett. After the arrival of another orphan, Maisie, an independent girl, Dick finds solace in her company. The two are separated when they are sent away to school, and both become artists. Dick eventually becomes a war correspondent as well, and, while covering the Gordon relief expedition in the Sudan, he is discovered sketching by Torpenhow, of the Central Southern Syndicate. Dick's pictures of soldiers and battles (subjects similar to those of Kipling's stories and poems) are published by the syndicate and achieve such popularity that Torpenhow calls Dick back to London, where prints of his sketches bring him financial success. Yet despite his popularity with the public there is the suggestion that Dick has compromised his artistic integrity.

In London he once again meets Maisie, still independent (and perhaps a lesbian). She is dissatisfied with her work, and, as Dick tries to help her (while unsuccessfully entreating her to marry him), it becomes apparent to the reader that she is essentially shallow. Dick also begins the painting that he hopes will be his masterpiece, a conception of Melancholia; but in the Sudan he had received a sword cut over one eye, a serious wound that took months to heal, and his eyesight begins to deteriorate rapidly. Struggling heroically, he completes the painting before the onset of total blindness, but a vengeful former model defaces the painting—a fact that his friends keep from him at first. He has been too proud to tell Maisie about his condition, but Torpenhow seeks her out in Paris, where she has gone to study, and brings her back to London.

Two versions of the novel were published in 1891. For *Lippincott's Monthly Magazine* (January 1891), Kipling wrote a happy ending; but he preferred the other ending, in which Maisie displays her weak character by refusing to stand by Dick, and the heartbroken young man, who has also discovered the fate of his masterpiece, returns to the battlefield, where he deliberately places himself in the line of fire and is killed.

The Naulahka is not even discussed in Kipling's autobiography. It reads more like one of Kipling's travel books than a novel; the depiction of the Indian scene is not as well done as it is in *Kim.* The main characters are an American man and woman. The man, through a certain naïveté and boldness, wins the rajah's treasure, only to be persuaded by the woman to return it. The ending is ambiguous as the sheer diversity of Indian life prevails over the Americans' efforts. The novel seems rather hastily and opportunistically concocted and suffers from lack of unity and design, perhaps as a result of the unwieldy nature of joint authorship.

Kipling's novel *'Captains Courageous'* (1897), published shortly after his return to England in 1896, is based on his observation of life in New England fishing ports. The profusion of technical detail in the novel illustrates Kipling's lifelong respect for competence, and, while the novel is marred by sentimentality, its depiction of brave men who undertook the dangerous task of fishing the Grand Banks off the coast of Newfoundland in the days before steam-powered fishing boats has won *'Captains Courageous'* admirers. Emphasizing the value of hard work in the development of character, the novel is the story of Harvey Cheney, a wealthy and spoiled fifteen year old who one May is washed overboard from an ocean liner bound for Europe, rescued by a fisherman, and taken aboard the schooner *We're Here,* captained by Disko Troop. The fishing season having just begun, Troop is unwilling to risk his season's profits by immediately taking the boy to

Honorary degree recipients at Oxford, 27 June 1907: 1) General William Booth, 2) Samuel Clemens, and 3) Rudyard Kipling. Other recipients were Auguste Rodin and Charles-Camille Saint-Saëns (Bodleian Library).

port. Harvey insists that his father is a millionaire who would pay handsomely for his immediate return to New York, but Troop, doubting the boy's tale of his father's wealth, refuses and says that he will hire Harvey as a member of his crew until they return to Gloucester in September. When the arrogant young man becomes insulting, Troop punches him in the nose, beginning his education about the harsh discipline aboard ship. Because of such treatment and because he is an intelligent young man, Harvey learns quickly and earns the respect and friendship of the crew. He especially values their acceptance because it is based on his merits as a crewman, rather than on his father's wealth, the stories of which only two, the captain's son Dan and the Negro cook, believe. After the ship has docked in Gloucester and Harvey's parents have come to take him home, his father, a self-made man, is pleased to see that his son has grown from a snobbish boy to a self-reliant young man who has learned how to make his own way through hard work and to judge people by their merits rather than by their bank balances. While *'Captains Courageous'* has the elements of a good sea tale and novel of maturation, it is flawed by episodic plotting, shallow characterization, and sometimes-dubious psychologizing. Kipling eventually rejected the novel as simply a "boy's story."

Kipling's best novel, *Kim,* was published in 1901. The glory of *Kim* lies not in its plot nor in its characters but in its evocation of the complex Indian scene. The great diversity of the land—its casts; its sects; its geographical, linguistic, and religious divisions; its numberless superstitions; its kaleidoscopic sights, sounds, colors, and smells—are brilliantly and lovingly evoked. The British are less sympathetically portrayed; as one character says, "the Sahibs have not all this world's wisdom," and they are wrong to try to change the ineluctably Indian nature of the country. Kim, "the little friend of all the world," represents a union of both cultures and ignores religious and caste prejudices. Kim was born Kimball O'Hara to an Irish mother who died giving birth to him, and an Irish father—formerly a member of a regiment called the Mavericks, who died of drinking and drugs, leaving his young son in the care of a half-caste woman. Growing up in the streets of Lahore, Kim becomes so tanned by the sun that he looks like an Indian boy, and, on meeting an old Tibetan lama searching for the River of the Arrow, which will wash away all sin, he decides to accompany the lama on his quest. Kim is also befriended by Mahbub Ali, a horse trader who, at first unknown to Kim, belongs to the British secret service.

Kim has been told that his life will change when he sees a red bull in a green field, and in their travels Kim and the lama come upon the Mavericks, whose regimental flag is a red bull on a green background. After a regimental chaplain opens an amulet Kim has worn around his neck and discovers Kim's baptismal certificate and a letter from his father asking that his son be cared for, it is decided Kim should be sent to school. The lama agrees and obtains the money from his order to pay for Kim's education at St. Xavier's, a school for British colonials. Kim dislikes his lack of freedom, but he is a good student and remains at the school for three years, traveling in the summer with Mahbub Ali, who, with other members of the secret service, educates Kim to play the "great game," as they call their work.

After leaving school, Kim, once again dressed as a street boy, travels with the lama to aid in his quest, while at the same time he uses their journey as a cover for his clandestine activities on behalf of the British, uncovering the existence of Russian spies in the north of India. The novel ends with the dying lama believing that he has found his river on the estate of a wealthy old woman who has aided them in the past, and with the assurance that Kim has performed well in the great game. This enigmatic ending (it is not made clear how Kim resolves the conflict between the Indians and the Sahibs) suggests a compromise between the pragmatic and the otherworldly, between the imposed British organization and the myriad, sprawling, resistant realities of India. As Kim realizes that his collaboration with the British contributes to the bondage of the native people he feels so close to, he faces a dilemma of allegience. Although he has favored the native life-style that he slips into whenever he can, the lure of the civilization through the British also appeals to him. *Kim* was Kipling's last novel. In the remaining thirty-five years of his life, he devoted himself to poetry and the short story.

Even though he described politics as "a dog's life without dog's decencies," between the end of the first decade of the 1900s and the outbreak of World War I Kipling wrote verses to support causes of Britain's political right wing; for instance, he attacked the home-rule movement in Ireland, inveighed, in "The City of Brass," against the ideals of liberalism, and, opposed to woman's suffrage, wrote a ballad which coined the phrase, "the female of the species is more deadly than the male."

On the subject of World War I Kipling's poems express a far wider and sympathetic range of feelings. To incite enthusiasm for the initial war effort Kipling wrote in 1914 "For All We Have And Are." It is a simple, clear, and tough rant that warns "The Hun is at the Gate!" As the title suggests, the poem uses very high and formal diction. Typically, Kipling was interested in writing poems about prosaic-seeming innovations in machinery, for instance, about "Mine-Sweepers" which "bear, in place of classic names, / Letters and numbers on their skin" ("The Trade"). Yet he did not shun the horror of the war's technical innovations, for example, comparing a soldier's thoughts at the onset of a mustard-gas attack to Christ's praying in Gethsemane that the "cup" of his suffering "might pass":

> It didn't pass—it didn't pass—
> It didn't pass for me.
> I drank it when we met the gas
> Beyond Gethsemane!

There are also the usual Kipling verses attacking what he considered political treachery. For instance, "The Question," written in 1916, urged the United States to delay no longer in entering the war; and "A Song at Cock-Crow" (first published in 1916), bitterly criticized the pope's efforts for a peace treaty on uncertain terms. "The Holy War" is a rather jaunty kind of homage to John Bunyan, who was in many ways surely a great influence on Kipling in his work. Kipling had been reading Bunyan's *The Holy War*:

> The craft that we call modern,
> The crimes that we call new,
> John Bunyan had 'em typed and filed
> In Sixteen Eighty-two.

Nevertheless, these are not Kipling's greatest poems on World War I.

In the autumn of 1915 Kipling's eighteen-year-old son, John, was wounded and reported missing in action. More than two years elapsed before there was confirmation that, as Kipling already believed, his son had been killed. Reflecting on the event, Kipling wrote, with a kind of cathartic restraint, "My Boy Jack":

> "Have you news of my boy Jack?"
> *Not this tide.*
> "When d'you think that he'll come back?"
> *Not with this wind blowing, and this tide.*
>
> "Has any one else had word of him?"
> *Not this tide.*
> *For what is sunk will hardly swim,*
> *Not with this wind blowing, and this tide.*

Kipling's best and most justifiably well-known poems on World War I are his "Epitaphs of the War." Although in retrospect he called them merely "naked cribs of the Greek Anthology," they are original, technically near-perfect, unadulterated emotional statements of powerful judgment. In 1917 he had become "Honorary Literary Advisor," the rhetorical consultant, to the Imperial War Graves Commission. In an address called "Literature," which he gave in 1906, Kipling had said that "the man with the Words shall wait upon the man of achievement, and step by step with him try to tell the story of the Tribe. . . ." Now many men of achievement in England had to be buried. In his official capacity he offered the standard epitaph to be posted at the veterans' cemeteries: "Their name liveth forevermore." His "Epitaphs of the War" far more decisively presented the awful death of particular—both blameless and culpable—members "of the Tribe." His son could be "The Beginner":

> On the first hour of my first day
> In the front trench I fell.
> (Children in boxes at a play
> Stand up to watch it well.)

While each of the thirty-five epitaphs, representing many different, willing and unwilling parties to the war, has its own strength, some are exceedingly powerful. For instance, "Common Form" reads: "If any question why we died, / Tell them, because our fathers lied." One of the biggest of such liars is "A Dead Statesman":

> I could not dig: I dared not rob:
> Therefore I lied to please the mob.
> Now all my lies are proved untrue
> And I must face the men I slew.
> What tale shall serve me here among
> Mine angry and defrauded young?

Unidentified civilian casualties are perhaps the most gruesome, as in an "Unknown Female Corpse":

> Headless, lacking foot and hand,
> Horrible I come to land.
> I beseech all women's sons
> Know I was a mother once.

Perhaps no two consecutive lines of English poetry compress more compassion, cruelty, terseness, elegance, horror, understatement, and drama than Kipling's epitaph for "The Coward": "I could not look on Death, which being known, / Men led me to him, blindfold and alone."

With a few exceptions, Kipling's major poems were written by 1918. After the war, he persisted in verse to express his concerns for a now new generation of veterans. He early recognized and wrote about the unprecedented and terrible psychological wounds which trench warfare inflicted. "The Mother's Son" is a "mad-song" about a soldier who "just because he had not died / Nor been discharged nor sick" must remain in the trenches "Longer than he could stick. . . ." "The Expert" presents another veteran, who, so brutalized by the experience of combat, can now only contemplate further heartless acts of violence, even though he is home: "For the past he buried brings / Back unburiable things—":

> "All the lore of No-Man's Land
> Steels his soul and arms his hand.
> . . . .
> And, in mirth more dread than wrath,
> Wipes the nuisance from his path!"

Yet Kipling was evenhanded and not all bleak in assessing the effects of World War I on the society which survived. He wrote warmly on the unique theme of veterans "whose education was interrupted by the War" and who now were asked to return to Cambridge as "The Scholars." Meanwhile, Kipling was also continuing to compose slight though amusing first-person parodies,

The Kiplings and their daughter leaving Buckingham Palace after a garden party, July 1921

which imagined how Geoffrey Chaucer, John Donne, Robert Herrick, Matthew Prior, William Wordsworth, Robert and Elizabeth Browning, and others would react to riding in automobiles.

Kipling's few important poems written after World War I evoke, yet further develop, familiar themes in his verse. Like "The English Flag," "We and They" attacks particularly British, self-righteous xenophobia. Here, however, Kipling's contempt is tempered by a comic spirit which sees such pathetic human failings also as universal in human nature: "all good people say, / All nice people, like Us, are We / And every one else is They." Kipling could not, though, be sure as he approached the end of his life whether humanity, with all of its comedy, would avert ultimate tragedy. World War I had made clearer than ever, although Kipling had also recognized the fact in his previous verses about the many ways that humans work, that there is no escape from "the twin-damnation— / To fail and know we fail" ("Hymn of Breaking Strain"). The strength of "stone and steel," "The stress that shears a rivet," "What traffic wrecks macadam," "What concrete should endure," is, through good effort, reasonably predictable. But there is "no set gauge" for how much reality—personal, psychological, spiritual—a human being can support, and, furthermore, life will "presently o'ertake us / with loads we cannot bear. / *Too merciless to bear*." Nevertheless Kipling hoped, reiterating Psalm 51—"The sacrifices of God *are* a broken spirit"—"That we. . . . In spite of being broken, / *Because of being broken, / May rise and build anew*." Still, for Kipling there was no presuming that whatever would "rise . . . anew" out of a ruined empire, England, United States, or Third World, would be any better than what had been replaced. Moreover, since no work of humanity can stand the test of the "Great Overseer," "Who has made the Fire / . . . who hast made the Clay" ("My New-Cut Ashlar"), people might even throw away such a standard. Instead of aspiring to make another Eden—of which Kipling seemed to believe the "good craftsman's brain" always capable—a society primordially alienated from its divine origin and creator may work merely for "The Gods of the Copybook Headings." And for Kipling such work has no hope:

As it will be in the future, it was at the birth of
  Man—
There are only four things certain since Social
  Progress began:—
That the Dog returns to his Vomit and the Sow
  returns to her Mire,
And the burnt Fool's bandaged finger goes wab-
  bling back to the Fire;
And that after this is accomplished . . .
          . . . as surely as Fire will burn,
The Gods of the Copybook Headings with terror
  and slaughter return!

The poet who was buried in Poet's Corner in Westminster Abbey in 1936, after suffering an intestinal hemorrhage resulting from an ulcer condition, had felt and written with unmistakable and austere clarity about what still seems to remain as the greatest fear of the twentieth century:

This is the midnight—let no star
Delude us—dawn is very far.
This is the tempest long foretold—
Slow to make head but sure to hold.

Bibliography:

James McG. Stewart, *Rudyard Kipling: A Bibliographical Catalogue*, edited by A. W. Yeats (Toronto: Dalhousie University Press / University of Toronto Press, 1959).

Biographies:

C. E. Carrington, *The Life of Rudyard Kipling* (London: Macmillan, 1955; Garden City, N.Y.: Doubleday, 1955);

Kingsley Amis, *Rudyard Kipling and His World* (London: Thames & Hudson, 1975);

Angus Wilson, *The Strange Ride of Rudyard Kipling* (New York: Viking, 1978; Harmondsworth, U.K.: Penguin, 1979);

Lord Birkenhead, *Rudyard Kipling* (London: Weidenfeld & Nicolson, 1978).

References:

Paul Beam, " 'A Most Bitter Harvest': Rudyard Kipling's South African Poetry," in *Four Decades of Poetry* (Toronto: University of Toronto Press, 1979), II: 153-173;

Harold Bloom, ed., *Rudyard Kipling* (New York: Chelsea House, 1987);

A. C. Bodelson, *Aspects of Kipling's Art* (Manchester: University of Manchester Press, 1964);

G. K. Chesterton, "On Mr. Rudyard Kipling and Making the World Small," in his *Heretics* (London & New York: John Lane, 1905);

Morton Cohen, *Rudyard Kipling to Rider Haggard: The Record of a Friendship* (London: Hutchinson, 1965);

Donald Davie, "A Puritan's Empire: The Case of Kipling," *Sewanee Review*, 87 (1979): 34-48;

Bonamy Dobrée, *Rudyard Kipling: Realist and Fabulist* (New York & London: Oxford University Press, 1967);

Ralph Durand, *A Handbook to the Poetry of Rudyard Kipling* (London: Hodder & Stoughton, 1914);

T. S. Eliot, Introduction to *A Choice of Kipling's Verse*, edited by Eliot (London: Faber & Faber, 1941; New York: Scribners, 1943), pp. 5-36;

Richard Faber, *The Vision and the Need* (London: Faber & Faber, 1966);

Elliot L. Gilbert, ed., *Kipling and His Critics* (London: Owen, 1965);

Roger Lancelyn Green, ed., *Kipling: The Critical Heritage* (New York: Barnes & Noble, 1971);

John Gross, ed., *The Age of Kipling* (New York: Simon & Schuster, 1972);

Kipling Journal, edited by Roger Lancelyn Green, 1927- ;

Phillip Mallett, ed., *Kipling Considered* (New York: St. Martin's Press, 1989);

George Orwell, "Rudyard Kipling," in his *My Country Right or Left, 1940-1943*, volume 2 of *Collected Essays, Journalism and Letters*, edited by Sonia Orwell and Ian Angus (New York: Harcourt, Brace & World, 1968), pp. 194-197;

Norman Page, *A Kipling Companion* (London: Macmillan, 1984);

A. L. Rowse, "Blowing Kipling's Trumpet," *Sunday Telegraph* (London), 19 December 1965;

Andrew Rutherford, ed., *Kipling's Mind and Art* (Stanford: Stanford University Press, 1964);

J. I. M. Stewart, *Eight Modern Writers* (New York & London: Oxford University Press, 1963), pp. 223-293;

J. M. S. Tompkins, *The Art of Rudyard Kipling* (London: Methuen, 1959).

Papers:
There are Kipling papers in many libraries, including the Houghton Library at Harvard University, the New York Public Library, the Library of Congress, and the Pierpont Morgan Library.

John Masefield

(1 June 1878 - 12 May 1967)

This entry was updated by Donald E. Stanford (Louisiana State University) from his entries in DLB 10: Modern British Dramatists, 1900-1945: Part Two *and* DLB 19: British Poets, 1880-1914.

John Masefield

SELECTED BOOKS: *Salt-Water Ballads* (London: Richards, 1902; New York: Macmillan, 1913);
Ballads (London: Elkin Mathews, 1903);
A Mainsail Haul (London: Elkin Mathews, 1905; enlarged edition, London: Elkin Mathews, 1913; New York: Macmillan, 1913);
Sea Life in Nelson's Time (London: Methuen, 1905);
On the Spanish Main (London: Methuen, 1906);
A Tarpaulin Muster (London: Richards, 1907; New York: Dodge, 1908);
Captain Margaret: A Romance (London: Richards, 1908; Philadelphia: Lippincott, 1909);
Multitude and Solitude (London: Richards, 1909; New York: Kennerley, 1910);
The Tragedy of Nan and Other Plays (New York: Kennerley, 1909; London: Richards, 1909);
The Tragedy of Pompey the Great (London: Sidgwick & Jackson, 1910; New York: Macmillan, 1910);
Ballads and Poems (London: Elkin Mathews, 1910);
Martin Hyde: The Duke's Messenger (Boston: Little, Brown, 1910; London: Wells, Gardner, Darton, 1910);
A Book of Discoveries (London: Wells, Gardner, Darton, 1910; New York: Stokes, 1910);
Lost Endeavour (London: Nelson, 1910; New York: Macmillan, 1917);
The Street of To-Day (London: Dent, 1911; New York: Dutton, 1911);
William Shakespeare (London: Williams & Norgate, 1911; New York: Holt, 1911);
The Everlasting Mercy (London: Sidgwick & Jackson, 1911; Portland, Maine: Smith & Sale, 1911);
Jim Davis (London: Wells, Gardner & Darton, 1911; New York: Stokes, 1912);
The Everlasting Mercy and The Widow in the Bye Street (New York: Macmillan, 1912);

The Widow in the Bye Street (London: Sidgwick & Jackson, 1912);
The Story of a Round-House and Other Poems (New York: Macmillan, 1912);
The Daffodil Fields (New York: Macmillan, 1913; London: Heinemann, 1913);
Dauber: a Poem (London: Heinemann, 1913);
Philip the King and Other Poems (London: Heinemann, 1914; New York: Macmillan, 1914);
John M. Synge: A Few Personal Recollections, With Biographical Notes (Churchtown, Dundrum: Cuala Press, 1915; New York: Macmillan, 1915);
The Faithful: A Tragedy in Three Acts (London: Heinemann, 1915; New York: Macmillan, 1915);
Good Friday and Other Poems (New York: Macmillan, 1916);
Sonnets (New York: Macmillan, 1916);
Good Friday: A Play in Verse (Letchworth: Garden City Press, 1916);
Sonnets and Poems (Letchworth: Garden City Press, 1916);
The Locked Chest; The Sweeps of Ninety-Eight (Letchworth: Garden City Press, 1916; New York: Macmillan, 1916);
Gallipoli (London: Heinemann, 1916; New York: Macmillan, 1916);
Lollingdon Downs and Other Poems (New York: Macmillan, 1917); republished as *Lollingdon Downs and Other Poems, With Sonnets* (London: Heinemann, 1917);
The Old Front Line (New York: Macmillan, 1917); republished as *The Old Front Line, or, the Beginning of the Battle of the Somme* (London: Heinemann, 1917);
Rosas (New York: Macmillan, 1918);
The War and the Future (New York: Macmillan, 1918);
Collected Poems and Plays, 2 volumes (New York: Macmillan, 1918);
A Poem and Two Plays (London: Heinemann, 1918);
St. George and the Dragon (London: Heinemann, 1919);
The Battle of the Somme (London: Heinemann, 1919);
Reynard the Fox: or, The Ghost Heath Run (New York: Macmillan, 1919; London: Heinemann, 1919);
Enslaved and Other Poems (London: Heinemann, 1920; New York: Macmillan, 1920);
Right Royal (New York: Heinemann, 1920; London: Heinemann, 1920);
King Cole (London: Heinemann, 1921; New York: Macmillan, 1921);
The Dream (London: Heinemann, 1922; New York: Macmillan, 1922);
Melloney Holtspur (London: Heinemann, 1922; New York: Macmillan, 1922);
King Cole and Other Poems (London: Heinemann, 1923); republished as *King Cole, The Dream, and Other Poems* (New York: Macmillan, 1923);
The Taking of Helen (London: Heinemann, 1923; New York: Macmillan, 1923);
A King's Daughter: A Tragedy in Verse (New York: Macmillan, 1923; London: Heinemann, 1923);
The Collected Poems of John Masefield, 2 volumes (London: Heinemann, 1923);
Recent Prose (London: Heinemann, 1924; revised, 1932; New York: Macmillan, 1933);
Sard Harker (London: Heinemann, 1924; New York: Macmillan, 1924);
The Trial of Jesus (London: Heinemann, 1925);
Collected Works, 4 volumes (New York: Macmillan, 1925);
Odtaa (New York: Macmillan, 1926: London: Heinemann, 1926);
Tristan and Isolt: A Play in Verse (London: Heinemann, 1927; New York: Macmillan, 1927);
The Midnight Folk (London: Heinemann, 1927; New York: Macmillan, 1927);
The Coming of Christ (New York: Macmillan, 1928; London: Heinemann, 1928);
Midsummer Night and other tales in Verse (London: Heinemann, 1928; New York: Macmillan, 1928);
Easter: a Play for Singers (New York: Macmillan, 1929; London: Heinemann, 1929);
The Hawbucks (London: Heinemann, 1929; New York: Macmillan, 1929);
The Wanderer of Liverpool (London: Heinemann, 1930; New York: Macmillan, 1930);
Minnie Maylow's Story and Other Tales and Scenes (London: Heinemann, 1931; New York: Macmillan, 1931);
A Tale of Troy (London: Heinemann, 1932; New York: Macmillan, 1932);
End and Beginning (London: Heinemann, 1933; New York: Macmillan, 1933);
The Bird of Dawning (London: Heinemann, 1933; New York: Macmillan, 1933);
The Taking of the Gry (London: Heinemann, 1934; New York: Macmillan, 1934);
The Box of Delights: or When the Wolves Were Running (London: Heinemann, 1935; New York: Macmillan, 1935);
Victorious Troy: or, The Hurrying Angel (London: Heinemann, 1935; New York: Macmillan, 1936);
Plays, 2 volumes (London: Heinemann, 1936);
A Letter from Pontus and Other Verse (London: Heinemann, 1936; New York: Macmillan, 1936);

Eggs and Baker (London: Heinemann, 1936; New York: Macmillan, 1936);

The Square Peg: or the Gun Fella (London: Heinemann, 1937; New York: Macmillan, 1937);

Dead Ned (New York: Macmillan, 1938; London: Heinemann, 1938);

Some Verses to Some Germans (London: Heinemann, 1939; New York: Macmillan, 1939);

Live and Kicking Ned (London: Heinemann, 1939; New York: Macmillan, 1939);

Basilissa: A Tale of the Empress Theodora (New York: Macmillan, 1940; London: Heinemann, 1940);

Some Memories of W. B. Yeats (New York: Macmillan, 1940);

In the Mill (London: Heinemann, 1941; New York: Macmillan, 1941);

Conquer: A Tale of the Nika Rebellion in Byzantium (London: Heinemann, 1941; New York: Macmillan, 1941);

Guatama the Enlightened and Other Verse (London: Heinemann, 1941; New York: Macmillan, 1941);

Natalie Maisie and Pavilastukay: Two Tales in Verse (London: Heinemann, 1942; New York: Macmillan, 1944);

Wonderings: Between One and Six Years (London: Heinemann, 1943; New York: Macmillan, 1943);

New Chum (London: Heinemann, 1944; New York: Macmillan, 1945);

Thanks Before Going (London: Heinemann, 1946); enlarged as *Thanks Before Going with Other Gratitude for Old Delight including A Macbeth Production and Various Papers Not Before Printed* (London: Heinemann, 1947; New York: Macmillan, 1947);

A Book of Both Sorts (London: Heinemann, 1947);

Badon Parchments (London: Heinemann, 1947);

A Play of St. George (London: Heinemann, 1948; New York: Macmillan, 1948);

On the Hill (London: Heinemann, 1949; New York: Macmillan, 1949);

St. Katherine of Ledbury and Other Ledbury Poems (London: Macmillan, 1951);

So Long to Learn: Chapters of an Autobiography (London: Heinemann, 1952; New York: Macmillan, 1952);

The Bluebells and Other Verse (London: Heinemann, 1961; New York: Macmillan, 1961);

Old Raiger and Other Verse (London: Heinemann, 1964; New York: Macmillan, 1965);

In Glad Thanksgiving (London: Heinemann, 1966; New York: Macmillan, 1967);

Grace Before Ploughing: Fragments of Autobiography (London: Heinemann, 1966; New York: Macmillan, 1966).

PLAY PRODUCTIONS: *The Campden Wonder,* London, Court Theatre, 8 January 1907;

The Tragedy of Nan, London, New Royalty Theatre, 24 May 1908;

The Witch, adapted from H. Wiers-Jenssen's play, London, Royalty Theatre, 10 October 1910;

The Tragedy of Pompey the Great, London, Aldwych Theatre, 4 December 1910; revised version, Manchester, Manchester University Drama Society, 1915;

Philip the King, Bristol, Theatre Royal, 26 October 1914; Convent Garden, London, Royal Opera House, 5 November 1914;

The Faithful, by Masefield, Rollo Peters, and Henry Herbert, Birmingham, Repertory, 4 December 1915; London: King's Hall, 13 April 1919;

The Sweeps of Ninety-Eight, Birmingham, Repertory, 7 October 1916;

Good Friday: A Dramatic Poem, London, Garrick Theatre, 25 February 1917;

The Locked Chest, London, St. Martin's Theatre, 28 April 1920;

Esther, adapted and translated from part of Jean Racine's play, Wootton, Berkshire, 5 May 1921;

Berenice, translated from Racine's play, Boar's Hill, Oxford, 24 November 1921;

A King's Daughter: A Tragedy in Verse, Oxford, Playhouse, 25 May 1923;

Melloney Holtspur: or, The Pangs of Love, London, St. Martin's Theatre, 10 July 1923;

The Trial of Jesus, Oxford, Music Room, 9 May 1925; London, Royal Academy of Dramatic Art, 28 March 1926;

Tristan and Isolt: A Play in Verse, Bayswater, London, Century Theatre, 21 February 1927;
The Coming of Christ, Canterbury, Canterbury Cathedral, 28 May 1928.

TRANSLATIONS: *Esther: a Tragedy, Adapted and Partially Translated from the French of Jean Racine* (London: Heinemann, 1922);
Berenice: a Tragedy Translated from the French of Jean Racine (London: Heinemann, 1922).

John Masefield rose to prominence during the first two decades of the twentieth century as the author of *Salt-Water Ballads* (1902) and of several popular narrative poems including *The Everlasting Mercy* (1911) and *The Widow in the Bye Street* (1912). He was also the author of more than twenty volumes of fiction, which included novels, books for children, and collections of short stories; of several historical books, which included *Sea Life in Nelson's Time* (1905); and of seventeen plays in prose and verse. During his poet laureateship from 1930 to 1967 he used his opportunity as a world-famous figure to carry those concerns expressed in his earlier work to an enlarged public audience: the suffering of the poor and exploited, respect for the common man, the preference for the simple rural life as contrasted with urban life, the hatred of excessive commercialism and industrialism fostered in our ugly cities, and the necessity for the human soul to recognize and respond to beauty in all its forms.

He was born 1 June 1878 in the town of Ledbury in a Victorian house known as Knapp, with vistas of the fields and woodlands of Herefordshire. In later years, recalling his childhood at Knapp with its orchard and garden, the poet referred to it in the autobiography *So Long to Learn* (1952) as "living in Paradise," and he describes an experience there which Constance Babington Smith in her *John Masefield: A Life* (1978) calls "the birth of creative imagination in him": "Then, on one wonderful day, when I was a little more than five years old, as I stood looking north, over a clump of honeysuckle in flower, I entered that greater life; and that life entered into me with a delight that I can never forget." It was a moment of euphoria similar to those recorded by other poets as diverse in time and temperament as Henry Vaughan, William Wordsworth, and Robert Bridges. The beauty of rural England, the beauty of music, and certain verses by Alfred, Lord Tennyson and other poets recited to him by his mother were also early and strong influences on his later poetry.

Masefield, in his Conway cadet uniform, with his sister, Nora. The telescope was a prize for winning an essay contest.

Masefield's mother died when he was six. The family moved to another house, the Priory, and at the age of ten the future poet became a boarder at Warwick School in Warwick. About this time he began writing his first juvenile verses. Upon the death of his father in 1891, Masefield, at the age of thirteen, joined the merchant-navy school ship H.M.S. *Conway*. He left the ship in 1894 as a senior petty officer and was taken on as an apprentice aboard the *Gilcruix*, belonging to the White Star line and bound for a thirteen-week voyage to Chile around Cape Horn. Masefield's graphic descriptions of the stormy rounding of the cape are to be found in his journal and later in his semiautobiographical poem *Dauber* (1913). Masefield suffered from bad health during the voyage and after the embarkation at Iquique, Chile. He was released from duty, put into a hospital at Valparaiso, and returned to the Priory in Ledbury in the autumn of 1894. In March 1895 he sailed to New York to ship aboard the *Bidston Hill*, but he jumped ship, stayed in New York, lived for a time as a vagrant, and took on various odd jobs including tending bar in a Greenwich Village hotel. In September of 1895 he obtained a job in a carpet factory in Yonkers, where he worked for the next two years. By the summer of 1897 he had returned to England, where, suffering from bad health, he lived in London in cheap lodgings and worked in a small office in the city.

In New York in September 1895, just before he went to work in the carpet factory, Masefield had come across a volume of Geoffrey Chaucer's verse in a neighborhood bookstore. The poetry stirred his imagination, and he quickly obtained volumes by John Keats and Percy Bysshe Shelley. The discovery of these poets marked the beginning of Masefield's serious efforts to become a poet. By the end of 1897 he had completed two collections of verse (never published), which he dedicated to a neighbor in London. In 1898 he became a bank clerk and kept the position for three years, during which time his first successful poem was published in the *Outlook* (in 1899), and he met William Butler Yeats and Lady Augusta Gregory (in 1900). The meeting with Yeats was of paramount importance in Masefield's career. He became a regular guest at Yeats's Monday evenings in Bloomsbury. Masefield, who was having poems published in the *Outlook*, the *Tatler*, and the *Speaker*, moved to Bloomsbury in late 1901. In 1902 Grant Richards published Masefield's now famous *Salt-Water Ballads*. The first edition of 500 copies sold out in six months.

Masefield's first volume shows the obvious influence of the early work of Yeats. Both poets had a fondness for the six-or seven-beat anapestic line. Masefield's best-known early poem, "Sea-Fever," which begins "I will go down to the seas again, to the lonely sea and the sky," perhaps echoes the first line of Yeats's well-known early poem, "The Lake Isle of Innisfree": "I will arise and go now, and go to Innisfree."

The Yeatsian influence is even more obvious in Masefield's second volume of poems, *Ballads* (1903), especially in such poems as "The Ballad of Sir Bors," which begins "Would I could win some quiet and rest, and a little ease, / In the cool grey hush of the dusk, in the dim green place of the trees." The second line, with its "Celtic Twilight" diction, could have been written by Yeats. And Masefield seems to have Yeats's symbol of the rose in mind when he continues "Would I could see it, the rose, when the light begins to fail / . . . / The red, red passionate rose of the sacred blood of the Christ." At least two other poems in *Ballads*—"Spanish Waters" ("Like a slow sweet piece of music from the grey forgotten years") and "Beauty," which ends "But the loveliest things of beauty God ever has shown to me, / Are her voice, and her hair, and eyes, and the dear red curve of her lips"—also remind one of the Yeats of the Celtic Twilight. But in Masefield's most characteristic early poems there are also marked differences from Yeats. The realistic or naturalistic diction of "Cape Horn Gospel—II" ("Jake was a dirty Dago lad, an' he gave the skipper chin, / An' the skipper up an' took him a crack with an iron belaying-pin") and of "Evening—Regatta Day" ("Your nose is a red jelly, your mouth's a toothless wreck, / And I'm atop of you, banging your head upon the dirty deck") is a far cry from the Celtic Twilight. These poems anticipate the diction, tone, and subject matter of the later *The Everlasting Mercy* and *The Widow in the Bye Street*. "One of the Bo'sun's Yarns," from *Salt-Water Ballads*, reveals Masefield's talent for telling a story in verse, which he developed in his later long narrative poems. Finally, the ever-present experience of the sea and of ships, whether treated realistically, as in the poems just mentioned, or romantically, as in "Sea-Fever," or both romantically and realistically, as in "Cargoes," is the most distinctive feature of Masefield's work throughout his career. Of his passion for sailing ships he wrote to Florence Lamont in 1926, "they were the only youth I had, and the only beauty I knew in my youth, and now that I am old not many greater beauties seem to be in the world."

Masefield had the gift of making quick but lasting friendships. By the time his second book was published he numbered among his literary acquaintances John Millington Synge and Laurence Binyon, as well as Yeats and Lady Gregory. It was at a party given by Binyon that he met his future wife, Constance Crommelin, whom he married in 1903. In that same year he stayed for a time with the painter Jack Yeats, brother of William Butler Yeats, and his wife in South Devon, where he composed a few "Theodore Ballads" for *A Broad Sheet*, edited by Jack Yeats. After Masefield's marriage on 23 July, the couple acquired a flat on Marylebone Road. He managed to eke out a slender living by reviewing books, doing some editing for the *Speaker*, and accepting

The Gilcruix, *on which Masefield sailed around Cape Horn in 1894. His experiences on the thirteen-week voyage were the basis for his long poem* Dauber *(National Maritime Museum).*

a temporary job as organizer of an art exhibit in Bradford. Soon after their first child, Judith, was born on 28 April 1904, the Masefields moved to a flat in Greenwich. In October, Masefield went to Manchester to work for C. P. Scott of the *Manchester Guardian*, but he gave up the position after five months. By the end of 1905 Masefield had had published a collection of short fiction, *A Mainsail Haul*, with a frontispiece by Jack Yeats, and a historical essay, *Sea Life in Nelson's Time*. He had also completed a ghost story, "Anty Bligh," which was praised by G. K. Chesterton in the *Speaker* after its pirated stage production. He had contributed articles to the *Speaker*, narratives to the *Manchester Guardian*, and poems to various periodicals. At this time he was also writing his next historical book, *On the Spanish Main* (1906), and editing the poems of Robert Herrick, Ben Jonson, and Francis Beaumont and John Fletcher. He edited an anthology of sea poetry, *A Sailor's Garland*, which was published by Methuen in 1906. His article on sea chanteys appeared in the *Manchester Guardian* on 16 August 1905; his descriptive article "Sea Songs" appeared in *Temple Bar* in 1906.

Masefield's expertise on sea chanteys caught the attention of Harley Granville Barker, who called him in to advise him on the use of sea chanteys in the production of George Bernard Shaw's *Captain Brassbound's Conversion* at the Court Theatre, an assignment that strengthened Masefield's interest in playwriting, which began in 1903 when he attended a performance of Ben Jonson's *The New Inn* in Chipping Camden. In the same year he discovered that John Millington Synge was his neighbor in Bloomsbury. They quickly became friends, and Masefield was present in Yeats's rooms at a reading from manuscript of Synge's *Riders to the Sea* and *The Shadow of The Glen*. There was a marked influence of the dramas of Yeats and Synge on Masefield as he began his career as a playwright.

After several false starts in which he wrote and destroyed a series of plays of which only the titles remain, Masefield set to work at his home, Diamond Terrace in Greenwich, toward the end of 1905 on his first surviving play, *The Campden Wonder* (1907). The work derives from a story that Masefield had heard several years previously in the town of Chipping Camden about the hanging, out of pure spite, of three innocent people. After a visit with Lady Gregory in her home at Coole Park, Ireland, a visit which must have further stimulated his interest in the drama, he was ready to settle down to what became his most serious literary occupational concern until the outbreak of World War I. He wrote in the introduction to his *Collected Poems and Plays* (1918), "I was a playwright, according to my power, for ten years during which the theatre of England was the main interest of my fellows and myself." During this period he completed ten plays, the most important of which are generally considered to be *The Tragedy of Nan* (1908) and *The Faithful* (1915). *The Tragedy of Pompey the Great* (1910) and *Philip the King* (1914) also received considerable critical attention, most of it favorable. Included in these ten early works is *The Witch* (1910), adapted from H. Wiers-Jenssen's play and published as *Anne Pedersdotter* in 1917.

Masefield followed *The Campden Wonder* with three plays, *Mrs. Harrison* (published in 1909), *The Sweeps of Ninety-Eight* (1916), and *The Locked Chest* (1920), all written at Greenwich in 1905 or 1906. In *Mrs. Harrison*, a sequel to *The Campden Wonder*, the protagonist learns that her drunken husband has been bribed for three hundred pounds to conspire in the hanging of three innocent men. She takes poison and dies while reading the Bible aloud as her husband is having a good visit with the parson in church. The play is an exercise in unrelieved naturalism. *The Sweeps of Ninety-Eight*, with a historical background but an original plot, is an amusing comedy about the outwitting of British naval officers by an Irish rebel of 1798. In this play Masefield was probably influenced by Lady Gregory. *The Locked Chest* is a trivial but suspenseful play about a wife who outwits her cowardly husband and the lord who had bribed him to betray their cousin.

The Tragedy of Nan was written at Greenwich from February to September 1907 and had successful runs in repertory theaters. It is somewhat less brutal in its naturalism than the murderous criminality of Masefield's earlier *The Campden Wonder*; even so, the play was brutal enough to arouse the antagonism of Storm Jameson and a few other critics, and yet compassionate enough in its depiction of the central character to win praise from most reviewers and readers. Pity for the poor and oppressed, together with a relentlessly honest presentation of their struggle and suffering, is the distinguishing characteristic of these early plays. The heroine of this "country tragedy," as Masefield called it, is Nan Hardwick, an orphan and charity girl whose father has been hanged for sheep stealing. She is forced to live with her greedy aunt and uncle who exploit and betray her by persuading the one consolation of her life, her lover Dick Gurvil, to break his troth with her and marry their daughter. The scene in which Nan is betrayed and then mocked by her relatives is perhaps the most poignant and terrible in all of Masefield's prose dramas. It is followed by the arrival of government officials who tell Nan her father was hanged by mistake and pay her fifty pounds compensation. Gurvil, realizing that he too has made a mistake, begins wooing Nan again, but the embittered girl stabs him to prevent his betrayal of other women and then drowns herself. The language of the play is that of the Gloucestershire-Hereford peasant early in the nineteenth century, a dialect well known to Masefield, but in the drama's most powerful moments the heroine achieves a credible eloquence which somehow transcends the diction of the peasant protagonist in a manner similar to that of Synge's *Riders to the Sea*, to which Masefield is indebted, although his play is dedicated to Yeats. Contributing to the drama's stage success was Masefield's friend Barker, who directed *The Tragedy of Nan* at its premier production, as he did several other plays by Masefield.

In *The Tragedy of Pompey the Great*, written in 1908-1909, first produced in 1910, and later revised, Masefield is employing one of his recurrent themes—the fall of a tragic hero who, in meeting his defeat with dignity and courage, wins a kind of spiritual victory. In his losing struggle with Caesar, Pompey is idealized (more, perhaps, than history warrants) as the victim of a patriotic desire to save Rome from civil war. Caesar himself does not appear, and for that reason the play is more a revelation of character and a vivid historical pageant than it is a dramatic struggle between two leaders of the Roman world.

The Faithful, composed at Hampstead and Great Hampden in 1913, is described by Masefield as "a pageant showing the tragedy of the 47 Ronin of Japan," who in loyally and successfully avenging the death of their nobleman master, Asano, by an upstart tyrant cheerfully meet their own deaths. The play has been widely praised for the eloquence of its style and the sublimity of its theme. It was begun as a verse narrative and changed to a prose play after Masefield saw Barker's productions of Shakespeare's *Twelfth Night* and *The Winter's Tale* in 1912. The beauty and pageantry of the Theatre Guild production in New York in 1919, with sets designed by Lee Simonson, was commended. Some reviewers criticized it for being pseudo-Japanese, but most readers and viewers agreed with the critic who wrote in the *New Republic*, "In this performance is a self-contained world that needs no historical support. . . . My own sense of *The Faithful* was one of unimpeded enjoyment."

Masefield's next play, his first drama in verse, was the one-act *Philip the King*, written in 1914 in Hampstead and Lollingdon and produced the same year. Philip II of Spain, awaiting news of the Spanish Armada, is forewarned by his daughter that God may humble the pride of Spain, and then, after being troubled in his sleep by the ghosts of those he murdered, he is given by a messenger a detailed account of the destruction of his fleet. This wholly static play then ends in a prayer by Philip. The writing of *Good Friday: A Dramatic Poem*, Masefield's second in verse, was interrupted by World War I and, according to Masefield, never finished. However, it was considered complete enough for publication in 1916 and for stage production at the Garrick Theatre the following year. It is the first of five biblical plays by Masefield and is noteworthy for the graphic and moving speech of Longinus in iambic couplets describing the crucifixion.

In 1909 the Masefields were living at Maida Hill West in the Paddington area of London, and they also secured a small country house, the Rectory Farm, in the village of Great Hampden, Buckinghamshire. By the end of this year Masefield's first two novels, *Captain Margaret* (1908) and *Multitude and Solitude* (1909), had been published; he had had his portrait painted by William Strang; and he had met the famous actress Elizabeth Robins, whose intimate friendship with him was broken off a year later. The year 1910 marked the appearance of his third book of poetry, *Ballads and Poems*, which showed little advance over his two previous collections. Most of the poems were of early date; many had appeared in *Salt-Water Ballads* and *Ballads*. His third novel, *The Street of To-Day*, was published in 1911, the year in which Masefield's fame as a poet was dramatically augmented with the publication of his narrative poem *The Everlasting Mercy*, which first appeared in England in the October issue of the *English Review*. It quickly achieved a succés de scandale. Some readers and reviewers were hostile to what they considered to be the poem's needlessly brutal naturalism. The word *bloody*, offensive to British taste, appeared eleven times—or rather in the *English Review* it was indicated by blank spaces eleven times. The word was not actually printed until book publication in November. According to the editor of the *English Review*, the uproar occasioned by the poem increased the magazine's circulation enough to save the publication from financial collapse.

Masefield had written his plays *The Tragedy of Nan* and *The Tragedy of Pompey the Great* before he started writing *The Everlasting Mercy*. In his play writing he had found it necessary in effectively moving the emotions of a theater audience of mixed education and social background to present scenes of dramatic physical action spoken in a colloquial style. He carried this technique over into his first long narrative poem, in which his protagonist, Saul Kane, engages in a fistfight, twice breaks up a pub, and arouses the whole town by roaring naked through the streets at night after ringing the fire bells.

The time of the action is mid-nineteenth century, the place is probably the town of Ledbury in Herefordshire, Masefield's birthplace. The poem opens with a provocation by Saul Kane, a rambunctious town character frequently given to poaching, whoring, and drunkenness. He reminds one of Yeats's Red Hanrahan. He insists on encroaching on the trapping territory of his poacher friend, Bill Meyers, and their argument leads to an exciting prearranged fight, graphically presented by a poet who was a boxing enthusiast. (In his youth he patriotically celebrated the victory of the British boxer Bob Fitzimmons over the American James J. Corbett in 1897.) According to the editor of the *English Review*, the Kane-Meyers fight scene was read aloud in English pubs. Kane wins by a fluke after Meyers sprains his thumb. He feels remorse and shame. He knows he is in the wrong, and his former friend refuses to make up and shake hands. Immediately after the fight Kane and his supporters find their way to the Lion pub, where Kane makes an assignation with Doxy Jane, the barmaid, indulges in a drunken orgy, and then is moved again by fierce remorse as he flings the window open and hears "the cold note of the chapel bell." In a fit of madness he smashes the glassware in the pub, tears off his clothes, rushes into the street brandishing two lamps, and rings the fire bells. When the fire engines arrive he seizes two hose nozzles and yells, "I am the fire." The next afternoon he breaks up the bar again, has a confrontation in

Masefield in his early twenties

the street with the parson, accusing him and his church of hypocrisy and social injustice, and then berates a mother in the marketplace for not properly looking after her child. After Doxy Jane fails to keep her appointment, he gets drunk again, but when a Quaker lady, making her nightly round of the saloons to preach temperance, seizes his drink and pours it on the floor, saying "every drop of drink accursed / Makes Christ within you die of thirst," Saul experiences a sudden spiritual enlightenment similar to that of his namesake on the road to Damascus. All is changed for Saul. Everything seems bathed in the glory of Christ. The conversion is completed when, after an all-night walk in the fields, he sees at dawn the farmer Callow plowing his field and recognizes him as a figure of Christ.

The poem, a study of sin and redemption, was begun in the spring of 1911 at Great Hampden shortly after Masefield had received what he considered to be two messages from the supernatural world. He wrote in *So Long to Learn* of his second experience, "I was in a state of great inner joy from a sight I had seen that morning" in the fields at dawn. As he surmounted a fence at the wood's edge he said to himself, "Now I will make a poem about a blackguard who becomes converted. . . . Instantly the poem appeared to me in its complete form." The morning scene, he tells us in his introduction to *The Everlasting Mercy*, was the sight of a plowman and a "breaking wave of red clay thrust aside by the share." The plowman was a friend of Masefield's, and he became the Christ figure, farmer Callow, at the end of the poem. *The Everlasting Mercy* was completed in June 1911 at the Rectory Farm, Great Hampden.

It should be noted that Kane's conversion experience is initiated at the beginning of the poem when he feels a sense of guilt after winning his fight against Meyers while knowing his cause is unjust. The working of God's grace on Kane's soul begins at this moment. His violent rebellion against grace and his eventual surrender to it are in the conversion tradition of Christian theology generally speaking, and specifically are in the evangelical revivalist tradition of mid-nineteenth-century England. The psychology and the language of the poem are revivalist. Although the story is told with graphic concreteness and particularity, it is successfully universalized so that Kane becomes a kind of Everyman figure, a type of sinner saved. Sanford Sternlicht in *John Masefield* (1977) calls the poem "a confession, a poor man's St. Augustine's," and Muriel Spark in a detailed and perceptive analysis in her *John Masefield* (1953) says the poem "is a document of a whole epoch in history. It characterizes the wave of revivalism which spread over rural England from the time of Wesley, mid-eighteenth century, right through the nineteenth."

The story is told from the first-person point of view, and Kane tells of his conversion after he has been saved. He therefore sometimes interrupts the action to reflect on its significance or to recall relevant scenes from an earlier time. Some of the best poetry occurs in these reflections, as when he recalls the legend of a visionary scene in church on Christmas Eve, brought to mind as he passes the church on his way to the drunken orgy in the Lion pub. The poem is written in tetrameter couplets varying in diction from the vulgar, coarsened violence of angry peasant epithets to a Blakean purity of tone, as when Masefield depicts the innocence of childhood:

And he who gives a child a treat
makes joy-bells ring in Heaven's street,
And he who gives a child a home
Builds palaces in Kingdom come,
And he who gives a baby birth,
Brings Saviour Christ again to Earth.

There are, in contrast, passages where Kane, speaking in his own colloquial tongue, utters sentiments which seem ridiculous: "I sometimes go without my dinner / Now that I know the times I've gi'n her." There is far too much facile writing in *The Everlasting Mercy*. The poem was parodied in Siegfried Sassoon's *The Daffodil Murderer* (1913) and elsewhere, and it has suffered a decline in reputation during the past fifty years.

In June 1911, after completing *The Everlasting Mercy*, Masefield began writing another poem which soon became well known, *The Widow in the Bye Street*, while on vacation with a new acquaintance, Robert Ross, later Sir Robert, a pioneer of tropical medicine, in Capel Curig. He then returned to Great Hampden to write the greater part of it. It first appeared in the *English Review* in February 1912. It was published in New York by Macmillan in an edition which also included *The Everlasting Mercy* in March 1912 and published separately in England in June by Sidgwick and Jackson in an edition of 3,000 copies with a second printing of 2,000 copies to meet demand. The Macmillan edition was reprinted in 1919 in an illustrated version of 2,000 copies, and in 1923 a Macmillan Leather Pocket Edition of 2,000 copies was released.

The Widow in the Bye Street is a Hardyesque tale of passion and fate played out against the countryside of Shropshire, serene and beautiful but indifferent to the human catastrophe for which it is the setting. Four persons, the widow Gurney, her son Jimmy, the shepherd Ern, and the beautiful femme fatale Anna, come together quite by accident at the October fair, and that chance meeting sets in motion a train of action that leads inevitably to the deaths of two of them and the madness of a third. The child Jimmy, living with a widowed mother whose love for him is possessive and obsessive, eventually grows to young manhood after his mother has half starved herself and worked her fingers to the bone by sewing (usually shrouds) to keep him strong and healthy. He gets a job as a laborer for a short time; there is money enough for both, and they are relatively happy until he meets Anna, a beautiful but profligate widow who had born two children, one of whom she has murdered, the other whom she has sent to the workhouse. Her fancy man is the shepherd Ern, married to a gentle and virtuous wife. At the October fair she is delayed from keeping her appointment with Ern, who in anger immediately takes up with the gypsy Bessie. Anna, arriving late, sees them together. Angry and jealous, she accosts Jimmy, who has just won a wrestling match with a ram. It is a case of love at first sight for Jimmy. During the next few weeks, he courts her by spending his hard-earned money on her instead of on his mother, but he gets nothing in return, for Anna is still interested in Ern and is using Jimmy's attachment to her as a means of arousing Ern's jealousy. On a Sunday afternoon Ern sees the two of them walk by his cottage and joins them. Anna hastily gets rid of Jimmy and that night welcomes Ern to her bedroom. Jimmy, mad with jealousy, spies on the lovers from an apple bough near the bedroom window, rushes to the house, picks a fight with Ern, and is knocked out by him. Jimmy quits his job, gets drunk with his terminal wages, picks up a plough bat, walks to Anna's cottage, where he finds Ern with Anna again. He hits Ern over the head with the plough bat, killing him instantly although it was not his intention to do so. Filled with remorse, Jimmy surrenders to the police, is tried, convicted, and hanged. His mother becomes mad, dreaming of her happy past at night and wandering the fields by day, singing the songs her son loved as a child.

Masefield's early admiration of Chaucer is evident throughout the poem, which is written in the rhyme-royal stanza used by Chaucer in "The Prioress's Tale," which, like Masefield's poem, depicts the relationship between a widow and a son who is eventually murdered.

In Masefield's poem there is considerable criticism of the English establishment. The chaplain who attends the hanging is caricatured, and the brutality of English justice and the frequent use of capital punishment are criticized by implication, as is the harshness of human relationships that occur, ironically, in rural England, a setting of great natural beauty. But the main theme, and here Masefield reminds us of Hardy, is the implacable fate, the tragic destiny which governs the lives of men. It is this theme and the brilliantly depicted scene of the country fair, where the characters come, by chance, so catastrophically together, and a few other descriptions of rural Shropshire that mitigate the sentimental melodrama of much of the poem.

In Great Hampden in the spring of 1912, Masefield began his third important narrative poem, *Dauber*, which first appeared in the *English Review* of October 1912 and in his book *The Story of a Round-House and Other Poems* published by Macmillan of New York in November 1912. The next year *Dauber* was published separately in England by Heinemann in an edition of 2,500 copies.

The poem opens with a scene in the tropics on the deck of a clipper ship, with Dauber, a would-be painter, watching the sunset alone. Alienated from the rest of the crew, he is considered good only for menial tasks and is jeered at for his continual daydreaming and attempts at painting. Forced to remove his paintings from the roundhouse, he hides them beneath a longboat. They are discovered and mutilated by members of the crew. Dauber protests vehemently, and he is told to take his troubles to the captain, but when he goes to the captain, he is reprimanded for not keeping the longboat clear of rubbish. He confides in an officer trainee named Si, telling him of a desire, inherited from his mother, to become a great painter, of his early love of clipper ships and the sea, and of his decision to go to sea to obtain experience and materials for his art. Si, because he is a gentleman and future officer, is reprimanded by the mate for talking with a common seaman, and Dauber's alienation is complete. As the ship moves toward Cape Horn, Dauber dreads the approaching storms, fearing he will not be able to cope with his assigned tasks in the rigging, yet resolving to play his part without flinching. At the same time he has a sudden insight into what he thinks will be his destiny—to depict the heroic battle of "naked manhood" against the sea, the power, tragedy, and misery of the common sailor which he will shortly experience himself as they round Cape Horn. Soon the air is filled with polar snow; a southwest gale almost capsizes the ship, but the crew saves it after a terrible struggle in which Dauber plays his part well. He has successfully met the test of manhood and is accepted by his mates as one of them. He makes it clear to them that he will continue his painting, but chance or fate determines otherwise. After the storm subsides and the sailors are about to repair the damage in calmer seas, an unexpected squall hits the ship. Dauber is the first to rush aloft to man the topsails. He is thrown to the deck by a blast of wind which tears the sail from his hands. The crew runs to assist him, but he dies and is buried at sea. From that time on, as the ship sails into port under fair skies, only one reference is made to the would-be painter: "Dauber was a Jonah," says a member of the crew. After the ship's arrival in safe harbor, its sails are furled during a lovely sunset, and that evening an eagle screams all night long from a mountain peak. The symbolic significance of the sunset and the eagle has been variously interpreted as indicating a kind of spiritual triumph for the artist or, obversely, as indicating the complete indifference of the natural as well as of the human world to the fate of Dauber. The reference to Dauber as a Jonah in seamen's language means that he was a bringer of bad luck and that when he was thrown overboard, all went well. But it should be remembered that in Christian typology, Jonah was considered a type of Christ, and Masefield may have intended this deeper significance.

Dauber may be considered a tragedy of wasted talent. As an artist Dauber, perhaps, would have accomplished something. As a seaman he succeeded in establishing his courage, but he was no better at seamanship than his mates and probably inferior to most of them. His sacrifice appears to have been useless. Even if he had succeeded as an artist, the men whom he tried so hard to equal in their skill as sailors would not have appreciated his painting. Muriel Sparks argues that Dauber's death "is an *alien* death," that the tragic error was Dauber's decision to go to sea and submit himself to a hostile environment. However, the decision is quite understandable. Dauber had become enamored of ships and the sea. He wished to use his life at sea as material for his art, to celebrate and validate the sufferings and the nobility of the common man. Furthermore, the sea gave him a chance to earn a living. Herman Melville made a similar decision when he went to sea, as did Masefield himself, who probably had *Moby-Dick* (a book he read and admired very early in his life) in mind as he composed the poem. In a powerful passage, the sound of the ship's foghorn (manned by Dauber) just preceding the storm is answered by the sound of the whales that surround the ship. The whale anticipates and signifies death as it does in Melville's romantic epic:

> Who rode that desolate sea? What forms were
>   those?
> Mournful from things defeated, in the throes

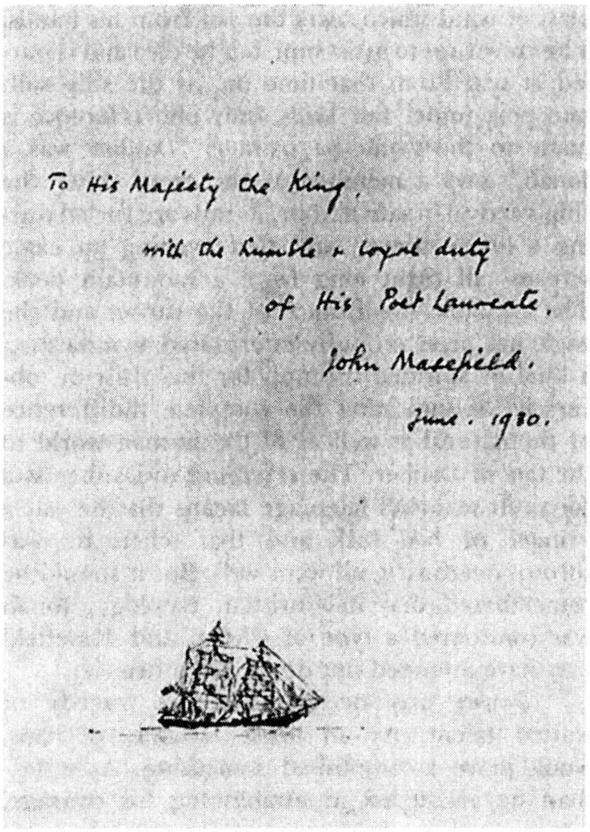

Inscription and title page in the copy of Reynard the Fox *presented to King George V (Windsor Castle Library, Collection of Her Majesty the Queen)*

Of memory of some conquered hunting-
ground,
Out of the night of death arose the sound.

. . . .

A wall of nothing at the world's last edge,
Where no life came except defeated life.

Dauber is one of Masefield's best poems both in the effectiveness of its poetic style—especially in the storm scenes, for Masefield is at his best when dealing with action at sea—and in its narrative suspense. Some of the power probably comes from the poem's being partly autobiographical. There is a good deal of the young Masefield in the character of Dauber, and much of Dauber's experience at sea was Masefield's. The description of the rounding of Cape Horn is derived from Masefield's journal which he kept when he rounded Cape Horn on the ship *Gilcruix* in 1894. The setting, all the detail about the ship's gear as well as Dauber's response to the sea, has the ring of authenticity. Like Dauber, Masefield considered becoming a painter and, like Dauber, he built model ships. Like him, he always showed admiration and compassion for suffering humanity. Like Dauber, Masefield took a ship bound for Chile, where his career as a seaman ended. Dauber's voyage ended in death, Masefield's in an almost fatal illness which invalided him home to England. He never went to sea again except as a passenger.

The ambiguity surrounding Dauber's ability as an artist can also be explained autobiographically. Masefield, like many other artists, was sure of his commitment to his art, but he sometimes doubted his ability to create literature of permanent value. The theme of the alienated artist or intellectual has become commonplace in the twentieth century. Combined with the theme of the self-doubt of the artist, it has given rise to other fine poems besides *Dauber*, such as Edwin Arlington Robinson's "Rembrandt to Rembrandt."

As in *The Widow in the Bye Street*, the stanza form of *Dauber* is the rhyme royal used by Chaucer, and the dramatic dialogue, the scenic presentation, and the sharp realism remind one of Chaucer. But there is also a power of image and symbol which Muriel Spark thinks may be the result of Masefield's close reading of Shakespeare just prior to his writing of the poem. Perhaps, too, the symbolic style (not commonly found in Masefield's poems) may owe something to Melville's *Moby-Dick*.

By the time the family moved to 13 Well Walk, Hampstead, in 1912, Masefield found himself famous. Three long narrative poems—*The Everlasting Mercy, The Widow in the Bye Street*, and *Dauber*, all published within a twelve-month period—had started the Masefield boom, although a few critics, including Rupert Brooke and J. C. Squire, dissented.

"Biography" and "Ships," both first published in the *English Review* in 1912, are of interest as a demonstration of Masefield's considerable skill in using the conventional heroic couplet. "Ships" appears to have been influenced by Robert Bridges's "Elegy: The Summer-House on the Mound" (1899), also written in heroic couplets and containing, like Masefield's poem, a fine description of ships at sea, individually named and described, as they are remembered from the poets' earlier years. There is also an echo of Bridges in one of Masefield's finest poems, "The Wanderer," first published in *Harper's* magazine in 1913. Bridges's line in "A Passer-by" (1879) which describes a sailing ship anchored in the South Seas—"so stately, and still thou standest"—is echoed in Masefield's line describing a ship in a southern port—"So stately and so still in such great peace."

The history of the *Wanderer*, a four-masted barque launched in 1860 and lost in 1907, is told in Masefield's much later book, *The Wanderer of Liverpool* (1930). (There are two pictures of the ship in Charles H. Simmons's *A Bibliography of John Masefield*, 1931.) Masefield first saw the *Wanderer* in Liverpool harbor when he was a boy. He was stirred by its beauty so deeply that it became for him a symbol of immortality, of the beauty which inspires creative activity, and of endurance which prevails in adversity. The narrator of Masefield's poem reports the luckless adventures of the ship through several storms and the difficulty of finding a crew to man her. He does not see her for a long time. One Christmas eve when he is near a southern port after a fierce gale, the sky suddenly clears, there is a bright dawn, and he experiences a mystical illumination similar to that Masefield had during childhood in Ledbury. In the poem Masefield writes:

> That soul was there apparent, not revealed,
> Unearthly meanings covered every tree,
> That wet grass grew in an immortal field,
> Those waters fed some never-wrinkled sea.

The narrator hears a ship's bell, recognizes it as coming from the *Wanderer*, rushes to the sea's edge, and beholds the *Wanderer* at anchor in the bay: "Come as of old a queen, untouched by Time, / Resting the beauty that no seas could tire." Recalling the frequent storm lashings that the ship had suffered, he states the theme of his poem in the final line: "The meaning shows in a defeated thing."

Another highly successful poem published in the *English Review* in the same year as "The Wanderer" is "The River," a short narrative poem which tells the story of a crew trapped in a vessel slowly sinking into a sandbar. The trapped men are momentarily expecting the arrival of a tugboat gone in search of explosives to clear the wreckage and release the crew. While they are awaiting rescue, a member of the crew identified only as "the digger" insists, against the objections of the men, on chipping away with his knife at the lead seal holding a manhole cover in place. The explosives do not arrive in time; the crew drowns—all except the digger, who escapes through the manhole and survives. It is a suspenseful tale of endurance and will to live. Especially graphic are Masefield's descriptions of the whirlpool and the sinking ship.

The Daffodil Fields was published in 1913, first in the *English Review*, then by Macmillan of New York (1,620 copies), and in London by Heinemann (3,000 copies). It is one of the weakest of Masefield's narrative poems and has been frequently condemned by critics; yet Masefield still demonstrates his storytelling ability. The action creates suspense. Furthermore, Masefield, as in his previous narrative poems, succeeds in evoking the beauty of the English countryside, where most of the action occurs, and the recurrent image of the daffodils gives a thematic unity to the poem. But the material is that of sentimental melodrama, and Masefield does not succeed in making his story believable, especially the sensational ending. The story begins with a love triangle in a small English town. Mary Keir loves Michael Gray. Lion Occleve, Michael's friend, loves Mary, who does not love him. Michael must go to Argentina for three years to seek his fortune. Before going, he discovers he is in love with Mary, and they plight their troth. Michael in South America forgets Mary, and lives with a Spanish woman. Mary, deeply in love with Michael, remains faithful to him and resists the advances of Lion, but for three years she receives no letters from Michael, and before the fourth year is finished, she marries Lion. Upon discovering that Mary has married Lion, Michael, sick with jealousy and with returning passion for his lost sweetheart, returns to England. Mary abandons her husband to live with Michael for a time. Eventually they both agree that Mary should return to her husband, but before they can inform Lion of their decision, he picks a quarrel with Michael. They fight and kill each other. Mary brings daffodils and other flowers to cover the bodies, then dies of a broken heart on Michael's breast. Besides the obvious incredibility of the story, there is a good deal of bad writing: forced rhymes, careless and padded lines, and sentimental romantic rhetoric.

In spite of the failure of *The Daffodil Fields*, Masefield continued to be a famous public figure. Frank Swinnerton in *The Georgian Literary Scene* (1911) had called him the first Georgian poet because he had broken with the Victorian upper-middle-class tradition and was being read by the common man. In 1912 he received the annually awarded Edmond de Polignac prize from the Royal Society of Literature. The next year he was caricatured by Max Beerbohm, and on 16 April 1913, he was invited to dine at Number 10 Downing Street to help celebrate the birthday of Violet Asquith, the prime minister's daughter. When the poet laureate, Alfred Austin, died in June 1913 there was considerable support for Masefield to succeed him, but Robert Bridges was given the honor. Upon England's entry into World War I, Masefield wrote his only war poem, "August 1914," at Lollingdon, the farmhouse he had just bought near Wallingford at the edge of the Berkshire Downs. Here Masefield farmed and wrote the sonnets published in *Lollingdon Downs and Other Poems* (1917). The family retained the Hampstead house in Well Walk. In April 1917, while her husband was in France, Mrs. Masefield supervised the move to Hill Crest on Boar's Hill near Oxford.

During the years 1915-1918 Masefield undertook four trips to France, one to the Middle East, and two to America—all on behalf of the war effort. On his first trip to France (March-April 1915) he went to Arc-en-Barrois as a Red Cross orderly to tend to the French wounded. His second trip in July 1915 was a two-week survey of the hospital area around Tours to guide him in his plan for setting up a new fresh-air hospital in France—a project which never materialized. From August to October 1916 he was in France again at the request of Sir Gilbert Parker of British Intelligence to ascertain the amount of American aid to the French ambulance and hospital units; his report was to be made available to America with a design for promoting further war efforts by the Americans. On his final visit to France during the war (February-May 1917) he was attached to Lord Lytton's group of French war correspondents to inspect the Somme area for a chronicle of the Battle of the Somme commissioned by General Douglas Haig, the commander in chief. From August to October 1915 he was sent by the Red Cross to tend to the wounded in the Gallipoli area. His experiences in France and the Middle East are graphically described in his letters to his wife, which have been excerpted by Constance Babington Smith in her biography of the poet. His motivation for undertaking these arduous tasks is stated in one of these letters: "It is a question of going through a little hardship to save the lives of beautiful human beings."

His first trip to America during the war (January-March 1916) was made ostensibly for the purpose of giving a series of lectures on English literature to American audiences, with the hope of strengthening cultural ties with the Americans who at that time were technically neutral. He was also asked to report to Parker on American attitudes toward the Allied cause. His second trip (January-August 1918), made after America had entered the war, was openly advertised as propaganda on behalf of the Allies. Toward the end of his stay, he visited the southern training camps to give lectures to the American soldiers.

Three books of prose resulted from Masefield's participation in the war effort: *Gallipoli* (1916), *The Old Front Line* (1917), and *The Battle of the Somme* (1919). *Gallipoli* was enthusiastically received in England and America, and it effectively aroused American support for England and the Allied cause. The other two war books were reduced by censorship to rather dull military reports. In his only poem dealing directly with the war, "August 1914," Masefield describes England's young men who, when war was declared:

> sadly rose and left the well-loved Downs,
> And so by ship to sea, and knew no more
> The fields of home, the byres, the market towns,
> Nor the dear outline of the English shore,
>
> But knew the misery of the soaking trench,
> The freezing in the rigging, the despair

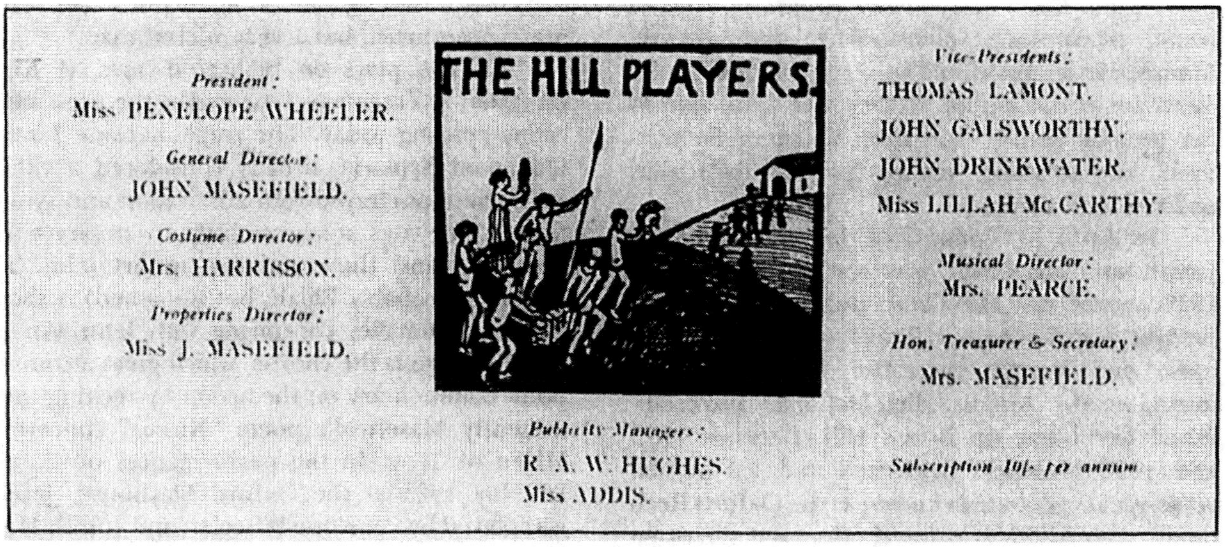

Flier for the Boar's Hill theater company that Masefield helped to organize in 1922

In the revolting second of the wrench
When the blind soul is flung upon the air,

And died (uncouthly, most) in foreign lands,
For some idea but dimly understood
Of an English city never built by hands
Which love of England prompted and made good.

During his first wartime lecture trip to America, Masefield met in New York City, after a lecture on 28 February 1916, Florence Lamont, wife of the financier and banker Thomas W. Lamont, a partner in the House of Morgan. The strong and enduring friendship which ensued lasted until her death in 1952. It is recorded in two thousand extant letters from Masefield to her, letters of wide-ranging interest including not only Masefield's opinions on literature, past and contemporary, but also opinions on British politics, two world wars, Anglo-American relations, and the social problems of England and America. In this important correspondence Masefield repeatedly expresses his compassion for the poor and his respect for the common man, the need (as he saw it) for Western man to return to simple country life and to reject the excessive commercialism of the ugly cities. He was an ardent royalist, and, during the abdication crisis of 1936, he took the side (together with Winston Churchill, but against the great majority of Englishmen) of Edward VIII and Wallis Simpson, saying that she "might have been the greatest Queen to the greatest King we ever had." Masefield was especially impressed by Edward VIII's determination to improve the lot of the Welsh coal miners.

Repeatedly expressed in these letters is the poet's passion for beauty wherever he found it—in nature, women, poetry, painting, music, sailing, ships—a passion reminiscent of that of his friend Robert Bridges, and, like Bridges, he frequently reveals his love for and knowledge of birds, flowers, trees, and the downs of England. The devastation wrought in parts of France by World War I is unforgettably depicted as he describes his tour of the battlefields of the Somme. The one good thing to come out of the war, he wrote to Florence shortly after his first American tour, was the improvement in Anglo-American relations: "We have wrangled with America ever since our German Court & King decided that America should be taxed. Well, it is time all that should end, & the very possibility of quarrel between us removed by an act of will. That is the thing I want to work at for the next few years." From this time on, Masefield usually had high praise for America. He wrote to Florence in 1923, "I like to see young Americans, for in them I look on the future of this civilized world."

Masefield was an indefatigable letter writer throughout his career, but especially in his later years, when he wrote hundreds of what Smith calls "affection-letters" to several women younger than himself, including Lucie Nicoll, the widow of a Hampshire farmer; Joyce King, editor of the *Malvern Gazette*; Rose Bruford, his protégée and a speaker of verse with whom he corresponded for forty-four years; Audrey Napier-Smith, a violinist; and others. Masefield's epistolary style is lively, picturesque, entertaining, and warmly human. His letters would be a contribution to the literature of his period if they were available to the general reader, but most of them lie scattered, unpublished, among private collections and research libraries.

In April 1917 Masefield, his wife, daughter Judith, and son Lewis, who was born on 4 July 1910, moved into Hill Crest, Boar's Hill, Oxford. Bridges and Sir Arthur Evans were their neighbors, and shortly thereafter Gilbert Murray moved nearby. Actress Lillah McCarthy also established her home on Boar's Hill. Between 1923 and 1929 Masefield organized and led annual verse-speaking contests known as the Oxford Recitations. But his chief cultural effort was the organizing of amateur theatricals in which his actress-daughter Judith took a leading part. Beginning in 1919 there were productions in the neighboring village of Wootton which included plays by Yeats, Anatole France, Shakespeare, and Euripides. In 1922 the Hill Players were formed. The list of vice-presidents included John Galsworthy and financier Thomas W. Lamont. In 1924, with the aid of Corliss Lamont and Thomas W. Lamont, a small theater was built close to Hill Crest which became known as the Music Room. Here until 1932 some noteworthy experimental plays, including Masefield's *Tristan and Isolt* and *The Trial of Jesus* and works by Yeats, Laurence Binyon, T. Sturge Moore, R. C. Trevelyan, and others were produced. Masefield's *A King's Daughter: A Tragedy in Verse* was performed at the nearby Oxford Playhouse in 1923.

Of Masefield's postwar plays, the most serious critical attention has been given to *Melloney Holtspur; or, The Pangs of Love*, a fantasy, melodrama, and ghost story concerned with the psychic and psychological influences of the misdeeds of the past generation on the present generation. Should the nephew of Melloney, a woman who had been betrayed in love by Lenda's father, be permitted to wed Lenda? The justice of imposing ancestral guilt on the young is fought out in this world and by the spirits of the departed. Critics praised Masefield for moving from naturalism toward "the romantic supernormalism of Barrie" and for his imaginative treatment of the theme of sin and atonement. But he was faulted for the too quickly achieved happy ending and for not facing up to the central ethical problem of the play—the interrelation of art and morality as stated by Melloney's description of her lover: "He was a marvellous artist, but a very wicked man."

Of the plays on biblical themes, *A King's Daughter: A Tragedy in Verse* makes the most interesting reading today. The tragic heroine Jezebel, Queen of Samaria, usually considered a villainess, is here portrayed with admiration and sympathy as she tries unsuccessfully to preserve her throne against the conniving upstart Jehu. The Prophet (probably Elijah, but unnamed) is shown as a troublemaker conspiring with Jehu. An unusual feature is the chorus, which gives a counterpoint commentary on the action by reciting intermittently Masefield's poem "Nireus" concerning Helen of Troy. In the performances on 25 and 26 May 1923 at the Oxford Playhouse, Jezebel was played by Penelope Wheeler, and Judith Masefield played the First Chorus.

Another work with a biblical theme is *The Trial of Jesus*, which was incorrectly attributed to George Bernard Shaw by the London press. After considerable trouble with the censor, the play was privately performed in 1925 at the Music Room, Boar's Hill, with Judith Masefield playing the part of Mary Magdalene. The work is written in prose and verse. The trial scene was criticized by some as being too realistic in its resemblance to a modern courtroom. Herod is portrayed as a skeptical sophisticate, Pilate as an able administrator reluctant to send Jesus to death but forced to do so for legal reasons. Jesus' humanity rather than his divinity is emphasized, which caused one reviewer to remark, "Masefield does not seem to have anything to tell the world about the divinity of Christ."

The high point of Masefield's experiments in religious drama was the performance of *The Coming of Christ* on 28 and 29 May 1928 in Canterbury Cathedral before audiences of six thousand. Written entirely in verse, the play was performed with music by Gustav Holst and costumes and design by Charles Ricketts. Spirits symbolizing Power, the Sword, Mercy, and Light attempt to dissuade Christ (here portrayed as Anima Christi) from assuming human form but support him after failing in their arguments. The play received widespread attention in the press, including stories of the rehearsals and performances and pictures in the London *Times*. Masefield's last play on a biblical subject, *Easter: A Play for Singers*, is, as its title suggests, more a tableau with music than a drama. Only fifteen pages in length, it is written in verse of mixed meters "for 12 voices and a quire of angels." After a lament

Masefield (left) and T. S. Eliot looking at the Caxton Chaucer (London Times)

over the corpse of Christ, there is a dialogue of two soldiers as they seal the grave, in which one states: "He had not any future but to die." A Resurrection scene follows.

Masefield, as well as reviewers, found flaws in the staging of *Tristan and Isolt: A Play in Verse* in 1927 by the Lena Ashwell Players in Bayswater. He wrote to Florence Lamont that it moved too slowly: "Passion isn't a funeral service." He went on to say, "The poetical theatre cannot be run on the lines of a commercial theatre. It needs a technique of its own." The *Times* reviewer considered Marc the most sympathetic character and criticized the author's harsh and unromantic treatment of Tristan and Isolt's lawless passion.

Masefield's verse play, *The End and Beginning*, which presents Mary Stuart's final day as a prisoner and her execution, was published in 1933. His last dramatic work, *A Play of St. George*, written in verse and prose, was published in 1948. Masefield modifies the legend somewhat. Saint George fights and kills the Sea Dragon, a pirate, thus freeing the princess who had been held for ransom. Saint George is killed on orders from Diocletian, but his spirit enters in the final scene on its way to paradise guided by spirits and dancers.

Armistice Day, 11 November 1918, found Masefield in London. Reunited with his family shortly thereafter at Boar's Hill, Masefield set to work on a series of long narrative poems. The first of these, *Reynard the Fox: or, The Ghost Heath Run*, was completed in May 1919 and published in October by Macmillan of New York in an edition of more than 2,000 copies and by Heinemann of London in an edition of 3,000 copies. Immediately successful, it was followed the next year by an illustrated edition of more than 3,000 copies in New York and in London by an illustrated edition of more than 5,000 copies.

Reynard the Fox is the most Chaucerian of all Masefield's narrative poems. It presents, like *The Canterbury Tales*, scenes and characters from various social levels of English country life, all described in loving detail, with compassion and humor, and with none of the bitterness and gloom of Masefield's four preceding narrative poems. The story ends happily. The protagonist escapes, and yet the hunters and hounds are satis-

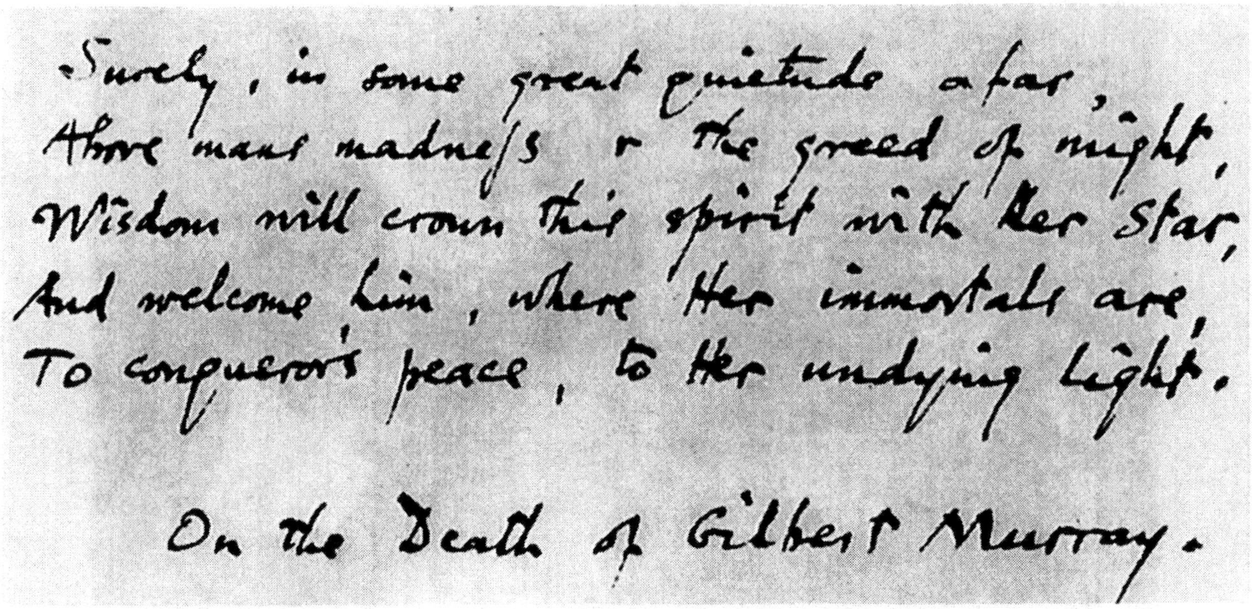
Surely, in some great quietude afar,
Above mans madness or the greed of might,
Wisdom will crown this spirit with Her Star,
And welcome him, where Her immortals are,
To conqueror's peace, to Her undying Light.

On the Death of Gilbert Murray.

Manuscript for "On the Death of Gilbert Murray" (Fisk University Library)

fied, for another fox with whom we are not emotionally involved is killed, the hunters believing that it is probably the fox they have been chasing throughout the day. Masefield said he chose this subject because "the fox-hunt gave an opportunity for a picture, or pictures, of the members of an English community. . . . At a fox-hunt and nowhere else in England, except, perhaps, at a funeral can you see the whole of the land's society brought together, focussed for the observor, as the Canterbury pilgrims were for Chaucer."

The poem is in two parts. Part one presents the preparations for the hunt at The Cock and Pye, a three-hundred-year-old inn, by means of a series of brilliant vignettes or thumbnail sketches of the participants. Part two presents the fox and describes the hunt. Among the participants and observers who assemble at the inn are huntsmen, grooms, stable hands, horse trainers, a publican, housemaids, a barmaid, children of various ages, several athletes including a former cricketer, gunners, beaters, a parson and his family, a clergyman, a doctor, a squire and other country gentry, several young ladies, a major, a colonel and several soldiers, a naval officer and a sailor, and many others. The characters are sharply and briefly individualized with Chaucerian precision and irony:

The parson and his sporting wife,
She was a stout one, full of life
With red, quick, kindly, manly face.
She held the knave, queen, king and ace,
She was no sister to the hen,
But fierce and minded to be queen.
She wore a coat and skirt of green,
A waistcoat cut of hunting red,
Her tie pin was a fox's head.

The parson was a manly one
His jolly eyes were bright with fun.
His jolly mouth was well inclined
To cry aloud his jolly mind
To everyone, in jolly terms.
He did not talk of churchyard worms,
But of our privilege as dust
To box a lively bout with lust
Ere going to heaven to rejoice.
He loved the sound of his own voice.

Reynard the Fox in his lair is introduced with the same picturesque precision:

there he berthed
Under the beech-roots snugly earthed,
With a roof of flint and a floor of chalk
And ten bitten hens' heads each on its stalk,
Some rabbits' paws, some fur from scuts,
A badger's corpse and a smell of guts.

The action begins when Reynard becomes aware of

A faint rank taint like April coming,
It cocked his ears and his blood went
drumming,
For somewhere out by Ghost Heath Stubs
Was a roving vixen wanting cubs.

Over the valley, floating faint
On a warmth of windflow came the taint,
He cocked his ears, he upped his brush,
And he went up wind like an April thrush.

Reynard is off to find the vixen; the hunters are off after Reynard; and a long and exciting chase follows through several counties, most of the story told from the viewpoint of the fox, with whom the reader identifies:

But the cry behind him made him chill,
They were nearer now and they meant to kill.
They meant to run him until his blood
Clogged on his heart as his brush with mud,
Till his back bent up and his tongue hung
flagging,
And his belly and brush were filthed from
dragging.
Till he crouched stone still, dead-beat and dirty,
With nothing but teeth against the thirty.
And all the way to that blinding end
He would meet with men and have none his friend.

Intense suspense is created when the hunters almost fail, and again when the fox is several times on the verge of death. The blackest moment for the hunters occurs when a rabbit hunter with his terrier crosses the trail and destroys the fox's scent. It is finally picked up again; Reynard, ready to drop with exhaustion, reaches his burrow only to find it blocked up with stone. He just staggers into a dark and thorny wood. The hounds come crashing after him, but they pick up the scent of another fox and Reynard is saved.

Reynard the Fox has been well received by critics and the reading public and is the most popular of Masefield's narrative poems. Sanford Sternlicht calls it an "exquisitely detailed and precise moving panorama of the English countryside at the turn of the century." The poem presents an unforgettable picture of English country life and an exciting chase, but there is another dimension to it. Written immediately after the devastation of World War I, *Reynard the Fox* is a poem about survival, about the survival of Western man as well as about the survival of a fox, as Masefield makes clear in his 1962 introduction to the poem. Yet Masefield's allegorical intention in no way lessens the interest in the surface story, the story of a fox who survived the worst assaults of his enemies.

Enslaved (1920) appeared within a year of the publication of *Reynard the Fox*. It is the story of a beautiful girl stolen by pirates from her home in rural England. Her lover follows the pirate ship and permits himself to be imprisoned as a galley slave so that he can be near his loved one. The girl is imprisoned in the harem of a caliph of Morocco, but the lover, with the help of a fellow prisoner, an Englishman named Gerard, escapes from confinement. Together they free the girl but are captured near the palace by the caliph and are condemned to torture and death. Gerard in an eloquent speech tells the story of the two lovers to the caliph, who, moved by compassion and admiration for the strength of the bonds of love and friendship among the foreign Englishmen, allows them to go free together with a fourth captive who had befriended them. The story is suspenseful, but somewhat sentimental and hardly believable. The poetry, written in a variety of meters, is not Masefield's best.

John Masefield, portrait by Sir John Lavery

Masefield's next narrative poem, *Right Royal* (1920), is the story of a horse race told with gusto and excitement. Charles Cothill, owner of the steeplechase horse Right Royal, is moved by a dream in which his horse, apotheosized "like a pearl on fire," speaks to him saying, "It is my day." He mortgages his home and bets all his money on his horse to win, although the odds are strongly against him. His fiancée, Emily, is distressed, for she is opposed to gambling because her father lost all his money on the races. Nevertheless, she loyally supports her lover. Cothill rides his own horse. The course is a dangerous one, more than three miles in length, with numerous obstacles, all of which are described in detail. Cothill suffers a fall that leaves him thirty lengths behind, and a collision with another horse that almost throws him again. But he perseveres until the end. The outcome, on which his marriage and his future happiness depend, is in doubt until the last second, when Right Royal wins. The poem is inferior to *Reynard the Fox* not because of its conception or its structure, but because of the mediocrity of the verse and the lack of a serious theme.

King Cole (1921), Masefield's last important long narrative poem, tells the fairy tale of the legendary King Cole who, granted life everlasting, has chosen to walk this earth bringing beauty and hope into the lives of downtrodden men. In Masefield's poem the king, disguised as a strolling musician—"His old hat stuck with never-withering green, / His flute in poke, and little singings sweet / Coming from birds that flutter at his feet"—transforms, by his magic, a down-at-heels small-town circus into a resplendent show, glittering with supernaturally imparted beauty and attended by the prince and queen. As always in Masefield's poetry, the narrative line is interestingly maintained, but the characterization is weak and the verse stereotyped.

In the 1920s Masefield's popularity rapidly increased. In 1922 he received an honorary degree from Oxford, and in the following year degrees from Aberdeen, Glasgow, and Manchester universities. According to Constance Babington Smith, the 1923 Heinemann edition of *The Collected Poems of John Masefield* sold eighty thousand copies. His novels *Sard Harker* (1924) and *Odtaa* (1926) were also popular. In May 1930 he was appointed poet laureate to succeed Robert Bridges, and that fall he gave his first speech as laureate at Hereford, where he was made freeman of the city. He continued to receive honorary degrees from the universities—Liverpool and St. Andrews in 1930, Cambridge in 1931, and Wales in 1932. In the spring of 1933 Masefield and his family left Hill Crest to move to a Cotswold Manor house, Pinbury Park. During the 1930s Masefield, who took his duties as poet laureate seriously, engaged in public lectures and poetry readings in England and abroad. His travels included trips to America, Australia, Europe, and the West Indies. In 1936 he delivered the Commemorative Ode at Harvard's tercentenary celebrations. He championed such causes as wildlife preservation at Hawksmoor Nature Preserve, and he gave poetry readings in Gloucestershire to raise funds for young vagrants. On his recommendation an annual award, The Royal Medal for Poetry, was established to be given for a first or second volume of verse or to a poet under the age of thirty-five. The Order of Merit was awarded to him in George V's birthday honors of 1935. He became president of the Society of Authors in 1937 and was awarded the Hanseatic Shakespeare Prize at the University of Hamburg in 1938. During this decade he had published at least eight novels, of which the two sea stories *The Bird of Dawning* (1933) and *Victorious Troy: or, The Hurrying Angel* (1935) are generally considered the best, and five volumes of verse including *The Wanderer of Liverpool* (essay and verse, 1930), *Minnie Maylow's Story and Other Tales and Scenes* (1931), *A Tale of Troy* (1932), *A Letter from Pontus and Other Verse* (1936), and *Some Verses to Some Germans* (1939). He also wrote a series of books for young people including *The Box of Delights: or When the Wolves Were Running* (1935). In the spring of 1939, the Masefields gave up their home, Pinbury Park, and moved to their final residence, Burcote Brook, in the village of Clifton Hampden, near Oxford.

The years of World War II were darkened for Masefield by the death of his only son, Lewis, who was killed in the African desert in 1942. The decade of the 1940s saw Masefield still active in writing and having published a variety of verse and prose, including three novels of medieval life—*Basilissa: A Tale of the Empress Theodora* (1940), *Conquer: A Tale of the Nika Rebellion in Byzantium* (1941), and *Badon Parchments* (1947)—and two autobiographical books—*In the Mill* (1941) and *New Chum* (1944). His new volumes of verse included *Guatama the Enlightened and Other Verse* (1941), *Natalie Maisie and Pavilastukay: Two Tales in Verse* (1942), and *Wonderings: Between One and Six Years* (1943), autobiographical verse.

In the 1950s Masefield continued his autobiographical writings with *So Long to Learn: Chapters of an Autobiography* (1952). Toward the end of this decade he took part in a pioneer experiment sponsored by the American Academy of Poets by reciting his long narrative poem *The Story of Ossian* for a long-playing phonograph record. During the final decade of his life, the poet laureate wrote obituary tributes in verse for President

John F. Kennedy and T. S. Eliot. For *The Bluebells and Other Verse* (1961) he received the William Fogle Poetry Prize. His *Old Raiger and Other Verse* (1964) was awarded a prize by the National Book League. His final autobiographical volume, *Grace Before Ploughing: Fragments of Autobiography*, was published in 1966. His last book, a volume of poems titled *In Glad Thanksgiving*, was published in 1966. Masefield died at his home, Burcote Brook, on 12 May 1967. His ashes were deposited in the Poet's Corner at Westminster Abbey.

With the Georgians, John Masefield effected a change in literary taste involving a reversion to the language and the experience of the common man similar to that preached but not always practiced by Wordsworth a century earlier. His most important contributions to the poetry of the twentieth century are several short lyrics—"Sea Fever," "Cargoes," "August 1914," and "On Growing Old"; the three long narrative poems—*The Everlasting Mercy, Dauber*, and *Reynard the Fox*; and at least two poems of medium length—"The Wanderer" and "The River." But not to be forgotten was the power for more than half a century of the personal presence of Masefield as an exemplar of the engaged poet, committed to teaching the young and improving their taste in poetry; committed also to arousing popular interest in poetry throughout the English-speaking world and to using the written and spoken word to protest social and economic injustice.

Letters:

Letters of John Masefield to Florence Lamont, edited by Corliss Lamont and Lansing Lamont (New York: Columbia University Press, 1979);

Letters to Reyna / John Masefield, edited by William Buchan (London: Buchan & Enright, 1983);

John Masefield: Letters to Margaret Bridges (1915-1919), edited by Donald E. Stanford (Manchester, U.K.: Carcanet Press, 1984);

John Masefield's Letters from the Front (1915-1917), edited by Peter Vansittart (London: Constable, 1984).

Bibliographies:

Henry Woodd Nevinson, *John Masefield: an Appreciation, Together With a Bibliography* (London: Heinemann, 1931);

Charles Herbert Simmons, *A Bibliography of John Masefield* (New York: Columbia University Press, 1931);

Geoffrey Handley-Taylor, comp., *John Masefield, O.M.: The Queen's Poet Laureate, a Bibliography and Eighty-First Birthday Tribute* (London: Crambrook Tower Press, 1960).

Biography:

Constance Babington Smith, *John Masefield: A Life* (Oxford: Oxford University Press, 1978).

References:

Francis Berry, *John Masefield: The Narrative Poet* (Sheffield, U.K.: University of Sheffield, 1967);

Fraser B. Drew, *John Masefield's England: A Study of the National Themes in His Work* (Cranbury, N.J.: Associated University Presses, 1973);

June Dwyer, *John Masefield* (New York: Ungar, 1987);

Margery Fisher, *John Masefield* (London: Bodley Head, 1963);

William Hamilton Hamilton, *John Masefield: a Critical Study* (London: Allen & Unwin, 1922);

Corliss Lamont, *Remembering John Masefield* (Rutherford, N.J.: Fairleigh Dickinson University Press, 1971);

John Edward Mason, *John Masefield* (Exeter, U.K.: Paternoster Press, 1938);

Muriel Spark, *John Masefield* (London: Nevill, 1953);

Sanford Sternlicht, *John Masefield* (Boston: Twayne, 1977);

Lionel Stevenson, "Masefield and the New Universe," *Sewanee Review*, 37 (July 1929): 336-348;

Leonard Alfred George Strong, *John Masefield* (London: Longmans, Green, 1952).

Papers:

Masefield's papers are in the Bodleian Library, Oxford; Harry Ransom Humanities Research Center, University of Texas, Austin; Houghton Library, Harvard University; Berg Collection, New York Public Library; Yale University Library; and in other libraries and private collections. See Constance Babington Smith's *John Masefield: A Life*, pp. 229-231, for a more complete list.

H. H. Munro
(Saki)

(18 December 1870 - 14 November 1916)

This entry was written by Maureen Modlish for DLB 34: British Novelists, 1890-1929: Traditionalists.

BOOKS: *The Rise of the Russian Empire* (London: Richards, 1900);

The Westminster Alice (London: Westminster Gazette, 1902; New York: Viking, 1929);

Reginald (London: Methuen, 1904; New York: McBride, 1922);

Reginald in Russia, and Other Sketches (London: Methuen, 1910);

The Chronicles of Clovis (London & New York: John Lane, 1912; New York: Viking, 1927);

The Unbearable Bassington (London & New York: John Lane, 1912; New York: Viking, 1928);

When William Came: A Story of London under the Hohenzollerns (London & New York: John Lane, 1914; New York: Viking, 1929);

Beasts and Super-Beasts (London & New York: John Lane, 1914; New York: Viking, 1928);

The Toys of Peace, and Other Papers (London & New York: John Lane, 1919; New York: Viking, 1928);

Reginald and Reginald in Russia (London: John Lane/Bodley Head, 1921; New York: Viking, 1928);

The Square Egg, and Other Sketches, With Three Plays (London: John Lane, 1924; New York: Viking, 1929).

Collection: *The Works of Saki,* 8 volumes (London: John Lane/Bodley Head, 1926-1927; New York: Viking, 1927-1929).

H. H. Munro (photograph by E. O. Hoppé)

Hector Hugh Munro (Saki), one of many British writers to perish during World War I, is thought to have died before his writing attained its full potential. While he wrote short stories throughout his career, he eventually turned to writing novels and plays as well, seeking a genre with a larger scope than that of the short story, which, as he conceived it, was too limited to allow either for character development or for the sustained treatment of issues, particularly the issue of Britain's national survival. The single situation that engages attention through clever plot turns and witticisms in his short stories becomes in his novels one of a series whose variety allows for more extensive development of character and theme in the novels.

Hector Hugh Munro was born in Akyab, Burma, the third child of Charles Augustus Munro, a career officer in the British army, and

Munro with his sister, Ethel; sister-in-law, Muriel; niece, Felicia; and brother, Charles, 1908

Mary Frances Mercer Munro, who died in winter 1872. Deciding that it was impossible to raise three small children in Burma, C. A. Munro left Ethel, Charles, and Hector with his widowed mother and two unmarried sisters at Broadgate Villa, a large house that he rented in Pilton, near Barnstaple in Devonshire. Broadgate's comforts, which included servants, a governess, gardens, and access to the coast of North Devon, were overshadowed for Hector by his sickliness and the presence of his aunts, from whose bickering and strict governance there was little relief.

By comparison to his childhood at Broadgate, Munro's attendance at Pencarwick, a boarding school in Exmouth, was pleasant. He "was very happy there," his sister wrote, but a year later at the age of fourteen he was sent to Bedford Grammar School in Bedfordshire, which was stricter but acceptable to Munro, who attended the school for four terms. Yet his public-school education, which confirmed his membership in the English upper class, did not modify his skepticism about its pretenses. Rather, his schooling contributed to a facility with language, which would enable him to cast his skepticism into stories the upper class would read. As J. C. Squire observes, "he polished his sentences with a spinsterish passion for neatness and chose his words as the last of the dandies might choose his ties." In his fiction, through deft turnings of plot and phrase, Munro assures that his upper-class characters will be found wanting in generosity, honesty, and common sense.

Having retired from service in the East, C. A. Munro took his children on several trips to Europe during the years 1887-1890, and in late 1890 the rest of the family went to live at Heanton Court in Devonshire, where, for the next two years, after their brother had left to join the Burmese police, Munro and his sister were tutored by their father. In June 1893 Munro went to Burma, where his father had procured a post for him in the military police. He seems to have been as unenthusiastic about it as the cynical young dandy, Comus, is about his West African post in *The Unbearable Bassington* (1912). After contracting malaria Munro resigned his post and in August 1894 returned to Devonshire for a lengthy convalescence, during which he had the leisure to consider the idiocies

Munro in the enlisted man's uniform of the 22nd Battalion, Royal Fusiliers

of colonial bureaucrats, who were destined to number among his characters, and to become more acquainted with the lore and superstitions of Devonshire, which influenced him in writing stories such as "The Music of the Hill." These features, together with his estimation of propriety as pragmatic rather than moral in motive and his ferocious irony, are prominent in many of his short stories.

In 1896 he left for London to become a writer. By 1899, after several false starts, he had begun his first project, a history of medieval Russia, an indication of his youthful ambitions as well as of his capacity for hard work. He wished to be acknowledged as a professional historian by other historians. Subsidized by his family, he spent hours reading books in Russian in the British Museum Reading Room, completing the history in 1899. But *The Rise of the Russian Empire* (1900), while well-enough received by lay reviewers, was dismissed by the professionals as confused, flippant about religion, and sarcastic, in short, bad historiography. It was his first and last venture into history, but from it he gained knowledge which would be useful to him when he became a foreign correspondent for the London *Morning Post.*

The heresies noted by the historians were to be turned on the class to which the historians belonged in the satires he began to write in 1900 to accompany the illustrations of the political cartoonist F. Carruthers Gould for the *Westminster Gazette.* For these satires he adopted the pen name Saki, the name of the cupbearer to the gods in the *Rubáiyát of Omar Khayyám.*

The *Westminster Alice* sketches, published in the *Gazette* in 1900 (eleven were collected in a book in 1902), were followed by another, less successful, series. The "Not So Stories," a series published in the *Gazette* in 1902, parodied Parliament by imitating the form of Rudyard Kipling's *Just So Stories* (1902). Midway through the series, the title was changed to "The Political Jungle Book," further strengthening the connection with Kipling. In 1903 Munro began the Reginald series. Reginald comments extend from political satire to broader criticisms of the upper class, but the Reginald sketches are remembered more for their witticisms than for their satire: "Why are women so fond of raking up the past? They're as bad as tailors, who invariably remember what you owe them for a suit long after you've ceased to wear it." As in his short stories, the wit of the satirist diverts attention from the objects of criticism to the cleverness of the critic. Saki's novels suffer less from this circumstance.

The Reginald sketches appeared in the *Gazette* while Munro was a foreign correspondent for the *Morning Post,* an assignment which took him to the Balkans in late 1902, to Serbia and Poland in 1904, and then to St. Petersburg, Russia, in autumn 1904. Remaining there until late 1906, he was a witness to the Bloody Sunday massacre in St. Petersburg on 22 January 1905 and to political intrigues of the kind he dramatized in his play *The Death Trap* (posthumously published in *The Square Egg,* 1924). On 10 May 1906 he reported on the first session of the Russian Duma, the newly constituted governing body of Russia, formed in the wake of the 1905 rebellion, before his transfer to Paris. The Balkans and Russia remained a part of his imagination, recurring through characters with Russian and Slavic names, and forming the substance of *Reginald in Russia* (1910).

After returning briefly to England in May 1907 to be at his father's deathbed, he went back

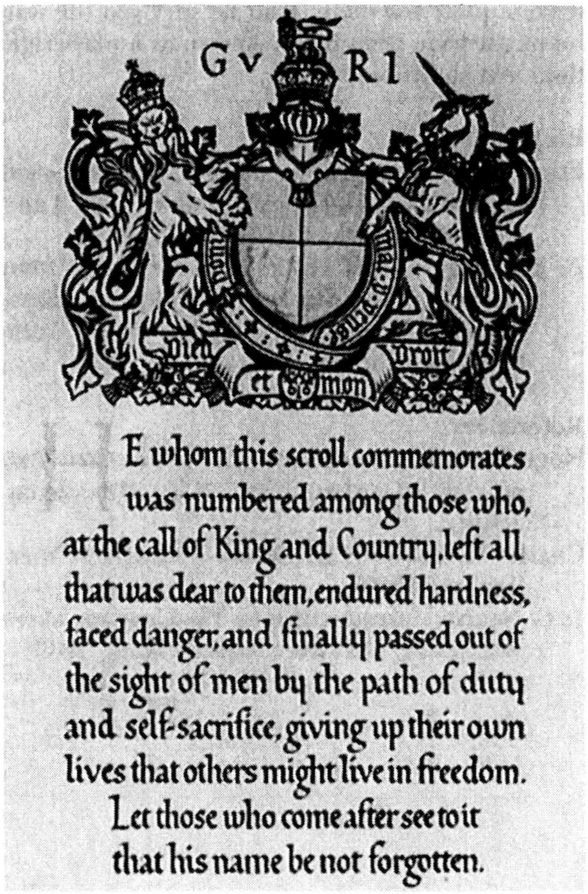

E whom this scroll commemorates
was numbered among those who,
at the call of King and Country, left all
that was dear to them, endured hardness,
faced danger, and finally passed out of
the sight of men by the path of duty
and self-sacrifice, giving up their own
lives that others might live in freedom.
Let those who come after see to it
that his name be not forgotten.

Memorial scroll sent by the king to Munro's family

to France, but in 1908 he resigned to become a free-lance writer. His stories became regular features in the *Gazette,* the *Morning Post,* and the *Bystander* until 1914. *The Chronicles of Clovis* (1912), one of several collections of his short stories, was followed by his first novel, *The Unbearable Bassington.* The title refers to Comus Bassington, and aptly describes him. Like many of Saki's upper-class characters, he is clever, cynical, self-indulgent, and self-destructive. The source of his decadence is suggested by the characterization of his widowed mother, Francesca Bassington, who "if pressed in an unguarded moment to describe her soul would probably have described her drawing-room." To assure her continued financial security, as well as her son's, she twice attempts to arrange suitable marriages for Comus, but each time his misbehavior ruins the match. She then attempts to find him suitable employment. A post is procured for him in West Africa, where he dies. Toward the end of the novel both Comus and his mother become dimly aware that their values have betrayed them, have undermined whatever potential there might have been for them to discover their importance to one another. In a final blow, Francesca learns that her Van der Meulen painting, the most prized of all the possessions in her drawing room, is a copy. Saki's critics, such as Charles H. Gillen, tend to regard this ending as gratuitously cruel.

When William Came (1914), while peopled with Saki's bores, politicos, cynics, and socially ambitious women, is distinctive among his works for its directness and seriousness. The malice with which Saki assails the English upper class seems less gratuitous in *When William Came* than in his short stories, in which the petty consequences of blundering and selfishness seem too unimportant to warrant Saki's violence. In this novel, however, the same upper-class proclivities have resulted in tragedy, the acquiescence of Britain to Germany. It is as if prior to its writing, Saki observed the inadequacies of the upper class but was unable to attribute dire consequences to them, at least unable to do so with conviction. The novel is set in the near future. Its upper-class protagonist, Murrey Yeovil, returns from Russia to England to learn the significance of England's conquest by Germany to language, art, daily activities, and to his own life. His wife, Cicely, as socially ambitious as ever, has begun to cultivate the conquerors. Her rationalizations and Yeovil's own apologies for retiring to the country rather than fighting the Germans are more subtly realized than anything else in Saki's writing. The Tory slant of the book is reminiscent of Tory arguments against financial interests and Tory anxieties about the decline of taste which surfaced during and after the accession of William and Mary in 1688. The novel has several minor heroic figures, each of whom gives to Yeovil his account of the conquest and response to it, and ends with unnamed heroes, the boy scouts who are supposed to honor the new king with a parade, but who do not appear. With England's involvement in World War I only a year away, the observation of a young clergyman, one of the novel's few heroic characters, seems appropriate: "I have learned one thing in life, and that is that peace is not for this world. Peace is what God gives us when He takes us into His rest. Beat your sword into a ploughshare if you like, but beat your enemy into smithereens first." For all its strengths *When William Came* is propaganda, and its causes and prejudices, which Saki forwards without question, are those of the upper class. His disagreement was not with the existence of the upper class, but with the failure of its members to take social responsibility more seriously than they took their privileges.

In 1914 he finished a collaboration with Cyril Maude on a play, *The Watched Pot,* a surprisingly lighthearted comedy of manners in the tradition of Richard Brinsley Sheridan, and fired a parting shot at George Bernard Shaw with *Beasts and Super-Beasts,* a collection of short stories. When war was declared in August 1914, Munro enlisted. He was killed in action on 14 November 1916.

Although he is best known for his fiction, drama seems to be the genre best suited to Munro's abilities. His plays show his strengths—witty dialogue, complexity of plot, and energetic pace—to advantage, while his weaknesses, which appear in his fiction as gratuitous witticisms and pompous asides in the narrative, are absent from his plays. In the traditional dramatic form there is no place for such weaknesses, and his extant plays give no indication that he was inclined to make a place for them. Had he survived the war, he might have been better known as a playwright than as a short-story writer.

Biographies:

Ethel Munro, "Biography of Saki," in *The Square Egg, and Other Sketches* (London: John Lane, 1924; New York: Viking, 1929);

A. J. Langguth, *Saki: A Life of Hector Hugh Munro with Six Short Stories Never Before Collected* (London: Hamilton, 1981; New York: Simon & Schuster, 1981).

References:

Noel Coward, Introduction to *The Complete Works of Saki* (Garden City, N.Y.: Doubleday, 1976);

Charles H. Gillen, *H. H. Munro (Saki)* (New York: Twayne, 1969);

J. C. Squire, Introduction to *The Complete Novels and Plays of Saki* (New York: Viking, 1945).

George William Russell
(Æ)

(10 April 1867 - 17 July 1935)

This entry was updated by Henry Summerfield (University of Victoria) from his entry in DLB 19: British Poets, 1880-1914.

George William Russell (Æ), 1923 (photograph by Simson)

SELECTED BOOKS: *Homeward: Songs by the Way* (Dublin: Whaley, 1894; Portland, Maine: Mosher, 1895);

The Earth Breath and Other Poems (New York & London: John Lane/Bodley Head, 1897);

The Divine Vision and Other Poems (London & New York: Macmillan, 1904);

Co-operation and Nationality (Dublin: Maunsel, 1912; New York: Norman, Remington, 1913);

Collected Poems (London: Macmillan, 1913; New York: Macmillan, 1915; enlarged, 1919; enlarged again, 1926; enlarged again, London: Macmillan, 1935);

Imaginations and Reveries (Dublin & London: Maunsel, 1915; New York: Macmillan, 1916);

The National Being (Dublin & London: Maunsel, 1916; New York: Macmillan, 1930);

The Candle of Vision (London: Macmillan, 1918; New York: Macmillan, 1919);

The Interpreters (London: Macmillan, 1922; New York: Macmillan, 1923);

Voices of the Stones (London: Macmillan, 1925; New York: Macmillan, 1925);

Vale and Other Poems (London: Macmillan, 1931; New York: Macmillan, 1931);

Song and Its Fountains (London: Macmillan, 1932; New York: Macmillan, 1932);

The Avatars (London: Macmillan, 1933; New York: Macmillan, 1933);

The House of the Titans and Other Poems (London: Macmillan, 1934; New York: Macmillan, 1934);

Selected Poems (London: Macmillan, 1935; New York: Macmillan, 1935);

The Living Torch, edited by Monk Gibbon (London: Macmillan, 1937; New York: Macmillan, 1938);

Selections from the Contributions to the Irish Homestead, 2 volumes, edited by Henry Summerfield (Gerrards Cross, U.K.: Colin Smythe, 1978);

The Descent of the Gods, Comprising the Mystical Writings of G. W. Russell, "A. E.," edited by Baghavan Iyer and Nandini Iyer (Gerrards Cross, U.K.: Colin Smythe, 1988).

Although George William Russell (who wrote under the pseudonym Æ) was a prolific writer in prose and verse, he is more often remembered as a cause of creativity in others than as a distinguished author. For about four decades his influence fertilized the Irish Literary Renaissance, and his promotion of the cooperative ideal contributed much to a noble attempt by Sir Horace Plunkett and his supporters to make Ireland at once more efficient and more humane. As a mystic, he described—more successfully in prose than in verse—his exploration of supersensible realms. Finally, the near perfection of his character has left its impress on many published memoirs.

Russell was born in Lurgan, County Armagh, the youngest of three children of Thomas and Marianne Russell, members of the (Episcopal) Church of Ireland. In 1878 the family moved to the more stimulating environment of Dublin. During his youth, George's overwhelming ambition was to become an artist, but equally significant were his questioning of Christianity and a certain spiritual awakening. At about the age of fourteen, it occurred to him that God had no right to penalize him for failing to do anything he had not agreed to undertake. Two or three years later, he began to see visions, some of them containing figures of almost inconceivable grandeur, recognizable as ancient Irish gods. These visions were associated with an adoration of nature which remained lifelong. A thinker by temperament, Russell brooded over his visions and became preoccupied with the character of the human soul. Combining his obsessions, he tried to paint a myth of his own invention representing the spiritual evolution of humanity. In mid 1884, in a class at the Metropolitan School of Art in Dublin, Russell met the young poet William Butler Yeats, who had similar preoccupations, and a year later he found himself moving in the newly emerged circle of young Dublin theosophists, among whom Yeats was one of the leading spirits. Russell, however, distrusted spiritual organizations and did not become a member of the Theosophical Lodge until 1889 or 1890. In 1888 he explained his views in a letter to the editor of *Lucifer* signed "Aeon": the printer could read only the first two letters, and so Russell acquired his pseudonym. His detachment from family life at this time is reflected in his complaint, when John Eglinton refused to join him on Christmas Day for their usual walk, that a Christmas dinner was a genuine example of tragedy in human life.

The years 1890 to 1897 form a distinct period in Æ's biography. In 1890 he took a job as a cashier at a Dublin drapery store named Pim's, and in 1891 he began, with several other dedicated theosophists, to reside at the Theosophical Lodge, which became known as "the Household." For seven years he devoted his days to business and his free time to spiritual study, meditation, and attempts to propagate the faith. His fellow theosophist H. F. Norman afterward recalled, "Æ was *aflame* with Theosophy then."

When Æ committed himself to Theosophy, he renounced the practice of the arts as tending to weaken the will, but, like Hopkins's renunciation, Æ's did not prove permanent. He was soon painting fine murals of spirit forms to adorn the walls of the lodge and contributing prose and verse to its monthly journal, the *Irish Theosophist*. In 1894 his friend Charles Weekes published Æ's first volume of lyrics, *Homeward: Songs by the Way*. It is prefaced by a brief prose statement: "I moved among men and places, and in living I learned the truth at last. I know I am a spirit, and that I went forth in old time from the Self-ancestral to labours yet unaccomplished; but filled ever and again with homesickness I made these songs by the way." The keynote of the book is struck at the beginning of the untitled prelude—

> Oh, be not led away,
> Lured by the colour of the sun-rich day.
> The gay romance of song
> Unto the spirit life doth not belong . . .

Æ sings of moments of visionary perception associated with nature and especially with dawn and dusk, and he explores the tension between the magnetism of the heavenly realms and the seductiveness of earthly pleasures. To some of his contemporaries, Æ's poems opened a new world, but for the most part later readers tend to find their rhythms monotonous, their poetic diction hackneyed, and their images repetitive and cloudy. Terms for the spiritual entities derived from the One, such as "the Mighty Mother" and "Light of Lights," seem unattractively vague, even though, like the Hindu names Æ also employs, they had for him exact theosophical meanings. In spite of these faults, however, each of Æ's collections contains a few pieces charged with a vitality that has not faded.

At the beginning of 1895, an American named James Pryse arrived at the Dublin Theosophical Lodge, and he rapidly became Æ's guru. Pryse not only gave him spiritual instruction, sometimes by mentally concentrating on certain images which his disciple could see and describe, but encouraged him in his poetry and painting.

Æ's March 1891 drawing of Charles A. Weekes, the friend to whom he dedicated his first volume of poems

A month or two after Pryse's arrival, Æ produced a theosophical interpretation of Gaelic mythology, which was published in the *Irish Theosophist* in March and April of 1895. This work was the first sign that he was beginning to take an interest in Irish culture. He and Pryse shared a preoccupation with ancient spiritual initiations, and they believed that the Druids had practiced them. In 1896, after Pryse had returned to America, Æ and his fellow disciples came to believe that an avatar, a mortal incarnation of a higher being, was about to appear in Ireland. Æ's new concerns are apparent in *The Earth Breath and Other Poems* (1897), in which he relates life and pain on earth to their meaning in the light of the godlike nature of man's hidden essence. Those poems, such as "The Robing of the King," which describe revelations of that essence in the form of heroic, many-colored figures fail to capture the grandeur of Æ's conception; but in the noble monologue "The Man to the Angel" he draws a fine contrast between the suffering, imperfect human and the flawless, yet limited, spirit who has never fallen. The poet seems more clearly aware of the solid earth than in *Homeward*, and occasionally the images take on a crisp clarity, as in these lines from "In the Womb":

> Still rests the heavy share on the dark soil:
> Upon the black mould thick the dew-damp lies:
> The horse waits patient: from his lowly toil
> The ploughboy to the morning lifts his eyes.

He begins, too, in such poems as "Illusion" and "Dream Love," to write of romantic passion, but always as a dazzling lure to be resisted. He had expected to remain celibate, but to his distress he found that he was falling in love with his fellow theosophist Violet North, and she with him.

In November 1897 Æ changed his way of life by accepting a full-time position in Horace Plunkett's Irish Agricultural Organization Society, whose function was to improve the lives of Ireland's poverty-stricken farmers by promoting cooperative societies of several kinds. Æ's first task was to travel in the west of Ireland and urge groups of uneducated, debt-ridden peasants to start cooperative credit banks. To accomplish this aim, he had to overcome his initial depression at the extreme poverty he encountered. The following spring, Plunkett promoted him to assistant secretary of the organization, a post which reduced the time he spent outside Dublin, and on 11 June he married Violet North at a registry office.

From 1898 to 1905, Æ led a richly varied private life. Having seceded from what he considered the degenerating Theosophical Society, he formed his own Hermetic Society in which to instruct the Dublin theosophists. Despite a certain disdain on the part of Yeats, he also fostered a large group of Irish writers including James Stephens, Padraic Colum, and Seamas O'Sullivan. (Among his discoveries in later years were Austin Clarke and Patrick Kavanagh.) When James Joyce brought him his poems, Æ noticed that this proud youth wrote "amazingly well in prose." Equally important was Æ's contribution to the development of the Irish National Theatre Society; here his organizational ability proved more valuable than his own play, *Deirdre*, produced in 1902. His cultural nationalism, which led him to support home rule for Ireland, found expression in his miscellaneous journalism, and he began to

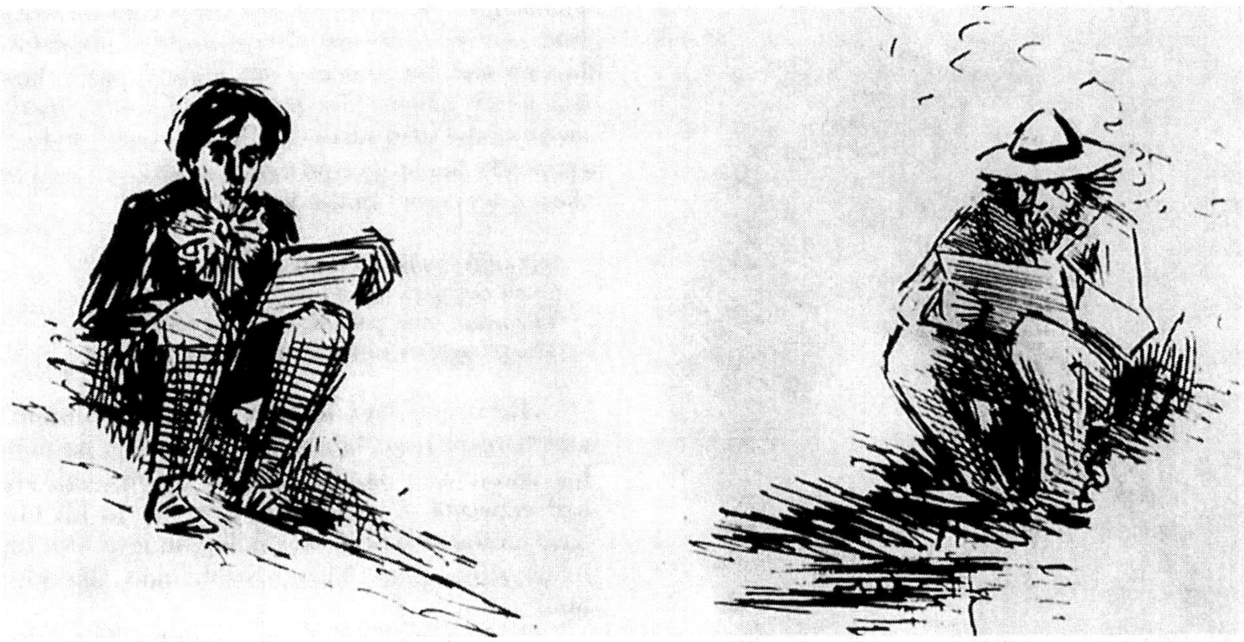

William Butler Yeats and Æ sketching; drawing by Æ (Sotheby Parke Bernet, 15 December 1982)

take an annual holiday in the west of Ireland, where he painted landscapes and the spirits of his visions. He found time to bring out his third collection of poems in 1904.

The Divine Vision and Other Poems reflects Æ's new experience of his native land and her people and the feeling he had acquired for her folklore and mythology. In all of these, he tries to perceive the spiritual core that theosophy tells him of and that his visions intermittently reveal to him, but in poems such as "The Voice of the Waters" he does not neglect to evoke the natural image which is the starting point of his meditation:

Where the Greyhound River windeth through
  a loneliness so deep,
Scarce a wild fowl shakes the quiet that the purple
  boglands keep,
Only God exults in silence over fields no man may
  reap.

In some ways Æ's pleasantest book of verse, *The Divine Vision* is limited in its achievement by drowsy, repetitive rhythms, though these occasionally awaken into a charming lilt. There are more love poems to Violet North, among which "Ordeal" is distinguished for its poignant expression of the reluctant lover's anguish.

In 1905 Æ was appointed editor of the *Irish Homestead,* the independent weekly which existed to support the agricultural cooperative movement. In his editorials and "Notes of the Week," he defended cooperative principles against hostile politicians and berated the less admirable farmers for vices ranging from the dishonesty that allowed them to adulterate their butter to the laziness that made them prefer pasturage to tillage. Gradually he developed a lucid, hard-hitting style and showed a surprising gift for satirical irony and humor. Incorporating many of the graver passages from his articles but omitting his vivid sketches of incidents from contemporary life, Æ compiled the short book *Co-operation and Nationality* (1912). In this tract he outlines a program for freeing the farmers from debt, imbuing them with self-reliance, and encouraging them to develop a rural civilization capable of stemming the drift to the cities. Four years later, he published *The National Being,* an expanded treatment of these ideas. In this longer volume, he calls for a union of rural and urban cooperators and proposes that each occupation should be governed by its own representative council, leaving the elected parliament to mediate between conflicting interests and control national affairs. This prescription for a combination of economic and political democracy in a form suited to the Irish national character was his most influential publication—in 1923 it was even reissued in India.

Æ's married life had begun happily, but it was soon marred by the deaths of his firstborn child—a son—in 1899 and of his only daughter in 1901. He began to drift away from his wife emotionally and left to her the task of bringing up their two surviving sons. In time, she became jealous of Æ's affection for Susan Mitchell, the witty assistant editor of the *Irish Homestead*.

Æ's well-established literary reputation made it worthwhile for Macmillan to publish his *Collected Poems* in 1913. The volume, which was received with much acclaim, comprised, with some omissions, the contents of the three earlier books and twenty-one hitherto uncollected pieces. Some of the new poems reflect Æ's sharpened awareness of life as it was lived in Dublin's slums—an awareness which made him risk his position in the strictly nonpolitical cooperative movement by writing to the press in defense of the workers participating in the great Dublin strike of 1913. The famous "On Behalf of Some Irishmen Not Followers of Tradition" defies, with fine clarity, obscurantist attachment to the Gaelic past. The most beautiful of the new lyrics, however, is "The Virgin Mother," a eulogy of the female principle written in four sentences, each consisting of a five-line stanza with its individual rhythmic pattern.

By this period, Æ was something of an institution in Dublin. While much of his poetry has faded in the eyes of posterity and his prose has been widely neglected, the near perfection of his character has inspired an astonishing quantity of tributes in the memoirs of wondering admirers. The radiant tranquillity which they praise was accompanied by a power to lift others into his own spiritual region and make them share his consciousness of a higher world, to them unseen, coexisting with the visible universe. To Henry Wallace, afterward vice-president of the United States, he seemed "A prophet out of an ancient age," while Katharine Tynan declared that "the peace of God which passeth understanding lies all about him," and to Constantine Curran he was "a tribunal before which the ignoble dwindles."

After the outbreak of World War I in 1914, Æ wrote in the *Homestead* imploring Irish farmers to produce sufficient food to feed the nation, while the London *Times* published his bitterly eloquent poems denouncing the conflict of perverted empires. Ireland's position became more complicated when a group of Republicans staged an abortive rising in Dublin at Easter 1916. The execution of their leaders won the sympathies of three-quarters of the country for the Republican cause, and in 1917 Æ was one of two ardent nationalists co-opted by Prime Minister David Lloyd George's government into a convention which tried unsuccessfully to draft a compromise constitution. The next year, Æ referred to the creative ferment in Ireland in *The Candle of Vision*, his finest book and the only one in which he succeeded in conveying the grandeur and strangeness of his visionary experiences. Combining autobiography, an exposition of meditation, and rational speculation, he recounts his visions of ancient battles, of a great leader yet to appear, and of Irish gods. Remembering marvelous airships he has beheld, he wonders whether they entered his visions from the past or the future. His fiery conviction that the material universe is only a small portion of reality coexists with an attractive freedom from rigid dogma. Whereas *The National Being* was based on the premise that ninety-nine out of one hundred people are what the social environment makes them, *The Candle of Vision* declares that all have the power, if they will only use it, to travel inward and discover that they are fallen spirits who can recover their lost greatness and wisdom.

Before World War I ended, fighting broke out in Ireland between British troops and Republican guerrillas. Æ, a nationalist and a pacifist, concentrated on trying to save the cooperative movement, but he also attempted by means of pamphlets to promote a peaceful settlement and to explain to Americans the Irish case for independence. The achievement at the end of 1921 of what amounted to dominion status for three-quarters of the country was followed by a civil war between the new Irish government and the minority who rejected anything less than a republic. Æ would leave his front door unlocked even when there was fighting in Dublin, and his moral stature was such that bitter enemies could meet peacefully in his presence. In print he urged the minority to draw back from bringing ruin on their country and the majority to impose their will on an irrational and undemocratic minority. During the civil war, he completed *The Interpreters* (1922), an intriguing exploration of the spiritual roots of political standpoints. The title refers to a group of rebels against the world state of the future and their involuntary companion, a devoted servant of that state arrested in error. As the rebels await their execution, they and their fellow prisoners analyze their ideals. The debate shows that there is some validity in all of them, because the socialist's dedication to brotherhood, the loyalist's belief in human solidarity, the anarchist's commitment to personal autonomy, and

G. K. Chesterton, William Lyon Phelps, and Æ

the poet's quest for beauty rooted in a cultural identity can each be traced to an impulse from one of three primal emanations that, according to theosophists, proceed from the Absolute.

Soon after the hard-pressed Republicans announced at the end of April 1923 that they would suspend their armed resistance, Æ took up the editorship of the *Irish Statesman*, a weekly of broader scope than the *Irish Homestead*, which it superseded. The new journal strongly supported the treaty with Britain, assembled economic and other advice for the inexperienced new government, and promoted the arts in Ireland. Æ wrote some of his best prose for the columns of the *Statesman* as he explored subjects ranging from the nature of myth to the nature of the state, and from Greek tragedy to contemporary Irish painting. With an equal mastery of noble imagery and of the language of rebuke, he praised good poets and exposed the weaknesses of bad ones. While he edited the journal, he continued to compose verse.

Voices of the Stones (1925) introduces a new phase in Æ's poetry. He adds to his earlier concerns an aging man's preoccupation with time, memory, and the destiny awaiting his soul, while he uses poetic diction more sparingly—though still obtrusively—and introduces more variety into his rhythms. The majority of the lyrics, however, are rather slight, and the most impressive piece is the concluding poem—the story, told in octosyllabic couplets, of a peasant participant in the Easter Rising whose heroism is intimately connected with a vision of the Gaelic heaven-world.

Early in 1928, Æ paid his first visit to the United States. While lecturing to raise money for the *Irish Statesman*, he was powerfully impressed by the grandeur of the cities and the energy of the people. In 1929 some of the *Statesman*'s Irish-American guarantors lost heavily in the stock market crash, and in April 1930 the paper had to cease publication.

By the end of the 1920s, Susan Mitchell was dead, and Æ's closest surviving friends—such as

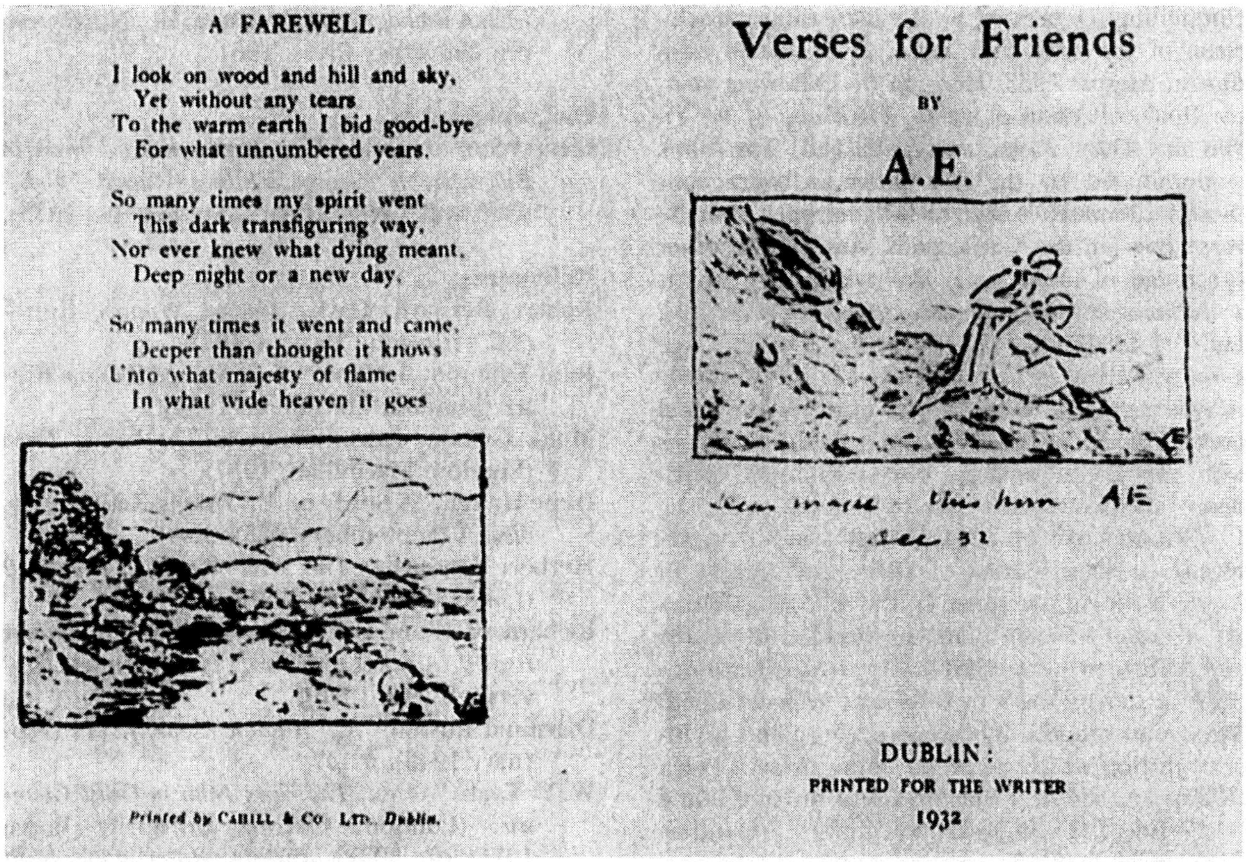
A FAREWELL

I look on wood and hill and sky,
Yet without any tears
To the warm earth I bid good-bye
For what unnumbered years.

So many times my spirit went
This dark transfiguring way,
Nor ever knew what dying meant,
Deep night or a new day.

So many times it went and came,
Deeper than thought it knows
Unto what majesty of flame
In what wide heaven it goes

Printed by Cahill & Co Ltd., Dublin.

Verses for Friends

BY

A.E.

DUBLIN:
PRINTED FOR THE WRITER
1932

One of the twenty-five copies of the pamphlet Æ decorated with crayon-and-ink drawings as gifts for friends in December 1932

James Stephens and James Pryse—were far away. His sons—the source of some domestic friction since the younger had been his father's favorite, the elder his mother's—had left home. In these circumstances, the aging couple were able to recover some of their former happiness in each other. After the collapse of the *Statesman*, Æ undertook a second American lecture tour, this time to earn money for Violet's medical treatment, and during the course of it he assembled another collection of poems.

Vale and Other Poems (1931) is a richer volume than *Voices of the Stones*. While the preoccupation with youth, age, and time persists, there are, alongside more characteristic poems, lyrics based on Æ's American journeys, a reminiscence of "the Household," and meditations on the spiritual standing of a drunkard and on the limitations of natural science. Several of these pieces are in competent blank verse, but finer than any of them is the stanzaic poem "Germinal," an expression of the poet's belief that each person's destiny is determined in infancy:

Amid the soul's grave councillors
A petulant boy
Laughs under the laurels and purples, the elf
Who snatched at his joy,
Ordering Caesar's legions to bring him
The world for his toy.

Æ returned to Dublin and during his wife's illness completed *Song and Its Fountains* (1932), a meditation on the relationship between the creation of poetry and the combination of selves within each human being. Despite the occurrence of dated poetic phrases, this is the most delightful of Æ's books. A kind of sequel to *The Candle of Vision,* it contains many autobiographical passages, describes visions and psychic experiences, and explains the recovery through a mental exercise of submerged memories, including some from past lives.

In February 1932 Violet died, and for more than a year Æ stayed on uncomfortably in Dublin working at *The Avatars* (1933), a spiritual romance based on the Dublin theosophists of the 1890s and their belief that the coming of a high incarnation was at hand. Unfortunately, despite its many pleasant passages, this tale lacks convincingly drawn characters, and the narrative is not compelling. Depressed by the increasing parochialism of the Irish Free State, Æ moved to London in August 1933. Here, in the following year, his final collection of verse, *The House of the Titans and Other Poems*, was published. The book is dominated by the title poem, a courageous though ultimately unsuccessful attempt at a blank-verse epic on the Gaelic gods. Among the other specimens of blank verse, the most noteworthy is a monologue put into the mouth of the Dark Lady of Shakespeare's *Sonnets*, but Æ's language is not powerful enough to make her passion fully convincing. The best of the lyrics is the final poem, "Farewell," in which the poet contemplates with superficial anxiety, but deep-down confidence, the posthumous fate of his soul.

At the end of 1934, Æ left London in response to an invitation to advise and lecture in America on rural reform. In the following February, finding himself ailing, he decided to return to London to be treated by his own doctor instead of moving back to Dublin as he had hoped. After some months of brave struggle against his illness, during which he prepared his *Selected Poems* (1935), he died at a Bournemouth nursing home on 17 July 1935 and was mourned by Ireland as a national hero.

Since his death, the reputation of Æ's poetry has greatly declined. While first his wartime poems, then *Voices of the Stones*, and finally *Vale* were added to new editions of his *Collected Poems*, no edition containing *The House of the Titans* was ever published. Today his verse is not widely read. Although as he grew older Æ became less addicted to outworn phrases and more adventurous in his choice of subjects and verse forms, he never found a style which enabled him to convey consistently the experience of a spiritual world that he rendered so powerfully in *The Candle of Vision*. The impassioned prose of that book and the vigorous modern prose of his *Homestead* and *Statesman* articles are more alive than all but a small portion of his verse.

Letters:

Æ's Letters to Minanlabain (New York: Macmillan, 1937);

Letters from Æ, edited by Alan Denson (London, New York & Toronto: Abelard-Schuman, 1961).

Bibliography:

Alan Denson, *Printed Writings by George W. Russell (Æ): A Bibliography* (Evanston, Ill.: Northwestern University Press, 1961).

Biography:

Henry Summerfield, *That Myriad-minded Man: a Biography of George William Russell "A. E."* (Gerrards Cross, U.K.: Colin Smythe, 1975).

References:

Robert Bernard Davis, *George William Russell ("Æ")* (Boston: Twayne, 1977);

John Eglinton, *A Memoir of Æ: George William Russell* (London: Macmillan, 1937);

Monk Gibbon, Introduction to *The Living Torch* (London: Macmillan, 1937);

Irene Haugh, "A Study of Æ," *Ireland-American Review*, 1 (September 1938): 36-49;

Herbert Howarth, *The Irish Writers 1880-1940* (London: Rockliff, 1958);

Richard M. Kain and James H. O'Brien, *George Russell (A.E.)* (Lewisburg, Pa.: Bucknell University Press, 1976);

Diarmuid Russell, "Æ," *Atlantic Monthly*, 171 (February 1943): 51-57;

W. Y. Evans Wentz, *The Fairy Faith in Celtic Countries* (London: Oxford University Press, 1911), pp. 59-66—the unnamed man whom the author interviews is Æ.

Papers:

Æ's papers are held by the following institutions: Armagh County Museum (letters, especially to Carrie Rea and Charles Weekes, and Æ's notebooks); the Berg Collection, New York Public Library (letters, especially to Lady Gregory, E. H. W. Meyerstein, James Pryse, John Quinn, and W. B. Yeats); the British Library (letters, especially to Bernard Shaw); Colby College Library, Waterville, Maine (copies of the letters which John Eglinton collected for his memoir); Houghton Library, Harvard University (letters and manuscripts of his poems); Lilly Library, Indiana University (letters to and from Æ, his Theosophical Diary from 1895-1896, and manuscripts, especially *Song and Its Fountains* and *The Avatars*); National Library of Ireland (letters); Plunkett Foundation, Oxford (letters to Horace Plunkett); University of Texas Library (letters, especially to Frank Harris, F. R. Higgins, Seumas O'Sullivan, and L. A. G. Strong, and manuscripts, especially of poems and of his unpublished comedy "Enid"); and University of Victoria Library, British Columbia (letters to John Eglinton).

Robert Louis Stevenson

(13 November 1850 - 3 December 1894)

This entry was written by Robert Kiely (Harvard University) for DLB 18: Victorian Novelists After 1885.

See also the Stevenson entry in DLB 57: Victorian Prose Writers After 1867.

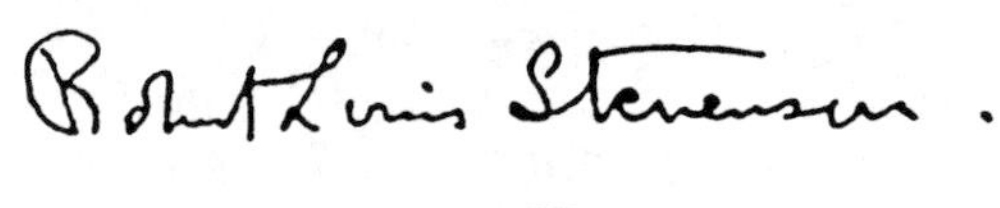

BOOKS: *The Pentland Rising* (Edinburgh: Privately printed, 1866);

An Appeal to the Clergy (Edinburgh & London: Blackwood, 1875);

An Inland Voyage (London: Kegan Paul, 1878; Boston: Roberts, 1883);

Edinburgh: Picturesque Notes, with Etchings (London: Seeley, Jackson & Halliday, 1879; New York: Macmillan, 1889);

Travels with a Donkey in the Cévennes (London: Kegan Paul, 1879; Boston: Roberts, 1879);

Virginibus Puerisque and Other Papers (London: Kegan Paul, 1881; New York: Collier, 1881);

Familiar Studies of Men and Books (London: Chatto & Windus, 1882; New York: Dodd, Mead, 1887);

New Arabian Nights (2 volumes, London: Chatto & Windus, 1882; 1 volume, New York: Holt, 1882);

The Story of a Lie (London: Hayley & Jackson, 1882); republished as *The Story of a Lie and Other Tales* (Boston: Turner, 1904);

The Silverado Squatters: Sketches from a Californian Mountain (London: Chatto & Windus, 1883; New York: Munro, 1884);

Treasure Island (London: Cassell, 1883; Boston: Roberts, 1884);

A Child's Garden of Verses (London: Longmans, Green, 1885; New York: Scribners, 1885);

More New Arabian Nights: The Dynamiter, by Stevenson and F. Van de G. Stevenson (London: Longmans, Green, 1885; New York: Holt, 1885);

Prince Otto: A Romance (London: Chatto & Windus, 1885; New York: Roberts, 1886);

Strange Case of Dr. Jekyll and Mr. Hyde (London: Longmans, Green, 1886; New York: Munro, 1886);

Kidnapped (London: Cassell, 1886; New York: Munro, 1886);

Some College Memories (Edinburgh: University Union Committee, 1886; New York: Mansfield & Wessels, 1899);

The Merry Men and Other Tales and Fables (London: Chatto & Windus, 1887; New York: Scribners, 1887);

Underwoods (London: Chatto & Windus, 1887; New York: Scribners, 1887);

Memories and Portraits (London: Chatto & Windus, 1887; New York: Scribners, 1887);

Memoir of Fleeming Jenkin (London & New York: Longmans, Green, 1887);

The Misadventures of John Nicholson: A Christmas Story (New York: Lovell, 1887);
The Black Arrow: A Tale of the Two Roses (London: Cassell, 1888; New York: Scribners, 1888);
The Master of Ballantrae: A Winter's Tale (London: Cassell, 1889; New York: Collier, 1889);
The Wrong Box, by Stevenson and Lloyd Osbourne (London: Longmans, Green, 1889; New York: Scribners, 1889);
Ballads (London: Chatto & Windus, 1890; New York: Scribners, 1890);
Father Damien: An Open Letter to the Reverend Dr. Hyde of Honolulu (London: Chatto & Windus, 1890; Portland, Maine: Mosher, 1897);
Across the Plains, with Other Memories and Essays (London: Chatto & Windus, 1892; New York: Scribners, 1892);
A Footnote to History: Eight Years of Trouble in Samoa (London: Cassell, 1892; New York: Scribners, 1892);
Three Plays: Deacon Brodie, Beau Austin, Admiral Guinea, by Stevenson and William Ernest Henley (London: Nutt, 1892; New York: Scribners, 1892);
The Wrecker (London: Cassell, 1892; New York: Scribners, 1892);
Island Nights' Entertainments: Consisting of The Beach of Falesá, The Bottle Imp, The Isle of Voices (London: Cassell, 1893; New York: Scribners, 1893);
Catriona: A Sequel to "Kidnapped" (London: Cassell, 1893; New York: Scribners, 1893);
The Ebb-Tide: A Trio and a Quartette, by Stevenson and Osbourne (Chicago: Stone & Kimball, 1894; London: Heinemann, 1894);
The Body-Snatcher (New York: Merriam, 1895);
The Amateur Emigrant from the Clyde to Sandy Hook (Chicago: Stone & Kimball, 1895, New York: Scribners, 1899);
The Strange Case of Dr. Jekyll and Mr. Hyde, with Other Fables (London: Longmans, Green, 1896);
Weir of Hermiston: An Unfinished Romance (London: Chatto & Windus, 1896; New York: Scribners, 1896);
A Mountain Town in France: A Fragment (New York & London: Lane, 1896);
Songs of Travel and Other Verses (London: Chatto & Windus, 1896);
In the South Seas (London: Chatto & Windus, 1896; New York: Scribners, 1896);

Stevenson's birthplace: No. 8 Howard Place, Edinburgh

St. Ives: Being the Adventures of a French Prisoner in England (New York: Scribners, 1897; London: Heinemann, 1898);
The Morality of the Profession of Letters (Gouverneur, N.Y.: Brothers of the Book, 1899);
A Stevenson Medley, edited by S. Colvin (London: Chatto & Windus, 1899);
Essays and Criticisms (Boston: Turner, 1903);
Prayers Written at Vailima, With an Introduction by Mrs. Stevenson (New York: Scribners, 1904; London: Chatto & Windus, 1905);
The Story of a Lie and Other Tales (Boston: Turner, 1904);
Essays of Travel (London: Chatto & Windus, 1905);
Essays in the Art of Writing (London: Chatto & Windus, 1905);
Essays, edited by W. L. Phelps (New York: Scribners, 1906);

Lay Morals and Other Papers (London: Chatto & Windus, 1911; New York: Scribners, 1911);

Records of a Family of Engineers (London: Chatto & Windus, 1912);

The Waif Woman (London: Chatto & Windus, 1916);

On the Choice of a Profession (London: Chatto & Windus, 1916);

Poems Hitherto Unpublished, 2 volumes, edited by G. S. Hellman (Boston: Bibliophile Society, 1916);

New Poems and Variant Readings (London: Chatto & Windus, 1918);

Poems Hitherto Unpublished, edited by Hellman and W. P. Trent (Boston: Bibliophile Society, 1921);

Robert Louis Stevenson: Hitherto Unpublished Prose Writings, edited by H. H. Harper (Boston: Bibliophile Society, 1921);

When the Devil Was Well, edited by Trent (Boston: Bibliophile Society, 1921);

Confessions of a Unionist: An Unpublished Talk on Things Current, Written in 1888, edited by F. V. Livingston (Cambridge, Mass.: Privately printed, 1921);

The Best Thing in Edinburgh: An Address to the Speculative Society of Edinburgh in March 1873, edited by K. D. Osbourne (San Francisco: Howell, 1923);

Selected Essays, edited by H. G. Rawlinson (London: Oxford University Press, 1923);

The Castaways of Soledad: A Manuscript by Stevenson Hitherto Unpublished, edited by Hellman (Buffalo: Privately printed, 1928);

Monmouth: A Tragedy, edited by C. Vale (New York: Rudge, 1928);

The Charity Bazaar: An Allegorical Dialogue (Westport, Conn.: Georgian Press, 1929);

The Essays of Robert Louis Stevenson edited by M. Elwin (London: Macdonald, 1950);

Salute to RLS, edited by F. Holland (Edinburgh: Cousland, 1950);

Tales and Essays, edited by G. B. Stern (London: Falcon, 1950);

Silverado Journal, edited by J. D. Hart (San Francisco: Book Club of California, 1954);

From Scotland to Silverado, edited by James D. Hart (Cambridge, Mass.: Harvard University Press, 1966);

The Amateur Emigrant with Some First Impressions of America, 2 volumes, edited by Roger G. Swearingen (Ashland, Oreg.: Osborne, 1976-1977);

A Newly Discovered Long Story "An Old Song" and a Previously Unpublished Short Story "Edifying Letters of the Rutherford Family," edited by Swearingen (Hamden, Conn.: Archon Books, 1982; Paisley, Scotland: Wilfion, 1982);

Robert Louis Stevenson and "The Beach of Falesá": A Study in Victorian Publishing with the Original Text, edited by Barry Menikoff (Stanford: Stanford University Press, 1984).

Collections: *The Works of R. L. Stevenson*, Edinburgh Edition, 28 volumes, edited by Sidney Colvin (London: Chatto & Windus, 1894-1898);

The Works of Robert Louis Stevenson, Vailima Edition, 26 volumes, edited by Lloyd Osbourne and Fanny Van de Grift Stevenson (London: Heinemann, 1922-1923; New York: Scribners, 1922-1923);

The Works of Robert Louis Stevenson, Tusitala Edition, 35 volumes (London: Heinemann, 1924);

The Works of Robert Louis Stevenson, South Seas Edition, 32 volumes (New York: Scribners, 1925).

One of the hallmarks of the Victorian literary achievement is genius wedded to industry and professionalism. One has only to think of Charles Dickens and Anthony Trollope or George Eliot and Matthew Arnold to recall the persistence, self-discipline, and patiently sustained labor that resulted in the steady accumulation of a body of works as firm and fixed as the building blocks of a great edifice. It is one of the many paradoxes in the life of Robert Louis Stevenson that, though he was a worker and craftsman of extraordinary skill, his literary image is that of a whimsical amateur, an aesthetic drifter. Not only did he move from place to place, scribbling on trains, dictating in bed, but he seems to have written a bit of everything.

In fact, though Stevenson wrote poetry, essays, travel books, hundreds of wonderful letters, and a few plays, his reputation as an author writing for adults rests on his short stories and novels. Furthermore, despite the frequent travel, the velvet jacket and careless manner, the illness and relatively early death at the age of forty-four, his output betrays Victorian industry. Robert Louis Stevenson was, as Henry James said, a "figure," but he was also a writer of great determination, seriousness, and ever-increasing scope.

Stevenson was born in Edinburgh on 13 November 1850 of middle-class Church of Scotland parents who expected him to become an engineer like his father, uncles, and grandfather. Like so many gifted Victorian children, Stevenson wanted to please his parents, Thomas and Margaret Isabella Balfour Stevenson, but found that he could not do so and remain true to himself. His early schooling was limited, partly because of ill health caused by lung problems and partly because his father doubted the value of an orthodox education. His education at Mr. Henderson's school on India Street, near his Edinburgh home, was frequently interrupted by illness between 1855 and 1861. His later attendance at the Edinburgh Academy, beginning at age eleven, was similarly disrupted by poor health and trips to the Continent in search of better climates. He spent a brief time at boarding school in Isleworth, but, unhappy, he returned to Edinburgh and attended Mr. Thompson's school. At Edinburgh University he studied first, engineering, then law, a compromise with his father after the son confessed his religious skepticism and desire for a literary career. Stevenson was called to the bar in July 1875. In some ways, the early signs of frail health were a good omen for his career as a writer, for they enabled his parents to "make allowances" for him, to let him go abroad for his health, to rest and to write rather than to pursue the rigors of a "manly" profession. Partly as a concession to their attitude, partly out of necessity and for the amusement of it, Stevenson approached the life of the writer as a long holiday.

Two of his earliest sustained pieces of writing are travel journals based on excursions in France. *An Inland Voyage* (1878) traces a somewhat damp, disappointing journey by canoe down the River Oise, and *Travels with a Donkey in the Cévennes* (1879) records a walking trip through the Cévennes mountains. Though these works are inevitably loose and discursive, they contain elements of local color and incidental vignettes that betray an early narrative gift. They also betray a tactic that Stevenson was to employ with particular effectiveness in his later suspense fiction: rococo dawdling. He never seems in a hurry, yet his delays are usually too rhetorically splendid, too entertaining in themselves to be irritating. After a while, one gives up worrying about the destination—which is precisely the state of mind Stevenson is trying to produce.

Stevenson shortly after being called to the bar in 1875

While still in his middle twenties Stevenson also began writing the occasional essays that eventually earned him a reputation as a popular philosopher. As William Wordsworth and Henry David Thoreau had been among his favorite models as nature writers, so Hazlitt and Charles Lamb inspired him to try his hand at the informal essay. In all of his writing, Stevenson liked moving from the personal, chatty, even frivolous to the elevated and moralistic. Though the pieces published in *Virginibus Puerisque and Other Papers* (1881), including "Aes Triplex," "Crabbed Age and Youth," "Ordered South," "An Apology for Idlers," and "Pan's Pipes," stand by themselves as complete and charming exercises, they, like his travel pieces, reveal the irrepressible traits of the future writer of fiction. Stevenson could not resist telling a story; and though in his essays he tries to fit his anecdotes to general observations, the tale is often superior to the moral tag to which it is applied. This does not necessarily mean, as some critics have asserted, that Stevenson was a hypocrite; rather it means that he came most naturally to terms with life through concrete and dramatic situations.

Readers of his own time were exhilarated by the freshness, the unexpected directness in the midst of luscious paragraphs in which he had seemed only to be marking time. Today the prose still sparkles in places, though the foot tapping seems less justifiable in exposition than in fiction and travel writing; the modern taste in essays demands that the writer get on with his point. But when, in fact, Stevenson does get on with his point, the twentieth-century reader is likely to feel let down: his observations about youth, age, marriage, work, suffering, play, and travel are rarely as original or stimulating as the fragmentary meditations, emotions, and incidents to which these themes are so loosely attached. In his essays, as in his life, Stevenson often challenges Victorian complacency, philistinism, and moral rigidity. Yet his antidotes are themselves deeply characteristic of the time: post-Romantic, personal, voluntaristic. His essays are sermons on self-help. He extols the imagination and the holiness of the heart's affections, but he also preaches duty, determination, self-reliance, and discipline.

If his essays reveal him to be a versatile and charming Victorian more than a truly rebellious or original thinker, they also show him developing and experimenting with a personal voice of considerable tonal range. Stevenson may not have created a new ethical system nor even cut very deeply into the faults of the existing one, but he learned in his essays to create a personality—or, more precisely, many personalities. Like other novelists who wrote essays—Joseph Conrad, D. H. Lawrence, and Stevenson's friend, Henry James—Stevenson often sacrificed logical coherence to those sudden shifts in voice, argument, or atmosphere so essential to great narrative.

As his essays and travel pieces show, Stevenson's personal charm derives in large part from his unabashed interest in and affection for other people. It sometimes seems that the less his acquaintances were like him, the more fascinated in and sympathetic toward them he became. Men as different as James, Sidney Colvin, Edmund Gosse, and, for a time, William Ernest Henley (who collaborated with him on several plays) were devoted to him. His friendships with women were equally unpredictable. In the summer of 1876 Stevenson went with his cousin to an artist's colony near Fontainebleau and there met Fanny Van de Grift Osbourne, an American eleven years older than he. She had left an irresponsible husband in San Francisco and had set off with her three children for Europe to study art. Not long after arriving on the Continent, her youngest child, Hervey, had died of tuberculosis; and by the time she met Stevenson, she was in a state of extreme depression. Despite all the apparent obstacles, the two became friends and gradually over a two-year period developed an unusual bond. When Fanny returned to America, Stevenson's parents assumed the "danger" was over, but his close friends knew better and were not surprised when Stevenson responded to a telegram by dropping everything and setting off for the New World.

Never one to lose an opportunity to translate experience into words, Stevenson kept a travel journal of what for a person of his limited means and fragile health was an arduous, even hazardous, journey. *Across the Plains, with Other Memories and Essays* (1892) and *The Amateur Emigrant from the Clyde to Sandy Hook* (1895) contain a good deal of the color and vivacity of the earlier travel books. Eccentric characters on shipboard, the mercantile bustle of the port of New York in 1879, the vast spaces of the American West, and the pioneer towns of California are presented with characteristic style. But no rhetorical polish is employed to conceal the fact that the trip was long, tedious, often painful, and, in the end, almost fatal to Stevenson. Though he had undertaken the voyage to save Fanny from ill health and a reckless husband, Stevenson literally collapsed on her doorstep in Monterey and was tenderly nursed by this woman who so often struck others as tough. During his eight months of illness and difficulty in California, he managed to write *The Amateur Emigrant from the Clyde to Sandy Hook* and to begin "A Vendetta in the West," an unfinished adventure novel. He was also working on such short stories as "The Pavillion on the Links" and contributing occasional pieces to the *Monterey Californian*, the local paper.

Once legally divorced from Osbourne, Fanny was free to marry Stevenson, and the wedding took place on 19 May 1880. Despite the fact that both had been ill, they were determined not to spend their honeymoon amid the comforts of San Francisco or Monterey but in the cabin of an abandoned mine at Silverado, more than two thousand feet up the slope of Mount Saint Helena.

Fanny Van de Grift Osbourne, Stevenson's American wife, whom he married in May 1880

During the weeks spent in this unlikely place, Stevenson not only gained in strength and equilibrium, but he returned to pieces he had begun during his travels and started on one of his most vivid and mature travel sketches, *The Silverado Squatters: Sketches from a Californian Mountain* (1883). Like his other American works, this one possesses a realism and confidence of tone missing in the earlier descriptions of his excursions in France. Stevenson was older, he had suffered and experienced more, and the American terrain, though challenging and often sublime, could not be trivialized or charmed into submission.

Though Stevenson's Scottish family and many of his friends adjusted to his unconventional marriage surprisingly well for the time, there is no doubt that some of his old associations, most particularly that with Henley, did not survive Fanny. From all accounts, she was a strong, protective, and opinionated woman, but it is difficult to deny that she and Stevenson loved one another or that from the time of their marriage his health and literary creativity took a marked turn for the better. In August 1880 they left the United States for a reunion with friends in Liverpool and London, a visit to Stevenson's family in Edinburgh, and a prolonged expedition to Switzerland. In the summer of 1881 Stevenson returned to Scotland, rented a cottage in Braemar, and there, surrounded by his American family and the rough and rainy beauty of his own land, began to write *Treasure Island* (1883).

Originating in a watercolor map Stevenson drew, *Treasure Island* describes the dangerous adventures of Jim Hawkins and his passage from adolescence to manhood. Set in the 1740s, the novel outlines Jim's discovery of a map to buried treasure in the possession of the pirate Billy Bones who, terrified by Blind Pew, dies in the inn run by Jim's mother and father. Under the leadership of Dr. Livesy and Squire Trelawney and with Jim as cabin boy, the *Hispaniola* sets sail in search of Treasure Island, somewhere off the Spanish Main (the coast of South America). The cook, however, is the one-legged Long John Silver, who, in league with the crew—mostly his cohorts—plans a mutiny. Jim learns of this, but before he can act, they sight the island. Smuggling himself on land, Jim meets Ben Gunn, once a pirate with Captain Flint, who buried the treasure. Suddenly, the mutiny breaks out, and Jim, with Dr. Livesy, the squire, and others, takes refuge in an abandoned stockade on the island. Courageously, Jim sneaks out to cut the *Hispaniola* adrift but is caught by the first mate, Israel Hands. They fight, and Jim proves his bravery; but upon returning to the island he is caught by the pirates and nearly killed. Long John Silver, however, protects him, and the pirates turn against them both. The pirates suspend their harmful actions while they search for the treasure, discovering only an empty chest. Returning to kill Silver and Jim, they are stopped by Ben Gunn and company, who free the two heroes. Escaping in the *Hispaniola* with the treasure Gunn had earlier dug up, the company travels to the West Indies; there, Silver leaves the ship, which finally returns safely to its home port, Bristol.

It is almost impossible to analyze the qualities of a classic of this kind without seeming to make an unnecessary academic fuss over an unpretentious adventure story. Yet to pass too quickly over *Treasure Island* would be to ignore a major turning point in Stevenson's career and an impor-

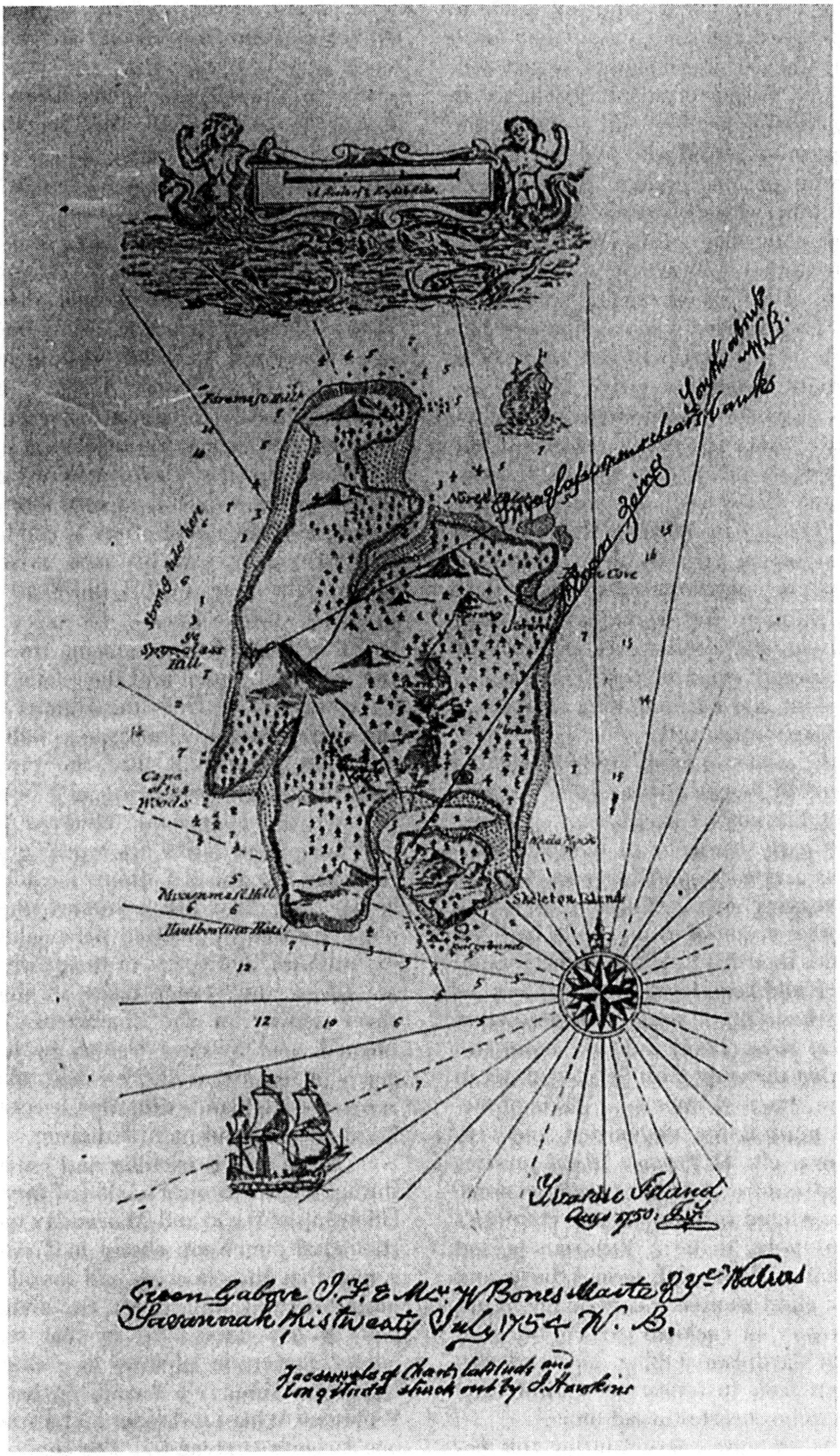

Map from the first edition of Stevenson's classic 1883 novel about pirates, buried treasure, and the adventures of Jim Hawkins and Long John Silver (Thomas Cooper Library, University of South Carolina)

tant key to his literary talent. Until the publication of this book, Stevenson's output had been promising but uneven: warm humor mixed with stiff sobriety and flashes of stylistic brilliance in the essays, increasing realism and irony in the travel sketches, interspersed with odd fantasies in the short stories of *New Arabian Nights* (1882). Aside from its other virtues, *Treasure Island* is a totally consistent, controlled, beautifully paced narrative; for the author, though obviously not for the characters, it is smooth sailing. Stevenson found a tone, a vocabulary, a convention and manipulated each with mastery. In one sense, it is the perfection of a familiar genre, but in another, it is a work of considerable originality. Most adventure books for young readers of the Victorian period are prosy, thick with schoolmaster's syntax, and heavy with the pieties of empire. To read *Treasure Island* today is still to find it fresh and exuberant, an absorbing imitation of a child's daydream, unhampered by adult guilt or moral justification. Jim Hawkins and Long John Silver do not smell musty even after a hundred years. Through them Stevenson succeeded in creating actions and emotions of a simple but timelessly comprehensible sort.

During the next two years (1882-1884), the Stevensons lived in France at the Chalet La Solitude in Hyères. Stevenson's health once again deteriorated; his early tendency to develop bronchial infections and correspondingly weak lungs led to hemorrhaging, and suffering acute weakness, he was often required to remain in bed. Yet it was during this time that he solidified his reputation as a writer and completed some of his most successful and best-known works. He finished *A Child's Garden of Verses* (1885) and once more created a classic that the critic must be careful not to crush or ignore. These rhymes show a side of Stevenson that is musical, fey, unguarded, and very much of his own era. If *Treasure Island* survives as a timeless adventure, *A Child's Garden of Verses*, though still reprinted in innumerable children's editions, seems today to be a Victorian period piece. The adult world is solid, serious, busy, and detached. The child is often lonely or ill, secure in his bed, nursery, or enclosed garden, but with little to do but daydream. Lilting, gay, and earnest, the poems seem to reflect not entirely successful efforts to be cheerful in sad times.

Most of Stevenson's energy during this period went into the writing of fiction. He wrote *More New Arabian Nights: The Dynamiter* (1885), his only book written in collaboration with his wife. These stories, like the earlier *New Arabian Nights*, combine melodrama and a touch of the eerie with outcomes that are often wildly ludicrous. With some exceptions, Stevenson had still not made up his mind when he wished to write mystery and when comic satire. Sometimes he gives the impression that he cannot take his own grotesqueries seriously and ends up laughing at what he had first thought to be terrifying.

Following the success of *Treasure Island*, Stevenson set out to write another adventure novel. Perhaps fearing that the earlier book had been too unhistorical, he tried, without much success, to give *The Black Arrow: A Tale of the Two Roses* (1888; published serially in *Young Folks* in 1883) a recognizable setting. Yet Stevenson himself called the work "tushery" (his own term) and admitted that he wrote it quickly to earn money. His more serious and successful effort at combining history with adventure was his next novel, *Kidnapped* (1886). The year is 1751 (no exact time is ever given in *Treasure Island*), the place is the Highlands. Scotland is experiencing the aftermath of the Jacobites' return and their failed effort to reclaim the throne from the Hanoverians. Stevenson evokes the wild landscape as well as clan rivalries with great skill. But the most important difference from *Treasure Island* is in his rendering of the main characters. Whereas Jim Hawkins and Long John Silver are types, larger and simpler than life, David Balfour, the adolescent Lowlander, and Alan Breck Stewart, the daring Jacobite, are sharply realized personalities with habits, attitudes, and voices of their own. As in *Treasure Island*, the reader takes an interest in the sheer activity of the characters. David is orphaned, sold to slave traders by his uncle, engages in mutiny, is shipwrecked, and then flees across the Highlands with Alan Breck to escape political enemies and natural disaster.

All of this is exciting and entertaining, but throughout the central section of the novel, the relationship of David and Alan adds a moral and psychological dimension absent in *Treasure Island*. It is true that Jim Hawkins had found much in the nasty Silver to admire, but the ambiguity of villainy is left unresolved in that story. In *Kidnapped*, Stevenson explores in greater depth and with some subtlety a friendship between a loyal Protestant Whig Lowlander and a rebellious Catholic Jacobite Highlander. The innocent and prudent younger man is attracted by the courage and impetuosity of the older. During their flight together, they form a complex bond of trust, ri-

Pencil sketch by Stevenson of Alison Cunningham ("Cummy"), his nurse, to whom he dedicated A Child's Garden of Verses *(1885) (Anderson Galleries, Inc., sale 2311, 22 January 1929)*

valry, and affection against which the political and religious conflicts of the times seem insanely simplistic and exaggerated. In some ways, the two characters seem to be in flight from the terrors of social reality, but, in the end, though the memory of their bond remains, they must return to the world of communal obligation. *Kidnapped* can be read as an adventure story; the historical detail is never so rich nor so deeply woven into the narrative as it is in Stendhal or Count Lev Nikolayevich Tolstoy or the best of Sir Walter Scott. Still, the daydream is no longer so free and pure as it had been in *Treasure Island*. The adult world encroaches both on the unsettled emotions of the young David and on the political ambitions of Alan Breck. In 1893 Stevenson wrote *Catriona: A Sequel to "Kidnapped"*. Uneven, the work is transitional between the completeness of *Kidnapped* and the experimental fragments of fiction he left behind at his death.

In 1884 the Stevensons moved back to England and settled at Bournemouth in Skerryvore, a villa overlooking the sea, named after a famous lighthouse designed by his uncle Alan Stevenson. There it was possible for family and friends such as Colvin, Henley, and William Archer to visit. From the literary point of view, the most important friendship that developed during this period

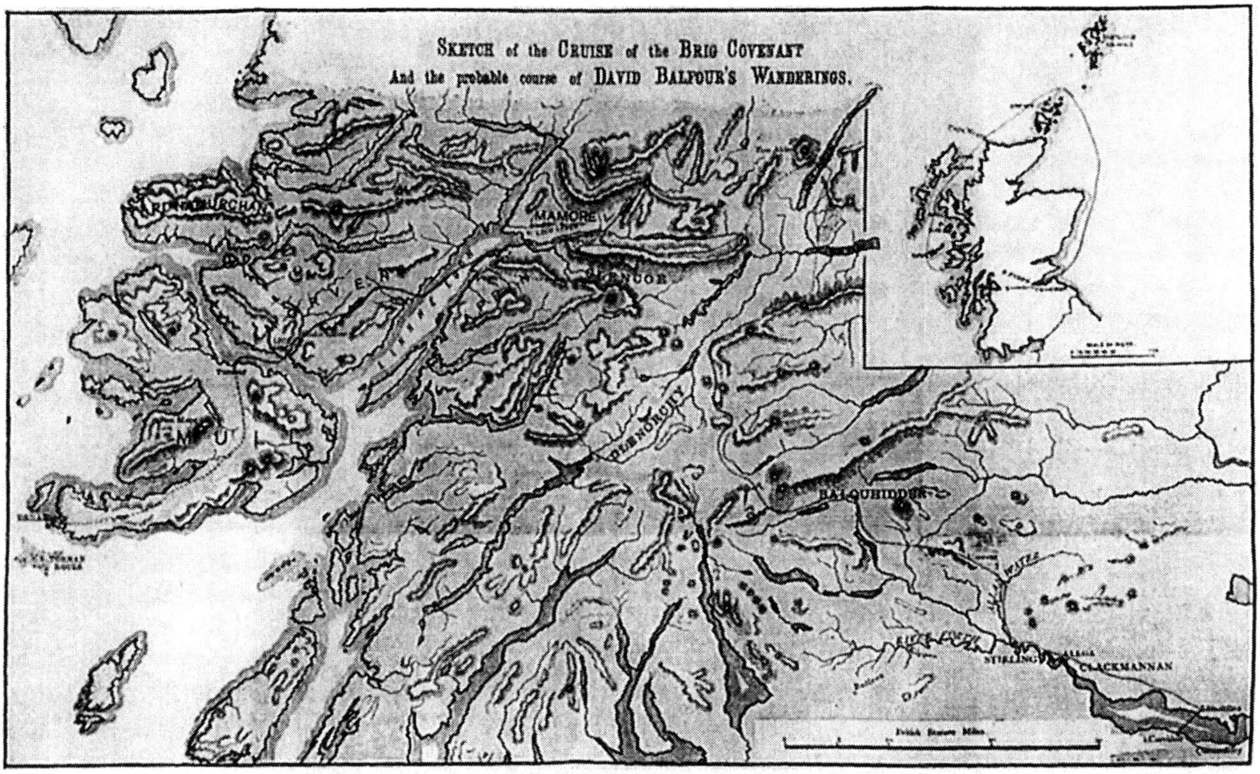

Map from the first edition of Kidnapped, *Stevenson's 1886 historical novel set in the eighteenth-century Scottish Highlands (Thomas Cooper Library, University of South Carolina)*

was that with Henry James. During 1884 *Longman's Magazine* published "A Humble Remonstrance," Stevenson's reply to James's "The Art of Fiction" and probably his single most important critical statement. James had argued for moral and psychological "realism" in fiction and insisted that in order to be taken seriously, literature had to "compete with life." With flare and apparent relish, Stevenson took the opposite view: "No art—to use the daring phrase of Mr. James—can successfully 'compete with life'; . . . To 'compete with life,' whose sun we cannot look upon, whose passions and diseases waste and slay us—to compete with the flavour of wine, the beauty of the dawn, the scorching of fire, the bitterness of death and separation—here is, indeed, a projected escalade of heaven . . . . Life is monstrous, infinite, illogical, abrupt, and poignant; a work of art, in comparison, is neat, finite, self-contained, rational, flowing, and emasculate." Anyone familiar with James's fiction and criticism will see how much, despite the apparent disagreement, he would have liked Stevenson's reply. Stevenson may seem to be reflecting an invalid's view of life and defending the literature of escape, but, more profoundly, he, like James, celebrates deliberate artistry, intelligent design, the craftsmanship of a work of art. Though many of their contemporaries might have spoken of poetry or painting and music in such terms, Stevenson and James were almost alone in treating the novel with such respect. While vacationing in Bournemouth, James visited the Stevensons regularly and formed a friendship with Stevenson which developed into one of the most lively and thoughtful literary correspondences of the period.

If Braemar is associated with *Treasure Island* and Hyères with *Kidnapped*, Bournemouth is the notorious birthplace of the *Strange Case of Dr. Jekyll and Mr. Hyde* (1886). Stevenson had been intrigued by the ambiguities of evil since the beginning of his career. Long John Silver and Alan Breck Stewart are attractive outlaws, and in two of his most important short stories, "Thrawn Janet," involving the Scottish fear of witchcraft and the Devil, and "Markheim," showing a murderer's confession and relief at turning to the Devil, he had probed the irrational specters of dream and the unconscious. Though he had abandoned literal adherence to the Calvinism of his parents, Stevenson's imagination and moral sensi-

Stevenson and some of the crew of the Casco, *the yacht in which he made his first Pacific cruise, in 1888*

bility had obviously been influenced by a vision of good and evil forever locked in combat. Furthermore, he was continually irritated by hypocrisy and especially by the self-righteous moral superiority of those who claimed to be above the fray. In the novel (the idea for which came to Stevenson in a nightmare), Dr. Henry Jekyll, long interested in the problem of dual personality, has invented a chemical that can alter his character from that of a kind physician to that of the violent, criminally minded Edward Hyde. Gradually, Dr. Jekyll loses his ability to shift at will from one personality to another; at the same time, he loses control over Hyde's violent behavior, which leads to murder. In the end, lacking any chemical to transform him from Hyde back to Dr. Jekyll, the protagonist kills himself after having written a letter that reveals all. This tale, narrated by a young lawyer, Utterson, achieves a large portion of its impact through the vivid contrast between reason and the irrational.

In one sense, *Dr. Jekyll and Mr. Hyde* can be taken as a satire of the times in which a respectable and educated man is forced so to repress his animal nature as to turn it into an uncontrollably violent beast. Yet there is much in the tale that does not allow such an interpretation to go unqualified. There is a wildness in Hyde that does not really lend itself to possible accommodations to a moral world, even one more liberal and permissive than that of the 1880s. Furthermore, as it progresses the story seems preoccupied less with social and moral alternatives than with the inevitable progress into vice. Part of the appeal of the tale is, as the title suggests, its strangeness. It has its own obsessive logic and momentum that sweep the reader along. Thus, though various morals can be drawn from it (warnings against intellectual pride, hypocrisy, and indifference to the power of the evil within), the continuing attraction of the *Strange Case of Dr. Jekyll and Mr. Hyde* is perhaps the exact reverse of that of *Treasure Island*: one is an almost perfect literary rendition of a child's daydream of endless possibilities, the other of an adult's nightmare of disintegration.

Searching once again for an ideal climate, the Stevensons set out for America in 1887 with his stepson and recently widowed mother in tow and settled temporarily in Saranac Lake, New York. Encouraged by his popularity in the United States, Stevenson began work almost immediately on a new novel of history and adventure. *The Master of Ballantrae: A Winter's Tale* (1889) departs even further than *Kidnapped* from the pure entertainment of *Treasure Island.* It is less well known than his earlier books and deserves more attention than it has received. Though, as in *Kidnapped,* the action turns on events connected with the Jacobite Rebellion of 1745, the political details and even the Scottish landscape are really secondary to a psychological and moral drama of rivalry and hatred between two brothers. At first glance, James and Henry Durrisdeer seem to be variants on Alan Breck Stewart and David Balfour. James, the older brother, is dark, handsome, reckless, a champion of the Stuart cause; Henry, the younger, is fair, mild, gentle, and cautious, a loyal Hanoverian. But whereas Alan and David brought out the best in one another and reflected the affinity and attraction of opposites, the Durrisdeer brothers drive one another to the worst extremes of their natural temperaments. As James becomes more and more flamboyant and brutal, Henry recedes into a near paralysis

The Stevensons' house at their estate, Vailima, in Samoa

Stevenson with his mother; his stepson, Lloyd Osbourne; Fanny; his stepdaughter, Isobel Strong; and servants on the porch at Vailima

of blandness. It is as though Stevenson is deliberately weaving together caricatured versions of the conventional protagonists of domestic and romantic fiction. One brother almost defeats the reader with tedium, the other risks exhausting him with overactivity. However, at its best, the novel is neither a parody nor an incoherent double narrative but a powerful drama of blood hatred. The plot is convoluted but includes a dramatic duel between the brothers in which the wounded James is smuggled off to India, where he makes a fortune. He returns with the mysterious Secundra Dass, an East Indian who, in league with James, pursues Henry and his family to America. In a dramatic conclusion, Henry conspires to have James killed in the wilderness of New York State while searching for treasure. James appears to die, but as Henry watches, James returns momentarily to life under the care of Secundra Dass—and the shock kills Henry. But Dass cannot restore James completely to life because of the frigid temperatures in the wilderness. James dies, and the two brothers lie buried in the barren land.

As might have been predicted, New York did not answer Stevenson's needs. Indeed, it becomes clearer and clearer that although health was the immediate reason for his numerous moves, his restlessness ran very deep, and it is unlikely that he would have led a settled life even had he been robust. In addition to being solicitous of his health, Fanny seems to have shared his wanderlust. In 1888 she chartered the schooner *Casco,* and in June, along with Fanny's son Lloyd, Stevenson's fifty-nine-year-old mother, and a family servant, they set sail for the Pacific islands, touching Nuku Hiva, the Paumotus, Tahiti, and Oahu in the Hawaiian Islands. During the next two years, on the *Equator* and then on the *Janet Nicoll,* they visited Australia and the Gilbert and Marshall islands and eventually bought 400 acres in Samoa, where they decided to build a house and establish themselves permanently. They named the estate Vailima, meaning "Five Rivers" in Samoan.

It is difficult to look at the photographs of the Stevenson clan in Samoa without reacting to the absurdity as well as the charm and spiritedness of their adventure. There they all are—Lloyd with his pince-nez, Fanny in a muumuu, Mrs. Stevenson wearing her widow's bonnet, Stevenson striking a pose in a funny hat. Like so much of Stevenson's life and writing, there is an impression of game playing, of flair and bravado, of an ultimate lack of seriousness. Yet, as in the case of the writing, if one looks carefully, the seriousness is there. In the first place, as his letters show, Stevenson never felt very far away from death. He continually suffered from the damp or cold climates of the various places he had tried to live. The warm sea air of Samoa did, for the first time in years, give him hope for a recovery, or at least a partial easing of his pain.

Furthermore, once he came to know the islands and their history, Stevenson's interest in them and their inhabitants was sincere and far more understanding and sympathetic than that of many of his Victorian contemporaries. His famous *Father Damien: An Open Letter to the Reverend Dr. Hyde of Honolulu* (1890) in defense of the memory of Father Damien, the Catholic missionary to the lepers of Molokai, is as much a defense of the native islanders as it is of their priest. Father Damien's "sin," according to the appropriately named Dr. Hyde, was that he had "gone native," did not maintain a proper distance from his flock, was not always clean, and may have befriended a native woman. Stevenson's attack on the hypocrisy of these accusations is combined with a ringing defense of the true spirit of Christianity that preaches the common humanity of all men and women.

Stevenson's letters and journals reveal a growing concern for the health and well-being of the island population and an increasing irritation with the political and economic exploitation of the natives by European and American colonists. He and his family were rare among the white settlers in that they wanted nothing more than to live with the Samoans. These attitudes are reflected in the fiction that deals with the Pacific: *The Wrecker* (1892), about murder and a treasure hunt to Midway Island; *Island Nights' Entertainments* (1893), a collection of short stories including "The Bottle Imp"; and *The Ebb-Tide* (1894), written with Osbourne, a story of three outcasts who descend on a small island where a miniature English society has been established. As in the earlier fiction, these narratives include strong elements of melodrama and high adventure, but they also contain searching studies of the behavior and motivation of the whites who are drawn to the islands and the destructive effects that their various searches for wealth and power have on the native populations. It is not too much to say that several of the narratives of this period, most particularly *The Ebb-Tide* and "The Beach of Falesá," anticipate Joseph Conrad. They are, in any case, far from the innocent dreams of *Trea-*

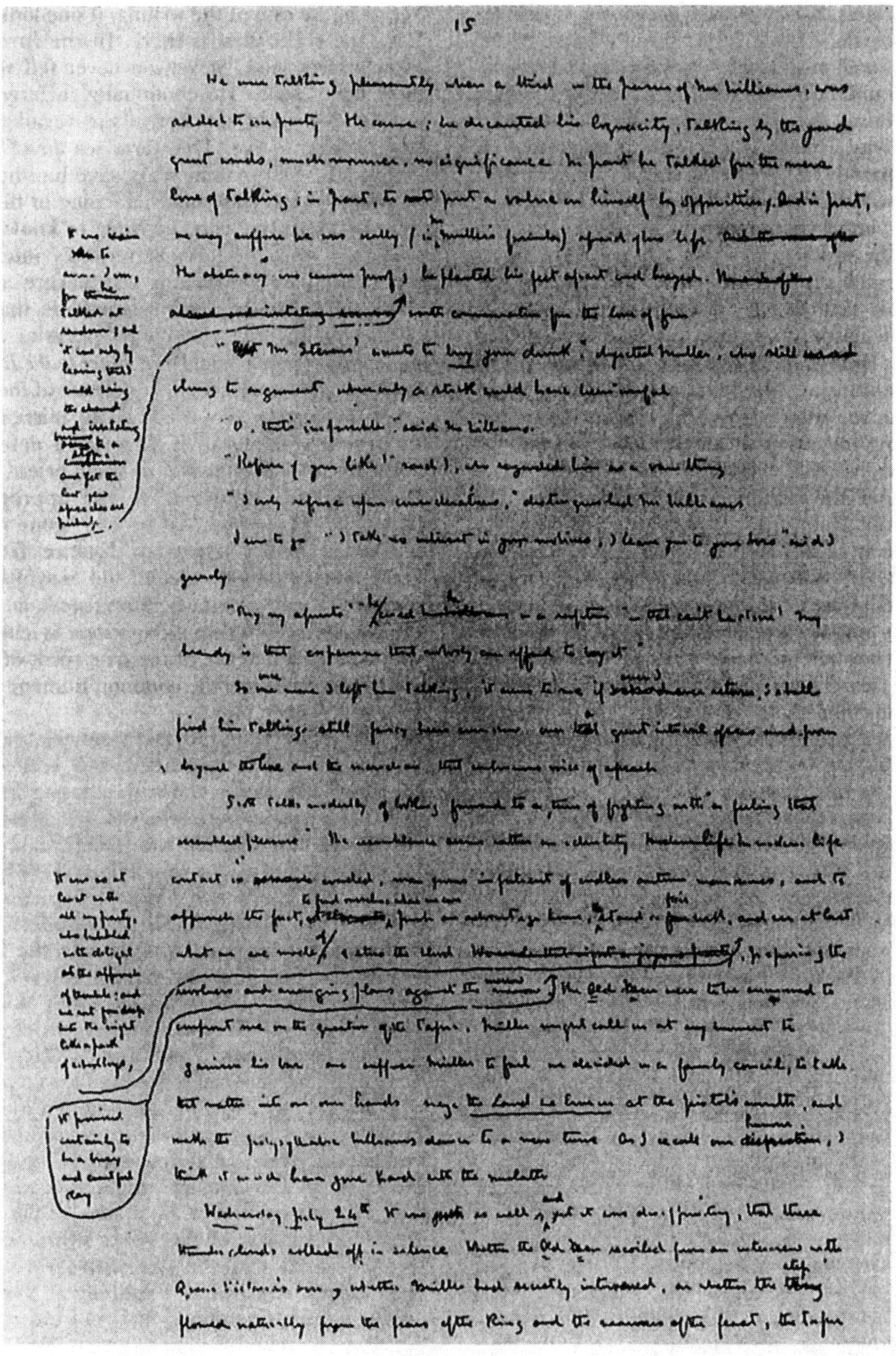

A manuscript page from one of the letters Stevenson wrote for newspapers to finance his Pacific cruises. Some of this material was published as In the South Seas *(1896) (American Art Association/Anderson Galleries, Inc., sale 4249, 9 April 1936).*

Stevenson presiding over a feast for a group of Samoan chiefs who had built a road to his house

sure Island, in which the search for gold is a game played in a world without mixed motives or long-range consequences.

Finally, though he did remain playful and boyish and impulsive, Stevenson understood, as no modern reader or writer can, the vast distance he had placed between himself and home by coming to Samoa. Beneath the excitement of seeing new places and adjusting to a new life was the growing realization that he had cut himself off from the cultures and lands that had frustrated but also nourished him. Stevenson's homesickness for Scotland became, even as his physical health seemed to improve, the major psychological preoccupation of his last years. It was in Samoa that he wrote *Catriona,* the sequel to *Kidnapped;* and his last work—and one that promised to be his greatest if he had lived to finish it—was *Weir of Hermiston* (1896), a book that is Scottish to the core.

In presenting the Hermiston family—the father who is a brilliant but merciless judge, his pious wife, and their sensitive, rebellious son—Stevenson combines all his best talents. The richness of social and political history and local color are perfectly blended with characterizations of powerful psychological penetration. Archie, the judge's son, is sent to Hermiston, a moorland estate, for protesting a hanging ordered by his father. There he falls in love with Kirstie Elliott, but a visiting former schoolmate maligns Archie to Kirstie and her family. A stormy meeting between the two lovers breaks off because of Stevenson's sudden death, but Sidney Colvin, in a postscript, summarizes the notes Stevenson made concerning the remainder of the novel. Archie kills his former friend for betraying him; he is then condemned to die by his father, but he is rescued by Kirstie's brothers and escapes with her to America. However, the ordeal of the trial and sentencing of his son is too much for the judge, and he dies. In some ways it seems appropriate that Stevenson, who loved new starts and mysterious conclusions, left readers to speculate about some of his most intriguing characters.

His death came swiftly and unexpectedly on 3 December 1894. In the morning, he had been dictating the latest section of *Weir of Hermiston* to his stepdaughter Isobel Strong, who had arrived in Samoa in 1891. That evening he complained of a headache to Fanny. He appears to have suffered a stroke, and within a few hours he was

The last photograph of Robert Louis Stevenson

dead at the age of forty-four. A burial procession of nearly sixty Samoans cut a path up a steep slope until they reached the summit of Mount Vaea, where he was laid to rest.

The manner of his living and dying, in conjunction with the variety and popularity of much of his writing, has had a mixed effect on Stevenson's reputation as a writer. Immediately after his death, he was almost canonized as a literary and moral genius who lived courageously in the face of affliction. Inevitably there was a reaction to this sentimental portrait, but it too was excessive. In the 1920s and 1930s critics suddenly found his style imitative and pompous, and biographers discovered that he was mortal after all and for two or three decades took an almost lewd pleasure in detailing the ways in which he was not perfect. Though his books always had some faithful defenders and his younger readers were oblivious to the opinions of adults, it was not until the 1950s and 1960s that his work, especially his fiction, was reconsidered by scholars in a relatively unbiased way. Few would now disagree that he was an essayist of great charm and versatility or that his fiction belongs with that of Scott, Edgar Allan Poe, Herman Melville, and Conrad in that compelling tradition where mystery and psychology, adventure and moral choice converge.

Letters:

Sidney Colvin, ed., *The Letters of Robert Louis Stevenson to His Family and Friends*, 2 volumes (London: Methuen, 1899; New York: Scribners, 1899);

De Lancey Ferguson and Marshall Waingrow, eds., *R. L. S.: Stevenson's Letters to Charles Baxter* (New Haven: Yale University Press, 1956; London: Oxford University Press, 1956).

Bibliographies:

J. H. Slater, *Robert Louis Stevenson: A Bibliography of His Complete Works* (London: Bell, 1914);

W. F. Prideaux, *A Bibliography of the Works of Robert Louis Stevenson*, revised edition, edited and supplemented by Mrs. Luther S. Livingston (London: Hollings, 1918).

Biographies:

Graham Balfour, *The Life of Robert Louis Stevenson* (New York: Scribners, 1901);

Janet Adam Smith, *Robert Louis Stevenson* (London: Duckworth, 1937);

David Daiches, *Robert Louis Stevenson* (Norfolk, Conn.: New Directions, 1947);

J. C. Furnas, *Voyage to Windward: The Life of Robert Louis Stevenson* (New York: Sloane, 1951);

Jenni Calder, *RLS: A Life Study* (London: Hamish Hamilton, 1980).

References:

Jenni Calder, ed., *Stevenson and Victorian Scotland* (Edinburgh: University of Edinburgh Press, 1981);

G. K. Chesterton, *Robert Louis Stevenson* (London: Hodder & Stoughton, 1927);

Edwin M. Eigner, *Robert Louis Stevenson and Romantic Tradition* (Princeton: Princeton University Press, 1966);

Harry M. Geduld, ed., *The Definitive Dr. Jekyll and Mr. Hyde Companion* (New York: Garland, 1983);

Lord Guthrie, *Robert Louis Stevenson: Some Personal Recollections* (Edinburgh: Green, 1924);

Stevenson's grave atop Mount Vaea, Samoa

J. A. Hammerton, ed., *Stevensoniana* (Edinburgh: Grant, 1910);

John R. Hammond, ed., *A Robert Louis Stevenson Companion: A Guide to the Novels, Essays and Short Stories* (New York: Macmillan, 1984);

Robert Kiely, *Robert Louis Stevenson and the Fiction of Adventure* (Cambridge, Mass.: Harvard University Press, 1965);

Paul Maixner, ed., *Robert Louis Stevenson, The Critical Heritage* (London & Boston: Routledge & Kegan Paul, 1981);

Nicholas Rankin, *Dead Man's Chest: Travels After Robert Louis Stevenson* (London: Faber, 1987);

E. B. Simpson, *The Robert Louis Stevenson Originals* (New York: Scribners, 1913);

Janet Adam Smith, ed., *Henry James and Robert Louis Stevenson: A Record of Friendship and Criticism* (London: Rupert Hart-Davis, 1948);

Isobel Strong and Lloyd Osbourne, *Memories of Vailima* (New York: Scribners, 1902);

Roger G. Swearingen, *The Prose Writings of Robert Louis Stevenson: A Guide* (Hamden, Conn.: Archon, 1980).

Papers:

Collections of Stevenson's papers are at the Beinecke Rare Book and Manuscript Library, Yale University; the Pierpont Morgan Library, New York; the Henry E. Huntington Library, San Marino, California; the Widener Library, Harvard University; the Edinburgh Public Library; the Silverado Museum, Saint Helena, California; and the Monterey State Historical Monument Stevenson House, Monterey, California.

Bram Stoker

(8 November 1847 - 20 April 1912)

This entry was updated by Brian Murray (Loyola College in Maryland) from his entry in DLB 70: British Mystery Writers, 1860-1919.

See also the Stoker entry in DLB 36: British Novelists, 1890-1929: Modernists.

BOOKS: *The Duties of Clerks of Petty Sessions in Ireland* (Dublin: Privately printed, 1879);

Under the Sunset (London: Low, Marston, Searle & Rivington, 1882);

A Glimpse of America: A Lecture Given at the London Institution, 28th December, 1885 (London: Low, Marston, 1886);

The Snake's Pass (New York: Harper, 1890; London: Low, Marston, Searle & Rivington, 1891);

Crooken Sands (New York: De Vinne, 1894);

The Man from Shorrox's (New York: De Vinne, 1894);

The Watter's Mou' (London: Constable, 1895; New York: Appleton, 1895);

The Shoulder of Shasta (London: Constable, 1895);

Dracula (London: Constable, 1897; New York: Doubleday & McClure, 1899);

Miss Betty (London: Pearson, 1898);

Sir Henry Irving and Miss Ellen Terry (New York: Doubleday & McClure, 1899);

The Mystery of the Sea (New York: Doubleday, Page, 1902; London: Heinemann, 1902);

The Jewel of Seven Stars (London: Heinemann, 1903; New York & London: Harper, 1904; revised and abridged edition, London: Rider, 1912);

The Man (London: Heinemann, 1905); abridged as *The Gates of Life* (New York: Cupples & Leon, 1908);

Personal Reminiscences of Henry Irving, 2 volumes (London: Heinemann, 1906; New York: Macmillan, 1906; revised, London: Heinemann, 1907);

Lady Athlyne (London: Heinemann, 1908; New York: Lovell, 1909);

Snowbound (London: Collier, 1908);

The Lady of the Shroud (London: Heinemann, 1909);

Famous Impostors (London: Sidgwick & Jackson, 1910; New York: Sturgis & Walton, 1910);

The Lair of the White Worm (London: Rider, 1911);

Dracula's Guest, and Other Weird Stories (London: Routledge, 1914; New York: Hillman-Curl, 1937).

PERIODICAL PUBLICATION: "The Censorship of Stage Plays," *Nineteenth Century & After*, 66 (December 1909): 974-989.

Though he was shy and sickly as a child, Bram Stoker grew up to be a man with many talents and interests, and a seemingly endless supply of energy. He was simultaneously an amateur athlete, a businessman, a journalist, and an impresario; he maintained countless friendships and read widely, particularly in subjects related to spiritualism and the occult. Stoker was also the author of nine novels, most of which are ignored today—and justifiably so. But Stoker's best book, the extensively researched *Dracula* (1897), effectively combines macabre atmospherics with high suspense, and not only set the standard for subsequent novels in the horror-mystery genre but also helped establish the vampire as one of the most recognizable figures in the popular arts.

Stoker—the third of seven children—was born in Clontarf, Ireland, north of Dublin Bay, on 8 November 1847. His father, Abraham Stoker, was a civil servant; his mother, Charlotte Thornley Stoker, was a social activist with a particular concern for impoverished women. Though the precise nature of his illness remains unknown, the young Stoker was so chronically weak that, until the age of seven, he rarely left his bed. He kept himself occupied with books from his father's well-stocked library and was frequently entertained by the grisly folktales involving spirits and plagues that his mother liked to tell. As a boy, Stoker wrote many poems and ghost stories and promised his family that one day he would enjoy literary fame.

In 1864 Stoker began his studies at Dublin's Trinity College, where he was named president of the Philosophical Society and the Historical Society, both of them prestigious undergraduate organizations. Now large and robust, he participated in a variety of sports and began to evince an increased enthusiasm for both the theater and Walt Whitman's verse. As a young man, Stoker sent Whitman a series of lengthy, unrestrained fan letters and continued to plan for a literary career of his own. Still, acceding to his father's wishes, Stoker, upon graduation, entered the Irish civil service and was soon promoted to inspector of petty sessions—a position that, perhaps not surprisingly, failed to develop into a consuming passion.

In 1871 Stoker began writing play reviews for the *Dublin Mail*; he also continued to work on making marketable his own plays and stories. In 1875 he sold to the *Shamrock* "The Chain of Destiny"—a lengthy, serialized tale that features, among other things, a phantom and a curse. In 1876 Stoker met the British actor Henry Irving, who was already famous for his interpretations of Shakespearean roles including—most notably—*Hamlet*. Stoker and Irving quickly became close friends, and in 1878 Stoker began to manage Irving's Lyceum Theatre in London. Stoker's association with Irving—which lasted until the actor's death in 1905—provided him with considerable stimulation. Traveling four times to the United States, Stoker met many prominent people, including Whitman and Theodore Roosevelt (then head of New York City's department of police).

On 4 December 1878 Stoker married Florence Balcombe, a stunning but apparently rather austere woman who—a year later—bore Stoker his only child, a son named Noel. Though his duties as theater manager and tour arranger for the mercurial Irving took up enormous amounts of his time, Stoker did not cease in his attempts to produce profitable fiction in the romance-adventure vein. His first published novel, *The Snake's Pass* (1890), features a dashing hero named Arthur who looks for treasure and competes for the heart of a virginal young woman in a region rich in "legends and myths" and "gloomy scenes." The wide success of *The Snake's Pass* encouraged Stoker to continue extensive research on a much more ambitious work, *Dracula*.

Dracula is constructed principally and masterfully of journal entries and letters written by several characters, including Jonathan Harker, an English real-estate agent who, in the book's opening chapters, describes his journey through Transylvania to the castle of Count Dracula, who wants to buy property in London. Transylvania, he observes, is a rugged, mysterious realm full of the descendants of "Attila and the Huns"; it is a country without maps—a place where "every known superstition in the world is gathered." Dracula, Harker discovers when they meet, is a tall old man with pointed ears, hairy palms, "massive" eyebrows, a "heavy" moustache, and "peculiarly sharp white teeth" which "protruded over the lips." Moreover, he shares his castle—which sits "on the edge of a terrific precipice"—with several alluring women endowed with "brilliant white teeth" and "voluptuous lips." They appear before Harker one bright moonlit night and—with a "deliberate voluptuousness which was both thrilling and repulsive"—hover about his neck, their "sweet" scent offset by a "bitter offensiveness, as one smells in blood." One of the women "licked her lips like an animal, till I could see in the moonlight the moisture shining on the scarlet

Cover for the first American edition (1899) of Stoker's 1897 novel, the culmination of years of research on vampires that Stoker began in 1890 after Professor Arminius Vambery, the model for Dr. Abraham Van Helsing in the novel, introduced him to some of the stories about these supernatural beings

lips and on the red tongue as it lapped the white sharp teeth."

Later, after realizing that his host steals infants, sleeps in a coffin, scurries "lizard fashion" up and down the castle wall, and in fact sucks blood "like a filthy leech," Harker flees Dracula's castle and returns to England and to his fiancée, Mina Murray, whom he describes as "so sweet, so noble, so little an egoist"—as "one of God's women fashioned by His own hand to show us men and other women that there is a heaven where we can enter, and that its light can be here on earth." But Dracula also makes his way to London, where he attacks Mina's close friend—Lucy Westenra—before finally sinking his fangs into Mina herself. As a result of her encounter with the count, Lucy becomes emaciated and dies; she returns, however, as an eerie and erotic ghoul and must finally be stopped with a tar-tipped stake through the heart. Mina also begins to behave weirdly but is in due course cleansed of her curse when—at the novel's well-paced, riveting conclusion—Dracula (her seducer and controller) is cornered near his Transylvanian castle and killed by a team of men that includes Harker and Dr. Abraham Van Helsing, a Dutch physician and hypnotist. Van Helsing is familiar with the habits of vampires and continually provides his fellow characters and the novel's readers with the facts necessary to anticipate and understand Dracula's actions. For example, he notes that vampires fear religious—particularly Christian—articles and symbols (such as the crucifix), and must periodically return to their native soil. Several critics have suggested that Stoker modeled Van Helsing on Professor Arminius Vambery, a Hungarian professor of Oriental languages who, around 1890, apparently introduced Stoker to some of the arcana regarding vampires and their haunts in eastern Europe and the Balkans. But

Dust jacket for the 1914 collection of short stories compiled by Stoker's widow. The title story was originally written as an early chapter in Dracula.

as Clive Leatherdale points out, "nothing is known of the content of Stoker's and Vambery's conversations or later correspondence, and if Vambery ever wrote on the subject of vampires, or a so-called Dracula, no record has survived."

A fascination with vampirism was not uncommon among European intellectuals and artists of the eighteenth and nineteenth centuries. In "The Bride of Corinth" Johann Wolfgang von Goethe writes of a young woman doomed to wander eternally from the grave, hoping to "seek the Good's long-sever'd link" while drinking "the life-blood" of the lover she has lost. Samuel Taylor Coleridge alludes to vampiric activity in "Christabel," as does Sir Walter Scott in *Rokeby* (1813), Lord Byron in *The Giaour* (1813), and Robert Southey in *Thalaba the Destroyer* (1801)—a verse fantasy set in the Orient that includes a vivid portrayal of a female "fiend" with "livid cheeks, and lips of blue." The literary male vampire—typically magnetic, brooding, and pale—made his first appearance in the form of a character called Lord Ruthven in John Polidori's *The Vampyre, A Tale* (1819), a work similar to such Gothic novels as Horace Walpole's *Castle of Otranto* (1764) and Ann Radcliffe's *The Mysteries of Udolpho* (1794). Perhaps even better known, however, was "Carmilla," an 1871 novella written by Joseph Sheridan Le Fanu, an Irishman who also studied at Trinity and who later produced numerous stories and novels with supernatural themes. Like *Dracula*, "Carmilla" includes the observations of a young male narrator who visits a "feudal residence" in an isolated region of eastern Europe; it features a female vampire who is at once a "playful, languid, beautiful girl" and a "writhing fiend" with a "horrible lust for living blood."

Stoker acknowledged a special fondness for "Carmilla," and—as surviving notes for *Dracula* clearly reveal—he had absorbed, at the British Museum and elsewhere, an extraordinary amount of information about the ways in which vampires have been portrayed in the literature and lore of various cultures. He knew then that accounts of creatures who sipped blood and stalked by night were common in ancient times; that European legends about a particularly monstrous aristocrat owed much to Voivode of Wallachia, a very real fifteenth-century Transylvanian landowner who became known as both Vlad the Impaler and "the son of the devil"—or Dracula—because of his fondness for indiscriminately torturing and murdering in a variety of horrific ways.

Still, Stoker was not a particularly deep thinker; it is unlikely that he viewed his own *Dracula* as anything more than a well-constructed and highly suspenseful story which features several memorable characters and a deft blending of the ghastly and the grotesque with a convincingly rendered normality. Indeed, the publicly prudish Stoker—who once wrote an essay calling for the censorship of works that exploit "sex impulses"—would probably be shocked to read much of the recent criticism of *Dracula*, which perceptively points to the many ways in which the novel not only plays to man's fear of disease and foreignness and his own animality but to the Victorian middle-class male's fear of women and female sexuality. *Dracula* repeatedly reveals an intense interest in a woman's capacity to extend and to receive physical pleasure but simultaneously reinforces the notion that, in the end, a man ought to settle for nothing less than an angel constrained and doting; that a woman who has attained carnal knowledge—especially illicitly—has been rendered unclean and thus much too tainted for the respectable bourgeois male. Lucy, for example, becomes diseased and monstrous after having been touched by unbridled sex, here symbolized by the rather satyric count; Mina can be redeemed only when she in effect renounces her bestial seducer and presents Harker, her husband, with a child.

Dracula received more than one unfriendly review: the *Athenaeum*, for instance, described it as "a mere series of grotesquely incredible events" that was "wanting in the constructive art as well as in the higher literary sense." But the novel was also enthusiastically praised by such influential publications as the *Bookman* and the *Pall Mall Gazette*. *Dracula* sold steadily and well and can certainly be credited with reigniting in both Europe and America a craze for vampires, which probably reached its peak in the 1920s and 1930s when Irish actor Hamilton Deane adapted *Dracula* into a highly successful stage play.

After *Dracula* Stoker remained as manager of the Lyceum and continued to devote a fair portion of his free time to the writing of fiction. His fourth novel, *The Mystery of the Sea* (1902), meticulously describes a hunt for lost treasure in Cruden Bay—and runs on, often laboriously, for nearly five hundred pages. Archie Hunter, the novel's hero, possesses a "big body and athletic powers" as well as a keen interest in occult matters. "The whole earth and sea, and air," he announces in an early chapter, "all that of which human beings generally ordinarily take cognisance, is but a film or crust which hides the deeper moving powers of forces." "These forces," he decides (and the novel's plot is structured to bear him out), do not clash arbitrarily; rather, "there was somewhere a purposeful cause of universal action. An action which in its special or concrete working appeared like the sentience of nature in general, and of the myriad items of its cosmogony."

The Lady of the Shroud (1909) opens with a lengthy, deadly dull discussion of the provisions of a will but becomes—by book 3—perhaps the best paced and most readable of Stoker's later novels. Structured, like *Dracula*, around a series of interconnected documents, this work focuses on a brawny and very earnest fellow named Rupert St. Leger and his attempts to discover the identity of a young, shroud-clad woman who visits him nightly in his room on the Adriatic estate where he is temporarily staying. St. Leger dubs his visitor "the Lady of the Shroud," and though he fears that she might be a vampire (she is not), he soon falls in love with her and begins a chain of thought and action that suggests the sexual tension and confusion that is so abundant in *Dracula*. Rupert kisses the very cushions where his mysterious lady rests her head; he admits that she has awakened in him a passion "quick, hot and insistent." Early on, he is shocked by her proposal that the two of them spend the night together holding hands by the fire and proclaims that, in the final analysis, nothing can be more "sweet" than "to restore the lost or seemingly lost soul of the woman you love!"

The title of Stoker's final novel, *The Lair of the White Worm* (1911), is a Freudian's delight. Put simply, the story focuses on Lady Arabella, "a girl of the Caucasian type, beautiful, Saxon blonde, with a complexion of milk and roses"—who is able to transform herself into a large and deadly snake. This book illustrates the principal characteristics and weaknesses of the bulk of Stoker's book-length fiction. It features stereotypical characters involved in utterly implausible adventures in an exotic setting; it has a strong boy-gets-girl subplot, and its muzzy occultism is paralleled by a sense that large white British males are the crowning achievement of all creation and can always be counted on to save the day. Thus, much of the ridicule that Stoker perhaps intended as comic relief is aimed at Lady Arabella's black servant, Oolanga. Stoker routinely refers to this character as "the nigger" and occasionally uses his appearance in the text to introduce racist slurs.

The Lair of the White Worm sold surprisingly well, but none of Stoker's other novels came close to achieving the popular or critical success of *Dracula*. Stoker, moreover, suffered a series of disappointments and setbacks in the later years of his life, beginning with the closing of the Lyceum in 1902 and the death of his idol Irving in 1905. According to Daniel Farson, Stoker contracted syphilis in the 1880s, and as a result suffered from a steady decline in his mental health—a fact that might explain the particular awfulness of his final novel. Leatherdale suggests that such an assertion is "far from proven," but concedes that the vague and ambiguous wording on Stoker's death certificate "was typical of that used to refer to certain sexually trasmitted diseases" at a time when, among members of "the respectable middle classes," syphilis was "virtually an unmentionable term."

Following her husband's death, Florence Stoker released a collection of his shorter fiction

Edward Van Sloan as Dr. Van Helsing and Bela Lugosi as Count Dracula in the 1931 Universal Pictures film version of Stoker's best-known novel

entitled *Dracula's Guest, and Other Weird Stories* (1914). In the vivid, strongly paced title piece—originally conceived as an early chapter of *Dracula*—Jonathan Harker again makes his way to the count's castle. This time he encounters, among other things, a very nervous coachman, a hailstorm, and a female vampire who turns into a wolf and spends the night nestled protectively against his chest. Even more curious, however, is "The Squaw," which begins with a detailed description of a carelessly tossed rock shattering out the "little brains" of a playful kitten and concludes with a scene in which one man's eyeball is gouged out; another is crushed inside a spiked torture device; and the narrator picks up a sword and cuts in half yet another cat. This brief story is so thoroughly gory that the reader is tempted to view it as a subtle parody of the horror genre, especially when—early on—the narrator matter-of-factly observes that the infamous Iron Virgin of Nuremberg (a torture device in which the victim is impaled on iron spikes) "has been handed down as an instance of the horrors of cruelty of which man is capable" and then adds that he and his wife had "long looked forward to seeing it." Stoker was not noted for his subtlety, and most evidence also suggests that he was not prone to take himself or his work lightly. "The Squaw" can be viewed only as the particularly fascinating, unsettling product of a late-Victorian gentleman writer oddly preoccupied not only with matters mysterious and frightening but with the brutal mutilation of innocent life: with impalements, gaping wounds, and great showers of blood.

Stoker's death attracted relatively little attention in the world's press. Today he remains far less famous than his best-known fictional character, who—at least in his Bela Lugosi guise—is probably as recognizable to most Americans as Mickey Mouse or Batman. Broadly and essentially, Stoker was himself the creator of prose cartoons. But *Dracula* is a marvel: its murky depths will surely keep readers and critics intrigued for many years to come.

Bibliography:

Richard Dalby, *Bram Stoker: A Bibliography of First Editions* (London: Dracula Press, 1983).

Biographies:

Harry Ludlam, *A Biography of Dracula: The Life Story of Bram Stoker* (London: Foulsham, 1962);

Daniel Farson, *The Man Who Wrote Dracula: A Biography of Bram Stoker* (London: Joseph, 1975; New York: St. Martin's Press, 1976).

References:

C. F. Bentley, "The Monster in the Bedroom: Sexual Symbolism in Bram Stoker's *Dracula*," *Literature and Psychology*, 22, no. 1 (1972): 27-33;

Joseph S. Bierman, "The Genesis and Dating of *Dracula* from Bram Stoker's Working Notes," *Notes and Queries*, new series 24 (1977): 39-41;

Charles S. Blinderman, "Vampurella: Darwin and Count Dracula," *Massachusetts Review* (Summer 1980): 411-428;

M. M. Carlson, "What Stoker Saw: An Introduction to the History of the Literary Vampire," *Folklore Forum*, 10, no. 1 (1977): 26-32;

Stephanie Demetrakopoulos, "Feminism, Sex Role Exchanges, and Other Subliminal Fantasies in Bram Stoker's *Dracula*," *Frontiers*, 2, no. 3 (1977): 104-113;

Radu Florescu and Raymond T. McNally, *Dracula: A Biography of Vlad the Impaler, 1431-1476* (New York: Hawthorn, 1973);

Carrol L. Fry, "Fictional Conventions and Sexuality in *Dracula*," *Victorian Newsletter*, 42 (Fall 1972): 20-22;

Donald F. Glut, *The Dracula Book* (Metuchen, N.J.: Scarecrow Press, 1975);

Mark M. Hennelly, Jr., "*Dracula*: The Gnostic Quest and Victorian Wasteland," *English Literature in Transition*, 20, no. 1 (1977): 13-26;

Eric Irvin, "Dracula's Friends and Forerunners," *Quadrant*, 135 (October 1978): 42-44;

Clive Leatherdale, *Dracula: The Novel and the Legend* (Wellingborough, Northamptonshire: Aquarian Press, 1985);

Elizabeth MacAndrew and Susan Gorsky, "Why Do They Faint and Die?—The Birth of the Delicate Heroine," *Journal of Popular Culture*, 8 (Spring 1975): 735-745;

Raymond T. McNally and Radu Florescu, *In Search of Dracula: A True History of Dracula and Vampire Legends* (New York: Warner, 1976);

McNally, ed., *A Clutch of Vampires: These Being Among the Best from History and Literature* (Greenwich, Conn.: New York Graphic Society, 1974);

Lowry Nelson, Jr., "Night Thoughts on The Gothic Novel," *Yale Review*, 52 (Winter 1963): 236-257;

Phyllis A. Roth, *Bram Stoker* (Boston: Twayne, 1982);

Harry A. Senn, *Were-Wolf and Vampire in Romania* (New York: Columbia University Press, 1982);

David J. Skal, *Hollywood Gothic: The Tangled Web of Dracula from Novel to Stage to Screen* (New York: Norton, 1990);

John Allen Stevenson, "A Vampire in the Mirror: The Sexuality of *Dracula*," *PMLA*, 103 (March 1988): 139-149;

Richard Wasson, "The Politics of *Dracula*," *English Literature in Transition*, 9, no. 1 (1966): 24-27;

Judith Weissman, "Women and Vampires: *Dracula* as a Victorian Novel," *Midwest Quarterly*, 18 (Summer 1977): 392-405;

Leonard Wolf, ed., *The Annotated Dracula* (New York: Ballantine, 1975);

Dudley Wright, *The Book of Vampires* (New York: Causeway Books, 1973).

Papers:

Seventy-eight pages of Bram Stoker's diagrams, notes, and outlines for *Dracula* are held by the Rosenbach Museum and Library, Philadelphia.

John Millington Synge

(16 April 1871 - 24 March 1909)

This entry was written by Susan Stone-Blackburn (University of Calgary) for DLB 10: Modern British Dramatists, 1900-1945: Part Two.

See also the Synge entry in DLB 19: British Poets, 1880-1914.

SELECTED BOOKS: *In the Shadow of the Glen* (New York: John Quinn, 1904);
The Shadow of the Glen and Riders to the Sea (London: Elkin Mathews, 1905);
The Well of the Saints (London: A. H. Bullen, 1905; New York: John Quinn, 1905);
The Playboy of the Western World (Dublin: Maunsel, 1907; Boston: Luce, 1911);
The Aran Islands (London: Elkin Mathews / Dublin: Maunsel, 1907);
The Tinker's Wedding (Dublin: Maunsel, 1908; Boston: J. W. Luce, 1911);
Poems and Translations (Dundrum: Cuala, 1909; New York: John Quinn, 1909);
Deirdre of the Sorrows (Dundrum: Cuala, 1910; New York: John Quinn, 1910);
The Works of John M. Synge, 4 volumes (Dublin: Maunsel, 1910);
John M. S.: Collected Works, 4 volumes, edited by Robin Skelton, Alan Price, and Ann Saddlemyer (London: Oxford, 1962-1968);
The Autobiography of J. M. Synge; Constructed from the Manuscripts, edited by Price (Dublin: Dolmen, 1965);
My Wallet of Photographs: The Collected Photographs of J. M. Synge, edited by Lilo Stephens (Dublin: Dolmen, 1971).

PLAY PRODUCTIONS: *In the Shadow of the Glen*, Dublin, Molesworth Hall, 8 October 1903, 3 [performances];
Riders to the Sea, Dublin, Molesworth Hall, 25 February 1904, 3;
The Well of the Saints, Dublin, Abbey Theatre, 4 February 1905, 7;
The Playboy of the Western World, Dublin, Abbey Theatre, 26 January 1907, 7;
The Tinker's Wedding, London, His Majesty's Theatre, 11 November 1909;
Deirdre of the Sorrows, Dublin, Abbey Theatre, 13 January 1910.

SELECTED PERIODICAL PUBLICATIONS—UNCOLLECTED: "A Story from Inishmaan," *New Ireland Review*, 10 (November 1898): 153-156;
"La Sagesse et la Destinée," *Daily Express*, 17 December 1898, p. 3;
"A Celtic Theatre," *Freeman's Journal*, 22 March 1900, p. 4;
"The Last Fortress of the Celt," *Gael* (April 1901): 109;
"La Vieille Littérature Irlandaise," *L'Européen*, 15 March 1902, p. 11;
"An Epic of Ulster," *Speaker*, 7 June 1902, pp. 284-285;
"Riders to the Sea," *Samhain* (October 1903): 25-33;
"Celtic Mythology," *Speaker*, 2 April 1904, pp. 17-18;
"In the Shadow of the Glen," *Samhain* (December 1904): 34-44;
A letter on "In the Shadow of the Glen," *United Irishman*, 11 February 1905, p. 1;
"In the Congested Districts," *Manchester Guardian*, 10, 14, 17, 21, 24, 28 June; 1, 5, 8, 19, 22, 26 July 1905;
"A Translation of Irish Romance," *Manchester Guardian*, 6 March 1906, p. 5;
A letter on "The Playboy of the Western World," *Irish Times*, 31 January 1907;
"In West Kerry," *Shanachie* (Summer 1907): 61-70; (Autumn 1907): 138-150; (Winter 1907): 233-243.

J. M. Synge is the most highly regarded dramatist of the modern Irish literary movement. His reputation as a major twentieth-century playwright was established by six plays, written in the last seven years of his life. Although Synge's early career showed few signs of what were to be his ultimate accomplishments, his plays with their distinctive blend of poetry and realism, both characteristically Irish and uniquely his own, are the most powerful of that remarkable dramatic movement led by William Butler Yeats in Dublin at the turn of the century.

Born on 16 April 1871 near Dublin, Edmund John Millington Synge was the youngest of five children. His father died the following year. The family was Protestant upper class, and Synge, his three brothers, and his sister were brought up by a fervently religious mother in comfortable financial circumstances. Beginning at age ten, he attended private schools for four years, but only intermittently because of ill health. He then studied with a private tutor at home. At seventeen he entered Trinity College in Dublin, where he applied himself to his studies sporadically but sufficiently to obtain a pass degree in December 1892. His particular interests there were Irish antiquities and languages; he took first place on prize examinations in both Irish and Hebrew during his third year. Much of Synge's energy during these years was poured into his musical training at the Royal Irish Academy of Music, where he studied violin, theory, and composition, winning a scholarship for advanced study in counterpoint. He was beginning to write poetry as well as music, but music was his primary interest.

Synge lived with his mother until 1893, but he did not fit altogether comfortably into life at home because of his mother's lack of enthusiasm for his plan to make a profession of music and because of his religious skepticism, which evidently took root in his early teens. His failure to embrace Protestant orthodoxy also blighted his first romance; Cherry Matheson came from a family as strictly religious as his own, and his pursuit of her during his visits home from Europe, where he studied for several years after receiving his B.A. from Trinity, ended finally in her refusal of his marriage proposal in 1896. In 1893 Synge went to Germany to pursue his musical studies, but his year there apparently convinced him that his extreme nervousness about performing before an audience made a musical career impossible. During that year he was still writing poetry and beginning to sketch out plays, and by the end of the summer of 1894 he had decided to move to Paris to study language and literature at the Sorbonne. Supporting himself by giving English lessons, Synge studied French until April 1895; then until the end of June he took courses at the Sorbonne in phonetics, medieval literature, and modern French literature. After spending the summer of 1895 in Ireland, he returned to Paris and went on to Italy, where he studied Italian and began reading Petrarch. In December 1896 he again enrolled for lectures in literature at the Sorbonne.

In Paris, on 21 December 1896, Synge met Yeats, who was to influence his career profoundly. Yeats was unimpressed with Synge's early writing, which, he later recalled in his preface to *The Well of the Saints* (1905), was "full of that kind of morbidity that has its roots in too much brooding over methods of expression, and ways of looking upon life, which come, not out of life, but out of literature." Synge's language, Yeats complained, was "that conventional language of modern poetry which has begun to make us all weary." Yeats, who had just been to the Aran Islands off the west coast of Ireland, where the Irish-speaking peasants lived harsh and primitive lives, urged Synge to forget Paris and go to Aran to find a different mode of expression for a different mode of life.

His acquaintance with Yeats renewed Synge's interest in Irish literature, and even more important for Synge's development as a writer, he eventually took Yeats's advice about experiencing life on Aran. In the spring of 1898 he stayed for several weeks on the islands, as he did in each of the next four years. At the time of his first visit to Aran, Synge's only published work was a sonnet that had appeared in his college magazine. During the next few years he continued to struggle with his writing, spending his winters in Paris and returning to Ireland in the summers. By the spring of 1902 he had had only half a dozen articles published, consisting of book reviews and pieces about Aran. However, these years, notably the summers spent in the Aran Islands and in Wicklow with his family, were to prove crucial to Synge's career, providing central ideas, settings, and characters for his plays as well as the rhythms and vocabulary which distinguish his characters.

The Aran Islands are rocky, dominated by the sea and isolated from the mainland. Synge recorded his observations on the primitive life there in photographs and in notebooks, finding "spiritual treasure" containing "every symbol of the cosmos" and noting in the expressions of some of the women's eyes "the whole external symphony of the sky and seas. They have wildness and humour and passion kept in continual subjection by the reverence for life and the sea that is inevitable in this place." The language spoken by the islanders, most of whom knew both Irish and English, was especially significant for Synge, who learned by recording their rhythmic, archaic, Irish-

John Millington Synge, drawing by James Paterson

flavored English to write the peasant dialect of his plays. He listened intently to stories told in the tradition of the ancient bards by men who impressed him with the extraordinary vitality of their recitations, and when he was stirred by recitations in Irish that he did not fully understand, he learned the emotional effect that euphony and cadence could have independent of meaning.

Synge turned his notes on his visits to the islands into a book, *The Aran Islands,* which he first offered for publication in 1901, but which remained unpublished until 1907, apparently because publishers doubted that its subject would have wide appeal. In 1901 he also completed his first play, *When the Moon Has Set,* which he later condensed into one act. The hero of this early work, which was not performed, is a young landowner, an atheist, who has fallen in love with a nun. She is affected by the pathetic ravings of a madwoman who long ago refused an offer of marriage from the man she loved, who was also an atheist. Fearing the same fate, the nun yields to the hero's plea to give up her religion and marry him. The play concludes with his paean to nature and all that is divine in the heroine, a pagan ceremony in which the bride wears green, and the groom pronounces their union in the name of the forces of nature. Synge's rebellion against orthodox religion and its connection with his failure to win Cherry Matheson are obvious factors in this first play, which is passionate but undramatic and unconvincing in characterization. Yeats found it "morbid and conventional though with an air of originality," and of course there was no possibility of Dublin audiences tolerating its blatant rejection of religious orthodoxy. The dialect spoken by all the characters of Synge's later plays appears only in the speeches of the maid and the madwoman. The dialogue of the main characters is not particularly interesting in diction, rhythm, or imagery, and the play rarely comes to life except in the madwoman's scene.

In the spring of 1902 Synge wrote two verse plays, only fragments of which survive. His diaries note that he had finished both in March and was revising them in April. One is a pastoral play which contains the poignant contrasts of youth and age, love and death that would continue to occupy Synge in his later work; its language is an uncertain mixture of elevated diction, formal verse rhythms, and a good deal of end rhyme, with occasional infusions of Irish rhythm and phrasing. The other deals with three fishermen who come from Spain with their wives to settle in Ireland but then drown. Synge had encountered the story a year and a half earlier in Geoffrey Keating's *The History of Ireland.* The anguish of birth, love, and death Synge depicts is not adequately conveyed by his formal language, though some passages describing the look of the sea show the direct impact of Synge's Aran experience on his writing. Synge's writing through the spring of 1902 constitutes his apprenticeship to the craft of playwriting.

In the summer of the same year, Synge was able to bring together effectively all the ingredients of his art: his formal study of literature, languages, and music was given significance and focus by his vivid impressions of the Aran islanders, and he found himself artistically in the rhythmic and colorful language, the simple and poignant lives of the peasant characters who appear in *In the Shadow of the Glen* (1903) and *Riders to the Sea* (1904). Both were written in the summer of 1902, which Synge was spending in the house his mother had rented in Wicklow. There, he was to recall in the preface to *The Playboy of the Western World* (1907), "I got more aid than any learning could have given me, from a chink in the floor . . . that let me hear what was being said by the servant girls in the kitchen." In them, as in the Aran islanders, Synge found the "rich and living" imagination and language which make it "possible for a writer to be rich and copious in his words, and at the same time to give the reality which is the root of all poetry, in a comprehensive and natural form."

Riders to the Sea owes its setting, its atmosphere, its characters, its dialogue, and its story to Synge's experience in Aran. Synge's dramatization of a mother's reaction to the drowning of her last two sons grew out of his observations of the power and constant threat of the sea that was such an inevitable part of the islanders' lives. In *The Aran Islands* Synge comments frequently on the apparent frailty of the *curaghs* (canvas canoes) and the risks taken by the men who must cross from one island to another or to the mainland. In the play, the last living son, Bartley, easily accepts the necessity of going to the mainland to sell horses at a fair, and his sisters agree with him, though less casually. His mother, Maurya, however, is obsessed with the fear that he will drown as his five brothers, his father, and his grandfather have drowned before him. In *The Aran Islands* Synge notes that in bad weather "a curagh cannot go out without danger, yet accidents are rare. . . ." Thus, the one-act play, remarkable for its distillation of emotion and concentration of events, is not a direct representation of Aran life, for all its realism. Yet Synge also noted in *The Aran Islands* that "often when an accident happens a father is lost with his two eldest sons, or in some other way all the active men of a household die together." This sense of family tragedy is the focus of the play, in which the emphasis is on the women in their anticipation of and response to the deaths of brothers and sons. The play is a poetic presentation of the elemental struggle between life and death and the high price one must pay for peace when life necessitates struggle.

In *The Aran Islands* Synge records two incidents that occurred during his third and fourth visits, which figure prominently in his play. He saw the mother of a man lost at sea weeping and looking out over the sea, heard the sister's attempts to match her recollections of her brother's things with the descriptions she has heard of those found on the body washed ashore in Donegal, and listened to her keening as she decides that the body is her brother's. The only change Synge made in dramatizing this episode is toward more immediate stage action; Nora and Cathleen actually receive the bundle of clothes, mull over the fact that the common material of the shirt makes a definite conclusion impossible, and then count the stitches of the stockings, remembering the stitches of each as it was knitted, to arrive at a positive identification of Michael. Maurya's vision preceding Bartley's death also came directly out of Synge's Aran experience. In *The Aran Islands* he described an account he heard of an incident that preceded a drowning: "When the horses were coming down to the slip an old woman saw her son, that was drowned a while ago, riding on one of them. She didn't say what she was after seeing, and this man caught the horse, he caught his own horse first, and then he caught this one, and after that he went out and was drowned." Maurya sees Bartley on a red mare leading a gray pony, and she has a vision of her son Michael, who has already drowned, on the gray pony. Later she learns that Bartley has in fact been knocked into the sea by the gray pony, washed into the heavy surf on the rocks, and drowned. Synge's observation that the Aran islanders "make no distinction between the natural and the supernatural" becomes part of the atmosphere of his play, where fate is embodied in the natural force of the sea, and Maurya's vision of death following Bartley proves truer than the priest's vain assurance that "God won't leave you destitute with no son living." The play ends with Maurya's poignant speeches of grief and resignation.

In the Shadow of the Glen, written at the same time, is different from *Riders to the Sea* in setting, tone, and theme, but there are resemblances in the simplicity of the characters' lives and in their language. This play is set in Wicklow, not Aran, but the story is one Synge heard from a storyteller he met on his first visit to the islands. In this story, which he records in detail in *The Aran Islands,* a traveler takes shelter from the rain in a house where a wife is keeping watch over her husband's body. When the wife goes out, the "dead" man informs the stranger that he is only shamming in order to catch his wife, whom he suspects of infidelity, in the act of betraying him. The wife comes back with a young man and is caught in bed with him. In Synge's play, Nora Burke's transgression is less explicit, but her conversation with the stranger and the young man clearly reveals her distaste for the sour old "dead" man who is her husband and the lonely life she has led with him. The young man's proposal of marriage elicits a burst of wrath from the husband, who drives Nora out of his cottage to a life on the road with the stranger, a tramp who offers to take her under his wing when it becomes evident that young Michael Dara is not so interested in Nora herself as he was in Nora with her husband's land and livestock. Unlike *Riders to the Sea, In the Shadow of the Glen* is a comedy, though its ending is more ironic than festive. Both plays deal with the shadow death casts over life, but *In the Shadow of the Glen* features not death but the comic mock-death of Nora's husband, Dan, and the more serious death-in-life he represents in his old age and in the life of loneliness that marriage to him imposes on Nora. For most of the play Nora is torn between the attraction of the materially secure but restrictive life for which she married Dan and the attraction of the free-spirited and full but primitive life in nature with the tramp that she embarks on at the end of the play. Although the natural life is forced on Nora, her exit with the tramp has the appeal of a new beginning. Synge's sympathy with the tramp's life is revealed most clearly in the power of the tramp's final two speeches, which contrast the glories of nature with the grimness of Nora's life with Dan.

In the fall Synge showed both plays to Yeats and Lady Gregory, who helped to promote his work in London and at home. *Riders to the Sea* was published in Yeats's occasional review, *Samhain,* in September 1903, the first piece of Synge's creative work to appear in print in the ten years after he published a poem in his college magazine. *In the Shadow of the Glen* was the first play to be staged (on 8 October 1903) by the Irish National Theatre Society, the repertory company which resulted in 1902 after the Irish Literary Theatre, founded in 1899 by Yeats, Lady Gregory, George Moore, and Edward Martyn, was deserted by Moore and Martyn. Yeats and Lady Gregory then formed a liaison with Frank and Willie Fay's National Dramatic Society. Yeats's *The King's Threshold* opened the program, *In the Shadow of the Glen* followed, and the evening concluded with Yeats's *Cathleen ni Houlihan.*

Yeats's plays were well received by the audience, the patriotic spirit of *Cathleen ni Houlihan* being particularly to its taste, but Synge's play drew boos as well as applause. Reviews showed a distaste for Synge's "slur on Irish womanhood." Public disapproval of the play was shared by some of the actors, two of whom had resigned from the company rather than take part in the play. Though Yeats's father, John Butler Yeats, heralded the play in a notice published the day of the performance as an attack on "our Irish institution, the loveless marriage," that vociferous segment of the Irish who thought that Irish theater should be primarily political and whose nationalism consisted of romantic idealization of every aspect of national life opposed Synge's ironic treatment of marriage—Irishwomen must by definition be virtuous; Nora was an inappropriate portrayal of an Irishwoman. Synge's realistic and sympathetic depiction of the effect on a young and vibrant woman of a lonely and frustrating life touched some and infuriated others. He took little part in the public discussion of the play, leaving Yeats to defend the artistic prerogatives of the playwright and the authentic Irishness of the play against accusations that there was nothing Irish about it, that the dialect was Synge's own contrivance, and that the story was taken from Petronius. The play weathered such criticisms, however. In 1904 it was revived in Dublin and taken on tour in England where it was well received; later it was translated into German and Bohemian and performed in Berlin and Prague in 1906. When the Irish National Theatre Society acquired the Abbey Theatre, which was to be the center of Ireland's dramatic movement for more than forty years, its opening in December 1904 was celebrated by Yeats's publication of an issue of *Samhain* which included the text of *In the Shadow of the Glen.* The opening program of plays at the Abbey included *In the Shadow of the Glen* along with *Cathleen ni Houlihan* and new plays by Yeats and Lady Gregory. Commentators on the play in the decades since its first performance have disagreed on the success of Nora's characterization and the effectiveness of the play's conclusion; on the whole, after the furor over the depiction of Irish womanhood abated, the play aroused less interest than most of Synge's others.

Riders to the Sea was fairly well received from the beginning, though Willie Fay apparently had some reservations about it which delayed its opening performance until 25 February 1904. Audience and press reacted favorably, if not rapturously, and the play's reputation has grown since. It attracted more attention than did *In the Shadow of the Glen* when the company produced both in London in March 1904, drawing high praise from leading critics William Archer and Max Beerbohm. The least controversial of Synge's plays, it was the most frequently played by Fay's company in the years to follow. Its international reputation is now firmly established; it has been called the most perfect one-act play in English and has been praised for its dramatic economy and emotional intensity. Because of its somber tone and its emotional power, critical attention has focused on its stature as tragedy: Is Maurya solely a victim of fate to be pitied and thus undeserving of full tragic stature, or does her stoic endurance, her ultimate acceptance of her fate, provide the catharsis of true tragedy? *Riders to the Sea* is the most consistently praised of Synge's plays, partly because of its merits and partly because it lacks the ambiguities and risky subject matter that make his other plays contentious.

Synge's plays lent themselves to and fostered the realistic style of presentation which the Fays were working toward in the Irish National Theatre Society. The uneasiness in audience response to *In the Shadow of the Glen* has been attributed in part to its realism, for which they were unprepared by traditional melodrama or by Yeats's poetic style of drama. Willie Fay and Synge were of the same mind about authentic detail in production, and the nationalistic desire of the actors to represent Irish life accurately, as well as Frank Fay's voice coaching when the music of Synge's peasant speech did not come easily to Dublin actors, contributed to the accuracy of detail in gesture, dialect, costume, and setting which constituted "the Abbey method" of production.

During the summer of 1902, while Synge was writing *Riders to the Sea* and *In the Shadow of the Glen,* he was also drafting *The Tinker's Wedding* (produced in 1909), which was completed in one act by the fall or early winter of 1903 and later expanded to two acts. It is pure farce, so the three plays together constitute an interesting experiment in tone, with the dark comedy of *In the Shadow of the Glen* occupying the middle ground between the somber mood of *Riders to the Sea* and the rollicking uproar of *The Tinker's Wedding.* Like *In the Shadow of the Glen, The Tinker's Wedding* is set in Wicklow, but it presents a different class of people, described in some of Synge's travel essays as vagrants who make their way by begging or making things to sell. They are "little troubled by laws" and often at odds with the police, but they lead a vigorous outdoor life that keeps them in good health and humor. In his essay "The Vagrants of Wicklow" (1906) Synge wrote of having seen fifty tinkers on a road: "all matchmaking and marrying themselves for the year that was to come.... [One], maybe, would swap the woman he had with one from another man, with as much talk as if you'd be selling a cow." Synge's three tinkers are Sarah Casey, a young woman who takes it into her head to arrange a proper marriage to her man despite her class's disdain for orthodox wedding vows; Michael Byrne, her young man, who is skeptical but willing after she arouses his jealousy by threatening to go off with another man if he refuses to cooperate; and his mother, Mary, an unregenerate drunken vagrant, who sees the plan as a crazy waste of money and hoots at the notion that the ceremony will make any difference at all if either of them decides to revert to the tinkers' traditional freedom. The plot is outlined in another essay, "At a Wicklow Fair," in which Synge tells of hearing about a tinker who asked a priest to marry him and his woman for half a sovereign; the priest agreed to the meager price on condition that they would make him a tin can as well. When they approached the priest again three weeks later, they claimed that the can they made had been kicked out of shape by an ass, and the priest, calling them rogues and schemers, refused to marry them at all. This is the essence of Synge's slender plot, except that he has Michael's mother steal the can to buy drink, replacing it with empty bottles, so that its disappearance is discovered only after Sarah and Michael present to the priest the bundle they believe contains the can.

The climactic episode, in which a priest is gagged, tied up in sacking, and threatened, made the play impossible to produce for Dublin audiences, as even Synge recognized. Negotiations with Elkin Mathews in London to publish *The Aran Islands* and the two one-act plays, begun late in 1903, resulted in some exchange of correspondence over *The Tinker's Wedding* as well. Synge gave Mathews the play, expanded to two acts, early in 1904, but took it back in the spring to make some alterations. In any case, Synge said he preferred to have *Riders to the Sea* and *In the Shadow of the Glen* brought out together (as they were in May 1905) without the third play, "as a character in 'The Tinker's Wedding' is likely to displease . . . a good many of our Dublin friends and would perhaps hinder the sale of the book in Ireland." More than a year later, in September 1905, Yeats wrote to Synge asking for the manuscript of *The Tinker's Wedding,* wanting to consider it for publication in *Samhain* and also for production during the Abbey Theatre's winter season. Both Yeats's comment and Synge's reply show a good-humored awareness of the play's hazards. Yeats observed, "We are rather hard up for new short pieces, and you have such a bad reputation now it can hardly do you any harm. But we may find it too dangerous for the Theatre at present." Synge explained his delay in sending the play to Yeats with "I have not got it with me, and I am afraid to set my pious relations to hunt for it among my papers for fear they would set fire to the whole." Ultimately, Yeats, Synge, and Willie Fay decided that it would indeed be unwise for their theater to face a Dublin audience with such a play, nor was it published in *Samhain.*

Never quite satisfied with the play, Synge was still revising it early in 1906, having offered it to Max Meyerfield for possible translation into German and performance in Berlin, and pronounced himself still "not wholly satisfied" when he finally sent it in April. Meyerfield decided against the play as "too undramatic and too Irish." The play was finally published by Maunsel and Company in January 1908 but never performed in Synge's lifetime. Harley Granville Barker showed considerable enthusiasm for it when Synge sent it to him in 1907 but decided that his company would be unable to capture the Irish atmosphere in such a way as to do the play justice. It is clear that Synge had similar doubts, as he noted when he sent Barker the manuscript (after making yet more alterations): "I do not think the 'T. Wedding' is altogether a satisfactory play and as what merits it has lie in a humorous dialogue that would have to be very richly and confidently spoken, I am not sure that it would be a very wise experiment for Mr. Barker to produce it." When it was finally produced in England on 11 November 1909 by the Afternoon Theatre Company at His Majesty's Theatre, Yeats found the production so unsatisfactory that he left before the second act, though the *Times* (London) review pronounced the play on the whole "a vivid and effective little work."

Synge's reservations about *The Tinker's Wedding* have been shared by critics since. The plot is too slender to carry two acts well, and character development is slight. The primary interest in the play, and a significant source of comedy, is the contrast between two sets of values, those of the tinkers, epitomized by Mary, and those of the orthodox world, represented by the priest. The ending is a problem, if not because its antiecclesiastical action offends audience sensibilities, then because the tinkers' treatment of the priest may alienate audience sympathy for them. Regarded as a high-spirited romp, a lighthearted disparagement of establishment morality, the play is simply good fun. Because it was conceived with Synge's earliest plays and he was still reworking it while he wrote *The Playboy of the Western World,* it is of interest as a transitional step between his early one-acts and his later full-length plays.

Synge's first three-act play was *The Well of the Saints,* which he began in 1903, about a year after he drafted the first version of *The Tinker's Wedding,* and finished early the following summer, about the time he was expanding *The Tinker's Wedding* to two acts. Well before *The Tinker's Wedding* underwent further, substantial changes, *The Well of the Saints* was completed and turned over to the Fays for production by the Irish National Theatre Society. The idea for the plot was prompted by a medieval French farce which Synge may have encountered in the medieval French literature course he took at the Sorbonne; it is described in a history of French

Sara Allgood, Barry Fitzgerald, and Arthur Shields in an Abbey Theatre production of The Playboy of the Western World

theater by his former professor, Petit de Julleville, which Synge was reading in 1903. The French farce is about a blind man who carries a crippled man on his back, each compensating for the other's handicap. When both are miraculously cured, the blind man is happy, but the cripple regrets the loss of his old, easy life. Synge makes use of the idea that a miracle which looks at first to be a blessing may in fact destroy happiness, but his play deals with a married couple, both blind, who, when their sight is miraculously restored, find that their happiness depended on illusions about themselves and each other which sight stole from them. The recovery of their blindness in the end restores the possibility for happiness. The play is set in western Ireland, across the water from the Aran Islands, where Synge had seen "an old ruined church of the Ceathair Aluinn (The Four Beautiful Persons), and a holy well near it that is famous for cures of blindness and epilepsy." The play's reference to "a place across a bit of the sea, where there is an island, and the grave of the four beautiful saints" clearly identifies the well.

Yeats was delighted with Synge's new play, which he called "the best thing that could have happened to" the dramatic society. It was accepted by the company immediately and went into rehearsal in the summer of 1904 while Synge was staying in county Kerry; he returned in early September to look in on a few rehearsals before making another trip, this time to North Mayo, where he had never been. Correspondence from Yeats and Willie Fay during the months of rehearsals, and Synge's replies, show that Synge was willing to make some minor changes to avoid being needlessly offensive, but most unwilling to violate his perception of the real Ireland to accommodate anybody else's. Fay had reservations about the truth of a line which describes Mary Doul's studied refusal to look at her husband Martin as "going by with her head turned the way you'd see a priest going where there'd be a drunken man in the side ditch talking with a girl." In reply, Synge reported witnessing "a young man behaving most indecently to a girl on the roadside while two priests sat near by on a seat looking out to sea and pretending not to see what was going on. . . . What I write of Irish country life I know to be true and I most emphatically will not change a syllable of it because A, B, or C may think they know better than I do. . . . I am quite ready to avoid hurting people's feelings needlessly, but I will not falsify what I believe to be true for anybody." In fact, although Synge's first response to criticism was often strongly indignant, he often relented on longer consideration, and many of his minor textual changes were in the direction of softening language or allusions which might be thoughtlessly offensive simply because of his unorthodox views. Synge goes on in his reply to Fay, for instance, to suggest that if there were passages in the saint's role that gave "unnecessary trouble," he would do what he could to alter them if someone would point them out to him. And he did change the simile describing the studied oblivion of the priests to "the way you'd see a sainted lady going where there'd be drunken people in the side ditch singing to themselves"—after all, the dramatically necessary point was not about priests, but about Mary's deliberate refusal to look at Martin. Fay had a more basic objection to the play, that every character in it is bad-tempered, and he was afraid the play might affect the audience the same way. His suggestion that at least the saint or Molly might be made good-natured and easygoing was ignored by Synge, who told Fay he wanted to write "like a monochrome painting, all in shades of one color."

The Well of the Saints opened in the new Abbey Theatre on 4 February 1905, and copies published by A. H. Bullen were sold in the theater. (In order to protect Synge's American copyrights, John Quinn, an American lawyer and book collector, published this and other plays by Synge in very small limited editions.) Press reaction was critical of the people Synge portrayed: these unattractive characters certainly could not properly be considered truly Irish. Of the play's cool reception, Yeats wrote to Quinn, "We will have a hard fight in Ireland before we get the right for every man to see the world in his own way admitted. Synge is invaluable to us because he has that kind of intense narrow personality which necessarily raises the whole issue. It will be very curious to notice the effect of his new play. He will start next time with many enemies but with many admirers. It will be a fight like that over the first realistic plays of Ibsen." Yeats's forecast was accurate, though even he could not have foreseen the effect of Synge's next play, *The Playboy of the Western World,* which was to be regarded as his masterpiece but was also to provoke extraordinary demonstrations from hostile Dubliners. Among Synge's admirers, unexpectedly, emerged George Moore, who had not supported the dramatic movement spearheaded by Yeats since the founders of the Irish Literary Theatre went their separate ways in 1901 and who had apparently not cared for what he saw of *The Well of the Saints* in rehearsal. Yet he wrote a letter to the editor of the *Irish Times,* praising *The Well of the Saints* and pointing particularly to "the abundance and the beauty of the dialogue, to the fact that one listens to it as one listens to music, charmed by the inevitableness of the words and the ease with which phrase is linked into phrase. . . . Mr. Synge has discovered great literature in barbarous idiom as gold is discovered in quartz, and to do such a lovely thing is surely a rare literary achievement." *The Well of the Saints* also gave Synge his first taste of recognition in Europe when it was translated into German and performed in Berlin in January 1906, though it was not particularly successful and closed after a few days' run.

Critics tend to be puzzled by *The Well of the Saints,* finding it difficult to align the play thematically with Synge's others. Martin and Mary's clear choice of illusion over reality would seem to be a choice with which Synge would have little sympathy, yet they are the central characters, and they are vagrants living close to nature, a type with whom Synge always seemed to feel a sympathetic bond. The thematic relationship between major and secondary characters, the various shades of color in Synge's "monochrome painting," is a related subject of interest. Though the rather sour view of humanity that is inescapable in the play may be found disturbing, the play is well constructed, the characterizations are convincing, and the attraction of the musical dialogue helps to compensate for the characters' bad humor.

Synge kept himself apart from the business of the Abbey Theatre until 1905. It was Yeats, seconded by Lady Gregory, who was absorbed in the practical side of the theater and they who encouraged Synge's work, forming the link between Synge and the theater which was the first to perform all but one of his plays. Synge was not writing his early plays with specific actors in mind, and he did not dominate rehearsals of his plays until *The Playboy of the Western World*, though he was often present and ready with suggestions about various aspects of the productions of his plays, from setting and costumes to actors' gestures and pacing. Synge did a good deal of traveling, and even when he was in Dublin, he did not necessarily feel drawn to engage actively in theater affairs.

In 1904 a music hall and an adjoining building on Abbey Street were acquired and renovated to create a new home for the Irish National Theatre Society; a patent for the production of plays was obtained; and in the last week of the year, the new theater opened. The work was largely Yeats's and the funding that of his patron, Miss Annie Horniman. Yeats's dramatic movement had weathered the defection of other founders and of leading actors. Yeats encouraged promising writers, notably Synge, and defended their work against attacks by the press. Synge had been content to stay on the sidelines, but in 1905 an internal reorganization of the society took place which resulted in a board of directors composed of Yeats, Lady Gregory, and Synge. Willie Fay, manager, and the actors, formerly amateurs, were now salaried, thanks to the generosity of Miss Horniman. The three directors were given the sole authority for choosing plays—and it was at this juncture that the decision against producing *The Tinker's Wedding* was made; Synge's responsibility for the fate of the Abbey Theatre was not necessarily in harmony with the playwright's desire to promote his own work. Resentment among the actors at their loss of voice in the selection of plays and political sentiments which opposed the directors' nonpolitical values caused the departure of a significant portion of the company's actors after the reorganization. The defectors formed their own rival company, and it was a difficult period for the Irish National Theatre Society, to which Synge, the only one of the directors who resided in Dublin, now devoted a good deal of time.

In addition to searching for new plays and advising Willie Fay on management problems, Synge frequently went along on the company's tours. In the process, he fell in love with Molly Allgood, a young actress. The younger sister of Sara Allgood, an established member of the company, Molly took the stage name of Maire O'-Neill and played a walk-on part in *The Well of the Saints,* then played Cathleen in a revival of *Riders to the Sea.* Early in 1906 she was playing Nora Burke in a revival of *In the Shadow of the Glen,* and both her great promise as an actress and Synge's attraction to her became evident to the company. She was fifteen years younger than he, a product of the working class with only a grade-school education, yet she was to hold a central position in the few remaining years of Synge's life, and it was she who first performed the roles of Pegeen Mike in *The Playboy of the Western World* and Deirdre in *Deirdre of the Sorrows* (1910). Marriage plans were repeatedly postponed by the fear of family opposition to the unlikely match, by their work, and by Synge's increasing illness with Hodgkin's disease, which proved to be terminal. Synge's emotional and physical ups and downs, his pattern of writing and rewriting, his concerns with structure and tone as he worked on *The Playboy of the Western World* and *Deirdre of the Sorrows* are documented in unusual detail in his frequent letters to Molly Allgood.

Synge's earliest work on *The Playboy of the Western World* was done before Molly Allgood entered his life. He must have begun developing his ideas for it after he finished *The Well of the Saints* in 1904, for sketches of three acts are to be found in the notebook where he was making notes on his visit to county Mayo that September. The play is set in Mayo, and it contains snippets of information and bits of dialogue recorded in Synge's notebooks from his travels all over the west of Ireland. In Aran he had first heard the story of a man from Connaught "who killed his father with the blow of a spade when he was in a passion, and then fled to this island and threw himself on the mercy of some of the natives with whom he was said to be related." Synge attributes an "impulse to protect the criminal" found throughout western Ireland to a primitive feeling "that a man will not do wrong unless he is under the influence of a passion which is as irresponsible as a storm on the sea." He may have transferred the story to Mayo out of the feeling that the miserable life there would lend itself particularly to the mentality he depicts in the play where the people exult in the daring overthrow of authority represented by a patricide. "In Mayo," he observed, "one cannot forget that in spite of the beauty of the scenery the people in it are debased and nearly demoralized by bad housing and lodging and the endless misery of the rain." A return trip to Mayo the following year with Jack Yeats, when Synge was commissioned by the *Manchester Guardian* to do a series of illustrated articles on life in this poor and crowded part of Ireland, reinforced Synge's views, though he always found something attractive and colorful in the lives of the poorest people.

Synge worked on *The Playboy of the Western World,* generally regarded as his masterpiece, in 1905 and wrote and rewrote steadily through 1906. The play depicts the reception given to Christy Mahon by Pegeen Mike and a few of the people who live near her when he arrives in their midst and admits to the impulsive murder of his domineering father. They embrace him as a lad of daring, a clever and fearless hero. Pegeen, who is on the brink of marriage to a colorless cousin until Christy arrives, and the Widow Quin, a lusty lady who likes to have a man around, vie for Christy's favor. He, at first timid and self-effacing, blooms under their admiration, growing quickly into their image of him. When he is in the full bloom of his newfound life and love, however, his father turns up, head bandaged, but very much alive. He is astonished to find his son, whom he has always thought "a dribbling idiot," being touted as "the wonder of the western world," cheered wildly as he wins at all the games and sports of the day. Pegeen, who has just pledged herself to Christy in a beautiful love scene, turns against him, as does the crowd; his demonstrated deeds of the day mean nothing once his initial claim to fame has been proved a lie. When the Mahons quarrel again, and again Christy lays his father out with a swing of the loy, seeing the deed in part at least as his last hope to win Pegeen, she and the rest are appalled; "the gallous story" of a patricide becomes simply "a dirty deed" when it is done before their eyes. The scene gets ugly as all turn on Christy, and Pegeen herself burns his leg with sod from the fire. When Old Mahon revives yet again, he and Christy unite against the "villainy of Mayo and the fools is here" and leave, with Christy masterfully taking command, to his father's obvious delight. The curtain falls on Pegeen's grief as she realizes what she has lost in Christy.

The many typescripts of various drafts of the play testify to Synge's determination to get it just right. He later explained his working method to John Quinn, who was offering to buy the play's manuscript: "I make a rough draft first and work over it with a pen till it is nearly unreadable; then I make a clean draft again, adding whatever seems wanting, and so on. My final drafts—I letter them as I go along—were 'G' for the first act, 'I' for the second, and 'K' for the third! I really wrote parts of the last act more than eleven times, as I often took out individual scenes and worked at them separately." In the summer of 1906 his letters to Molly Allgood suggest that he felt he was well on the way to finishing the play, and it was originally scheduled to open on 19 December. By the end of October he was getting desperate with the problems involved in perfecting it; he wrote to Molly, "I don't know what will become of me if I don't get the *Playboy* off my hands soon. I nearly wrote to them last night to ask them to put on *The Well of the Saints* instead of it in December so that I might have a few months more to work at it, but I don't like the thought of having it hanging over me all this winter when I ought to be so happy. Parts of it are the best work, I think, that I have ever done, but parts of it are not structurally strong or good. I have been all this time trying to get over weak situations by strong writing, but now I find it won't do, and I'm at my wit's end." A little over a week later he reported the play "very nearly ready" and wrote to Lady Gregory to arrange a reading. When the day came, only the first two acts were ready to read to Yeats and Lady Gregory and the Fays. He continued to agonize over the third act, illness plagued him, and he finally asked to have the opening of *Playboy* postponed. He read them the third act on 28 November, but remained dissatisfied and continued revising all through December and into January, when the play went into rehearsal.

Lady Gregory described Synge's presiding over rehearsals as "a tiger with its cub." He agreed to minor alterations, mostly cuts to reduce offensive language, but he kept the text intact for publication. Rehearsal cuts included a passage in which Pegeen accuses the Widow Quin of having "reared a black ram at your own breast, so that the Lord Bishop of Connaught felt the elements of a Christian, and he eating it after in a kidney stew," and another in which Pegeen's father enthusiastically describes the flow of drink at a wake resulting in five or six men at the funeral "stretched out retching speechless on the holy stones."

Though everyone was somewhat apprehensive about what public response opening night, 26 January 1907, would bring, there was no expectation of serious trouble. However, *The Playboy of the Western World,* on which Synge had lavished so much anxious care, provoked the most violent reaction in the history of Dublin theater. The audience was quiet for two acts but began hissing during the third, and the play finished in a noisy tumult of mixed applause and reprobation. The line which appeared to cause most offense was Christy's insistence that he wants only Pegeen and would not be tempted even by "a drift of chosen females, standing in their shifts itself." Willie Fay, playing Christy, apparently substituted "Mayo girls" for "chosen females" that night, but the reaction to a common name for an undergarment probably would have been much the same in any case. Irish nationalistic feelings were high, and Synge's plays had caused offense before among those who felt that Ireland and the Irish should always be depicted with decorum on the stage. The reviews of the Saturday night opening in the Monday papers ranged from the observation in the *Irish Times* that the dialogue was full of indiscretions which brought "what in other respects was a brilliant success to an inglorious conclusion" to the *Freeman's Journal*'s revulsion at the "squalid, offensive production," the "unmitigated, protracted libel upon Irish peasant men and worse still upon Irish peasant girlhood," by means of "the barbarous jargon, the elaborate and incessant cursings of these repulsive creatures" who peopled the play. Monday's performance drew a full house which was predisposed to create an uproar. The noise was so great that the play appeared to be largely a dumb show, and the action was stopped altogether twice during futile attempts to restore order.

The directors, led by Yeats, considered the public's reaction a challenge and announced to the press that the play would continue until it had "been heard sufficiently to be judged on its merits"; though it had been scheduled for only a week, they would, if necessary, perform it all the following week as well. With Synge's permission, Lady Gregory, in consultation with the actors, cut a good many objectionable phrases in addition to the few which had been omitted during rehearsals, and the play was performed through the rest of the week under heavy police protection. Nightly, arrests were made; daily, Yeats testified against rioters who were duly lectured and fined by a magistrate. By Thursday the rioting diminished, and the play was heard on Friday and Saturday. The following Monday, Yeats held a public debate on the freedom of the theater. Synge, ill with influenza following exhaustion and anxiety, did not attend, but Yeats stood up to the hostile crowd, insisting, as he had to the rowdy third-night audience, that "every man has a right to hear" a play "and condemn it if he pleases, but no man has a right to interfere with another man hearing a play and judging for himself. The country that condescends either to bully or to permit itself to be bullied soon ceases to have any fine qualities."

John Millington Synge

Even after *The Playboy of the Western World* closed, the controversy raged on in the press and erupted again over a revival in 1909 and on the company's New World tour in 1911. Opposition to the play came from all sides and in all forms, encouraged by Maunsel Press's publication of the play, which sold two hundred copies in the first week. Resolutions condemning it were passed by councils in Clare, in Kerry, even in Liverpool. The Gort Board of Guardians prohibited workhouse children from picnics on Lady Gregory's estate. The architect who designed the Abbey Theatre and supported the company loyally thought Synge got what he deserved from the hostile audience, whose disapproval of "the glorification of murder on the stage" he shared. William Boyle, a fellow playwright, publicly withdrew his three plays from the Abbey's repertoire. Another playwright, Padraic Colum, wrote to Synge that he had been twice to see *The Playboy of the Western World,* and though his dislike of the last act was less intense the second time, partly because Pegeen's burning of Christy's leg had been omitted, he remained dissatisfied with the play, feeling that Pegeen should have stood by her man. George Moore wrote that he admired the play very much, but he too took exception to the end, finding the burning of Christy's leg especially intolerable and suggesting what he thought was a more appropriate conclusion for a comedy. Synge had already tried Moore's suggested conclusion, along with practically every other possible ending to the play, and rejected it. His various sketches and drafts of act 3 include a considerable range of possibilities: Pegeen might marry Shawn, her cousin, or Old Mahon or Christy; Christy might marry Pegeen or the Widow Quin; Old Mahon might be really killed in the third act encounter. Synge settled ultimately for the conclusion which would best emphasize the loss suffered by Irish people like Pegeen who have dreams of better lives than those dictated by social convention such as the loveless marriage or by domineering authority figures such as Christy's father, but have not the courage to bring the dream to fulfillment. Christy does; he subdues his father finally, though—appropriately for comedy—he does not kill him. He does not marry Pegeen, who proves herself unable to cut the bonds of social convention, but he is transformed into "a likely gaffer in the end of all" and exits triumphantly to "go romancing through a romping lifetime from this hour to the dawning to the judgement day." Pegeen must be a heroine attractive enough to make an audience feel her loss of Christy in the end, but she has to deserve the loss: thus her cruel betrayal of Christy when she is faced with the ugly reality of an act which, as a safely distant story of daring, she praised.

Of the three most frequent objections to *The Playboy of the Western World,* one, to such "filthy" language as the word *shift,* was provincial and unimportant. The other two, to the central idea of a heroic murderer and to the lack of a conventionally happy ending for a comedy compounded by the ugliness of the climactic scene, are more universal objections, yet these elements grow out of the very essence of Synge's conception of the play, which was not meant to be simply light entertainment. In answer to the criticism that, unlike his earlier work, the play was "unduly grotesque" and "superfluously coarse," Synge agreed that there was a difference of which he was perfectly conscious. "The romantic note and a Rabelaisian note are working to a climax through a great part of the play, and . . . the Rabelaisian note, the 'gross note,' if you will, *must* have its climax no matter who may be shocked."

The Playboy of the Western World eventually became a cherished classic even in Ireland. George Moore, who had objected to the third act, acknowledged fifteen years later that "the letter I sent to Synge was superficial." He admired Synge's strength in refusing to change the play to fit anyone else's notion of what a play should be: "if the play had been altered we should all have been disgraced." When the company went on tour in Scotland and England in May and June of 1907, Yeats and Lady Gregory persuaded them to try *The Playboy of the Western World* again, but at intellectual centers only, not in the towns where there were large numbers of Irish people who were likely to react badly. Yeats had both his speech at the debate on the freedom of the theater and a new defense of the play printed for sale to the audiences. The cast was understandably nervous about the performance at Oxford, but, the *Oxford Times* reported, the play found there "a warmth and enthusiasm that appeared to surprise the company." Four days later, the play was performed in London, with Synge present to reap the rewards of its great success. Literary London made much of him; the play which brought him the most notoriety at home was also the play that brought him fame abroad.

The Playboy of the Western World is generally considered to be Synge's best play, in terms of both its stageworthiness and its literary merit. Its language draws special praise, particularly Christy's speeches in his love scenes with Pegeen.

The language is especially important because Christy is often seen as the poet in a play about the relationship between imagination and reality; his imagination and increasingly effective language create a new reality. In *The Playboy of the Western World* Synge was examining not only the assumptions of conventional society but also the assumptions about artistic conventions and the role of the poet in society. Critics have also commented on the play's mythic quality, relating Christy's story to Christ's and to Oedipus's in particular, as well as to more general mythic patterns.

Synge's last play, still not completed to his satisfaction at his death, was in some ways a radical departure from his earlier work. Part of the reason for this change was undoubtedly the hostility aroused by *The Playboy of the Western World,* as well as by the perceptions of contemporary Irish people that Synge had set forth in his earlier plays. Certainly Synge was not indifferent to the hostility. His hard work and anxiety over the production of *The Playboy of the Western World,* coupled with the strain of the riots, led to an illness which kept him in bed for more than two weeks. He had a relapse in early March, and while he was still feeling ill, he received word that Charles Frohman, a New York producer, was coming to select plays for an American tour of the company. Synge was furious to find that Frohman was to be shown several of Yeats's plays and five or six of Lady Gregory's, but only one of his: *Riders to the Sea.* In answer to Synge's letter of complaint about the short shrift his plays were given by the company, Frank Fay reminded him that writers could always turn to the reading public, but professional actors were dependent on the good will of theatergoers and could not simply play whatever they liked. *Riders to the Sea,* he pointed out, had been staged "very frequently, and when you write uncontroversial pieces you will get plenty of show." Synge accepted Fay's argument, and he was beginning to be intrigued with the notion of getting away from contemporary subject matter, wondering whether "drama as a beautiful thing" was a lost art.

In fact, Synge had been thinking of doing a different sort of play well before the riots over *The Playboy of the Western World.* In December 1906, before the play went into rehearsal, he wrote to Molly Allgood, "My next play must be quite different from the P. Boy ... I want to do something quiet and stately and restrained and I want you to act in it." Still earlier, in August, when *The Playboy of the Western World* was far from finished, he was in the woods of Kerry, writing to her, "It is good for anyone to be out in such beauty as this and it stirs me up to try and make my Irish plays as beautiful as Ireland—I wonder if you could act a beautiful part? . . . We must try you." Her beautiful part was to be that of Deirdre from the heroic legends of Ireland's past; the "quiet, stately and restrained" play, *Deirdre of the Sorrows.* Synge's thoughts of the possibilities for such a play were from the beginning entwined with his thoughts of Molly Allgood. In November he asked her to get a copy of Lady Gregory's *Cuchulain of Muirthemne* and read in it "The Sons of Usnach." Synge had reviewed the book, a retelling of medieval Irish legends in Anglo-Irish dialect, with enthusiasm in 1902, and was now, with his thoughts of Irish beauty and his love for Molly, focusing on its most famous love story. According to the legend, King Conchubor had Deirdre reared from her childhood to be his queen. Free-spirited and unwilling to be tied down to a staid life with an old king, Deirdre ran away with the youthful, brave, and handsome Naisi, despite her knowledge that she was falling into the doom which had been foretold for her at her birth: that her unequaled beauty would bring tragedy to herself, to Naisi, and to Ireland. Obsessed with Deirdre, Conchubor eventually succeeded in luring the lovers back to Ireland and killing Naisi, and rather than marry Conchubor, Deirdre killed herself.

Though Synge was thinking of a Deirdre play before the end of 1906, illness delayed his work. The illness that struck him after the *Playboy* riots lingered through the spring, and the glands in his neck began to enlarge. He had needed surgery on a gland in his neck in 1897, probably the first manifestation of the Hodgkin's disease which would finally prove fatal, though its symptoms did not recur for nearly a decade. Now his doctor said that Synge ought to have the enlarged glands removed before his wedding to Molly Allgood. After the company's tour in England and a summer holiday in Wicklow with Molly Allgood, Synge had the operation in September. He convalesced cheerfully, planning his marriage and beginning work on *Deirdre of the Sorrows.*

The greatest difficulty Synge contemplated in dealing with legendary heroic characters was to find a way to make them as vivid and real as his contemporary peasant characters. In September 1907, just before his operation, he wrote to an Irish-American correspondent, "I am a little afraid that the 'Saga' people might loosen my grip on reality." More than a year later, in the heat of revisions, he was still very conscious of this problem, as he wrote to John Quinn, who was publishing twelve copies of act 2 of *The Playboy of the Western World* to protect the American copyright: "I don't know whether I told you that I am trying a three-act prose 'Deirdre', to change my hand. I am not sure yet whether I shall be able to make a satisfactory play out of it. These saga people, when one comes to deal with them, seem very remote; one does not know what they thought or what they [ate] or where they went to sleep, so one is apt to fall into rhetoric. In any case, I find it an interesting experiment, full of new difficulties, and I shall be the better, I think, for the change."

In the fall and winter of 1907-1908 Synge did a great deal of work on *Deirdre of the Sorrows.* Toward the end of October he reported to Molly Allgood that he had written the first ten pages of dialogue "in great spirits and joy," and a couple of weeks later he wrote that he had finished a second rough draft of the whole, after "working at *Deirdre* till my head is going round. I . . . got her into such a mess I think I'd have put her into the fire. . . . Since yesterday I have pulled two acts into one, so that if I can work it the play will have three acts instead of four." By the end of November, the frenzy of creating *Deirdre of the Sorrows* had crowded even wedding preparations out of his life, as he wrote to Molly, who was on tour with the company, "I'm squirming and thrilling and quivering with the excitement of writing Deirdre and I *daren't* break the thread of composition by going out to look for digs and moving into them at this moment. . . . Let me get Deirdre out of danger—she may be safe in a week—then marriage in God's name." By the first of December he had completed a seventh draft of act 3; the first week of January found him working to strengthen the structure of act 1 and give it more dramatic impact.

He was busy too in his role as director of the theater company, which was undergoing another crisis, culminating in the resignation of Frank and Willie Fay. He did find a flat in the middle of January 1908, and he moved into it in early February, but his wedding to Molly Allgood was never to take place. By the time they were ready to set a definite date, Synge's doctor ordered him back into the hospital, and on 4 May he underwent further surgery, this time on a lump in his side. The doctors informed Synge's family afterward that his condition was incurable, but Synge and Molly Allgood were not told. He was able to leave the hospital in July, and although he was depressed at how slow his recovery seemed, he went back to work on *Deirdre of the Sorrows* in August, fretting over difficulties in the second act and thinking of cutting the play down to two acts. He was also much taken up with plans to publish some of his poetry. In October he made a trip to Germany, and when he returned to Dublin in November he went back to work on the edition of his poems and on *Deirdre of the Sorrows,* of which he reported to Molly Allgood on 22 December, "I've pretty nearly gone on to the end of *Deirdre* and cut it down a little. It is delicate work—a scene is so easily spoiled." On 3 January 1909 he wrote to Lady Gregory that he felt there was still "a good deal to be done with the dialogue, and some scenes in the first Act must be re-written to make them fit in with the new parts I have added. I only work a little every day as I suffer more than I like with indigestion and general uneasiness inside—I hope it is only because I haven't got over the shock of the operation—the doctors are vague and don't say much that is definite." A month later he was back in the hospital. He took the play with him, hoping to be able to work on it, but he weakened steadily, and when he died on 24 March 1909, *Deirdre of the Sorrows* was still not completed to his satisfaction, though he had worked his way through nine drafts of act 1, eleven of act 3, and had the fifteenth of act 2 under way.

During his illness Synge had asked that Yeats and Lady Gregory complete the play for him if necessary. When he saw it early in 1908, Yeats observed that there was "nothing grotesque" in *Deirdre of the Sorrows* "and an astonishing amount of sheer lyrical beauty. However, by the end of the year, Synge had decided that he was not satisfied with sheer lyrical beauty; he wanted a thread of the grotesque woven through the play. With this in mind, he introduced into act 2 Owen, a character who commits suicide after having been driven mad by his hopeless love of Deirdre and his awareness of the evil which will befall her. Synge wanted him worked into act 1 as well. Yeats, Lady Gregory, and Molly Allgood went through the various typescript drafts to arrive at a final version of the play, and after attempting to write a few passages that would introduce Owen into the first act, they decided instead to have the play performed and published as Synge left it. Molly Allgood directed the play, which was performed on 13 January 1910, and played the title role as Synge intended. The play had a mixed reception (the best that can be said for any of Synge's plays except perhaps *Riders to the Sea*). It was thought less stageworthy than *The Playboy of the Western World,* though Molly's performance as Deirdre was admired. Both Synge's supporters and his detractors agreed that he accomplished what he set out to do; it was the appropriateness of the goal that was in question: "His idea seems to have been to wrest the legend from its exalted plane and breathe the commonplaces of everyday life into it—in fact, to vulgarize the beautiful legend. . . . That he succeeded in doing this is only too true," wrote one contemporary commentator, who did not share Synge's taste for realism.

Because *Deirdre of the Sorrows* has been classified as "unfinished," it gets less critical attention than it might otherwise. Yet the play does not seem incomplete, and perhaps the qualification to Yeats's praise in his preface to the play is unnecessary. Had Synge lived to complete the revisions he intended, Yeats wrote, "*Deirdre of the Sorrows* would have been his masterwork, so much beauty is there in its course, and such wild nobleness in its end, and so poignant is an emotion and wisdom that were his own preparation for death." Even "unfinished," *Deirdre of the Sorrows* deserves to be ranked with *The Playboy of the Western World* and *Riders to the Sea.* Critics agree that the skill with which Synge met the challenge of humanizing his heroic-poetic characters is remarkable, and the realism enhances the dramatic value of the play. The language of the play is a dignified version of the peasant dialect he used in his other plays. It is both beautiful and earthy, perfectly appropriate to his Deirdre, who is both a child of nature and a queen among women, both a woman who loves and fears and quarrels and a heroine who deliberately chooses to sacrifice immediate joys to the eternal beauty of her legend. The blend of poetic beauty and dramatic effect in the play is usually judged successful. Purely as a stage piece, the play is thought less effective than *The Playboy of the Western World,* but the mood of tragic inevitability, of serene triumph even in the face of loss of love and life, is generally admired. As an artist Synge was still growing in depth and technical proficiency, reaching in new directions as he wrote his last play. There is considerable interest in the play's development of the themes of love and death, both in relation to Synge's earlier plays and in relation to the facts of his own life: his romance with Molly Allgood and his acute consciousness of his own mortality. Deirdre's death provided a means of avoiding the ugliness of old age and the pain of diminishing love, a means of perpetuating a story of her life and love that will be "a joy and triumph to the ends of life and time."

The passage of eight decades has changed the perspective from which Synge's drama is viewed. What shocked Dubliners in the first decade of the twentieth century no longer shocks. Language that was "filthy" then is "colorful" now. Synge's metaphors are no longer offensive, but they are still striking; the individual turn of phrase and the rhythms of the peasant dialect still arrest the ear, now without disturbing the listener's sense of propriety. The Irish, once enraged by Synge's perception in the Irish character of something other than unsullied virtue, now give him credit for capturing the individuality of the nation, recognizing the positive qualities of the joy and variety Synge sought to depict in his peasants, as well as the truth of his portrayal of the strictures of poverty and social convention. Synge's place in the history of Irish drama is similar to Anton Chekhov's in Russian and Bernard Shaw's in English; they follow Henrik Ibsen's lead in the transition from the conventionality and artificiality of nineteenth-century drama to the realism of the early twentieth, suffering the effects of the public outrage that any innovator suffers, and establishing the taste for honesty and individuality of expression which has since influenced innumerable twentieth-century dramatists. In his time, Synge was noted for his realism. Since, though the realism is acknowledged, the other pole of his art, the poetic imagination, is rightly receiving its share of attention. Synge achieved what he set out to achieve: drama in which life is honestly pictured but also transcended by the artistic imagination. His plays exemplify his belief that "what is highest in poetry is always reached where the dreamer is leaning out to reality, or where the man of real life is lifted out of it," and he fits his own description of the greatest of poets: "They are supremely engrossed with life, and yet with the wildness of their fancy they are always passing out of what is simple and plain."

Letters:

Letters to Molly: John Millington Synge to Maire O'Neill 1906-1909, edited by Ann Saddlemyer (Cambridge, Mass.: Harvard University Press, 1971; London: Oxford University Press, 1971);

Synge to Lady Gregory and Yeats, edited by Saddlemyer (Dublin: Cuala, 1971).

Bibliographies:

Weldon Thornton, "J. M. Synge," in *Anglo-Irish Literature: A Review of Research*, edited by Richard J. Finneran (New York: Modern Language Association of America, 1976), pp. 315-365;

Thornton, "J. M. Synge," in *Recent Research on Anglo-Irish Writers*, edited by Richard J. Finneran (New York: Modern Language Association of America, 1983), pp. 154-180.

Biographies:

Donna Gerstenberger, *John Millington Synge* (New York: Twayne, 1964);

David H. Greene and Edward M. Stephens, *J. M. Synge 1871-1909* (New York: Macmillan, 1959; revised, New York: New York University Press, 1983).

References:

Maurice Bourgeois, *John Millington Synge and the Irish Theatre* (London: Constable, 1913);

J. B. Bushrui, ed., *Sunshine and The Moon's Delight: A Centenary Tribute to John Millington Synge 1871-1909* (Gerrards Cross, U.K.: Smythe, 1972; Beirut: American University, 1972);

Nicholas Grene, *Synge: A Critical Study of the Plays* (London: Macmillan, 1975);

Maurice Harmon, ed., *J. M. Synge Centenary Papers 1971* (Dublin: Dolmen, 1972);

Weldon Thornton, *J. M. Synge and the Western Mind*, Irish Literary Studies, 4 (Gerrards Cross, U.K.: Smythe, 1979).

Papers:

The Library of Trinity College, Dublin, contains Synge's manuscripts and typescripts, notebooks and diaries, correspondence and photographs.

Francis Thompson

(16 December 1859 - 13 November 1907)

This entry was updated by Robert Beum (University of Saskatchewan) from his entry in DLB 19: British Poets, 1880-1914.

SELECTED BOOKS: *The Life and Labours of Saint John Baptist de la Salle* (London: Sinkins, 1891);

Poems (London: Elkin Mathews & John Lane, 1893; Boston: Copeland & Day, 1894);

Sister Songs: An Offering to Two Sisters (London: John Lane, 1895; Boston: Copeland & Day, 1895);

New Poems (London: Constable, 1897; Boston: Copeland & Day, 1897);

Health and Holiness (London: Burns & Oates, 1905; St. Louis: Herder, 1905);

Ode to English Martyrs (London: Privately printed, 1906);

Shelley: An Essay (London: Burns & Oates, 1909; New York: Scribners, 1909);

Saint Ignatius Loyola, edited by J. H. Pollen (London: Burns & Oates, 1909);

A Renegade Poet and Other Essays (Boston: Bell, 1910);

Poems (Portland, Maine: Mosher, 1911);

The Works of Francis Thompson, 3 volumes (volume 1, London: Burns & Oates, 1913; volumes 2-3, London: Burns, Oates & Washbourne, 1925);

The Collected Poetry of Francis Thompson (London: Hodder & Stoughton, 1913);

Uncollected Verses (London: Privately printed, 1917);

Youthful Verses (Preston: Halewood, 1928);

Poems of Francis Thompson, edited by Terence L. Connolly (New York & London: Century, 1932; revised edition, New York & London: Appleton-Century, 1941);

Literary Criticisms Newly Discovered and Collected, edited by Connolly (New York: Dutton, 1948);

The Man Has Wings: New Poems and Plays, edited by Connolly (Garden City: Hanover House, 1957);

The Real Robert Louis Stevenson and Other Critical Essays, edited by Connolly (New York: University Publishers, 1959).

Francis Thompson

Francis Thompson is best known for his ode "The Hound of Heaven" and for a short quatrain poem, "In No Strange Land" (or "The Kingdom of God"). Defying all cultural changes and literary reassessments, these two pieces have retained a place not only in British but in world literature, both as memorable poems and as expressions of religious thought and feeling at the deepest and most sincere levels. Though Thompson wrote a fairly large body of religious poetry, it is mainly these two remarkable achievements that have prompted such claims as John Davidson's that Thompson is "perhaps the greatest of English Roman Catholic poets of post-

Reformation times." Today most readers would probably reserve such a title for Gerard Manley Hopkins. Nevertheless, such estimates of Thompson have often been rendered and ought to keep us from being too complacent about the usual designation of Thompson as a "minor" poet. How is it that a poet can be minor and yet write several major and at least two great poems? It is more sensible to think of Thompson as a badly flawed yet major writer. His poems are extremely uneven (as are William Wordsworth's and Thomas Hardy's) and in certain ways distinctly limited. But there is nothing minor about his productivity (almost four hundred poems in eight years, which compares favorably with W. B. Yeats's composition of about the same number over about fifty years) and nothing minor about either of his characteristic subjects—religious experience and intense spiritual suffering—or his preferred verse form, the grand ode, which from ancient times to the present has been held as a genre lower only than epic and tragedy.

Thompson's orthodoxy, real piety, and unusual innocence have also contributed to his fame, particularly, of course, among Roman Catholics. It is probably not far from the mark to say that he is overvalued by a very small (and proportionately ever-shrinking) Catholic contingent and undervalued by everyone else, including most Catholic readers. For several decades his reputation has remained at the low level to which it sank in the early 1920s, partly as the result of a mounting reaction against all things Victorian and partly as the consequence of a shift in literary fashion away from soft romantic poetry and toward a "harder"—a drier, more ironic, less effusive—type.

It is unlikely that Thompson will ever regain the wide and enthusiastic readership his work as a whole enjoyed between the late 1890s and World War I. But the fact remains that, despite his faults, he is a rewarding poet and when all is said and done still stands as the author of several poems distinguished by greatness of scope and insight, if not at every point by complete artistic success. By consensus, this group includes at least the following: "The Hound of Heaven," "In No Strange Land," "An Anthem of Earth," "The Mistress of Vision," "A Fallen Yew," "From the Night of Forebeing," "All Flesh," and "Contemplation." Some of his other poems, including "Daisy," "To Daisies," "To a Snowflake," "Any Saint," "Arab Love-Song," "The Nineteenth Century," "Of Nature: Laud and Plaint," "To the English Martyrs," and "Nocturn," achieve, if not greatness, memorable charm or resonance. "Nocturn," a deeply felt lyric that attains perfection of form, has been, for no apparent reason, almost universally ignored.

Thompson's short life is a legend of dereliction: poverty, drug addiction, solitariness, and chronic illness. The life lends no credence to the environmentalist and psychoanalytical views which see unpropitious surroundings and childhood traumas as the root causes of later psychic troubles.

The poet was born in Preston, Lancashire, on 16 December 1859. His mother, Mary Morton Thompson, and father, Charles Thompson, zealous converts to Catholicism and loving and generous parents, provided him with a stable home, as well as excellent schooling and other opportunities of which Francis took small advantage. At first he studied for the priesthood (St. Cuthbert's College, Ushaw, 1870-1877). Bright and intuitive, but dreamy, dilatory, and pathetically weak-willed, he was rejected in 1877 as hopelessly unsuited for clerical duties. The sense of inadequacy and guilt resulting from this failure may have exacerbated Thompson's seemingly congenital melancholy, apathy, and morbidity of temper. As a medical student at Owens College in nearby Manchester he showed no improvement in self-discipline and was dismissed in 1884. His chief legacy from Manchester was addiction to laudanum (a legal and popular opiate tincture), taken at first, on prescription, to alleviate the pain of a serious lung infection.

In December 1885, without money and without any immediate or long-range purposes, he arrived in London and began three years of destitute wandering. From near-starvation, exposure, worsening tuberculosis, and unbroken addiction, he was rescued by Wilfrid and Alice Meynell, Catholic poets and journalists who were the indefatigable editors of the leading literary journal of the "Catholic revival," *Merry England*.

Under the solicitous care of the Meynells and later of the Premonstratensian brothers at their monastery infirmary in Surrey, Thompson achieved, in 1889, a bitterly painful and temporary but important remission of the drug habit and also some stabilization of general health. The "cure" was followed by what may be the greatest outpouring of impressive poetry ever recorded. In fact, all but a handful of Thompson's poems, and virtually all his important ones, were composed between 1889 and 1897.

Thompson's addiction to laudanum may well be more than a superficial fact of biography or "life-style" (his years of addiction were certainly years of life without style). Contrary to fashionable mythology, all evidence points to the fact that opium is the enemy, not the friend, of imagination and productivity. In any event, when Thompson reverted to the laudanum bottle he reverted to poetic sterility. But the issue is more complex. Except for the relatively brief cure, his addiction covered about the last two decades of his life; and his dosage levels were, characteristically, close to the level of maximum tolerance, a fact which suggests that for long periods the poet was cut off from the normal responses of the sensibility and experienced on the one hand the bizarre phantasmagoria of hallucination, on the other an illusory sense of independence and world mastery. His rehabilitation was effected in the most brutal way: he was simply removed from all opiates. He was thus plunged into a complex nervous agony which included intense craving, acute depression, and all but unbearable physical pain. It seems likely that the addiction and the cure, considered together, are responsible for much that is wrong with Thompson's poems: for some of the obscurely motivated gloom and outcry, and for some of the strained imagery and metaphors which seem to have no relationship either to general human experience of reality or to the particular experiences the poems are trying to present and evaluate, and which may be remembered sights and sounds from hallucinatory experience.

Throughout his last decade, Thompson's creations were mostly in prose. All of it is readable, much of it interesting, some of it touched by Thompson's genius. Perhaps the best thing in it is *Health and Holiness* (1905), a piquant, good-natured, and sensible little book endorsing the dignity of the body (Brother Ass) and tactfully disposing of the traditions of violent asceticism.

Interestingly, "The Hound of Heaven," conceived in 1888 but not completed until May 1890, was one of the very first products of Thompson's spiritual maturity and release from opium. The poem treats the highest possible theme—a universal truth of man's secret experience, his harried but stubborn flight from the truth of the soul, from God—and deals with it at the deepest possible psychic level. And though this poem of genuine mysticism may not be without aesthetic blemish, Thompson's artistry is here equal to the task, so that the poem becomes as clear and moving as it is cosmic. Much of the power stems from the basic figure: that of an awful power tracking man like some relentless, sure-scented beast. Like much of the best work of other romantic poets, "The Hound of Heaven" supports Longinus's belief (expressed in *On the Sublime*) that the literary works ultimately held to be the most fascinating and powerful are those whose intellectual and emotional intensities produce the effect of wonder. That literary modernists have not taken to the poem reflects to some extent the fact that its poetics and values have been arbitrarily excluded or evaded rather than seriously considered and finally rejected. On the other hand, the mature W. H. Auden, usually a fair-minded arbiter, flatly calls the poem "no good." In any event, it is important to see that the poem is by no means, as some have suggested, mere "Catholicism set to meter." The word *God* does not appear in it, and whatever God may mean or be, the pursuer in this poem is personified, at last, as Love. Leone Vivante, commenting on the ode, says rightly that Thompson "does not especially extol a reality outside time . . . does not emphasize the infinite as the unintelligible, the unknowable," but "searches into it without tracing it necessarily either to a transcendent Deity or to a relatively transcendent influence."

Publication of the poem in the July 1890 issue of *Merry England* went a long way toward establishing Thompson's reputation among his fellow communicants. It was reprinted in 1893 in the poet's first collection, *Poems*. This volume was warmly received in most quarters, though several reviewers (including Coventry Patmore) objected to the poet's preciosity in word choice, and to what seemed a lack of restraint.

Only two more collections were published in Thompson's lifetime: the slight *Sister Songs: An Offering to Two Sisters* in 1895 and the splendid *New Poems* in 1897. *New Poems* extended Thompson's fame to quarters it had not yet reached. But even before 1897 Thompson sensed a loss of poetic vitality and predicted that he would thenceforth achieve very little in poetry.

Many readers have claimed that "An Anthem of Earth," a long ode in irregular blank verse, is in its own way as powerful a poem as "The Hound of Heaven." It sees human life as a doomed innocence, a helpless dependence born to inexorable extinction by an all-devouring earth. But the poem's darkness is a darkness of grandeur. One critic, R. L. Mégroz, says that the poem's rhythm, "Carrying tremendous images . . . gives to the poem the force of a thunderbolt."

More obscure, but more songlike and symbolically inventive, is "The Mistress of Vision," a suggestive poem which, with its rich imagery, indirectly affirms Christian renunciation, the constant seeking for God, and poetic creativity. The poem's lady, the mistress of vision, is, according to Terence L. Connolly, "Queen of the triple realm of Heaven, of Grace and of Poetry." Immensely helpful for an understanding of this worthy but difficult poem is the commentary by John O'Connor (reprinted in Mégroz's study of Thompson).

Far simpler and closer to ordinary experience, but equally rich and poignant, is "A Fallen Yew" (probably written in 1891), a meditation on a felled, quite ancient yew tree Thompson had known at Ushaw. The tree had had a secret heart, a sheltering and preserving force:

But bird nor child might touch by any art
Each other's or the tree's hid heart,
A whole God's breadth apart.

Similarly in man, as J. C. Reid puts it, "there is a hidden, unplumbable mystery, the essence of his particular personality, his deep-hid secret self."

"In No Strange Land," discovered after Thompson's death from tuberculosis in 1907, is probably the last poem the poet wrote and has long been considered one of the great short poems in English. It articulates the poet's spiritual vision in its final selfless maturity. Reid says of it: "Now brought unforgettably together are the experience of the streets and the experience of the heart, the certainty of the continual Incarnation. . . . Thompson had emerged from the dark forest of his life with a vision we may call truly mystical; and he expressed it here in language purged of . . . elaborations, with the plain poetic beauty of his true self."

Poetry is at once vision and craft. The great poets are those who have depth and range and have mastered the technical skills that turn insight into compelling communication. What the poet faces is the necessity of inventing or appropriating images and symbols that tend both to objectify, or universalize, the subjective perception and experience, and to encompass it—that is, to render it accurately and completely rather than partially.

Francis Thompson possessed neither the sustained imaginative fertility and instinct for the universal of great poets such as Geoffrey Chaucer, Dante, and William Shakespeare, nor the passion for perfection in form of a talented minor artist such as Austin Dobson. Thompson does not have Alfred, Lord Tennyson's fine-tuned ear; he lacks John Keats's facility for creating vivid but always controlled pictures and richly sensuous atmosphere. Reid and others have pointed out that though Thompson is capable on occasion of fine or even brilliant acoustic and rhythmic effects, more often, even in his best poems, he misses opportunities to harmonize sound with sense, and quite often arranges misalliances. Usually his poems read better on the page than aloud.

Drawing of Thompson by Everard Meynell

By endowment inventive in image and figure, and committed to a poetics of ornateness, Thompson typically crams his poems with images and metaphors, to the point of overlushness. And, again, though some of his word choices and figures are both individually interesting and well integrated—at times they are not unworthy of Shakespeare or Rainer Maria Rilke—far too often one finds, as Reid says, a poet of wild and capricious images, the poems proceeding "from image to image with scant regard for their congruity," providing "a series of illustrations by a virtuoso rather than creating a poetic experience."

In short, Thompson is outstanding in only a single area of poetic creativity: the generation of image and figure. But this capacity requires, if it is to become reliable, hard discipline and a taste purified by the development of self-critical habits.

The conclusion we are led to is, first, that sheer intensity of belief and feeling—impassioned insight—coupled with inventiveness in image and figure may in itself carry the poet to success and even, at times, to greatness; second, that much as Thompson wanted to be recognized as a poet, he was a mystic first, a poet second. His intuitive apprehension of an unseen spiritual world within the seen, together with his intense but innocent and unobtrusive desire for personal righteousness and for his and his fellows' salvation, is ultimately more important to him than even the beloved muse. Indeed, the poems often turn into, or come close to turning into, prayer—and are more of an achievement in that sphere than in poetics.

In other words, the psychological—and quite paradoxical—problem confronting Thompson was that though his religious intensity was his principal aesthetic strength—the main generative principle that carried him toward success in poetry—it also, at the same time, indisposed him to sacrifice religious feeling, concept, and image in order to make large gains, through an earthier spirit, on the imaginative and aesthetic levels. His religious intensity is his poetic intensity; but in the fullness of poetry, as in the fullness of life, there are other valid and important sources of intensity: the intensity of the dramatic, or confrontational; the intensity of the moralist or satirist; of the student of character; of the artist in storytelling; of the builder of erotic realities or fantasies; of the earthy or bawdy humorist. Most of these sources of inspiration and emotional and intellectual vigor are altogether absent from Thompson. The mystic search, the idealism of the religious impulse, remains paramount and will make only passing concessions to such secular interests as characterization or inspiriting earthy observation. All, or nearly all, is staked upon that idealism. It is worthy; but it does to some extent censor Thompson's imagination and limit his interests.

If a good many of Thompson's poems are distinguished more by reverential attitude than by the memorableness that comes when every rift is loaded with ore, many others were written not as a form of prayer but as a form of therapy. Writing them gave Thompson the relief of expression, a relief made all the more necessary by his personality and circumstances: by his extreme shyness and guilt, by his three years of humiliation on the London streets, and later by the long periods of relative isolation necessitated by illness. Such "confessional" poems enervate—or simply bore—the reader. They vindicate Matthew Arnold's proscription of "passive suffering" (suffering that admits of no relief) as a subject for poetry. Thompson's self-consciousness and self-pity are no less tedious than anyone else's. All such poetry has to be referenced to the poet's self rather than to an audience, for the ineluctable fact is that reading, like love, is voluntary, and that readers read for excitement, discovery, or escape, not to take upon themselves the burdens imposed by the writer's mere "self-expression."

Like all other English writers of his generation, Thompson was born at a time generally unpropitious for poetry. The reinvigoration of English poetry toward the end of the eighteenth century and in the early years of the nineteenth was made possible by the triumph of the Romantic outlook; by mid century the spirit of Romanticism had lost its freshness and vigor. The unique inward and unrhetorical spirit, the seminal force, that operates in William Blake, Robert Burns, Samuel Taylor Coleridge, the early Wordsworth, Keats, and Percy Bysshe Shelley appears only intermittently in the Victorian poets despite their immense productivity. Reid states very ably the general artistic problem that confronted Thompson: "The Romantics' exploitation of connotations and their stress upon secondary meanings gave the poetry at the beginning of the century a new freshness and ambience. But . . . the connection between connotation and denotation became gradually looser, and associations rather than meanings were given greater emphasis in poetry, resulting in diffuseness. . . . That precision which is at the heart of poetry fades. . . . Thompson tried to create a special language for poetry as far removed as he could make it from the ordinary vocabulary of prose. . . . Where there is a choice, he nearly always chooses the more exotic and sensational word."

Similarly, Thompson's melancholy or morbidity reflects not only his individual temperament and personal circumstances but the pessimism and enfeebled élan of the end of the century. The main body of that era's literary production is accurately described as literature of decadence, and Thompson, as Reid notes, is "a typical decadent poet . . . his language is artificial and affected, sensation concerns him more than emotion, his images, in their bookishness, operate at a couple of removes from life; and the general tone of his early poetry is morbid, spiritually inert, in the minor key."

Poets learn from other poets, develop their interests and styles partly out of the models provided by predecessors or contemporaries. Thompson was strongly indebted to Thomas De Quincey, Shelley, Blake, Richard Crashaw, Dante Gabriel Rossetti, and, in his later poetry, also to Alice Meynell and Coventry Patmore. One is tempted to say that, on balance, only the influence of Patmore was markedly beneficial. There is evidence that De Quincey's glowing accounts of the opium dream helped confirm Thompson's attraction to morphia, and that the earlier writer's stylistic ornateness catered to Thompson's tendency toward overelaboration. In Shelley and Crashaw, Thompson found models of certain types of grandeur but also models of effusiveness and figurative incoherence. Thompson admired Rossetti's verbal "stunners," his whimsical anachronisms and neologisms, all too uncritically.

The chief obstacle, then, to an adequate appreciation and a juster estimate of Thompson than exists at present is not the reigning secular spirit, or anti-Catholicism, or even literary modernism, but the quite simple fact that to reach the poet's really fine performances, the reader must plow through a mass of mediocre and sometimes bad verse. And Thompson is not the beneficiary of historical and cultural accidents like those that have continued to motivate us to endure the long journey through the works of Wordsworth and Walt Whitman.

Nevertheless, Thompson remains one of the many victims of an age more committed to social than to literary justice. His genius is unique and, as such, immensely rewarding; that it should remain lost to so many is a misfortune, an impoverishment. He and Hopkins are the most impressive devotional poets in English since George Herbert and are able to render something which, as Malcolm M. Ross points out in *Poetry and Dogma*, is generally missing even from Anglo-Catholic devotional poetry, the sense of a "living exchange between the Church Militant and the Church Triumphant . . . of an actual and active communion between the temporal and eternal orders."

Any serious attempt to restore Thompson to his rightful place will, after freely acknowledging his many general limitations and particular mistakes, give serious consideration to certain fundamental possibilities. First, that Thompson is not a minor but a flawed major poet, a poet abounding with insight and with intellectual and emotional power even though he often fails to effect perfect harmonization of his material. Second, that though Thompson was notably weak-willed, impractical, and ineffectual in daily life, he was not a weak-minded or fuliginous thinker but a clearheaded, intellectually precise mystic in the great tradition of St. John of the Cross and Baron Friedrich von Hügel. A charitable but not overly palliative judgment would be that his reputed "vagueness" and "looseness" are not much more prevalent than one would expect from a notably nonmaterialist, nonnaturalistic temper devoted to the symbolization of complex and elusive spiritual realities, regions for whose delineation the diction and figures of everyday were not devised. Third, that Thompson's reputed preciosity has been much exaggerated and misunderstood, and that it seriously mars relatively few of his poems and very few of his greater ones. Finally, that though Thompson is unmistakably Catholic, not one of his best poems demands from the reader either detailed instruction in, or pronounced sympathy with, Catholic doctrine or tradition; that, in other words, most of these poems achieve a statement which is consonant with but not narrowly dependent upon Catholicism.

The attempt is worth making not only because it serves justice (and mercy) but also because any widening of Thompson's readership simply means more and more people discovering poems that, in Peter Butter's words, "open new horizons, give a sense of exhilaration, and enhance the feeling of wonder."

Bibliography:

C. A. and H. W. Stonehill, *Bibliographies of Modern Authors*, second series (London: Castle, 1925).

Biographies:

Beverly Taylor, *Francis Thompson* (Boston: Twayne, 1987);

Brigid M. Boardman, *Between Heaven and Charing Cross: The Life of Francis Thompson* (New Haven: Yale University Press, 1988).

References:
R. L. Mégroz, *Francis Thompson: The Poet of Earth in Heaven* (London: Faber & Gwyer, 1927; New York: Scribners, 1927);
Viola Meynell, *Francis Thompson and Wilfrid Meynell: A Memoir* (London: Hollis & Carter, 1952);
J. C. Reid, *Francis Thompson: Man and Poet* (Westminster, Md.: Newman Press, 1960);
Leone Vivante, "Francis Thompson," in his *English Poetry* (London: Faber & Faber, 1950; Carbondale: Southern Illinois University Press, 1963).

Papers:
Terence L. Connolly's *An Account of Books and Manuscripts of Francis Thompson* (Newton, Mass.: Boston College, c. 1937-1938) catalogues the Boston College library's extensive holdings of Thompson's books and manuscripts.

Oscar Wilde

(16 October 1854 - 30 November 1900)

This entry was updated by Karl Beckson (Brooklyn College, City University of New York) from his entry in DLB 10: Modern British Dramatists, 1900-1945: Part Two.

See also the Wilde entries in DLB 19: British Poets, 1880-1914; DLB 34: British Novelists, 1890-1929: Traditionalists; *and* DLB 57: Victorian Prose Writers After 1867.

SELECTED BOOKS: *Ravenna* (Oxford: Shrimpton, 1878);
Vera; or the Nihilists (London: Privately printed, 1880);
Poems (London: David Bogue, 1881; Boston: Roberts Brothers, 1881);
The Happy Prince and Other Tales (London: David Nutt, 1888; Boston: Roberts Brothers, 1888);
The Picture of Dorian Gray (London, New York & Melbourne: Ward, Lock, 1891); original version, edited by Wilfried Edener (Nuremberg: Hans Carl, 1964);
Intentions (London: Osgood, McIlvaine, 1891; New York: Dodd, Mead, 1891);
Lord Arthur Savile's Crime and Other Stories (London: Osgood, McIlvaine, 1891; New York: Dodd, Mead, 1891);
A House of Pomegranates (London: Osgood, McIlvaine, 1891; New York: Dodd, Mead, 1892);
Salomé: Drame en un acte (Paris: Librarie de l'Art Indépendant / London: Elkin Mathews & John Lane, Bodley Head, 1893);
Lady Windermere's Fan (London: Elkin Mathews & John Lane, Bodley Head, 1893);
Salome: A Tragedy in One Act, translated into English by Alfred Douglas (London: Elkin Mathews & John Lane / Boston: Copeland & Day, 1894);
The Sphinx (London: Elkin Mathews & John Lane, Bodley Head, 1894; Boston: Copeland & Day, 1894);
A Woman of No Importance (London: John Lane, Bodley Head, 1894);
The Soul of Man (London: Privately printed, 1895);
The Ballad of Reading Gaol (London: Leonard Smithers, 1898);
The Importance of Being Earnest (London: Leonard Smithers, 1899); original version (New York: New York Public Library, 1956);
An Ideal Husband (London: Leonard Smithers, 1899);
De Profundis, edited by Robert Ross (expurgated edition, London: Methuen, 1905; New York: Putnam's, 1905);
First Collected Edition of the Works of Oscar Wilde, edited by Ross, volumes 1-11, 13-14 (London: Methuen, 1908; Boston: J. W. Luce, 1910); volume 12 (Paris: Charles Carrington, 1908);
Second Collected Edition of the Works of Oscar Wilde, edited by Ross, enlarged, volumes 1-12 (Lon-

don: Methuen, 1909); volume 13 (Paris: Charles Carrington, 1910); volume 14 (London: John Lane, 1912);

Literary Criticism of Oscar Wilde, edited by Stanley Weintraub (Lincoln: University of Nebraska Press, 1968);

The Artist as Critic: Critical Writings of Oscar Wilde, edited by Richard Ellmann (New York: Random House, 1969).

PLAY PRODUCTIONS: *Vera; or the Nihilists*, New York, Union Square Theatre, 20 August 1883, 7 [performances];

Guido Ferranti: A Tragedy of the XVI Century, New York, Broadway Theatre, 26 January 1891, 21;

Lady Windermere's Fan, London, St. James's Theatre, 20 February 1892, 156;

A Woman of No Importance, London, Haymarket Theatre, 19 April 1893, 118;

An Ideal Husband, London, Haymarket Theatre, 3 January 1895, (transferred 13 April 1895 to Criterion Theatre), 124;

The Importance of Being Earnest, London, St. James's Theatre, 14 February 1895, 86;

Salomé, Paris, Théâtre de l'Oeuvre, 11 February 1896; London, New Stage Club at Bijou, 10 May 1905;

A Florentine Tragedy, by Wilde, with opening scene by T. Sturge Moore, London, King's Hall, 10 June 1906.

Together with George Bernard Shaw, Oscar Wilde transformed British drama in the late nineteenth century by expressing a new, "modern" sensibility. By the mid nineteenth century, the British theater, though rich in various theatrical forms, such as verse drama, melodrama, farce, and burlesque, had produced little of lasting value. In the 1860s, however, Thomas William Robertson's realistic, sentimental "cup and saucer" plays pointed to a new form of entertainment; in the 1870s the plays of William Gilbert (and especially his later librettos for Arthur Sullivan's operettas) revealed a new, ironic treatment of social mores and classes. In addition, the influence of the French "well-made play" elevated the quality of popular British melodrama and farce by introducing carefully designed plot structure dependent upon such theatrical devices as the secret that is ultimately revealed and the compromising letter that brings about the villain's downfall. By the 1880s Arthur Wing Pinero and Henry Arthur Jones were writing melodramatic problem plays involving social conflict and revealing the influence of the well-made play, but these playwrights, though effective craftsmen, expressed conventional and respectable views. When Wilde turned to the writing of social comedy, he made deliberate use of the theatrical conventions of his day but introduced a quality of epigrammatic wit, paradox, and irony that had not been seen in such brilliant profusion on the London stage since the late-eighteenth-century comedies of Richard Sheridan.

Though Wilde is known today primarily as a playwright and as author of *The Picture of Dorian Gray* (1891)—his only novel—he also wrote poetry, fairy tales, essays, and criticism, all of which express his aesthetic approach to life and art. Indeed, he was the most articulate and popular spokesman in the late nineteenth century advocating the doctrine of aestheticism, which insisted that art should be primarily concerned with "art for art's sake," not with politics, religion, science, bourgeois morality, or other intrusions. "All art," he said, "is quite useless," a view denying any utilitarian function that could be pressed upon art, since its appeal was fundamentally aesthetic. Such ideas had, of course, been current in France ever since Théophile Gautier's famous introduction to his novel *Mademoiselle de Maupin* (1835), but Wilde expressed them with striking wit and a daring designed to startle readers.

A major influence on Wilde was Walter Pater's *Studies in the History of the Renaissance* (1873), which urged its readers to cultivate an aesthetic sensibility from the experience of art and to "burn with a hard gemlike flame"—that is, to live life with passionate intensity. Wilde later wrote that Pater's work had had a "strange influence" over his life; undoubtedly, he was fascinated by Pater's chapter on Leonardo da Vinci, whose life is described as one of "brilliant sins and exquisite moments." Wilde called Pater's work "the very flower of decadence." From the French Decadents, Wilde absorbed the idea that art was superior to life and that the one obligation was to transform life into art—to be as "artificial" as possible. Central to Wilde's life and art was the idea of the dandy as the embodiment of the heroic ideal as well as of the aesthetic temperament hostile to bourgeois sentiment and morality—a view compounded from such writers in France as Charles Baudelaire and Jules Amédée Barbey d'Aurevilly, in England from such figures as Beau Brummell and Benjamin Disraeli. Indeed, Wilde's life as an artist—as supreme individualist

Oscar Wilde in the United States, 1882

and aesthete—was fostered, in part, by the circumstances of his early family life.

Oscar Fingall O'Flahertie Wills Wilde was born in Dublin on 16 October 1854 to parents who were prominent in Ireland's cultural life. His father, Dr. William Ralph Wills Wilde, was a leading ear and eye surgeon who had founded a hospital a year before Wilde's birth and who had received the appointment of Surgeon Oculist in Ordinary to the Queen, an honorary position especially created for him in recognition of his international reputation. His *Aural Surgery* (1853) was the standard textbook on the subject in Britain and America. In 1864 he was knighted in recognition of his work as director of the medical census in Ireland. Despite professional obligations, he was an author of considerable distinction, writing some twenty books on such topics as Irish antiquarian topography, archaeology, and ethnology; his book on Jonathan Swift attempted to demonstrate that Swift was not mad in his final years. A notorious philanderer, Dr. Wilde was the father of at least three illegitimate children.

Wilde's mother, Jane Francesca Elgee Wilde, some nine years younger than her husband, was known in literary and political circles as "Speranza," a name she adopted in the 1840s to give hope to Irish nationalists and activists in the woman's rights movement. In 1848 she achieved sudden fame when, in an article in the *Nation*, a revolutionary weekly, she urged young Irishmen to defend their country by force; as a result, the periodical was suppressed and the editor prosecuted. In the course of her long life, she had many volumes of essays, stories, and poems and collections of folklore published.

Wilde received an education appropriate to his station in life. When he was ten, he was sent to Portora Royal School (founded by King Charles II) in Enniskillen, Ulster, where his elder brother, Willie, was a student. At school, Wilde did not distinguish himself until his final year, when he won prizes for Greek testament and a gold medal in classics. Much of the time he spent reading English novels, poetry, and, as he later wrote, books on the "wonder and beauty of the old Greek life." In October 1871 he matriculated on an entrance scholarship at Trinity College, Dublin, where he distinguished himself by winning various prizes and medals, particularly for his learning in the classics. In June 1874 he won a scholarship, the Classical Demyship, to Magda-

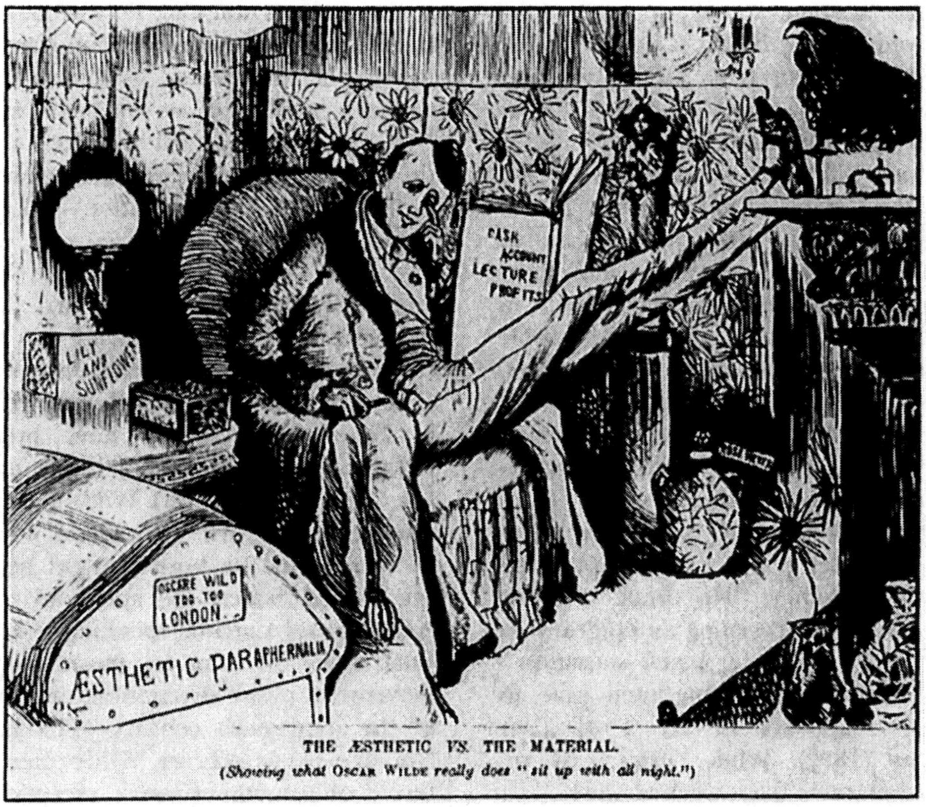

THE ÆSTHETIC VS. THE MATERIAL.
(*Showing what* OSCAR WILDE *really does "sit up with all night."*)

American cartoon inspired by Wilde's 1882 tour of the United States

len College, Oxford University, after completing his third year at Trinity College. He had been urged to try for it by his tutor in ancient history, John Mahaffey, who reinforced Wilde's interest in Hellenism. In the summer of 1874 Wilde spent much time at Mahaffey's seaside house in Dublin reading proofs and suggesting revisions of Mahaffey's *Social Life in Greece from Homer to Menander* (1874), which acknowledges Wilde for "having made improvements and corrections all through the book."

At Oxford, Wilde developed the manner of the poseur and was widely recognized by his fellow students as a brilliant talker. In the summer of 1875 he traveled with Mahaffey and a friend through northern Italy, which inspired poems that were published in Irish magazines. In April 1877 he went with Mahaffey and friends to Italy and Greece, which provided him with further inspiration for poems. In June 1878, in his fourth year at Oxford, Wilde won the prestigious Newdigate Prize for his lengthy poem *Ravenna* (1878), which brought him twenty guineas and was published as a pamphlet of sixteen pages. In November 1878 he was awarded the B.A. degree, having taken a first class in classical moderations, known as "mods." While at Oxford, Wilde attended lectures by Walter Pater and John Ruskin, both of whom impressed him with their conviction that the full life was possible only through a devotion to art, though Ruskin believed that art should lead to moral and spiritual elevation, whereas Pater urged aesthetic gratification in sensory experience.

Wilde was granted a demyship for a fifth year in order to permit him to read for the Chancellor's English Essay Prize, the subject of which was "Historical Criticism among the Ancients." He failed, however, to win the prize with his essay (first published in its entirety in 1909 as "The Rise of Historical Criticism" in *Essays and Lectures*, which was contained in the *Second Collected Edition of the Works of Oscar Wilde*). Later that year, Wilde took rooms on Salisbury Street, off the Strand, with his friend, the artist Frank Miles, where they entertained "beautiful people," such as the actresses Lillie Langtry (to whom he wrote a poem, "The New Helen"), Ellen Terry, Helena Modjeska, and numerous writers and artists. Visitors noted that the reception room was filled with white lilies, photographs of Lillie Langtry, paintings, and peacock feather screens—a most appropriate aesthetic setting. In 1880 Wilde and Miles moved to Tite Street, Chelsea, across the street from American artist James Whistler, who, with increasing acrimony, accused Wilde of pretentiousness and plagiarism.

At this time, Wilde was at work on his first play, *Vera; or the Nihilists* (1880), the subject of which came from current newspaper reports of Russian terrorist activities. The drama—more precisely, melodrama—is bombastically heroic in pseudo-Shakespearean diction expressing noble sentiments; as a result, characterization suffers. Vera's self-sacrifice in the final act, when she stabs herself to save the new czar, whom she had loved but had pledged to murder, is difficult to accept. The play contains elements of epigrammatic wit and dandyism that Wilde developed more fully in his later plays. For example, one character says of another, "He would stab his best friend for the sake of writing an epigram on his tombstone or experiencing a new sensation." The line "Experience, the name men give to their mistakes" reappears in act 3 of *Lady Windermere's Fan* (1892). Wilde customarily reused his better epigrams from work to work.

Wilde had the play privately printed in 1880 and sent copies to several actors and actresses, including Ellen Terry, hoping for a production. The assassination of Czar Alexander II on 13 March 1881 provided Wilde with an unexpected opportunity. The English actress Mrs. Bernard Beere agreed to play the leading role in a planned production at the Adelphi Theatre in December 1881; three weeks before the premiere, however, the production was canceled, for since the new czarina was the Prince of Wales's sister-in-law, it was believed Wilde's play might be offensive.

During 1881 Wilde was writing art reviews and poems and establishing himself in fashionable London circles. The result was that the British humor magazine *Punch* began caricaturing the self-styled aesthete in the characteristic attitude of the intense young man gazing at lilies or admiring the beauty of blue china. (At Oxford, Wilde had decorated his rooms with blue china, the current aesthetic craze, and had achieved notoriety with his reported remark, "Oh! would that I could live up to my blue china!") When Gilbert and Sullivan's *Patience* opened on 23 April 1881, many associated the central characters, both aesthetes—one a "fleshly" poet, the other an "idyllic" poet—with Wilde, though they were also obvious caricatures of such poets as Dante Gabriel Rossetti and Algernon Charles Swinburne, both associated with the new aesthetic movement. Capitalizing on the unexpected publicity, Wilde arranged to have published, at his own expense, *Poems* (1881), which received a mixed response from the critics, who detected the strong influence—indeed, some said "imitation"—of such poets as Rossetti and Swinburne.

As a result of his notoriety, Wilde was engaged by impresario Richard D'Oyly Carte (whose production of *Patience* was then running in New York) to lecture in America in the costume of the aesthete Bunthorne, the fleshly poet in *Patience*—that is, in knee breeches, velvet jacket, and a sunflower or lily in his buttonhole. On Christmas Eve 1881 Wilde sailed from Liverpool for New York. He carried with him a copy of *Vera*, which he hoped might be produced in the United States. He spent an entire year in America and Canada, speaking in large cities and small towns for some ten months on the aesthetic movement, house decoration, and the Irish poets of the nineteenth century—125 lectures in all. Not an exciting lecturer, Wilde often had an indifferent or sometimes satiric reception from audiences and reviewers; nevertheless, he often drew large crowds in the larger cities, and the publicity he generated was extraordinary. In addition to many government officials, Wilde met such writers as Walt Whitman, Henry James, and Oliver Wendell Holmes. After departing from New York in late December 1882, Wilde concluded that "America is a land of unmatched vitality and vulgarity. . . ."

He arrived in London early in January 1883 then left for Paris to live and write while he supported himself from the money he had earned on his lecture tour. While there, he met such writers as Victor Hugo, Emile Zola, Edmond de Goncourt, and Paul Verlaine, and such artists as Edgar Degas, Camille Pissarro, and John Singer Sargent. Wilde returned to London in the middle of May, having completed negotiations for an American production of *Vera* and having completed his second play, *The Duchess of Padua*, which he sent to actress Mary Anderson in New York. (The play, which she rejected, was finally produced in 1891 as *Guido Ferranti*.) It was collected in 1908 under its original title.

In early 1883 Wilde was writing to American actress Marie Prescott, who was to play the title role of Vera. Informing her that he would not remove, as she had requested, any of the play's comic lines, he assured her that laughter in serious drama would not destroy its effect but relieve tension (a well-known idea derived from Thomas De Quincey's essay on the porter's monologue in Shakespeare's *Macbeth*). In July he wrote approving of her thoroughness in carrying out his directions with respect to costumes and scenery, including a "yellow satin council-chamber" that was "sure to be a most artistic scene." He promised to bring enough vermilion silk for her costume in the final act. Of the play, he wrote: "I have tried in it to express within the limits of art that Titan cry of the peoples for liberty, which in the Europe of our day is threatening thrones. . . . But it is a play not of politics but of passion. It deals with no theories of government, but with men and women simply; and modern Nihilistic Russia . . . is merely the fiery and fervent background in front of which the persons of my dream live and love."

Wilde departed from Liverpool on 2 August 1883 and arrived in New York on the eleventh. He attended all rehearsals, and on the opening night (20 August), he took a curtain call and delivered a brief speech, as was the custom of the times. The reviews that appeared the following morning in the leading newspapers were most unfavorable: the *New York Times* reviewer, noting that Wilde's "labor [was] altogether out of proportion to his reputation," found the play "unreal, longwinded, and wearisome"; the *New York Herald* critic, agreeing with most of the other reviewers, concluded that *Vera* was "long-drawn, dramatic rot." The *New York Mirror* critic, the lone dissenting voice, said that *Vera* "takes rank among the highest order of plays," but his review seems designed to atone for abuse which had been heaped on Wilde by American newspapers during his lecture tour. When the play closed after a week, *Punch* concluded that, from all reports, Wilde's play must have been "Vera Bad."

Returning to England, Wilde undertook an eighteen-month lecture tour of the British Isles on the subjects of "Impressions of America" and "The House Beautiful." Following the tour, he married Constance Lloyd, whom he had known since 1881 and whose brother he had known at Oxford. In a letter to Lillie Langtry, he described Constance as "a beautiful girl . . . a grave, slight, violet-eyed little Artemis." After a brief honeymoon in France, Wilde eventually settled with his bride at 16 Tite Street, Chelsea, not far from the previous house he had shared with Frank Miles.

In addition to lecturing, Wilde became a regular reviewer for the *Pall Mall Gazette* over the next two years. His income from such sources, however, was at best precarious. In April 1887 he became editor of the *Woman's World*, which had been titled the *Lady's World* since its inception the year before; Wilde persuaded Cassell, the publisher, to change its title before the appearance of the first issue with Wilde as editor in November 1887. The *Times*, reviewing the *Woman's World*, acknowledged that it "has taken a high place among the illustrated magazines." Not long after this impressive beginning, he began to lose interest in the daily routine of editing a popular magazine. He stopped writing "Literary and Other Notes" after the fifth issue, and no other contributions by Wilde appeared for the next eight months. When circulation began to wane, he again began to contribute notes and reviews, but by July 1889 the publisher decided to let him go. During this period, Wilde had published his first book of fairy tales, *The Happy Prince and Other Tales* (1888), which drew praise from Pater, to Wilde's delight.

In July 1890 Wilde's first major literary work, *The Picture of Dorian Gray*, appeared in its entirety in one issue of *Lippincott's Monthly Magazine*. As the most famous novel of the British Decadence, it echoes such works as Pater's *Studies in the History of the Renaissance* and Joris-Karl Huysmans's *À Rebours* (1884, usually translated as *Against the Grain* or *Against Nature*). The plot involves the youthful Dorian, a "young Adonis . . . made out of ivory and rose leaves," and the dandy Lord Henry Wotton, who urges him: "Live! Live the wonderful life that is in you! Let nothing be lost upon you. Be always searching for new sensations. . . . A new Hedonism—that is what our century wants. You might be its visible symbol." Like the hero of Huysmans's *À Rebours*, Dorian cultivates the pleasures of art and artifice to the exclusion of morality and nature. His callous rejection of the actress Sybil Vane and her consequent suicide affect him only briefly. Dorian's progressive moral decline leads him to transform Lord Henry's "new Hedonism"—faint echoes of Pater—into his personal vision of self-destruction: "There were moments when he looked on evil simply as a mode through which he could realize his conception of the beautiful."

The central symbol of the novel is the magical picture that embodies Dorian's fallen soul (his burden of conscience and guilt) while his physical appearance over a twenty-year period remains strikingly youthful. Behind him are lives that he has destroyed (never explicitly discussed by Wilde). Basil Hallward, the painter of the portrait, confronts Dorian with the intriguing question: "Why is your friendship so fatal to young men?" But Hallward, who had himself refused to exhibit the painting that revealed his own fatal attraction to the young man, is himself murdered by Dorian. The painting, now horribly disfigured, eventually becomes the object of Dorian's rage. When he plunges a knife into the canvas, the innocence and beauty of the picture are miraculously restored, whereas Dorian ages and dies, his hideous-looking body symbolically reflecting the decadence of his life.

Widely reviewed, the novel generated considerable distaste, even revulsion, among many reviewers by its suggestion of homosexuality, though it is never specified in either the novel or the reviews. The *Daily Chronicle* referred to the work as "a tale spawned from the leprous literature of the French *Décadents*—a poisonous book . . . [of] unbridled indulgence in every form of secret and unspeakable vice." The *Athenaeum* regarded the novel as "unmanly, sickening, vicious. . . ." (The words *vice* and *unmanly* were Victorian code words usually implying homosexuality.) Wilde complicated matters by first denying that his novel had a moral. But in response to an unfavorable review in the *St. James Gazette*, he wrote to the editor that, in fact, the moral was that "all excess, as well as all renunciation, brings its own punishment." However, he added—as one might expect from an Aesthete—that this "terrible moral" was the "only [artistic] error in the book." For the book version, which appeared in 1891, Wilde added six additional chapters and made many revisions. He also added a preface, which lists some of his aesthetic principles, such as "No artist has ethical sympathies" and "The artist is the creator of beautiful things." William Butler Yeats praised the novel as a "wonderful book," and Pater saw "a very plain moral pushed home . . . that vice and crime make people coarse and ugly."

In January 1891 *The Duchess of Padua*, retitled *Guido Ferranti* to emphasize the leading role performed by Lawrence Barrett, opened in New York. Subtitled *A Tragedy of the XVI Century*, the play employs a pseudo-Elizabethan style mixing prose and blank verse with a melodramatic plot and even specific lines echoing Shakespeare, especially *Hamlet*, as well as the plays of Victor Hugo (a son, raised without the knowledge that he has been dispossessed of his hereditary rights, must avenge his father's murder). The bloody conclusion—a double suicide involving the hero, Guido, and his beloved duchess (whose husband, the duke, is the murderer of Guido's father)—is melodramatic rather than tragic, for motivation is arbitrary and characterization is superficial—hardly a major advance over *Vera*. The reviewers were not as devastating with *Guido Ferranti* as they had been with Wilde's previous attempt. The *New York Times* acknowledged "a number of well-imagined and skillfully wrought scenes," and the *New York Daily Tribune* found the play "deftly constructed" and the verse "always melodious, often eloquent," yet the reviewer concluded that the play is a melodramatic "drama of situation." The play closed after twenty-one performances but was taken on the road in repertory with five other plays. In July 1898 Wilde wrote to Robert Ross, later his literary executor, that the play was "unfit for publication—the only one of my works that comes under that category. But there are some good lines in it."

Wilde's productivity, as revealed by his publications in 1891, was impressive. In addition to the expanded version of *The Picture of Dorian Gray*, Wilde produced *Intentions*, a collection of critical essays that had been published during the past two years. "The Critic as Artist" and "The Decay of Lying," his best-known essays, argued that criticism itself was an art (following Pater) and that art was superior to nature (indeed, nature imitated art far more than art imitated nature). With these two major works through the press, there were two more published before the end of the year: *Lord Arthur Savile's Crime and Other Stories* and *A House of Pomegranates* (a volume of fairy tales). Though Wilde was demonstrating his extraordinary versatility, he had yet to be spoken of as a major figure in the literary world.

Early in 1891 he began writing a modern society comedy that would establish him as the wittiest writer for the London stage; the play was eventually titled *Lady Windermere's Fan*. He continued working on it through the year until he had completed a draft in the autumn. He then went to Paris to complete work on another play, *Salomé*, which he had begun while still engaged on *Lady Windermere's Fan*. While there, he met such writers as Remy de Gourmont, Catulle Mendès, Marcel Proust, and André Gide, who later recalled that Wilde "did not converse; he narrated. . . . He knew French admirably. . . . He had almost no accent." Wilde wrote *Salomé* in French, and it

Salomé, *scene from the 1931 London private production when the play was still banned*

was revised and corrected by Stuart Merrill (an American poet who lived most of his life in France), Adolphe Retté, and Pierre Louÿs. Another writer, Marcel Schwob, corrected the proofs when *Salomé* was published in 1893.

On 20 February 1892 *Lady Windermere's Fan* opened in London to a fashionable audience, which also included many of Wilde's friends. Wilde himself was there with his wife, Constance. The play combines conventional melodrama with Wildean wit within the structure of the well-made play. The plot device of the hero caught between a young woman, Lady Windermere, and a mature woman with a past, Mrs. Erlynne (the mother of Lady Windermere, who is unaware of their relationship), is borrowed principally from the plays of Alexandre Dumas fils. Significantly, Wilde's borrowings are those that provide the melodrama; his wit, however, is original in those scenes that make his play a strikingly new contribution to British theater. The basic situation in the play involves Mrs. Erlynne's attempt to be readmitted into fashionable society and the self-sacrifice she endures to save her daughter from eloping with Lord Darlington, Wilde's first dandy in his society comedies, much like Lord Henry Wotton in *The Picture of Dorian Gray*. Both men appear to be wicked but express their unorthodox views in epigrams. Lord Darlington's famous line, "I can resist everything except temptation," is the wit of the amoral dandy, who, in embodying the artistic ideal, is principally concerned with the beauty and perfection of phrasing rather than with its truth or moral vision. Wilde's inclusion of such a dandy in his melodrama reveals the fundamental conflict between the aesthetic and moral positions of its characters—in short, between dandyism and philistinism.

The audience received the play with enthusiasm, and shouts for the author filled the theater. The reviews on the following days were, however, quite mixed. A. B. Walkley, drama critic of the *Speaker*, acknowledged the borrowings but also recognized a striking new talent expressing the "style of the Age of the Dandies." Henry James, who attended the first performance, wrote to a friend: "there was so much drollery—that is 'cheeky' paradoxical wit of dialogue, and the pit and gallery are too pleased at finding themselves clever enough to 'catch on' to four or five of the ingenious—too ingenious *mots* in the dozen, that it makes them feel quite *'decadent'*. . . ." Despite that fact that Wilde did not always succeed in his epigrams, "those that hit," wrote James, "are very good indeed. This will make, I think, a success—possibly a really long run." Clement Scott, who invariably reviewed Wilde's work vitriolically, condemned the play in the *Illustrated London News*, referring to its "cynicism," and the audience's acceptance of "smart things." "Meanwhile," he wrote, "society at large will rush to see his play." Indeed, it did for four months. For the first time in his career, Wilde was well off, for he earned seven thousand pounds from the first production.

In the same year, Wilde seized upon the opportunity of staging *Salomé* with Sarah Bernhardt in the title role. In London at the time, she agreed to engage an all-French cast; rehearsals proceeded at the Palace Theatre. When, however, the play was submitted in June to the lord chamberlain's office for licensing, it was rejected because it contained biblical characters, forbidden on the British stage since the Protestant Reformation (the original intent of the prohibition was to prevent the old Catholic mystery plays from being performed). Of the few to protest the lord chamberlain's action, critic William Archer wrote a letter, published in the *Pall Mall Gazette* on 1 July 1892, condemning the censor's power in suppressing "a serious work of art" and adding, "Mr. Wilde's talent is unique. We require it and we appreciate it—those of us, at any rate, who are capable of any sort of artistic appreciation." Wilde thanked him for the letter, "not merely for its very courteous and generous recognition of my work, but for its strong protest against the contemptible official tyranny that exists in England in reference to the drama."

In the summer and autumn of 1892, Wilde was at work on his second society comedy, to be titled *A Woman of No Importance*, for actor-manager Herbert Beerbohm Tree, elder half brother of critic and caricaturist Max Beerbohm. When Wilde read it to him, Tree was enormously pleased, later calling it "a great modern play." In November, Wilde took his family (he now had two small sons) to spend the winter at Babbacombe, near Torquay in southwest England, where he planned to write two plays, one in blank verse. There, he completed most of *A Florentine Tragedy* (never produced in his lifetime), a one-act verse drama with the familiar Renaissance setting but with dialogue less Elizabethan than that of *Vera* or *The Duchess of Padua*. The simple plot concerns the killing of a nobleman by a merchant who is outraged by the duke's attentions to his wife. The play is a melodrama with a minimum of wit, though the psychology of the characters is of interest. The curtain line following the duel between the merchant and the duke is striking, for when the wife, suddenly embracing her husband, says, "Why did you not tell me you were so strong?" the merchant responds, "Why did you not tell me you were so beautiful?"

At Babbacombe, he also worked on another one-act play, "La Sainte Courtisane; or The Woman Covered with Jewels," only a fragment of which has survived (no evidence exists that he completed any more than this). Like *A Florentine Tragedy*, this play seems to have been derived from stories Wilde had told to friends. The king's daughter has sought out Honorius, the "beautiful young hermit" who lives a life of abstinence in a cave—reminiscent of countless stories of the femme fatale encountering a holy man, such as that in *Salomé*. In tempting Honorius, she succeeds in converting him to a life of sexual pleasure, but, ironically, she embraces a life of holiness. When he asks why she has tempted him, she replies: "That thou shouldst see Sin in its painted mask and look on Death in its robe of Shame"—hence, the significance of Wilde's title involving the sinful woman who is saintly. The irony of the conversion reveals the nature of Wilde's individualism, for at the beginning of the play, one of the characters says that "when you convert someone else to your own faith, you cease to believe in it yourself "—an indication of how individualism, one's uniqueness, is destroyed. In *Lady Windermere's Fan*, Lord Darlington holds the same view: "Ah! you are beginning to reform me. It is a dangerous thing to reform anyone, Lady Windermere."

In February 1893 *Salomé*, dedicated "*A mon ami Pierre Louÿs*," was published simultaneously in Paris and London. Its French sources of inspiration are derived from such nineteenth-century works as Théophile Gautier's *Une Nuit de Cléopâtre*, Gustave Flaubert's *Herodias*, Joris-Karl Huysmans's *À Rebours*, and Maurice Maeterlinck's *La Princess Maleine*, whose Symbolist style is hypnotically repetitive. In *Salomé*, Wilde makes use of the Symbolist device of the moon as a unifying, recurring symbol to suggest the presence of mysterious, transcendent forces associated with Salomé's perversity. Wilde attempted to shock his audience by depicting her lust for Jokanaan, particularly her bizarre final moments when she holds his severed head and kisses its lips. In 1893 Arthur Symons defined Decadence in literature as "an intense self-consciousness, a restless curiosity in research, an oversubtilising refinement upon refinement, a spiritual and moral perversity." In England, *Salomé* was one of the few supremely Decadent works of the 1890s.

As might be expected, *Salomé* created a sensation. The *Times* (London) called it "morbid, *bizarre*, repulsive," though admitting that it was "vigourously written in some parts." Wilde, still at Babbacombe, wrote to a friend, "I hear London [is] like some grey monster raging over the publication of *Salomé* . . . ," and to another correspondent, he referred to himself as a "famous French author." He had his defenders, however. Archer, in *Black and White*, cited Maeterlinck as a major influence on *Salomé* but saw "far more depth and body" in Wilde's work: "His characters are men and women, not filmy shapes of mist and moonshine. His properties, so to speak, are far more various and less conventional. His palette . . . is infinitely richer. Maeterlinck paints in washes of water-colour; Mr. Wilde attains the depths and brilliancy of oils. *Salomé* has all the qualities of a great historical picture. . . ."

On 19 April 1893 Wilde's second comedy, *A Woman of No Importance*, opened at the Haymarket Theatre. Once again, Wilde turned to Dumas fils, specifically his play *Le Fils naturel* (1858), for inspiration, if not direct borrowings. Indeed, the central element of Wilde's plot is taken from Dumas's play. It involves a wronged woman whose son is secretary to an illustrious figure, who, unknown to the young man, is his father. When he discovers the truth, the son rejects the father in defending his mother. Wilde's major contribution is, of course, the creation of the father, Lord Illingworth, a dandy who, unlike other Wildean dandies whose amorality is a pose, is a true villain. Like Wilde's other society comedies, *A Woman of No Importance* is concerned with a secret that is exposed (in this case, the mother, Mrs. Arbuthnot, has sinned but remains pure in heart, like Mrs. Erlynne in *Lady Windermere's Fan*). The philistine view, as expressed by various characters in both plays, is that sinners should be punished, but Wilde opposes such a view by revealing the sinners' essential goodness, a sentimental quality that pervades his comedies.

Though *A Woman of No Importance* is structurally weaker than *Lady Windermere's Fan*, the critical response was generally more enthusiastic. Archer, in the *World*, contended that Wilde's work "stands alone . . . on the very highest plane of modern English drama," but he insisted that Wilde's "pyrotechnic wit" was one of his defects that "he will one day conquer when he begins to take himself seriously as a dramatic artist": "It is not his wit, then, and still less his knack of paradox-twisting that makes me claim for him a place apart among living dramatists. It is the keenness of his intellect, the individuality of his point of view, the excellence of his verbal style, and above all the genuinely dramatic quality of his inspirations." In the *Speaker*, A. B. Walkley concluded: "The point is, that he has worked out his ideas with true dramatic instinct, not shirking a single one of the scenes which they involve—the series of battles between man and woman, of explanations between mother and son—and giving them to us at the right moment." But Walkley and Archer had their opponents, according to Max Beerbohm, who wrote to his friend Reggie Turner: "How the critics attack gentle Oscar! Have you, though, read Archer's very true and just critique? Walkley also is to the point, but the rest have scarcely tried to write on the play at all. They have simply abused Oscar."

In the summer of 1893 at Goring-on-Thames, Wilde began work on his next comedy, *An Ideal Husband*. At the same time, he was reading proofs of his long poem *The Sphinx* (1894), on which he had been working sporadically since his Oxford years. In the autumn, he was preparing *Salomé* for publication in English translation, which Lord Alfred Douglas (or "Bosie," as everyone called him) had completed but which Wilde improved. Bosie, whom Wilde had met in 1891, was seventeen years younger than Wilde. The young, handsome, effeminate aristocrat was a homosexual and a poet, the central love and inspiration of Wilde's life. At the same time, Bosie was a destructive force, indeed, Wilde insisted, "the true author of the hideous tragedy" of his life. In later years, Wilde wrote: "My genius, my life as an artist, my work, and the quiet I needed for it, were nothing to him when matched with his unrestrained and coarse appetites for common profligate life: his greed for money: his incessant and violent scenes: his unimaginative selfishness. . . . I curse myself night and day for my folly in allowing him to dominate my life." But Wilde was also self-destructive, for his progressively compulsive homosexuality in the 1890s, arising from a need for inner stability but resulting in increasing guilt and inner division, led him into experiences with "renters" (male prostitutes) as well as casual pick-ups. It was, he said, like "feasting with panthers. The danger was half the excitement."

For the remainder of 1893, Wilde was at work on *An Ideal Husband.* In November, *Lady Windermere's Fan* was published, as was *Salomé* in February 1894. In the spring, he spent time with Bosie in Paris and Florence, where he worked on *A Florentine Tragedy.* But when he returned to London, he had an idea for a new society comedy, which was to be *The Importance of Being Earnest.* He worked on the play during August and September at Worthing, on the south coast, not far from Brighton. (He used the name of the seaside resort for his central character, John Worthing, Wilde's habitual device of using place names for his characters.) At the same time, he was completing *An Ideal Husband* for production early in 1895.

An Ideal Husband, which opened 3 January at the Haymarket Theatre, was an instant success. The theatrical machinery of stolen state secrets, blackmail, a stolen bracelet, and a misunderstood letter is apparently drawn from Dumas fils's *L'Ami des femmes* (1864) and Victorien Sardou's *Dora* (1877), though Wilde denied that the latter had been an influence. The central character, Sir Robert Chiltern, like Mrs. Erlynne and Mrs. Arbuthnot, has committed a sin, for which he craves forgiveness. Like Lady Windermere, Lady Chiltern is a puritan who represents moral perfection; inevitably, she will come to understand and forgive. Wilde's "flawless dandy," Lord Goring, one of the wittiest figures in all of Wilde's plays, insists that "To love oneself is the beginning of a lifelong romance," which, to be sure, reflects Wilde's narcissism. Other characters in the play, including Lord Goring's butler, Phipps, who is described in a stage direction as representing the "dominance of form," speak as though they were dandies also. Clearly, Wilde was anticipating *The Importance of Being Earnest,* his supreme achievement, in which the world consists entirely of dandiacal characters.

Despite the audience's delight with *An Ideal Husband,* most of the critics either grudgingly praised it or condemned it. Archer, who had championed Wilde's work, had doubts about Wilde's "epigram factory" that "threatens to become all trademark and no substance." Walkley, citing the theatrical devices of nineteenth-century melodrama and the well-made play, called the reduction of international politics to trivial drama "not only poor and sterile but essentially vulgar." However, Shaw, though temperamentally different from Wilde in personality and social vision, enjoyed the play. "Wilde," he wrote, "is to me our only thorough playwright. He plays with everything: with wit, with philosophy, with drama, with actors and audience, with the whole theatre." On 2 February, a month after *An Ideal Husband* opened, Henry James, having seen a performance, wrote to his brother, William: "I sat through it and saw it played with every appearance (so far as the crowded house was an appearance) of complete success, and *that* gave me the most fearful apprehension. The thing seemed to me so helpless, so crude, so bad, so clumsy, feeble and vulgar, that as I walked away across St. James's Square to learn my own fate [James's play *Guy Domville* closed that night at the St. James's Theatre] . . . I stopped in the middle of the Square, paralyzed by the terror of this probability—afraid to go on and learn more. 'How *can* my piece do anything with a public with whom *that* is a success?' "

While *An Ideal Husband* was in production, Wilde was completing *The Importance of Being Earnest,* which he had constructed in four acts. Actor-manager George Alexander, who had played in *Lady Windermere's Fan,* urged Wilde to compress acts 2 and 3 into one act (thus eliminating an entire scene where a solicitor comes to arrest Ernest for an unpaid debt). Wilde resisted at first but eventually submitted to Alexander's judgment, which proved sound. At first reading, the actors believed that the play would be too subtle for the audience. Wilde attended rehearsals, but when he continually made suggestions on how the play should be acted, Alexander informed him privately that unless the actors were uninterrupted, the play would never open on schedule. Heeding his suggestion, Wilde left London in mid January with Bosie for Algiers. On the eve of his departure, Wilde reportedly said in an interview in the *St. James's Gazette* that his forthcoming play expressed the "philosophy"—clearly dandiacal—that "we should treat all the trivial things of life very seriously, and all the serious things of life with sincere and studied triviality." Wilde subsequently subtitled his play "A Trivial Comedy for Serious People." To a friend he wrote, in his char-

Oscar Wilde and Lord Alfred Douglas, 1894

acteristically ironic manner, that it was a "trivial play . . . written by a butterfly for butterflies."

In Algiers, Wilde and Bosie admired the boys and took hashish. They returned to London in time for the 14 February opening of *The Importance of Being Earnest,* Wilde's greatest theatrical triumph. Novelist and satirist Ada Leverson (whom Wilde playfully called "the Sphinx") wrote of Wilde as he appeared at the opening: "He was on this evening at the zenith of his careless, genial career. . . . He was dressed with elaborate dandyism and a sort of florid sobriety. . . . He held white gloves in his small pointed hands. On one finger he wore a large scarab ring. A green carnation, echoing the colour of the ring, bloomed in his buttonhole. . . . He seemed at ease and to have the look of the last gentleman in Europe." The artificial green carnation, symbol of Decadence, had become associated with Wilde, who wore it on special occasions as an emblem of his individualism and presumably his perversity; it had been the central image of Robert Smythe Hichens's brilliant satiric novel *The Green Carnation* (1894), in which Wilde and Bosie appear, thinly disguised. Wilde thought the novel "clever" but protested when the *Pall Mall Gazette* suggested that he was the author of the anonymously published work: "I invented that magnificent flower. . . . The flower is a work of art. The book is not."

The audience on opening night of *The Importance of Being Earnest* responded to the play, as Hamilton Fyfe, London correspondent for the *New York Times,* cabled, with "unrestrained, incessant laughter from all parts of the theatre, and those laughed the loudest whose approved mission it is to read Oscar long lectures in the press on his dramatic and ethical shortcomings." Actor Allan Aynesworth, who created the role of Algernon Moncrieff, later said, "In my fifty-three years of acting, I never remember a greater triumph than the first night of *The Importance of*

Being Earnest. The audience rose in their seats and cheered and cheered again."

Though *The Importance of Being Earnest* is his most original society comedy in conception and wit, Wilde, who was an excellent classical scholar, drew directly upon the ancient Greek dramatist Menander for the device of the misplaced baby. But within the absurd world that Wilde created, the device is transformed through the use of the mock-heroic style into a matter of the utmost comic solemnity, for there is here a breach of proper form: "To be born," says Lady Bracknell, "or at any rate bred, in a handbag, whether it has handles or not, seems to me to display a contempt for the ordinary decencies of family life that reminds one of the worst excesses of the French Revolution." Unlike Wilde's other society comedies, *The Importance of Being Earnest* contains characters—male and female alike—who all speak like dandies, concerned with the dominance of form, so that philistine and puritan are always subjected to satire and aesthetic judgment. Indeed, as Joseph Wood Krutch has stated, Wilde has "created a mythological realm of perfect dandyism." For Wilde—in life as in art—and for other great dandies before him, dandyism was the last heroic gesture against the increasingly vulgar world of the late nineteenth century; the dandy's superiority and individualism were his only codes of manners and morality.

The Importance of Being Earnest, with its pun on "earnest," is concerned with two friends who are unaware that they are actually brothers. The elder, Jack Worthing, has invented a profligate younger brother named Ernest who lives in town, to whose aid he professes to go in order to escape from the country (when he is in town, Jack assumes the name of Ernest); in order to escape social obligations, Algernon Moncrieff has invented an invalid named Bunbury, to whose assistance he professes to go. (Wilde's ironic use of the double, or doppelgänger, perhaps unconsciously parallels the psychological division within himself.) Gwendolen and Cecily, the young women in love with Jack and Algernon (who, in act 2, pretends to be the wicked brother, Ernest), believe that they are both engaged to an Ernest, the cunning Jack and the pretending Algernon. These deceptions, on being exposed, will complicate the plot and produce the discoveries that Jack and Algernon are, in fact, brothers and that Jack's given name is actually Ernest.

Unlike certain characters in Wilde's preceding comedies, those in *The Importance of Being Earnest* are in no need of forgiveness for a sinful secret (not even Miss Prism, who had misplaced Jack when he was a baby), for in the dandiacal world, bourgeois morality does not exist, only the code of the dandy. As Gwendolen says, "In matters of grave importance, style, not sincerity is the vital thing." Gwendolen's wish to marry a man named "Ernest" reveals her dandiacal concern with form and an unconcern with Jack's character. Cecily, who is Gwendolen's double, is delighted when Algernon appears as the wicked Ernest, for she is concerned with the beauty of the name, not with the philistine horror of wickedness. When Algernon protests that he is not really wicked, she responds: "If you are not, then you have certainly been deceiving us all in a very inexcusable manner. I hope you have not been leading a double life, pretending to be wicked and being really good all the time. That would be hypocrisy."

The critical response to Wilde's most brilliant play was, by far, the most enthusiastic since *Lady Windermere's Fan.* In the *Pall Mall Gazette,* H. G. Wells, who had thought that *An Ideal Husband* was "fairly bad," now congratulated Wilde "unreservedly on a delightful revival of theatrical satire." Archer wrote in the *World* that the play was "an absolutely wilful expression of an irrepressibly witty personality." In the *Speaker,* Walkley wrote that Wilde was "an artist in sheer nonsense.... It is of nonsense all compact, and better nonsense, I think our stage has not seen." Shaw, less impressed, wrote in the *Saturday Review*: "I cannot say that I greatly cared for *The Importance of Being Earnest.* It amused me, of course; but unless comedy touches me as well as amuses me, it leaves me with a sense of having wasted my evening. I go to the theatre to be moved to laughter, not to be tickled or bustled into it; and that is why, though I laugh as much as anybody at a farcical comedy, I am out of spirits before the end of the second act, and out of temper before the end of the third, my miserable mechanical laughter intensifying these symptoms at every outburst."

Though Wilde had indeed reached the zenith of his career with two successes in West End theaters, he was simultaneously on the verge of disaster, for since early 1894 Bosie's father, the unstable marquess of Queensberry, had determined to save his son and disgrace Wilde. Shortly after the opening of *The Importance of Being Earnest,* Queensberry left a calling card at Wilde's club on which he wrote: "For Oscar Wilde, posing

Somdomite," misspelling "sodomite." Instead of ignoring the card, Wilde lied to his solicitor that he was entirely innocent. A warrant was consequently requested for the arrest of Queensberry, who was charged with libel; Bosie, seeing the chance of punishing his father, provided Wilde with money to cover the expenses of the trial, which opened on 3 April.

Wilde's performance as a witness was extraordinary. Convinced that he had control of the situation, he delighted the spectators with his banter and wit. However, Queensberry had beforehand hired private detectives to gather information against Wilde, who, when he saw the evidence going against him, dropped his libel suit, on the advice of counsel, on the morning of 5 April. Instead of fleeing the country, as his friends urged him to do, he remained with Bosie at the Cadogan Hotel, where he was arrested on the same day. His deep psychic divisions had paralyzed him. To flee the country was, to be sure, degrading; to remain was, on the other hand, to enact the double life that he had depicted in his plays (which, incidentally, continued their run but with Wilde's name removed from the programs).

The trial, with Wilde now as defendant, opened on 26 April, but the jury could not reach a verdict; a second trial was ordered. Released on bail, Wilde was again urged by friends to leave the country, but he refused to betray friends who had provided the bail money, and he reportedly had promised his mother that he would behave like a gentleman. He was convinced, moreover, that he would be acquitted. As the trials brought forth damaging evidence, he grew less witty and more uncertain. His second trial, convened on 20 May, resulted in his conviction and a sentence of two years at hard labor.

Most of that time was spent at Reading Gaol, where he wrote his lengthy, bitter letter to Bosie outlining the events that had brought him there and accusing Bosie of being the major cause of the disaster. Yet the letter (first published in 1905 in expurgated form, with all references to Bosie removed, as *De Profundis*, edited by Robert Ross) is at the same time an attempt at reconciliation. The years at Reading Gaol were spent in solitary confinement for twenty-three hours a day, with one hour reserved for recreation or chapel. Wilde was fed poor food and forced to live under primitive sanitary conditions; he slept on a wooden plank bed and suffered bleeding fingers from picking oakum (involving the untwisting of old rope, sometimes treated with tar). His imprisonment would have been unendurable had he not had access to books and writing paper (on which he wrote *De Profundis*) provided to him by a humane prison governor who had taken charge in Wilde's second year there.

Despite the fact that he had applied for early release, Wilde was required to serve the entire two years. Accordingly, on 19 May 1897 he was released from Pentonville Prison (having been transferred from Reading the day before), now bankrupt and permanently separated from his children. His library and manuscripts at his Tite Street home having been either auctioned or stolen after his arrest, Wilde possessed only the clothes he wore. Some friends were there to meet him on his release and arranged for his journey to France; he never returned to England. Once on the Continent, he adopted the pseudonym Sebastian Melmoth (the name derived from the third-century Christian martyr Saint Sebastian and the central character of the Gothic novel *Melmoth the Wanderer* [1820], written by Wilde's great-uncle Charles Maturin). The martyred, cursed wanderer had now become Wilde's personal myth.

Wishing to acquaint the general public with the abominable prison conditions that dehumanized inmates, especially children (who were housed with hardened criminals), Wilde wrote a letter that appeared in the *Daily Chronicle* on 28 May 1897; in another lengthy letter, published on 24 March 1898, at the time when a prison reform bill was under consideration, he pleaded for an improvement in living conditions for prisoners and the amendment of prison regulations that restricted visitors to four visits a year (twenty minutes a visit) and the writing or receiving of four letters a year.

In May 1897 Wilde settled in Berneval, near Dieppe, France, to begin writing his lengthy poem *The Ballad of Reading Gaol*, which depicts the hell of prison life and suggests his self-destructive impulses: "For each man kills the thing he loves." In August he was reunited with Bosie, and in the autumn they were together for several weeks in Naples and Capri. Of Bosie, Wilde wrote to a friend: "I love him, and have always loved him. He ruined my life, and for that very reason I seem forced to love him more: and I think that now I shall do some lovely work." As a result of this meeting, Wilde's allowance—granted by Constance on the condition that he refrain from associating with "disreputable persons" —was stopped by her solicitor. Wilde's final years were filled with constant anxieties over money (though his allowance was partially restored and friends continually assisted him).

In February 1898 *The Ballad of Reading Gaol* was published under the pseudonym C.3.3 (Wilde's prison cell block number at Reading); the poem was an instant success. In the seventh edition, his name appeared for the first time, though the poem's author had been widely known since its initial publication. This was Wilde's final literary work, though he had numerous plans for other works. He could not, however, concentrate on any of his proposed projects. To Ross, he wrote: "I don't think I shall ever really write again. Something is killed in me."

In April 1898 Constance died after an operation on her spine (her death deeply affected Wilde); his brother Willie, a journalist, died a year later; his mother, Lady Wilde, had died in 1896, when he was at Reading. During his last two years, Wilde lived mostly in Paris on the money from Constance's renewed payments (she had been impressed with *The Ballad of Reading Gaol* and reinstituted his allowance), money from Bosie in repayment for expenses incurred by the trials, and payments for publication of his plays. His sexual life remained unchanged: he entertained young boys he picked up on the boulevards, and he saw Bosie on occasion. Despite the fact that his world had collapsed and that he was widely regarded as an object of pity, Wilde, wrote Shaw, retained "an unconquerable gaiety of soul" that sustained him.

In October 1900, following a trip to Rome, Wilde was ill with an ear infection that developed into encephalitis. On 10 October he underwent an operation to relieve the condition, but his health continued to deteriorate. On the day before his death, Wilde received baptism and extreme unction while in a semicomatose state. Thus, he died a Roman Catholic, the fulfillment of a desire he had had since his Oxford days, on 30 November at the age of forty-six. His tomb, sculpted by Sir Jacob Epstein, is in Père Lachaise Cemetery, Paris.

Wilde's reputation and influence, from the time of his death to the present, have undergone considerable change. In the early years of this century, he was admired in England and America by a few critics, such as Max Beerbohm, who, in 1900, wrote that Wilde's death was a "lamentable loss to dramatic literature." Because moral condemnation or defense of his homosexuality often accompanied literary evaluation, his importance and influence on drama were for many years insufficiently appreciated. However, on the Continent, particularly in Germany, Wilde's reputation at the time of the publication of *De Profundis* in 1905 rose dramatically. He was ranked by some critics with Shakespeare and Byron.

Since the 1950s, many important evaluations have appeared. Eric Bentley, for example, attributed to Wilde a new conception of comedy, a "variant of farce," in which "witticisms are, not comic, but serious relief." Bentley concludes that Wilde's doctrine of masks has significant implications for modern drama: "If Wilde seems shallow when we want depth, if he seems a liar when we want truth, we should recall his words: 'A Truth in Art is that whose contradictory is also true. The Truths of metaphysics are the Truths of masks.' These words lead us to Pirandello."

Other critics have recently explored Wilde's importance in the dramatization of an absurd world, particularly in *The Importance of Being Earnest,* in which, as Dennis J. Spininger suggests, "language is substituted for reality": "His last play, in which melodrama is a target of the wit and wit itself is the play's essence, evokes a nihilistic spirit that places Wilde closer to Beckett than to Shaw." Indeed, Samuel Beckett's work would seem to be the logical conclusion of Wilde's play of masks, in which the purely aesthetic realm contains the only possibility of attaining order—accompanied by a desperate kind of tragic wit and humor—in a world seemingly chaotic. Rodney Shewan's view that *The Importance of Being Earnest* is a "highly original fusion of Wilde's idiosyncratic redemptive comedy and his basically anarchic assumptions" containing elements of "comic autobiography and parody confessional" suggests, finally, that Wilde is less the late Victorian than the startlingly innovative modern dramatist.

Letters:

The Letters of Oscar Wilde, edited by Rupert Hart-Davis (New York: Harcourt, Brace & World, 1962);

More Letters of Oscar Wilde, edited by Hart-Davis (New York: Vanguard Press, 1985).

Bibliographies:

Stuart Mason, *Bibliography of Oscar Wilde* (London: T. Werner Laurie, 1914);

Abraham Horodisch, *Oscar Wilde's "Ballad of Reading Gaol": A Bibliographical Study* (New York: Aldus, 1954);

E. H. Mikhail, *Oscar Wilde: An Annotated Bibliography of Criticism* (Totowa, N.J.: Roman & Littlefield, 1978).

References:

Karl Beckson, ed., *Oscar Wilde: The Critical Heritage* (London: Routledge & Kegan Paul, 1970);

Eric Bentley, "*The Importance of Being Earnest*," in his *The Playwright as Thinker* (New York: Reynal & Hitchcock, 1946), pp. 172-177;

Alan Bird, *The Plays of Oscar Wilde* (New York: Barnes & Noble, 1977);

Harold Bloom, ed., *Oscar Wilde* (New York: Chelsea House, 1985);

Bloom, ed., *Oscar Wilde's The Importance of Being Earnest* (New York: Chelsea House, 1988);

J. E. Chamberlin, *Ripe Was the Drowsy Hour: The Age of Oscar Wilde* (New York: Seabury, 1977);

Richard Ellmann, "A Late Victorian Love Affair," in his and John Espey's *Oscar Wilde: Two Approaches* (Los Angeles: Clark Memorial Library, University of California, 1977), pp. 1-21;

Ellmann, *Oscar Wilde* (New York: Knopf, 1988);

Ellmann, "Romantic Pantomime in Oscar Wilde," *Partisan Review*, 30 (Fall 1963): 332-355;

Ellmann, ed., *Oscar Wilde: A Collection of Critical Essays* (Englewood Cliffs, N.J.: Prentice-Hall, 1969);

Donald Ericksen, *Oscar Wilde* (Boston: Twayne, 1977);

Regina Gagnier, *Idylls of the Marketplace: Oscar Wilde and the Victorian Public* (Stanford: Stanford University Press, 1986);

Arthur Ganz, "The Divided Self in the Society Comedies of Oscar Wilde," *Modern Drama*, 3 (May 1960): 16-23;

Ganz, "The Meaning of *The Importance of Being Earnest*," *Modern Drama*, 6 (May 1963): 42-52;

H. Montgomery Hyde, *Oscar Wilde: A Biography* (New York: Farrar, Straus & Giroux, 1975);

Hyde, *Oscar Wilde: The Aftermath* (New York: Farrar, Straus, 1963);

Hyde, *The Trials of Oscar Wilde* (New York: Dover, 1973);

Norbert Kohl, *Oscar Wilde: The Works of a Conformist Rebel* (New York: Cambridge University Press, 1990);

Lloyd Lewis and Henry Justin Smith, *Oscar Wilde Discovers America* (New York: Harcourt, Brace, 1936);

E. H. Mihail, ed., *Oscar Wilde: Interviews and Recollections*, 2 volumes (New York: Barnes & Noble, 1979);

Ellen Moers, *The Dandy: Brummell to Beerbohm* (London: Secker & Warburg, 1960);

Vincent O'Sullivan, *Aspects of Wilde* (London: Constable, 1936);

John Allen Quintus, "The Moral Implications of Oscar Wilde's Aestheticism," *Texas Studies in Literature and Language*, 22 (1980): 559-574;

Edouard Roditi, *Oscar Wilde* (Norfolk, Conn.: New Directions, 1947);

Epifanio San Juan, Jr., *The Art of Oscar Wilde* (Princeton: Princeton University Press, 1967);

Rodney Shewan, *Oscar Wilde: Art and Egotism* (New York: Barnes & Noble, 1977);

Dennis J. Spininger, "Profiles and Principles: The Sense of the Absurd in *The Importance of Being Earnest*," *Papers on Language and Literature*, 12 (1976): 49-72;

Terence de Vere White, *The Parents of Oscar Wilde: Sir William and Lady Wilde* (London: Hodder & Stoughton, 1967);

Katharine Worth, *Oscar Wilde* (New York: Grove, 1984).

Papers:

The William Andrews Clark Memorial Library of the University of California at Los Angeles contains the largest library collection of manuscripts and letters by and related to Wilde. Major collections of letters and manuscripts are held at the New York Public Library (Berg Collection and Arents Collection); the J. Pierpont Morgan Library; the Beinecke Library, Yale University; the British Library; and the Harry Ransom Humanities Research Center, University of Texas, Austin. Other significant collections are at Magdalen College, Oxford University; the Rosenbach Museum, Philadelphia; the Houghton Library, Harvard University; and the University of Edinburgh Library.

William Butler Yeats

(13 June 1865 - 28 January 1939)

This entry was updated from an entry by B. L. Reid (Mount Holyoke College) in DLB 19: British Poets, 1880-1914.

See also the Yeats entries in DLB 10: Modern British Dramatists, 1900-1945: Part Two *and* DLB 98: Modern British Essayists: First Series.

William Butler Yeats

SELECTED BOOKS: *Mosada: A Dramatic Poem* (Dublin: Sealy, Bryers & Walker, 1886);

The Wanderings of Oisin and Other Poems (London: Kegan Paul, Trench, 1889);

John Sherman and Dhoya, as Ganconagh (London: Unwin, 1891; New York: Cassell, 1891);

The Countess Kathleen and Various Legends and Lyrics (London: Unwin, 1892; Boston: Roberts / London: Unwin, 1892);

The Celtic Twilight (London: Lawrence & Bullen, 1893; New York & London: Macmillan, 1893; revised and enlarged edition, London: Bullen, 1902; New York: Macmillan, 1902);

The Land of Heart's Desire (London: Unwin, 1894; Chicago: Stone & Kimball, 1894; revised edition, Portland, Maine: Mosher, 1903);

Poems (London: Unwin, 1895; Boston: Copeland & Day, 1895; revised edition, London: Unwin, 1899; revised again, 1901, 1912, 1927);

The Secret Rose (London: Lawrence & Bullen, 1897; New York: Dodd, Mead / London: Lawrence & Bullen, 1897);

The Table of the Law; The Adoration of the Magi (London: Privately printed, 1897);

The Wind Among the Reeds (London: Elkin Mathews, 1899; New York: John Lane / Bodley Head, 1902);

The Shadowy Waters (London: Hodder & Stoughton, 1900; New York: Dodd, Mead, 1901);

Cathleen ni Houlihan (London: Bullen, 1902);

Where There Is Nothing (New York: John Lane, 1902; London: Bullen, 1903);

Ideas of Good and Evil (London: Bullen, 1903; New York: Macmillan, 1903);

In the Seven Woods: Being Poems Chiefly of the Irish Heroic Age (Dundrum: Dun Emer Press, 1903; New York & London: Macmillan, 1903);

The Hour-Glass: A Morality (London: Heinemann, 1903);

The Hour-Glass and Other Plays (New York & London: Macmillan, 1904); republished as *The Hour-Glass, Cathleen ni Houlihan, The Pot of Broth* (London: Bullen, 1904);

The King's Threshold (New York: John Quinn, 1904);

The King's Threshold and On Baile's Strand (London: Bullen, 1904);

Stories of Red Hanrahan (Dundrum: Dun Emer Press, 1905);

Poems 1899-1905 (London: Bullen / Dublin: Maunsel, 1906);

The Poetical Works of William B. Yeats, 2 volumes (New York & London: Macmillan, 1906, 1907; revised, 1912);

Deirdre (London: Bullen / Dublin: Maunsel, 1907);

Discoveries; A Volume of Essays (Dundrum: Dun Emer Press, 1907);
The Unicorn from the Stars and Other Plays, by Yeats and Lady Gregory (New York: Macmillan, 1908);
The Golden Helmet (New York: John Quinn, 1908);
The Collected Works in Verse and Prose of William Butler Yeats, 8 volumes (Stratford-upon-Avon: Shakespeare Head Press, 1908);
The Green Helmet and Other Poems (Dundrum: Cuala Press, 1910; New York: Paget, 1911; enlarged edition, London: Macmillan, 1912);
Synge and the Ireland of His Time (Dundrum: Cuala Press, 1911);
The Countess Cathleen, revised edition (London: Unwin, 1912);
The Cutting of An Agate (New York: Macmillan, 1912; enlarged edition, London: Macmillan, 1919);
Stories of Red Hanrahan, The Secret Rose, Rosa Alchemica (London & Stratford-upon-Avon: Bullen, 1913; New York: Macmillan, 1914);
Poems Written in Discouragement 1912-1913 (Dundrum: Cuala Press, 1913);
Responsibilities: Poems and a Play (Dundrum: Cuala Press, 1914);
Reveries over Childhood and Youth (Dundrum: Cuala Press, 1915; New York: Macmillan, 1916; London: Macmillan, 1916);
Responsibilities and Other Poems (London: Macmillan, 1916; New York: Macmillan, 1916);
The Wild Swans at Coole (Dundrum: Cuala Press, 1917; enlarged edition, London: Macmillan, 1919; New York: Macmillan, 1919);
Per Amica Silentia Lunae (London: Macmillan, 1918; New York: Macmillan, 1918);
Two Plays for Dancers (Dundrum: Cuala Press, 1919);
Michael Robartes and the Dancer (Dundrum: Cuala Press, 1921);
Four Plays for Dancers (London: Macmillan, 1921; New York: Macmillan, 1921);
The Trembling of the Veil (London: Laurie, 1922);
Later Poems (London: Macmillan, 1922; New York: Macmillan, 1924);
Plays in Prose and Verse, Written for an Irish Theatre, by Yeats and Lady Gregory (London: Macmillan, 1922; New York: Macmillan, 1924);
The Player Queen (London: Macmillan, 1922);
Plays and Controversies (London: Macmillan, 1923; New York: Macmillan, 1924);
Essays (London: Macmillan, 1924; New York: Macmillan, 1924);
The Cat and the Moon (Dublin: Cuala Press, 1924);
The Bounty of Sweden (Dublin: Cuala Press, 1925);
Early Poems and Stories (London: Macmillan, 1925; New York: Macmillan, 1925);
A Vision: An Explanation of Life Founded upon the Writings of Giraldus and upon Certain Doctrines Attributed to Kusta Ben Luka (London: Laurie, 1925); substantially revised as *A Vision* (London: Macmillan, 1937; New York: Macmillan, 1938);
Autobiographies: Reveries Over Childhood and Youth and The Trembling of the Veil (London: Macmillan, 1926; New York: Macmillan, 1927);
October Blast (Dublin: Cuala Press, 1927);
Stories of Red Hanrahan and The Secret Rose (London: Macmillan, 1927);
The Tower (London: Macmillan, 1928; New York: Macmillan, 1928);
Sophocles' King Oedipus: A Version for the Modern Stage by W. B. Yeats (London: Macmillan, 1928; New York: Macmillan, 1928);
The Death of Synge and Other Passages from an Old Diary (Dublin: Cuala Press, 1928);
A Packet for Ezra Pound (Dublin: Cuala Press, 1929);
The Winding Stair (New York: Fountain Press, 1929);
Stories of Michael Robartes and His Friends. An Extract from a Record made by his Pupils; and a play in prose (Dublin: Cuala Press, 1932);
Words for Music Perhaps and Other Poems (Dublin: Cuala Press, 1932);
The Winding Stair and Other Poems (London: Macmillan, 1933; New York: Macmillan, 1933);
The Collected Poems (New York: Macmillan, 1933; London: Macmillan, 1933);
Letters to the New Island, edited by Horace Reynolds (Cambridge: Harvard University Press, 1934; London: Oxford University Press, 1970);
The Words Upon the Window Pane (Dublin: Cuala Press, 1934);
Wheels and Butterflies (London: Macmillan, 1934; New York: Macmillan, 1935);
The Collected Plays (London: Macmillan, 1934; New York: Macmillan, 1935);
The King of the Great Clock Tower (Dublin: Cuala Press, 1934; New York: Macmillan, 1935);
A Full Moon in March (London: Macmillan, 1935);
Dramatis Personae (Dublin: Cuala Press, 1935);
Poems (Dublin: Cuala Press, 1935);
Dramatis Personae 1896-1902, Estrangement, The Death of Synge, The Bounty of Sweden (New

York: Macmillan, 1936; London: Macmillan, 1936);

Nine One-Act Plays (London: Macmillan, 1937);

Essays, 1931 to 1936 (Dublin: Cuala Press, 1937);

The Herne's Egg: A Stage Play (London: Macmillan, 1938);

The Herne's Egg and Other Plays (New York: Macmillan, 1938);

New Poems (Dublin: Cuala Press, 1938);

The Autobiography of William Butler Yeats, Consisting of Reveries Over Childhood and Youth, The Trembling of the Veil and Dramatis Personae (New York: Macmillan, 1938); republished, with *Estrangement, The Death of Synge,* and *The Bounty of Sweden,* as *Autobiographies* (London: Macmillan, 1955);

Last Poems and Two Plays (Dublin: Cuala Press, 1939);

On the Boiler (Dublin: Cuala Press, 1939);

Last Poems and Plays (London: Macmillan, 1940; New York: Macmillan, 1940);

If I Were Four-and-Twenty (Dublin: Cuala Press, 1940);

Poems of W. B. Yeats, Definitive Edition, 2 volumes (London: Macmillan, 1949);

The Collected Plays of W. B. Yeats (London: Macmillan, 1952; New York: Macmillan, 1953);

The Variorum Edition of the Poems of W. B. Yeats, edited by Peter Allt and Russell K. Alspach (New York: Macmillan, 1957);

Mythologies (New York: Macmillan, 1959);

Senate Speeches, edited by Donald R. Pearce (Bloomington: Indiana University Press, 1960);

Essays and Introductions (New York: Macmillan, 1961);

Explorations (New York: Macmillan, 1962);

The Variorum Edition of the Plays of W. B. Yeats, edited by Russell K. Alspach, assisted by Catherine C. Alspach (London & New York: Macmillan, 1966);

Uncollected Prose, 2 volumes, edited by John P. Frayne (New York: Columbia University Press, 1970);

Memoirs: Autobiography, first draft, transcribed and edited by Denis Donoghue (London: Macmillan, 1972);

The Collected Works of W. B. Yeats, edited by Richard J. Finneran and George Mills Harper (New York: Macmillan, 1989-).

OTHER: *Fairy and Folk Tales of the Irish Peasantry,* edited by Yeats (New York: Boni & Liveright, 1888; London: Scott, 1893);

Drawing of Yeats by John Singer Sargent (The Anderson Galleries, sale 1820, 17-20 March 1924)

The Works of William Blake, Poetic, Symbolic, and Critical, 3 volumes, edited by Yeats and Edwin John Ellis (London: Quaritch, 1893);

Augusta, Lady Gregory, *Vision and Belief in the West of Ireland,* includes two essays and notes by Yeats (New York & London: Putnam's, 1920);

The Oxford Book of Modern Verse, edited by Yeats (Oxford: Clarendon Press, 1936; New York: Oxford University Press, 1936);

The Ten Principal Upanishads, put into English by Yeats and Shri Purohit Swami (London: Faber & Faber, 1937; New York: Macmillan, 1937).

William Butler Yeats, probably the twentieth century's greatest poet in English and certainly one of its most complex men, was born in the Dublin suburb of Sandymount on 13 June 1865. He was the eldest of the four surviving children, all brilliant, of a brilliant and problematical father, the painter-philosopher John Butler Yeats, and his muted and problematical wife, Susan Pollexfen Yeats. It was John Butler Yeats who spoke what his son called in his autobiography "the only eulogy that ever turned my head": "by marriage with a Pollexfen, we have given a tongue to the sea cliffs." W. B. Yeats's impassioned mystique of lineage, of name and place and history, is found at its most concentrated in the dedicatory lines beginning "Pardon, old fathers . . . " of his 1914 volume *Responsibilities.* There Yeats phrased his grief and shame over the case that a "barren passion," his long hopeless pursuit of Maud Gonne, unnamed, had left him at forty-nine with "no child . . . nothing but a book. / Nothing but that to prove your blood and mine."

Yeats was proud to belong in both strains of his blood to the Anglo-Irish Protestant minority that had produced over several centuries in Catholic Ireland an astonishing list of men of genius and power in arts and politics. The Yeats line had been settled in Ireland since the seventeenth century; they began as merchants, but later generations were Trinity College scholars and Church of Ireland clergymen, Yeats's great-grandfather having been rector of Drumcliff in County Sligo, where the poet would be buried at last under his own famous epitaph, *"Cast a cold Eye / On Life, on Death. / Horseman, pass by!"* His mother's family, comfortably fixed Pollexfens and Middletons, were shipowners and millers in and about Sligo, where remnant Yeatses also lived. The hills and lakes and fens about the busy West of Ireland seaside town, with Ben Bulben to the north and Knocknarea, topped by Queen Maeve's cairn, to the south of a tidal river, became Yeats's spiritual home in childhood and remained so all his life.

John Butler Yeats was trained for the law, but he did not like the trade and resolved to make a living out of his gift for drawing and painting, especially for portraiture. The gift was real, but he never learned to exploit it; he could never let a painting go, preferring to repaint, while talking. He remained a delightful and indiscriminately productive failure, and poverty became a fact of life for his family. To put himself to school as a painter, J. B. Yeats carried his young family in 1868 to London, where they lived in Fitzroy Road, Regents Park, for the next seven years, during which four other children were born. Robert died in childhood, but Jack B. Yeats and his sisters Lily and Lollie survived to become notably original persons and to form with their father and brother one of the world's brilliant families.

In the 1915 portion of his autobiography, *Reveries over Childhood and Youth,* Yeats wrote: "Indeed I remember little of childhood but its pain. I have grown happier with every year of life as though gradually conquering something in myself. . . . " The gauzy, veiled effects of visual observation down past the turn of the century in Yeats's writings, and indeed to a degree all his life, doubtless owed something to poor eyesight: both eyes were weak, the left almost useless. Still, like a great half-blind Englishman, Samuel Johnson, and another half-blind Irishman, James Joyce, he always seemed to be able to see what mattered to him. Much of the time in any case his essential seeing was more visionary than visual. Yeats recalled hardly anything of his first London years; his early memories are obsessed with scenes and persons in Sligo, particularly his uncle George Pollexfen, horseman and astrologer, "That could have shown how pure-bred horses / And solid men, for all their passions, live / But as the outrageous stars incline / By opposition, square and trine," and his grandfather William Pollexfen, the "silent and fierce old man" who always reminded him of Lear, whom as a child he confused with God and to whom he traced his lifelong "delight in passionate men."

The boy Yeats was dreamy and introspective but by no means housebound. He rode about the Sligo countryside on a red pony, with a black dog and a white, alert to flora and fauna, and beginning to steep himself in the fairy lore of the local peasants. His formal education would never be better than spotty. He wrote in *Reveries over Childhood and Youth:* "Because I had found it difficult to attend to anything less interesting than my thoughts, I was difficult to teach." He was so slow in learning to read that he was thought to be simple, and he would be tone deaf all his life. When he began to read he was mystified as to why the church choir took three times as long as he did to reach the end of a hymn. Back in London, where his father pursued his endless apprenticeship, Yeats would remember Sligo "with tears." He spent five inconsequential years at Godolphin, a day school in Hammersmith, a poor student, absentminded, more interested in collecting moths and butterflies than in his daily task. The people who interested him were his father's friends, painters of the second rank under Pre-Raphaelite influence. He hated London and survived spiritually on annual holiday visits to Sligo.

In 1880 the family returned to Ireland, settling first on the hill of Howth, the north horn of the crescent of Dublin Bay, later sacred as the scene of the lyrical consummation of the love of Molly and Leopold Bloom. Howth was a "gentle" spot (an ancient resort of fairy folk), and pursuit of such lore and of entomology occupied Willie much more than his formal studies. He was now a tall, gaunt lad, very dark skinned, with sheaves of black hair falling over his eyes. He rode the train into the city daily, accompanying his father, who quizzed and harangued him on the "passionate" portions from the English poets that he spent much time in reading aloud. Willie was now enrolled in Erasmus High School in Harcourt Street. His thinking moved slowly away from amateur science and toward literature, and he began to see himself in the guise of various heroic solitaries, doomed and melancholy: Hamlet, Manfred, Athanase, Alastor. At seventeen he began to write poetry that pointed gradually toward *The Wanderings of Oisin and Other Poems* (1889), lyrics and ballads founded mainly on tales, scenes, atmospheres of Howth and Sligo, where George Pollexfen had become an affectionate confidant.

Money being short and his chances of passing entrance examinations being judged poor, Yeats was sent next not to Trinity College but to the Metropolitan School of Art nearby in Kildare Street. His talent in art was as weak as his eyes, and he never progressed beyond a primitive amateur level. In any case his head was now full of the language of his own romantic poems and plays, Percy Bysshe Shelley and Edmund Spenser being his chief models. He had made *Prometheus Unbound* his "sacred book." At the art school he formed a friendship that would be troubled but lifelong with a tall young Ulsterman, George William Russell (AE), who as poet, painter, journalist, and mystic would come to stand second only to Yeats among Irishmen of genius in their generation. Russell could soon quote every word of young Yeats's writings, which now included his first two published poems that appeared in the *Dublin University Review* in March 1885.

In the same year, moved by a reading of A. P. Sinnett's *Esoteric Buddhism,* by a general fascination with Eastern mysticism, and by an innate love for closed, secret circles, Yeats and a few friends formed a Hermetic Society in Dublin. In his autobiography he traced to his early studies in "psychical research and mystical philosophy" his first decisive movement away from the influence of his father's humanist rationalism. He was also deeply impressed by the teaching of a visiting Bengali Brahmin, Mohini Chatterji: "It was my first meeting with a philosophy that confirmed my vague speculations and seemed at once logical and boundless." Within this atmosphere Yeats composed a dramatic poem, *Mosada,* published as a pamphlet in 1886, and a half-dozen "Indian" poems such as "The Indian to His Love," soft, sad matter like all his earliest work, pleasingly mellifluous but boneless in thought and rhetoric.

By contrast, Yeats was also frequenting several disputatious politically oriented societies about Dublin, and he began to play a part in their debates. "I wished to become self-possessed," he wrote in his autobiography, "to be able to play with hostile minds as Hamlet played, to look in the lion's face . . . with unquivering eyelash." Influenced in part by his new friendship with the noble old Fenian John O'Leary, recently returned from twenty years of prison and exile, a man he judged to be "of Plutarch's people," Yeats was rapidly turning self-consciously "Celtic"—nationalist and anti-English—though his base was less political than cultural and literary. It pleased him to be having his verse published in two Catholic periodicals, the *Irish Monthly* and the *Irish Fireside,* among other poems the haunted and haunting lyric "The Stolen Child." Pursuing "self-possession," he began to speak regularly at meetings of the Young Ireland Society. "From these debates," he reflected many years later, "from O'Leary's conversation, and from the Irish books he lent or gave me has come all I have set my hand to since."

Near the end of *Reveries* Yeats described his early dream of a nationalism that would bring together the political nerve and fervor of Catholic Ireland with "the good taste, the household courtesy and decency" of Anglo-Ireland, and his thought that "we might bring the halves together if we had a national literature that made Ireland beautiful in the memory, and yet had been freed from provincialism by an exacting criticism, an European pose." He gave much thought to a fit style, for oratory but also for prose and verse. He argued with his father, who favored declamation and "drama": "We should write out our own thoughts in as nearly as possible the language we thought them in, as though in a letter to an intimate friend." He worked hard at this simplifying discipline but found results slow to come, particularly in his poetry: "when I re-read those early poems which gave me so much trouble, I find little but romantic convention, unconscious drama.

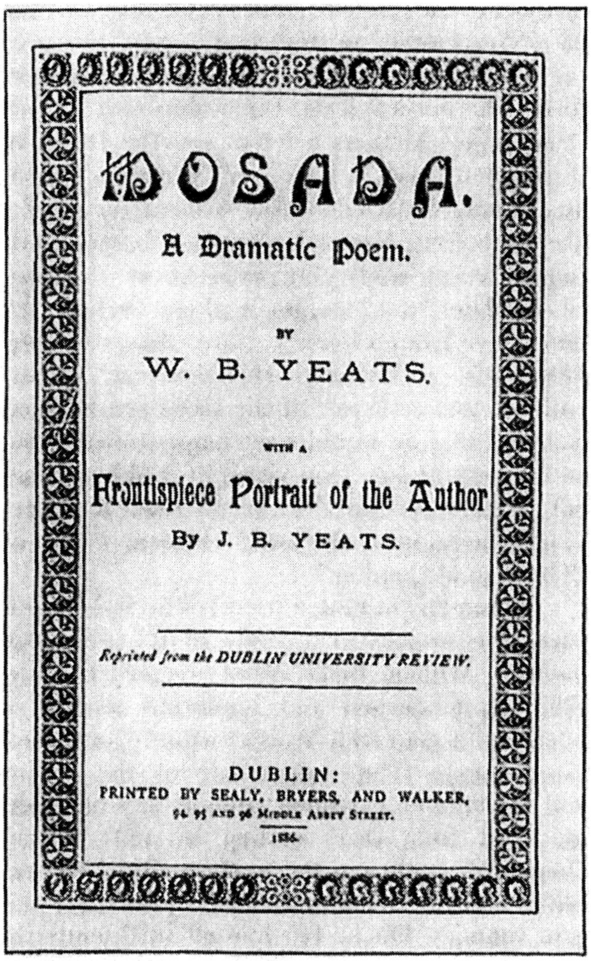
MOSADA.

A Dramatic Poem.

BY

W. B. YEATS.

WITH A

Frontispiece Portrait of the Author

By J. B. YEATS.

Reprinted from the DUBLIN UNIVERSITY REVIEW.

DUBLIN:

PRINTED BY SEALY, BRYERS, AND WALKER,

94, 95 AND 96 MIDDLE ABBEY STREET.

1886.

Front cover for Yeats's first book, which reflects his interest in Eastern mysticism

It is so many years before one can believe enough in what one feels even to know what the feeling is."

The mystical side of Yeats's thought also took a new turn in 1886 when a friend in Dublin took him to his first spiritualist séance. He proved a frighteningly apt subject: "my whole body moved like a suddenly unrolled watch-spring, and I was thrown backward on the wall," and his hand banged the table with such violence that he broke the table. In his terror he tried to pray but could think only of the first lines of *Paradise Lost:* "Of Man's first disobedience and the fruit / Of that forbidden tree. . . . " Did those spirits come from within or without? It was years before he dared again to tempt them so directly, though when he recovered his nerve he kept at it till the end.

In 1887 J. B. Yeats carried his family again to London, where they settled into a better house than they could afford in Bedford Park, a community where the Pre-Raphaelite movement was "at last affecting life." Willie and Jack painted the ceiling of Willie's room with a map of Sligo. Their mother suffered a stroke, then another, and declined into premature senility. Times were hard, with Willie and his father eking out pittances by hackwork. Yeats edited for Dublin and London publishers *Poems and Ballads of Young Ireland* (1888), including four poems of his own, and *Fairy and Folk Tales of the Irish Peasantry* (1888), and contributed letters on Irish affairs to two American papers. His first poem to be published in England appeared in the *Leisure Hour;* "The Madness of King Goll" is notable for showing already installed his lifelong mastery of a refrain: "*They will not hush, the leaves a-flutter round me, the beech leaves old.*" Yeats judged himself to have been at this stage "in all things Pre-Raphaelite"—meaning apparently, though not clearly, romantically elaborate, stylized, antiquarian. He continued to make and unmake his complex aesthetic. He saw himself as a young man naturally religious, needing to believe, deprived of his childhood religion by science and rationalism, forming in recoil "a new religion, almost an infallible church of poetic tradition, of a fardel of stories, and of personages, and of emotions, inseparable from their first expression, passed on from generation to generation by poets and painters with some help from philosophers and theologians."

Early working of that religion was visible in *The Wanderings of Oisin* (Ossian, Usheen), completed in the summer of 1888 during a visit to Sligo. It was Yeats's longest and most ambitious work to date, a dramatic dialogue, mostly monologue, of thirty pages, a thousand lines, in a mixture of meters, much of it in rhymed couplets. Saint Patrick quizzes the battered but unrepentant pagan Oisin, "bent, and bald, and blind, / With a heavy heart and a wandering mind," who tells him the story of three hundred ecstatic and tortured years in Fenian fairyland with his demon lady, "white-bodied" Niamh. It was Yeats's first decisive venture into Celtic myth, even more important for his plays to come than for his poetry. Reading it to George Pollexfen in Sligo, Yeats broke down, overcome by labor and feeling.

The long poem gave bulk and a wavering backbone to Yeats's first published volume of verse, *The Wanderings of Oisin and Other Poems,* published in 1889 by Kegan Paul, Trench, on the strength of subscriptions mostly collected by the loyal John O'Leary. The general response was approving if not ecstatic, and it brought Yeats the obsession of a lifetime, the keenest and most durable of his raptures and his tortures, his love for Maud Gonne. The young woman whom George Bernard Shaw called "outrageously beautiful" appeared in Bedford Park with an introduction from John O'Leary and word that *The Wanderings of Oisin* had made her weep. The enchanted vagueness of the mere paragraph Yeats gave to their meeting in the autobiography suggests the power of her magic. In "The Arrow" a few years later he recalled his first vision of Maud Gonne in the light of a window full of apple blossoms in sun: "Tall and noble but with face and bosom / Delicate in colour as apple blossoms." He thought of her in the line of heroic legendary beauty, as his Helen, his Leda, his Phoenix, his "woman Homer sung," his "Pallas Athene in that straight back and arrogant head." His bitter late image of her as "an old bellows full of angry wind" was a long way off, and it was regularly offset by images that remembered more fairly his early sexual starvation and the enchantment of her presence. In 1889 he was discovering the passion of her commitment to radical Irish nationalism and allowing her to lead him toward a mask that proved a bad fit, that of the man politically engagé.

Yeats continued to find friends among older men, notably now William Morris, whom he soon called "my chief of men," and W. E. Henley, editor of the *Scots Observer* (later the *National Observer*) and a generous, contentious man of whom he wrote: "I disagreed with him about everything, but I admired him beyond words." Henley published, often with alterations by himself, what Yeats called "my first good lyrics and tolerable essays"; prose pieces later collected in *The Celtic Twilight* (1893) and such poems as "A Cradle Song," "The Man Who Dreamed of Faeryland," and the one that became and remained his most famous, "The Lake Isle of Innisfree." At Henley's he met Oscar Wilde, as yet untouched by scandal, and found him not only brilliant but warmly hospitable and openhearted.

Yeats's fascination with the occult grew ever more intense. He frequented the theosophical fellowship of the London Lodge, amused and impressed by Madame Blavatsky's massive "peasant" humanity and stirred by her doctrine and her discipline. "A great passionate nature, a sort of female Dr. Johnson," he called her, and admired her "air of humour and audacious power." As a member of the "esoteric" inner circle of devout initiates, Yeats joined in studies of oriental charts of correspondences among soul, body, planetary forms, the musical scale. Friendship with Liddell (MacGregor) Mathers led him into the Order of the Golden Dawn, a society of "Christian Cabbalists" whose ritual embodied Western forms of a like symbolism. Under Mathers's influence Yeats "began certain studies and experiences" that convinced him "that images well up before the mind's eye from a deeper source than conscious or subconscious memory." He was in reach, apparently, of that reservoir of the race's accumulated emblems that he would later name *Anima Mundi* and *Spiritus Mundi*. One vision evoked by a symbol of Mathers's stayed in Yeats's mind for thirty years, emerging as the awful climactic image of "The Second Coming."

When Edwin Ellis, a friend of his father's, invited him to join in a study of the prophetic books of William Blake, Yeats accepted happily. Ellis was a spirited and humorous scholar, a poet, and a man with Yeats's own gift for mysterious visions. The transcribing of the poems and the editors' extended commentary occupied much of four years ending in 1891. When Quaritch brought out the work in 1893 Yeats received no cash, only thirteen sets of the three elegant volumes; but he felt himself sufficiently rewarded by his steeping in Blake's symbolic system and his verse, and by much instruction in the craft of poetry from Ellis and Blake, including a decisive negative insight: "I had learned from Blake to hate all abstraction."

While Yeats's speculative thought was growing bolder and more expansive, his aesthetic thought was turning harder, more concentrated, more empirical and exacting. His romantic instinct, deep in character and temperament, sustained his leaning to the Pre-Raphaelite, the Celtic, to soft feeling and lush textures; at the same time he began to ask harder things of his art: sharper outlines, tighter structures, simpler, more natural diction, a firmer grounding in familiar experience. Romantic and classical impulses would contend in Yeats's spirit all his life. The great poetry of his maturity would express a brilliant peacemaking, a control of opposites in tense counterpoise. Now, although he had learned from Blake "to hate all abstraction," he was still "full of thought, often very abstract thought, longing all the while to be full of images." The conflict tore his life while shaping it.

Yeats in an 1894 photograph by fellow Rhymers' Club member T. W. Rolleston

Yeats was trying to find a way to marry art to life. Being Irish, and personally and ethnically ambitious, aspiring, he was churning complex elements of art and history, polity, nationhood, art and egotism, personality, selfhood. He wanted to be at once timely and timeless, personal and impersonal, representative: "I wanted to create once more an art where the artist's handiwork would hide as under those half-anonymous chisels or as we find it in some old Scots ballads, or in some twelfth- or thirteenth-century Arthurian Romance. That handiwork assured, I had martyred no man for modelling his own image on Pallas Athena's buckler. . . ." He struggled to express "those simple emotions which resemble the more, the more powerful they are, everybody's emotion," and he was "soon"—in fact always—"to write many poems where an always personal emotion was woven into a general pattern of myth and symbol." He sought an art of largeness, significance, but also of wholeness, of "Unity of Being"; myth and symbol seemed to offer a terrain, a climate, an understood generalness in which to situate the particular: "I delighted in every age where poet and artist confined themselves gladly to some inherited subject-matter known to the whole people, for I thought that in man and race alike there is something called 'Unity of Being,' using that term as Dante used it when he compared beauty in the *Convito* to a perfectly proportioned human body. . . . I thought that all art should be a Centaur finding in the popular lore its back and strong legs. . . . Have not all races had their first unity from a mythology that marries them to rock and hill?"

Very soon he began to suspect that we would find such wholeness as we were to be granted in this life (or in any other life) in dividedness: in imperfection, opposition, in what he later called comprehensively "the antinomies." It was our excruciating and exhilarating fate to be forever torn. Yeats's mind began "drifting vaguely," as he put it, toward master images that would be permanent counters in his thought: the "Mask" or "anti-self" and "the Daimon," shapes that emblematized his conviction that we must find our troubled peace in conflict, in endless stress. Imperfection was a condition of being, a definition of humanity, as Christians had said—though Yeats did not credit them with the idea, for him self-discovered: "Nations, races, and individual men are unified by an image, or bundle of related images, symbolical or evocative of the state of mind, which is of all states of mind not impossible, the most difficult to that man, race, or nation; because only the greatest obstacle that can be contemplated without despair rouses the will to full intensity." It is the role of the Daimon or "Gate-keeper" to bring the creature and his will to that strenuous confrontation. Yeats put it all together in the most shattering of his statements: "We begin to live when we have conceived life as tragedy."

Loving costume and theater, Yeats often dressed the poet in these years—in a flowing loose tie, a brown velveteen jacket, and an old Inverness cape abandoned by his father twenty years earlier. Loving cabals and exclusiveness, he joined the Welshman Ernest Rhys in 1891 in founding the Rhymers' Club, which for some years was to meet almost every night in an upper room of an old inn in the Strand, the Cheshire Cheese: "We read our poems to one another and talked criticism and drank a little wine." The shifting membership included Lionel Johnson, Ernest Dowson, John Davidson, Richard Le Gallienne, Edwin Ellis, Arthur Symons, and Oscar Wilde, several of whom he would later group as "The Tragic Generation." Johnson and Symons were Yeats's closest comrades. He noticed that when he began to talk his "philosophical ideas" to the Rhymers "a gloomy silence fell upon the room."

In the same interval Yeats was founding in London the Irish Literary Society and in Dublin the National Literary Society. In Dublin in the summer of 1891 he spent all possible time with Maud Gonne; he proposed marriage and was sweetly refused. He had been feeling that the time was ripe for doing something fundamental about Irish culture, "that Ireland would be like soft wax for years to come," and the downfall and heartbroken death of Ireland's great hero in Westminster, Charles Stewart Parnell, whose coffin ship Yeats met at Kingstown pier in October, brought his Irish resolutions to a point. First and most personally, he wanted to create an Irish theater, and he wanted it to perform *The Countess Kathleen* (later *Cathleen*, 1892), his first stage play, with which he had been wrestling, with Maud Gonne in mind as both mythic heroine and principal actress.

But his general ambition was much grander: to lift the whole level of Irish thought and discourse, to give it both poetry and solidity. He assigned his Irish literary clubs, for example, the task of creating a "standard of criticism," an Arnoldian current of true and fresh ideas. Revolted alike by Protestant crassness and Catholic self-deceiving sentiment, sick of "convivial Ireland with the traditional tear and smile," of belonging to "a race intemperate of speech, declamatory, loose, and bragging," he wished to attack those vulgarities and to offer the race higher motives, more adult consciousness, and an answerable style, beginning with what he called "the applied arts of literature": literature rising out of myth and popular lore and in close touch with music, speech, dance, and painting, gradually moving a whole culture toward Unity of Being. The question of style seemed to him fundamental: style in thought, art, personality. He looked toward "manner at once cold and passionate, daring long premeditated act." He wanted Ireland to join him in conceiving life as tragedy and so beginning to live; then the bitter Irish might find themselves of all races "nearest the honeyed comb." Paradox, oxymoron, "the antinomies" stirred in his mind; "cold and passionate" was a characteristic formula, and it looked all the way ahead to his self-composed epitaph. The antinomies in tension composed the organism. At this point in his autobiography Yeats quoted the final stanza of "Another Song of a Fool" of 1919: "Like the clangour of a bell, / Sweet and harsh, harsh and sweet, / That is how he learnt so well / To take the roses for his meat."

Yeats traveled about Ireland founding branches of the National Literary Society, surprised at his own readiness in argument and persuasive powers. Notable men came to his support: O'Leary, Russell, Douglas Hyde, Standish O'Grady. But his dream had been all too grand, and it remained for a corollary movement, Hyde's Gaelic League, to effect real change in the texture of Irish life. Indeed it was ten years before the hardening of Yeats's aesthetic worked any real change in his own style. When Fisher Unwin brought out *The Countess Kathleen and Various Legends and Lyrics* in 1892, his "fitful Danaan rhymes" still brooded richly in fairyland and legendary Ireland, choosing to "sing of old Eire and the ancient ways," to find subjects in fragments of "Eternal beauty wandering on her way." The beauty is real, and the volume contains a half-dozen first-rate neoromantic lyrics: "The Lake Isle of Innisfree," "When You Are Old," "The Man Who Dreamed of Faeryland," "The Two Trees," and "Who Goes with Fergus?" Yeats's drenched nostalgia for a life that never was gave the volume its pitch and tone. "The Lake Isle of Innisfree" enchanted many people, and critics praised its mastery of vowel sounds—at a time when, as Yeats noted, he hardly knew what a vowel was. He kept his own respect for the poem as "my first lyric with anything in its rhythm of my own music," and he recognized the hesitantly transitional place of such poems in the forming of his style: "I had begun to loosen rhythm as an escape from rhetoric, and from that emotion of the crowd that rhetoric brings, but I only understood vaguely and occasionally that I must for my special purpose use nothing but the common syntax." "Who Goes with Fergus?," set to music, moved the mother of Stephen Dedalus to tears when he sang it to her, and it stayed in the mind of that bitter and envious young man for that reason and because it had authentic grandeur and mystery, a wildness in touch with chaos, at its heart: "For Fergus rules the brazen cars, / And rules the shadows of the wood, / And the white breast of the dim sea / And all dishevelled wandering stars." Self-indulgence was beginning to move out.

For Yeats the remainder of the 1890s was a period of mixed purposes, divided energies, though hardworking and productive as all his life would be. His deepest personal tendencies, to sensuality and mysticism, colored all he did. "Sex and the dead," he would write much later, were the only fit subjects for a serious mind. Yeats was

Coole Park, the home of Lady Gregory

happier, easier, more personally attractive with women than with men, and by 1895 he was on terms of sympathetic intimacy with many able, active, handsome young women. Katharine Tynan, the talented daughter of a Wicklow farmer, had been his good comrade in Ireland for ten years. In 1890 he had been first enthralled by the mastery of gesture, the low thrilling voice, and the "incomparable" sense of rhythm of a beautiful young minor actress, Florence Farr. He made her his intimate friend and his model for the "ideal" effects he sought in stage performances: a stylized, poetical art, physically restrained, almost static, directing all attention to the beauty of language. Olivia Shakespear, whose daughter Dorothy was to marry Ezra Pound, was another beautiful and intelligent young woman, caught like Florence Farr in an unsatisfactory marriage. It is probable that both became Yeats's lovers, and certain that they remained his dear friends as long as they lived.

Maud Gonne probably never became his mistress, but she, remained his enchantress, at once scattering and concentrating his energies, moving him constantly to poetry. In Dublin she refused to be his "hostess" as she refused to be his wife. She said her "social life" was to be in Paris, where she frequented a Boulangist coterie of political journalists and schemed to turn French opinion against the common enemy, England. She lived and even traveled in a menagerie of dogs, monkeys, and birds that included a full-grown Donegal hawk. Yeats made himself her willing cavalier in Ireland, England, and France, seeing her off with her cages of birds and beasts. Together they were a famous and amazing sight, both tall, sweeping in vestment and gesture, too preoccupied with their own impassioned chatter to notice the sensation they caused.

A woman from a calmer world, whom he met in 1896, offered Yeats the most serviceable friendship of his life. Augusta, Lady Gregory was a chunky little brown woman of forty-five, widow of a distinguished British Foreign Service officer. Romantically but not hopefully attracted to Yeats, fifteen years her junior, she offered indispensable mothering and sistering. Her house, Coole Park, near Gort in the West of Ireland, was an ancient family estate, a great house, big and plain, stuffed with the trophies of generations of wealth, travel, and accomplishment, with an avenue of arching limes, extensive woodlands, and a small lake whose swans Yeats would make illustrious. The snob in Yeats, his deep-seated grand seigneur instincts, rose swiftly to the appeal of this paradigm of aristocratic Anglo-Irishry. Lady

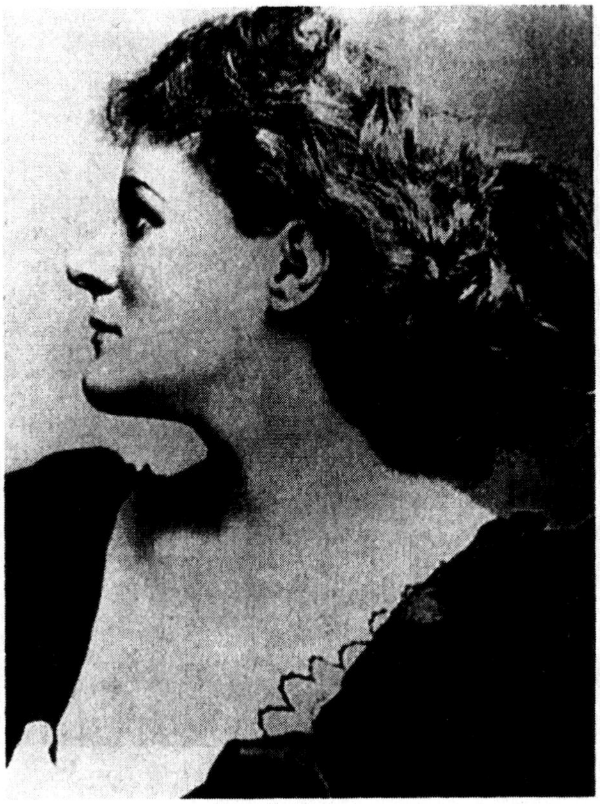

Maud Gonne

Gregory saw that he was needy and unwell. She housed and fed him, approved his dreams, took him about the countryside to share in the collecting of folklore upon which both were already embarked. Until his marriage in 1917 Yeats was to spend parts of every year at Coole, a beloved guest. If Lady Gregory had not saved his life she had made it healthier, firmer, more elegant, given him the first stability he had known.

For his important atmospheric acquaintance with the French symbolists and decadents Yeats was indebted chiefly to Arthur Symons, learned in their language and lore. In February 1894 Yeats made his first trip to Paris, staying with the unregenerate cabalist MacGregor Mathers and his wife, a sister of Henri Bergson's, and seeing as much as possible of Maud Gonne. Symons took him to call upon Paul Verlaine, whose English was sufficient for conversation; and with Maud Gonne he saw a performance of a famous period piece, the *Axël* of Villiers de L'Isle-Adam. Yeats's French was primitive, but Maud Gonne's was good enough to carry him through the play, which Yeats at once installed among his "sacred books" as a guide to what Joseph Hone calls "a dramatic art where symbol replaces character, events are allegories and words keep more than half their secrets to themselves."

At London's Avenue Theatre in March 1894 occurred the first performance of a Yeats play, *The Land of Heart's Desire,* a harmless bit of fairy fluff, which was brought on as a curtain raiser to Shaw's new comedy *Arms and the Man.* Yeats's piece went well enough to survive Shaw's long run, and in the first weeks he haunted the theater, watching the workings on stage narrowly. In *Ave* (1911) George Moore preserved Yeats's restless louring figure in long cloak, sombrero, and flowing tie, all black.

Being penniless, fond of his uncle and his second-sighted servant Mary Battle, and anxious to add to his stock of folktales, Yeats paid a visit to George Pollexfen in the summer that was stretched to half a year. An autumn impression of the Gore-Booth sisters of Lissadell bore fruit nearly forty years later in one of his most magical cadences: "The light of evening, Lissadell, / Great windows open to the south, / Two girls in silk kimonos, both / Beautiful, one a gazelle." That was sex, beautifully sublimated. The dead were active too. Yeats "plunged without a clue into a labyrinth of images," and he and his uncle made many experiments with magic and symbolism, and emerged with intensified convictions. Yeats "knew" himself "face to face with the Anima Mundi described by Platonic philosophers." Two years earlier he had defended his occult studies against John O'Leary's misgivings: "The mystical life is the centre of all that I do and all that I think and all that I write. . . . I have always considered myself a voice of . . . a greater renaissance—the revolt of the soul against the intellect—now beginning in the world." He summed up the facts of his case and their psychology in a very straight passage in his autobiography: "I had not taken up these subjects willfully, nor through love of strangeness, nor love of excitement, nor because I found myself in some experimental circle, but because unaccountable things had happened even in my childhood, and because of an ungovernable craving. When supernatural events begin, a man first doubts his own testimony, but when they repeat themselves again and again, he doubts all human testimony." It would not do to suppose that Yeats's mystical life was a matter of play.

Yeats was thirty when he first took up quarters of his own, rooms in the Temple connected by that passageway to rooms of Arthur Symons's that was his real avenue into the Continental literature of the 1890s. Symons helped him to read works by contemporary French poets, though the great influence on his prose was still Walter Pater, to whom he had been led by Lionel Johnson. Soon Yeats moved to two rooms in Woburn Buildings in Bloomsbury; eventually he occupied most of the house, and it became his London place for many years. Local children called him "the toff in the Buildings."

Fisher Unwin brought out *Poems* (1895), containing Yeats's two plays and the lyrics that still pleased him from his first two volumes. The book was a success and was to be reprinted fourteen times down to 1929, bringing Yeats a steady small annual royalty. Over the years he constantly revised these poems, some to the point of transformation, but he never abjured them. "Early Yeats" was the best poetry in English in late Victorian times; but they were bad times. Early in 1896 the *Savoy,* with Yeats's friends Symons and Aubrey Beardsley as editor and art editor, picked up the fallen banners of the *Yellow Book* and continued the war of the decadents upon the moral and aesthetic stuffiness of entrenched Victorianism. Yeats's prose and verse appeared often in the *Savoy.*

In the summer of 1896 Yeats took Symons on a visit to Ireland that would be full of consequences. Their party was soon joined by Symons's ribald friend George Moore and Moore's cranky, God-haunted friend Edward Martyn. They traveled the West Country and the Aran Islands, and at Coole Park near Gort they met Martyn's neighbor Lady Gregory. Unknowingly Yeats had collected the directorate of his coming theater movement, lacking only its resident genius, John Millington Synge. Him he duly discovered a few months later under the eaves of his hotel in Paris, where Yeats had gone to consult with Mathers and Maud Gonne about designing a ritual for an Order of Celtic Mysteries that he hoped to found. He dreamed of setting up the sanctum of the order in an enchanted spot, an abandoned "castle" that filled a little island in Lough Key. For ten years, he wrote in "Hodos Chameliontos" (book 3 of *The Trembling of the Veil,* 1922), his "most impassioned thought" was of the philosophy of his Order. He foresaw that "invisible gates would open" as they had done for Blake, Emanuel Swedenborg, and Jakob Böhme; then, he thought, he must turn "difficult, obscure."

Hampered by penury, exhaustion, trouble with his eyes, Yeats worked in London and, in-

Yeats (left), Æ (front), and John Millington Synge fishing on Coole Lake, drawing by Harold Oakley (Sotheby Parke Bernet, 15 December 1982)

vited by Lady Gregory, at Coole on the Marmorean tales of *The Secret Rose* (1897) and the *Stories of Red Hanrahan* that would be added to the text of *The Celtic Twilight* in 1902. Working "with laborious care and studied moderation of style," he was avoiding the bourgeois and aiming at high and low, at an "aristocratic" literature with its feet in folklore. "The noble and the beggarman" would hold hands in his art for the rest of his life, as they did in his plan for an Irish theater as an instrument of national culture. His indispensable supporter, early and late, was Lady Gregory.

It was she who collected money and patrons to launch the Irish Literary Theatre, the germ of the Abbey, in the autumn of 1898 with Yeats, Moore, and Martyn as directors. The first bill was to be composed of *The Countess Cathleen* and Martyn's strong realist play *The Heather Field.* During early stages of rehearsal and promotion affairs were hectic, with the officious Moore clashing with the doctrinaire Yeats. The two would snipe at each other, wittily and extravagantly, for the rest of their lives. Yeats's play, in which his heroine sells her soul to "demons" to preserve the peasants from starvation, opened on 8 May 1899 and ran into trouble with the church on grounds of rumored heresy. The performances went forward, but with such tumultuousness as to provide the university student James Joyce with an Irish-symptomatic episode for *A Portrait of the Artist as a Young Man* (1916).

With an almost perverse appropriateness, the lyric poet Yeats closed out the nineteenth century with the most Victorian and Pre-Raphaelite of his collections, *The Wind Among the Reeds* (1899). These poems have a cameo effect: small, shapely, stylized—beautifully formed and spoken but soft, unreal, manneristic. Yeats seemed to be demonstrating how easily and expertly he could write "early Yeats." The poems fall into suites of related attitudes, the titles of which read like captions for serial illustrations, as if one were turning the pages of a very fine old parlor emblem book, the scenes done by Edward Burne-Jones or G. F. Watts. But there is nothing absurd or cheap about these rich conventions. The finest poems are two in which Yeats moved through and past the convention into the stereotyping of full myth. "The Cap and Bells" is a piece of pure Pre-Raphaelite medievalism, controlled by primary colors and sharp outlines and acidified by wit: the lady finally succumbs to the emblems of the jester's ridiculousness, his cap and bells. "The Song of Wandering Aengus" is an unforgettable brief visionary poem which conveys a lifetime's obsessed enchantment by a magical telescoping of time and a surrealistic linking of images.

In the first years of the new century Yeats was constantly and somewhat erratically busy. He shifted publishers restlessly before settling on A. H. Bullen, a scholarly and bibulous friend of his family's. He moved back and forth between London and Dublin and spent most of his summers at Coole. Maud Gonne's French machinations had collapsed in spectacular circumstances, and she had settled back into Dublin and the new Sinn Fein movement. When Yeats spoke of marriage she discouraged him: both of them had better things to do, she argued. It was "a miserable love affair," he wrote in *Dramatis Personae* (1935), and he might as well have been offering his heart "to an image in a milliner's window, or to a statue in a museum."

His other major preoccupation was with the new theater and the series of poetico-mythical short plays he was trying to write for it. *The Shadowy Waters* (1900) was followed in 1901 by *Diarmuid and Grania*, fruit of a quarrelsome collaboration with Moore, produced in October but never published by either author. *Cathleen ni Houlihan*, in which Lady Gregory had helped with dialogue and style, was performed in April 1902 with Maud Gonne a great success in the title part, an old woman who embodies "Ireland herself." Yeats thought she "made Cathleen seem like a divine being fallen into our mortal infirmity." *The Pot of Broth* and *The Hour-Glass* were produced in 1902 and 1903 and published in 1904.

By this time Yeats's group had joined hands with two young Dublin workingmen, the brothers Frank and Willie Fay, brilliant amateur actor-producers, and the company had metamorphosed into the Irish National Theatre. By now Synge too was on the scene, having at last obeyed Yeats's instruction to get out of Paris and dig down to his own Irish roots, and having spent a long interval in the Aran Islands, a country Yeats described as so bleak that men reaped with knives between the stones. The National Theatre's early polity was clumsily "democratic," with all members of the company discussing and voting on all questions of casting and production. After months of squabbling, Yeats, Synge, and Lady Gregory took control as a governing troika.

With his wife now dead, with Willie and Jack leading independent lives, J. B. Yeats decided to return yet again to Dublin, and he and his daughters took a house in Dundrum on the south side of the city. Lily and Lollie had trained in fine textiles and printing in William Morris's Kelmscott workshops, and in Dundrum they settled into Dun Emer Industries. The family had been still in London, however, when John Quinn, a rising young New York corporation lawyer, came abroad for his first whirlwind visit in the late summer of 1902. Quinn was Irish-American, prosperous, and acquisitive. J. B. and Jack Yeats showed him about London and showed examples of their own work. Quinn bought a dozen paintings and commissioned others. In a letter to Willie, J. B. Yeats called him "the nearest approach to an angel in my experience." In Dublin, Quinn met William Yeats and most of his friends, bought paintings, books, and manuscripts, and crossed to the West, where he met the Moore-Martyn-Gregory enclave and carved his initials in the great signatory copper beech at Coole. He proposed to Yeats an American lecture tour and offered also to secure American copyrights by getting out small private editions of new works by the Irish writers. He even effected a temporary reconciliation between Yeats and Moore, who had been involved in another wrangling "collaboration." But Yeats tired of the struggle and dictated a five-act "tragedy" on their common theme to Lady Gregory, called *Where There Is Nothing* (produced in London in 1904 and later rewritten and retitled *The Unicorn from the Stars*, 1908).

A better play, his strongest to date, the little Cuchulain play *On Baile's Strand* (produced in Dublin in 1904), was combined with a dozen recent lyrics in the summer of 1903 to form *In the Seven Woods*. It would be the first volume in the eventually long and distinguished list of handprinted books to come from Lollie Yeats's Dun Emer Press (later Cuala Press). The little book seemed a poor show for four years' work, but considering the manifold forms of Yeats's busyness one wonders, as he often wondered, how he found any time for mere verse. Nor did metrical composition come easy. A lyric commonly began with a few words or phrases or a couple of sentences of the flattest kind of prose; and the shaping of that germ into a half-dozen half-perfected lines needed a hard day's work. The real validation of the volume lay in the quality of the poems. The old softness lingered, but here Yeats took the first steps toward the imposing and exhilarating poetry of his maturity, audible in a new hardness and economy and the sound of an identifiable daily world.

No doubt Yeats's world had changed, as well as his sense of it. Beardsley, Dowson, Johnson, Wilde, the "tragic generation," were all tragically dead, and the 1890s had passed in fact and in spirit; Victoria was gone at last; the Boer War had shaken a great many complacencies. The general air was tenser, dryer, troubled, more soberly empirical, at once less confident and more soberly resolute. Yeats later described his sense of the passing of an era: "Everybody got down off their stilts; henceforth nobody drank absinthe with his black coffee; nobody went mad; nobody committed suicide; nobody joined the Catholic Church or if they did I have forgotten." John Quinn had introduced Yeats to "that strong enchanter" Friedrich Wilhelm Nietzsche, and he had been reading him with fascination, finding in Nietzsche's terms Dionysiac and Apollonian names for his own sense of the soul's two primary "movements": to transcend form, to create form. Now he wrote to Quinn: "I think I have to some extent got weary of the wild god Dionysus, and I am hoping that the Far-Darter will come in his place." "Apollonian" would be one way to describe the new economical shapeliness in Yeats's

John Quinn and William Butler Yeats

poems. In Ireland, in a sense, as always nothing had changed; it was still a case of "Tara uprooted, and new commonness / Upon the throne"; but Yeats was addressing the state of things even there with a new rigor.

Yeats's new manner was clearest in three poems in which Maud Gonne is at last addressed as a real presence, still a goddess but more than a dream. If one's beloved is an incarnated Diana one can expect real shafts in one's heart, as in the tiny poem "The Arrow": "I thought of your beauty, and this arrow, / Made out of a wild thought, is in my marrow." "The Folly of Being Comforted" employs the dialogue structure that would become a favorite form. In answer to a kind friend who "comforts" with advice of "patience," noting that his love is losing her first beauty, "Heart cries, 'No, / I have not a crumb of comfort, not a grain. / Time can but make her beauty over again.' " "Adam's Curse" reinvokes an evening in London when Yeats, Maud Gonne, and her almost equally beautiful sister had talked of poetry and the beauty of women and the general curse of being human, caught in labor, time, mutability. The tone and much of the language are familiar from early Yeats, but this is a tighter poetry; the luxuriousness is gone. The scene feels actual, the rhythm is that of a mind moving, the language sounds like real talk. Perhaps his work in the theater was making a difference.

Quinn had organized his promised American lecture tour, and Yeats gave four months to the enterprise in the fall and winter of 1903-1904. He appeared at most of the major American colleges and universities and at many clubs and societies, especially those of a "Hibernian" cast. Quinn judged he had been the most impressive Irishman to conduct a "mission" to America since Parnell. Confounding friends and enemies who expected him to enact the dream-crossed poet, he made trains, kept appointments, sized up audiences and interviewers expertly, talked good sense. Exhausted but also exhilarated, he returned with a good deal of money in his purse, badly needed. Until he was fifty Yeats regularly earned less than two hundred pounds in a year.

In the preceding winter Yeats had been stunned by the news of Maud Gonne's marriage in Paris to John MacBride, an event that he later preserved in "Reconciliation" as "the day / When, the ears being deafened, the sight of the eyes blind / With lightning, you went from me. . . ." He had easily forgiven her when she produced a beautiful illegitimate girl-child, *la belle* Iseult (who usually passed as her "niece"), credited by many to him but actually fathered by her French coconspirator Lucien Millevoye; but this marriage was something else. Yeats was not only staggered by it as a fatally separating fact, but insulted, angered, and frightened that the woman who had repeatedly refused him should give herself to a brute. MacBride was an Irishman of courage who had led an Irish Brigade against the British in the Boer War, but as a civilian he was a man of no standing or achievement and of crude, even depraved behavior, "a drunken vainglorious lout," as Yeats still called him in "Easter 1916" in the act of forgiving him as a hero who had helped create the "terrible beauty" of the Easter Rising. Now he saw MacBride as an outright miles gloriosus and saw the marriage as a disaster not only to himself but to Maud Gonne. In that he was right; the union was soon dissolved by legal separation—on grounds considered unspeakable—after producing a son, Sean MacBride, who would become a statesman of international eminence.

In the Irish National Theatre things were going better. An English admirer and fellow cabalist, Miss A. E. F. Horniman, a woman of moderate wealth, had offered to "give" Yeats a theater: to provide a building and an annual subsidy of eight hundred pounds for what became the famous Abbey Theatre. *On Baile's Strand* went into rehearsal, and Yeats was also preparing two other plays, *The King's Threshold* (1904) and *Deirdre* (1907). He did not want his Theatre of Beauty to lack matter. Yeats was absorbing the lesson, important to his lyrics as well as to his plays, that for conviction, poetic speech needed to be simplified and braced by common idiom.

Yeats, circa 1905 (photograph by G. C. Beresford)

Synge's rough, loving, satirical Irish visions had caused trouble in the theater from the beginning, and Yeats had defended him stoutly when *In the Shadow of the Glen* and *The Well of the Saints* were attacked. Yeats was lecturing in Scotland late in January 1907 when the performance of Synge's comic masterpiece *The Playboy of the Western World* brought on a week of "riots" in the Abbey, with offended and defensive Irishmen drowning out the lines with hisses, boos, and stamping, and the players eventually turning upon them to join the general slanging match.

Called home by a telegram from Lady Gregory, Yeats threw open the theater to "debate" the issues of the play and the question of whether the theater was to be silenced by a vulgar censorship. Taking the stage in full evening dress, he harangued the generally hostile crowd: "The author of *Cathleen ni Houlihan* addresses you," he announced, and assured them: "You have disgraced yourselves again." The play, he said, was not a travesty upon Irish morality but a celebration of Irish vitality and imaginativeness. Interrupted often by shouted questions and objections, he explained his aspiration for the theater as an instrument to articulate and enrich the national life. J. B. Yeats supported his son onstage, and his grand moment was recalled thirty years later in "Beautiful Lofty Things": "My father upon the Abbey stage, before him a raging crowd: / 'This Land of Saints,' and then as the applause died out, / 'Of plaster Saints'; his beautiful mischievous head thrown back."

In the spring of 1907 Yeats joined Lady Gregory and her son, Robert, for his most elegant holiday to date, a tour of several weeks among the cities of northern Italy: Venice, Florence, Milan, Urbino, Ferrara, Ravenna. He returned with his head full of new and permanent images of beauty and vitality accomplished by a union of aristocracy and genius that made it all the harder to tolerate the crassness and petty passions of Dublin. But the race was his own, and he did not mean to repudiate it. He wrote to Miss Horniman: "I understand my own race and in all my work ... I have thought of it.... I shall write for my own people—whether in love or hate of them matters little—probably I shall not know which it is."

It was still "theatre business, management of men" that filled his days; he was writing little poetry. In the fall of 1907 he was systematically revising his published prose and verse for *The Collected Works in Verse and Prose* to be published by A. H. Bullen, supported by a subsidy of fifteen hundred pounds from Miss Horniman. For his elegant edition Bullen ordered portraits of the poet by his father and by Sargent, Mancini, Augustus John, and Yeats's old friend Charles Shannon. Yeats enjoyed the company of these men of the world, particularly that of the madcap John, and he was fascinated to see their very different images of him. At forty-two he was young for a collected edition, and looked a good deal younger. Enemies and envious rivals wondered if he intended to lay down his pen. Bullen's eight handsome volumes came out in 1908 under the Shakespeare Head imprint.

Another preoccupation and a constant grief was the illness of Synge, a victim of the incurable Hodgkin's disease, as yet undiagnosed. Coming out of the ether after the first operation on his throat, Synge had delighted his doctor by intoning: "May God damn the English, they can't even swear without vulgarity." The difficult, inward-looking Synge idolized Yeats but was shy in his great-man presence. Yeats visited him often now, particularly to discuss the text of Synge's masterly play *Deirdre of the Sorrows*, not quite finished when he died at thirty-seven in March 1909. He had made Yeats his literary executor and begged him to polish the play for production, and Yeats humbly did so.

Maud Gonne had moved back to France and was living nonpolitically in a house on a bluff above the sea at Colville in Normandy with her little son; young Iseult, already heartbreakingly lovely, was being educated in a convent. Yeats crossed to see them whenever he was free. To that old passion grown ruminant, forgiving, and a bit autumnal are owed the best poems in *The Green Helmet and Other Poems* (1910) from Lollie Yeats's newly named Cuala Press. For the first time fairyland is missing, and the simplifying and empiricizing tendencies in Yeats's style continue and intensify. He sums up the manner himself in "The Coming of Wisdom with Time," an example of the spare explosive quatrains that became one of his hallmarks: "Though leaves are many, the root is one; / Through all the lying days of my youth / I swayed my leaves and flowers in the sun; / Now I may wither into the truth." Several of the Maud Gonne poems express a reflection in Yeats's journal: that she had never really understood what he was trying to do and say in Ireland, but her very incomprehension had stirred him productively in art and life, to prove and explain himself. "Words" reasons that way but turns the irony bitter at the end: had she ever met his mind, he "might have thrown poor words away / And been content to live." In "A Woman Homer Sung" the note of middle age, of loss and forgiveness, is sounded frankly, then gives way to ecstatic recollection of the old enchantment. His Helen had been a fated creature, a prisoner of her own heroic nature, and ordinary men must expect to be trampled: "Why should I blame her that she filled my days / With misery, or that she would of late / Have taught to ignorant men most violent ways, /

Tom Lalor cartoon of Yeats addressing the audience at the Abbey Theatre about Synge's The Playboy of the Western World *(National Library of Ireland)*

Or hurled the little streets upon the great, / . . . / Why, what could she have done, being what she is? / Was there another Troy for her to burn?" ("No Second Troy"). In such poems the grand classical context and the heightened rhetoric are justified by the power of the feeling and the mastery of the verse. But the old unsubduable love is latent in all these elaborate devices, and it emerges pure in the exquisite little song that closes the volume: "Ah, penny, brown penny, brown penny, / I am looped in the loops of her hair."

In Yeats's friendships, this period was one of losses and new acquisitions. Late in 1907, his father at sixty-seven crossed to New York on the strength of a purse made up by friends in Ireland. Thereafter he could never quite bring himself to return, and he was to stay on till his death in 1922, a vivid talkative figure at his "French" boardinghouse, surviving on the generosity of Quinn and on occasional small fees for pictures, articles, or lectures. He sent back to his son a stream of nourishing and delightful letters, sometimes several in a day, full of news, ideas, argument. George Pollexfen died in Sligo in the autumn of 1910, on the night after Lily Yeats (and others) heard the banshee cry. Synge was a dreadful loss to the Abbey, as was Miss Horniman, who angrily withdrew her support (amounting in all to ten thousand pounds) when the theater, under Lennox Robinson, alone among theaters in the United Kingdom, failed to close on the day of the death of Edward VII. In England Yeats's acquaintance in social, artistic, and political circles was wide and influential, including Prime Minister Asquith, Mrs. Patrick Campbell, Bernard Shaw, Robert Bridges, Wyndham Lewis, and Ezra Pound.

The Yeats-Pound coalition seemed odd, but it was warm and important to both men. Yeats was by now an eminent and elegant person, but Olympian only when he saw a need, not ordinarily humorless or hard to approach. He described Pound as "a headlong rugged nature," and he was charmed, amused, and instructed by the energetic, untidy, and irreverent young American (Pound called Robert Bridges "Rabbit Britches"). He also respected Pound's mind, seething with wide half-learning—classical, Oriental, medieval,

Continental, "modern." Pound was the most generously helpful man of his time to other artists; to Yeats he was an unlikely but necessary angel, an astringent influence, pulling him down to earth, urging clarity and directness in imagery and language, opening doors to broader, stranger cultures but wishing them controlled within a frame of history and common sense.

Late in 1910 Yeats's financial problems were eased somewhat by a crown pension of £150 a year, awarded after representations by Lady Gregory, Edmund Gosse, and Augustine Birrell. Once he had satisfied himself that the grant implied no promise of political loyalty, Yeats accepted it gratefully.

Yeats was lecturing often in England and Ireland, raising funds to replace Miss Horniman's former capital. He formed a close friendship with the brilliant young stage designer Gordon Craig and brought his work into Abbey productions. Audiences in Dublin were shrinking, owing in part to Yeats's stubborn loyalty to the works of Synge and to the manner of his Theatre of Beauty; but the company was a success in England, and they were invited to make their first American tour in the fall and winter of 1911-1912. Yeats went with the players but quickly returned, to be replaced, as arranged, by Lady Gregory, and it was she who bore the brunt of riotous receptions from American Irishmen in New York, Boston, and Philadelphia who loyally re-created the Dublin *Playboy* disorders of 1907. On the complaint of a local publican Synge's exuberant chaste comedy was stopped in Philadelphia and the players arrested on charges of indecency. Quinn rushed down from New York and made mincemeat of the man and his charges, but life was difficult.

Back home, Yeats was working at a new play, *The Player Queen* (1922), rewriting *The Countess Cathleen* once more as a kind of stylized masque, and doing a "translation" of *Oedipus Rex* with a better Greek scholar at his elbow, trying to turn the Jebb version into good stage talk. In London he grew intimate with the Bengali poet Rabindranath Tagore, helped him with translations into English, and wrote an introduction to his *Gitanjali* (1912). He was still very close to Olivia Shakespear, who was to provide wives for both Yeats and Pound. In Devon she introduced him to Georgiana Hyde-Lees, the daughter of her brother's wife by her first marriage. Georgiana would become Mrs. "George" Yeats in 1917.

In the winter of 1912-1913 Yeats was drawn into a Dublin quarrel that would drag on for years. Lady Gregory's dear nephew Hugh Lane had offered to give his notable collection of modern French paintings to the city, but he demanded that the Corporation display them in a new pedestrian bridge over the Liffey, to be designed by an English architect, Sir Edward Lutyens. The scheme was both novel and expensive, and it met entrenched opposition on the usual Dublin mixture of grounds, personal, aesthetic, economic, political, religious. By the time Lane, angry and exhausted with the wrangle, had thrown up his hands and sent his collection on loan to the National Gallery in London, Yeats had been stirred not only to a great deal of passionate lobbying and letter writing but to a series of rancorous and brilliant new poems.

With Lennox Robinson in charge of the Abbey and moving it gradually toward a more popular realistic and contemporary taste, Yeats was freer to think and write than he had been for a dozen years. The thirty-one poems of his 1914 collection *Responsibilities* show the gusto with which he had been using his time after a long fallow period. Here we move fully into middle Yeats. He summed up his own sense of the matter quite simply in a letter to his father in August 1913: "I thought your letter about 'portraiture' being 'pain' most beautiful and profound.... Of recent years instead of 'vision,' meaning by vision the intense realization of a state of ecstatic emotion symbolized in a definite imagined region, I have tried for more self portraiture. I have tried to make my work convincing with a speech so natural and dramatic that the hearer would feel the presence of a man thinking and feeling."

After the majestic "Introductory Rhymes" ("Pardon, old fathers . . .") come the half-dozen harshly sardonic poems inspired by the Lane controversy. In a note on these poems Yeats listed the controversies over Parnell, *The Playboy of the Western World*, and Lane's gift as the three Irish quarrels that had most exasperated him, and he blamed all of them mainly upon a crass, jealous, and unimaginative middle class. Like William Hazlitt, Yeats was "a good damner," and it was not safe to stir his wrath. The poem entitled with a wicked cumbersomeness "To a Wealthy Man Who Promised a Second Subscription to the Dublin Municipal Gallery If It Were Proved the People Wanted Pictures" reduces the cautious donor a full half-class by linking him to "Paudeen" and "Biddy" hoarding their greasy

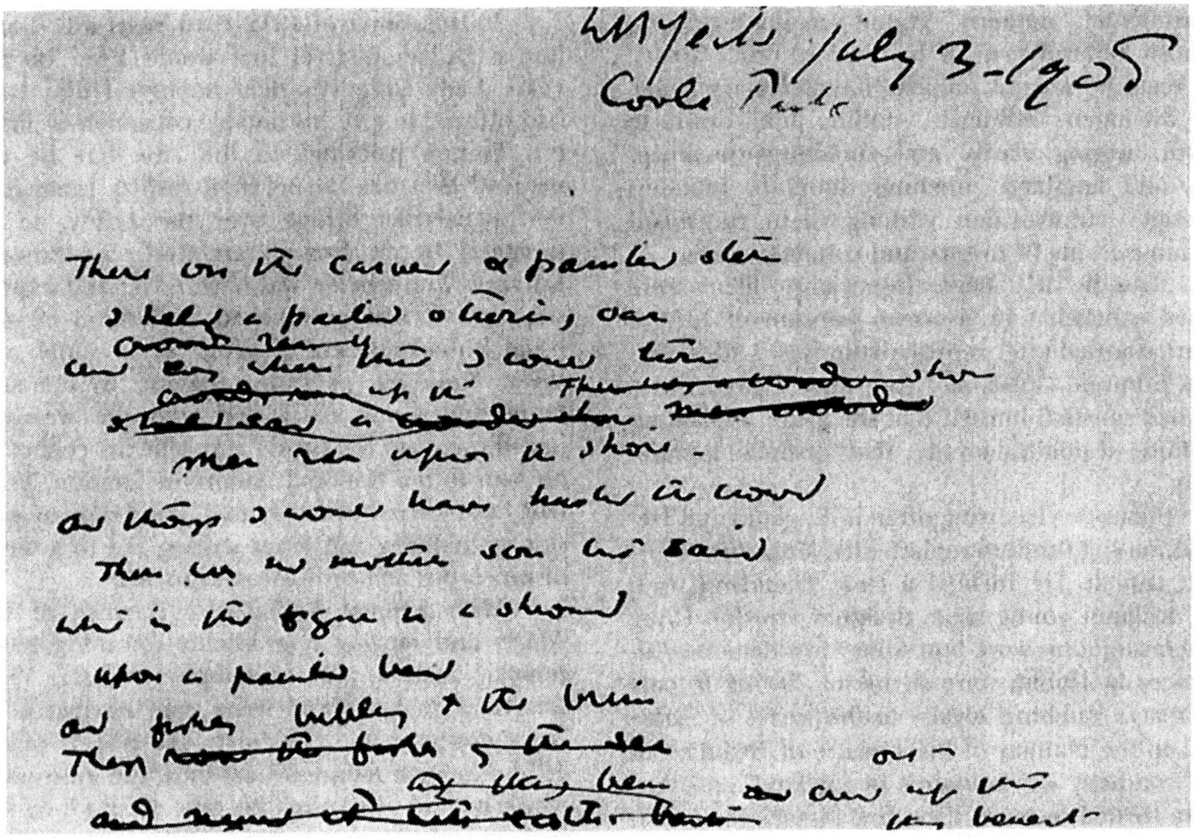

Page from a draft of "His Dream." The heading, upper right, was written by Lady Gregory (Sotheby Parke Bernet, 15 December 1982).

pence. Yeats chides the rich man for making his gift contingent upon such darkened taste and invites him to consider the example of the old open-handed Italian princes: "And when they drove out Cosimo, / Indifferent how the rancour ran, / He gave the hours they had set free / To Michelozzo's latest plan / For the San Marco Library. . . ." Think more bravely, he commands: "Look up in the sun's eye and give / . . . the right twigs for a eagle's nest."

In "Paudeen" the good man receives his own little poem saluting his "fumbling wits, the obscure spite," and "September 1913" sets Paudeen's motto, "For men were born to pray and save," against a past that produced Edward FitzGerald, Robert Emmet, and Wolfe Tone, and against the stanzas' refrain lament: "Romantic Ireland's dead and gone, / It's with O'Leary in the grave." Yet in the terse, contemptuous little poem "When Helen Lived," where the Lane affair is only a part of the trouble, Yeats makes the cultural guilt not only a class issue but a racial one in which he shares: "Yet we, had we walked within / Those topless towers / Where Helen walked with her boy, / Had given but as the rest / Of the men and women of Troy, / A word and a jest."

The grandest of the Lane poems is "To a Shade," in which the ghost, the "thin shade" of the heroic Parnell, is imagined as revisiting "the town" and being shown that "they are at their old tricks yet"—treating Lane as they had treated him, set on by Parnell's old enemy Martin Murphy, proprietor of the two most popular Dublin papers and incidentally a leader of the lockout in the current bitter labor strife in the city. Nobody is named but identities are clear enough. High and colloquial rhetoric mingle resonantly: "A man / Of your own passionate serving kind who had brought / In his full hands what, had they only known, / Had given their children's children loftier thought, / Sweeter emotion, working in their veins / Like gentle blood, has been driven from the place, / And insult heaped upon him for his pains, / And for his open-handedness, disgrace; / Your enemy, an old foul mouth, had set / The pack upon him." The ghost is advised to give it up and return to the grave, to "gather the

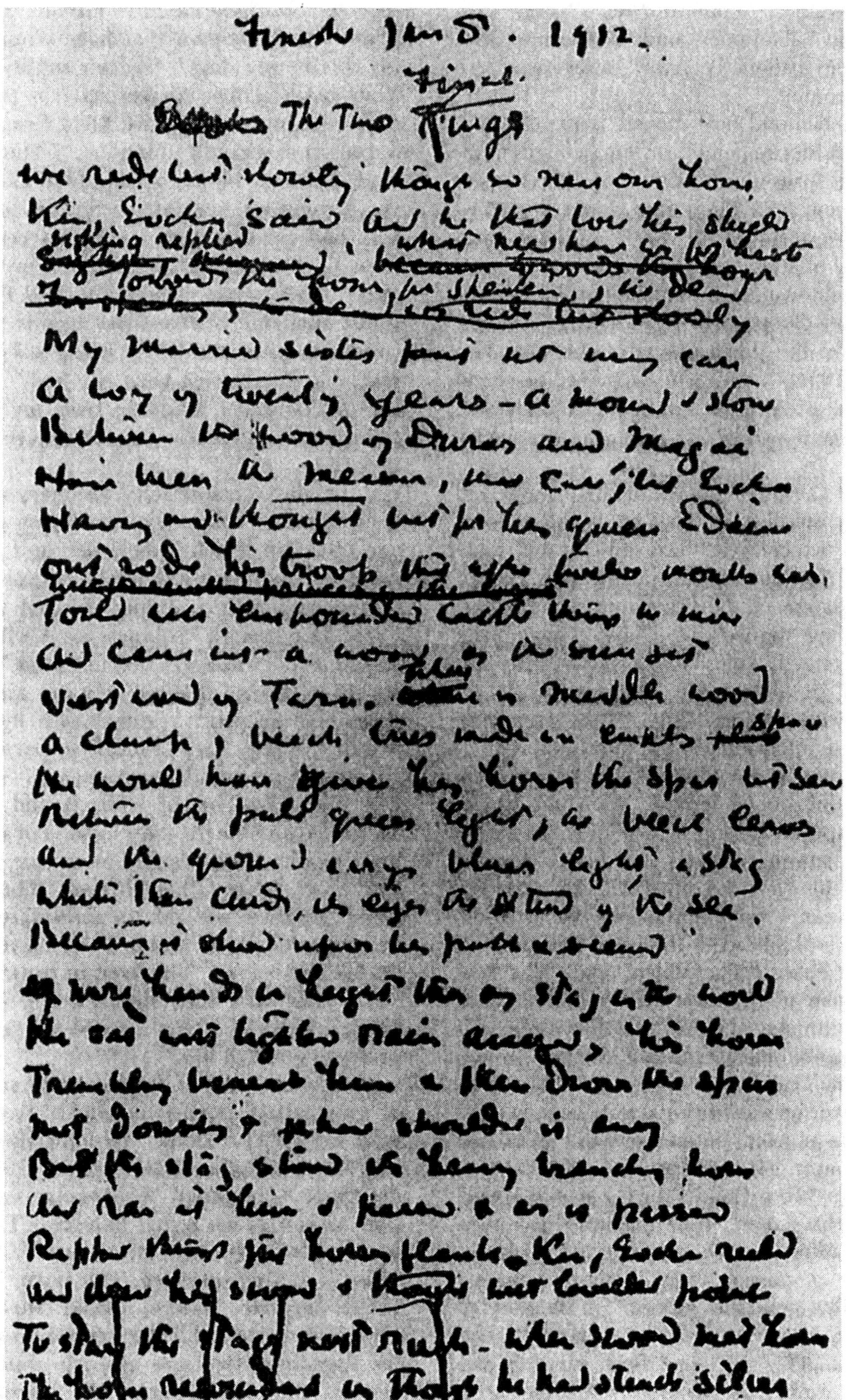
Finished Jan 8. 1912.
Final
The Two Kings

First page of the manuscript for "The Two Kings" (The Anderson Galleries, sale 1820, 17-20 March 1924)

Glasnevin coverlet / About your head till the dust stops your ear." The poem ends in an imperative Shakespearean cadence: "Away! away! You are safer in the tomb."

A related mood now moved Yeats to a little bit of expert decapitation, or emasculation, inspired by the preceding controversy, the *Playboy* riots. The poem, "On Those that Hated 'The Playboy of the Western World,' 1907," is based on a journal entry of some years earlier in which Yeats wrote that Synge's enemies made him think of people turned lewdly prudish by "a certain surgical operation." In the poem eunuchs who have run through hell "met / On every crowded street to stare / Upon great Juan riding by: / Even like these to rail and sweat / Staring upon his sinewy thigh."

Most of the other poems of this volume fall similarly into small suites that show the concentration with which Yeats was mining his daily thought and feeling. Several poems treat one of his lifelong personae, the Fool: outcasts, isolatoes, road-wandering figures of whom Crazy Jane would come to be the most staggering—filthy, passionate, old or deformed, crack-pated but in touch with wild wisdom. "The Three Hermits," for example, is a balladlike bit of tight-metered anarchy, bitter and funny. Two of the old men talk sense, but the poem centers upon the third, whose only speech is song, apocalyptic rhapsody: "While he'd rummaged rags and hair, / Caught and cracked his flea, the third, / Giddy with his hundredth year, / Sang unnoticed like a bird." Such poems look ahead to the great half-mad visions of *Last Poems*. "The Witch" and "The Peacock" are a pair of explosive little poems set back to back in a dimeter anapestic rhythm; bare, epigrammatic, poised in easy tension, they are fundamental middle Yeats.

Whenever he was writing poetry with concentration, Yeats noticed, sooner or later it turned into love poetry. Here a pair are addressed to Iseult Gonne: "To a Child Dancing in the Wind" and "Two Years Later"; then a suite of five turn helplessly to Maud Gonne, ruminating the old obsession with a passion that is more complex than ever. The generally gloomy "A Memory of Youth" partly recovers spirits in a magical, enigmatic final image: "And had been savagely undone / Were it not that Love upon the cry / Of a most ridiculous little bird / Tore from the clouds his marvellous moon." "Fallen Majesty" is a brief elegiac recollection of Maud Gonne's early beauty and its effect on men: "a thing . . . that seemed a burning cloud." "Friends" is written to praise "three women that have wrought / What joy was in my days." We can supply the names Yeats omits: Olivia Shakespear for the "delight" of her mind's meeting his; Lady Gregory for her "strength that could unbind / . . . Youth's dreamy load" and free him to work; Maud Gonne for the very cruelty of her grip, a tyranny over his life that had never ceased to be an ecstasy: "And what of her that took / All till my youth was gone / With scarce a pitying look? / How could I praise that one? / When day begins to break / I count my good and bad, / Being wakeful for her sake, / Remembering what she had, / What eagle look still shows, / While up from my heart's root / So great a sweetness flows / I shake from head to foot."

In the extraordinary visionary poem "The Cold Heaven" that ecstatic suffering calls up images that approach apocalypse and sets Yeats's mind moving upon a question central to the mystical speculations collecting toward *A Vision* of 1925. The specific "coldness" and wild "passion" of this poem's imagery are not what Yeats meant earlier by a "cold passion." Phrases such as "rook-delighting heaven," "riddled with light," "injustice of the skies" are immune to paraphrase, but one would never call them opaque. A much quieter poem, one of the shortest and simplest of the group, may be the most moving of all. Developing a single death-wishing metaphor, in trimeter with an exquisite falling rhythm, "That the Night Come" makes peace with the sorest fact of the relationship: that Maud had preferred a violent political life to his love: "She lived in storm and strife, / Her soul had such desire / For what proud death may bring / That it could not endure / The common good of life."

Near the end of *Responsibilities* stands a pair of enigmatical poems on which Yeats's note is little help. "The Dolls," sardonically humorous, may be among other things a parody upon the Virgin Birth. "The Magi" Yeats explains only as a vision he saw in an actual blue sky. The vision is hauntingly intense and clear, visually, and cast in a single driving sentence. The poem shows what Yeats's mature passion could do with Pre-Raphaelite material. The composite image and the haunting effect are again in touch with the "system" of *A Vision*, part of the matter coming to him from "that reed-throated whisperer / Who comes at need" whom he salutes in this volume's "Closing Rhyme," the one who brings news of "companions / Beyond the fling of the dull ass's hoof." One of the most splendidly simple and explicit of Yeats's great short poems, "A Coat," tells the whole story of the career of his style and tells us how he intends to work forward from his fiftieth year. The poet compares his early style to "a coat / Covered with embroideries / Out of old mythologies," but others have imitated him and worn the coat "in the world's eyes / As though they'd wrought it." Thus, the poet concludes, "let them take it, / For there's more enterprise / In walking naked."

In the winter of 1912-1913, when Yeats was ill and out of sorts in London, the athletic Pound taught him to fence. In the following autumn the two settled into Stone Cottage at Coleman's Hatch in rural Sussex and worked together on Japanese Noh materials in the notebooks of the scholar Ernest Fenollosa, whose widow had made Pound her husband's literary executor. Pound was still "a learned companion and a pleasant one." Yeats worked also at his verse and on lectures for another American tour, forthcoming in the new year with a guarantee of five hundred pounds. The tour was a success, and it also put an end to the estrangement with Quinn that had embarrassed their many mutual friends (in 1909 the two had quarreled bitterly, apparently over a mistress of Quinn's). Quinn noticed Yeats's gray hair but thought him otherwise as robust and humorous, "charming and agreeable" as ever. Yeats found his old father healthy and happy but in debt. He paid off the debts and at Quinn's suggestion worked out an arrangement for Quinn to buy Yeats's manuscripts as available and remit the sums to J. B. Yeats for his use.

As he had been doing all his life, Yeats looked toward a system that would form for "a churchless mystic" a satisfying religion, a composite myth of personality and history, a diagram of the soul's movement in time and the symbols of the motives that impelled it. He read Johann Wolfgang von Goethe and reread Blake and Emanuel Swedenborg. In the United States and Canada, as in London, he would attend the séance of any promising spiritualist medium. In spring 1914 he traveled with Maud Gonne and Everard Feilding of the Psychical Research Society to Mirabeau, near Poitiers, to investigate reports of a "bleeding" oleograph of the Sacred Heart. Results were inconclusive, but the process was fascinating, and to Yeats deadly serious. He was shaken by a message for him that the old priest of the place said he had heard while praying at four in the morning: "He is to become an apostle; he must use his intelligence. If he does not our Lord will take away his intelligence and leave him at the mercy of his heart." Yeats must have felt that his own deepest monitory mind had spoken.

With Maud and Iseult Gonne nursing the wounded in French hospitals, Yeats spent the first autumn of World War I in Coole, finishing *Reveries over Childhood and Youth,* then traveling to Dublin to read it to Lily Yeats. At Coole and in London he worked at the first of his "Plays for Dancers," *At the Hawk's Well* (1916), inspired by Pound's exposition of the Noh. The form, Greek-Japanese, drew Yeats powerfully for its union of the arcane and aristocratic and the primitive and fabulous. Being terse, symbolic, pictorial, it was a final astringency of his ideal of "poetic" theater. With settings and transitions evoked by the folding and unfolding of a cloth and the beating of a drum, such plays hardly required scenery or even a theater; they could be played in a drawing room or a barn, he said: noble and beggarman again. In fact the play was tried out in Lady Maud Cunard's drawing room.

It was she who lobbied for a knighthood for Yeats, which he now refused; he was grateful but unable to reconcile the image with his lifelong definition of himself as an Irish patriot. He wrote to Lily Yeats: "I do not wish anyone to say of me 'only for a ribbon he left us.' " At about the same time he joined in Ezra Pound's successful plea for a crown grant of one hundred pounds to James Joyce, harried and hard up in Zurich.

In May 1915 Hugh Lane went down on the *Lusitania.* The controversy over his pictures boiled up again, for Lane had changed his mind again before going to America and written a codicil to his will consigning the collection to Dublin. The codicil was unwitnessed and so carried no legal force, but Yeats and Lady Gregory argued the moral imperative in London for the next several years.

Preparations for the Easter Rising in Dublin had been managed by a small radical cadre of the IRB with an efficient secrecy untypical of Irish rebels, and when the firing began in April 1916 nearly everyone was taken by surprise. Yeats in England complained that he had not been consulted. He had known some of the rebel leaders personally: Padraic Pearse, Thomas MacDonagh, Joseph Plunkett, James Connolly, and Constance Gore-Booth, now the Countess Markiewicz. The rising, its quick and bloody suppression by English troops, and especially then

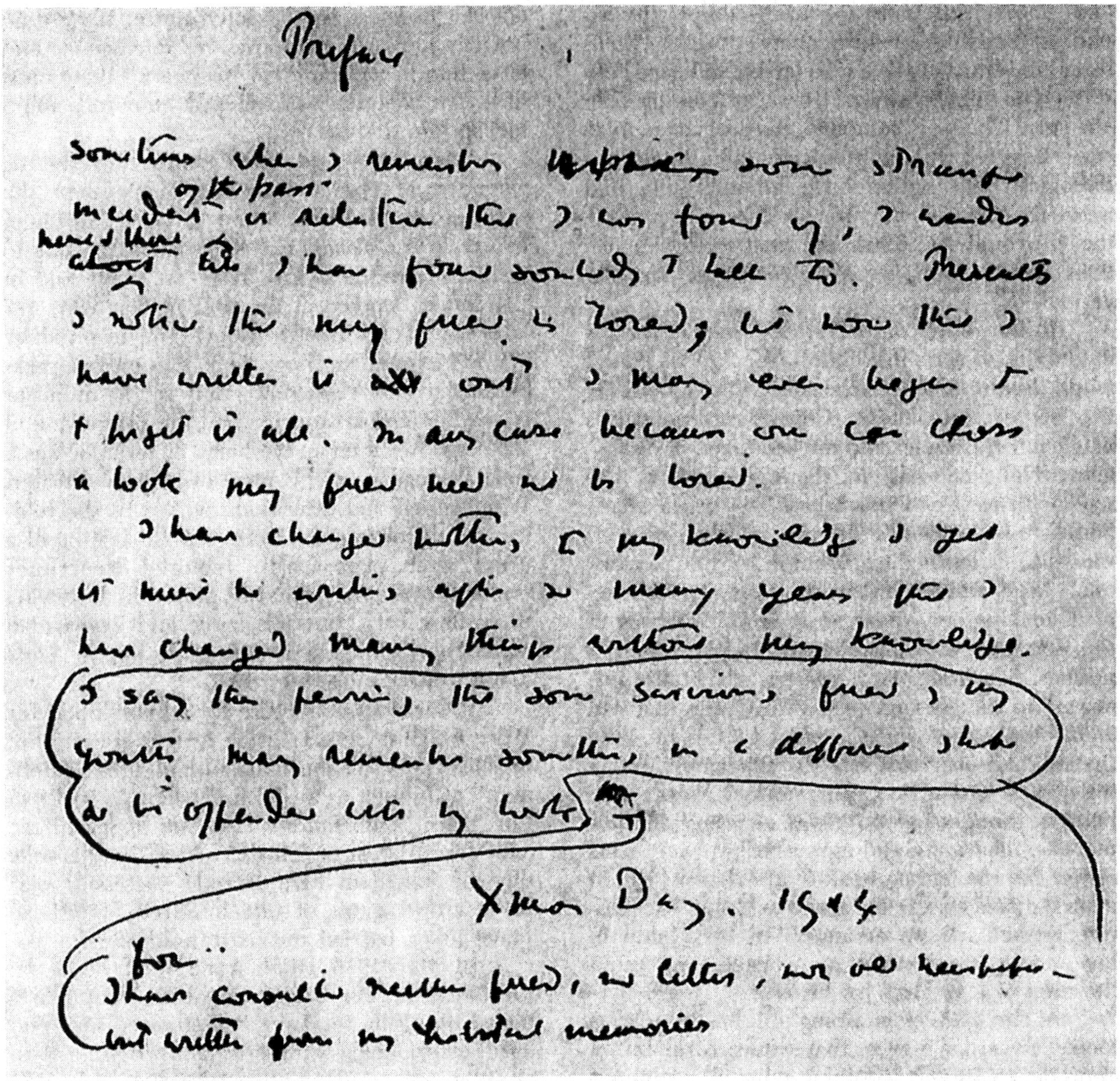

Manuscript for the preface to Reveries over Childhood and Youth *(The Anderson Galleries, sale 1820, 17-20 March 1924)*

the agonizing serial executions of the leaders stirred Irishmen to the heart. With his accumulated disillusionment, Yeats had been half-consciously cutting his ties to Ireland; now his old affection welled up again in a flood, stirred by an enterprise that he saw as brave and mad. Two weeks after Easter he wrote Lady Gregory of "the heroic, tragic lunacy of Sinn Fein." At the end of his life he was still wondering with doubt, pride, and perturbation if his early writing had helped to seed the rising, to "send out / Certain men the English shot" ("The Man and the Echo"). Now he quickly composed the memorial that would be his best-known poem after "The Lake Isle of Innisfree," the incantatory "Easter 1916," with its famous refrain, "A terrible beauty is born."

When he read the poem to Maud Gonne in Normandy she thought it too highfalutin, not nearly hard enough in the revolutionary way. John MacBride had been one of the sixteen men executed after the rising, and her new legal freedom encouraged Yeats to propose marriage once more; but she was feeling a strong call back to

Irish politics, and she would not listen to him. Yeats returned to London and completed a little book of philosophical speculations, *Per Amica Silentia Lunae* (1918), a sort of finger exercise for *A Vision*, and another "Play for Dancers," *The Dreaming of the Bones*. Then in the summer of 1917 he went back to Normandy, and this time he proposed not to Maud Gonne but to her daughter, Iseult, one-third his age. Iseult refused and wept over her "selfishness" in wishing to love him only in the old way of friendship. The situation was heartbreaking in the way of high comedy, and the principals were miserable and exalted. Yeats got passports for the family and saw them back to London, but there Maud Gonne was forbidden to go to Ireland under provisions of the Defense of the Realm Act.

Yeats was clearly determined to marry before it was too late, and he now thought again of Georgiana Hyde-Lees, merely half his age, to whom he had already mumbled occasionally of marriage. He now frankly proposed, and she accepted; they were married in simple style in London in October 1917 with Ezra Pound as best man. Pound approved the marriage with the young woman who was his own wife's good friend and shared the nourishing connection with Olivia Shakespear; but other friends viewed the general hustle with some amusement, Charles Shannon, for example, remarking: "it all seems very sudden and suggests that she is furniture for the Castle."

The Castle, renamed by Yeats Thoor Ballylee and soon to become a central emblem in his poetry, was a very old stone structure in Norman style on the bank of a stream near Gort, a square pile of four big superimposed rooms connected by a winding stone stairway, with one cottage attached and another ruinous one in an orchard beyond a road that crossed the bridge at the base of the tower—all formerly part of Lady Gregory's demesne. Yeats had coveted it for a long time, and he had been able to buy it from a public board a few months earlier for thirty-five pounds.

There was no need to worry about Yeats's marriage. George, as he immediately renamed her, was small and animated, with a dark gypsy beauty, humorous, high-spirited, both intelligent and levelheaded, and moreover already considerably learned in his own magical systems. Yeats wrote Lady Gregory from Woburn Buildings, where they settled first: "My wife is a perfect wife, kind, wise, and unselfish." He organized repairs at the tower, and soon he composed his marvelous little epithalamium, "To Be Carved on a stone at Thoor Ballylee," which was indeed cut into a big flat stone set in the wall next to the door to the winding stair: "I, the poet William Yeats, / With old mill boards and sea-green slates, / And smithy work from the Gort forge, / Restored this tower for my wife George; / And may these characters remain / When all is ruin once again."

But the general good feeling was rudely undercut in February 1918 by news that Robert Gregory, a major in the British air force, had fallen to his death in Italy, leaving his wife and three young children, as well as his mother, stunned for the second time by the war. Yeats grieved for her and for himself, for he had admired and loved the young man.

All his life Yeats heard voices in his ear, and when he was about twenty he heard one say: "Hammer your thoughts into unity." That was to be a process of impassioned thought that would go on all his life. Yeats was a philosophical artist and a sensuous one, and it was the union of those powers at the pitch of genius that made him one of the half-dozen greatest poets in the history of English. At fifty-two Yeats had been laboring for thirty years, with a discipline and stubbornness rare in poets, and often in the teeth of ridicule, toward a system that could satisfy his need for a religion that would sustain and inspire him, intellectually and emotionally. His constantly emerging "churchless mystic's" system would "remember many masters": the pre-Socratic philosophers, Plato himself, Plotinus and the neo-Platonists, the Christian Kabala, the Eastern mystics, folklore, myth, and legend, alchemy, astrology, magic, spiritism, Böhme, Blake, Swedenborg, symbolism ancient and modern; but the fusion was his own, original and infinitely complex.

Yeats burned not only to know Anima Mundi but to verbalize it and spread it abroad, to share the wealth. His autobiographical writings, his recent poems, and the little high-ruminant essays of *Per Amica Silentia Lunae* were expressions of his urge to make his forming system audible and visible. If he was to be "an apostle," as the old Abbé of Mirabeau had said, he would be an apostle to the Christians, and to the rationalists who had deprived him of Christianity.

Soon after his marriage in 1917, indeed during the honeymoon, Yeats's mystical thought received a sudden strange intensification. After try-

Thoor Ballylee, near Gort, County Galway (Irish Tourist Board)

ing and succeeding at automatic writing, Yeats solemnly assures us, his young wife suddenly began speaking in tongues—began to babble at great length, in a state that seemed half sleep, half trance, of arcane matters in a voice not her own. Yeats had heard his own "reed-throated whisperers"; but this was something far more continuous, baffling, and exhilarating. These "teachers" or "communicators" seemed to be speaking directly to the hoarded content of his mind, trying to clarify it (in perverse moods to confuse it), to supply it with order and symbols. When the flabbergasted poet offered to spend the rest of his life in organizing the early script, the "unknown writer" responded: "No, we have come to give you metaphors for poetry." One is grateful for that view of the case, but it is only one side of the story; the other side is belief: religion.

"Ego Dominus Tuus" forms one of these "systematic" grand tropes or master metaphors. It is a poem of the kind that Yeats said he had composed in part illustratively, as "texts for exposition." It is true that he did intend to go on and treat the ideas discursively in prose; but the poems are also tropaic precipitates of ideas held long in solution. "Ego Dominus Tuus," for example, is a didactic-dramatic formulation of the principles of Mask and Daimon that had moved in Yeats's mind for twenty-five years; and the dialogue structure incarnates the oldest and deepest of his convictions, that of the bifurcation of personality and of its life in time. The condition is both a torture and a glory; it is in any case human, real, and necessary, a prerequisite to fertility. "No mind can engender till divided into two," he wrote in *The Trembling of the Veil* (1922), and in his notes on that work: "All creation is from conflict, whether with our own mind or with that of others, and the historian who dreams of bloodless victory, wrongs the wounded veterans."

One of the most compact definitions of the Mask, or anti-self, runs as follows: "Nations, races, and individual men are unified by an image, or bundle of related images, symbolical or evocative of the state of mind, which is of all states of mind not impossible, the most difficult to that man, race, or nation; because only the greatest obstacle that can be contemplated without despair rouses the will to full intensity." The Daimon is a sort of benign but exacting hovering genius, "personifying spirits . . . Gates and Gatekeepers," whose function is to force us to confront the antinomy, to "bring our souls to crisis, to Mask and Image. . . . They have but the one purpose, to bring their chosen man to the greatest obstacle he may confront without despair." He would put the matter tersely in *A Vision*: "All the gains of man come from conflict with the opposite of his true being." It is this principle of Mask or conflicting Image summoned by Daimon that underlies Yeats's statement in *Per Amica Silentia Lunae*: "We make out of the quarrel with others, rhetoric, but of the quarrel with ourselves, poetry." The statement continues: "Unlike the rhetoricians, who get a confident voice from remembering the crowd they have won or may win, we sing amid our uncertainty; and, smitten even in the presence of the most high beauty by the knowledge of our solitude, our rhythm shudders." The true poet, that is, will be one who has "begun to live" because he has "conceived life as tragedy," who is "no longer deceived, whose passion is reality."

"Ego Dominus Tuus" thus dramatizes a governing principle of Yeats's system. On a moonlit night, pacing the low bank of the stream at the base of the tower, two speakers, Hic and Ille ("This One" and "That One"), gravely debate the issue of self and anti-self. They are spokesmen of the basic types of personality, objective and subjective, that Yeats would name in *A Vision* the two "Tinctures" of Primary and Antithetical. The dominant voice, that of the subjective-antithetical Ille, is certainly the voice of the poet (Ezra Pound called the speakers "Hic and Willie"). Hic speaks first, in quiet derision: "you walk in the moon, / And, though you have passed the best of life, still trace, / Enthralled by the unconquerable delusion, / Magical shapes." Ille explains his quest: "By the help of an image / I call to my own opposite, summon all / That I have handled least, least looked upon." Hic counters with his own simpler motive: "and I would find myself and not an image." That, says Ille, is just what has drained the energy from art: "by its light / We have lit upon the gentle, sensitive [Christian] mind / And lost the old [classical] nonchalance of the hand," turning artists into men, such as Matthew Arnold, who are "but critics, or but half-create."

Now the speakers bandy examples, each seeing great poets in the light of the bias of his own "tincture." Hic cites Dante but Ille at once claims him: "I think he fashioned from his opposite / An image that might have been a stony face / Staring upon a Bedouin's horsehair roof / From doored and windowed cliff, or half upturned / Among the coarse grass and the camel dung. / He set his chisel to the hardest stone." Hic objects: "Yet surely there are men who have made their art / Out of no tragic war, lovers of life, / Impulsive men that look for happiness / And sing when they have found it." Ille corrects him, dismissing the world-snared Primary type and applying his formula from *Per Amica Silentia Lunae*: "The rhetorician would deceive his neighbors, / The sentimentalist himself; while art / Is but a vision of reality." Hic instances the "love of the world" and "deliberate happiness" of Keats; again Ille beats him down: "I see a schoolboy when I think of him, / With face and nose pressed to a sweet-shop window, / For certainly he sank into his grave / His senses and his heart unsatisfied, / and made—being poor, ailing and ignorant, / Shut out from the luxury of the world, / The coarse-bred son of a livery-stable keeper— / Luxuriant song."

The exasperated Hic returns to personal derision, chiding Ille for his obsession with arcane matters and advising more pragmatical behavior: "A style is found by sedentary toil / And by the imitation of great masters." Ille stubbornly recapitulates, invokes Daimon and Mask, and glides out in mystical enchantment in lines that concentrate the sibylline character of the whole poem: "I seek an image, not a book. / Those men that in their writings are most wise / Own nothing but their blind, stupefied hearts. / I call to the mysterious one who yet / Shall walk the wet sands by the edge of the stream / And look most like me, being indeed my double, / And prove of all imaginable things / The most unlike, being my anti-self, / And, standing by these characters, disclose / All that I seek; and whisper it as though / He were afraid the birds, who cry aloud / Their momentary cries before it is dawn, / Would carry it away to blasphemous men."

A half-dozen of these speculative "systematic" poems, at once "texts for exposition" and digests of long thinking, are grouped at the end of Yeats's 1919 edition of *The Wild Swans at Coole*. They vary in form and mood, but all are marked by profound thought, a reined-in excitement of feeling, a sometimes weird luminousness in imagery, and a general sophisticated humorousness. Central to the whole enterprise is "The Phases of the Moon," which would be incorporated as an outright text in *A Vision* in 1925. It is a grand example of the "metaphors for poetry" coming, currently coming, from the reed-throated whisperers, their most fundamental and one of their earliest communications. The master metaphor of the Great Wheel of the twenty-eight phases of the moon is an infinite refining and geometrizing of Yeats's old bifurcating vision, dividing and defining men and their destinies, and the poem

Georgiana Yeats (Underwood and Underwood)

alone, quite apart from its intricate rationalization in *A Vision,* is long and complex. Two old men, Aherne and Robartes, creatures of Yeats's earlier imagination, returning worn from long wandering stand on the dark bridge and amuse themselves at the plight of the poet in the tower, whose burning lamp attests his endless quest for insight. Why don't "you who know it all" straighten the poor fellow out, asks Aherne—at least tell him enough to show his quest is hopeless. No, says Robartes, the lamp-burner has earned his misery: "He wrote of me in that extravagant style / He had learnt from Pater, and to round his tale / Said I was dead; and dead I choose to be." Well, says Aherne, at least tell the tale to me: "Sing me the changes of the moon once more; / True song, though speech. . . ."

Robartes obliges by chanting the litany of the "changes," the diagram of dark-light-dark shiftings in the moon's disk that record the rhythm of the soul's metamorphosis; "Twenty-and-eight the phases of the moon, / The full and the moon's dark and all the crescents, / Twenty-and-eight, and yet but six-and-twenty / The cradles that a man must needs be rocked in: / For there's no human life at the full or the dark." The last clause is among the most important: the rich logic there being that the "full" (phase 15) and the "dark" (phase 1), being expressions of absolutes, perfections, cannot accommodate man, whose very being is granted on condition of conflict, imperfection—"tragedy."

The soul begins its journey at the dark in primal innocence, and seeks the subjective or Antithetical, first by happy "adventure" then by pursuit of "whatever whim's most difficult" among those possible. The full is a self-canceling state of perfect intellectuality, hence suspended, "cast out," alien to being: "All thought becomes an image and the soul / Becomes a body: that body and that soul too perfect. . . . / Estranged amid the strangeness of themselves, / Caught up in contemplation. . . ." In the primary phases of the "crumbling of the moon" (phases 16-28) the achieved personality turns more and more from "self" to "world," from "whim" to "task," and welcomes duty, service, "the coarseness of the drudge," an impersonalization that culminates in deformity: "Hunchback and Saint and Fool are the last crescents." At the end of this weird, funny, majestic poem the old cronies move off cackling over their superior wisdom, a bat circles and squeaks, and the light in the tower goes out.

"The Cat and the Moon," the bijou poem set next in the collection, is equally magical but tighter, playful in a less solemn way. Black Minnaloushe dances in the grass while the moon overhead goes about its deterministic business: "The cat went here and there / And the moon spun round like a top." The cat cannot comprehend the influence, but his "animal blood" is "troubled," his body is moved, and his pupils flick like a camera lens in unconscious response to the heavenly manipulation: he "lifts to the changing moon / His changing eyes." Yeats has brilliantly compacted his manifold emblem of the phases and brought it down to earth to be dealt with by wit, as comedy as well as fate. In the curtain poem, "The Double Vision of Michael Robartes," Yeats returned to full "systematic" seriousness. Robartes is now a Yeats speaker, doubleness and vision are embedded, and the particular vision is situated in an Irish sacred place: the ruined medieval house of Cormac MacCarthy at Cashel in Tipperary; the body is set in history and legend. It is a very difficult poem, perhaps impossible to explicate satisfactorily. Yeats called it "a supreme moment of self-consciousness, the two halves of the soul separate and face to face." The "two halves," the "double" figures are creatures of the anarchic extreme phases neighboring phase 1 and phase 15: perfections of instinct, intellect, love. In the long run the dominant image is the mediating figure of the dancer: "And right between these two a girl at play / That, it may be, had danced her life away, / For now being dead it seemed / That she of dancing dreamed." She seems both supernatural and notably human, dead and alive, entranced and purposeful, a union of dream, art, and flesh. The stylization of this triple artifact, Sphinx-Buddha-dancer, feels statically poised, Oriental: "O little did they care who danced between, / And little she by whom her dance was seen / So she had outdanced thought. / Body perfection brought / . . . . / In contemplation had those three so wrought / Upon a moment, and so stretched it out / That they, time overthrown, / Were dead yet flesh and bone." But the girl of the vision feels mortal and compound. She is Helen ("Homer's paragon"), she is a long-recurrent dream figure ("that girl my unremembering nights hold fast"), and no doubt she is Iseult Gonne dancing on a beach in Normandy. In any case she is a reconciler and an animator, one who makes conflict, system, stasis potent and tolerable. The final feeling of Robartes-Yeats is one of gratitude: "And after that arranged it in a song / Seeing that I, ignorant for so long, / Had been rewarded thus / In Cormac's ruined house." That rich quiet feeling is the same as that Yeats expressed in his quatrain of fifteen years later, "Gratitude to the Unknown Instructors."

These seven "systematic" poems of *The Wild Swan at Coole* constituted less than a third of what was surely the noblest volume of English verse in many years and one of the widest in range. The famous title poem expresses a theme that invades a half-dozen poems, that coming-on of age that Yeats lamented all his life. He later pointed out the comedy in the fact that he had begun to "curse" old age in *The Wanderings of Oisin,* written when he was just past twenty. In "The Wild Swans at Coole" the voice of false menopause mourning antiquity at fifty feels rather slack with self-pity, but its biographical absurdity by no means robs the idea of power in the volume as a whole. It takes a tonic form in resolute moods in which the poet vows to sustain a dynamic old age. He would not "wither into eighty years, honoured and empty-witted," as he wrote cruelly of Wordsworth in *Per Anima Silentia Lunae;* his models would be men who stayed passionate and creative to the end, he would "dine at journey's end / With Landor and with Donne." "The Balloon of the Mind" faces and welcomes age as an intellectual imperative: "Bring the balloon of the mind / That bellies and drags in the wind / Into its narrow shed." The great small poem "A Deep-Sworn Vow" faces another emotional constant, a condition unhealed by marriage, "that monstrous thing / Returned and yet unrequited love" (as he called it in "Presences").

The love poems form the largest group in the volume, turning helplessly about Maud Gonne, with interpolations of Iseult. Mother and daughter were closely joined in "To a Young Girl," for example. The theme of love blends several times with the theme of age, as in "Broken Dreams." And the old obsession began to be linked to Yeats's "systematic" ideas and images. In *The Trembling of the Veil* he wrote of his belief in a process of reincarnation or "dreaming back" after death as a standard movement in the rhythm of the lives of the soul; it was one of his oldest convictions: "When we are dead ... we live our lives backward for a certain number of years, treading the paths that we have trodden, growing young again, even childish again, till some attain an innocence that is no longer a mere accident of nature, but the human intellect's crowning achievement." In "On Woman" he applies the imagery of "return" to the past, present, and future of his love: "But when, if the tale's true, / The Pestle of the moon / That pounds up all anew / Brings me to birth again— / To find what once I had / And know what once I have known. . . ." He will be glad enough, he says, once more to "live like Solomon / That Sheba led a dance."

That imagery of mysterious "return" appears also in a poem that has been undervalued by critics, the pastoral "Shepherd and Goatherd," one of four poems of elegiac purpose in *The Wild Swans at Coole* (1917). Three of the four were tributes to Robert Gregory, intended to honor and assuage his mother's grief. The young man recently dead is imagined on the soul's new travels which are also its old travels: "He grows younger every second / . . . . / Jaunting, journeying / To his own dayspring, / He unpacks the loaded pern / Of all 'twas pain or joy to learn / . . . . / Knowledge he shall unwind / Through victories of the mind, / Till, clambering at the cradle-side, / He dreams himself his mother's pride, / All knowledge lost in trance / Of sweeter ignorance."

"In Memory of Major Robert Gregory" is one of Yeats's greatest poems, probably the noblest English elegy since *Lycidas.* W. H. Auden,

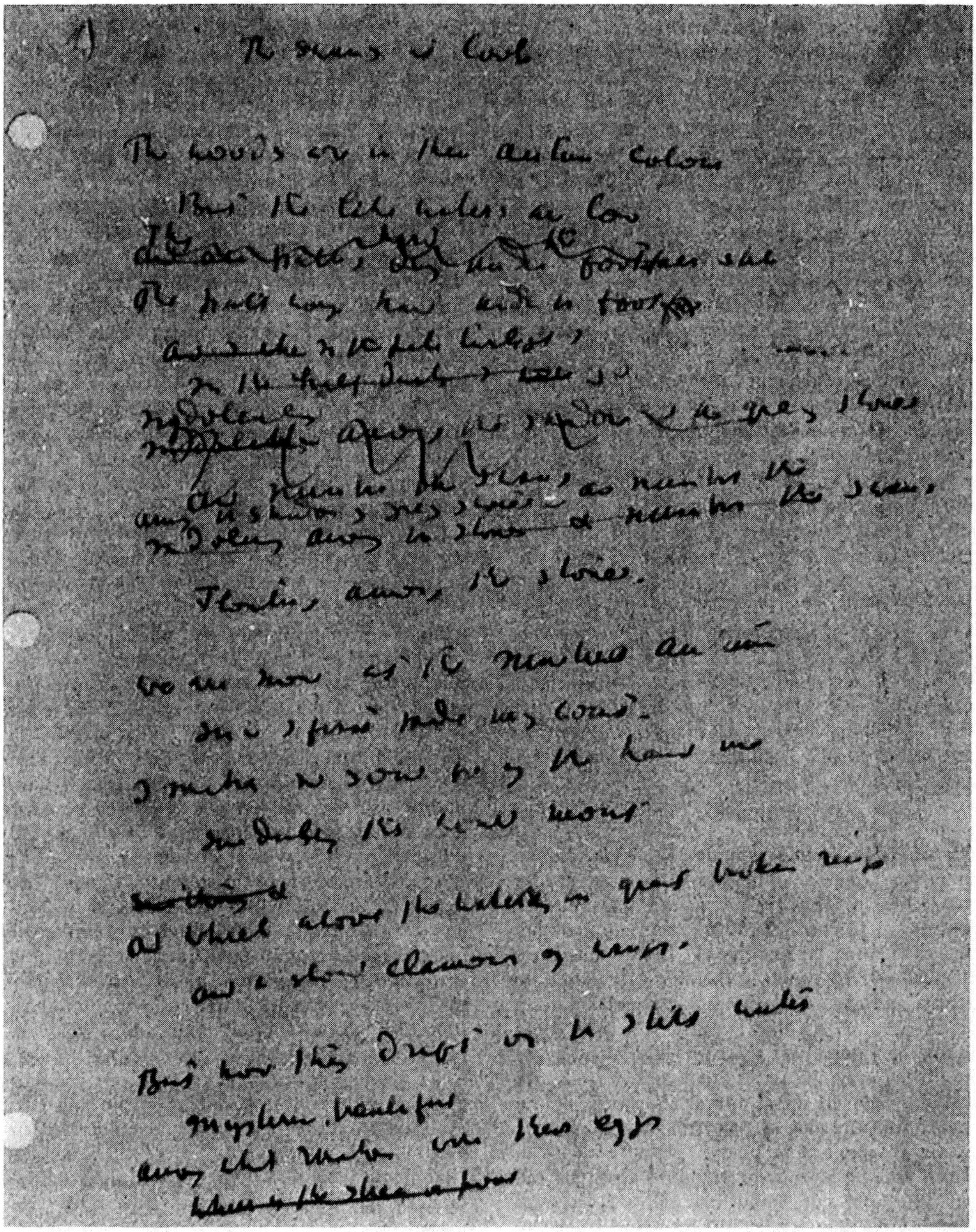

Pages from two drafts for "The Wild Swans at Coole" (National Library of Ireland)

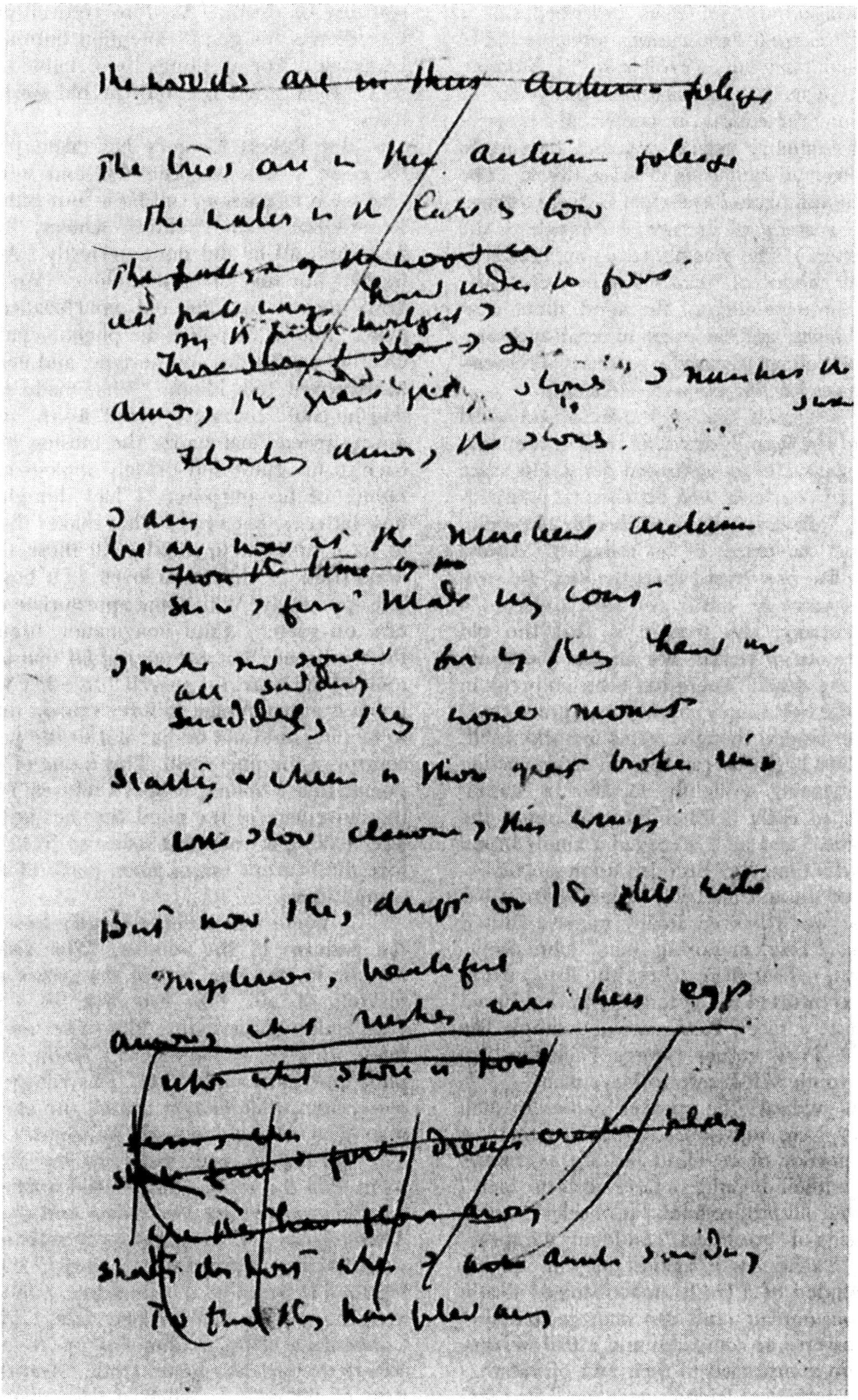

no uncritical admirer of Yeats, described it as a work that "restored the occasional poem to life in English"—and set out to rival it in "In Memory of W. B. Yeats." Yeats organizes the poem in twelve numbered stanzas, in iambics, mostly pentameter, resembling ottava rima but rhymed in two couplets and four lines of brace rhyme. (The variety, the tuning, and the vigor of Yeats's rhyming needs a study of its own; he is one of the great masters.) The poem's structure combines two major modes of Yeats's mature verse: the poem of the movement of the mind, thought itself in dynamics; and the poem of recall and summation, roll calling, summoning a series of remembered figures for address and celebration.

The setting is that of the newly occupied tower, and the form is dramatic monologue: only the poet speaks, to an unnamed guest. His voice is grave and courteous and his rhetoric polished-colloquial, following sadly and flexibly the seemingly casual movement of his thoughts. "Always we'd have the new friend meet the old," he says, and he is sorry he could not have collected a larger company; the trouble is that the old friends are out of reach: "For all that come into my mind are dead." There has been no break in the tone; the host simply continues his grave courtesy; the unbidden thought seems to speak itself. Now the host begins to call the roll of his missing friends, meaning evidently to allot a stanza-paragraph to each. "Lionel Johnson comes the first to mind," and he is accorded a kindly brutal pun: "much falling he / Brooded upon sanctity"—his habit of sin and his habit of falling from bar stools that was rumored finally to have caused his death. "That enquiring man John Synge comes next, / That dying chose the living world for text," comforted in the tomb by having found in the West "a race / Passionate and simple like his heart." Then ensues George Pollexfen, "In muscular youth well known to Mayo men."

Now, midway, the speaker pauses to sum up: "They were my close companions many a year, / A portion of my mind and life, as it were, / And now their breathless faces seem to look / Out of some old picture-book." (Consider the rhetorical daring of "breathless.") Suddenly the speaker's voice catches, as if against its will; he has been reminded of a fresh, unaccustomed death. Only a consummate craft can manage this kind of thing in verse, so compactly and withal so naturally: "I am accustomed to their lack of breath, / But not that my dear friend's dear son, / Our Sidney and our perfect man, / Could share in that discourtesy of death." As if to recover poise, the host directs his guest's attention outward to the landscape: "For all things the delighted eye now sees / Were loved by him: the old storm-broken trees."

But Robert Gregory has taken possession, the poem is now his. The next four stanzas, at a new pitch of passion, call back "our Sidney," our Renaissance man: "Soldier, scholar, horseman, he, / And all he did done perfectly / As though he had but that one trade alone." We see what Yeats meant by "the old nonchalance of the hand." Stanza 11 poises the phenomenally gifted Gregory against his countertype, and ends with a heartbroken folk idiom: "What made us dream that he could comb grey hair?" In the marvelous down-turned final stanza the musing host turns back to his guest and gravely apologizes for the failure of his purpose: "I had thought, seeing how bitter is that wind / That shakes the shutter, to have brought to mind / All those that manhood tried, or childhood loved, / Or boyish intellect approved, / With some appropriate commentary on each; / Until imagination brought / A fitter welcome; but a thought / Of that late death took all my heart for speech." In other words the poem is a triumphant failure, a poem that meant to be but could not be but still is: the poem took control of the poet's will. This is one of the great poems (like "Among School Children") in which the movement of the mind becomes its own subject, making a work that seems to form itself before the hearer's eye, a poem made of the *act* of composition.

A poem that stands austerely isolated amid the patterns of the volume, "The Fisherman," may be in the long run of the career most significant of all. This evocation of a freckled Connemara fisherman, "this wise and simple man," an artist in his way, is a vision of the simplest and most basic kind. The rough trimeter verse clumps stubbornly ahead, the speech of a man glad enough to walk in country brogues. The old-idealist poet sums up his disenchantment with the Irish: "What I had hoped 'twould be / To write for my own race / And the reality." Then comes the invigorating compensatory vision: "Maybe a twelvemonth since / Suddenly I began, / In scorn of this audience, / Imagining a man, / And his sun-freckled face, / And grey Connemara cloth, / Climbing up to a place / Where stone is dark under froth, / And the down-turn of his wrist / When the fly drops in the stream; / A man who does not exist, / A man

The Abbey Theatre Company's dinner to honor Yeats on his reception of the Nobel Prize: 1) Sean O'Casey, 2) Barry Fitzgerald, 3) Arthur Shields, 4) Lennox Robinson, 5) Yeats, 6) George Yeats

who is but a dream; / And cried, 'Before I am old / I shall have written him one / Poem maybe as cold / And passionate as the dawn.' " The "cold and passionate" conjunction encapsulates the other Yeats, the passionate realist who walked alongside the mystical philosopher and shaped the language of both poets. Certainly Yeats saw the fisherman as an ideal auditor. He kept remembering the advice of Aristotle to think like a wise man but to express oneself like one of the common people.

When their first child, Anne Butler Yeats, was born in Dublin in February 1919, George Yeats's horoscope for her predicted "good looking and lucky." Soon they were able to take the baby to Ballylee, where repairs to the cottage, with handmade furnishings in a homely, massive country style, had made the place barely habitable in warm dry weather. The ceremonious Yeats promptly composed the long poem "A Prayer for My Daughter," which has been overpraised and is most notable for a newly bitter view of Maud Gonne: "Have I not seen the loveliest woman born / Out of the mouth of Plenty's horn, / Because of her opinionated mind / Barter that horn and every good / By quiet natures understood / For an old bellows full of angry wind?" The tower still lacked a sound roof; Yeats called it "half dead at the top" ("Blood and the Moon"). To finance further repairs he undertook a third American tour in the winter and spring of 1919-1920, leaving Anne with Lily and Lollie Yeats and taking George along to meet his father and American friends. His most popular performance was "My Own Poetry with Illustrative Readings," confined to early work always beginning with "The Lake Isle of Innisfree."

In the summer they were back in Oxford, where Yeats thought the Bodleian "the most friendly comfortable library in the world and . . . the most beautiful." He saw much of Bridges, Masefield, Sturge Moore, and Edmund Dulac and often visited the Morrells at Garsington. Joseph Hone has described a walking party headed by Yeats and his famous hostess: "The two in front made a marvellous pair, striking the villagers with speechless amazement: W. B. Y. tall and stately, gesticulating, his hair ruffled in the wind, and Lady Ottoline, in period lilac silk, large picture hat and shoes with high red heels, listening to him and nodding, her long face alight with animation. They looked like beings from some pageant outside time."

Overshadowed as it is by its grander neighbors, *The Wild Swans at Coole* of 1919 and *The Tower* of 1928, Yeats's small 1921 volume, *Michael Robartes and the Dancer,* contains poems of high distinction. The new poems are marked in manner by an ever more confident and natural ease of movement, and in matter by a nonchalant induction of ideas, emblems, and even the cant terminology of his forming system. In the gaudy comedy of "Solomon and the Witch," for example, Solomon, described as one "who understood / Whatever has been said, sighed, sung, / Howled, miau-d, barked, brayed, belled, yelled, cried, crowed," discusses with "that Arab lady," Sheba, their lovemaking of the preceding night, so intense that Sheba had cried out in a voice not her own. Solomon thinks the voice must have been that of a voyeur-cockerel, crowing because he thought the completeness of their union signaled the end of the world: "he thought / Chance being at one with Choice at last, / All that the brigand apple brought / And this foul world were dead at last."

Yeats wrote often of sexual passion, as ecstasy and torture, one of God's greatest half-gifts to tragic man. "All things fall into a series of antinomies in human experience," he wrote in *A Vision,* and "my instructors identify consciousness with conflict, not with knowledge." He saw sexual union as the nearest thing to perfected oneness available in familiar experience, and he was haunted by the fact that it must always fall short. Hence he was enchanted by Swedenborg's idea that the lovemaking of angels would take the visible form of incandescence, a great fire or light. The great love of Solomon and Sheba had fooled the cockerel by its approximation of Unity of Being. "Chance" and "Choice," forms of Body of Fate and Will among the four Faculties of the system, have almost coalesced, but not quite, these lovers not being angels. Solomon explains what happens when the thing is perfect, and he uses the Swedenborgian image: "the world ends when these two things / Though several, are a single light, / When oil and wick are burned in one." "Yet the world stays," Sheba points out. Yes, says Solomon, they have made a distinguished failure—not supernal, but not bad for mortals: the cockerel "thought it worth a crow." Sheba exclaims: "O! Solomon! Let us try again."

There is precious little comedy in the great tragic lyric that forms the centerpiece of this volume. "The Second Coming" moves with an equally confident mastery, but here the vision is sweeping and apocalyptic, the rhetoric formal, grand, full of power, the structure that of two stately, violent blank-verse paragraphs. This too is a "systematic" poem, but its awful clarity of action and image is such that one hardly need know *A Vision* to feel and understand it. Yeats is dramatizing his cyclical theory of history: that whole civilizations, like men but on far grander scale, live in antinomy, every culture "perning" or wheeling in a "gyre" of about two thousand years, undergoing birth, life, and death and preparing all the while the life of its opposing successor—two cultures in immense rhythmical alternation "living each other's death, dying each other's life." The critical period of the "interchange of tinctures," when one era struggles to die and its "executioner" struggles to be born, will be violent and dreadful.

Yeats with his children, Michael and Anne

In 1920 the Christian era nears the end of its "Great Year" of two thousand calendar years; it is "turning and turning in the widening gyre," reeling in centripetal drunkenness. One may, perversely, recall the opening of Hopkins's "The Windhover"; but the "hurl and gliding" flight of the Christian poet's hawk was very different, and the god and the yearning spirit were in stretched contact. Yeats's poem remembers war and revolution and inhabits an apocalyptic climate in which "the falcon cannot hear the falconer": man has lost touch with God, with any center of order. The landscape is alternately grimly graphic and splendidly vague: "Things fall apart; the center cannot hold; / Mere anarchy is loosed upon the world, / The blood-dimmed tide is loosed, and everywhere / The ceremony of innocence is drowned; / The best lack all conviction, while the worst / Are full of passionate intensity."

"Surely some revelation is at hand," exclaims the appalled spectator; and his mind instinctively calls up the revelation promised by scripture: "Surely the Second Coming is at hand." But the Christian image is immediately dispossessed by an unbidden pagan form that rises out of the storehouse of timeless symbols: "Hardly are those words out / When a vast image out of *Spiritus Mundi* troubles my sight," a huge polymorphic figure that recalls the Sphinx of pre-Christian Egypt. Its movement is sluggish, sensual, insolent, cruel, irresistible. The flight of the birds helplessly follows the path of the widening gyre: "somewhere in sands of the desert / A shape with lion body and the head of a man, / A gaze blank and pitiless as the sun, / Is moving its slow thighs, while all about it / Reel shadows of the indignant desert birds." The lens of vision closes, but the horrified viewer knows that he has seen the rearisen god of a new and old barbarism, waking to keep his appointment with time: "The darkness drops again; but now I know / That twenty centuries of stony sleep / Were vexed to nightmare by a rocking cradle, / And what rough beast, its hour come round at last, / Slouches towards Bethlehem to be born?"

The rocking-cradle image is one that recurs in these late-middle poems, to emblematize the seesaw rhythm of the interlocking gyres, in the single life as in the collective life. When the rough beast slouches off to Bethlehem to wedge his heartless, mindless bulk into the cradle of Christ, the massive accuracy of the nonchalant verb is enough to show how and why Yeats was a great poet. He wrote in *The Trembling of the Veil:* "One thing I did not foresee, not having the courage of my own thought: the growing murderousness of the world"; and later in that text: "After us the Savage God." If he had not foreseen him, he had certainly found him in Spiritus Mundi, and enabled us to see him unforgettably.

The Yeatses spent most of 1920-1921 in Oxford, away from the Black and Tan violence in Ireland. Yeats led a busy social life, with a salon "evening" of his own on Mondays, worked at his poetry and his memoirs, and moved deeper into his system. A son, William Michael Yeats, who would be like his father a senator of Ireland, was born in August 1921. Yeats's *Four Plays for Dancers* in the Noh style came out in October 1921. In December came the treaty with England, establishing an Irish Free State in the South but excluding, with heavy consequences, the six counties of Ulster in the North, carefully gerrymandered to insure a Protestant majority and attached to England. Lady Gregory wrote describing the "purr" of the Dublin crowds as they watched the departure of the Black and Tans, signaling the end of seven hundred years of English occupation. In early 1922 John Butler Yeats died in New York at eighty-two, comparatively swiftly and painlessly, attended by Quinn and other friends. The self-portrait for Quinn on which he had worked for twelve years was still unfinished.

Yeats wished to bring up his children in Ireland, and in early 1922 George found a fine, tall Georgian house at 82 Merrion Square, an elegant address and close to everything that mattered in central Dublin. Yeats felt "very grand" when he recalled an old ballad about the Duke of Wellington: "In Merrion Square / This noble hero first drew breath / Amid a nation's cheers." But he feared that the political situation was "a whirlpool of hate." Diehard Republicans led by Eamon De Valera scorned the "Partition" Treaty and the Provisional Government of Arthur Griffith and Michael Collins, raised an army of Irregulars, and in April set off civil war that was small in scale but murderous in style and detail. The family was able to spend spring and summer of 1922 at Ballylee, idyllically happy with the place but mildly troubled by visits from detachments of the ragtag contending armies. Finally the Republicans blew up the bridge at the base of the tower, having given Yeats time to take the children to the top room.

In the fall Yeats was chosen one of the sixty members of the new Irish Senate, a largely honorary body, though some of its debates concerned issues of importance. Yeats had always taken his politics seriously, and he was pleased now to have a share in what he called "the slow exciting work of creating institutions—all coral insects but with some design of the ultimate island." He had long mistrusted the whimsicality and vulgarity of democracy, and his votes usually supported the more conservative Government party. The Irregulars were burning the houses of senators, and "82" had an armed guard to whom he lent the detective stories to which he had grown addicted. Civil war came to an end in 1923.

For Yeats the crowning event of the year, probably of his life, was the award of the Nobel Prize for Literature, an official international homage proclaiming him for the moment the world's most distinguished man of letters. "I covet honour," he wrote in his autobiography. It pleased him that the first congratulatory telegram to reach him came from James Joyce. Yeats and his wife traveled to Stockholm for the presentation early in December. With his deep drawing to ceremony, elegance, distinction, he loved every minute of the affair, dinners, toasts, speeches, applause, rooms full of royalty and eminence in full dress. He was gratified to be told later that the royal family had preferred him to every other Nobel Prize winner because he "had the manners of a courtier."

Yeats kept an amplified diary of the Nobel events which he entitled "The Bounty of Sweden" and eventually incorporated into his autobiography. Although he honored his lyric poetry highest of his own work, he felt glumly that his verse would always be known only to "a meagre troop," and it was his work in the theater that had made him known as "the representative of a public movement" and brought him the Nobel award; hence he chose "The Irish Theatre" as the subject for his own speech before the Swedish Academy. He spoke without notes and let his voice follow the track of his reverie. His first thought was simple and generous: "When your King gave me medal and diploma, two forms should have stood, one on either side of me, an old woman sinking into the infirmity of age and a young man's ghost. I think when Lady Gregory's name and John Synge's name are spoken by future generations, my name, if remembered, will come up in the talk, and if my name is spoken first their names will come in their turn because of the years we worked together. I think that both had been well pleased to have stood beside me at the great reception at your Palace, for their work and mine has delighted in history and tradition." Earlier he had studied his Nobel medal, a French design in the style of the 1890s showing a young man listening to a muse standing "young and beautiful with a great lyre in her hand," and had reflected, "I was good-looking once like that young man, but my unpractised verse was full of infirmity, my Muse old as it were; and now I am old and rheumatic, and nothing to look at, but my Muse is young. I am even persuaded that she is like those Angels in Swedenborg's vision, and moves perpetually 'towards the dayspring of her youth.' " Another considerable comfort was the cash value of the prize, seventy-five hundred pounds, the largest sum ever to reach him in a lump, and enough, invested, to provide a strong hedge against old age.

As Yeats neared sixty he looked robust, almost portly, but in fact his health was turning fragile in ways that would alter the rhythm of his remaining life. Shortness of breath and high blood pressure sent him to Sicily, Capri, and southern Italy for three months in the winter of 1924-1925. He returned in fine fettle, anxious to resume his Senate duties and particularly to argue the Protestant case for a liberalization of divorce in a forthcoming debate. He was stirred by the issue of personal liberty, and he closed with sweat pouring off his face: "We [Anglo-Irish] are no petty people. We are one of the great stocks of Europe. We are the people of Burke; we are the people of Grattan; we are the people of Swift, the people of Parnell. We have created the most of the modern literature of this country. We have created the best of its political intelligence." He was agitated now, as always, by the problem of how to unite Gaelic nationalism, more prickly and defensive than ever with the coming of independence, with the aristocratic and intellectual instincts of the old Protestant ascendancy.

At the Abbey Theatre, Yeats had become a sort of honorary but by no means impotent chairman of the board. He still read every play before production, attended all meetings, and cast a deciding vote when so moved; and he continued to write for the theater, though more slowly. His major energies in this period were concentrating toward two forthcoming capital works, the philosophical prose of *A Vision* and his great verse collection *The Tower*. Since 1917 when he and George joined their mediumship, Yeats had felt that he lived in a spirit-drenched atmosphere, a climate of miracle: "All things hang like a drop of dew / Upon a blade of grass." To give it form and validation he was reading not only his old masters but a broader range of philosophy, history, biography, political theory. It was partly his and Pound's fascination with Benito Mussolini's bustling new fascism that led him to the Italians, Giambattista Vico, Benedetto Croce, Giovanni Gentile; but he also went on to Immanuel Kant and Georg Wilhelm Friedrich Hegel, back to Nietzsche, back to George Berkeley. As always the rationalists and realists were the enemy: David Hume, John Locke, Charles Darwin, Herbert Spencer.

When *A Vision* came out in a private edition from Werner Laurie at the end of 1925, causing very little stir, Yeats was already making notes toward a revision. At the tower in the spring and summer of 1926 he was writing some of the greatest poems of his life. One of his many rich letters of these years to Olivia Shakespear combined two of the already fused themes of the coming volume: "as always happens, no matter how I begin, it becomes love poetry before I am finished with it. . . . One feels at moments as if one could with a touch convey a vision—that the mystic way and sexual love use the same means—opposed yet parallel existences. . . ." His other major theme, the encroachment of age, was also a property of both life and art. In October, Yeats developed "congestion" of the lungs, with high fever and delirium. He and George crept off to Spain, but there he suffered hemorrhages from the lung. Moving slowly toward the Pounds in Rapallo, Yeats was ill again for weeks in Cannes. In Rapallo he soaked in the sun and slowly recovered; in the evenings he walked with Pound, around whom collected the street cats who knew he carried meat and chicken bones.

Michael and Anne Yeats had been placed in school in Switzerland, and, as Yeats had been warned to winter in the sun henceforward, he and George reluctantly decided to sell 82 Merrion Square and engaged a flat of their own in Rapallo for the coming winter. In the spring of 1928 they were back in Dublin, and in the summer Yeats completed his Senate service, having decided not to seek reelection. *The Tower* was out and a quick success, selling two thousand copies in its first month. When he reread it, Yeats wrote Olivia Shakespear, he was "astonished at its bitterness"; yet, as he recognized, "that bitterness gave the book its power and it is the best book I have written." He might have claimed more. In range, beauty, and power *The Tower* surely dwarfs every other volume of poetry since its day; the only rival that comes to mind is Yeats's own *Last Poems* (1940). Passions of sexuality, mystical vision, war, and age occur and recur, superbly phrased and ordered.

Age and vision dominate the opening poem, "Sailing to Byzantium," set in four tight ottava rima stanzas. The old speaker cries his sad curse upon a land where creatures of teeming biological life, unaware that they are "dying generations" and obsessed with the "sensual music" of the flesh, pay no courtesy to "monuments of unageing intellect." Accepting in stanza 2 the fact that an old man is "a tattered coat upon a stick," a scarecrow, "unless / Soul clap its hands and sing, and louder sing / For every tatter in its mortal dress" (the image recalled Swedenborg's vision of ecstatic angels in paradise), the speaker has willed his own exile, to a place that Yeats thought approached, in history, Unity of Being.

In the great third stanza the old man addresses illuminated spirits who are at once creatures of the purgative Condition of Fire of *A Vision* and man-made Christian icons, artifacts, themselves "monuments of unageing intellect"; he implores them to spin ("perne") his purgation from flesh and time: "Consume my heart away; sick with desire / And fastened to a dying animal / It knows not what it is; and gather me / Into the artifice of eternity." Finally he envisions his coming transfiguration into the immortal passiveness of supreme art, then retransfigured into prophetic song: "Once out of nature I shall never take / My bodily form from any natural thing, / But such a form as Grecian goldsmiths make / Of hammered gold and gold enamelling / To keep a drowsy Emperor awake; / Or set upon a golden bough to sing / To lords and ladies of Byzantium / Of what is past, or passing, or to come."

The longer title poem treats old age in a wider range of tones that are powerful but perhaps imperfectly unified. In setting and in some aspects of structure "The Tower" recalls the Robert Gregory elegy: it too calls a roll, but of figures who are fabricated or semilegendary; and it ends with a long testamentary flourish. The three numbered sections are quite different in length and shape, but all are more or less colloquial in movement. Throughout, the aging poet speaks in propria persona, and he makes another poem in which the drama is the movement of the mind. At the outset the speaker puts to his "troubled heart" the question that excites the whole poem: how to make peace between a newly potent imagination and a newly impotent body, "this caricature, / decrepit age that has been tied to me / As to a dog's tail." Must he abandon bodily and imaginative passion and retreat into sedentary musings?

The long second section is composed of thirteen Gregory-style stanzas. Dragging its battered kettle, the restless body paces the tower top, pausing to allow the "excited, passionate, fantastical" imagination to call up "images and memories" from the landscape. In the will-making part 3 the verse changes abruptly to blunt trimeter lines, in alternating rhyme with many brilliantly casual off-rhymes, arranged in loose paragraphs. The old poet makes his beneficiaries on the model of his Connemara fisherman: "I choose upstanding men / That climb the streams until / The fountain leap, and at dawn / Drop their cast at the side / Of dripping stone." He bequeaths them first his "pride," of a kind they will understand, the old Anglo-Irish pride, "bound neither to Cause nor to State," of the "people of Burke and of Grattan." (Yeats wrote in his autobiography: "I love proud and lonely things.") His "faith," which he offers next, turns out to be a stunning humanist dogma, defying even the greatest of his masters, asserting the power of man to make both his own mortality and his own immortality.

In the closing paragraphs the mind settles back and down, sadly and with some bitterness, into reverie, resignation, resolution. Yeats sets his own decrepit body alongside that of his vigorous fisherman heir: "Being of that metal made / Until it was broken by / This sedentary trade." The final resolution is executed in an exquisite and strong diminuendo rhythm. If he must decline into study, Yeats vows, he will study with passion and he will move toward exaltation.

Yeats had long understood that a poem should not ride the high horse all the way, that tension profits from the relief of words or phrases that are neutral or even dull in feeling. "Meditations in Time of Civil War" contains a good many areas of such slackness, yet the general effect is one of concentrating intensity. The poem is actually a cycle of seven poems of ordinary lyric length, separately titled and varying in form. Yeats wrote the poem at Ballylee in 1922, at the height of Ireland's brief but savage civil strife, and the title is precise. He arranges his meditations in an order that moves in general from comparative peacefulness through violence and emerges in wild apocalyptic vision—though all three moods are implicitly present all the time. "Ancestral Houses" evokes the life of the great house, "the inherited glory of the rich," but it soon wonders whether its proper emblem is "the abounding glittering jet" of the garden fountain, or something like a gyre, importing disorder and impermanence: "some marvellous empty seashell flung / Out of the obscure dark of the rich streams." Yeats imagines the house as founded by "some violent bitter man, some powerful man" who sought to "rear in stone" a fabric of "sweetness"; that paradoxical union, he suspects, may still shake the troubled House of Ireland: "But take our greatness with our bitterness."

Similarly the second poem, "My House," describes the tower in detail, then settles in the study where a peaceful thinker arrives at images of violence: "*Il Penseroso's* Platonist toiled on / In some like chamber, shadowing forth / How the daemonic rage / Imagined everything." He suspects that he in his turn will leave to his heirs "befitting emblems of adversity" found in contemplation; not peace but a sword. A real sword forms the emblem of meditation in "My Table": lying on his study table a great Samurai sword "curved like a new moon," given to Yeats in America in 1920 by a young Japanese admirer, Junzo Sato, in whose family it had been passed down for five hundred years. The artifact is perfect, and Yeats reflects that the culture that produced it was said to have possessed Unity of Being: "Soul's beauty being most adored, / Men and their business took / The soul's unchanging look." Yet Yeats knows that perfect works are produced only by men in temporal torture: "only an aching heart / Conceives a changeless work of art"; and when he describes the old Japanese he surely has his own image in mind as well: "That he, although a country's talk / For silken clothes and stately walk. / Had waking wits. . . ."

"My Descendants" explores the mysteries of lineage. Having, as he feels, inherited "a vigorous mind / From my old fathers," Yeats "dreams" of passing on that strength to his own children: "leave a woman and a man behind / As vigorous of mind." But experience has proved the mutability of things, and he wonders if his children will not turn out ordinary failing folk "through natural declension of the soul, / Through too much business with the passing hour, / Through too much play, or marriage with a fool?" The last stanza accepts the overarching power of the gyres, counts the blessings of friendship (Lady Gregory) and love (George), and takes sad comfort in the survival of the emblematic house: "The Primum Mobile that fashioned us / Has made the very owls in circles move; / And I, that count myself most prosperous, / Seeing that love and friendship are enough, / For an old neighbour's friendship chose the house / And decked and altered it for a girl's love, / And know whatever flourish and decline / These stones remain their monument and mine."

The fifth and sixth poems evoke the war directly. In "The Road at My Door" Yeats is visited first by a Republican soldier, "an affable Irregular, / A heavily-built Falstaffian man," and then by a Free State officer, "a brown Lieutenant," and in both cases he is astonished at their nonchalant courage, "cracking jokes of civil war." Shamed by his sedentary trade, the poet-philosopher returns to his drab solitude, "caught

Lady Gregory

/ In the cold snows of a dream." The gloom of "The Stare's Nest by My Window" is still more bitter and comprehensive. The tower is failing as a shelter of the troubled spirit: "My wall is loosening," and bees and starlings nest in the cracks of the masonry—a metaphor of the Irish state. The air is full of horror: "A man is killed, or a house burned, / . . . . / Last night they trundled down the road / That dead young soldier in his blood"—a polite way to say that recently nearby a young man had been dragged behind a car until his body was dismembered, his mother recovering only his battered head. Irish hatred, even self-hatred, took appalling forms. The refrain line, inviting the honeybees to "come build in the empty house of the stare," forms a despairing prayer for the return of sweetness.

The final lyric, "I See Phantoms of Hatred and of the Heart's Fullness and of the Coming Emptiness," is another of Yeats's poems of the movement of the mind. It is an envelope structure, in five of the eight-line Robert Gregory stanzas with long lines given an additional foot; three separate visions are framed by an opening and a closing stanza that carry the poet's narrative of objective and subjective movement. From his tower top the poet looks out upon a swirling mist that shrouds the landscape under the light of a moon shaped like Sato's sword. A puff of wind scatters the mist into "glimmering fragments" that drive the mind into phantasmagoria. The first vision, "of Hatred," begins with the battle cry of "Vengeance for Jacques Molay," the Grand Templar, but its violence is so mad that it turns anonymous and timeless, an archetype out of *Spiritus Mundi* that is also contemporary Ireland. "In cloud-pale rags, or in lace, / The rage-driven, rage-tormented, and rage-hungry troop, / Trooper belabouring trooper, biting at arm or at face, / Plunges towards nothing, arms and fingers spreading wide / For the embrace of nothing." In one of the most stunning of all Yeats's stanzas, the second vision, "of the Heart's Fullness," presents creatures from his phase 15, the full of the moon, a phase too absolute to accommodate mortal beings: "Their legs long, delicate and slender, aquamarine their eyes, / Magical unicorns bear ladies on their backs. / The ladies close their musing eyes. No prophecies / Remembered out of Babylonian almanacs, / Have closed the ladies' eyes, their minds are but a pool."

These two visions "Give place to an indifferent multitude, give place / To brazen hawks." The third vision, "of the Coming Emptiness," presents the anarchic inhuman landscape of the dark of the moon: "Nothing but grip of claw, and the eye's complacency, / The innumerable clanging wings that have put out the moon." At last the air clears and with it the mind. In the final stanza of flat and powerful anticlimax Yeats turns back down the stairs, away from the gaudiness of violence and vision, heading back to his study, wondering once more why he could not have lived an ordinary serviceable public life. But no, he must go on being fatally himself: "The abstract joy, / The half-read wisdom of daemonic images, / Suffice the ageing man as once the growing boy."

Yeats dated the composition of "Nineteen Hundred and Nineteen" in the year of the title, and the outrage and disgust that dominate the voice seem to stem mainly from the guerrilla warfare of the Black and Tan terror, though the images are shockingly applicable to the all-Irish warfare that ensued. The fourth of the great ottava rima stanzas, for example, cites specific Black and Tan atrocities but at the end makes its image from a kind of timeless and nonspecific Irish malice and lust for blood: "Now days are dragon-ridden, the nightmare / Rides upon sleep: a drunken soldiery / Can leave the mother, murdered at her door, / To crawl in her own blood, and go scot-free; / The night can sweat with terror as before / We pieced our thoughts into philosophy, / And planned to bring the world under a rule, / Who are but weasels fighting in a hole." The same image reappears in the apparently "Irish" later quatrain: "We, who seven years ago / Talked of honour and of truth, / Shriek with pleasure if we show / The weasel's twist, the weasel's tooth." And the "us" and "we" of the bitter litany of mockery that forms part 5—"Come let us mock at the great. / . . . / let us mock at the wise. / . . . / let us mock at the good. / . . . / Mock mockers after that / . . . for we / Traffic in mockery"—seems to be spoken by an Irish voice bent on genocide followed presumably by suicide. It is a poem of heartbreak, rage, and despair, and the poet does not spare himself in the general destructiveness: "The swan has leaped into the desolate heaven: / That image can bring wildness, bring a rage / To end all things, to end / What my laborious life imagined. . . ."

The poet's despair often works itself out in images of great beauty. The gyre formed by a troupe of American dancers is not less beautiful because it is a type of the cosmic remorselessness: "When Loie Fuller's Chinese dancers enwound / A shining web, a floating ribbon of cloth, / It seemed that a dragon of air / Had fallen among dancers, had whirled them round / Or hurried them off on its own furious path; / So the Platonic Year / Whirls out new right and wrong, / Whirls in the old instead; / All men are dancers and their tread / Goes to the barbarous clangour of a gong." The terrifying apocalyptic vision of the closing part 6 is also barbarously beautiful, as the last few lines will show: "But now wind drops, dust settles; thereupon / There lurches past, his great eyes without thought / Under the shadow of stupid straw-pale locks, / That insolent fiend Robert Artisson / To whom the love-lorn Lady Kyteler brought / Bronzed peacock feathers, red combs of her cocks." And along the way in the poem Yeats has pronounced the simplest and most traditionally lovely of all his statements of tragic temporality: "Man is in love and loves what vanishes, / What more is there to say?"

The Tower is full of complex fusions, as in "Two Songs from a Play" (*The Resurrection*), set in a pair of two-stanza lyrics. Here the birth-death-rebirth of Dionysus, ushering in the Antithetical Greco-Roman era, blends, conflicts, alternates with the birth-death-resurrection of Christ and his Primary Christian age. Then in his great final stanza Yeats abruptly dismisses all his elaborate cyclicality, throws over it the fabric of his overarching romantic humanism, accepts the fatality of failure, asserts the primacy of passion: "Everything that man esteems / Endures a moment or a day. / Love's pleasure drives his love away, / The painter's brush consumes his dreams. / The herald's cry, the soldier's tread / Exhaust his glory and his might: / Whatever flames upon the night / Man's own resinous heart has fed."

In "Leda and the Swan" the fusion is literal and carnal and stranger still. In his notes Yeats poised this poem and "Two Songs" as poems of Annunciation, of God bringing his spiritual and sexual news to man. There is no Christian matter in "Leda and the Swan"; Yeats turns entirely to pagan myth, and the news Zeus brings to Leda is that of the birth of the classical age. For Yeats myth was a branch of history, and in "Leda and the Swan" he was proposing the reality, the carnality of a mythical event. The poem is intensely, magnificently sensual (his typist refused, in tears, to copy it).

His point of view is that of an amazed and awed accidental bystander, elected voyeur and granted powers of empathy with Leda's physical experience and with some part of her mental experience. The physical event occupies the octave of the sonnet, the first line of the sestet, and the final clause of the poem. The poem, like the event, comes out of nowhere with a crash: "A sudden blow: the great wings beating still / Above the staggering girl . . . " (in the extra half-syllable, the rhythm staggers organically with the girl—an effect repeated several times later). It plunges straight ahead until the god in the swan has worked his will in this exalted rape. The two questions that form the second quatrain are spoken, as it were, both by Leda and the empathizing spectator, as the girl submits, even cooperates, in the grip of the brutal and beautiful divine power: "How can those terrified vague fingers push / The feathered glory from her loosening thighs? / And how can body, laid in that white rush, / But feel the strange heart beating where it lies?" In phrases such as "dark webs," "feathered glory," "white rush," Yeats's beautiful shorthand or ellipsis fuses that other mysterious fusion at the center of the experience.

Consummation, of a singularly complex sort, comes at the beginning of the sestet. Orgasm is also conception, birth, and long future history: conceiving Helen and Clytemnestra, Leda conceives the Trojan War, Homer, Aeschylus, Greek civilization: "The broken wall, the burning roof and tower, / And Agamemnon dead." When Yeats boldly breaks his eleventh line he breaks, graphically, the body of Leda, the roofs of Troy, the body of Agamemnon, and the hearts of many men and women. In the final lines Yeats, or his voyeur persona, wonders comprehensively about the relationship of men and gods: "Being so caught up, / So mastered by the brute blood of the air, / Did she put on his knowledge with his power / Before the indifferent beak could let her drop?" The poem offers no answer to its question, and if any is implied it is more likely in the negative. If Leda took on any divine knowledge it was not because the god willed it so. His beak is indifferent not only on grounds of satiety: notice the barbaric wit of the off-rhyme in "up" / "drop."

One wearies of one's own superlatives, but it would be silly to call "Among School Children" anything other than a great poem, perhaps Yeats's most perfect union of simplicity and loftiness, of passion and control, of personal life as fact and emblem. In fact the poem is "about" unity, about the relation of the singular to the plural, the universal, of person to person and to race, of youth to age and to immortality, of part to part and to whole. Cast in eight of Yeats's favorite ottava rima stanzas, the shape has the feeling of a perfect square. The action is basically simple. W. B. Yeats, an Irish senator in an Arnoldian function, visits an elementary school and allows his mind to follow the progress of what he sees and thinks. The result is the richest of his many poems of the movement of the mind.

The opening stave is curiously toneless—flat, mechanical (one soon sees that the effect was deliberate; Yeats was not the kind of poet who is dull unintentionally): "I walk through the long schoolroom questioning; / A kind of old nun in a white hood replies." The nun drones the curriculum; the seated children look up at the visitor: "the children's eyes / In momentary wonder stare upon / A sixty-year-old smiling public man." Moved by that impulse of self-consciousness, in stanza 2 the mind abruptly takes over from the public body. The children make him think not merely of children, but of a beautiful mature woman, Maud Gonne, talking of her own childhood: "I dream of a Ledaean body, bent / Above a sinking fire, a tale that she / Told of a harsh reproof, or trivial event / That changed some childish day to tragedy." Yeats's mind has run all the way back to the turn of the century; the lines are a re-recollection of the scene in "Adam's Curse." Now he recalls, as if present, the poignancy of his sympathetic feeling on that distant day; then, seeking an equivalent in the universal, the mind calls up, only to reverse, Plato's only half-humorous account of how the sexes came to be two—a smooth bisexual whole divided into halves that thenceforth seek reunion: "it seemed that our two natures blent / Into a sphere from youthful sympathy, / Or else, to alter Plato's parable, / Into the yolk and white of the one shell." Leda and Plato remain in the mind, and will be called back.

In stanza 3 the body goes back to work, but the mind carries its new burden of feeling and image. The children become Maud Gonnes; Maud Gonne becomes a child, becomes Leda again, becomes Leda's daughter Helen; the children become the ugly ducklings who may turn into swans: "For even daughters of the swan can share / Something of every paddler's heritage." Now memory and image-making are displaced by outright vision: "And thereupon my heart is driven wild: / She stands before me as a living child."

The time-ranging mind is in control now. Having already seen Maud Gonne as a mature woman and an imagined child, Yeats now abruptly calls up the real Maud Gonne of the current day: "Her present image floats into the mind," worn by time and contentiousness, "Hollow of cheek as though it drank the wind," an image that might have been made by a "Quatrocento finger." (In the first printings of the poem Yeats tried out "quintocento" and "DaVinci," then apparently rejected the rounder modeling of the high Renaissance in order to get the gaunt effect of the earlier art.) Now of course Yeats must set himself alongside Maud Gonne, and in double guise: the youthful and the antiquated, the final image shared with "Sailing to Byzantium" and the wit similarly rueful, self-mocking and self-defensive: "And I though never of Ledaean kind / Had pretty plumage once—enough of that, / Better to smile on all that smile, and show / There is a comfortable kind of old scarecrow."

The poem has come exactly halfway. In the second half the mind's movement settles onto a single plane, a complex reverie upon time and its human ravages, asking again the question of "Nineteen Hundred and Nineteen": "But is there any comfort to be found?" Grammatically stanza 5 is a single question, and it manipulates a single awful conceit, that of the young mother who is forced to see her child as infant and old man in a single vision: "What youthful mother, a shape upon her lap / Honey of generation had betrayed / . . . . / Would think her son, did she but see that shape / With sixty or more winters on its head, / A compensation for the pang of his birth, / Or the uncertainty of his setting forth?" Stanza 6 seems disjunct at first, but a little thought brings it into the scheme. Yeats sent an early version of the stanza to Olivia Shakespear in September 1926, describing it as "a fragment of my last curse upon old age." He juxtaposes in capsule form the systems of three great Greeks—Plato, Aristotle, Pythagoras—who embody three notions of primary value—Spirit, Nature, Art—and abruptly mocks all three masters by holding up the mirror of his scarecrow image: "Old clothes upon old sticks to scare a bird." This gnomic stanza Yeats glossed simply enough for Mrs. Shakespear: "It means that even the greatest men are owls, scarecrows by the time their fame has come."

The nun of the first stanza and the mother of the fifth are brought together in stanza 7 as worshipers of "images" or icons: of immortal beings, of a time-free ideal child. Both kinds of images "break hearts"; they are "mockers of man's enterprise" because they offer ideal images to real people caught in real time: they are "self-born" because they are absolutes, out of the order of nature.

The final twelve lines of the poem form a lofty extended rhapsody composed of five flowing apostrophes, beginning with "O Presences" and "O self-born mockers" of stanza 7 and continuing into three more apostrophes in stanza 8 without even a break in syntax. Yeats is asking again his ultimate question about Unity of Being, and in the last stanza proffering mortal equivalents, or approximations, where alone there is "comfort to be found." Only a pure and impassioned spirit can save "enterprise" from exhaustion and "despair": "Labour is blossoming or dancing where / The body is not bruised to pleasure soul, / Nor beauty born out of its own despair, / Nor blear-eyed wisdom out of midnight oil." In the grand climax, apostrophes shape two ecstatic self-answering questions: "O chestnut-tree, great-rooted blossomer, / Are you the leaf, the blossom, or the bole? / O body swayed to music, O brightening glance, / How can we know the dancer from the dance?" Unity, in nature, in art, is made by achieved organic wholeness in which part is part and whole, and form is inseparable from function and spirit.

The big house in Merrion Square was sold in the summer of 1928, and in the following healthy happy winter the Yeatses took up their own flat in Rapallo. Through Pound, Yeats formed new friendships with Gerhart Hauptmann and George Antheil, the modernist pianist and composer, who helped stimulate him to compose songlike poems. Having been genuinely disturbed by his own bitterness in *The Tower,* he was trying to write "more amiable" poetry. At Rapallo he also wrote "A Packet for Ezra Pound" and "The Great Wheel," which would introduce the second, corrected *A Vision* (1937) and would tell for the first time, with her permission, the story of George Yeats's communications with the spirit instructors. Lollie Yeats at Cuala Press found these pages so strange that she asked the advice of AE (no stranger to spirits), who reassured her: "My opinion is that *anything* Willie writes will be of interest now and later on." To their great sorrow the Yeatses had now abandoned Thoor Ballylee; it was simply too demanding in Yeats's state of health. He was ill throughout the winter of 1929-1930, coughing up blood in London and nearly dying in Rapallo of what was finally diagnosed as Malta fever. As he slowly recovered he resumed work on *A Vision* and returned to his central visionary manner in such poems as the second "Byzantium." At sixty-five his formerly gray-brindle hair had become a great shock of pure white. Elegantly dressed and ceremonious in manner, he was a highly distinguished figure.

In Dublin, Yeats kept a regular "evening" on Mondays, receiving old and new friends and especially pleased by visits from the rising young. To stay in reach of Lady Gregory in her old age and ill health, Yeats risked the winter of 1930-1931 in a furnished house above the Bay of Killiney, south of Dublin. He was working toward a new *Collected Poems* (1933). "Months of rewriting," he wrote Mrs. Shakespear, "What happiness!" In May, Yeats was made an honor-

William Butler Yeats, 1930

ary D.Litt. of Oxford University. The summer brought him an important new friend, the Italian philosopher and scholar of Berkeley and Swift, Mario Rossi, whose subjects were much on Yeats's mind. He hoped to send Rossi home with "a faultless Dublin accent." Much later Rossi sent Joseph Hone a moving account of their meetings: "He had no philosophy to offer by chapter and verse. He offered poems—and asked for philosophical theories, for an explanation. . . . He asked and listened, and asked and listened again. His slow voice, which he had deliberately trained on the psaltery, might have seemed pontifical. But he was not proud of himself. He was proud of poetry, of the great things to which he gave voice. . . . He wanted to solve his problems. He wanted to come in clear about his own mind. He wanted to connect thing and image. . . ." At Coole, Yeats and AE drew up plans, in which they were later joined by Shaw, for an Academy of Letters, aiming to institutionalize and preserve the Irish intellectual "movement" over which they had presided for thirty-five years.

With Lady Gregory visibly failing, Yeats virtually lived at Coole in the winter and spring of 1931-1932. He reread Honoré de Balzac and Percy Bysshe Shelley and added poems to his raffish "Crazy Jane" series; then, "to exorcise that slut . . . whose language has become unendurable," he worked at anticipatory elegiac verse that would express his drenched feeling for Lady Gregory, her house, and her kind of noble-beggarman lineage. Called to Dublin by Abbey affairs, he was not present at her death on 22 May, but he was much moved to walk through her house on the following day conducting a Dublin sculptor, dressed like a workingman, who had called "to pay his respects" and who, looking about the rooms full of portraits, said quietly: "All the nobility of earth."

In the autumn of 1932 Yeats made his last American lecture tour. His health held up, he enjoyed himself, and he made money for himself as well as seven hundred pounds for the theater from Depression America. Money was needed for settling into another house, Riversdale, which George Yeats had found in the suburban village of Rathfarnham, giving easy access to the city and far enough out to discourage "most interviewers and the less determined travelling bores." The "little creeper-covered farm-house" was a modest, two-story eighteenth-century structure set in four acres beautifully planned and tended by the previous tenant, with fruit trees, flower and vegetable gardens, and lawns, including a velvety croquet ground where Yeats liked to perform. Two rooms were combined to make a long, light drawing room and study, with walls of lemon yellow lined with books and pictures. Yeats thought it the perfect place for his last years. "We have a lease for but thirteen years," he wrote Olivia Shakespear, "but that will see me out of life." He had no intention of "withering into eighty years, honoured and empty-witted." *The Tower* must remain Yeats's richest single volume, his densest accumulation in the high-horse manner; but in his last decade he not only remained a poet but became several different kinds of new poet. His must be the greatest old-poet's work in the language.

The Winding Stair and Other Poems of 1933 contained no fewer than sixty-four poems in a wide range of form and tone. Mrs. Edmund Dulac wrote to thank Yeats for the dedication to her husband: "It is good to see that you have come thro' the Tower and discovered another passion on the other side. . . . No other poet I have ever heard of has done this. . . . to go on with rich life and vigour and fullness of power to a third is I think unknown except to you." The volume opens with the beautiful romantic rhapsody "In Memory of Eva Gore-Booth and Con Markiewicz," addressing the horse-riding Gore-Booth sisters of his Sligo youth, remembered as "Two girls in silk kimonos, both / Beautiful, one a gazelle," but now known as "withered old and skeleton-gaunt" with time and political passion. The poem ends in an ecstasy of acceptance and defiance of tragic reality in which Yeats does not separate his own history from theirs: "Dear shadows, now you know it all, / All the folly of a fight / With a common wrong or right. / The innocent and the beautiful / Have no enemy but time; / Arise and bid me strike a match / And strike another till time catch; / Should the conflagration climb, / Run till all the sages know. / We the great gazebo built, / They convicted us of guilt; / Bid me strike a match and blow."

"A Dialogue of Self and Soul" appears almost to reverse certain of Yeats's usual values. "Self" sounds like his usual "Mask," and "Soul" very nearly becomes his usual "self," and the new Mask-self has much the better of the argument. Soul speaks first: "I summon to the ancient winding stair," the ascent to inwardness, contemplation, transcendence. Self counters with his own symbol, Sato's sword, "still razor-keen." Soul wonders why an aging man should fix his mind upon a thing "emblematical of love and war"; far better to look beyond passional life to a state that can "deliver from the crime of death and birth." Self stubbornly proffers again the sword and its embroidered sheath "for emblems of the day against the tower / Emblematical of the night." But in the beatitude of the Soul's night, the other insists in terms borrowed from *A Vision,* the mind will be so free of conflict that it need no longer distinguish "*Is* from the *Ought,* or *Knower* from the *Known.*" Yeats now abruptly silences Soul, and for the remaining four eloquent stanzas Self develops a single defiant assertion: awful as it is, I take life: "I am content to live it all again / And yet again, if it be life. . . ."

This grave, beautiful poem with its climax in "sweetness" is best read in the company of the still more complex "Vacillation." The brief first section again defines life as conflict, antinomy, moving toward states of bodily and spiritual crisis, then turns to confront the puzzling condition it calls simply "joy." How to explain the mysterious encompassing feeling of the tragic-happy man who "may know not what he knows, but knows not grief"? In part 3 Yeats tells us quite directly how, antinomies apart, to live well in order to die well, in stoic-rhapsodic acceptance: "No longer in Lethean foliage caught / Begin the preparation for your death / And from the fortieth winter by that thought / Test every work of intellect or faith, / And everything that your own hands have wrought / And call those works extravagance of breath / That are not suited for such men as come / Proud, open-eyed and laughing to the tomb." Part 4 records an experience of his own in which, sitting alone in a London tea shop, he felt his mind and heart drenched by an inexplicable wave of pure beatitude—the "joy" of part 1: "While on the shop and street I gazed / My body of a sudden blazed; / And twenty minutes more or less / It seemed, so great my happiness, / That I was blessed and could bless."

Part 7 presents a compact dialogue between the "Soul" and the "Heart," with Heart speaking specifically for man as artist. Here the "reality" advocated by Soul is the Platonic ideality, and Heart counters with "sin," meaning what the other dialogue meant by "life": the dynamics of stressful living. "What theme had Homer but original sin?" runs Yeats's great inclusive question; it is easy to see what lineage he means to join.

The marvelous swooping final stanza is spoken in the voice of one of the bold new poets Yeats was becoming in old age. In one of his periods of recuperation from illness he called out to his wife at night: "I feel I am becoming Christian and I hate that." This stanza originated in that rueful half-serious feeling. It opens with a breezy, expansive rhetorical question addressed to the German Catholic theologian Friedrich Von Hügel, seen as spokesman of Christian mysticism and by extension, of all mysticism, a mode of vision that Yeats admits he has deeply shared, but one which in this bold empirical mood he must put aside, in spite of its beauty and richness. "Must we part, Von Hügel, though much alike, for we / Accept the miracles of the saints and honour sanctity? / The body of Saint Teresa lies undecayed in tomb, / Bathed in miraculous oil, sweet odours from it come, / Healing from its lettered slab. Those self-same hands perchance / Eternalized the body of a modern saint that once / Had scooped out Pharaoh's mummy." "I," says Yeats at the end, though feeling the pull of available creature comfort, "did I become a Christian man," "play a predestined part," the part of secular man involved in pagan myth and passionate experience: "Homer is my example and his unchristened heart." Still, one feels as Yeats does the Christian threads that adhere in that last great negative adjective. When he dismisses the theologian it is with much fellow-feeling kindness: "So get you gone, Von Hügel, though with blessings on your head." The bravery and the gaiety of the speech are quintessential Yeats.

The emblems of the tower and Sato's sword keep recurring in this volume. In the tiny poem candidly called "Symbols" the tower carries its usual connotations of withdrawal, contemplation, arcane study, and the sword blade is violently active, "all-destroying." Yeats is both the tower's "blind hermit" and the "wandering fool" who carries the sword. But the tower is also the house of the marriage bed, and the phallic sword's housing is the feminine "gold-sewn silk" of the scabbard. So the final couplet couples the coupling of all the emblems: "Gold-sewn silk on the sword-blade / Beauty and fool together laid."

In "Blood and the Moon" Yeats abruptly alters the symbolic value of the tower, makes it "my symbol," and emblematic of a self that is specifically Irish, involved in historical time and in the conflicting spiritual values that divide real personalities. "Quarrel in Old Age" of this volume describes Dublin offhandedly as "this blind bitter town," and "Remove for Intemperate Speech" (his own speech) puts in capsule form the compacted bitterness that Yeats had long seen as genetic in Irish character: "Great hatred, little room, / Maimed us from the start." In "Blood and the Moon" his scene is contemporary Ireland, against which he erects his roofless tower: "In mockery of a time / Half dead at the top."

It is the sublime rant of part 2 that makes this poem unforgettable. It begins innocently with a quick catalogue of famous towers: Alexandria's beacon, Babylon's celestial observatory, Shelley's lofty study. Then in the second stanza it all begins to go a bit mad, at least frenzied, as Yeats seizes and rides his symbol and makes it "ancestral" and Anglo-Irish, hence personal and familial and genetic to his own small distinguished fragment of the Irish race, which he gives its own pantheon. Yeats's verse swoops and soars with his mind: "I declare this tower is my symbol; I declare / This winding, gyring, spiring treadmill of a stair is my ancestral stair; / That Goldsmith and the Dean, Berkeley and Burke have travelled there."

What distinguished those eighteenth-century saints of Anglo-Irishry was their grand sweet humanism: intellectual and spiritual generosity, a common hatred of that vulgar spirit which in a neighboring poem, "The Seven Sages," Yeats named "Whiggery" and spat upon as "a levelling, rancorous, rational sort of mind." Yeats looses his periods, his rhythm, and his images to roll, crash, and accumulate in sympathy with the torrent of his feeling. He begins with Swift, the heartbroken priest, and goes on to pile up the free-associated images of his own visionary passion: "Swift beating on his breast in sibylline frenzy blind / Because the heart in his blood-sodden breast had dragged him down into mankind, / Goldsmith deliberately sipping at the honey-pot of his mind, // And haughtier-headed Burke that proved the State a tree, / That this unconquerable labyrinth of the birds, century after century, / Cast but dead leaves to mathematical equality; // And God-appointed Berkeley that proved all things a dream, / That this pragmatical, preposterous pig of a world, its farrow that so solid seem, / Must vanish on the instant if the mind but change its theme." Then Yeats casually demonstrates that the paroxysm of his visionary rage was under control after all, unified within the comprehensive "savage indignation" of Swift's self-composed Latin epitaph.

In the sad, solemn, majestic poem "Coole Park and Ballylee, 1931" Yeats combines his symbolic tower with another symbolic place, and sets both against his general Irish disenchantment. He was in a mood to see symbols everywhere: "Another emblem there!" he exclaims midway. At the outset he stands musing at his tower window, turning the stream at its base into a metaphor of the flowing history of the soul: "Run for a mile undimmed in Heaven's face / Then darkening through 'dark' Raftery's 'cellar' drop, / Run underground, rise in a rocky place / In Coole demesne, and there to finish up / Spread to a lake and drop into a hole. / What's water but the generated soul?" In the second stanza he has moved to the familiar lake at Coole where he finds another soul emblem in the "sudden thunder of the mounting swan" which rises to poise against the sky.

When he moves inside the house of Lady Gregory, old and ill, the sound of her toiling movement overhead calls up an anatomy of the signs of a rich, traditionary, aristocratic culture. Against that elegance and high-mindedness he sets the small peevish indecisiveness, "like some poor Arab tribesman and his tent," of contemporary Ireland in his view of it. The famous opening of his peroration, "We were the last romantics," groups himself and his old friends as common aspirers, common dupes of an implacable vulgarity; he defines his term: "Traditional sanctity and loveliness; / Whatever's written in what poets name / The book of the people; whatever most can bless / The mind of man or elevate a rhyme." The close at once grimly accepts the case and reasserts the grandeur of the displaced "romantic" classicism: "But all is changed, that high horse riderless, / Though mounted in that saddle Homer rode / Where the swan drifts upon a darkening flood."

The strange, spectral roll-calling "All Souls' Night," written at Oxford in 1920 but then preserved to stand as epitaph to *The Tower* (1928) and to *A Vision* (1925, 1937), introduced a "mummy" image, used three times in the poem and repeatedly thereafter. Yeats was apparently fascinated by contemporary excavations in Egypt, yielding not only human mummies but edible mummified grain (in "Conjunctions" he wrote, "If Jupiter and Saturn meet, / What a crop of mummy wheat!"), and these images, surviving from an ancient stargazing culture, stayed in his mind as metaphors of cosmic secrecy and recurrence, of time past but come again: "Wound in mind's wandering / As mummies in the mummy-cloth are wound."

A note of 1930 at Portofino shows that the mummy image was fundamental to the conception of "Byzantium," the second of the two great poems on the sacred place of Unity of Being: "Describe Byzantium as it is in the system towards the end of the first Christian millennium. A walking mummy, flames in the street corners where the soul is purified, birds of hammered gold singing in the golden trees." In theme and in structure the poem counterpoises the most inclusive antinomies: human and superhuman, body and spirit, entrapment and transcendence. The great dome of Santa Sophia, a perfected monument to a timeless faith, rises above the "unpurged" forms of quotidian living: "A starlit or a moonlit dome disdains / All that man is, / All mere complexities, / The fury and the mire of human veins." In stanza 2 Yeats calls up the death-freed spirit and uses the wrapping of the mummy to create a "perning" action in which the figure spinning in transcendence "unwinds" the complexities of its earthly life: "For Hades' bobbin bound in mummy-cloth / May unwind the winding path."

The third stanza places transcendence in art, calling back the inspired artifact that sang the end of "Sailing to Byzantium." Here that "miracle, bird or golden handiwork" has power in its perfection to "scorn aloud" the untidiness of mortal forms, "all complexities of mire and blood." Stanza 4 loops back to imagine the actual beginning of the body's transfiguration, as the dancing figure begins to "pern" its bobbin of spirit time, the mummy-wound figure that will be empowered to unwind mortal time.

Still, it is humanity that has the last word in the poem. In the gorgeous imaginings of the final stanza the dolphins of myth, traditional porters of the soul, swim in to the shore bearing "spirit after spirit" to its purgation. The "golden smithies of the Emperor" will work their transfiguring will; but the spirits do keep coming: "Those images that yet / Fresh images beget." And in the barbarically mysterious and beautiful last line, "That dolphin-torn, that gong-tormented sea," the sea, torn by the dolphins of passage and tortured by the gong that proclaims the power both of spirit and of time, is still the sea of mortal being, of the impassioned life of the body.

Words for Music Perhaps (1932) runs to twenty-five poems, most of them short and songlike but not uniformly simple. Yeats's Crazy Jane (originally Cracked Mary) was modeled upon a bitter-tongued old country woman of his acquaintance, much given to satirizing her neighbors, a figure who could have come straight out of Synge (or Shakespeare). She dominates the first seven of the lyrics, the most staggering of which is "Crazy Jane Talks with the Bishop." Meeting her upon the road the bishop reproves her bluntly for her loose life: "Those breasts are flat and fallen now, / Those veins must soon be dry; / Live in a heavenly mansion, / Not in some foul sty." She rails back uncowed: " 'Fair and foul are near of kin, / And fair needs foul,' I cried." Her harridan language, as it becomes more dignified, rounds into fundamental Yeatsian doctrine, dismissing ceremonious gentility—"A woman can be proud and stiff / When on love intent"—in favor of a deep instinctual wisdom that senses sublime ironies (covertly Christian): the nearness of loftiness to lowness, the necessity of suffering to sanctity: "But love has pitched his mansion in / The place of excrement; / For nothing can be sole or whole / That has not been rent." Here are the antinomies in basic passional form. It is anatomically, psychologically, and spiritually true that "Love has pitched his mansion in the place of excrement." The brilliant punning images of "pitched"

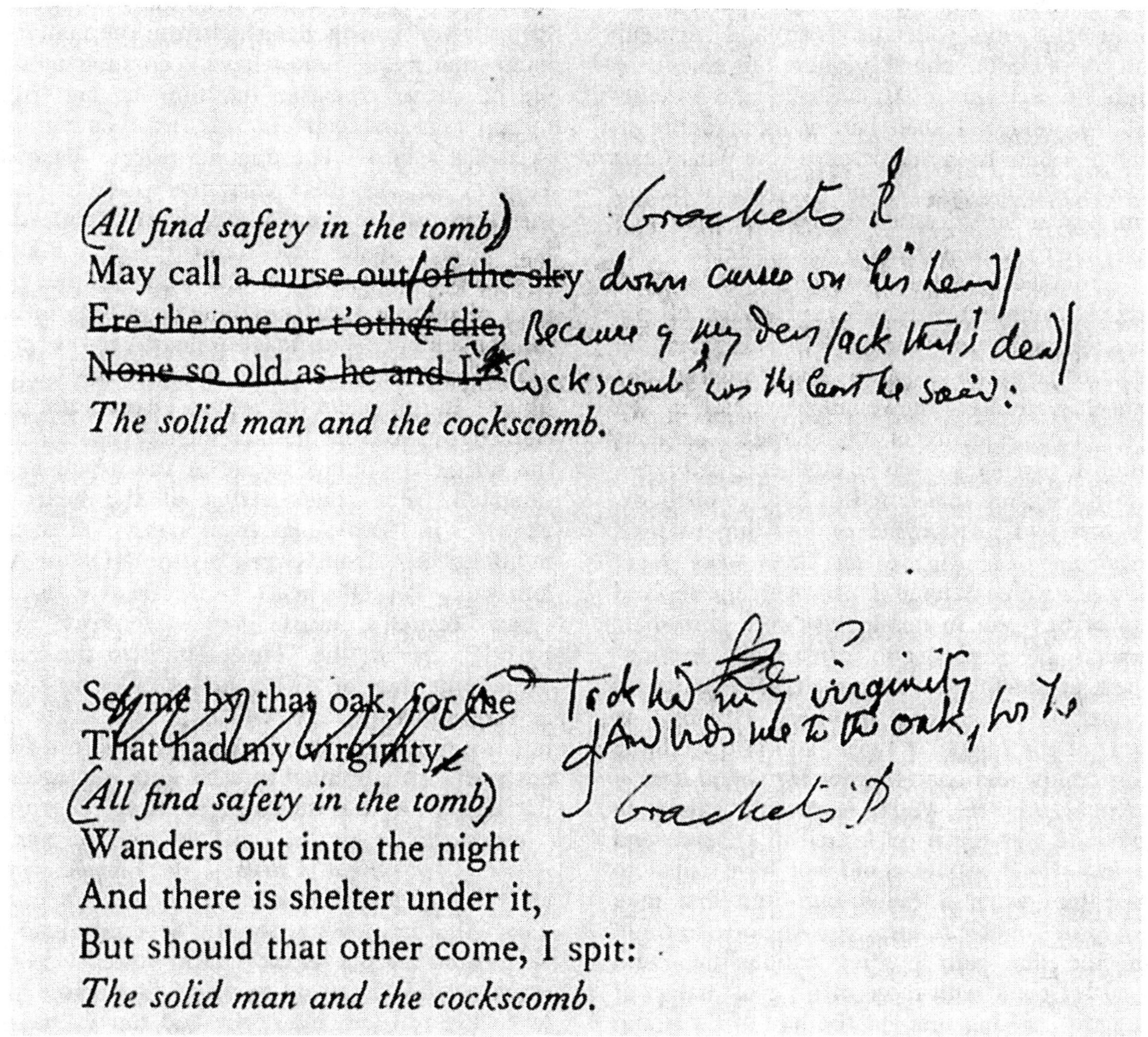
(All find safety in the tomb)
May call a curse out of the sky
Ere the one or t'other die,
None so old as he and I:
The solid man and the cockscomb.

Set me by that oak, for he
That had my virginity,
(All find safety in the tomb)
Wanders out into the night
And there is shelter under it,
But should that other come, I spit:
The solid man and the cockscomb.

Corrected proofs, circa 1931, for two verses of "Crazy Jane Talks with the Bishop" (from Allan Wade, A Bibliography of the Writings of W. B. Yeats, *1968)*

(erected, thrown down, tarred) and "mansion" (tent, grand house) make Yeats's point linguistically. Of course what is most moving is to hear all this wisdom in the cracked folk voice of the battered and defiant old woman—instructing her spiritual adviser. It is what Yeats meant at the end of "The Seven Sages" when he said that "wisdom comes of beggary"—giving the word a satirical off-rhyme to "Whiggery."

It is appropriate to end an overview of this great late volume by merely quoting one of the grave, rich, simple poems of a kind he might have written at any point in his fifty-year career, poems on the order of "When You Are Old" or "A Deep-Sworn Vow," spoken so quietly that the voice hardly rises above a whisper. "After Long Silence" is spoken to Olivia Shakespear: "Speech after long silence; it is right, / All other lovers being estranged or dead / . . . / That we descant and yet again descant / Upon the supreme theme of Art and Song: / Bodily decrepitude is wisdom; young / We loved each other and were ignorant."

Lady Gregory had been Yeats's last link to his beloved West of Ireland. In his remaining years his Irish life centered in Riverside, and when health allowed he spent more and more time in England, drawn particularly to the houses of new women friends, Lady Gerald Wellesley, Ethel Mannin, and Edith Shackleton Heald, and as always seeing much of Olivia Shakespear in London. National and international politics agitated his mind in grandiloquent, sardonic, irresponsible ways. The note of his only half-humorous flirtation with the Irish and amateur form of fascism, the Blueshirt movement, is caught in a letter to Mrs. Shakespear of July 1933: "Doubtless I shall hate it (though not so much as I hate Irish democracy). . . ." What Yeats hated was demagoguery, and his political dream form was an aristocratic oligarchy. It took him some time to see that fascism was not that.

Troubled as always by "the sexual torture," perhaps complicated now by problems of potency, Yeats abruptly decided in the spring of 1934 to cross to London and undergo the Steinach glandular "rejuvenation" operation. An apparent consequence of the operation, or of its optimistic psychology, was an ebullience and fertility in his writing that lasted as long as his body. The half-wild metaphysics of his "Supernatural Songs" and *The King of the Great Clock Tower* (1934), in which Salome dances with the severed head of St. John in her hands, were immediate products. He worked also, often while "resting" in bed, at the *Dramatis Personae* (1935) section of his memoirs, centering on Lady Gregory, at proofs of the revised *A Vision,* and at the editing of his cranky and controversial *The Oxford Book of Modern Verse* (1936). Yeats's seventieth birthday in June 1935 was much celebrated in Ireland, and the *Irish Times* tribute could not have failed to please him when it called him "the first man since Swift . . . able to bring the Anglo-Irish tradition into line with positive nationalism," and joined his name with those of his great haters of Whiggery, placing him "in the line of Swift and Goldsmith, Berkeley and Burke, while clinging to his inheritance as a successor of the Irish bards." The writer was obviously ventriloquizing Yeats himself.

The small volume of 1935, *A Full Moon in March,* is late Yeats and essential Yeats. Nearly all the poems are short and nearly all are "songs"; but the defining note of these and later poems is sounded in a poem of different form, "A Prayer for Old Age": "God guard me from those thoughts men think / In the mind alone; / He that sings a lasting song / Thinks in a marrow-bone; // . . . // I pray—for fashion's word is out / And prayer comes round again— / That I may seem, though I die old, / A foolish, passionate man." Prayer was also *credo.* From now on Yeats would be a fool for the song's sake, a foolish, passionate man thinking marrow-bone thoughts.

At end as at beginning of his career, Yeats's instinct turned to balladry, song, and one sign of that was a long list of spectral, mummy-thought refrains, often weirdly detached from the matter in hand, that might almost have been sung by that old hermit of an earlier day who, having "rummaged rags and hair" for his flea, "sang unnoticed like a bird." The opening poem, "Parnell's Funeral," reaches back forty-five years to recall the death of the great leader in the scene that had always made Yeats (and Joyce) think of Goethe's denunciation of the Irish people as a pack of hounds forever pulling down one or another noble stag. The image appears here as "popular rage, / *Hysterica passio* dragged this quarry down." In this poem the refrain effect is not outright but evoked in the incremental repetition of the image of salutary eating of the hero's heart (imitated from Zeus's eating of the heart of Dionysus in "Two Songs from a Play," in turn a motif imitated from Greek myth): "Had de Valera eaten Parnell's heart. / . . . / Had Cosgrave eaten Parnell's heart. / . . . / Had even O'Duffy. . . ." In the "Three Songs to the Same Tune" (the tune of "O'Donnell Abu"), composed as rallying rhymes for O'Duffy's Blueshirts but much too esoteric for any popular use, a different refrain is amplified in each song into a four-line chorus; here is the strangest of the choruses: " *'Who'd care to dig 'em,' said the old, old man, / 'Those six feet marked in chalk? / Much I talk, more I walk: / Time I were buried,' said the old, old man."* The "Alternative Song for the Severed Head in 'The King of the Great Clock Tower' " offers three seven-line stanzas in which lines three and seven are refrains, metrically and tonally haunting as are all the great late refrains: *"What says the Clock in the Great Clock Tower? / . . . . / A slow low note and an iron bell."*

The twelve "Supernatural Songs" occupy most of the short volume. The most astonishing of these mummy matters is the first, "Ribh at the Tomb of Baile and Ailinn." The legendary lovers, "purified by tragedy" and thereby "transfigured" into "pure substance," make love on top of their own tomb on the anniversary of their death and of their first embrace; their performance validates Swedenborg's vision: "For the intercourse of angels is a light / Where for its moment both seem lost, consumed." By that light the ninety-year-old monk Ribh reads his Christian breviary: "I turn the pages of my holy book." Tragedy would be omnipresent in Yeats's thought from now on—but it had always been so. He must have chuckled wickedly when he gave "The Four Ages of Man" to the principal of his old high school to print in his school paper. Its mere four couplets composed a gnomic biography, a spiritual history, of Yeats and of Everyman: "He with body waged a fight, / But body won; it walks upright." When he struggles with his heart, "Innocence and peace depart," and when he struggles with his mind, "His proud heart he left behind." Finally, the poet concludes, "Now his wars on God begin; / At stroke of midnight God shall win."

In the summer of 1935 George Russell died in Bournemouth and was brought back to Dublin for burial. He and Yeats had been friends for more than fifty years, and in spite of frequent exasperation the two men had loved each other. Yeats was hard hit. George Yeats said to him: "AE was the nearest to a saint you or I will ever meet. You are a better poet but no saint. I suppose one has to choose." In the winter of 1935-1936 Yeats stayed in Palma de Mallorca with Shri Purohit Swami, resting but also working with the Indian scholar on a translation of the Upanishads. All went well at first, but then Yeats became seriously ill with a dropsical condition attended by pain, breathlessness, and edema. His bad heart was growing worse, but he kept making remarkable recoveries, and he continued to work, often in bed and often from four in the morning till noon or after. Frank O'Connor has described the sadness of watching him climb the stairs to the Abbey boardroom in Dublin, pausing on every step to get his breath.

Beginning in October 1936 Yeats presided over a series of broadcasts for BBC on the subject of modern poetry, his own and others'. He worked fanatically to secure the precise oral effects he heard in his head, whether he or another was doing the reading; "his ear for the sound of speech was so sensitive that it outran comprehension," wrote an associate. The enterprise occupied Yeats intermittently for a year, and he expanded his trips to London to include visits of some length with his English friends, particularly his women friends. In October 1938 he lost another of his dearest, Olivia Shakespear. He wrote Dorothy Wellesley: "You would have approved her.... She was not more lovely than distinguished—no matter what happened she never lost her solitude." In August he had made what would be his last public appearance in Ireland when he spoke briefly to the audience at the Abbey following the curtain of his one-act play *Purgatory*.

The Yeatses returned to the Riviera for the winter of 1938-1939, taking rooms in a hotel at Cap Martin. For the most part it was a happy time, with good friends nearby: Dermod O'Brien, W. J. Turner, Lady Gerald Wellesley, Edith Shackleton Heald. Yeats was able to visit and be visited, but his doctor told him his heart was very bad. On 4 January 1939 he wrote to Lady Elizabeth Pelham: "I know for certain that my time will not be long." Yet in the same letter he described himself as "happy, and I think full of energy . . . I had despaired of," and he talked of the work he intended to do next. He died in the afternoon of 28 January 1939. Yeats was buried first in Roquebrune, as he had suggested should he die in France. But nine years later he was given his first choice when his body was carried on an Irish naval vessel back to Ireland for reinterment, with full ceremonies, in Drumcliff churchyard near Sligo, under an epitaph in his own words: *"Cast a cold Eye / On Life, on Death. / Horseman, pass by!"*

Yeats's letters, like his poetry, grew only more brilliant in his last years, and certain statements in the letters help one to deal reasonably with the often nonreasonable events of *Last Poems*. Correcting proofs of recent poems, he wrote to Dorothy Wellesley in January 1938: "I have got the town out of my verse. It is all nonchalant verse. . . ." To Edith Heald he wrote in February: "Intensity is all. I want to be some queer man's companion." On 15 March: "My recent work has greater strangeness and I think greater intensity than anything I have done. I never remember the dream so deep." To Dorothy Wellesley in July 1935: "The lasting expression of our time is . . . in a sense of something steel-like and cold within the will, something passionate and cold." On 4 December: "my poetry all comes from rage or lust." On 23 December: "We that are joyous need not be afraid to denounce. . . . Joy is the salvation of the soul. . . . love is not pity. It does not desire to change its object. It is a form of the eternal contemplation of what is." To Ethel Mannin on 4 March (1935?): "Our traditions only permit us to bless, for the arts are an extension of the beatitudes. Blessed be heroic death (Shakespeare's tragedies), blessed be heroic life (Cervantes), blessed be the wise (Balzac). . . . There are three very important persons (1) a man playing the flute (2) a man carving a statue (3) a man in a woman's arms." To Dorothy Wellesley on 4 May 1937: "In my own life I never felt so acutely the presence of a spiritual virtue, and that is accompanied by intensified desire. . . . You must feel plunged, as I do, into the madness of vision, into a sense of the relation of separated things that you cannot explain, and that deeply disturbs emotion."

A simple listing of Yeats's major terms in these credo-statements is enough to show their extraordinary range and yet their complex unity: nonchalant, intensity, dream, cold, passionate, rage, lust, joy, contemplation, beatitude, heroic, spiritual, madness, vision. Perhaps the best way to pull them together is with another quotation, this from a letter to Olivia Shakespear of May 1933: "we long for an age which has the unity which Plato somewhere defined as sorrowing and rejoicing over the same things." It is all "a form of the eternal contemplation of what is." Plato also suspected that poets were a bit mad and not to be trusted, and Yeats knew that too, hence "madness of vision."

Last Poems (1939), containing fifty-seven poems written between 1933 and 1939, was one of the strangest and strongest of his collections. The dominant notes are those of resignation, defiance, sensuality, prophecy, all familiar in his poetry; what is new is the intensity and extravagance everywhere. He had written Mrs. Shakespear in 1929 that he wanted his late poetry to be "all emotion and all impersonal." Poems would rise out of personal action and feeling, hence be emotional, passionate, and they would achieve coldness, impersonality by making the self not an ego but an archetype, a human case—perhaps, now, that of the "foolish, passionate man" who does his thinking "in a marrow-bone." Several of the late poems lay out that program explicitly.

The little poem "An Acre of Grass" begins with two quiet stanzas that place the old poet in weary retirement at Riversdale; then the closing stanzas write another poem: the verse hardens and heightens, and Yeats summons his archetypes of inspired old age and commands himself to join them: "Grant me an old man's frenzy, / Myself must I remake / Till I am Timon and Lear / Or that William Blake / Who beat upon the wall / Till Truth obeyed his call; // A mind Michael Angelo knew / That can pierce the clouds, / Or inspired by frenzy / Shake the dead in their shrouds; / Forgotten else by mankind, / An old man's eagle mind." Yeats knew old men were supposed to be sexless and peaceful, but he felt neither way, and he named his anachronistic passions defiantly in a notorious quatrain, "The Spur": "You think it horrible that lust and rage / Should dance attention upon my old age; / They were not such a plague when I was young; / What else have I to spur me into song?" Yeats's raffish old rambler puts his sexual case to the young woman in "The Wild Old Wicked Man": "Who can know the year, my dear, / When an old man's blood grows cold?" With his emblematic "stout stick under his hand," he goes on to acknowledge the standard tragic and spiritual formulas, and then falls back on passional life: "But a coarse old man am I, / I choose the second-best, / I forget it all awhile / Upon a woman's breast."

In "Why Should Not Old Men Be Mad?" Yeats addresses the "craziness" of his late poems in direct autobiographical terms; he has earned his craziness by heartbreak. He recalls the fate of Iseult Gonne, then that of her mother: "A girl that knew all Dante once / Live to bear children to a dunce; / A Helen of social welfare dream, / Climb on a wagonette to scream." Rage induced by thwarted lust, no doubt; but then the personal case turns grandly general; his examples are just that, examples of a representative condition, the racial failure that maddens any thinking man: "No single story would they find / Of an unbroken happy mind, / A finish worthy of the start. / Young men know nothing of this sort, / Observant old men know it well; / And when they know what old books tell, / And that no better can be had, / Know why an old man should be mad."

The sexual theme is given an exquisitely spectral and elegiac form in the seven ballad-songs that make up the suite of "The Three Bushes." The first narrative song tells the whole story in eleven stanzas. A lady deeply in love, mindful of her lover's need but kept chaste by "shame," sends her chambermaid to the lover, having ordered him to keep his room unlit: " 'So you must lie beside him / And let him think me there, / And maybe we are all the same / Where no candles are, / And maybe we are all the same / That strip the body bare.' / *O my dear, O my dear.*" This love by proxy goes on for a year, then the lover is killed by a fall from his horse, and the lady seeing it happen falls dead herself. The chambermaid lives on and tends the graves, planting two rose trees that blend into one. Before she dies she tells the story to her priest, and he being "a good man" who "understood her case" orders her buried next to the lovers under her own rose tree. The three bushes intertwine so that "now none living can. / When they have plucked a rose there, / Know where its roots began." Yeats gives the lady three closing songs, the lover one, the maid two. "The Chambermaid's First Song" is representative: "How came this ranger / Now sunk in rest, / Stranger with stranger, / On my cold breast? / What's left to sigh for? / Strange night has come; / God's love has hidden him / Out of all harm, / Pleasure has made him / Weak as a worm."

The poem sardonically titled "News for the Delphic Oracle" gives Yeats's sexual theme a blatant and gorgeous investment in a bay-shore community called simply "There," a sort of carnal Earthly Paradise where the only business is love-making: let copulation thrive. The point, apparently, is to assert the awful vitality of sex, its habit of pricking all our sublimations. For the celebration Yeats invents a stanza of twelve trimeter lines wildly off-rhymed. In the first stanza his old heroes loll about awaiting developments. In stanza 2 a school of dolphins swims into the bay carrying the Innocents from Herod's slaughter. Here they find a welcome but no grieving sympathy; the action is brisk and businesslike, and it is implied that these souls have come not for the purgation of "Byzantium" but for sexual initiation. Stanza 3 forms a visionary quatrocento landscape setting the exquisite sensual entrancement of Peleus and Thetis against a seascape torn with copulating bodies: "Slim adolescence that a nymph has stripped, / Peleus on Thetis stares. / Her limbs are delicate as an eyelid, / Love has blinded him with tears; / But Thetis' belly listens. / Down the mountain walls / From where Pan's cavern is / Intolerable music falls. / Foul goat-head, brutal arm appear, / Belly, shoulder, bum, / Flash fishlike; nymphs and satyrs / Copulate in the foam."

In these late poems Yeats's mind ran much upon the past, trying to call back before his eye the things that mattered most in his memory. The title of one such poem, "Beautiful Lofty Things," evokes the general mode of feeling. The only action in the poem is recollection. Yeats simply calls up and caresses a series of five dearly remembered images of noble being; Maud Gonne for example: "Maud Gonne at Howth station waiting a train, / Pallas Athene in that straight back and arrogant head." He might almost be holding in mind the exclamation of the ragged Dublin sculptor looking about Coole: "All the nobility of earth." That is the force of his closing line: "All the Olympians; a thing never known again."

"The Municipal Gallery Revisited" developed the same motive in an ampler, more formal mode. Yeats sent copies of the poem to the group of Irish-Americans who had contributed to a fund intended to insure his comfort in old age. It is one more roll-calling poem, set in seven of his favorite ceremonial stanzas, the ottava rima. In this corporate elegy the feeling is at first temperate as Yeats's eye roams the walls in the ordinary way of gallery-goers; but then the eye begins to pick out those images he had held in his heart of hearts, and emotion suddenly collects in an unbidden spasm: "Heart-smitten with emotions I sink down, / My heart recovering with covered eyes; / Wherever I had looked I had looked upon / My permanent or impermanent images." We have had a sudden glimpse of the most moving and endearing side of the man and the poet: the power in him of naked, vulnerable feeling.

The rest of the poem is listing and reflection: Robert Gregory, Hugh Lane, Hazel Lavery, Augusta Gregory, John Synge. Mancini's portrait of Lady Gregory inspires two stanzas and more. Yeats wonders if any brush could do justice to "all that pride and that humility," and in effect he offers a prayer to her memory: "My medieval knees lack health until they bend." Reflecting on the dissolution of the house where he had "all lacking found" he comforts himself bitterly: "No fox can foul the lair the badger swept," and traces the image to high art and folklore: "(An image out of Spenser and the common tongue)." The final fifteen lines, centering on his father's portrait of Synge, join again the trinity of the theater he had named in his Stockholm speech as embodiments of an ideal union of loftiness and simplicity: "John Synge, I and Augusta Gregory thought / All that we did, all that we said or sang / Must come from contact with the soil, from that / Contact everything Antaeus-like grew strong. / . . . / Dream of the noble and the beggar-man. / . . . / You that would judge, do not judge alone / This book or that, come to this hallowed place / Where my friends' portraits hang and look thereon; / Ireland's history in their lineaments trace; / Think where man's glory most begins and ends, / And say my glory was I had such friends."

A gnomic couplet in the little poem "A Nativity" runs as follows: "What made the ceiling waterproof? / Landor's tarpaulin on the roof." The image is less cryptic than it seems: the power of

Yeats's grave, Drumcliff, County Sligo

passion in high art to seal against time and terror. In the long run that is the heart of the matter, for the later as for the earlier Yeats. A key phrase, only apparently paradoxical, is the "tragic joy" that appears in the first of the *Last Poems,* "The Gyres," and recurrently thereafter. The poem is Yeats's last formal salute to the matter of *A Vision,* and it has a hail-and-farewell feeling, an air of ceremony grateful but almost dutiful, as if Yeats were getting the system out of his system, in order to fall back upon the more empirical tragic wisdom that had been bedrock all the time. He had written of his work in general to Olivia Shakespear in June 1932: "The swordsman throughout repudiates the saint, but not without vacillation."

After an exclamation of apocalyptic excitement: "The gyres! the gyres!" one named Old Rocky Face is commanded to "look forth." The mysterious image is surely related to that of "The Man and the Echo" of this volume ("O Rocky Voice, / Shall we in that great night rejoice?"), but both may reach all the way back to the Mask of Dante in "Ego Dominus Tuus": "a stony face / Staring upon a Bedouin's horse-hair roof / From domed and windowed cliff "; and for that matter it would do no harm to remember the noise from Pan's cavern in "News for the Delphic Oracle," or even the tongue given to the sea cliffs by the union of Yeats and Pollexfen: "When all is in the wine-cup," Yeats had written long ago, "the grapes begin to stammer." Old Rocky Face is a Mask of Yeats as of Dante.

What he is summoned to view is the anarchic landscape of "The Second Coming," but the tonality is subtly different and the response sharply so: "Irrational streams of blood are staining earth: / Empedocles has thrown all things about; / Hector is dead and there's a light in Troy; / We that look on but laugh in tragic joy." What had at first sounded like a rage to end all things has merged into an ecstatically bitter welcome. "What matter?" the next two stanzas ask four times, answering the opening exclamation: "What matter? Out of cavern comes a voice, / And all it knows is that one word 'Rejoice!' " To the colossal gyres of the beginning the final stanza opposes the humbler cyclicality of the human will; the empirically passionate friends of Rocky Face will resurrect the battered lofty things of their own indomitable gyre: "What matter? Those that Rocky Face holds dear, / Lovers of horses and of women, shall, / From marble of a broken sepulchre, / Or dark betwixt the polecat and the owl, / Or any rich, dark nothing disinter / The workman, noble and saint, and all things run / On that unfashionable gyre again."

"Those Images" puts the tragic-humanist case in imperative terms. It commands: "Call the Muses home," and proceeds to name suffering symbols drawn from the humbler *Spiritus Mundi* of familiar vision, daily available: "Seek those images / That constitute the wild, / The lion and the virgin, / The harlot and the child, // Find in middle air / An eagle on the wing, / Recognise the five / That make the Muses sing."

On 6 July 1935 Yeats wrote Dorothy Wellesley of a gift he had recently received: "I notice that you have much lapis lazuli; someone has sent me a present of a great piece carved by some Chinese sculptor into the semblance of a mountain with temple, trees, paths and an ascetic and pupil about to climb the mountain. Ascetic, pupil, hard stone, eternal theme of the sensual east. The heroic cry in the midst of despair." On 26 July he sent another comment evidently inspired by the Chinese artifact: "To me the supreme aim is an act of faith or reason to make one rejoice in the midst of tragedy. An impossible aim; yet I think it true that nothing can injure us." It took these meditations exactly a year to produce the poem that he judged "almost the best I have made of recent years." "Lapis Lazuli" offers the most inclusive and eloquent images of the principles of "tragedy," "joy," and "gaiety" that dominate *Last Poems*. The first of the five irregular verse paragraphs scoffs in a breezy colloquial way at the "hysterical women" who protest the gaiety of poets at a time of crisis when "everybody knows or else should know / That if nothing drastic is done / Aeroplane and Zeppelin will come out, / Pitch like King Billy bomb-balls in / Until the town lie beaten flat."

In the great second stanza the sound of a colloquial voice continues but rises, generalizes, solemnizes, as Yeats reflects upon the paradoxical effect of joy, "gaiety" at the heart of Shakespearean tragedy: "All perform their tragic play, / There struts Hamlet, there is Lear, / That's Ophelia, that Cordelia; / Yet they, should the last scene be there, / The great stage curtain about to drop, / If worthy their prominent parts in the play, / Do not break up their lines to weep. / They know that Hamlet and Lear are gay; / Gaiety transfiguring all that dread." In the third stanza the frame extends to include all historical time, all artists, all decay and joyous recurrence: "On their own feet they came, or on shipboard, / Camel-back, horse-back, ass-back, mule-back, / Old civilisations put to the sword. / Then they and their wisdom went to rack. / . . . / All things fall and are built again, / And those that build them again are gay."

Now the poet turns quietly to his emblem, turns the carved stone in his hands, describes it first literally, then philosophically. The object becomes an all-sufficing symbol, a natural element whose casual forms blend organically with the artist's making. The stone is a palimpsest of the spirit: nature blended with man, time, journey, animal, art; the art of music incorporated within the art of living, both preserved by the art of the carver: "and I / Delight to imagine them seated there; / There, on the mountain and the sky. / On all the tragic scene they stare. / One asks for mournful melodies; / Accomplished fingers begin to play. / Their eyes mid many wrinkles, their eyes, / Their ancient, glittering eyes, are gay." What ties it all together, gives it Unity of Being, is human: genius, will, courage, humor. We are back at the end of "Among School Children."

To sense the brave swings of Yeats's athletic final muse, one should set the rich grave reflection of "Lapis Lazuli" against the mad business of "High Talk," a poem that his critics have strangely ignored. Here Yeats clearly enjoyed taking extravagant liberties with the sonnet form, rhyming fourteen fifteen-syllable lines in couplets. His speaker, surely a wild form of the poet himself, is a stilt walker dedicated to making crazy shows because people after all delight in thrilling sensations: "Because piebald ponies, led bears, caged lions, make but poor shows, / Because children demand Daddy-long-legs upon his timber toes, / Because women in the upper storeys demand a face at the pane, / That patching old heels they may shriek, I take to chisel and plane." He is not ashamed of his mere fifteen-foot stilts; after all, "no modern stalks upon higher." (Is Yeats naming his station in the hierarchy of English Literature?) He is "Malachi Stilt-Jack / . . . / All metaphor, Malachi, stilts and all." The poet metaphor, surely, is an image of nerve, gaiety, folk-loftiness, transcendence. The poem's closing vision is high, strange, ecstatic: "A barnacle goose / Far up in the stretches of night; night splits and the dawn breaks loose; / I, through the terrible novelty of light, stalk on, stalk on; / Those great sea-horses bare their teeth and laugh at the dawn."

Yeats chose "Under Ben Bulben," ending with the lines on his gravestone, to be his epitaphic poem; but "The Circus Animals' Desertion" serves that purpose better. There he called the roll of his career as poet and dramatist, subsuming the work of more than fifty years in a design of antinomy. The self is the subject, and the work of the poem is to identify the self of the self. One can imagine his circus animals in a procession led by Daddy-long-legs upon his timber toes; in the upshot he leads them out of sight. The first stanza presents the old poet groping for a theme, falling back on simple passion, lamenting the higher talk of earlier days and grander atmospheres: "Maybe at last, being but a broken man, / I must be satisfied with my heart, although / Winter and summer till old age began / My circus animals were all on show, Those stilted boys, that burnished chariot, / Lion and woman and the Lord knows what." The three central stanzas ask a common question: "What can I do but enumerate old themes?" Yeats lists those mythic creatures, Oisin, Cathleen, Cuchulain, Fool, Blind Man, and gives them fair play: "Heart-mysteries there." But at the end, night coming on, he has to face the fact that it was always the mere humanity, the familiar being of his symbolic figures that had made him feel and write: "It was the dream itself enchanted me: / Character isolated by a deed / To engross the present and dominate memory. / Players and painted stage took all my love, / And not those things that they were emblems of." The magnificent and humble final stanza puts all together. *Spiritus Mundi* is stocked from a Dublin junk shop, and the ladder of inspiration rests on earth and flesh: "Those masterful images because complete / Grew in pure mind, but out of what began? / A mound of refuse or the sweepings of a street, / Old kettles, old bottles, and a broken can, / Old iron, old bones, old rags, that raving slut / Who keeps the till. Now that my ladder's gone, / I must lie down where all the ladders start, / In the foul rag-and-bone shop of the heart."

Letters:

Letters on Poetry from W. B. Yeats to Dorothy Wellesley (London, New York & Toronto: Oxford University Press, 1940);

Some Letters from W. B. Yeats to John O'Leary and His Sister, edited by Allan Wade (New York: New York Public Library, 1953);

W. B. Yeats and T. Sturge Moore: Their Correspondence, 1901-1937, edited by Ursula Bridge (London: Routledge & Kegan Paul, 1953);

Letters of W. B. Yeats to Katharine Tynan, edited by Roger McHugh (Dublin: Clonmore & Reynolds, 1953; London: Burns, Oates & Washbourne, 1953; New York: Macmillan, 1953);

The Letters of W. B. Yeats, edited by Wade (London: Hart-Davis, 1954; New York: Macmillan, 1955);

Ah, Sweet Dancer: W. B. Yeats and Margot Ruddock, A Correspondence, edited by McHugh (London & New York: Macmillan, 1970);

The Correspondence of Robert Bridges and W. B. Yeats, edited by Richard J. Finneran (London: Macmillan, 1977);

Theatre Business. The Correspondence of the First Abbey Directors: William Butler Yeats, Lady Gregory, and J. M. Synge (University Park: Pennsylvania State University Press, 1982);

The Collected Letters of W. B. Yeats, edited by John Kelly (Oxford: Clarendon Press, 1986-).

Bibliographies:

Allan Wade, *A Bibliography of the Writings of W. B. Yeats,* revised and edited by Russell K. Alspach (London: Hart-Davis, 1968);

K. P. S. Jochum, *W. B. Yeats: A Classified Bibliography of Criticism, Including Additions to Allan Wade's Bibliography of the Writings of W. B. Yeats and a Section on the Irish Literary and Dramatic Revival* (Urbana, Chicago & London: University of Illinois Press, 1978).

Biographies:

Joseph M. Hone, *W. B. Yeats, 1865-1939* (London: Macmillan, 1942);

A. Norman Jeffares, *W. B. Yeats, Man and Poet,* second edition (New York: Barnes & Noble, 1966);

William M. Murphy, *The Yeats Family and the Pollexfens of Sligo* (Dublin: Dolmen Press, 1971);

Micheal MacLiammóir, with Eavan Boland, *W. B. Yeats and His World* (New York: Viking, 1972);

Murphy, *Prodigal Father: The Life of John Butler Yeats, 1839-1922* (Ithaca, N.Y.: Cornell University Press, 1978);

John Harwood, *Olivia Shakespear and W. B. Yeats. After Long Silence* (Basingstoke, U.K.: Macmillan Press, 1989).

References:

Hazard Adams, *Blake and Yeats: The Contrary Vision,* Cornell Studies in English, no. 40 (New York: Russell & Russell, 1968);

Daniel Albright, *The Myth Against Myth: A Study of Yeats's Imagination in Old Age* (London: Oxford University Press, 1972);

James L. Allen, *Yeats's Epitaph: A Key to Symbolic Unity in His Life and Work* (Washington, D.C.: University Press of America, 1982);

John Bayley, *The Romantic Survival* (London: Constable, 1957);

Harold Bloom, *Yeats* (New York: Oxford University Press, 1970);

Curtis B. Bradford, *Yeats at Work* (Carbondale & Edwardsville: Southern Illinois University Press, 1965);

David R. Clark, *Yeats at Songs and Choruses* (Amherst: University of Massachusetts Press, 1983);

Denis Donoghue, *William Butler Yeats* (New York: Viking, 1971);

Una Mary Ellis-Fermor, *The Irish Dramatic Movement* (London: Methuen, 1954);

Richard Ellmann, *Eminent Domain: Yeats Among Wilde, Joyce, Pound, Eliot, and Auden* (New York: Oxford University Press, 1967);

Ellmann, *The Identity of Yeats* (New York: Oxford University Press, 1954);

Ellmann, *Yeats: The Man and the Masks* (New York: Macmillan, 1948);

Richard Finneran, ed., *Yeats. An Annual of Critical and Textual Studies* (Ann Arbor: University of Michigan Press, 1983-);

Monk Gibbon, *The Masterpiece and the Man: Yeats As I Knew Him* (New York: Macmillan, 1959);

Oliver St. John Gogarty, *William Butler Yeats, A Memoir* (Dublin: Dolmen Press, 1963);

Warwick Gould, ed., *Yeats Annual* (Atlantic Highlands, N.J.: Humanities Press International, 1982-);

Stephen L. Gwynn, ed., *Scattering Branches: Tributes to the Memory of W. B. Yeats* (New York: Macmillan, 1940);

James Hall and Martin Steinmann, eds., *The Permanence of Yeats* (New York: Collier, 1961);

Thomas R. Henn, *The Lonely Tower: Studies in the Poetry of W. B. Yeats* (London: Methuen, 1950; New York: Barnes & Noble, 1965);

Daniel Hoffman, *Barbarous Knowledge in the Poetry of Yeats, Graves and Muir* (New York: Oxford University Press, 1967);

A. Norman Jeffares and A. S. Knowland, *A Commentary on The Collected Poems of W. B. Yeats* (Stanford: Stanford University Press, 1968);

Jeffares, ed., *Selected Criticism of W. B. Yeats* (London: Macmillan, 1964);

Jeffares and K. G. W. Cross, eds., *In Excited Reverie* (New York: Macmillan, 1965);

Frank Kermode, *Romantic Image* (London: Routledge & Kegan Paul, 1957; New York: Random House, 1964);

Maud Gonne MacBride, *A Servant of the Queen* (Dublin: Golden Eagle, 1950);

Louis MacNeice, *The Poetry of W. B. Yeats* (London: Oxford University Press, 1941);

Philip L. Marcus, *Yeats and the Beginning of the Irish Renaissance* (Ithaca, N.Y.: Cornell University Press, 1970);

Giorgio Melchiori, *The Whole Mystery of Art* (New York: Macmillan, 1961);

Liam Miller, ed., *The Dolmen Press Yeats Centenary Papers,* 30 volumes (Dublin: Dolmen Press, 1965-1968);

Virginia Moore, *The Unicorn: William Butler Yeats's Search for Reality* (New York: Macmillan, 1954);

James Olney, *The Rhizome and the Flower: the Perennial Philosophy, Yeats and Jung* (Berkeley: University of California Press, 1980);

Thomas Parkinson, *W. B. Yeats, Self-Critic and The Later Poetry* (Berkeley & Los Angeles: University of California Press, 1971);

Stephen Maxfield Parrish, ed., *A Concordance to the Poems of W. B. Yeats,* programmed by James Allan Painter (Ithaca, N.Y.: Cornell University Press, 1963);

Benjamin L. Reid, *The Man from New York: John Quinn and His Friends* (New York: Oxford University Press, 1968);

Reid, *William Butler Yeats: the Lyric of Tragedy* (Norman: University of Oklahoma Press, 1961);

Lennox Robinson, *Ireland's Abbey Theatre: A History 1869-1951* (London: Sidgwick & Jackson, 1951; Port Washington, N.Y.: Kennikat Press, 1968);

George B. Saul, *Prolegomena to the Study of Yeats's Poems* (Philadelphia: University of Pennsylvania Press, 1957);

Robin Skelton and Ann Saddlemyer, *The World of W. B. Yeats* (Victoria, B.C.: University of Victoria Press, 1965);

Jon Stallworthy, *Between the Lines: Yeats's Poems in the Making* (Oxford: Clarendon Press, 1963);

Stallworthy, *Visions and Revisions in Yeats's Last Poems* (Oxford: Clarendon Press, 1969);

A. G. Stock, *W. B. Yeats: His Poetry and Thought* (Cambridge: Cambridge University Press, 1961);

Helen H. Vendler, *Yeats's "Vision" and the Later Plays* (Cambridge, Mass.: Harvard University Press, 1963);

Thomas R. Whitaker, *Swan and Shadow: Yeats's Dialogue with History* (Chapel Hill: University of North Carolina Press, 1964);

F. A. C. Wilson, *W. B. Yeats and Tradition* (New York: Macmillan, 1958);

Wilson, *Yeats's Iconography* (London: Gollancz, 1960);

John Butler Yeats, *Essays Irish and American* (Dublin: Talbot Press / London: Unwin, 1918);

John Butler Yeats, *Letters to His Son, W. B. Yeats, and Others*, edited, with a memoir, by Joseph Hone (London: Faber & Faber, 1944).

Papers:

The National Library of Ireland in Dublin houses the largest collection of Yeats papers. Copies of its papers are at the State University of New York at Stony Brook, which also has a copy of the collection of Michael B. Yeats in Dalkey. Other collections are housed in the Berg Collection of the New York Public Library, and at Cornell University, Harvard University, the University of Chicago, and the Huntington Library.

Index to Volume 5

Index

This index includes proper names: people, places, and works mentioned in the texts of entries for Volume 5. The primary checklists, which appear at the beginning of each entry, are not included in this index. Also omitted are the names London and Dublin, because they appear so frequently. Volume 8 of the *Concise Dictionary of British Literary Biography* includes a cumulative proper-name index to the entire series.

Cumulative Index of Author Entries for Concise Dictionary of British Literary Biography

Cumulative Index of Author Entries

ISBN 0-8103-7985-6

90000>

9 780810 379855